Emp

Alternatives, Consequences and

STEPHEN J. PERKINS AND GEOFF WHITE

The CIPD would like to thank the following members of the CIPD Publishing editorial board for their help and advice:

- Pauline Dibben, Sheffield University
- Edwina Hollings, Staffordshire University Business School
- Caroline Hook, Huddersfield University Business School
- Vincenza Priola, Keele University
- John Sinclair, Napier University Business School

Employee Reward

Alternatives, Consequences and Contexts

Stephen J. Perkins and Geoff White

Chartered Institute of Personnel and Development

Published by the Chartered Institute of Personnel and Development,
151 The Broadway, London, SW19 1JQ

This edition first published 2008
© Chartered Institute of Personnel and Development, 2008

Typeset by Fakenham Photosetting Ltd, Norfolk

Printed in Spain by Graphycems

British Library Cataloguing in Publication Data

A catalogue of this publication is available from the British Library

ISBN 978 1 84398 156 5

The views expressed in this publication are the author's own and may not necessarily reflect those of the CIPD.

The CIPD has made every effort to trace and acknowledge copyright holders. If any source has been overlooked, CIPD Enterprises would be pleased to redress this in future editions.

Chartered Institute of Personnel and Development,
151 The Broadway, London, SW19 1JQ
Tel: 020 8612 6200
E-mail: cipd@cipd.co.uk
Website: www.cipd.co.uk
Incorporated by Royal Charter.
Registered Charity No. 1079797

Contents

List of figures and tables

Chapter 6 Variable Pay Schemes

Chapter 7 Benefits

Chapter 8 Pensions

Chapter 9 Non-financial Rewards

Chapter 10 Regarding Directors and Executives

Chapter 11 International Reward Management

Chapter 12 Employee Reward within 'HRM"

Foreword

Employee reward is an area that can provoke a great deal of controversy, which in some cases spills out well beyond the organisation. What we do to reward people in organisations, and how we do it, has strategic, practical and symbolic implications. If we stop paying people in ways that broadly match their economic value and expectations, we're unlikely to be successful in the war for talent. If we pay in excess we can materially impact on the financial performance of organisations. But pay and other elements making up 'total reward' also send powerful messages to recipients. Total reward can serve as a clear message about not only who but what kinds of contribution the organisation's leaders value – and that is why the mode of delivery can be just as crucial as the financial level of the reward 'package'.

Interpreting the contexts for reward determination and thinking through the consequences of choices of instruments and approaches is a complex undertaking. The theory of the employment relationship, with reward for effort at its core, is by definition subject to contested ideas and behaviours. In addition at the practical level there is a multiplicity of factors influencing design and implementation of total rewards and a number of solutions (some better, some worse) for any set of circumstances. A thinking performer recognised as a chartered professional needs to be aware of how we have learned to conceptualise employee reward – just like any other aspect of joined-up people management today – and to diagnose, recommend and implement justifiable actions which are robust in ever-changing conditions.

Narrow functional knowledge of reward is not enough. To be effective in this field, HR people need to command a thorough understanding of the business, political, legal and environmental conditions which shape our approach to reward. In addition HR professionals need to recognise the sociology and psychology of reward in the work place, where employee perceptions and sense of fair play in reward is a vital key to their engagement and performance.

The authors of this new text worked to a brief from CIPD Publishing that they should set the knowledge bar at a level that is accessible but challenging. Using it effectively, students and other readers should be able to equip themselves to make a difference in organisations, involving both strategic and practical operational decisions about people management and its reward dimension.

Vicky Wright
President, CIPD

Acknowledgements

A major project such as the production of this volume involves the creative energies of a large number of people. As authors, we are proud that the cover carries our joint names. But we are very aware that there is a body of people without whom the title now before you could not have seen the light of day. It is we, of course, who are responsible for errors or omissions in the text. But we wish to acknowledge here at least some of the people who we have benefited from, as key informants and supporters.

First, we wish to thank Ruth Lake for commissioning the work in the first place, and then extend our appreciation to other colleagues at CIPD Publishing for shepherding the work to completion, particularly Kirsty Smy, Jenna Steventon, and Caroline Windle.

Secondly, there is a host of colleagues who have generously shared ideas, experience, and of course their time, in particular during the formative stage of the text. During that phase, we were seeking stimulation to our imagination of what a 21st century 'employee reward' text for an English-speaking but, at least, European audience should look like.

Thanks are due to many, and especially to Paul Bissell, Duncan Brown, John Campbell, Cecile de Calan, Mark Childs, Charles Cotton, Marion Festing, Richard Greenhill, Alastair Hatchett, Prof. Chris Hendry, Dr. Ian Kessler, Karel Leeflang, Helen Murlis, Don Mackinlay, Susan Milsome, Jean-Pierre Nöel, Steve Palmer, Sandy Pepper, Michael Rose, John Shields, Natarajan Sundar, Angela Wright and Clive Wright. And we sincerely acknowledge a further debt, to our anonymous reviewers, for the supportive criticism to make the text more fit-for-purpose than it otherwise might have been.

Third, among colleagues in the HRM community, there is a special thanks to Vicky Wright, not only for creative input at the outset, but also for kindly writing the book's Foreword; and to Tim Fevyer for invaluable input to our discussion of the 'total reward journey', contributing information and experiential insights that bring the ideas to life.

Finally, we would acknowledge the benefits of a collaborative effort: working with one another, contributing what we hope readers will regard as complementary ideas, experience, and styles, has been a developmental process in itself. We should add a special closing thank you to our spouses, Erica and Jan – for putting up with us, whether the writing is flowing or seemingly blocked…

Book plan

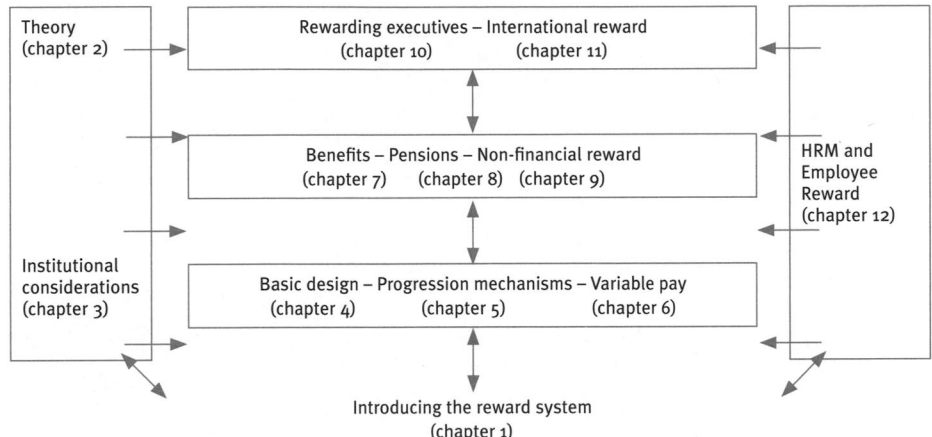

Theory
(chapter 2)

Rewarding executives – International reward
(chapter 10)   (chapter 11)

HRM and
Employee
Reward
(chapter 12)

Benefits – Pensions – Non-financial reward
(chapter 7)   (chapter 8)   (chapter 9)

Institutional
considerations
(chapter 3)

Basic design – Progression mechanisms – Variable pay
(chapter 4)   (chapter 5)   (chapter 6)

Introducing the reward system
(chapter 1)

Introducing Employee Reward Systems

CHAPTER OBJECTIVES

At the end of this chapter you should understand and be able to explain the following:

- Definitions of employee reward and the 'effort bargain', and managerial approaches advocated as part of a 'new organisational logic'.

- The concept of a 'reward system', and the alternatives and consequences for managing employee reward, accounting for the corporate, national, and international context(s) for situating 'effort–reward' bargaining.

- Structure of the book and how to use it to grasp concepts and themes intended to help navigate this complex and contested field of study.

CIPD STANDARDS COVERED IN THIS CHAPTER:

To be able to understand and explain:

- The employee reward 'contribution'.

- The concept of an employee reward system and its component processes, practices, structures, schemes and procedures.

- The factors that influence orientations to a reward system, such as equity, fairness, consistency and transparency, accounting for the corporate, national and international context.

Employee reward, as the accompanying media extracts vividly illustrate (Box 1.1), can hardly be described as simple or its application lacking in controversy. Moreover, the choices made by managements and people in employment relationships have consequences that reach across society. For the 'reflexive' HR specialist (the social actor who has learned to be self- and contextually aware), it's a far from dull aspect of the professional role; and for the expert in demand it can be highly rewarding both intellectually and materially, albeit with a more challenging 'client' base. One remuneration committee member of our acquaintance, an individual known for his candour, is reported as stressing the demands for 'more rigorous explanation' of intelligence presented to 'top pay' decision-makers, who know they are working in a transparent environment (Perkins and Hendry, 2005: 1156–7). Given that context, as Shields cautions:

> *reward management is fraught with peril … Perhaps more so than other facets of human resource management [it] is an attitudinal, emotional and behavioural minefield. Ill-chosen, badly designed or poorly implemented [managerial approaches] can communicate entirely the wrong messages [and] an ill-conceived reward system … may give rise to endemic organisational misbehaviour.* (2007: 6)

Entering the field of employee reward, it seems, is not for the faint-hearted.

BOX 1.1 JUST FOR STARTERS . . .

ISSUES IN REWARD

… Mr Deputy Speaker, the flexibility I propose – in employment, in pay, in the liberalisation of capital, labour and product markets generally, flexibilities important for competitiveness in the global economy and our engagement in Europe – is not bought at the cost of fairness to families but is underwritten by policies for full employment … And these are measures that combine the flexibility – too often undervalued in Europe – that is essential for enterprise with the fairness – too often undervalued in the US – that is essential for social cohesion: making Britain a leader for those who see enterprise and fairness advancing together. (Budgetary statement by Gordon Brown, Chancellor of the Exchequer, reported in *The Times*, 10 April 2003)

Research by the salary comparison site PayFinder suggested that female British workers earn on average 27% less than their male counterparts. … The figures were compiled from submissions to the site by 40,000 workers between August 2004 and 2005. … The imbalance in salaries is higher in private companies, but employers in the public services should not expect comfortable reading. Earlier this year Heather Wakefield, head of local government at the Unison trade union, identified a 'Grand Canyon-sized pay chasm' between men and women in the public sector. (*Sunday Times*, 4 September 2005)

The gender pay gap is growing for women in senior jobs, according to new figures showing female directors are paid up to 26% less than men. A woman director in a service sector role such as retail or business services earns an average of £57,000, compared with more than £70,000 for a man, the survey by the Institute of Directors revealed. The IoD's director general, Miles Templeman, yesterday described the findings as 'extremely disappointing'. The IoD said it struggled to explain the figures, which did not tally with its own impression of an improving pay picture in senior roles. (*Guardian*, 8 November 2007)

The minimum wage will rise in October, [2005] benefiting more than 1m people, the government has announced.

Adults must be paid at least £5.05 an hour, up from £4.85, while 18 to 21 year olds will be paid £4.25. The recommendations came from the Low Pay Commission which said the number of jobs had continued to grow since the minimum wage was introduced in 1999. Businesses wanted it frozen, warning more rises could damage competitiveness but the unions want a £6 rate. ... According to the commission, many businesses had found the last two significant increases in the minimum wage 'challenging'. 'We have therefore recommended only a slight increase above average earnings, and concentrated it in the second year to allow business more time to absorb the impact,' said chairman Adair Turner. The government says most of those on the minimum wage are women – with many working in cleaning, catering, shops and hairdressing. (BBC News, 25 February 2005, bbc.co.uk)

There are about 1m temporary and contract workers in Britain. ... One estimate suggests that agency workers contribute £24.8 billion to the nation's economy each year. The public sector depends on them. Richard Ratcliff ... 58-year-old English and religious education teacher works two or three days a week, filling in for absent staff at secondary schools ... The rest of his week is spent gardening or visiting cultural sites. 'I'm semi-retired, but this way I get to keep my hand in while avoiding that rat-race element you find in most full-time jobs,' he said. 'It's quite stressful but very fulfilling.' Bill Hooper's career is just beginning. Within days of contacting the recruitment agency Manpower, the 26-year-old IT worker started in a temporary position doing electronic file management for Hertfordshire County Council. 'I needed employment quickly and temporary work let me get my foot in the door,' he said.

'The only downside is the lack of security, but the longer you are in a position, the more chance there is that it could become a permanent job,' he said. While some agency workers are paid less than their permanent colleagues, both Ratcliff and Hooper receive the going rate. (*Sunday Times*, 18 November 2007)

Who is the greediest and most ruthless executive in the FTSE? To find the answer, you need only look at one business: Cable & Wireless, the publicly listed company that is doing for income inequality what the stretched Hummer is doing for global warming. For the answer is either John Pluthero, who runs C&W's businesses, or Richard Lapthorne, the group's chairman. ... Hefty executive pay is a good thing. Big payouts to top executives, when linked to performance, encourage competitiveness, wealth creation, economic growth and, ultimately, further employment and prosperity. C&W's shareholders are, quite rightly, applauding [the firm's chairman and its chief executive]. They may be taking tens of millions in pay, but they are returning billions in value to investors. However, there is a broader issue that goes beyond C&W. The concentration of reward to the top executives – without personal risk and without long-term social benefit either to the business, its customers or its employees – threatens the credibility of capitalism. (*The Times*, 14 November 2007)

On August 6th Chrysler ... unveiled a new boss, Bob Nardelli. ... The choice could hardly have been more controversial. Mr Nardelli was last sighted leaving Home Depot under a cloud of controversy in January, carrying $210m in his swag bag thanks to a fantastically generous severance clause in his contract. ... His huge pay packet at Home Depot was mentioned by Ron

Gettelfinger, the head of the United Auto Workers Union (UAW), when the two men met for the first time recently. The UAW has been a fierce critic of soaring executive pay in corporate America. (Economist.com, 7 August 2007)

Boardroom pay has been brought back under the spotlight after it emerged that chief executives of FTSE 100 companies received on average almost £3.2 million last year. ... The findings also highlight the narrowing gap between American and British pay settlements. (*The Times*, 29 October 2007)

Employees of the largest UK companies are finally starting to contribute a decent amount to money purchase, or defined contribution, pensions, Watson Wyatt, the leading pension advisers, said yesterday. Historically, employers have tended to put much less into the defined contribution pensions that have now largely replaced final salary schemes for new employees – typically only 6–7 per cent of salary. But Watson Wyatt's annual survey of FTSE 100 companies shows that the average combined contribution of employers and employees has now risen to 14.7 per cent of pay. Of that, the employer typically is paying two-thirds, Paul Macro, a senior consultant with the firm said ... 'tantalisingly close to the 15 per cent of salary that is generally accepted as being the level of contribution needed to provide a decent income in retirement', he said. (*Financial Times*, 14 November 2007)

In the past six years, the mail systems pioneer Pitney Bowes has acquired more than 65 companies, all on the watch of Michael Critelli, chief executive at the time and now executive chairman. ... Now the intention is to integrate the new businesses seamlessly into Pitney Bowes' central systems ... 58-year-old Mr Critelli, with six patents to his name and more pending, is himself no stranger to technology ... His background, however, is law. ... His first substantial contact with IT, however, was in 1990. Having been promoted to General Counsel, he also took on responsibility for safety, the environment and human resources. The human resources department was changing systems, from what he describes as an 'outsourced and very paper-driven benefits process' to a flexible benefits programme which gave staff considerably more choice. It involved the integration of personnel data, medical benefits data and payroll. He was also involved in improving storage and retrieval systems for the legal department. (*Financial Times*, 13 June 2007)

... Both economic strength and social justice are advanced when parents can balance work and family life and are able to make real and effective choices. (Budgetary statement by Gordon Brown, Chancellor of the Exchequer, reported in *The Times*, 10 April 2003)

From the small selection of media stories cited in Box 1.1, it is evident that reward associated with employment is newsworthy. The area is also swathed in prescriptive ('how should' / 'how to') commentary – with an ample dose of managerial fads and fashions. Cataloguing that material could quite easily turn a book like this into an encyclopaedia of what's been 'hot and not' over the past quarter century or so. Employee reward is also subject to contestation. The problem facing the novice or even the seasoned practitioner is where to begin and how to navigate this potentially overwhelming field of study, mastery of which is unlikely to follow rote learning of a bulleted list of 'dos and don'ts'. In our view, as we have approached the construction of this text, what is needed is an introduction to concepts and ways of framing employee reward issues that will enable the reflexive HR practitioner (or, to use a favoured CIPD term, 'thinking performer') to interpret and then weigh the alternative approaches to employee reward and its management, mindful of the anticipated consequences, located firmly in particular contexts (see the 'plan of the book' diagram, located on page xv, for an image of how this maps onto the content of this text).

Some of those 'contexts' and ideas on acting on and within them, as well as information on the consequences of choices exercised, are illustrated in the media sound bites presented earlier. Unpacking these kinds of issues and commenting on how the derived problems may be considered in depth is the subject of the chapters that follow. But here we will briefly remark on phenomena close to the surface and commanding attention, before we go on to summarise the scope of the chapter to complete this opening section. Doing so will help us defend our choice of a focus on concepts and themes, illustrated by reported contemporary practice, rather than being driven solely by 'technical' description.

INTERESTS IN EMPLOYEE REWARD

The opening and closing quotes in Box 1.1 above, from a UK Government Budget speech in 2003, indicate macro-level *interests* in employment and its reward, locating these in the economics of 'flexibility' for global competitiveness, while defending choices that weigh 'market forces' considerations against political and 'social justice' issues, balancing 'enterprise' and 'fairness'. The character and intended purpose of reward in these considerations appears to be widely drawn, raising issues around expectations between the various constituents party to an employment system. The media reports cited also foreground contentious issues surrounding rewards enjoyed by employment system segments: executives and professionals, as well as those working at or close to 'minimum wage' levels; those working on non-standard contracts (eg part-time agency employees), where gender as well as other workforce diversity characteristics are in play. As in dual goals of flexibility and fairness these carry ethical and moral connotations too.

Shifting the focus to the micro-level interests of the firm and other organisations, these comparative factors are not limited to the domestic employment system but may stretch across international borders, even where the workforce segment concerned is not necessarily required to be geographically mobile. Ideas concerning the merits of 'flexibility' are not limited to job tenure or work pattern, and can have significant consequences at the work-life interface. They are also concerned with pay, non-pay and non-financial 'benefits' as well as 'deferred pay', in the form of pensions in retirement, and who should bear the primary burden of financing them.

The question of utilising technology to enable flexibility of administration, as well as a medium for control, is also discernible in the Box 1.1 cameo quotations we presented to whet the reader's appetite for more detailed review in what follows.

BOX 1.2 EMPLOYEE REWARD DECISIONS AND NATIONAL INCOME DISTRIBUTION

What are the consequences flowing from the decisions employers throughout the economy make about salaries and wages paid to the people who work for them? The 2007 Annual Survey of Hours and Earnings (ASHE) published by the UK Office for National Statistics reveals that, at the median, annual earnings for all employee groups amounted to £19,943. Using this form of statistical average tells us that half of those represented in the data set are paid above this level and half below it. Breaking this 'average' down by selected occupational categories, the survey data informs us that people classified as 'managers and senior officials' earned a median of £34,000 annually.

Of course, as we shall see in Chapter 10, this figure does not capture the nuances of those found at the top end of the range of earnings from employment – such as the chief executives of large companies whose shares are quoted on the London Stock Exchange where a gross 'package' of annual salary and related 'incentive' awards amounting to more than £10m is possible (IDS, 2006). This stands in contrast to the position of an individual paid at the national minimum wage of £5.52 per hour for those aged 22 and over, effective October 2007 (HM Revenue & Customs, 2007).

Falling somewhere in between these extremes, median annual earnings are reported in the ASHE (2007), for example, covering 'heath professionals' (£47,448); 'business and public service professionals' (£31,508); 'science and technology associate professionals' (£24,999); 'skilled trades occupations' (£24,871); 'process, plant and machine operatives' (£19,648); 'administrative and secretarial occupations' (£15,542); 'caring personal service occupations' (£11,156); and sales and 'customer service occupations' (£9,093).

Alternatives in setting the amount and composition of employee reward may thus be viewed as extending beyond disinterested technical calculation – decision-taking carries with it social consequences, and may be viewed as signalling judgements on the perceived relative economic worth of an individual and the activity undertaken, as well as possibly the politically loaded symbol of what certain groups and individuals are able to secure in the context of an employment relationship. The outcome may be subjected to scrutiny on both functional and ethical grounds, therefore, going to the heart of debates about income distribution, fairness and values across society.

INFLUENCES ON EMPLOYEE REWARD THINKING

Much of the literature concerning employee reward is informed by the twin disciplines of economics and psychology. The hints in the foregoing remarks, however, signal the presence not only of phenomena concerned with macro-economic market transactions and/or individual micro-perceptions and responses but also of ethical, moral, political, social and technological factors – as well as managerial strategies and responses from employment system parties including finance capital investors, governments, trade unions, and other 'stakeholders'. Interest groups may adopt a variety of starting points too, in examining notions of 'employee reward' and the way it can be objectively discovered and determined or subjectively interpreted and socially constructed and deconstructed. The consequence of this is that not only do reflexive 'employee reward' actors find themselves confronted with conflicting prescriptions on how to derive effective consequences from investment decisions, they also encounter alternative ways of thinking about the subject – whether these feature explicitly in the commentary or lurk implicitly below the surface.

Given the range of factors complementing and supplementing economic and psychological issues, the search for guidance on how to navigate potentially conflicting, sometimes contradictory, 'best practice' techniques may be usefully supported by literature assembled by employee relations and HRM analysts, political scientists, sociologists, strategic management writers and so on. These ideas and concepts will need careful interpretation and evaluation. But they may help to situate alternative employee reward principles and practices mindful of the context in which they have been fashioned and to which the exhortation is to apply them.

That is the case whether the context is spatial and/or temporal, related to organisation and workforce – as well as managerial – characteristics, and cultural and/or institutional factors, not forgetting philosophical considerations that set the scene for what decision-makers and their advisers think is being observed and acted on, and how knowledge to inform the process is itself constituted. Observing these principles, it seems to us, the reader will be able to adopt a thematic and theoretically grounded orientation to the subject, rather than one overly reliant on 'techniques' (even when technical commentary is informed by reports of what 'works' and what does not, gathered in 'real world' settings).

CHAPTER SCOPE

The remainder of this chapter is organised to satisfy three main objectives. First is to clarify meaning(s) attached to employee reward and the contribution expected managerially in securing an organisationally effective set of relations around employment, accounting for chosen orientation(s) towards workforce members. Secondly, to scrutinise repeated references to 'reward systems', and then appraise the utility of long-standing 'systems' thinking to help assemble and interpret material on the alternatives, consequences and contexts for employee reward. Thirdly, fleshing out the 'plan of the book' diagram located on page xv, to outline the structure and content of the subsequent four parts arranged over another 11 chapters making up the book.

EMPLOYEE REWARD: DEFINITIONS, RELATIONS AND CONTRIBUTION POTENTIAL

Employee reward represents one of the central pillars supporting the employment relationship (Kessler, 2005). How it is perceived varies across contemporary society, whether the observer is the proverbial 'person in the street' or a specialist commentator (Milkovich and Newman, 2004). Employee reward is therefore a complex and potentially confusing area to study and practice (Gerhart and Rynes, 2003).

> **DEFINITION**
>
> Employee 'compensation', 'remuneration' or 'reward' (terms that may be used interchangeably in the literature, although 'compensation' tends to predominate in US commentary) may be defined as 'all forms of financial returns and tangible services and benefits employees receive' (Milkovich and Newman, 2004: 3).

Employee 'reward(s)' may, however, be differentiated between:

extrinsic, tangible or 'transactional' reward for undertaking work in employment, on the one hand, and

intrinsic reward derived from work and employment, on the other hand.

Extrinsic reward – in the form of salary, incentive pay and benefits – serves the purpose of directly recognising the comparative value of organisational roles and the contribution individuals may make in performing them. Extrinsic employee benefits and 'perks' delivered in a non-cash form (eg company cars, paid holiday and healthcare), or 'deferred remuneration' (eg predefined occupational pension benefits or equity share-based rewards that may be financially realised at a future date), may reflect managerial efforts to keep rewards competitive, intended to recruit and retain sufficient employees of the right calibre, and to secure work accomplishment for the organisation. Benefits may also reflect an employer's interest in employee wellbeing. The nature and combination of extrinsic reward is dynamic: for example, present-day contributions to an employee's 'portable' retirement income fund may be offered in place of a 'company pension', reflecting the increasingly 'flexible' employment relationship.

Intrinsic reward may be further subdivided (Kessler, 2001). On the one hand, 'environmental rewards' may be manifested in the physical surroundings in which work is performed, combined with other factors, such as the values displayed in the workplace by organisational leaders and work supervisors, and perceptions of their leadership quality. On the other hand, 'development-oriented rewards' that tend to be more individually directed may be offered to recognise employee aspirations to receive learning and development opportunities, and to gain acknowledgement of outstanding work and build feelings of accomplishment – wherever possible consolidated tangibly through career advancement (Milkovich and Newman, 2004). It is agued that extending the features of employee reward beyond those specified in the 'economic contract' may help to secure employees' discretionary effort (Wright, 2005: 1.2.2). This 'intrinsic' or 'psychological' contract in work relationships (Levinson *et al*, 1962; Schein, 1965; Rousseau, 1989, 1995) features in commentary advocating attention to the 'total reward' proposition (see Chapter 9).

Theoretical frameworks for interpreting and weighing extrinsic and intrinsic reward are introduced in Chapter 2; approaches to structuring and managing extrinsic forms of 'fixed' and 'variable' reward in the form of pay are the subject of discussion in Part Two; and detailed consideration of the 'total reward' concept is undertaken in Part 3, Chapter 9 (see Figure 9.1 for a diagrammatic illustration of the factors in play and their holistic aggregation).

EMPLOYEE REWARD LEVELS VS 'LABOUR COSTS'

Pfeffer (1998) sought to correct what he termed certain myths that he suggested managers may incorrectly embrace in thinking about rewarding people employed in organisations. He was at pains to point out that *rates* of employee reward are not the same as the *costs* of employing someone. It is possible to pay higher rates of reward to employees compared with a competitor and yet have employment costs – as a proportion of the total costs of running an organisation – that are relatively lower. The key ingredient is *productivity* – that is, what the employer is able to achieve in terms of efficient and effective output from the workforce for each component of a person's capacity to work.

Pfeffer (1998) gave as an example the comparative position of two steel mills where one pays higher wages than the other but keeps the overall cost of employment at a managerially acceptable level by requiring significantly fewer person-work hours to produce a similar amount of steel. He added that those managers who subscribe to the first 'myth' tend to embrace a second misconception – that by cutting salary and wage rates they can reduce their labour costs. However, as he argued:

> *I may replace my $2000 a week engineers with ones that earn $500, but my costs may skyrocket because the new lower-paid employees are inexperienced, slow, and less capable. In that case I would have increased my costs by cutting my rates.* (Pfeffer, 1998: 110)

ISSUES IN REWARD

BOX 1.3 THE EMPLOYMENT RELATIONSHIP BARGAIN

'Payment systems are at the core of the employment relationship. Work under an employment relationship is undertaken in return for pay' (Rubery and Grimshaw, 2003: 12). But the nature of this *'exchange* relationship' (Steers and Porter, 1987: 203, emphasis in original) implies more than an economic transaction.

Situating it in a socio-economic context, employee reward may be perceived as an 'effort-bargain' (Behrend, 1957; Baldamus, 1961; Kessler, 2001) between the parties to the employment relationship, needing to be continuously renewed on either side.

In simple terms, three reasons are generally given for the managerial importance of employee reward: the underlying idea is to help organisations and those who lead them to secure, retain and motivate people (CIPD, 2006a). Employers, or managers and supervisors acting on the employer's behalf, whether they are in 'for-profit' organisations, government agencies or other 'not-for-profit' enterprises, offer reward(s) that may be counted as representing the 'price' for employing 'labour', moderated by particular economic market conditions. But the employment relationship has a complex character. Employees are not selling 'their souls' as a labour market commodity (Rubery and Grimshaw, 2003: 2), but a capacity for and willingness to work. The relative value of economic recognition it is deemed legitimate for an individual to expect in employment is mediated through principles of fairness, equity, justice and respect for the human condition.

Because reward is about a relationship, the outcome of which is open to the striking of a bargain, employee reward may be perceived as dynamic and not wholly subject to unitary managerial design or control. A formal contract may be entered into between the parties – effort for reward – but the precise details of whether and to what extent employee effort matches managerial expectations remain indeterminate (Mardsen, 1999). Managerially, 'performance management' arrangements may be introduced to try to order the process, but the extent of employees' willingness to co-operate in terms of not only 'membership behaviour' (a decision to join and stay with an employer), but also 'task behaviour' (complying with managerial expectations over completing assigned work tasks), and 'organisational citizenship behaviour' (voluntarily and altruistically acting in ways that exceed membership and task compliance) is ultimately a function of employee choice (Shields, 2007).

'Normative' commentary (ie telling decision-makers what they *should* do, rather than 'positive' analysis, which focuses on the results of decisions and outcomes) argues that contemporary forms of employee reward need to complement and reinforce a 'new logic' of organising (eg Lawler, 2000). Under this reasoning, employee reward and its management need to match the criteria for judging an organisation as 'effective' (ie that it achieves a fit between the need for capabilities in co-ordinating and motivating behaviour matched to economic market demands, on the one hand, and competencies that distinguish the organisation from its competitors, on the other). Simultaneously, effectiveness implies that employee reward policies and processes are attuned to environmental conditions while also retaining a focus on enactment of a specific corporate strategy.

 SELF-ASSESSMENT EXERCISE*

Draw up a list of factors that employers and employees may hold in common in terms of employee reward, and highlight areas where there is scope for interests to diverge. What are the implications for day-to-day effort–reward bargaining?

* This is the first in a series of two types of activity we invite *Employee Reward* readers to engage in, to help them in actively thinking through and assessing argument and evidence presented. This 'self -assessment exercise' is something that may be undertaken as part of private study; a second set of themes presented at various points throughout the book under the heading 'student exercise' may be appropriate as a classroom session or, outside the formal learning environment, informally in conversation with peers or 'learning sets'.

ORIENTATIONS TOWARDS WORKFORCE MEMBERS

To develop proficiency in thinking about and practising employee reward, it helps to make connections systematically between the alternative approaches available to practitioners and the consequences of the choices exercised, paying attention to the context in which decisions will be taken and acted upon. Given the need to continuously renew the 'effort bargain', as defined above, one contextual influence on choices between alternative reward approaches and their consequences concerns the dynamic interaction between expectations among those involved regarding the character of their relationships. Explicit and implicit managerial orientations towards workforce members signal to employees how to perceive how their employer regards them. While it is possible the approach may be standardised across an organisation, it is likely that it will differ to some extent at least between different workforce segments/locations/times. The commentary organised in Table 1.1 works through these basic orientations, suggesting possible consequences for the managerial reward agenda.

The commentary in Table 1.1 illustrates the nature and implications of regarding workforce members as assets or liabilities on a 'human capital balance sheet'. It also casts them in the guise of 'customers' for the 'employment propositions' an organisation might market, or potential allies in a reciprocal partnership (even if

Table 1.1 Orientations towards the workforce: reward management implications

Interpretation	Issues	Reward agenda
'Employees are "our greatest asset" ... they need to be used effectively'		
Employees are valuable objects, but devoid of feeling, which are operated by the owner or agent for maximum utility.	How do we source compliant objects? How do we keep them in prime shape to do our bidding? Pump-priming, instrumental relationship.	Buy on 'contingency terms'. Service regularly (by service agent?). Run to breakdown: refurbish or write off and replace. Utility (exploitative) orientation?
'Employees are a liability ... they need to be controlled'		
Employees are 'debts' for which one is liable, or troublesome responsibilities, and therefore need to be limited, assiduously policed or expunged.	How do we minimise our 'debts'? How do we keep them under close surveillance? Wary, possibly antagonistic relationship.	Minimise cost of 'debt'. Arm's-length relations. Ensure ability to write off liability at earliest opportunity. Resigned-utility orientation?
'Employees are "customers" ... understand and serve them'		
Employees are independent beings; they exercise choices based on logic *and* emotion. They will offer loyalty to a 'supplier' of employment/ reward if they believe the promise and see results.	What 'customers' do we want? What can we (afford to) supply? What are the alternatives? Active supplier role to continuously renew an employee-centred relationship.	Understand 'customer' preferences Honest and transparent response with specification available. Regular client relationship review. Service orientation?
'Employees are "corporate allies" ... develop a mutual success agenda'		
Employees are independent beings; they exercise choices based on logic *and* emotion. They will offer commitment to organisational partners if they believe in them and see results in the substance and process of the effort–reward bargain.	What allies do we need and desire? What can we (afford to) trade? What are the alternatives? Active partner role to continuously renew a mutually profitable employment relationship.	Understand allies' needs and priorities. Honest and transparent response: accommodation available? Regular alliance relationship dialogue. Reciprocal commitment orientation?

in the final analysis the employer retains residual rights over the economic value created).

In the first two orientations, employees appear to be viewed either as emotionally inert, despite recognised potential to add value to organisational activity. Or they are perceived as a source of unwelcome intrusion into an organisational model that management would rather do without – perhaps to replace workers with mechanisation through investment in physical technology. A third orientation follows the conceptual thread that if people really do represent 'our greatest assets', the consequence is that the employer needs to find ways of 'selling' an employment 'brand', implying that employees hold the upper hand in the transaction. A fourth orientation towards the workforce signals that, while the employer recognises the latent value in people who may be persuaded to work for the organisation – still carrying a risk that the relationship may become employee-dependent (see eg Pfeffer and Salancik, 2003) – both parties have choices open to them.

A mixture of economic and socio-psychological factors may condition the choices. Rather than risk extrinsic or intrinsic contractual promises the rhetoric of which may fall short of the reality, owing to unplanned circumstances – for example, changes in investment or trading conditions that might undermine the 'ability to pay' – an employer may signal an orientation in which each party to the employment relationship focuses on the process of reaching an accommodation, involving continuous and transparent mutual reflection on an holistic 'deal'. As Herriot and Pemberton (1995) argue, this may in turn require a 'renegotiate or exit' orientation on the part of the employee. But the task open to managerial initiative is one of setting clear 'rules of engagement' and, by actions rather than words alone, communicating the potential for an employment relationship, founded on mutual trust and respect. Such 'employment alliances' imply the scope for conflicting positions to arise between the parties – perhaps acknowledged as inevitable – with a willingness to explore the room for compromise and (possibly short-term) trade-off to secure the long-term benefits with which the 'partnership' ideal is imbued by stakeholders.

This may all sound rather esoteric: fine in principle – but what about the practice? Two examples may help illustrate issues to be weighed in considering alternatives and consequences in employer orientations towards employees.

PERIPHERY TO CORE

One of the authors served on a large UK National Health Service Trust board of directors, overseeing a new hospital building project under public/private partnership commercial terms. To the great concern of employees working in 'support' services associated with keeping the hospital running day to day (catering staff, 'domestics' and other ancillary workers), the project plans involved the TUPE-transfer of their employment to the new private management partner. A potentially damaging employment relations dispute was averted when the senior hospital administrators explained to groups of employees affected that, being honest, they would always find themselves as peripheral workers – in effect, 'liabilities' or 'second-class', when viewed against the Trust's clinicians and nursing professionals. Without necessarily compromising the psychological contract they believed they had entered into in joining the NHS, they would remain members of a 'healthcare partnership', but enhanced by transition to 'core workforce' status in their new employment relationship.

The implication was a basis for effort–reward bargaining where their interests were potentially advanced, not only in extrinsic reward but also in terms of scope for recognition, personal and career development, and the sense of 'involvement'. Irrespective of what transpired, the point is that an employer may find decisive action – in this case transferring a workforce segment into an outsourced arrangement – a more satisfactory option on both sides of the effort bargain than one hampered by half-hearted managerial commitment.

PROMISE MEETS PRACTICE

The same author undertook an enquiry for a sub-set of the European partners of a large professional services firm. During the transformation the organisation was undergoing at the time, an announcement was made by its corporate leadership with great fanfare on both sides of the Atlantic that, with the explicit intention of creating conditions in which the firm's managerial and professional employees would adopt the highest quality service orientation towards clients, the firm would treat its people as 'clients' too in their employment relationship. The investigation involved focus group discussions with a cross-section of managers and professionals across a fairly wide geographical base, one telling remark from which might be interpreted as necessitating caution when top managers consider 'talking up' the employment promise. The partners 'treat us as no more than money-making machines', the researchers were told. Clearly, although no doubt well-intentioned from the 'bridge', at 'deck' level 'crew members' received a distorted 'orientation signal'.

 SELF-ASSESSMENT EXERCISE

Two case cameo illustrations have been provided covering the 'liabilities' and 'customers' segments in Table 1.1. To test your understanding, search for some company annual report and accounts statements in which the seemingly ubiquitous 'people as greatest assets' statement appears in the chairman's statement or similar commentary. Then look for statements embedded in reports, or in other sources of corporate information (eg company websites and/or analysts' appraisals). To what extent do you find these consistent with the 'assets' principle, or are there indications of more partnership orientations? You might conduct a similar 'audit' of your own organisation or one known to you.

Discussion to this point has signalled that management faces a series of alternatives for approaching employee reward – as do employees. Various consequences follow on from adopting one or other mode of engagement with this complex aspect of organisation and people management. The consequences flowing from employee reward choices, whether conditioned by tradition or 'new' logic for organising, may be viewed in terms of the nature of expectations the parties hold, the quality of the relationships and the underlying principles regulating their interaction. In the following section, we introduce the basis on which for the purpose of this book commentary has been organised to guide readers in navigating and interpreting the mass of reported evidence on the ways in which alternative employee reward approaches are discussed and operate in practice, and the consequences that have been observed by employment researchers, paying attention to context. We do so by reference to the habitually mentioned but rarely specified notion of the 'reward system'.

EMPLOYEE REWARD: A SYSTEMS APPROACH

Commentary in the human resource management literature frequently refers to reward (or compensation, pay or remuneration) *systems* (eg Boxall and Purcell, 2008; Heery and Noon, 2001; Kessler, 2005, 2007; Marchington and Wilkinson, 2005; Milkovich and Newman, 2004; Ulrich, 1997). But we can find little in the debates among management and social science commentators that explicitly justifies why a 'systems' view of employee reward is appropriate, or using ideas featuring in 'general systems theory' (von Bertalanffy, 1969).

While pursuing a search for underlying regularities that characterise the world in general, Ludwig von Bertalanffy, a biologist and the founding father of general systems theory, adopted the 'system' as 'an organising concept' to help overcome differences between different academic disciplines (Burrell and Morgan, 1979: 58). A system is formed from 'elements and parts that are organised and interdependent' (Holmwood, 2006: 587). Systems can be either 'closed' or 'open'. Closed systems are exemplified by conventional physics that isolates systems from their environments, for example, the 'controlled experiment' where phenomena are exposed to testing but isolated from the places in which such phenomena naturally occur. Closed systems, von Bertalanffy (1969) argues, will by definition become independent from their environment, but this will undermine attempts to understand the system as a dynamic phenomenon in continuous interaction with other, contextually linked, systems.

In direct contrast to a closed system, an 'open systems' approach draws attention not just to the structure or substance of phenomena but to the processes that impact on the system, and its impact in turn on those other systems with which it interacts. Open systems 'engage in transactions with their environment, "importing" and "exporting" and changing themselves in the process', continuously 'building up and breaking down ... component parts' (Burrell and Morgan, 1979: 59). Thus, open systems theory offers a route for studying 'the pattern of relationships which characterise a system and its relationship to its environment in order to *understand* the way in which it operates' and so to 'discern different types of open system in practice' (Burrell and Morgan, 1979: 59, emphasis in original).

It is possible to consider a reward system as 'closed' or self-contained. As will be discussed in Chapter 2, classical economics theory on wage determination assumes away environmental factors (or context), using the 'all other things being equal' clause. Treating reward systems as 'open' may be more realistic in the context of the contemporary economy. Organisations and their sub-systems interact with an increasingly interconnected division of labour across a capitalist 'world system' (Wallerstein, 1983), in which organisations of different sizes and stages of development enter into a diversity of employment relationships with people in locations that are also at various stages of development and change.

Moreover, consistent with the integrationist 'HRM' approach, as discussed in Chapter 12, within the organisation itself reward systems may be deliberately located as in continuous interaction with internal 'environmental conditions' derived vertically from corporate strategies and horizontally from other people management structures and processes. Depending on the viewpoint of the commentator, the direction of influence vertically and horizontally is debatable. Nonetheless, ideas from open systems theory may help encourage reflexivity around employee reward: whether or not specifically goal-directed, a reward system may evolve, regress or disintegrate, not only experiencing change itself but also possibly influencing changes to an organisational environment, possibly spilling over into an external employment system in the process.

An example of this may be the arrival of a large multinational corporation in a developing or transforming economy, where the inward investors and their managerial agents may introduce practices that begin to reshape a competitive environment for effort–reward bargaining. Choosing between a closed or open systems perspective has important consequences for the underlying assumptions accompanying the theories that help to interpret and understand how and why reward systems function. Theorists debate alternative explanations for adaptation within and between non-static systems, including provisions for addressing conflict and creating consensus among the actors within the system, underscored by the institutional context for employee reward (see below).

CRITICISMS OF SYSTEMS THINKING

Despite the influence that the 'systems approach' has had on various branches of management and social science since the mid-twentieth century, systems theory may be criticised when its users do little more than propose the reduction of complex phenomena to elements that may be observed and where possible experimented on, while promising not to forget that in reality the parts need to be considered 'holistically' and in 'interaction' (Burrell and Morgan, 1979).

Within the social sciences, 'grand theory'-building attempts to explain modern society in systems terms by American sociologist, Talcott Parsons, in the 1950s, have been dismissed as assuming common values among populations which, given the diversity of people within and across the world's nations, lack empirical grounding (Abercrombie et al, 2000). A prediction that societies would come to mirror the industrial and employment system characteristic of the USA (Kerr *et al*, 1964) has remained controversial. Important criticisms are associated with the potential of analysts to confer a self-determining (or 'reified') status on socio-economic systems, over-emphasising *systems* while neglecting *action* (Holmwood, 2006). In Chapter 2, for example, we take a critical look at the classical labour economist's view that vests ultimate authority in market forces in regulating the employee reward system.

Another important criticism has been the argument that social systems theory is couched in conservative ideology, and lacks the capacity to deal adequately with the presence of conflict and change in social life. This latter point may be answered to some extent by reference back to the more sophisticated project on which von Bertalanffy embarked. Attention may be paid to sources of influence, for example, in settling the terms of the effort–reward bargain: the necessity for individuals to interpret aspects of both the extrinsic and intrinsic employment relationship implies that, while management, as the 'keepers' of organisational and employment resources, may enjoy a 'dispositional' advantage in framing the offer (Edwards, 1986; 2003), the position remains indeterminate (Shields, 2007). Managers may not be assumed to act consistently, and employees may interpret their roles in ways that have unforeseen consequences in line neither with the intended corporate strategic nor a lateral HRM direction.

For the purposes of shaping discussion in the present book, while not ignoring the limitations of systems thinking as this may be applied to *reward* systems, it seems appropriate to remain sensitive to the ways in which reward design elements interact with one another, and with other systemic features observable at various levels of environmental analysis (eg those connected with managerial strategy and with other human resource management designs and activity inside the organisation; and with economic markets, and other institutions, such as the law, shareholders, trade unions, etc, located externally). The ways in which reward system actors may seek to regulate the effort–reward bargain, processing information and learning from feedback mechanisms within an open system setting, to modify and refine their orientation to the employment relationship, generate themes that, we would argue, deserve the attention of what the CIPD terms 'thinking HR performers' (CIPD, 2007).

 STUDENT EXERCISE

Discuss the benefits of approaching the analysis of employee reward systems as proposed above. Considering the criticisms we have sketched, why do you think a systems approach may have been popular among social analysts?

A FEW WORDS ON OUR TRIPARTITE TAXONOMY

This book reviews theory and practice associated with employee reward systems interacting with the employment relationship and concomitant effort–reward bargain. To create a thematic focus for the discussion of material assembled, the emphasis throughout is on the alternatives that call for decision-making, carrying consequences in each case, which may be interpreted in and conditioned by particular and changing contexts. Before concluding the chapter with a summary of the book's overall content and structure, at this point a short statement is appropriate on what the authors intend to convey through the 'alternatives, consequences and context' refrain.

An **alternative** is located in a proposition containing two (sometimes more) statements, or offer of two (or more) things, the acceptance of one of which involves the rejection of the other(s). Alternative possibilities, alternative statements of some position, may exist, open to the exercise of choice by social actors. Decision-takers are required to make selections between alternatives, electing for one course of action over one or more alternatives. Exercising 'choice' (the 'act of choosing'), involves 'preferential determination between things proposed'. A choice may be exercised managerially, for example, to reward employees for time they commit to the employer or on their performance. Each of the parties has a choice of how to approach the effort–reward bargain, and this is likely to be influenced by the assumptions and priorities they bring to the interaction and the nature of the relationship involved.

Being positioned to exercise choice locates decision-takers socially relative to others and implies, among other things, making judgements to secure the most favourable (or fit-for-purpose) outcome, to attain something that is worthy of being chosen, having *special* value relative to other available options. Choices are logically followed by consequences: it is an open question whether or not the decision-takers base their selection between alternatives either on logically conjectured projections or by reference to empirical evidence of past outcomes, to assist the process of judgement in pursuit of a preferred outcome (ie one that is anticipated and accords with the project being pursued by the chooser). Actors called to exercise choices in terms of the effort–reward bargain (managers and/ or employees) may be influenced by reference to 'benchmark' data on practice reported elsewhere or experience over time during the course of a particular employment relationship or employment relations in general. They may also be faced by ideas from advisers and other opinion-formers about what is deemed fitting or cost-effective in the circumstances.

A **consequence** may be described as something that follows as an action or condition, effect or result, from something preceding or antecedent to that consequence. A consequence following a particular act of choosing may be considered as *predetermined* (ie located within a cause-and-effect relationship). Where social relations are involved, as in the case of weighing alternatives in effort–reward bargaining, the situation is unlikely to be so clear-cut, however. While consequences may form a logical sequence starting with a specific choice, opening them to logical deduction from certain premises, a caveat is necessary.

That the consequence of an action, or decision to act, may be logically inferred (involving the exercise of judgement) is suggestive of a position where absolute certainty may be open to question. Hence, logical deductions may usefully be tested drawing on an existing pool of relevant empirical knowledge.

Adopting an alternative definition, choices may lead to outcomes that are 'of consequence': that is, they are endowed with importance ('assumed consequentiality'). They have an impact (positive or negative) on the people and circumstances in which the choice plays out. The corollary of this assertion is that scope for systematic reflection on inferred consequences – prior to action – merits the attention of parties involved in effort–reward bargaining, and those whose role is to advise them, whether as employees, managers, national/supranational government policy-makers, or other stakeholders in the complex field of employee reward. At minimum, systemic-looped feedback reflection and learning may help improve the quality of judgement exercised under emergent conditions.

Selection decisions between alternative effort–reward bargain approaches do not occur in isolation. In systems terms, the selections between alternatives by groups of decision-takers interact with the choices exercised by others, and in each case their choices may be viewed as reflecting particular interests. For example, managerial decisions to select one 'reward strategy' and thus reject others will interact with decision-taking by other groups of managers, as well as employees who may be the targets of such decision-taking. How alternatives are weighed and acted on, and the consequences that follow, are open to influence from the context (or environment) in which organisations are situated and how it is interpreted by the parties to the effort–reward bargain.

Interaction between the elements perceived as systematically regulating the employment relationship and effort–reward bargain may be theorised as 'context-bound' or 'context-free'. Reference to **context** describes action to weave or sew together 'contexted' phenomena to facilitate interpretation and possibly explanation. If something is contextual the implication is of a situation belonging to the context – if not standing in a dependency relation with then at least influenced *systematically* by the context.

The context for employee reward and the alternatives and consequences associated with its determination may be framed in terms of corporate, national and international systems. Managerially, the scale and sector of an organisation, its predominant technological make-up (affecting the balance of emphasis in the capabilities required to resource operations), its history and the predisposition of those who lead and make up the general membership may be viewed as bounding to some extent employee reward policy alternatives deemed legitimate. Adopting an open systems perspective, external to the organisation, context is likely to reflect the nature of its ownership, and the influence of the various stakeholders and other institutions with whom the organisation's members may be perceived to have a relationship – such as business partners, investor groups, state regulators representing a 'public interest', trade unions and so on. Also, the competitive environment, for sources of investment and revenue (not forgetting employee 'talent'), is likely to influence profitability and the disposition of management to invest in the effort–reward bargain.

It has been remarked that, over two decades, two themes – 'abiding confidence in the march of globalisation and progress' – have remained in the foreground (Franklin, 2006). While uncritical acceptance of this position is to be discouraged, beyond the internal organisational setting and its immediate context, as noted earlier, an increasingly significant influence on organisation systems, and on HRM and employee reward systems, is attributed to the 'global context'. A recurring theme in the literature is the question of whether or not approaches to employment regulation are converging internationally or whether they remain divergent, owing to the influence of culture and institutional factors within particular national systems (Anakwe, 2002; Katz and Darbishire, 2000; Sparrow, 1999).

Whether or not the organisation employs people across geo-ethnic borders, it may be argued that regional and global employment systems need to be factored in to attempts to evaluate the alternative ways of approaching the effort–reward bargain. A common governance architecture for contemporary 'business systems' may be assumed (Whitley, 2000), that is, capitalist principles inform the basis on which actors will seek to arrange the affairs of organisations and those of the national and international systems within which they are situated (Coates, 2000; Furåker, 2005).

Even if it is accepted that capitalism provides the dominant organising logic, however, alternative 'varieties of capitalism' (Albert, 1992; Hall and Soskice, 2001) have been postulated, reflecting the institutional basis for reaching 'social peace' as an antecedent of successful economic production (Roe, 2003: 1). Although a 'directional convergence' around particular sets of policies and practices for the management of organisations, including effort-bargaining orientations, may be open to perception, 'final convergence' may not be reliably assumed (Tregaskis and Brewster, 2006). Detailed policies and practices may reflect different interpretations of the opportunities and limitations of the global, national and organisational settings in which choices between alternatives are being made. The accent may vary according to the systematic interaction between economic, historical, legal, political, social and technological factors, in turn affected by cultural and psychological factors – that is, the influence of socialisation on decision-makers' interpretations of perceived opportunities and limitations.

The institutional context for employee reward is discussed in Chapter 3 and, specifically in the case of executive reward, in Chapter 10. In-depth treatment of the transnational context for corporate governance and knowledge mobilisation features in Chapter 11.

In short, it is our position that understanding employee reward will be assisted by attention to themes systematically arising as the parties evaluate and act on the range of alternative courses of action open to them and reflection, conceptually and empirically, on consequences that may follow from these choices. In the case of both alternatives and consequences the influence of the open systemic context in which alternatives occur and are weighed and consequences are played out is something that needs to be accounted for in drawing conclusions, which may in turn inform policy and practice.

 STUDENT EXERCISE

Consider the argument that, owing to the scale of western multinationals, their preferences for determining reward systems will tend to prevail across the countries in which they set up operations. To what extent can you build an alternative, or 'divergence', perspective? Are the tendencies polar opposites?

KEY LEARNING POINTS AND CONCLUSIONS

To summarise, in this chapter, we have defined employee reward, reflecting on its various manifestations, and introduced the concept of the effort–reward bargain and the consequences of applying this theoretical notion when trying to make sense of interaction between the parties to the employment relationship. We have introduced a model encouraging reflection on the orientations employers may adopt towards their employees when evaluating reward alternatives and the consequences implied, positing four possible scenarios. We have also briefly appraised the merits and criticisms of applying systems thinking when conceptualising employee reward. Commentary on developments in the corporate, national and international context for employee reward has been briefly appraised to situate alternative employee reward designs and the consequences that may follow from selected applications.

For postgraduate students following a specialist module in Employee Reward, the book can be used sequentially. Chapters have been written mindful of the CIPD Employee Reward Professional Standards, appropriate extracts from which are summarised at the beginning of each chapter. We have designed the content and style of the book as a text to support CIPD-related students in particular but also, we hope, to be of relevance to other readers interested in this important subject associated with people at work and their management. Students of general management and those following final-year undergraduate and postgraduate HRM programmes may find it beneficial initially to engage with Part One, in order to locate selective engagement with subsequent content, depending on specific interests or assigned work. Throughout the book, commentary is illustrated using calls for 'self-assessment' and other exercises, to inform discussion of issues raised. The intention is also to assist readers' preparation in addressing examination questions. Case study material appears at various points to illustrate conceptual arguments. To conclude the present chapter, a summary follows setting out a plan of the overall text.

PLAN OF THE BOOK

The book is structured in four parts over 12 chapters, including this introduction.

Part One deals with concepts, theory and the institutional context for employee reward alternative approaches and consequences.

While conceptual and theoretical frameworks inform the treatment of employee reward throughout the book, in **Chapter 2** particular attention is devoted to the principal attempts to theorise the subject. Acting as a reference point for what follows in subsequent chapters, models may be identified drawing on a multidisciplinary academic literature – principally (labour) economics, industrial/organisational psychology, employment relations, management strategy, and the sociology of organisations and work. Emerging themes include the extent to which employee reward is something open to 'management'; assumptions about people and work motivation under conditions of employment; and the social and political interactions around the effort–reward bargain.

A complementary foundational discussion – this time covering the legal and employment relations environment – is presented in **Chapter 3**. The material includes the impact of principal legislation and related regulatory developments affecting employee reward determination, beyond economic market influences, along with the role of collective bargaining where applicable. The increasing impact of European legislation on UK reward systems design is specifically considered, illustrating the dynamic nature of the institutional environment for employee reward.

Part Two introduces and evaluates structures and processes for extrinsic reward determination, describing some of the practicalities of their design and operation.

The basic architecture of pay systems is the focus of **Chapter 4**. Descriptions of and arguments for applying 'pay structures' are examined, including alternative types of pay structure, and conditions affecting their design and operation. Many pay structures are underscored by an aspiration to create the conditions for 'internal equity'. The objective has become even more important with the development of anti-discrimination regulatory frameworks. The concept, role, alternative approaches and administration of 'job evaluation' are discussed together with its impact on pay structures. Debate surrounding 'job' or 'role' analysis as the basis for structuring pay, as well as questions and practicalities regarding alignment of pay structures with external markets for jobs and people, is appraised.

Alternative approaches to 'base' pay determination, salary progression management and their consequences are reviewed in **Chapter 5**. Wages systems and salary systems are compared, as are 'seniority-' or 'service'-related pay versus pay 'contingent' on inputs (eg skills) or outputs (eg pre-set target achievement) or combined under the rubric of 'contribution-based pay'. The critical part played by 'performance management' and the centrality of line managers to the process of managing contingent pay systems is reviewed. The role of 'compensatory payments' for working 'flexibly', in particular beyond contracted 'basic' hours, administered either in piecemeal form or by applying alternatives such as 'annualised hours', is assessed. The practice of augmenting pay using concepts such as 'premiums' related to specific employment markets is also discussed.

Beyond time-based systems, the notion and variety of 'variable pay' (as a performance-motivating 'incentive' or 'reinforcement' device) is reviewed in **Chapter 6**. Short-term and long-term, individual, team and organisational 'bonus' payments, including profit-related pay and profit sharing, gain-sharing, as well as equity (share) based 'financial participation' initiatives that may be applied to some or all workforce segments are described and evaluated. The discussion includes 'sales bonuses' and other incentives for particular workforce segments.

Part Three reviews principles, policies and frameworks for 'non-cash benefits', 'deferred remuneration' and 'intrinsic rewards'.

Employee benefits and allowances, and policies for their application, are the subject of **Chapter 7**. Typologies of benefits – 'welfare', 'compensatory' or 'status'; types of benefits; 'single status' and 'harmonisation', flexible (or 'cafeteria') systems – are appraised. The principal employee benefits that may be applied beyond salary and wages and their roles (eg legal minima versus 'perks') are discussed. The interrelationship between employee benefits and taxation and social insurance systems – which vary significantly according to the national context – is reviewed.

Given its increasingly contentious and 'strategic' role within employee reward, **Chapter 8** is devoted to debates around pensions – a 'deferred' form of remuneration. Consideration begins with a discussion of the development and role of 'superannuation schemes', situating the topic in historical perspective, moving to examination of the contemporary and contested role of the state vs employers vs private insurance providers in employee 'retirement' provision. The main types of pension scheme are introduced, linked to their role within a reward management programme. Government policy intervention and the future of pensions provision are also analysed.

The increasing attention directed towards forms of 'non-financial reward' focuses discussion in **Chapter 9**. The concept is defined and related to notions of 'total reward', the 'employment proposition' and emerging ideas around 'employee engagement', aligning extrinsic reward with the 'psychological contract'. The question of why this factor may be of increasing importance in reward policy is investigated, accounting for issues such as 'employee recognition', 'workforce diversity' and its consequences for reward management, as well as 'career management' and 'employee involvement' initiatives.

Part Four gives specific attention to rewarding employees who have a direct influence on corporate governance, as well as the employee reward implications of organisational expansion requiring transnational knowledge mobilisation. Finally, attention turns specifically to questions around alignment between organisational strategy, HRM and employee reward management.

Rewarding corporate executives and directors is discussed in **Chapter 10**. Ideas on the composition and management of reward for employees occupying senior managerial roles are reviewed. This discussion is complemented by engagement with the corporate governance and 'top pay' debate, including the role of remuneration committees and advisers; 'executive incentives' (short-term and longer-term approaches, cash- and/ or equity-based); executive benefits and perquisites; contractual conditions; compliance and public disclosure requirements.

Developments in international reward management are appraised in **Chapter 11**. Factors impacting on the design of transnational reward systems are assessed. Questions around 'globalisation' and corporate structure propositions, focused on 'knowledge mobilisation', are considered, along with the extent to which these give rise to standardisation in employee reward management practice across 'multi-local' environments, as well as the part played by reward systems in supporting employee expatriation programmes. Expatriate–local reward management opportunities and threats in the competitive climate for multinational enterprise are also critically reviewed. The emerging role of information technology in communicating and calibrating international reward practice is introduced.

To conclude the book on an integrative and thematic note, **Chapter 12** covers the role of reward within 'HRM'. The growing importance of a strategic approach to people management in general and reward in particular, with a focus on vertical integration along one dimension, complementing horizontal integration along another, to ensure consistency across the range of people management policies and practices, is highlighted. Contested literature, where universalism and 'best practice' (including 'The New Pay' ideology and its impact on practice) meet more 'contingency-based' and 'critical' commentary, is reviewed. Roles attributable to the managerial parties to employee reward systems, in particular the interface between specialists and line managers under the HRM rubric, are appraised.

EXPLORE FURTHER

For a discussion comparing and contrasting prescription, empirical evaluation, critical materialist and post-structuralist commentary, see Shields, J. (2007) *Managing Employee Performance and Reward: concepts, practices, strategies.* Cambridge, Cambridge University Press.

For a critical appraisal of debates around the imperatives of 'reward strategy' as though this were an alternative to managing equity-based factors implicit in the effort–reward bargain, see Kessler, I. (2007) 'Reward choices: strategy and equity', in Storey, J. (ed.) *Human Resource Management: a critical text*, 3rd edn London, Thompson: 159–76.

For a treatment of employment systems contexts, see Rubery, J. and Grimshaw, D. (2003) *The Organization of Employment: an international perspective.* Basingstoke, Palgrave Macmillan.

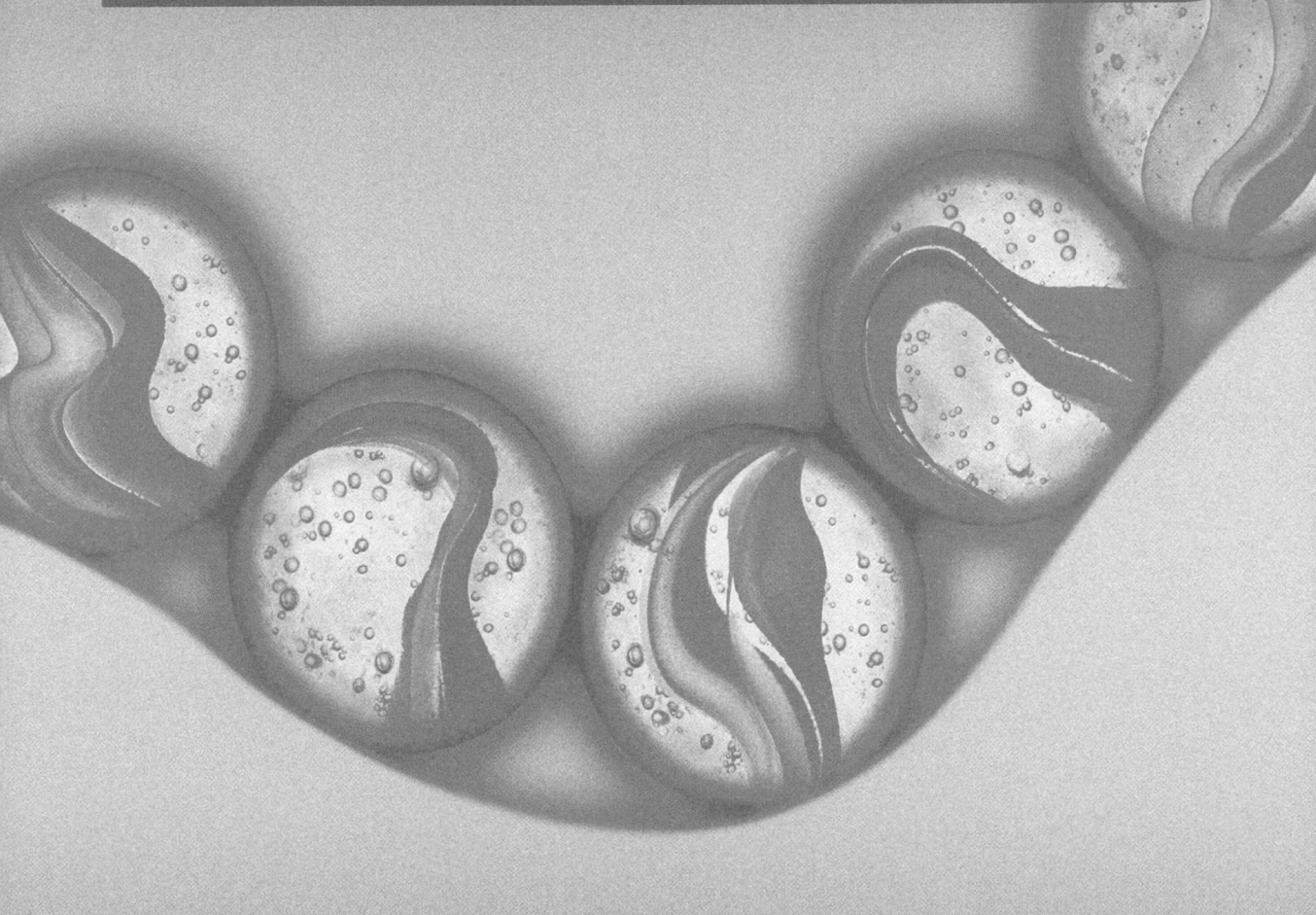

PART ONE

In Part One we engage with concepts, theory and the institutional context for employee reward alternative approaches and consequences. The initial chapter reviews the range of theory that informs ideas and practice on employee reward, to help students to grasp frameworks likely to help them when addressing subsequent aspects of the book's coverage. In the chapter that follows, issues are considered around the institutional context for contemporary employee reward systems.

CHAPTER 2

Conceptual and Theoretical Frameworks

CHAPTER OBJECTIVES

At the end of this chapter you should understand and be able to explain the following:

- Key concepts and theories to help interpret expectations, relationships and regulation among the parties to the effort–reward bargain.

CIPD STANDARDS COVERED IN THIS CHAPTER:

To understand and explain:

- The concepts of reward system, reward structure and reward levels.

- The key economic, psychological and motivational theories that influence reward policies and practices.

- The factors that influence employee satisfaction with their rewards and the reward system, such as equity, fairness, consistency and transparency.

INTRODUCTION

In Chapter 1 we introduced the 'effort–reward bargain', giving rise to some basic questions between the parties. From the **employer/managerial** perspective, drawing on Milkovich and Newman (2004), two strategic problems are:

1 how do we set the *necessary* level of expenditure on employee reward, and

2 how can the substance and process of employee reward be used, if at all, to influence employee work attitudes and behaviours?

To describe something as 'strategic' implies that it involves the exercise of *choice* among alternatives, where limited resources are being committed, with consequences that are likely to apply beyond the short term.

From the **employee** viewpoint, the issues include what return can be obtained for making available to an employer skills and experience (or 'human capital') – as well as time and contribution to value-creating activities – that is both fair and equitable. Thus both practical and ethical considerations apply.

Applying our 'systems' conceptualisation, in this chapter we examine alternative approaches to interpreting and addressing these basic employee reward questions, and the consequences of choosing between the alternative explanations on offer. In other words, we evaluate conceptual and theoretical knowledge that, explicitly or implicitly, interacts with practical action on the part of individuals representing themselves and their organisations.

There is, of course, a danger in addressing the 'applied' problems associated with employee reward at levels abstracted from 'real-world' contexts. Theoretical frameworks can give no more than a partial picture of the world; and 'seemingly neutral concepts may carry hidden value assumptions' (Furåker, 2005: 2). Thus, before we embark on an excursion into alternative ways of thinking about employee reward and their consequences in context, we address the question, why use theory at all? We also explore the assumptions and frames of reference informing ideas about 'reward strategies' and their expected outcomes.

WHY IS THEORY IMPORTANT?

Responses to the basic questions about employee reward posed above are likely to be influenced by whom you ask. Over the years, debate on employee reward has been 'heavily informed and structured by conceptual, analytical and theoretical frameworks from various disciplines' (Kessler, 2001: 206). The ways questions are framed and answered reflect the contrasting assumptions and priorities of these disciplines, as well as debates among commentators within them. Practising managers, who have their own assumptions and preoccupations in relation to employee reward, may find the resulting outpouring of commentary – whether prescriptive (how *should* we determine employee reward) or analytical (how *do* we actually determine it according to research) – confusing and/or downright irritating.

In the face of all this inconclusive discussion, it seems reasonable to ask 'why get involved in theory at all?' Employee reward is an applied field – whether the interested parties are employers or employees, or their representatives, or state policy-makers. Why not simply follow 'practical' steps to work out what is the best course of action on the basis of trial and error? Indeed, it could be argued that people management practice in Britain largely gets along without explicit models and frameworks to guide people management. For example, the WERS 1998 study found only 14 per cent of workplaces applied the 'HRM model' (eg that outlined by Guest, 1987) comprehensively (Cully *et al*, 1999).

From the viewpoint of the HR 'thinking performer', however, it may be wise to treat the concept of employee reward, and strategies for managing it, as problematic. And in addressing this employee reward 'puzzle', 'there is nothing so practical as a good theory' (Lewin, 1947, cited in Caldwell, 2006: 49). In short:

Theory deals with concepts and their interrelationships and is aimed at helping us understand and explain how and why things happen in the world. (Furåker, 2005: 2)

THE MAJOR THEORETICAL UNDERPINNINGS TO EMPLOYEE REWARD

While there are prescriptions on offer implying 'one best way' to manage reward, the range and contested nature of theory implies that this is a complex process. Each approach comes with underlying assumptions about the nature of people and organisations, about how social and management science may be mobilised to 'know' those environments, and about the methodologies for gathering and interpreting data to develop that knowledge (Burrell and Morgan, 1979). Assumptions underlying alternative theories for making sense of reward systems extend to the expectations of the parties, and the legitimacy with which their relationships may be regulated. Like other systems, 'systems of thought' evolve, regress or disintegrate, importing and exporting ideas and organising models within and between them.

Academic disciplines through which employee reward may be theorised include economics, industrial relations, occupational psychology, political science, organisational sociology and strategic HRM. Each of these emphasise different aspects of the reward relationship between employers, employees and other stakeholders (such as the state). For example:

- An economist might concentrate on how 'market forces' bring employers and employees into contact and sanction wage rates. The emphasis tends to be on determinants rather than consequences of employee reward: an economist's question might be, why do wage differentials exist?

- A traditional industrial relations focus might be on how wage rates may be 'marked up' owing to the presence of institutions such as employer associations and trade unions, engaged in forms of collective bargaining.

- The occupational psychologist might direct attention to the human 'drives' or internalised preferences leading people to seek out extrinsic and intrinsic forms of reward and recognition, or processes by which an individual's motivation to work may be influenced positively or negatively.

- Those interested in political forces at play in work organisations might position the analytical spotlight on the relative power to extract effort and to establish the criteria for reward distribution among individuals and groups within economic value-creating environments.

- Organisational sociologists might encourage exploration of the values and orientations employees bring to the workplace as both individuals and groups, and the likely impact on how they perceive the fairness or 'equity' of the employment relationship.

- Strategic HRM commentators might seek to identify and measure the systematic alignment of employee reward designs with business aims, other people management practices and organisational performance.

These varying agendas mean that explanations and priorities may be in competition with one another for decision-makers' attention. The law (eg on minimum wage levels and on equal pay for work of equal value) also has a role to play in approaching employee reward policy and practice, as discussed in Chapter 3. The 'systems orientation' selected also may be seen as influencing priorities for specifying and answering questions. Closed system thinking may pay little attention to the behaviour of individuals and groups, saying markets or instincts will settle pay outcomes and associated behaviour. More open systems analysis, in contrast, may offer increased scope for goal-directed managerial interventions in employee reward. This may, however, be more historically or more future-focused, more individual- or more group-oriented, or accented more towards manipulation or regulation of the reward relationship.

The 'basic' questions with which we began this chapter may thus be approached in a variety of ways. Different theoretical approaches to employee reward may be grouped in terms of either their emphasis on structuring reward, on the one hand, and on the process of reward determination, on the other. A long-standing debate exists too around whether or not extrinsic reward (a term defined in Chapter 1) will directly influence work behaviour or is merely one among a number of influences. Kohn (1993), in fact, sets out 'the case against rewards', at work and in other environments (eg at school), which he regards a form of bribery, with the consequence that 'people who are trying to earn a reward end up doing a poorer job on many tasks than people who are not' (1993: 49). Table 2.1 summarises the ways alternative theories derived from various disciplines may be used to address the three basic employee reward questions we posed at the start of the chapter. The range and interplay of theory around these issues is explored in detail over the following sections of the chapter.

Table 2.1 Employee reward theory and the 'basic questions': a selective overview

Issue	Theory	Source	Comment
'Necessary' expenditure on employee reward			
Labour market allocation and associated wage level determination	Market clearing	Neoclassical economics	Closed system model – external influences are regarded as 'noise'
Employee attraction and retention in high-skill contexts	Human capital	Institutional economics	Premium attracted by valuable experience/skills
Secure control over employee labour power and retain core skills	Exchange theory Efficiency wages	Institutional economics	Bargains to limit instrumental behaviour by employees that carries greater costs to employers

Issue	Theory	Source	Comment
Maintain stability of production + avoid spot market 'deals' (financed by monopoly profits)	Internal labour market Rent-sharing/ gift exchange Wage-gap/union mark-up	Institutional economics Industrial relations	Generally a feature of large private firms or public sector organisations
Create an incentive for those at or close to top of hierarchy	Tournaments and winner-take-all regimes	Management economics	Assumes top talent creates supernormal corporate profits
Managerial influence on work attitudes and behaviour from investment employee reward			
Job/role design to delimit employee discretion	Role	Sociology	Predictive capacity limited by interpretative complexities
Managerial control	Agency	Labour economics/ Strategy	Align employee/employer interests – monitor activity
Employee needs satisfaction	Drive theories (eg two-factor theory; hierarchy of needs theory)	Managerial psychology	Research bias undermines reward-related validity; more useful in focusing attention on job enrichment programmes
Harnessing ability to learn	Reinforcement theory	Managerial psychology	Sensitivity required to avoid harming implicit contract
Providing incentive for future-facing effort	Goal theory Expectancy theory	Managerial psychology	Care needed that signals are perceived as informational rather than attempted control
Controlling or informational signals to employees	Cognitive evaluation theory	Managerial psychology	Adults in work environments engage reflexively with their supervisors in continuous effort–reward bargaining
Fair returns for investment of human capital with an employer			
Perceptions of organisational justice	Distributive justice Procedural justice Interpersonal justice	Political science/ Sociology	Attention to process as much as the substance of employee reward
Trust in employer to respect implicit expectations	Psychological contract theory	Managerial psychology	Care needed to avoid damaging employees' implicit expectations

LABOUR MARKET THEORY

A major concept the employee reward student needs to understand from the start is the concept of a 'labour market'. This term implies that there is competition for labour in the same way that, within a capitalist society, goods and services are traded in a 'market'. Hence employers seek to purchase labour at the best price and workers seek to sell their labour within this market at the best price. Below we consider the main economic theories concerning reward. We begin by looking at classical labour market theory, which has dominated management thinking for over two centuries.

CLASSICAL LABOUR MARKET THEORY

The notion of rational choice by the parties to the effort–reward relationship underpins 'classical' labour market theory. The assumption is that pay will be fixed in the labour market where the demand for workers equates exactly to the supply, known as 'market clearing' (Black, 2002). So when the supply of labour meets employers' demands, employers will have to offer work at that price and workers will have to accept work at that price: this is the 'value of the marginal product of labour' (see Figure 2.1). Taken to its logical conclusion, this theory suggests that there is little point in employers attempting to differentiate themselves from their competitors by paying different (higher) wages as, in the final analysis, everyone has to pay the same as everyone else. 'The only "effective" policy is to pay what others do' (Gerhart and Rynes, 2003: 15). And

Figure 2.1 Wage determination in a perfectly competitive employment market, balancing supply of workers willing to sell a capacity to accept employment (S) with employers' demand for labour (D)

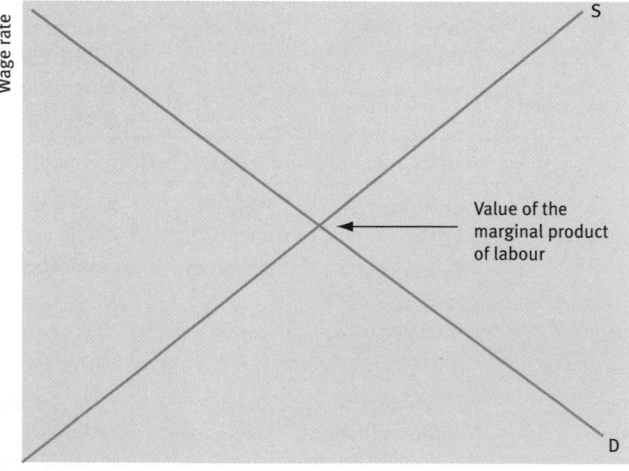

Quantity of labour

since the theory indicates that pay policies will always tend towards equilibrium (or a state of balance), there is little point investigating what other employers do in setting their pay policies and practices. Essentially, employers should expect to pay, and employees should expect to accept, wages for labour determined by an external market. Theoretically, the market regulates the employment relationship: employees make a rational choice to forgo leisure to make themselves available for work. Labour is perceived as a commodity that has a price just like any other.

This self-regulating model of the employment system – attributed to eighteenth-century Scottish economist Adam Smith – and its 'neoclassical' restatements by late nineteenth-century European economists such as Jevons, Menger and Walrus (Watson, 2005) – assumes that each of the parties is free to choose between work and leisure (employees) and to hire or not (employers). Employers will compete for labour with other employers, and employees will compete for paid work with other employees. It is also assumed that each party will be comprehensively informed ('perfect information', in the economist's jargon) about the present state of the market. For employees this means knowing about where work is available and the rewards on offer. For employers this means knowing how many and where the employees are available to work and the 'price' at which they are being acquired. The parties will, it is assumed, *instinctively* seek to maximise their individual interests, with supply and demand across the labour market tending to be stable over time, all other things being equal.

Rationally seeking 'maximum utility', employees will assess jobs by weighing the overall economic merits of different jobs. Thus jobs that are less pleasant than others, or those that carry more risk, or that are more difficult to attain mastery of, will require higher pay than those whose characteristics are the reverse. The model indicates limited discretion for employers in wage setting, as short-run attractiveness will tend to be eroded over the longer term, as abstract 'market forces' compel employers to offer jobs of roughly similar attractiveness or else fail to secure the labour to resource their organisations. Employers who pay above the market rate will be forced to charge higher prices for their goods, which, if not matched by competitors, in theory will lead to reduced revenues as customers buy more cheaply elsewhere. The result will be either bankruptcy for the employer or cuts in costs – specifically wage costs or reduced employment.

Even neoclassical labour economists recognise, however, that such a theory may be too simplistic. They sound a note of caution regarding the effects of 'market distortions' arising from political interventions in the labour market. For example, state regulations governing minimum wage levels, or the presence of employees acting collectively through trade unions, may act to disrupt the natural order of the market. Provided such distortions are minimised (and this is a job the neoclassical school allocates to governments), then even though from time to time there may be a shift in labour wage rates, this will be temporary. Any change in wage rates may be attributed to rises and falls in labour supply and demand, or to changes as new employers and/or employees enter the market or existing employers and/or employees exit. Instrumentally oriented, the tendency will be for parties to conclude that 'marginal utility' derived from the employment exchange relationship (the additional unit of labour power exchanged in return for each small increase in compensation for lost leisure opportunities) is best maximised by compliance with the 'free' functioning of market forces.

CRITICISMS OF THE CLASSICAL LABOUR MARKET

Since the middle of the twentieth century, research has indicated that the labour market does not operate in such a simple fashion as advocated by classical economics. Nonetheless, the influence of neoclassical labour economists on reward systems thinking has been remarkably durable. As Gerhart and Rynes (2003) argue, apologists for alleged recent excesses in executive reward have pointed to the effect of 'market forces'. Executives are simply being paid what the market demands (see Chapter 10 for a detailed discussion). The economic purist will argue in defence of criticism that any departure from market 'norms' will be self-adjusting over time. Or it may require the removal of 'market distortions' – eg co-operation by members of an employers' association in fixing rates of pay for an industry sector; or by political administrations setting minimum wage rates for the economy; or through employees combining in trade unions to improve wage rates relative to other groups of workers.

That defence notwithstanding, it is controversial to assume that employees have 'perfect' knowledge of competing types of work, and that the socio-economic costs for employees to transfer between employers are not prohibitive. Once the neoclassical assumptions are compared with social and political, let alone economic, reality the model becomes less reliable as a basis for predicting labour allocation. For example, Rees (1973) points out that the 'competitive model' uses the individual as its unit of analysis. Employment systems may be regulated in part by factors that locate individuals in their wider social context – as members of a household where, for example, domestic commitments limit availability to participate in the labour force as an employee, or as individuals undergoing education and other forms of 'work'. Such phenomena may inhibit the rational decision-making implied under the neoclassical economic model.

The notion of a self-regulating employment system is undermined by the fact that it is not limited to the actions of current and prospective employees. Employers, for example, a multinational joint venture company, may be able to dominate certain employment systems, with the resources to outbid local firms for labour on terms that are attractive to the employer compared with relative rates of pay in the employer's country of origin. Another example of this phenomenon, known by economists as 'monopsony' (ie there is effectively only one buyer in the market), is the National Health Service in the UK, which is by far the major employer of certain health occupations, including doctors and nurses. If such health professionals wish to work at their chosen occupation they have little choice, in the final analysis, in who employs them or the pay levels on offer (which are set nationally). Their only alternative is to seek promotion to improve their pay or to change occupations.

Decisions to recruit or supply labour, including decisions between competing employment opportunities, are, therefore, more complicated than simple decisions around trading paid work for leisure, and vice versa. In summary:

> *The more a firm or a business sector approaches the conditions of full and effective competition, the more likely it is that the competitive theory will provide useful pointers. But where competition, whether in the product market or in the labour market, is restricted, the greater the departure from competitive theory that is required to explain empirical observations or to analyse the consequences of alternative strategies for remuneration.*
> (Beaumont and Hunter, 2000: 46)

In fairness to Adam Smith's original conceptualisation, the influence of 'total net advantage', not price alone, on an employee's choice to enter or remain outside the labour market, and to move between employers or stay put, has been set aside by subsequent economic theorists. To locate pricing of labour in the economic market, other economists have assumed away all non-pecuniary aspects – premised on 'all else being equal' (Rottenberg, 1956, cited in Gerhart and Rynes, 2003). And, as Watson (2005: 64) puts it, in pursuit of elegant conceptual models, neoclassical economists set aside 'the learning processes through which actual conduct is formed' – habits acquired through repeated human interaction. The influence of history and learning is emphasised by postclassical social science theorists, as we shall see when discussing psychological theory below.

Whether or not to supply their labour to employers is not the sole economic issue for the employee. There is also the question of the amount of effort individuals will make available to the employer, once employed (Rees, 1973). Over the years average hours of work in industrialised economies have declined substantially. Employers would set hours of work and in theory employees have to accept these. Those employees with domestic responsibilities, however, have demonstrated their willingness to opt between employments where hours of work are more in keeping with other demands on their time. And individuals may be willing to make trade-offs between more acceptable hours and the level of pay or 'work-life balance available' (we take up this discussion in Chapter 9 related to the notion of 'total reward'). Of course, legislation, as well as market forces, may affect the hours of work undertaken by workforce participants. Introducing a comparative dimension, in countries where there are traditional family-related calls on individuals' time – eg where agriculture remains a significant family concern – there may be seasons where employers have difficulty in securing the required supply of labour as their employees may absent themselves to undertake work that cannot be delayed, such as the annual olive harvest in countries on the southern periphery of the European Union. Institutional factors therefore appear to merit attention.

SELF-ASSESSMENT EXERCISE

What reasons do you think explain the continuation of the classical labour market model of pay determination, despite the evidence from the real world of employment?

ALTERNATIVE ECONOMIC THEORIES OF REWARD

There are a number of alternative economic theories to the classical labour market approach. **'Institutional labour economics theory'** redefines the market-clearing model in order to explain differentials between wage levels, contingent on institutional factors. While the general assumption is kept that employers' and employees' expectations will rest on maximising their economic interests, a more open systems view is evident. Factors arising from the environmental and organisational context are introduced (eg culture and values, initiatives by governments and other organisations and interest groups), that may be associated with differential employee reward levels across the labour market. Such 'contingencies' may result in employment relationships that still tend towards a primarily individualised orientation, or they may open the way for bargaining activity along a collective dimension. Substantive labour market contingencies may be cited, such as the scale of organisations, the industry sector or the stage of economic development in a particular employment system. Economists have cited these contingencies as one explanation for what has been termed 'stickiness' in wage levels: if market-clearing theory applies, why in practice do wage levels rarely appear to fall?

This reframing of external labour market-clearing systems thinking opens the potential for employers to seek positive answers to the second basic question: how can employee reward investments enable managers to influence employee attitudes and behaviours in the workplace? The scope is introduced for a 'strategic' regulatory role for management to act in ways that compensate for market imperfections (at least in the short run). Vertical alignment between business strategy focused on competing for revenue through product or service quality, or on price alone, may be cascaded into decisions to offer a wage premium or on efforts to achieve pay compression (ie the narrowing, over time, of pay differentials between people in the same job or between people in different, usually adjacent, grades).

The assumption of perfect information on the part of employers and employees influencing labour supply and demand is discarded within institutional economics theorising in favour of more 'bounded rationality'. In particular, in assessing how individual workers perceive the overall attractiveness of employment opportunities in a labour market, the institutional economist may consider that employees may find it more rational to ignore higher short-term rewards in favour of longer-term considerations, such as the social costs of changing employers (eg loss of workplace environment, contacts, knowledge of an organisation's production system, etc). In terms of strategic initiatives, theorists such as Williamson (1975) have suggested that managers enter into contracts designed to minimise the economic costs of organising productive activity – including putting labour power to work to create value in the most efficient way. Rationality and instrumentalism between the parties in the nature of their expectations and underlying relationship remain important **transaction cost theory assumptions**. In other words, both employers and workers make complex decisions about the employment relationship weighing up, with the scope for trade-offs between, multiple issues affecting their interests in the transaction.

An alternative **resource-based theory of the firm** carries the assumption that economic efficiency and effectiveness will be achieved through managerial initiatives to take advantage of distinctive organisational resources (combining people with physical resources and processes to create valuable outcomes). Employee reward, horizontally aligned into unique bundles with other HRM practices (Kessler, 2001; Purcell, 1999), is deployed to help form and sustain a distinctive organisational culture. While a managerial emphasis on 'resource leverage' may be advocated as more rational over simple cost containment, Kessler (2001) points to tensions at the heart of the resource-based view. This relates to the problem of disentangling the complex series of steps to achieving effective vertical and horizontal bundling processes, making the cause–effect linkages somewhat problematic.

Instead, a **new institutional approach** to strategy theory, paying attention to the various political and social pressures confronting people in organisations, both internal and external to the organisational system, may facilitate more effective employee reward decision-making. Over time, employers and employees in specific contexts may build a shared history of effort–reward determination. This may involve accumulated learning on how to interpret factors such as internal norms and values, as well as external indicators (eg comparisons with other employers, from state legislation and from trade union interventions). The common understandings reached carry with them a shared legitimacy regarding employee reward-setting processes and outcomes. Underlying differences of interest may be held in check (Rubery, 1997) as the parties trust one another given common experience to follow 'rules of engagement' that are slow to change.

STUDENT EXERCISE

Discuss the factors managers need to weigh in attempting to create alignment vertically between corporate strategy and employee reward, and horizontally between reward management policies and processes and other HRM initiatives.

HUMAN CAPITAL THEORY

Another economic theory relevant to employee reward is **human capital theory**. This theory is based on the fact that individuals accumulate human capital by investing time and money (including deferred earnings) in education, training, experience and other qualities, that increase their productive capacity and thus worth to an employer (Abercrombie *et al*, 2000). While all employees bring some skill and experience to the performance of their tasks, accumulated educational attainment and experience give rise to differentiation in the level of reward necessary to secure and retain certain people. Competition among organisations across national boundaries – as more goods and services contain a higher marginal labour value content in terms of the skills, knowledge and accredited specialist experience needed – introduces a need for employee reward system regulation beyond simple market-clearing mechanisms.

> *The proposition that a trained worker, like a machine, represents a valuable investment is a very old one in the history of economics. In both cases making the investment requires a sacrifice of current consumption in order to increase future output.* (Rees, 1973: 35)

Human capital theory (developed by Schultz and Becker in the 1960s) distinguishes between expenditures on labour representing consumption and those representing investment in (human) capital. Human labour is, however, unlike capital equipment in that it is not generally sold but 'rented out for work' (the exception is work relations based on slavery). The market is for the *services* of the capital, not the capital stock itself.

Hendry (2003: 1433) argues that to satisfy a universal imperative to secure skills cost-effectively, managers must balance 'two considerations involving skills and costs …'. Managerial discretion may be exercised in various ways to create employment systems, first, to achieve the basic HRM tasks of getting, keeping, motivating and developing people. Secondly, to 'secure skills' also implies controlling them in different ways and to different degrees depending on how important they are to achieving organisational goals.

Exchange theory is premised on the notion that, under capitalist relations of production, employers and employees enter into an agreement whereby the employer contracts to pay wages or other extrinsic rewards to the employee in return for a willingness on the part of employees to give up their right to leisure and to accept the direction of the employer over their labour services. The employer then has to convert rented labour power into labour that has an economic value. Issues around the relative value of different skills and the transaction costs in harnessing them partly explain the segmentation of the workforce into core and peripheral 'employment systems' (Atkinson, 1984; Kalleberg, 2003). Employers will generally invest more in the 'core' permanent workforce than the 'peripheral' workforce that can be dispensed with when times are hard.

EFFICIENCY WAGE THEORY

A related line of argument within the institutional economics tradition is the idea of **'efficiency wage'** payments: a managerial strategy to achieve more 'efficient' employment contracts over the medium term. If employers assume that employees will use their human capital to secure alternative work at enhanced pay rates, but their loss to the employer would incur transaction costs greater than paying above market rates, paying higher reward levels is a rational employer response to sustain an ongoing relationship. Efficiency wages are thus an investment in firm-specific or idiosyncratic skills and knowledge, to maximise loyalty and minimise opportunistic employee behaviour.

The exercise of managerial discretion to regulate reward levels may also be a function of firm size. If the organisation is more complex to monitor, higher levels of reward are offered to employees in the expectation that people will see it as an incentive to perform better than the (possibly underperforming) external market norm. As noted above, the market-clearing mechanism takes no explicit account of the amount of effort individuals will supply to transform their labour power into organisationally valuable outputs.

Efficiency wage theory also indicates a potential disciplinary aspect, addressing what economists have labelled 'soldiering' (withholding full effort) on the part of the employee. The argument is that, if people feel better paid, they will not only be inclined to work harder but also their performance will be conditioned by a fear of losing employment with above-market pay. Here the transaction focuses on offsetting higher wages against the possibility of incurring replacement costs due to voluntary employee resignations (or 'wastage' effects). More positively, efficiency wage levels may theoretically introduce a 'sorting effect'.

Organisations whose operating strategies require higher human capital levels may find it more efficient to use above-market wage levels to signal their wish to attract above-average quality workers. The need for close supervision within the system may be reduced. This relates to the **'responsible autonomy'** policy identified by Friedman (1977, 1984), where management perceives the need to respond to inherent limitations on their ability to exercise 'direct control' over some workers, and turn to alternative strategies intended to align employee effort with managerial priorities. Internalised discipline on the employee's part, reinforced by above-market reward for the core workforce, may be a less costly option than funding additional supervision (Rubery, 1997). This view may have important implications for employing 'knowledge workers'.

Efficiency wages may be consistent, for example, with the bundles of HRM practices accompanying resource-based strategy. By contrast, given the emphasis in strategic approaches informed by transaction cost theorising to minimise organisational costs, paying an efficiency wage may be criticised as carrying an inherent risk. Assumptions may be misplaced that employee compliance will follow above-market reward investments. While a resource-based orientation may assume unity of interests between employers and employees, under transaction cost theory – consistent with a rationale of economic self-maximisation on either side – the nature of the employment relationship is viewed as one in which the principal party (the employer or management representative) assumes that the agent it employs will pursue interests that inherently differ from those of the principal. More explicit monitoring controls over employee effort, or tangible incentives that limit the principal's risk, may logically follow.

PRINCIPAL–AGENT THEORY

Also known as 'agency theory', this introduces the notion of *deferred* payment mechanisms. Rynes and Gerhart (2000) identify agency theory as having emerged within economics and management as the dominant basis for examining pay determination processes and outcomes. Pay rates may be set below market-'guaranteed' levels but workers are offered the opportunity to earn above-average total remuneration, contingent on higher performance. An agency-based approach to reward strategy may be associated with notions of incremental pay progression as individuals ascend internal job ladders, reasoning that the expectation of earning a full return on their human capital investment only over a lengthy employment career will encourage people to stay beyond the below-market paid phase in the early period of employment. Assuming organisational stability, an investment in seniority-building increases the individual's economic worth to the employer, while acting to mitigate divergence in the interests of employees and other stakeholders over the longer term. Approaches to pay progression are considered in detail in Chapter 5.

Alternatively, in particular where stable employment relationships may not be assumed, agency-based theorising may emphasise outcome-based deferred rewards such as profit-sharing, gain-sharing and long-term, stock ownership-based incentive plans – especially those designed for senior staff (see Chapters 6 and 10 for empirically informed discussion). The size of the deferred reward offered may be linked to the level of complexity (and associated transactional cost to principals) in monitoring agents' behaviour. Gaining prominence in recent years, alongside corporate governance reforms, agency theorists (eg Jensen and Meckling, 1976; Jensen and Murphy, 1990; Jensen *et al*, 2004) reason that alignment of interests between employed agents and other stakeholders (and shareholders, in particular) will require employees to share the risks associated with the organisation. This risk-sharing can be achieved by making a significant amount of employees' potential total earnings dependent on their own contribution to the organisation's financial success.

Forms of contingency or 'at risk' pay administered on a short-term basis are not new, of course. Piece-rate forms of payment were associated with manual work before the industrial revolution. They have been in use since the sixteenth century and were associated with the rise of merchant capitalism and home-working/ cottage industry (Smith, 1989). Transforming practice into theory, the 'scientific management' approach of early American management consultants, such as F.W. Taylor (1911), emphasised the role of the 'piecework bonus' as a motivational financial reward which, combined with a paternalistic management style, was intended to sustain labour productivity levels and to discourage workforce unionisation.

Managerial discretion to pay differentially may also be linked to job or – in less bureaucratic contexts – role design. Roles have been important constructs for sociologists in analysing organisations. Roles are viewed as socially determined signals to individuals about what is expected of them. They form the collective basis of institutions such as workplaces. And, as bundles of socially defined attributes and expectations, theoretically these elevate the role beyond the characteristics of the individual. The idea is that people will conform to what is expected of the position that they occupy. **Role theory** is applied to predict how behaviour is socially influenced: thus an engineer in a firm is likely to behave in ways expected of the role of engineer rather than the individual role occupant. There remains an interesting balance to be struck in how a role is paid and how the individual's contribution to organisational performance is reflected in reward. Playing a systemic role, pay rates based on the job or role contain signals of how individuals are expected to align themselves with the overall work system (see Chapter 4 for an empirically informed discussion of the issues involved).

The problem of unravelling the complexity inherent in organisation–people 'resource bundles', and the 'agency' problem of monitoring behaviour, were raised above. The socially determined effort–reward assumptions within role theory as a source of managerial control may be questioned in each of those contexts. For example, to what degree is individual performance important: what messages will be given to direct and reinforce the way the individual should behave in discharging responsibilities rather than simply executing the role 'objectively'? Is the level or role-position in the hierarchy important? How free is the worker under the organisation's operating rules to innovate and be creative? Is such creativity predominantly inward-facing (say, in the R&D environment) or required of even the most junior, customer-facing, role?

Extrinsic reward for performing job tasks strictly to the role description may send out messages that may be inappropriate to a position that requires the exercise of discretion. How do organisations send out the correct balance of informational and controlling signals through reward policies and practices? Is role-making a function of prescription – where behaviours are explicitly signalled in job design – or something that emerges through the process of trial and error as the individual interacts with peers and supervisor(s) to secure understanding of what is deemed to be value-added, reinforced over time through reward outcomes? It may be hypothesised that process issues may be as important as substantive ones.

INTERNAL LABOUR MARKETS

Where organisations seek a stable relationship with their workforces, a '**structured internal labour market**' (ILM) (Kerr, 1954, cited in Hendry, 2003) may be created and maintained to insulate some or all the organisation's employees from the vagaries of external market forces impacting on an organisation's ability to retain its employees. Doeringer (1967: 207, cited in White, 2000) comments that:

> *The theoretical construct of the internal labour market … may be more precisely defined as an administrative unit within which the market functions of pricing, allocating and often training labor are performed. It is governed by a set of institutional rules which delineate the boundaries of the internal market and determine its internal structure. These institutional or administrative hiring and work rules define the 'ports of entry' into the*

internal market, the relationship between jobs for purposes of internal mobility, and the privileges which accrue to workers within the internal market.

Entry portals from the labour market are restricted, limiting access to 'career ladders' (Doeringer and Piore, 1971; Thurow, 1975). Some current examples of internal labour markets would be the armed forces or the police where entry is restricted to particular grades (eg private and lieutenant for the armed forces and constable for the police service). It is not possible to enter the organisation at other levels than those proscribed (eg one cannot join as a sergeant or major in the armed forces or a superintendent in the police). Contrasting with reliance on sourcing employees based on external labour market competition, an ILM affords management greater knowledge about candidates. It also substitutes for potentially costly 'spot bargaining' or haggling over wage rates with individuals about their market value. It has also been deployed defensively as a union avoidance strategy.

In the United States the development of internal labour markets dates from after the First World War, and was a product of both demands for equity from trade unions and the development of modern personnel management with its emphasis on long-term planning (Cappelli, 1995). In Britain, in contrast, it has been noted that 'most British employers did not build strong internal labour systems, but relied more on market mechanisms for obtaining labour' (Gospel, 1992: 179). In systems terms, rather than being a theoretical assumption, ILMs represent an intended strategy with consequences including transaction costs. The question of the affordability of ILM-based employee reward management, and recent countervailing tendencies, is discussed below.

Under ILM, wage rates are attached to jobs rather than to workers (Williamson, 1975). Employees are rewarded by clear, long-term and guaranteed career trajectories rather than purely financial incentives. Labour pricing and allocation are governed by corporately determined rules and procedures (Gerhart and Rynes, 2003), whereby jobs are arranged hierarchically and reward rates are attached to jobs rather than to individuals (Beaumont and Hunter, 2000). An ILM may be a response to adoption of a resource-based strategy: seeking to preserve the idiosyncratic collection of skills and related processes internal to the organisational system as a basis for sustainable competitive advantage. In terms of employee expectations and the character of the relationship offered by management, a reputation for internal promotion signals an incentive and retention effect – at least to those classified as part of the 'core' workforce. The downside, of course, is sacrificing access to a wider talent pool.

ILMs are, on the face of it, expensive fixtures: the question arises of how employers can afford to commit to insulating segments or all workforce members from external market clearing processes. So-called **'rent-sharing'** or **'ability-to-pay' theories** have been advanced to address this issue. An 'economic rent' is a return for doing something (selling a good or service, for example) based on the perceived value to the user that they are willing to pay to the current holder of a resource that is 'in excess of the minimum needed

Figure 2.2 A multifaceted pay-setting framework

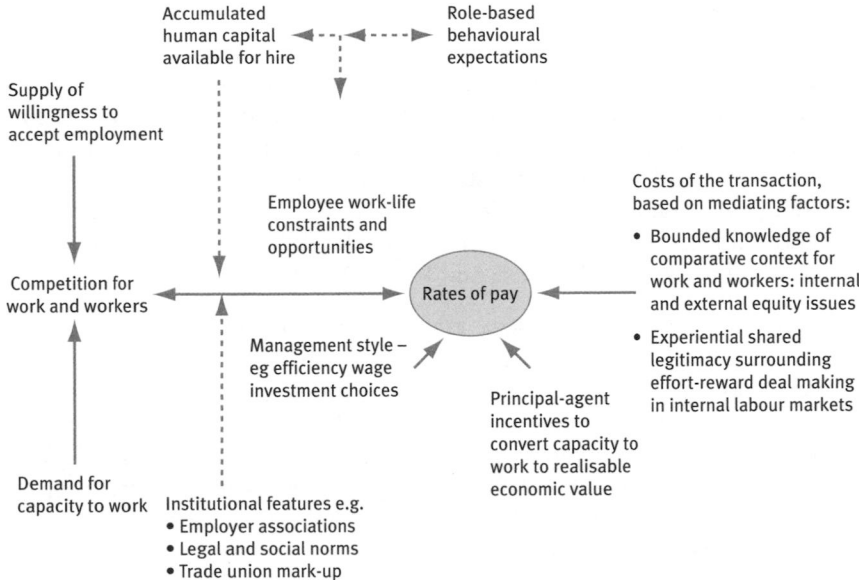

to attract the resources to that activity' (Milgrom and Roberts, 1992, cited in Gerhart and Rynes, 2003). In other words, firms making above-normal profits, whether owing to monopoly power or effective competitive organisation, may share these 'rents' with employees in the form of above-market-clearing rates of reward. Transaction cost assumptions may apply, as in efficiency wage theory: the ILM-determined employment rates are intended to reduce risks to continuous production by the workforce.

An alternative but not dissimilar theoretical approach may be perceived in the **gift-exchange** variant of institutional economics, whereby the employer gifts to employees higher than market average rewards, signalling a relationship regulated by a mutual expectation of reciprocity (ie that employees will 'gift' discretionary effort to the organisation in return). A link may be posited here with the notion of a 'psychological contract' discussed later in the chapter. Employer 'gift' wages may be funded by supernormal profits, or forward investment in anticipation of limiting future transaction costs through unplanned employee turnover, shirking or possible trade union encroachment on managerial discretion. Whether these theoretical assumptions are borne out is an empirical question that empirical research has found difficult to substantiate. As with the resource-based strategy position, internalised labour market system complexities are difficult to unravel analytically in pursuit of cause-and-effect associations.

WAGE-GAP (OR UNION MARK-UP) THEORY

Rent-share funding for ILMs associated with a business strategy based on consistent, high-quality production, attracting premium product prices/revenues, may be reversed under price-sensitive, low-pay strategies. The capacity of workers, however, to use 'episodic advantage' (eg skilled labour shortages in particular locations) around the 'frontier of control' over workplace relations (Edwards, 1990), and to 'hold other stakeholders hostage' in terms of halting production, has attracted the attention of industrial relations writers seeking explanations for the differences in average wage levels between unionised and non-unionised workplaces (Gerhart and Rynes, 2003).

While ILMs may feature in a trade union avoidance strategy, another neo-institutionalist approach, **'wage-gap theory'**, attributes agreement by employers who enjoy some degree of monopoly power in their product markets to share part of the higher than normal profits with the workforce, in return for agreement by employee representatives for continuity of production. The outcome is a 'trade union mark-up' over competitive market rates (see Heery 2000). Zweimüller and Barth (1992) investigated indications that wage rates across six OECD countries (Austria, Canada, Germany, Norway, Sweden and the USA) remained similar, controlling for labour quality. Efficiency wages paid in response to human capital factors were found to be less significant than the incidence of trade unions and collective agreements. In particular this reflected co-ordinated bargaining across industries, where differentials between wage payments across the industry sectors surveyed reflected a union mark-up.

A summary illustration of the ways in which neoclassical wage determination modelling may be expanded, drawing on the range of neo-institutional theory discussed in this section of the chapter, influencing the character and outcome of reward systems, is presented in Figure 2.2. While lacking the parsimonious elegance of the neoclassical model (Figure 2.1), it may offer a more accurate reflection of the dynamics encountered by managers and employee in practice.

CRITICISM OF NEO-INSTITUTIONALIST ARGUMENTS

Rubery (1997) criticises the attribution of a functional role to employee reward structures and levels in mainstream social science theorising (whether at economy or organisational level). She argues that, as management has sought to regulate employment relationships on more 'flexible' terms (eg shifting the risk from employer to employees through performance-contingent forms of pay), to support business product market-competitive strategies and/or to maximise the investment returns to shareholders, income has been redistributed in favour of the higher paid (see the empirical data presented in Chapter 10).

During the 1980s and 1990s, institutional processes designed to reward people with 'fair wages' and alignment with reward levels enjoyed by workers of similar productivity (the 'going rate') were substantially reduced, encouraged by government exhortations that pay should be based simply on firms' ability to pay. This change may also be attributed to the decline of trade union power and the prevalence of collective bargaining (Chapter 3). If internalising reward determination within the organisation was 'developed to overcome various forms of market failure, might it not be that, as the labour market itself undergoes change, this device will be less important?' (Beaumont and Hunter, 2000: 54).

Existing reward determination theory is found deficient in its overriding emphasis on stability and consensus-building, even where a plurality of interests in the employment relationship is recognised. Rubery (1997) argues for labour market regulation theory to be reconsidered. She argues that more attention should be paid to the potential for conflict, as value is redistributed between organisational stakeholders to privilege finance capital over human capital – and the scope for discretionary, random or opportunistic decisions on the part of the principals to the effort–reward relationship. Expectations between the parties, the nature of their relationships and the balance of regulatory influence have decisively shifted in favour of management, amplifying tendencies already inherent in the substance and process of employee reward management. While these trends may be significant, Rubery (1997) emphasises the social nature of wage markets, in which employers cannot legitimately act in ways that wholly ignore social expectations, even though former checks and balances associated with collective wage bargaining may have been eroded. This topic is one to which we return when considering variable, pay-for-performance approaches (Chapter 6).

TOURNAMENT THEORY AND WINNER-TAKE-ALL REGIMES

Where managerial 'cadres' are needed to support strategy execution, introducing 'tournaments' and 'winner-take-all' regimes may be preferred to opening up the system to the discipline of the external market. The theory is that discipline from the outside product and investment markets is imported to ILMs. Contrary to the original ILM approach, where pay progression over the course of a career is offered to motivate employees to remain within an organisation, tournament theory focuses attention on jobs and the relative gaps between the reward attached to particular jobs. In place of steady upward progress, careers are perceived to involve 'kinks', where promotion between hierarchical levels is the defining feature, with major 'prizes' for 'winners'.

As further discussed in Chapter 10, however, empirical evidence of the operation of tournaments usually comes from the arts and sport, such as the argument that networked TV enables widely dispersed populations to watch the 'world's best' without ever having to share the same physical space. Those who are the greatest draw will attract the largest 'prize money'. The 'war-for-talent' argument has extended the analogy into the conventional business world, but evidence of theory-in-practice is limited.

Prize levels vary between levels in the hierarchy, increasing in value the higher individuals progress up the organisation. This reflects the reduction in the remaining progression opportunities (Conyon and Peck, 1998; Lazear, 1995, 1999). Messages regarding orientation towards particular individuals and workforce segments are conveyed from this structuring of pay within the organisation. Management may choose either to compress reward hierarchies, indicating a more collective orientation to performance achievement, or to reverse the principle, based on the view that a few stars are likely to produce most value and therefore need higher extrinsic signals that the organisation wishes to recognise and retain them. Rather than emphasising group co-operation, individuals are encouraged to compete for prizes under winner-take-all rules of the game.

Under **winner-take-all theorising** (broadly similar to **tournament theory**), it is assumed that defining differences exist between the very best and next best (Frank and Cook, 1995). Small differences in 'core talent' ability may be worth a lot to employers, and the argument is made that market forces tend to reward these differences handsomely. The top job (CEO) arguably needs the highest relative reward, with the largest gap over subordinate roles, given that there is nowhere else to go internally. This does not imply intent to motivate CEO performance: arguably, high performance by the individual is not important. Instead, the idea is to encourage subordinate levels to continue to compete in the earlier 'elimination rounds'.

To sum up at this point, the basic questions, presented in economic terms, of how much an employer needs to pay, and what expectations employees may realistically hold on their ability to secure returns on their human capital, may be addressed in a variety of ways. Once exclusively market-regulating approaches are confronted with institutionally sensitive frameworks (ie a more open systems orientation), alternatives for gaining some 'employer leverage' on their reward investment aligned with various strategic considerations come into consideration. In drawing on economics and sociology of work theory it should be clear from the range of approaches introduced here that there is no generally accepted 'one size fits all' answer. And more radical evaluation indicates that basic assumptions regarding the functional consequences of mainstream thinking may be open to challenge from a variety of directions as employment systems continue to evolve.

In the next part of the chapter we consider theories associated in particular with psychological 'motivation' to perform in work situations. We also turn attention to the processes impacting on whether or not employees perceive their reward from work as fair, equitable and just.

STUDENT EXERCISE

Discuss the possible relationship between human capital assumptions, efficiency wages and internal labour markets. Would employers be more or less likely to establish and maintain an internal labour market where collective bargaining relations contribute to a 'mark-up' on the external rate for the job?

What might be the consequences of attempting reward system 'reform' following a tournaments approach?

ALTERNATIVE PERSPECTIVES ON EMPLOYEE MOTIVATION AND REWARD

It may appear self-evident that, in the words of Bowey and Thorpe (2000: 81), 'To be effective, remuneration systems need to be based on a sound understanding of how people at work are motivated.' But motivation theory has been dogged by popularisation of conclusions from laboratory or pseudo-experimental research designs, as well as an 'open systems effect' derived from the influence of the prevailing management and political ideologies and philosophies of particular eras. Moving between a variety of fairly extreme positions, the search continued throughout the twentieth century for 'one-best-way' to address the second and third questions cited at the start of this chapter, namely, the role of reward as a managerial 'lever' for employee performance, and the sense individuals might share of receiving 'just reward' for their skills and effort. The result has been faddishness in the adoption and discarding of policies intended to offer incentives and recognition for workers, possibly based on what Pfeffer (1998) labels 'dangerous myths'.

Bowey and Thorpe (2000) argue that the low level of understanding of how reward systems affect employee behaviour can be blamed on a combination of factors: the degree of opposition between theoretical positions; conflicting real-life examples of what seems to work; and poorly disseminated research findings (see Guest's (2007: 1020) evidence-based discussion of 'the challenge of communicating scientific knowledge to practitioners'). Although psychologists and other social scientists may dismiss ideas as unsubstantiated, certain nostrums have passed into individuals' experience portfolio and into general management folklore. Hence, organisation leaders may be seen confidently acting in a manner explicitly or implicitly informed by simplistic motivation theories (or simplistic interpretations of them). In short, much 'old' motivation theory has not 'died and gone away ... the great majority of managers in Britain, the United States and, quite worryingly, Central and Eastern Europe (as well as other developing countries) believe there is one best way to motivate employees to work well' (Bowey and Thorpe, 2000: 81–3).

DEFINITIONS OF MOTIVATION

Ideas surrounding motivation – a word derived from the Latin *movere*, 'to move' – have their roots in 'hedonism' in ancient Greek philosophy: that is, the principle that humans seek to maximise pleasure and minimise pain. *Movere* is also credited as the Latin source of the modern English word 'emotion' – clearly a mainstream interest for psychologically inclined investigators.

Hedonism is not something that is easily subjected to objective measurement – and, indeed, most aspects of motivation have to be inferred from observable behaviour (assumed to be in response to some actual or perceived energising force(s) external to the individual). When psychology began interacting with management science, psychological investigations that had previously

Although consensus around the precise meaning of the term is elusive, even between psychologists (Kleinginna and Kleinginna, 1981), human motivation can be broadly defined as stimuli acting on, or within, a person that cause the arousal, direction and persistence of goal-directed, voluntary effort. In other words, motivation is concerned with what gets someone to make a choice to act, selecting between alternatives (including no action), and the sustained focus of that action. Motivation theory is thus, in general, concerned with explaining why and how behaviour is activated and sustained. If this understanding can be ascertained, it follows that, in relation to employee motivation, better-informed performance and reward management may be undertaken.

concentrated on experimental situations involving animals stood in contrast to some of the underlying theories that appeared to guide managerial practice (and still do in some cases).

Early theorising on motivation, frequently informed by laboratory experiments using animals, concentrates on 'content' aspects (or perceived 'needs' – see below) or **what** motivates somebody. An accent on 'process' aspects – **how** people are motivated – becomes more pronounced when psychological theorising interacts with other thought systems such as anthropology, sociology and political science, as perceptions of equity and social justice in human relationships are factored in.

Thematically, discussion has included attempts to distinguish between *intrinsic* and *extrinsic* human motivation. Herzberg's **two-factor theory** (alternatively referred to as the **'motivation-hygiene' theory**) argues that intrinsic and extrinsic factors are wholly separate phenomena (Kohn, 1993), or at least arranged as a **hierarchy of needs** (Maslow, 1954, cited in Hollyforde and Whiddett, 2002). Once a fair level of pay is established, for example, money ceases to be a significant motivator for long-term performance. Factors such as salary levels and working conditions demotivate (by being poor) rather than motivate (by being good). While two-factor theory was discredited as an academic theory relevant to employee performance management four decades ago (House and Wigdor, 1967, cited by Rousseau, 2006), this distinction has had important consequences for employee reward systems design. Emphasis on extrinsic aspects (such as pay and other tangible employment benefits) has been juxtaposed with intrinsic sources of motivation (such as feelings within the person or group when participating in inherently satisfying work). Discussion on the design and application of pay progression systems, variable pay and incentive plans (Chapters 5 and 6), as well as the 'executive incentives', informed by agency theory presupposing the salience of economic motivators (Chapter 10), should be read mindful of this disputed psychologically grounded territory.

The psychological motivation literature shifts the emphasis on economic incentives and penalties found in economic theory towards biological and psychological 'predispositions' and to 'drives', to 'working environment' and to the quality of social relationships around production – in each case with recipes for managerial action. While trailblazers of particular approaches may appear to have great success in applying their prescriptions, subsequent empirical evidence indicates a more mixed scorecard. More reflexive motivation theory has lessened tendencies towards a binary (either/or) emphasis, putting the individual subject of motivation back in, as an active participant in design and application of organisational policies and practices with non-static and diverse characteristics. Thus expectations of each of the main parties to the effort–reward bargain have been more equally placed in the foreground, and relationships and regulatory processes refocused along the lines of active and reciprocal co-determination.

The implications of themes within motivation theory may be traced in a similar way to approaches within economic theory. These range from closed systems reasoning where scope for managerial initiative is constrained, to more open systems logic that accounts for institutional factors. The prescriptions vary between an accent on modifying employee behaviour to one in which it is the organisational environment that managers should act upon, to enable employee potential to be released. In the first case the assumption is that individuals need to be persuaded to perform; in the second case, that people enter the work relationship actively wishing to do a good job. These ideas are 'unpacked' below.

INSTINCTS, LEARNED BEHAVIOURS AND EXPECTANCY

In psychology, the 'scientific' assumption is that human motivation should not be perceived simply on the basis of individuals rationally pursuing self-interest. Instead, writers such as James and McDougall argue that internal cues lead individuals to behave in certain ways owing to 'automatic predispositions' (cited in Steers and Porter, 1987). The problem with substituting instinct for hedonistic rationality to explain human motivation is the number of discernible factors that may apply. Lists of instincts can grow into the thousands (Steers and Porter, 1987). And their variation in intensity and motive may not always lead to action/behaviour.

Freudians (ie those following the teachings of neurologist Sigmund Freud, 1856–1939) argue that such instinctive forces may be unknown even to the individual – they are a product of the subconscious mind. Given a stance not unlike the closed system economists, an emphasis on the inner aspects of the individual psyche and notions of predisposed unconscious behaviour leaves little room for positive managerial intervention. Individuals striving to fulfil unconscious desires that are unknown to them are unlikely to be discernible in the course of normal manager–employee interaction.

If instinctive or objectively rational behavioural tendencies are deemed inadequate in explaining human motivation, attention turns to the capacity of humans to learn from experience. Active managerial interventions may be premised on the theory that 'history counts', and if people have learned that needs will be satisfied arising from certain types of behaviour and its outcomes, active steps can be taken to reinforce the attractiveness of reproducing activities consistent with managerial goals.

Drive and **reinforcement** theories take up the notion of learning over instinct, so that subjects find themselves motivated to behave in certain ways owing to habit. Allport (1954) used the term 'historical hedonism' to describe this form of motivation. This argument follows the logic that subjects learn from the consequences of their actions and tend to repeat those that attract positive outcomes and abandon those that result in negative consequences. Woodworth (1918) introduced the notion of physiological 'drives' – specific 'energisers' such as thirst, hunger, reproduction, etc – towards or away from certain goals. Cannon (in the 1930s) used the term 'homeostasis' to describe a situation where arousal is triggered and the subject is driven to satisfy it, thus restoring equilibrium, thus a feeling of thirst motivates the subject to drink. Cannon assumed that organisms exist in a permanently dynamic state, their drives changing in response to 'disequilibriums' in their environment. Certain drives may come to the surface at various times and, once satisfied, decline. An individual who is out of work, for example, may be driven (or energised) to restore equilibrium in having the means of financial self-support by seeking out employment, based on previous experience that this attracts payment – that is, the means of achieving the goal of restoring equilibrium of being financially secure (Steers and Porter, 1987). Maslow (1954, cited in Hollyforde and Whiddett, 2002) contends that not satisfying employee expectations of a fair return on human capital may inhibit 'higher order' motivation taking place.

In response to criticisms that historical hedonism is insufficient to explain human behaviour that involves conscious choice, a further factor has been added, namely, that subjects require a psychological **incentive** to influence their expectation of what will occur in the future. This may be different from and not just a repetition of past outcomes (Hull, 1952). The anticipated effect on behaviour of the size of reward anticipated is thus factored in.

Reinforcement theory (Skinner, 1953) extends notions of learned behaviour and locates it in social encounters. Under this conceptualisation, the managerial role becomes central in motivational encounters ('social learning'). The assumption of this theory is that people seek positive reinforcement for their actions. Reinforcement theory may in fact be viewed as less a motivational theory and more concerned with subjects' responses to social encounters. Managers 'educate' employees in what is required to secure the desired reinforcement for their actions, and the task of management is to find out what will act to reinforce desired behaviour among subordinates and then monitor and appraise accordingly. Under this theory, differentiating between employees' individual performance outcomes will reinforce the learned connection between action and reward. Under reinforcement theory, people's mental state is ignored (Steers and Porter, 1987). The emphasis is on learning about how particular ways of 'operating on the environment' (another way of describing behaviour) lead to rewarding outcomes, reinforcing the aim for favourable rewards to be achieved and to avoid situations that carry penalties.

An alternative, 'cognitive' approach to motivation theory – where it is assumed that employees are thinking individuals who make rational choices based on experience – offers a corrective to instinct and drive-based theory. Here, rather than 'hedonism of the past', grounded in habit, a form of 'hedonism of the future' is postulated. Employee behaviour may be perceived as purposeful and goal-directed, grounded in beliefs and expectations surrounding future events. **Goal-setting theory** (Locke *et al*, 1981) and **expectancy theory** (Vroom, 1964) influence thinking about employee performance management (Mabey *et al*, 1998). Instead of understanding human motivation in terms of stimulus–response, the focus becomes human subjects' conscious evaluation of courses of action, to select the one that is most valued by the individual. Past events are not discounted entirely. However, they are perceived as only important as influences on today's values and expectation – they are not directly linked to behaviour, as the drive theorist would contend.

Although distinguishing between notions of 'general excitement' triggering behaviour and selectivity towards the 'positively valant', Atkinson (1964) argues that theories of motivation based either on learned habits or on goal-directed behaviour share many of the same concepts. Both anticipate the presence of some reward or outcome that is desired and sought. And 'both theories include the notion of a learned connection between the central variables; drive theory posits a learned stimulus–response association, while cognitive theories see a learned association between behaviour and outcome' (Steers and Porter, 1987: 14).

This kind of thinking may be perceived as influencing Sean Wheeler, people development director with hotels group Malmaison, to motivate business unit managers to act as 'boutique brand guardians' during a time of rapid expansion of the portfolio, reinforced by more internal promotion opportunities, outlined as a case cameo in Chapter 12.

Figure 2.3 Valance-Instrumentality-Expectancy (VIE) model developed by Porter and Lawler, displayed by Pinder (1987)

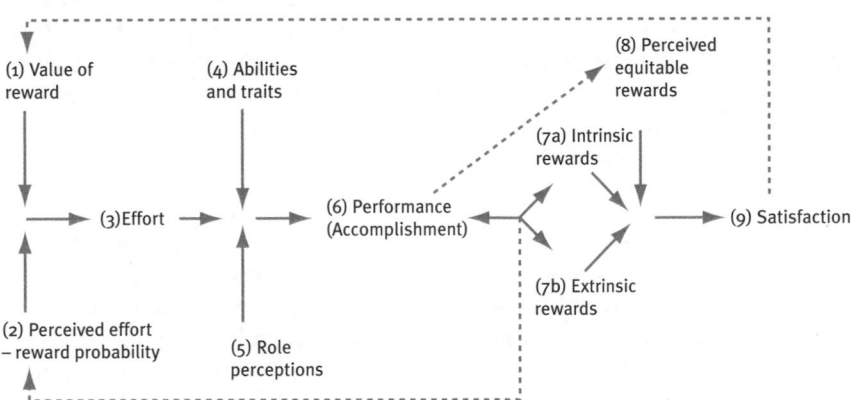

Source: Pinder, C. (1987) 'Valence-instrumentality-expectancy theory' in Steers, R.M. and Porter, L.W. (eds) *Motivation and Work Behaviour*, 4th edn. San Francisco: McGraw Hill (69–89) Reproduced with kind permission from McGraw Hill

Goals pursued by employees may play an important role in motivating superior performance in that, while following them, employees examine the consequences of their behaviour (Locke, 1968, cited in Mabey *et al*, 1998). If their estimation is that current behaviour will not support goal attainment, people are likely either (a) to modify their behaviour, or (b) to choose more achievable goals. Managers and supervisors may engage with employees in the goal-setting process to facilitate the best way to enlist employee co-operation in ways likely to serve organisational aims. Building on a theory of 'path-goal' approaches to work performance, developed by Georgopoulos *et al* (1957, in Mabey *et al*, 1998), Vroom's (1964) approach may be perceived as interfacing with goal theory, highlighting perceptions of future events as the basis on which performance is governed – that is, future expectations influence current behaviour. Perceptions among workers that high productivity will result in personal goal achievement are hypothesised as resulting in highly productive workers, with the reverse also being true.

Identification of these influences by work psychology researchers led to a specification of expectancy theory based on a combination of three factors (Galbraith and Cummings, 1967, cited in *Mabey* et al, 1998: 130–1):

1 the 'expectancy' factor, or an individual's own assessment of whether performing in a certain way will lead to a measurable result;

2 the 'instrumentality factor', or perceived likelihood by a person that such a result will, in turn, presage the attainment of a given reward; and

3 the 'valance' factor, or the individual's assessment of their likely satisfaction with the reward obtained.

Expectancy theory indicates that, 'if a person sees that performing in a certain way will bring about a reward which he or she values, then this individual is more likely to attempt to perform in that way than if the relationship between effort and measured performance, or measured performance and rewards, is slight or uncertain' (Mabey *et al*, 1998: 131). The model was further refined in the light of research by Porter and Lawler (1968, cited in Pinder, 1987), to include the motivational influence of active self-reflection on the individual's abilities and other traits, the perceived nature of the role to be performed, and the degree of equity attributed to both *extrinsic and intrinsic* reward likely to result from the endeavour. The nine-factor 'VIE' position is summarised visually in Figure 2.3.

In empirical tests of goal setting and expectancy theories, evidence suggests that, to achieve predicted outcomes, goal specification is all-important. This places significant demands on managers to establish relatively small numbers of fairly concrete objectives. In practice, in today's fast-moving multifaceted organisational climate, this exhortation may prove difficult to comply with. Also, as Whittington (2001) has pointed out, drawing on the work of writers such as Henry Mintzberg, advance planning and goal specification frequently give way to forms of strategy that is emergent, where aims and objectives (especially at the level of the individual employee) are liable to modification as people and organisations and socio-economic open systems environment interact. Vertical and horizontal alignment of people and performance initiatives are discussed in Chapter 12.

THE PSYCHOLOGICAL CONTRACT AND REWARD

Critical evaluations of goal-setting and expectancy theories draw attention to the notion of a **psychological contract**, a phenomenon that reflects the package of reciprocal obligations implicitly constituting an employee–organisation exchange relationship (Morrison and Robinson, 1997). The psychological contract has been defined as 'a set of beliefs about what each party is entitled to receive, and obligated to give, in exchange for another party's contributions' (Levinson *et al*, 1962, cited in Morrison and Robinson, 1997: 226). For Rousseau and Tijoriwala (1998: 679) it constitutes '… an individual's belief in mutual obligations between that person and another party such as an employer (either a firm or another person)'. Drawing inspiration from psychology and organisational behaviour rather than economics, the emphasis of psychological contract theory is that employment is a relationship in which the mutual obligations of employer and employee may be imprecise but have nevertheless to be respected. According to the CIPD (2003), which has sponsored surveys of 'the state of the psychological contact' in UK workplaces since the mid-1990s (see Guest and Conway, 2004), 'the price of failing to fulfil expectations may be serious damage to the relationship and to the organisation'.

There is evidence that employee reward system designs have consequences for the organisation–employee psychological contract (Guest, 2004; Rousseau and

Figure 2.4 A model of the psychological contract
Adapted from Guest and Conway (2004)

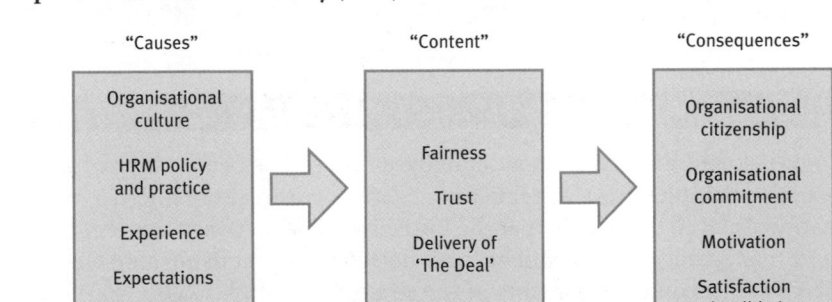

Source: Guest, D.E. and Conway, N. (2004) *Employee well-being and the Psychological contract* London: CIPD

Greller, 1994). If this is the case, the argument runs, it should also have an impact on the *type* of the psychological contract. Rousseau (1995) differentiates between 'relational', that is, open-ended employment relationships characterised by a high mutual interest, and 'transactional' psychological contracts, encapsulated in the statement: 'A fair day's work for a fair day's pay' (Rousseau, 1995: 91).

Described by Mabey *et al* (1998: 133) as 'a rich and nuanced collection of shared understandings built up over time', containing 'subtle structures of tacit but critical employee commitment', psychological contracts are at risk of being undermined by managerial interventions that emphasise a limited number of performance dimensions only. If the theoretical assumptions hold, it may be reasoned that insensitive handling of the psychological contract may encourage individuals to focus on instrumentally prescribed task activity (ie 'working to [explicit] contract'), sacrificing whole-job pride, to the detriment of long-term contribution to overall organisation performance.

The summary psychological contract dynamics in Figure 2.4 illustrate a systems orientation: contract inputs or 'causes', which are in turn affected by open system factors such as expectations and experience of work and alternative employment opportunities beyond the organisation, interact as throughput institutionalised in terms of inter-party trust and perceived fair dealing in both substance and process. In turn, system outputs follow: not only motivated performance, but also 'citizenship' behaviours beneficial to the organisation (ie working 'beyond contract', in Fox's (1974) phrase), accompanied by employee satisfaction and sense of wellbeing at work. Specific applications of the psychological contract notion are discussed in Chapters 9 and 12.

 STUDENT EXERCISE

Debate the arguments that managers may need to evaluate when considering competing motivation theories. Is it necessary to decide between either extrinsic or intrinsic approaches to motivating employees? Does reward have a large or a limited role to play in aligning the workforce with managerial objectives?

INDIVIDUALS, INSTITUTIONS AND STRATEGIC ALIGNMENT

Psychology-inspired theorising about employee reward has been criticised in the management literature for remaining overly focused at the micro (organisational) level. The risk is that the 'brokering role' between academic debate and managerial practice will become detached as practising managers focus their interests on developments in the strategy literature (Kulik, 2001). Guest (1997) contends that, in place of reliance on normative commentary on specific 'low-level' behavioural theories, further attention is needed on the more sophisticated (strategic) interplay between the multiple factors involved (an implicit argument for open systems thinking). Taking just one example, expectancy theory should be perceived not as a theory of motivation alone. Theoretical links need to be made between motivation and performance.

Guest (1997, 2001) puts forward 'HRM', with its emphasis on aligning every aspect of organisation and people management, as a candidate for a theoretical framework to link behavioural theories and HR practices, with the emphasis on performance. He advocates attention to contingencies. In linking with strategy it is necessary to be able to theorise when HRM matters most in achieving business goals. For example, service sector business environments may require a greater strategic emphasis on HRM factors. As previously indicated, the accent is on alignment at both the vertical and horizontal levels – that is, between people management and corporate goals, and between the elements of HRM policy and practice, reflecting holistic systems thinking. (We explore these issues in detail in Chapter 12.)

The 'traditional' managerial approach to motivating workers may be described as reliant on the threat of direct sanctions or punishment of the sub-ordinate by the superior party in a master-server relationship. Insubordinate sailors in Nelson's navy, for example, faced a flogging or worse. However, such an orientation has tended to be associated with work relationships based on some sort of mutual obligation between the parties, as under feudalism, for example. Emerging in the era of late industrialisation, **'scientific management'** may be perceived as a critique of inefficient managerial organisation rather than of the workforce. Taylorism is complemented by a moral view that fair treatment of workers will (and should) be achieved by specifying precisely what tasks are to be performed, and how they are to be performed, and training the workforce accordingly. Reward is to be tied to task/output attainment, provided this is exactly in accordance with managerial specifications.

In contrast with economics-based motivation under scientific management theory, what became known as the **'human relations'** school of thought, popularised by Elton Mayo (1949), adopts a more holistic view of the person performing a job. The source of employee satisfaction derives from the social relations surrounding work. Instead of simply specifying fragmented job tasks, the managerial role is to make employees at work feel important – by permitting some limited task discretion and by enhancing manager–employee communications. Some recognition is also given to teamwork rather than the atomised individual – in pay system terms reinforcing this with 'gain-sharing' and similar collectively based variable pay plans (see Chapter 6). But the human relations school faces criticism that the work design itself remains 'deskilled', and the emphasis is still on ensuring direct compliance with managerial authority. Motivation is socially located with the intention of securing managerial aims without attention to aligning these with the goals of workforce members themselves.

'Human resources' models have been articulated as the basis on which, while retaining the unitarism of human relations thinking, more satisfying work itself may be designed by management, for example McGregor's **'Theory X – Theory Y'** perspective (1960, cited by Smith, 1995). Theory X, conditioned by ideas from the scientific management school (not unlike the agency theory featuring in mainstream corporate governance-linked executive reward initiatives discussed in Chapter 10), charges management with actions intended to *modify the worker*, on the assumption that this is the only way to enlist employees in productive activity. The more employee-centred Theory Y approach to work design and motivation (which assumes that the average person likes work and wants to contribute in performing job tasks) contrasts with scientific management work design, not adequately corrected for the limited discretion offered under human relations management. Again a parallel might be drawn with the 'stakeholder' variant of agency theory advanced by Buck *et al* (1998): see Chapter 10.

Human resources models tend to see motivation as driven by a complex amalgam of interrelated factors, such as money, need for affiliation, need for achievement and desire to find meaning in work activities (Miles, 1965). Under this view, rather than being reluctant workers, needing incentives to trade leisure for work, employees are perceived as reservoirs of talent that management has to find ways of tapping (Steers and Porter, 1987). Employees, it is assumed, are 'pre-motivated' to perform positively in pursuit of satisfaction in the work they undertake and the self-esteem that may be obtained by recognition for a positive contribution to organisational success.

As Steers and Porter comment: 'In contrast to the traditional and human relations models, management's task is seen not so much as one of manipulating employees to accept managerial authority, as it is of setting up conditions so that employees can meet their own goals at the same as meeting the organization's goals' (Steers and Porter, 1987: 18). Employees are recognised and rewarded for their ability and willingness to make significant and rational decisions previously reserved to management.

Contingency theory (eg Child, 1975; Donaldson, 2003) draws attention to the structural context for managerial action, rather than encouraging the importation of universal (one-best-way) ideologies. Following this logic, managers should make judgements about which approach or combination of approaches intended to motivate a diverse workforce best fits with the observable organisational circumstances. Under a contingency approach, ideas about employee motivation from the scientific management, human relations and human resources schools of thought may all be used at one time (Steers and Porter, 1987).

The manager's task is to diagnose the situation to be managed and, not swayed by particular 'solutions' for application organisation-wide, apply the approach that appears most likely to align with the prevailing combination of organisation, technology, competitive and people conditions, context by specific context. Employee reward here becomes a more finely tuned signalling feature within the vertical and horizontal alignment matrix. Its use is neither to induce the 'self-maximising agent' of economic theory to concentrate efforts on exceeding production quotas nor to relegate it to the status of a 'hygiene factor', sharply differentiated from 'motivators' implicit in the work itself.

Managerially, it is not an 'either-or' situation, rather one of combination and balance: working out which situation calls for which blend of extrinsic and intrinsic motivational factors. Recent developments in **Cognitive Evaluation**

Theory indicate that, while prior commentary argued that managerial attention to extrinsic reward gave subjects the wrong signals, the position is subtler than that (Gerhart and Rynes, 2003). Subjects of early cognitive motivation experiments – frequently children – lacked maturity. Adults in work/employment environments have a more refined capacity – based on experience – to read the signals from those overseeing their work and its recognition. While they were likely to be aware of attempts to exercise control over their endeavours, positive *informational* indicators were received as helpful to individuals in judging to what extent pursuit of their goals (and hence performance) was in tune with organisational expectations of them.

Carefully managed extrinsic rewards may therefore serve as signals that individuals may use to guide their own behaviour, potentially increasing their intrinsic interest in work. The risk of manipulation remains, but active engagement in the effort–reward bargaining process as a dynamic exercise between the parties, where self-evidently the individual has an influence on outcomes, implies a more balanced relationship around productive activity. The model illustrated in Figure 2.3 may be revisited bearing this in mind.

The strategic alignment orientation among HRM theorists stresses the need for greater managerial attention to the diverse reactions (as well as dynamic priorities associated with work and reward) among employees. Based on the premise that employees make sophisticated judgements about the messages being signalled to them through reward, and other HRM initiatives, the focus shifts from one of structure to one placing greater stress on process issues. In particular, in place of top-down initiatives, this involves employees as active participants in reward design, and the capacity to draw on a flexible range of extrinsic combined with intrinsic sources of reward and recognition as part of what Herriot and Pemberton (1995) label 'new deals'.

Individuals may focus less on the content of reward and more on comparing the informational signals regarding relative recognition they receive against organisational peers (Chen *et al*, 2002). Equity and comparability are factors that may not actively motivate – but they may be anticipated to have a depressing effect on the motivational influence associated with extrinsic rewards for employment and performance in the job if mismanaged.

Distributional justice theory – how people assess the relative outcomes of reward allocation among peers – and **procedural justice** – how the process is managed, including the capacity of the individual to have their voice heard in reward system design and application – are also factors flagged for management attention (eg Cox, 2004). 'Decision-making is said to be procedurally just when those affected have an opportunity to influence decisions and when they are treated with neutrality, trustworthiness, and respect' (Tepper *et al*, 2006: 103). When the reverse situation is observable, targets of procedural injustice may be motivated to retaliate against those who are seen as blameworthy, based on a sense of resentment.

Additionally, some organisational justice theorists draw attention to **interpersonal justice** – the way that the interaction between the superior and subordinate, the quality of the relationship they enjoy and its perceived character relative to other organisational members, is handled (Olkkonen and Lipponen, 2006). Smith (2005: 6) thus encourages the location of extrinsic reward within 'a complex web of relationships'. In short, socio-psychological contract quality may be expected to modify employee perspectives on management in particular settings, positively or negatively influencing work orientations and pre-motivation to perform, with consequences for managerial potential to achieve corporate goals.

SELF-ASSESSMENT EXERCISE

What are the main cognitive processes by which employees may be expected to evaluate extrinsic reward opportunities, and how do these interact with intrinsic factors that are expected to lead to job satisfaction and motivation to exercise discretionary effort on the employer's behalf? In what ways may managers influence the processes positively or negatively?

KEY LEARNING POINTS AND CONCLUSIONS

Theory underlies action, whether implicit or explicit. In order to undertake systematic consideration of the alternatives, consequences and contexts of employee reward, a grasp of the range of theories that have developed from within the social and management sciences is a prerequisite. Analytical models and prescriptions addressing the propensity of individuals and groups to make their labour power available, and to accept direction and commitment to managerial aspirations, are available in abundance. As discussed in this chapter, some approaches privilege material factors – where it is assumed that employment relationships, expectations among the parties, and regulation of reward systems may be investigated and understood primarily in terms of factors associated with economic exchange. Others may place greater emphasis on behavioural and ideological phenomena, taking intrinsic dimensions into account.

- Economics theory may be abstract in the extreme, adopting a closed systems perspective, and in a similar vein psychological theory may concentrate attention on more biological factors, where managerial intervention may be regarded as of limited influence on outcomes.

- More institutionally inclined economics theory and similarly institutional and more cognitive approaches to psychology articulate roles for active managerial initiatives, alternating between efforts intended to modify employee behaviour or to create the environmental conditions in which employees may direct their own efforts to act in ways that may satisfy managerial goal-directed aspirations.

- Managerial practice may appear to the casual observer to be reliant on a non-theoretical approach, or at least theory that is unarticulated and may be almost subconscious, based on practitioners' socialisation and habit. More clearly developed thinking may be discerned, however, impacting on the ways alternative approaches and their anticipated consequences are weighed. In some cases this means adopting a position that managerial practice in the efficient pursuit of employee co-operation may best be served by matching the approach to the environmental contingencies observable in particular cases. This may involve mixing and matching thinking and concomitant approaches to employee reward management (aligned to people management more generally), perceiving available policy and practice as situated along a range or spectrum, rather than assuming a polarisation of approaches to choose from, in pursuit of universal 'best practice'.

Reflection on these considerations may help to inform HR thinking performers and general managers alike in gaining a better understanding of the possible courses of action at the effort–reward nexus. In the chapters that follow we return to the theoretical foundations for reward management, introduced and reviewed in this chapter, to help evaluate empirical evidence informing alternatives, consequences and contexts.

EXPLORE FURTHER

To gain an appreciation of economic theory as this contributes to the understanding of employee reward, see Beaumont, P. and Hunter, L. (2000) 'Labour economics, competition and compensation', in Thorpe, R. and Homan, G. (eds) *Strategic Reward Systems*. London, FT-Prentice Hall: 45–62.

For an overview of theories on motivation, see Hollyforde, S. and Whiddett, S. (2002) *The Motivation Handbook*. London, Chartered Institute of Personnel and Development.

An interesting discussion weighing alternative strategy models and their consequences for reward systems is to be found in Kessler, I. (2001) 'Reward system choices', in Storey, J. (ed.), *Human Resource Management: a critical text*, 2nd edn. London, Thomson: 206–31.

CHAPTER 3

The Legal, Employment Relations and Market Context

CHAPTER OBJECTIVES

When you have completed this chapter you should understand and be able to explain the following:

- The importance of both legal and employment relations regulation in the design of reward systems.

- The changing political agenda affecting reward.

- The major employment laws governing the reward relationship.

- The role of collective bargaining as a means to joint regulation of the reward relationship.

- Determining pay levels – keeping in line with the market.

CIPD STANDARDS COVERED IN THIS CHAPTER:

Learning outcomes:

- Participate as a team member in consultation or bargaining about the design, implementation and operation of a pay system.

- Help to analyse a pay structure to assess whether it contains sex or other discrimination and suggest ways of making a job evaluation scheme free of bias.

To understand and explain:

- The factors that affect reward philosophies, strategies, policies and levels of pay, including pay determination through collective bargaining.

- The concept of a market rate in local and national labour markets.

INTRODUCTION

Any reward strategy has to be placed within the context of the legal, employment relations and labour market environment within which the organisation operates. Indeed, with the increasing globalisation of business, human resources managers may need to know not just the details of their own country's regulatory framework and labour market but those of many other countries. National culture may also play a vital role in the design of reward systems, although the balance between national and corporate cultures may differ according to circumstances. We deal in more detail with the issue of international reward management in Chapter 11 and the influence of corporate culture in Chapter 2, but suffice to say here that the legal, employment relations, cultural and business context can vary greatly between countries, especially between developed, developing and undeveloped economies.

In most developed industrial economies, the employment relationship is governed by both specific legislation and a framework of accepted social norms governing the employment relationship, including acceptance of the employees' right to trade union membership and recognition for the negotiation of pay and conditions. The most regulated economies – both by law and through established collective bargaining systems – are those of the European Union, followed by Australia, New Zealand, Canada, the USA and Japan. In less developed countries, especially those without the benefits of democratic political systems, employment rights may be more minimal for employees and trade unions may be banned. Even in less developed countries, however, there are often minimum rights, such as limits on working time, minimum wage laws and the prohibition of child labour. Most countries have at least some legislation affecting pay and conditions of employment, usually setting out minimum standards that constrain employers in designing their own reward systems.

In this chapter we consider the major legal and employment relations constraints concerning reward matters upon employers, employees and trade unions in the UK. As the UK is part of the European Union, much of the employment legislation affecting reward increasingly relates to Europe-wide Employment Directives but there is also a considerable raft of domestically initiated legislation, including the UK National Minimum Wage and Rights to Trade Union Recognition for Collective Bargaining Purposes. We begin by examining the development of regulation of the reward relationship before going on to examine in more detail the key areas of UK law affecting pay and conditions of service, and the uses and processes of collective bargaining. We also consider the major levels at which pay may be determined and the pros and cons of decentralised versus centralised systems. Lastly, we consider how pay is determined more widely in terms of relating to the external labour market.

REGULATING THE REWARD SYSTEM

There are three main ways in which employer choice in reward strategy is constrained:

1 By legal regulation of remuneration terms and conditions.

2 By voluntary agreements to jointly regulate the relationship via the process of consultation and negotiation with trade unions known as 'collective bargaining'.

3 By the reality of the external labour market.

The balance between legal and voluntary regulation shifted substantially in the UK over the course of the twentieth century. At the start of the twentieth century both employers and trade unions were agreed – for different reasons – that the law should be kept out of the employment relationship as much as possible. Instead, non-legally binding agreements were reached between the two parties through the process of what became known as voluntary or 'free' collective bargaining (Clegg, 1976). Under this process, rather than the employer seeking to agree pay and conditions with individual employees, the organisation agrees to negotiate or 'bargain' with representatives of the workforce through recognised trade unions.

The logic behind collective bargaining – from the trade union perspective – is that, because the employment relationship is an unequal one between the buyers and sellers of labour, individual employees are stronger when able to negotiate as a group, rather than as individuals. There are, however, also advantages to employers in determining pay through collective bargaining, with which we deal later in this chapter. Unlike many other countries, in the UK the agreements reached through this negotiating process are non-legally binding contracts between the parties, unless the two parties expressly agree that such agreements are legal contracts. The content of such agreements, however, can be incorporated into individual contracts of employment that then become legally binding.

The development of collective bargaining in the UK was a slow and uneven process (Milner, 1995). Over half of the UK workforce was covered by collective bargaining arrangements by the 1970s, however, either directly or indirectly (ie employers without recognised trade unions chose to follow the collective agreements). Since the 1980s, however, there has been a significant decline in the use of collective bargaining as the major method of pay determination, reflecting large-scale changes in the labour market. The period of the 1980s and 1990s also saw new legislation restricting the rights of trade unions to organise in the workplace, which impeded their ability to maintain collective bargaining. Today around seven million (or a third) of UK employees are covered by collective agreements on pay and conditions, either directly or indirectly (Grainger and Crowther, 2006).

It is worth noting here that, while the decline of collective bargaining in the UK has been mirrored in several other developed countries such as the USA, Japan and New Zealand, in many European countries it still remains the most

Table 3.1 Union density and bargaining coverage in selected OECD countries

Country	Union density %			Bargaining coverage %		
	1970	1980	1994	1980	1990	1994
Australia	50	48	41	88	80	80
Austria	62	56	42	98	98	98
Belgium	46	56	54	90	90	90
Canada	31	36	38	37	38	38
Denmark	60	76	76	69	69	69
Finland	51	70	81	95	95	95
France	22	18	9	85	92	95
Germany	33	36	29	91	90	92
Italy	36	49	39	85	83	82
Japan	35	31	24	28	23	21
Netherlands	38	35	26	76	71	81
New Zealand	–	56	30	67	67	31
Norway	51	57	58	75	75	74
Portugal	61	61	32	70	79	71
Spain	27	19	19	76	76	78
Sweden	68	80	91	86	86	89
Switzerland	30	31	27	53	53	50
United Kingdom	45	50	34	70	47	47
United States	23	22	40	72	70	68
Average	43	47	40	72	70	68

Source: Freeman (1988) and OECD (1997), cited in Aidt and Tzannatos (2002)

important determinant of pay and conditions. For example, in countries such as Austria, Sweden, Finland, France and Denmark, collective agreements continue to be the major form of pay determination (Aidt and Tzannatos, 2002). Furthermore, the coverage of collective bargaining does not necessarily correlate with poor trade union membership levels (known as 'union density'). For example, unions in France have only 9 per cent of their potential membership but coverage by collective agreements is 95 per cent (see Table 3.1 above). In three countries (Denmark. Japan and Sweden) union density is higher than collective bargaining coverage. This is explained by the fact that in these countries people may belong to trade unions even where they do not represent them at work.

This variation in collective bargaining coverage largely reflects the differences in economic and political agendas between those countries that espouse the 'social market' and those that favour economic liberalism (Hall and Soskice,

2001). The former countries adhere to the concept of 'social partnership' between the major stakeholders in society – the government, employers' and workers' representatives. These nations believe that it is the role of government to ensure that inequalities of wealth are kept to a minimum; that citizens have certain rights to consultation over their employment conditions; and that both employers and trade unions have a role to play in the management of national economies. This belief is often manifested in national labour codes that lay down the rights and duties of employers and workers (eg France and Belgium), enforceable through labour inspectorates, although there are examples where this is achieved more through collective agreements than through law (eg Denmark).

In contrast, the economic liberals favour a limited regulation of the labour market with the emphasis upon the rights of individual employers and workers, rather than statutory collective rights and protection (eg the USA, Australia and the UK). In the USA, the doctrine of 'employment at will' predominates (ie the legal presumption is that the employment relationship is voluntary and indefinite for both employer and employee, and either side can end the relationship with impunity). This means that there are few laws protecting workers from wrongful dismissal or workplace unfairness in the USA. In Australia, protection against unfair dismissal currently does not apply to organisations employing fewer than 100 workers.

In the UK, since the 1970s, employment law has become much more important than collective bargaining as the major form of regulation of the reward relationship between employers and workers. Up to the 1970s there was relatively little legislation governing pay and conditions of service in the UK but by the end of the twentieth century a raft of new protective legislation had been passed. This new raft of laws covered rights to equal pay between men and women, compensation for loss of job, a national minimum wage, minimum sick pay and holiday entitlement, maximum working hours and time off work for maternity, paternity and carer duties. It is important to remember, however, that while EU Directives have played an important role in creating more uniformity of employment legislation across Europe, there have also been important domestic initiatives by UK governments such as the national minimum wage and rights to trade union recognition for collective bargaining purposes.

While much of this growth in legal regulation represents a reaction to the decline of collective determination of employment rights and the need for more individual protection, some of this change was a result of government policies to deregulate the UK economy. During the 1980s and early 1990s various new laws governing trade unions and their memberships were passed, reducing legal protection for trade unions, not least in terms of rights to recognition (Kessler and Bayliss, 1995). There was no major change, however, in the legal status of collective agreements, despite earlier calls for them to become legally binding on the parties involved. Moreover, during this period the Conservative government also won an important concession from the European Union in being able to 'opt out' of the Charter of Fundamental Rights of Workers (known as the 'Social Charter') passed in 1989.

This allowed the UK to ignore legislation aimed at harmonising European employment law and setting certain minimum standards (such as minimum leave entitlement, maximum working hours and rights for part-time workers). At the same time, the UK government passed new UK-based legislation aimed at emphasising the individual employment relationship, such as increasing financial participation by employees in their companies through various employee share ownership schemes, profit-sharing and profit-related pay. It did this by granting tax relief on such initiatives. The Conservative government also changed the law affecting state sickness benefit by transferring the major role for paying this minimum state benefit from the government to individual employers.

The most significant changes in employment legislation affecting reward, however, came with the election of the Labour government in 1997. The Labour Party promised to reverse the 'opt out' from the 'Social Charter' of the EU (the Charter of Fundamental Rights of Workers, 1989), thus opening up UK employment legislation to a whole new series of reforms. It also had a manifesto commitment to introduce a national minimum wage and pass legislation guaranteeing trade unions limited rights to recognition for the purposes of collective bargaining.

THE IMPACT OF ANTI-DISCRIMINATORY LEGISLATION

A major change in the regulation of reward systems has been the increasing concern to outlaw various forms of discrimination at work. This has been most prominent in the gender field, but in more recent times there has also been concern about the rights of part-time workers, fixed-term contract workers and agency workers. Laws against discrimination on grounds of race, ethnic origin, nationality, religion and sexual orientation have also had effects on some aspects of reward systems. Most recently, new legislation outlawing age discrimination have begun to have an effect on reward policies – for example, seniority-based pay and service-related conditions of service.

 ## SELF-ASSESSMENT EXERCISE

To what extent do you think that the reward relationship should be governed by law? Is non-legal voluntary collective bargaining a better way for employers and employees to reach agreement on their terms and conditions? Or should employers have total discretion in setting pay and conditions for their employees?

LEGAL REGULATION OF REWARD SYSTEMS

As mentioned above, the basis for the design and maintenance of any reward system in any country is the underpinning legal framework. While employers may wish as far as possible to create reward strategies for their own particular circumstances, the starting point will always be what the law allows or requires. In this section we examine the major areas of UK legislation affecting the reward relationship between employer and employee.

The major areas of law affecting reward are as follows:

- contracts of employment
- the national minimum wage
- hours of work, holidays and paid time off
- equal pay for work of equal value
- law covering discrimination in pay and conditions on other grounds, such as race, employment status or age
- law affecting the employee benefits package, including sick pay entitlement
- law affecting share ownership and profit-sharing schemes
- law affecting pension schemes.

It is important to stress here that the strong relationship between pay and working time means that the legislation does not just cover the levels, processes or content of remuneration systems but also the periods of time to which the remuneration relates.

CONTRACTS OF EMPLOYMENT

As discussed in Chapter 1, the exchange of money for work done (known as 'consideration') is the central feature of the employment contract. If no money changes hands, it is highly unlikely that a contract of employment will exist. A contract of employment exists as soon as an employee accepts the offer of employment (see Lewis and Sergeant, 2004 for a fuller explanation of the contract of employment). A contract of employment does not need to be in writing, and in the past the details of payment might have been purely verbal. However, under the terms of the Contracts of Employment Act 1963, employers are required to state the terms on which the contract is made. The Employment Rights Act 1996 requires employers to provide a written statement of further particulars of the contract. These include (among other requirements) the following:

- the rate of remuneration, how it is calculated and the interval at which it is to be paid;
- the terms and conditions relating to hours of work, holidays and holiday pay, and sick pay;
- terms relating to pension arrangements; and
- details regarding any collective agreements that directly affect the employee's terms and conditions of employment.

For the purposes of the Employment Rights Act 1996, 'wages' are defined as including 'any fee, bonus, commission, holiday pay or other emolument' referable to in the contract of employment, whether payable under the contract or otherwise (ERA, 1996). Certain other payments are also covered by this definition of 'wages', such as statutory sick pay and statutory maternity pay, but pension payments and redundancy pay are expressly excluded. Benefits in kind are not treated as 'wages', except where they can be exchanged for money, goods or services (such as vouchers or stamps).

In the past, manual workers ('wage workers') had a statutory right to be paid in cash (under the Truck Acts), but today the form of payment is agreed under the contract of employment. Employers are also constrained by the law in what can be deducted from an employee's pay. In general the only deductions that an employer has an absolute right to deduct from an employee's wages or salary are those required by statute, such as income tax and National Insurance contributions.

THE NATIONAL MINIMUM WAGE

While many countries have had a national floor to wages for decades, in the UK there was only limited legal control of wage levels in specific industries. For a period between 1993 and the passing of the National Minimum Wage Act in 1999 virtually no regulation of minimum wage levels existed. Previous attempts to ensure that pay levels could not fall below a legal minimum were in the form of Statutory Wages Councils. These covered specific sectors of employment where it was felt that employees did not have the protection of collective agreements through trade unions, and so various minimum rates were set at industry level. These Wages Councils also set basic minimum conditions of employment, including working hours and the premium rates to be used for overtime hours. Wages orders were considerably simplified under reforms in 1986 and, after the final abolition of the Wages Councils in 1993, only agricultural workers were covered by such minimum rates (LPC Report, 1998).

Income inequality in the UK has remained at historically high levels since the 1980s when there was a large increase in the gap in household incomes between the lowest-paid and the highest-paid. One academic commentator argued in 1999 that earnings inequalities 'between the rich and the poor have widened since the late 1970s, with wage inequality reaching the highest levels experienced in the twentieth century' (Machin 1999: 185). Machin argued that this growth in inequality had been largely fuelled by above-inflation earnings growth among the highest-paid. This trend was not mirrored in other EU countries, except Ireland.

More recent research by the Institute for Fiscal Studies (IFS, cited by ONS, 2007a), however, argues that this income gap developed in the 1980s for a number of reasons. First, the gap between the wages of the skilled and unskilled increased. This is explained by both the impact of technological change, with fewer jobs for unskilled workers, and a decline in the power of trade unions among such lower-skilled workers. Second, male participation in the labour market declined, especially in households where there was no other earner. Conversely, female participation increased. As men generally earn more than women this impacted on the income distribution. The IFS also found that the income tax cuts of the late 1980s worked to increase inequality (IFS, cited by ONS, 2007a).

There has been a major change, however, with the passing of the National Minimum Wage Act 1998 and the National Minimum Wage Regulations. From April 1999, all employers in the UK have had to pay at least the national minimum wage to their employees. Before the legislation was passed, fears were expressed that setting such a floor to pay would lead to increases in unemployment, increased price inflation and increased overall earnings growth. However, to date, these fears have not been realised. The inflationary effect was minimal; employment continued to grow (especially in some low-wage sectors such as hospitality and retail); and the effect on wage differentials, and hence earnings growth, was minor (Dickens and Manning, 2003).

ISSUES IN REWARD

BOX 3.1 THE NATIONAL MINIMUM WAGE: KEY POINTS

The minimum wage is calculated as an hourly rate based on a worker's pay over a fixed period (the 'pay reference period) divided by the number of hours worked. There are currently three main rates – an 'adult' rate for those aged 22 and above; a 'development' rate covering those aged between 18 and 21, and those workers aged over 22 undergoing training within the first six months of a new job; and a rate for those aged 16 and 17.

The national minimum wage (NMW) applies throughout the UK, and there are no variations or exclusions based on region, size of employer, occupation or industry. The definition of earnings for the NMW is that all 'standard' pay (ie basic pay plus all payments based on output, productivity and performance, including bonuses, PRP and tips paid through the payroll) can count towards the calculation of the wage. This definition excludes all premium pay (such as overtime, shift and special allowances and pay supplements), all benefits (including benefits-in-kind with the exception of a maximum offset for those employees receiving free accommodation), and all tips not paid through the payroll (ie which attract NI contributions) (DTI, 2004).

The minimum wage is up-rated periodically by the Low Pay Commission (LPC), an independent body set up by the government to make recommendations on the level, detail and enforcement of the minimum wage. The Commission is constituted on a tripartite basis, with representatives from employers, trade unions and independent academics. Since its first report in 1999, the LPC has produced a further seven reports, the latest to date being in 2008.

When the NMW was introduced in April 1999, the adult rate was set at £3.60 per hour. The latest increase took the adult rate to £5.52 per hour from October 2007. While increases in the rate were kept more or less in line with the growth in average earnings from 1999 to 2001, from 2002 the LPC has pushed the rate ahead of average earnings. Between 2002 and 2006 the NMW adult rate increased by 27.4 per cent compared to an increase in average earnings of 17 per cent.

Table 3.2 National Minimum Wage rates per hour, April 1999 to October 2007

Adult rate (for workers aged 22+)		Development rate (for workers aged 18–21)		16–17-year-olds rate	
1 Apr 1999	£3.60	1 Apr 1999	£3.00	–	–
1 Oct 2000	£3.70	1 Oct 2000	£3.20	–	–
1 Oct 2001	£4.10	1 Oct 2001	£3.50	–	–
1 Oct 2002	£4.20	1 Oct 2002	£3.60	–	–
1 Oct 2003	£4.50	1 Oct 2003	£3.80	–	–
1 Oct 2004	£4.85	1 Oct 2004	£4.10	1 Oct 2004	£3.00
1 Oct 2005	£5.05	1 Oct 2005	£4.25	1 Oct 2005	£3.00
1 Oct 2006	£5.35	1 Oct 2006	£4.45	1 Oct 2006	£3.30
1 Oct 2007	£5.52	1 Oct 2007	£4.60	1 Oct 2007	£3.40

Source: Low Pay Commission

Figure 3.1 Growth in adult NMW compared with average wages and price inflation

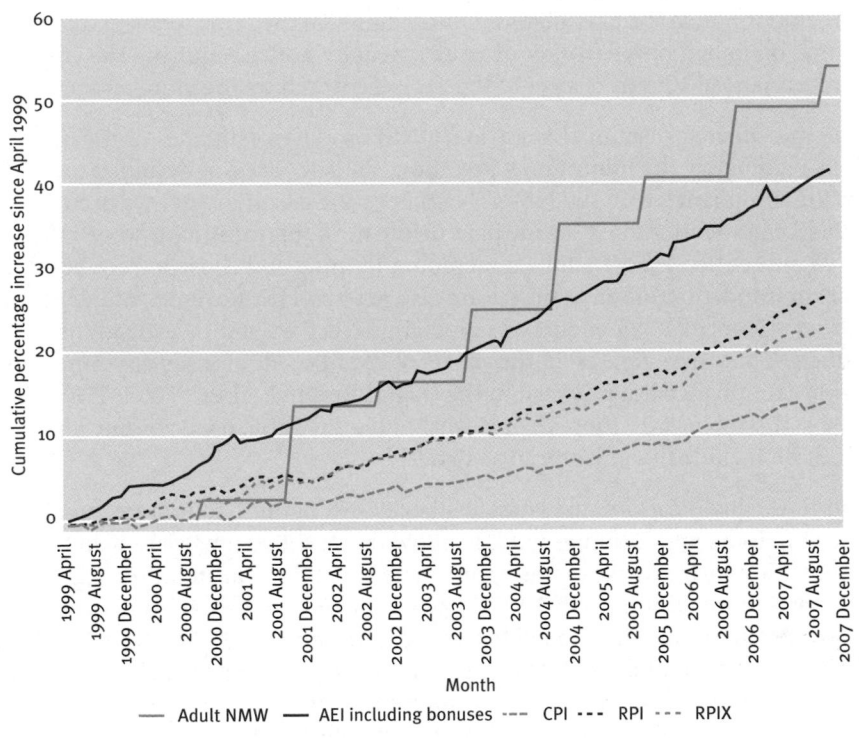

Source: LPC estimates based on ONS data.

The minimum wage is enforced, unusually compared to other UK employment law, through two mechanisms (Skidmore, 1999; Simpson, 1999). Employees can enforce the law themselves through a County Court or Employment Tribunal but this is not the primary means for enforcement (Simpson, 2004). In addition HM Revenue and Customs has a team of Compliance Officers whose enforcement role is to follow up workers' complaints and to conduct investigations of both 'at-risk' places of employment and random visits to employers' premises.

Deliberate refusal to pay the NMW is a criminal offence. There are six criminal offences relating to the NMW, with a fine for each. These six offences are as follows:

- refusal or wilful neglect to pay the NMW
- failing to keep NMW records
- keeping false records
- producing false records or information
- intentionally obstructing an enforcement officer
- refusing or neglecting to give information to an enforcement officer.

Enforcement notices are issued where (a) an employer agrees to rectify non-compliance but subsequently fails to correct the deficiency or (b) an employer refuses to rectify the matters following a further visit or telephone call from the compliance team. If an employer still does not comply with the enforcement notice the Compliance Officer can take the issue to an Employment Tribunal on behalf of the worker or issue a penalty notice requiring the employer to pay a financial sum in respect of the period covered by the enforcement notice.

While the Office for National Statistics (ONS) produces estimates of the number of jobs paid below the minimum wage, these statistics are not designed to monitor compliance with the NMW. Neither of the earnings surveys used by the ONS can identify those legally paid below the adult minimum wage rate, such as apprentices, those adults undergoing training and those in receipt of the accommodation offset. Statistics are also kept by HM Revenue and Customs on the numbers of NME enquiries, complaints received and investigations conducted, but these figures, in the words of the LPC, 'do not say anything about the non-compliance not reported to the Inland Revenue' (LPC, 2003: 158). Nor do the statistics pick up those people working in the informal economy and who will not be included in any official statistics.

Given these qualifications, the latest available ONS figures from the Annual Survey of Hours and Earnings (ASHE) show that 292,000 jobs were held by people with hourly pay below the appropriate statutory minimum (or 1.2 per cent of the total number of UK jobs) (ONS, 2007b). Jobs held by part-time workers and women are more likely to fall below the minimum wage than those held by full-time workers and men. Research by Croucher and White (2007) showed that, while in general enforcement of the minimum wage appeared to be working, there remained problems in workers receiving their full entitlement from employers. A major problem remains the lack of awareness of the law among both employers and employees and the reluctance of low-paid workers to enforce their rights.

The minimum wage has had a clear impact upon pay inequality. Between 2001/02 and 2004/05 there was a fall in inequality in disposable income as earnings at the bottom increased faster than those further up the pay distribution. This was partly due to the NMW increasing faster than average earnings and partly to the introduction of tax credits, which increased the income of households with children in the lower part of the earnings distribution. In 2005/06, however, income inequality increased again (ONS, 2007a). The minimum wage also had a major effect upon gender inequality when it was introduced, reducing the gender 'pay gap' by a full one per cent.

As the minimum wage has been increased it has increasingly become the lowest grade rate in many sectors. While at the start the level of the wage set affected only the very lowest-paid workers, it now has a major influence on pay levels in many sectors. Many employers do not wish to be seen as minimum wage employers and hence increase their minimum rates to stay ahead of the statutory minimum.

Full details of the requirements of the National Minimum Wage Regulations are laid out in the DTI Guide, available online from the Department for Business Enterprise and Regulatory Reform (http://www.berr.gov.uk/files/file11671.pdf).

SELF-ASSESSMENT EXERCISE

What do you think are the main arguments in favour of a statutory minimum level of pay? Should employers be able to pay what they like? What do you think might be the effects of such a policy on employment levels, inflation and earnings growth? Have any of these fears been realised?

HOURS OF WORK, HOLIDAYS AND PAID TIME OFF

While some workers are paid entirely by output (and hence create a problem for calculating any minimum wage entitlement), and yet other workers increasingly work to a professional contract requiring them to work flexibly and without fixed hours of work, most employment contracts stipulate some, at least notional, hours of attendance. Many workers are paid an hourly rate or weekly wage, while those on annual salaries will have their pay divided up into monthly instalments. Time is therefore normally of the essence in calculating an employee's pay. Because pay and time at work are so intrinsically linked together, any legislative framework affecting reward is likely to include some limits on working time and rights to holidays and time off. In general, manual workers have traditionally worked longer hours than non-manual, but this pattern has been changing in recent years. There has been a move to harmonise the working hours of all employees within an organisation, and of course there has been a trend towards increasing unpaid working time for many professional staff.

In the past, working time was controlled largely through industry-level collective agreements rather than through the law. There were, however, some limits on working hours for female employees and young persons under 18 in terms of the Factories Act 1961. Working time is now regulated through the Working Time Regulations 1998, introduced as a result of an EU Directive, which lays down a maximum working week of 48 hours (averaged over a 17-week period) with stipulated rest breaks. Many collective agreements (and even some employers who are not party to such agreements) lay down that workers should be compensated for working additional hours or unsocial hours, such as shift working or at night. Some workers, such as key maintenance personnel, may also be paid for being 'called out' from home to deal with urgent work problems or may be given an 'on-call' payment for being available out of normal working hours. There is no legislation in the UK requiring an overtime premium, a shift premium or an 'on call' or 'call out' payment, but in the USA there is such a requirement to pay overtime for certain classes of worker covered by collective bargaining.

Until the passing of the Working Time Regulations in 1998 there was no statutory entitlement to any paid holiday in the UK. Such entitlement was purely down to the individual contract of employment. While the Holidays with Pay Act 1938 allowed statutory wage-fixing bodies, such as the Wages Councils, to set minimum holiday entitlement and the level of holiday pay, other workers were not covered by this entitlement. Most collective agreements, however, did agree holiday entitlement, and by the end of the Second World War at least five days' holiday (in addition to customary and Bank Holidays) was universal; by the 1950s this had increased to 10 days (Clegg, 1976: 218). Holiday entitlement has increased since then to an average of around 25 days (IDS, 2007), and today there is a statutory minimum of 24 days for full-time employees under the Working Time Regulations (rising to 28 days from April 2009). This minimum statutory entitlement is not service-related and begins on day one of employment.

Employees are also entitled to time off work for other reasons. These include:

- maternity leave
- paternity leave
- adoption leave
- parental leave
- time off work to look after dependants
- time off work for public duties
- time off work for trade union duties.

Some of this leave is paid (at least at minimum rates and/or for minimum periods), but in some cases this is not required. In recent years there has been a significant improvement in the provision of such special leave for family-friendly reasons.

EQUAL PAY FOR WORK OF EQUAL VALUE

Until the passing of the Equal Pay Act in 1970 it was perfectly legal to pay women less than men for doing the same job. The gap between the average earnings of full-time men and women workers was 31 per cent in 1970. The 1970 Act was a major breakthrough in the journey towards greater equality between men and women. Since then the law covering equal pay has become increasingly complex, especially as gender inequality has become a major concern of the EU. Despite such interest and political action by government, the gender pay gap in the UK for full-time employees remains stuck at 17.2 per cent (ie full-time women's average hourly earnings were 82.8 per cent of full-time men's) in 2007 (ONS, 2007c). In the case of part-time female employees the gap is even wider (at 36 per cent).

Walby and Olsen (2002) identify several reasons for the gender pay gap. These include: differences in the patterns of male and female employment (ie differences in the jobs they do); their previous employment histories; levels of qualifications; and unequal pay where it exists (ie the extent to which women are being treated unfairly, and not being paid the same amount for the same, similar or equal-value jobs). The research identified the most important factors behind the gender pay gap as discrimination and other factors associated with being female (29 per cent of the problem) and the years of full-time employment experience (26 per cent). Interruptions to the labour market owing to family care accounted for 15 per cent, and occupational segregation (ie the different patterns of employment for men and women) for 13 per cent.

In recent years there have been two major government-commissioned reports on women's pay and employment. The Kingsmill Report (2001: 6) concluded that 'the scale and persistence of the gender pay gap in Britain reflects a failure in human capital management that is neither good for the economy nor in the interests of the majority of employers or employees'. The report made 14 recommendations aimed at improving the management of human capital and hence tackling the gender pay gap. Kingsmill found that the concentration of women in poorly paid part-time work was a significant factor in the scale and persistence of the gender pay gap. The Women and Work Commission's report (CLG, 2007), which followed the Kingsmill Report, called on employers to tackle all the causes of the gender pay gap, not just pay discrimination. Access for women to better-paid occupations, and especially better-paid part-time work, were seen as key.

Today inequality in reward on the basis of gender is covered by three pieces of legislation:

- the Equal Pay Act 1970 (as amended by the Equal Pay (Amendment) Regulations 1983)
- the Sex Discrimination Act 1975
- the Pensions Act 1995.

The Equal Pay Act 1970 outlawed unequal pay for men and women doing the same jobs. Employers were given a five-year period in which to bring women's pay up the same level as men's. This measure did not take account, however, of the fact that women's employment tends to be concentrated in particular sectors and occupations, and that their pay was therefore usually lower than for jobs of the equivalent value for men. This was because their jobs were seen as 'women's work' and hence innately inferior to men's work, rather than based on any genuine assessment of their content and value.

To deal with this inequality of treatment, the concept of pay for equal work of equal value was born. This concept has been part of European Union legislation since the original Treaty of Rome in 1957 included Article 119, which guaranteed equal pay for work of equal value. After the UK joined the EU in 1973, the 1970 Act – which was UK domestic legislation – needed to be brought into line with EU law on work of equal value. The result was the Equal Pay (Amendment) Regulations 1983. These Regulations require employers to ensure that their pay structures do not discriminate in terms of valuing the work of men and women employed by them. In order to defend themselves against equal-pay claims, employers must be able to prove that their grading structures are based on the principle of equal pay for work of equal value. This means that different jobs within the grading system must be equally valued according to the content of those jobs rather than the gender of the person doing them. While the law does not require this, the orthodox method of ensuring this is through job-evaluating all jobs.

The definition of 'pay' under the Equal Pay Act includes wages and all other contractual entitlements, such as holiday pay, discounts, vouchers and subsidies, but in the case of a discretionary payment or allowance the claim must be brought under the Sex Discrimination Act 1975. More recent legislation – the Pensions Act 1995 – requires that employers' pension schemes do not discriminate on the grounds of gender.

ISSUES IN REWARD

BOX 3.2 LOCAL AUTHORITIES TO BORROW MILLIONS FOR EQUAL-PAY CLAIMS

Government pushes for negotiations over legal action

Local authorities will be able to borrow £500 million to pay off thousands of equal pay disputes, the government has announced. The plan will allow the 46 councils with the largest number of claims to negotiate individual agreements and reduce threats of legal action. Public-sector union Unison welcomed the move. 'It clearly demonstrates a commitment towards the principles of equal pay,' said a spokeswoman. 'We have always maintained that collective bargaining, rather than lengthy court action, is the best way to ensure equal pay to all,' she added.

The announcement comes after comments made by Jenny Watson, chairman of the Equal Opportunities Commission, who warned that no-win no-fee lawyers were encouraging the number of women challenging employers over equal pay. The tribunal service heard 44,103 cases from men and women last year, an increase of 155 per cent on the previous year. TUC general secretary Brendan Barber said: 'This is a welcome first step towards ending the stalemate in securing equal pay settlements for local government workers.' He continued: 'However, this alone will not end the funding problems local authorities face in paying back female staff who have suffered unequal pay for many years.'

Source: Laura Chubb, *People Management*, 3 October 2007

Equal pay for work of equal value has become a major issue in reward management, especially in the public services where the risk of claims has been one of the driving forces behind new 'pay modernisation' agreements in local government, the NHS and higher education.

Equal pay is particularly an issue in the public services for three main reasons: because reward practices are generally more transparent compared to the private sector; because government has encouraged the public services to set an example of good practice; and because there have been clearly identified cases of gender discrimination in pay practices (eg males in jobs such as refuse collection having access to significant incentive earnings whereas female cleaners and catering staff have not, despite being on the same grade). In recent years attempts to remedy this situation through new pay agreements with the trades unions have been compromised by so-called 'no win, no fee' lawyers encouraging individual women to take legal action against their employers (and unions in some cases).

The problems in local government (see Box 3.2 above) demonstrate the impact that legislation can have on reward practice. The major issue in the public services is retrospective compensation for past inequality. Where, under job-evaluation exercises as part of 'pay modernisation', women are found to have been discriminated against they can claim retrospective 'back pay' for up to six years, adding considerably to the cost of implementing new 'equality-proofed' pay structures.

There has been a huge increase in the number of equal-pay claims in recent years. The figures indicate that in 2005/06 the number of cases lodged with employment tribunals more than doubled to 17,268 from 8,229 in 2004/05. The major reason for this growth was the number of multiple claims brought in the public sector against local councils and health authorities.

Since 6 April 2007, UK public authorities are also covered by a general duty to demonstrate that they treat men, women and transgender people fairly by eliminating unlawful discrimination and harassment on the grounds of sex and promoting equality of opportunity between men and women. In England, specific duties include the need to include objectives to address the gender pay gap.

 SELF-ASSESSMENT EXERCISE

What are the main ways in which equal pay law might influence the design of pay systems? Is it right that the law should play such an important role in the design of pay systems? Consider the case of UK public services.

AGE DISCRIMINATION

While discrimination on the basis of age has been unlawful in the USA and elsewhere for some time, it is only recently that an EU Directive has required member states to introduce age discrimination legislation. In the UK this has been implemented through the Employment Equality (Age) Regulations 2006. This legislation may have some important effects upon reward systems, not least the use of age-related pay rates and service-related entitlement to benefits. The Regulations may also affect the use of long, seniority-based pay scales (although the recent ECJ case of *Cadman v HSE* [2004 EWCA (civ) 1317] under equal pay legislation, described below, may also have implications here too).

A number of areas of potential unlawful pay discrimination on the basis of age have been identified (Armstrong and Murlis, 2007). These include the common practice of setting recruitment salaries in line with previous salaries. The problem emerging is that, in terms of job weight, there may be no difference between the job of the new recruit and those already employed or others being recruited. This is a particular problem if those benefiting from a premium from their previous salary are largely males and those not benefiting are females, but it may also pose a problem in terms of older versus younger workers. In this circumstances there is a clear risk of gender or age discrimination. Starting salaries therefore need to be set in line with objective and justifiable criteria and any anomalies dealt with. An audit or review of the distribution of salaries within each grade by gender and age will be one method of checking on this.

A second potential problem is the linking of salary level or benefits entitlement to service (for example, where pay progression is based on annual increments or where holiday entitlement increases with service). The Regulations allow for a five-year exemption period for such service-related rewards, so that service up to five years can be counted as a criterion for either incremental movement through a grade or for benefits entitlement. Service-related entitlements beyond five years will need to be justified in terms of a business need. Clearly, long-service requirements can discriminate against younger employees and females, who are more likely to have shorter service.

The *Cadman* judgment from the European Court of Justice (ECJ) also concerns the risk of unfair discrimination through service requirements, but was taken under equal-pay legislation. Cadman, who worked for the Health and Safety Executive (HSE), brought a claim under the Equal Pay Act after discovering that four of her (male) colleagues in the same grade were paid more than her. This was because, although carrying out the same level of work, the males had longer service and hence were ahead of Ms Cadman in the service-based incremental scale. The HSE argued that longer service equated to more experience. In dismissing Cadman's claim, the ECJ ruled that service was an appropriate criterion for rewarding experience, but went on to warn that such service-based progression needed to be objectively justified, particularly where an employee provides evidence raising serious doubts about the utility of such a criterion. There is no doubt that a victory for Cadman would have placed the continued use of service-based incremental pay progression in jeopardy.

OTHER DISCRIMINATION LAW AFFECTING PAY

It is also unlawful to discriminate, in terms of treatment under reward systems, against employees on grounds of race, ethnicity, religion or belief, disability, sexual orientation and age, but these areas, unlike gender pay discrimination, are not covered by specific legislation on remuneration. Rather they are covered as part of the overall duty of employers not to engage in unfair discrimination at work.

LAW AFFECTING BENEFITS

The major field of law covering employee benefits is not employment law but legislation governing the treatment of pay and conditions for tax and National Insurance purposes (Armstrong and Murlis, 2007), and the provision of certain statutory benefits, such as sick pay and redundancy pay. There is also legislation governing employer-run occupational pension schemes.

Perhaps one of the most important changes to the legislation in recent times was the decision of the Conservative government to transfer the provision of state sickness benefit from the state to employers through the Statutory Sickness Pay (SSP) Scheme introduced in 1983. Initially employers were allowed to recoup most of the cost of these payments from their PAYE income tax and National Insurance receipts, but from April 1995 employers have only been able to recoup payments where costs exceed 13 per cent of gross National Insurance Contributions (Smith, 2000). In effect this means that there is now a minimum level of sick pay that employers must provide for a minimum period.

Salaries, fees, wages, perquisites or profits are described in law as 'emoluments' from employment. 'Emoluments' are defined as rewards for 'services rendered, past, present or future' or, more broadly, payments made 'in return for acting as, or being, an employee' (Armstrong, 2002: 416–17). Most employees earning over £8,500 per year are likely to be taxed on any benefits received from the employer, in addition to paying tax on their annual salary. In addition, certain benefits count towards National Insurance (NI) contributions. A major role of reward managers in the 1980s and 1990s was the achievement of 'tax efficiency' (as opposed to tax avoidance) for their benefits packages. This means seeking to use the tax and NI system to ensure that both the employer and employee make maximum use of the tax relief possible on those benefits. The tax treatment of benefits has been tightened up significantly in recent years so that 'tax efficiency' has become much less easy for compensation and benefits managers in the UK.

FINANCIAL PARTICIPATION SCHEMES

As mentioned earlier in this chapter, a major development in the 1980s and early 1990s was the development of a new tax regime to encourage organisations to allow employees to participate financially in the success of their organisations. While tax relief only applied to private sector organisations (because the public sector has no shares or profits to distribute), these initiatives provided important incentives to the growth of the 'share-holding democracy' advocated by the Conservative Party (Hyman, 2000; Keef, 1998). Indeed, some of the schemes – especially Profit Related Pay – were so successful that the tax loss to the Exchequer finally spelt their death-knell in 2000 when the government decided to phase out tax relief on such schemes.

The major two forms of employee financial participation in the UK currently are:

- profit-sharing or gain-sharing schemes, where employees receive a share of any profits made by the organisation, and
- share option or ownership schemes.

In terms of share ownership schemes, the major vehicle available to cover an employer's entire workforce is the Share Incentive Plan (SIP). Other forms of financial participation scheme are savings-related schemes (also known as Save-as-you-earn schemes or Sharesave schemes); enterprise management incentives; and company share option plans (CSOPs). See Chapter 7 for further details. For directors and senior executives there are also various share options available.

PENSIONS

Most occupational pension schemes are administered under trust law, with the control of their funds vested in a board of trustees. Tax relief on contributions is available to employee members of those schemes approved by HM Revenue and Customs. The Revenue lays down limits on the maximum benefits available with this tax relief. The employer can also recover the tax on its contributions and the income tax payable on investment income from UK investments. See Chapter 9 for further details.

SELF-ASSESSMENT EXERCISE

What are the main sources of law affecting the design and implementation of a reward benefits package?

COLLECTIVE BARGAINING

In the preceding section we laid out the framework of UK law impinging on the reward system. But, as discussed earlier, regulation of the reward system is not done entirely through legislation. In many organisations, the design and outcomes of the reward system are contested through the process of collective bargaining. In this section we define collective bargaining and consider its advantages and disadvantages as a means to determining pay. We also look briefly at the coverage of collective agreements and how this has changed in recent years. We also consider the levels at which pay determination may take place.

COLLECTIVELY BARGAIN OR NOT?

A major decision for employers is to decide the scope for, if any, employee involvement in the reward determination process – so-called 'employee voice'. Employers may choose to consult with individual employees or groups of employees about the design and any changes to the reward system, or they may decide that it is management's prerogative to decide on these matters. On the other hand, where an employer recognises a trade union this normally implies that there will be a more formal relationship, including collective bargaining over pay and conditions. Indeed, formal recognition of a trade union by an employer for collective bargaining purposes will imply negotiations over pay and conditions. Even in workplaces without any formal employee representation or consultation arrangements, however, the reward system remains a contested area of the employment relationship, and any changes will require careful handling by the employer.

Gennard and Judge (2002: 41) define collective bargaining as 'a method of determining the "price" at which employee services are bought and sold – a system of industrial governance whereby unions and employers jointly reach decisions concerning the employment relationship'. In practice, collective agreements are applied to all employees, whether union members or not. It is also the case that organisations that do not recognise trade unions may still follow the collective agreement applying to workers in their sector or industry (eg in the construction and printing industries). For this reason, collective bargaining covers a larger proportion of the workforce than trade union membership.

Four prerequisites for collective bargaining have been observed (Gennard and Judge, 2002: 272): first, there must be organisation on the part of the buyers and sellers of labour; secondly, there must be a substantive agreement to bargain; thirdly, there must be a procedural agreement; and, finally, both the buyers and sellers of labour must be able to impose sanctions (costs) upon each other so that they can reassess their positions towards each other in terms of the demands they make of each other. At the extreme this may mean the temporary withdrawal of all or part of their labour by employees (known as industrial action or a 'strike') or a 'lock out' by employers where the employer tells staff not to come to work unless prepared to work normally. There is some protection for employees taking industrial action in that employees may not be dismissed when taking industrial action for the first 12 weeks of the dispute. Employers also cannot selectively dismiss workers taking action. It is worth noting here that the top reason for employees taking industrial action is over pay and conditions, with 73 per cent of disputes concerning this issue (Hale, 2007).

The choice for employers in whether to bargain collectively with trade unions is often circumscribed. In certain parts of the economy, especially in the public sector, trade unions are well represented among the workforce, and even managers may be union members. In certain cases, union representation in the pay determination system is embedded and accepted, even if not welcomed, by management. In the public sector, trade unions are an accepted part of the independent Pay Review Body system (discussed later), with evidence being submitted by and discussed with the unions.

Elsewhere, the decision to recognise unions may not be an employer's choice. Where unions use the union recognition rights under the Employment Relations Act 1999 to claim representation on behalf of the workforce, there are legal duties placed on employers. If the unions can demonstrate that 40 per cent of those in the 'bargaining unit' (the group for which recognition is sought) wish to be represented, then the recognition is automatic. With recognition rights goes the duty of the employer to engage in negotiations with the union about pay and conditions.

But many employers voluntarily recognise trade unions for collective bargaining purposes. There may be advantages in having reward determined formally through the process of negotiation with employee representatives. In general terms, some employers welcome the opportunity to involve their staff in decisions about reward – even if these are limited to the composition of the pay package and the processes of reward rather than the levels of pay. We discussed in Chapter 2 the more general advantages of having employee voice in the reward design process. Suffice to say here that many employers make a clear choice to recognise trade unions and negotiate about reward.

One significant advantage for employers of collective bargaining over individual negotiation is that a collective agreement can avoid having to reach a separate agreement with each employee. Under the employment contract, once terms have been agreed through the process of collective bargaining, any pay changes can be incorporated into individual terms and conditions without having to seek individual agreement with each worker. This can make pay determination considerably simpler in the longer term.

Whether employers favour recognition or not is often a matter of organisational culture and/or management style. According to the 2004 Workplace Employment Relations Survey (WERS), union recognition is much more likely in larger organisations than small – hence the prevalence of collective bargaining in the public sector (Kersley *et al*, 2006: 179). WERS data showed that around a quarter of workplaces set pay for at least some employees through collective bargaining. Almost two-thirds of workplaces with 500 or more employees set some pay through collective bargaining. Even in workplaces with fewer than 25 employees, a fifth used collective bargaining for at least some employees. In the public sector around four-fifths of workplaces used collective bargaining to determine pay.

The WERS data also indicated that collective bargaining is less likely to be found where the workplace was family-owned and in standalone workplaces. Conversely, bargaining was more likely to be found where no individual or family had a controlling interest and where the workplace was part of a larger organisation. It is interesting to note that, while there is no difference in the prevalence of bargaining between domestic (UK) and foreign-owned workplaces, the proportion of employees that are covered by bargaining is much higher in foreign-owned workplaces.

 SELF-ASSESSMENT EXERCISE

Write down a list of advantages and disadvantages for having collective bargaining in an organisation. Consider how these might affect the reward system in your own organisation or one with which you are familiar.

THE DECLINING COVERAGE OF COLLECTIVE BARGAINING

Over the period since 1984, the proportion of UK workers covered by collective agreements has significantly declined. Workplace Employment Relations Survey (WERS) data indicate that in 1984 some 70 per cent of workers in workplaces employing 25 or more people were covered by collective bargaining. The latest figures from the 2004 WERS indicate that coverage has stabilised at around 40 per cent – it was 39 per cent in 2004, but the difference from 1998 is not statistically significant. Nonetheless, if we look at the figures more closely it appears that there has been some increase in coverage in the public sector – up to 77 per cent. The private sector, however, continues to decline. In private services, collective bargaining coverage was down to 21 per cent in 2004 and in private manufacturing down to 38 per cent.

Table 3.3 Aggregate collective bargaining coverage, 1998 and 2004

	% employees		Average annual change (%)
	1998	2004	
All workplaces	38	35	−1.1
Broad sector			
Private manufacturing	43	34	−3.5
Private services	20	18	−1.4
Public sector	66	75	+2.1
Industry			
Manufacturing	43	35	−3.0
Electricity, gas and water	90	86	−0.6
Construction	32	24	−4.2
Wholesale and retail	21	13	−7.2
Hotels and restaurants	12	4	−16.2
Transport and communication	58	61	+0.9
Financial services	49	35	−5.0
Other business services	12	9	−3.7
Public administration	83	80	−0.6
Education	44	49	+1.9
Health and social work	40	55	+5.1
Other community services	36	40	+2.0
Any recognised unions	66	73	+1.4
Workplaces with 25 or more employees			
All	41	39	−0.7
Private manufacturing	46	38	−2.6
Private services	23	21	-1.1
Public sector	66	77	+2.5

Source: Kersley *et al* (2006: 187)

Collective bargaining coverage varies between industrial sectors. In the private sector coverage of employees is highest in electricity, gas and water (87 per cent); transport and communications (63 per cent); and financial services (49 per cent). In other sectors it is low: in hotels and restaurants it is only 5 per cent and in 'other business services' 12 per cent.

There is some indication that pay in workplaces covered by collective bargaining (the so-called 'union mark-up') is higher than elsewhere (Blanchflower and

Bryson, 2003), although this premium appears to be diminishing. In terms of outcomes, workplaces covered by collective bargaining appear to have more compressed pay distribution (ie a smaller gap between the lowest- and highest-paid). Employees covered by collective agreements are also less likely to be low-paid (Kersley *et al*, 2006). In general, workplaces with collective agreements also tend to provide better basic conditions of service such as holiday entitlement, pensions and sick pay (Forth and Millward, 2000). While WERS 2004 suggests that dissatisfaction with pay is more common where there are union members present, this is not the case for collective bargaining.

ISSUES IN REWARD

BOX 3.3 UNIONS FORCED TO BECOME WATCHDOGS

Research finds shift from pay bargaining to role in helping individual employees enforce legal rights such as the minimum wage

Globalisation and competitive pressures are forcing unions to take a new role in the workplace as a legislation watchdog, according to new research. A study by William Brown and Sarah Oxenbridge from Cambridge University identified a sea change in UK labour relations. Brown said they found that unions were moving away from traditional areas such as pay bargaining to a role as an industry watchdog, focused on helping individual employees enforce existing rights such as the minimum wage.

'Because of competitive pressures, companies no longer have the room to make concessions. If unions try to force a pay deal, the company may simply choose to relocate to a different country. These changes have led to an era of historically low strike records,' said Brown, professor of industrial relations at the University of Cambridge.

The study, which looked at factors that led to a long-lasting employer–union relationship, found the relationship was almost entirely dependent on the extent to which management wanted to work with the unions. 'If management refuses to get involved in negotiations there is nothing unions can do,' added Brown. Unions that negotiated on traditional areas, such as pay, had to demonstrate independence of management and had less influence in the workplace, the study found.

But where unions negotiated on non-pay issues, such as flexible working and training, broader relationships with management were established. Brown said this new role was leading to a partnership approach, enabling employers and unions to forge successful longer-term relationships.

Commenting on the findings, TUC general secretary Brendan Barber said: 'National-level collective bargaining and pay determination still flourish in the public sector. But the research does show though that unions are ready and able to adapt to different circumstances in different industries and to represent their members effectively, whether through collective bargaining or through individual representation.'

Source: Katie Hope, *People Management*, 16 September 2004: 7

ALTERNATIVE PAY DETERMINATION METHODS

By far the most common form of pay determination at workplace level in 2004 was unilateral pay-setting by management (Kersley *et al*, 2006), with some 70 per cent of workplaces setting pay in this manner. Other methods include negotiation with individual employees or through consultation and information (but not negotiation) with employees (eg via a company council). Some 13 per cent of workplaces set pay through individual negotiation with employees. According to WERS 2004 data, another 7 per cent of workplaces set pay by some 'other unspecified method'. A surprisingly small proportion of employers consult with employees about pay. Some 5 per cent of workplaces consulted with employees and 6 per cent informed employees about decisions taken.

In the public sector a common method of pay determination for major groups of public servants (such as school teachers in England and Wales, doctors and dentists, NHS staff, the armed forces and the prison service) is the independent Pay Review Body (PRB). Under this system, pay is determined through the decisions of a committee of independent individuals sitting in judgment on evidence provided by the main parties (government, the employers and the trade unions). The PRBs make recommendations to government on pay increases and other pay structure decisions (Horsman, 2003; White, 2000; White and Hatchett, 2003). According to WERS 2004 (Kersley *et al*, 2006), some 6 per cent of workplaces had their pay set through this process.

 SELF-ASSESSMENT EXERCISE

How is pay determined in your organisation or one with which you are familiar? At what level are decisions taken about the structure of reward and the pay levels for particular jobs? Is there any consultation with employees about either the pay system or increases in pay?

LEVELS OF PAY DETERMINATION

There are important issues for employers about the level at which pay is determined. Where collective bargaining exists, there have been important debates, in terms of management strategy and economic outcomes, about whether centralised bargaining (at industry or sector level) is better than decentralised (at organisation or workplace level) (see Arrowsmith and Sisson, 1999; Calmfors and Driffill, 1988; Purcell and Ahlstrand, 1994; White, 2000).

According to the CIPD (Palmer, 1990), the advantages of centralised bargaining are as follows:

- It reflects the nation-wide organisation of most trade unions.
- It relieves small employers of the need to negotiate on terms and conditions.
- It centralises resources and hence can be cost-effective.

- It ensures equitable treatment of employees across a sector and hence assists labour mobility.
- The absence of such centralisation can, where trade unions are powerful, lead to the playing off of strong employers against the weak.

The disadvantages of such centralised bargaining are that:

- It reduces the ability of individual employers to negotiate organisation/workplace deals.
- 'Something for something' productivity bargaining (eg changes in working practices) can only really be discussed at lower levels.
- Some employers are forced to pay more than they can afford.

Table 3.4 Pay determination methods (workplaces)

% of workplaces						
	1998			**2004**		
	Public sector	**Private sector**	**All**	**Public sector**	**Private sector**	**All**
Single method of collective bargaining						
Only multi-employer	28	2	8	36	1	7
Only single-employer	19	4	7	12	4	5
Only workplace-level	0	1	1	1	1	1
Single other method						
Only set by management, higher level	9	24	21	7	23	20
Only set by management, workplace	1	32	25	1	43	35
Only set by individual negotiations	0	6	5	0	5	4
Only other methods	4	3	3	1	0	1
Pay Review Body	-	-	-	1	0	1
Mixture of methods	39	28	31	41	23	26
All methods	100	100	100	100	100	100
Any collective bargaining	79	17	30	77	11	22
Any set by management	21	81	69	28	79	70
Any individual negotiations	1	16	13	2	15	13
Any other methods	39	8	14	32	2	7
Pay Review Body	-	-	-	32	0	6

Source: Kersley *et al* (2006: 184)

- National rates of pay ignore variations in labour market conditions locally and can mean employers pay more than they need to.

The issue of centralised bargaining in the public sector has been an ongoing political issue for government. Both Conservative and Labour governments have argued for more regional determination of pay in the public services, proposing that public organisations need to reflect regional variations in labour markets in their pay-setting mechanisms. A counter-argument has been that pay variations are small outside the regions clustering around London (largely London and the South East) and that regional pay-setting would be too simple a tool to deal with complex local, regional and national labour markets for public servants (IDS, 2006).

According to the latest WERS 2004 data, where employers engaged in collective bargaining, negotiations were most likely to take place at sector or industry level and then at single employer level. Bargaining at workplace level was least common. However, this picture was almost entirely influenced by the prevalence of large sector-wide agreements in the public sector. In the private sector it is much more common for employers to bargain at organisational or workplace level.

The arguments about whether to centralise or decentralise collective bargaining levels may be of reducing interest (except perhaps in the public sector) as coverage declines. But there are still important strategic issues for all employers about where decisions are taken about pay matters, irrespective of whether or not they have collective bargaining. In 35 per cent of workplaces pay was set by management at the workplace and in 22 per cent by management higher in the organisation (eg at head office level). The WERS 2004 data indicates that the biggest change in the 2004 survey was the growth in the proportion of workplaces where management at workplace level set all pay. This was the sole method of pay determination in over two-fifths of private sector workplaces.

THE IMPACT OF THE LABOUR MARKET

The third constraint on the reward system is the labour market. As discussed in Chapter 2, while employers may attempt to defend themselves against competition for their labour through asserting internal labour market (ILM) principles, with emphasis upon equity and fairness, the external market for labour always exerts a countervailing pressure. While job evaluation may help to provide a 'felt fair' hierarchy of jobs within the enterprise, under which jobs of equal weight are graded the same, there are always different market rates for different occupations and skills.

This tension between establishing internal differentials for different jobs, on the one hand, and ensuring that specific occupations or skills can be recruited from the external labour market and retained, on the other, is a constant threat to any attempt at rationality in pay structures. The price of labour in the external market, which will depend on both broader economic conditions and the individual stocks of particular skills and occupations available, is a key constraint on what an organisation does internally. As Kessler (2007: 167) states, 'external equity is an organisational imperative'.

The notion of 'market pay' has become very much in fashion over the last decade or so, reflecting the shift to more individualised payment systems and growing emphasis on the external market, rather than internal equity. Surveys of reward practice by the CIPD (eg CIPD, 2007) have consistently shown in recent years that achieving and maintaining market competitiveness is a key objective for organisations. As IDS (2004) argues, however, linking salary levels to what other organisations in the same labour market are paying is nothing new. In fact, 'it is practised more or less universally, in one form or another, although the language used to describe it may be very different' (IDS, 2004: 8). The shift to more market-related pay-setting has been linked to tighter labour markets as unemployment has fallen and dissatisfaction with performance-related pay among employers has grown. It has also reflected the environment of low inflation that has reduced the scope for significant individual performance-related pay increases.

Government has echoed the renewed emphasis on the external market in the private sector in its attempts to contain increases in public sector pay. In 2003, the Chancellor of the Exchequer changed the remits of the independent pay review bodies to include a stronger local and regional dimension. In the government's view, national pay structures for public servants do not provide sufficient matching to local and regional pay levels, and can end up underpaying for some jobs and overpaying for others. This is despite the fact that government earnings statistics show there is little variation in pay levels between regions outside London, the South East and the East (see Box 3.4, below).

Among manual workers, where pay rates are often single 'spot' grade rates, often known as 'the rate for the job', linking pay levels to those for the same trades or skill level in the local geographical area has been common for decades. In many cases, the 'rate for the job' was enforced by the trade union within a specific locality. The Coventry Tool Room Agreement, whereby a rate for a skilled toolmaker was established for all engineering companies within the city of Coventry, was a classic example (Croucher, 1999).

In more recent years, however, the term has been used more to describe the benchmarking of both salary structures and individual salaries for non-manual staff against external market comparators. This might be the mid-point of the salary band, the 'market median' or 'market indicator' (IDS, 2004). The term normally refers to the rate for the job at full competence and should be distinguished from a 'market supplement' paid on top of base salary as a recruitment and retention device in tight labour markets. Under market-based pay, the market rate determines the level of base pay.

Research indicates that 'the extent to which market benchmarking determines pay levels and their subsequent up-rating can be very different' (IDS, 2004: 8). In some cases, employers will use market benchmarks alongside other factors such as inflation, performance, skills or experience to set the pay level, but in other cases, employers set their pay levels almost entirely in line with market medians. The latter approach is often associated with broad-banded pay structures or job families. In smaller organisations, with less formalised pay structures, setting pay for individual workers through reference to external pay rates for the same job is common.

This growing emphasis on the external market and decentralised pay decision-making has led to a rapid growth in the amount of information relating to pay and benefits levels and practices (White, 2000). There is a wide range of salary surveys from various providers available to the reward manager (see Chapter 4).

BOX 3.4 WHAT NEXT FOR LOCAL PAY?

ISSUES IN REWARD

The government appears to have made an about-turn in its drive towards local public sector pay-setting, the result perhaps of a growing awareness of the pitfalls of localisation

Should public sector pay reform take place within national structures or is local variation the way forward? This issue has been hotly debated over the past year but, in guidance issued last month, the Treasury appears to have made a U-turn in its previous advocacy of localised pay.

So what has happened? Over the past two years, the Treasury – encouraged by economists rather than reward specialists – has pursued a policy of seeking to encourage local variations in pay levels and pay determination in the public sector. Its economic advisers see local pay across the country as the answer to recruitment and retention problems. In 2002, Treasury advisers told the pay review bodies to avoid 'deadweight costs from high settlements in low cost areas', an unsubtle way of suggesting lower pay rises outside London and the South East.

But advocates of local pay have not really understood a number of issues: first, the sheer size of the pay modernisation programme in the public sector, and its emphasis on fairness, equity, transparency and job evaluation. Pay reform in the NHS, local government and further and higher education is firmly based on new national structures, simplified, harmonised pay spines and a commitment to equal pay.

Where there is scope for local variation or recruitment and retention allowances, these are invariably within national frameworks. There is also the Treasury's mistaken belief that pay in the private sector is set at a local level. Yet most large, national, multi-site organisations such as banks and retailers, have operated with national structures. On top of these they have built allowances or pay zones for areas with a higher cost of living – London and the South East (see panel). The focus therefore is not on myriad local pay levels set in local labour markets; rather it is on getting basic pay right and only having local variation where necessary.

Private companies use pay benchmarking to set pay levels and relativities in their organisations, using salary surveys and pay clubs. Job evaluation may well be used in larger companies to check for job weight or job rankings, or perhaps specifically to conduct an equal-pay audit. Such measures have a countervailing pressure on local market-based pay determination.

Reward in such companies is set mainly in relation to skill level, qualifications, competencies and responsibilities, rather than geography. And they take central decisions on pay bill costs, particularly where zonal or regional variation has been introduced to respond to recruitment and retention difficulties.

Incomes Data Services' research has dispelled the following myths about regional and national pay:

Myth 1: There is a significant amount of regional variation in pay outside London and the South East. In fact, the regional average earnings data show that differences are minimal and owe more to industrial history than to geography.

Myth 2: Pay in large private sector companies is set by myriad individual-level decisions, when in fact there are national structures and systems. Firms frequently allow variation from the norm, under certain controls, but within defined systems and budgets.

Myth 3: There is minimal influence on pay from collective bargaining, with most pay decisions set at management's discretion, based on local cost-of-living factors. In fact, unions have significant influence in large organisations.

Myth 4: Local cost-of-living factors now outweigh skill levels or competencies. In fact, managers look at skill levels and grading across their organisations rather than just locally. There are complex versions of what in the past might have been termed a 'rate for the job', whether set by job evaluation or job weight, or by sectoral or national benchmarking.

Myth 5: Pay in the public sector is set by rigid national agreements, with no scope for flexible interpretation. In reality, there is scope for local flexibility to deal with recruitment and retention issues, although these have not always been well funded. Some of the new measures in London, such as pay spines for school teachers, are an example. The recent report of the Local Government Pay Commission found there was adequate flexibility in local determination within a national framework.

Over the past year the Treasury has obviously listened to some critics of its previous views on localisation. And last summer the Chancellor changed policy by saying that local variation should occur 'within national frameworks'. In the autumn the education secretary also reversed his advocacy of local pay in the school system by asking the review body to make no recommendations on this as it might create 'an unwelcome new source of turbulence in schools' budgetary arrangements'. Meanwhile the School Teachers' Review Body has developed its own innovative changes by introducing new pay spines in inner London, outer London and certain parts of the South East, specifically targeted at retaining teachers in the job who might otherwise leave teaching or London.

In new guidance on regional pay issued in January, the Treasury demonstrated growing awareness of the pitfalls of localisation: 'In practice, extremely devolved arrangements are not desirable.

'There are risks of workers being treated differently for no good reason other than subjective variation in judgement or local affordability. There could be dangers of leapfrogging and parts of the public sector competing with each other for the best staff. The administration and bargaining costs of a large number of separate units inventing their own pay and conditions systems, and engaging in manifold separate bargaining sessions, would be substantial. Such costs tie up management capacity and would not be available for improved public services.'

Now that the government's drive for localism is on the retreat, the focus will turn back to using London allowances and higher rates of pay in the South East. Perhaps we will also see a rise in more innovative pay structures.

Source: Alastair Hatchett, *People Management*, 12 February 2004: 14

Alastair Hatchett is head of pay services at Incomes Data Services www.incomesdata.co.uk

CRITERIA FOR PAY INCREASES

Employers consider a range of criteria in setting pay levels, irrespective of whether or not they engage in collective determination of pay with trade unions. Three main factors affecting the level of pay have been identified by Milkovich and Newman (1996): labour market pressures (supply and demand); product markets (level of competition and product demand); and organisational factors (such as the industry, technology, size and business strategy). In contrast, Armstrong and Murlis (2007) list six main factors: the intrinsic value of the job in terms of its content (eg responsibility or skill level required); internal relativities (how the job relates in 'size' to other jobs in the same organisation); external relativities (how the job relates to similar jobs in other organisations); the rate of inflation or changes in the cost of living; business performance (or 'ability to pay'); and trade union pressures.

In the past, pay comparisons with the wider labour market have been a key criterion in setting public sector pay, especially where independent pay reviews have been involved. Comparability remains a key concern of the trade unions, even though the government now stresses recruitment and retention and 'ability to pay' (ie government public spending limits) as more important criteria (White and Hatchett, 2003).

There is little up-to-date research on the relative importance of the criteria used to set pay levels. In 1990, WIRS (Millward *et al*, 2000) showed that the cost of living was the most important factor; analysis of the CBI Pay Databank (Ingram *et al*, 1999) confirmed this. WIRS found that in the private sector three other factors were important: labour market conditions; ability to pay; and comparisons with another pay settlement. The fact that inflation was the most important factor in 1990 was not surprising, given the high level of inflation at the time. In the 1990s, there was increasing emphasis by employers on internal factors (profits, orders, productivity, recruitment and retention) but Ingram *et al* (1999) argued that their research showed that external influences – especially the level of inflation and comparability with other pay awards – continued to be important.

Around half of all firms said that some form of comparability was a contributing factor in pay determination.

Research in four industrial sectors by Arrowsmith and Sisson (1999) found that business results were the most important single factor affecting pay decisions, but that inflation and comparisons with market competitors were also important. They concluded that the pay award 'seems to be the outcome of a complex process which simultaneously involves issues of "ability to pay" and assessments of the external "going rate", mediated by labour market pressures' (Arrowsmith and Sisson, 1999: 60).

The latest CIPD research (CIPD 2008) found that the key factors, in rank order, used to determine annual general rises were organisational performance, followed by inflation, movement in market rates and the going rate of pay awards elsewhere. Other factors were recruitment and retention and the level of government funding or guidelines.

SELF-ASSESSMENT EXERCISE

Read the article by Alastair Hatchett on local pay above. Answer the following questions:

● What are the arguments against national pay structures?

● How do large private sector employers determine their pay levels?

● What are the dangers of locally determined pay?

● Why might national pay structures be particularly common in the public services?

KEY LEARNING POINTS AND CONCLUSIONS

In this chapter we have considered the major regulatory and contextual limits on the design of the reward system. Clearly, an employer's options for alternative reward strategies will be limited by these constraints. While employers have little choice in whether to follow legal requirements, there are very real alternatives available in terms of other forms of regulation. There are also clear consequences that arise from these alternatives. Collective bargaining has explicit consequences in terms of sharing reward decisions with employees through their trade union organisations. But the limitations of the labour market will also have implicit consequences. Failure to respond to labour market changes will leave organisations at a disadvantage competitively, while trying to 'buck the market' may also have risks.

As we have noted, the law plays an increasingly important role in reward management in Europe. Reward managers need to continually keep up to date with legal changes in the field. In many ways, these legal limits increasingly circumscribe the freedom of employers within the EU to design reward systems along American 'new pay' lines, but this will vary according to the type and size of organisation. Certainly in the public sector and among larger private sector employers, issues of equal pay and discrimination are being taken increasingly seriously – not least because of the very high financial liabilities that can accrue from getting it wrong. Clearly, a major skill for reward specialists is being able to implement strategy within the constraints of the law.

At the same time, other forms of regulation are in decline, especially the use of collective bargaining to determine pay systems and levels. Nonetheless, pay-setting through negotiation with trade unions remains important for many large organisations, especially in the public sector. Even in workplaces where unions are not recognised, these agreements may have an important influence upon pay levels because they may set industry 'norms'. Reward specialists also need to be aware that the use of collective bargaining varies substantially between countries and, particularly where global reward strategies are being considered, the role of unions can be very important.

The final environmental constraint on employers is the state of the wider economy, especially the cost of living and the labour market. Employers are increasingly speaking of 'market pay', whereby individual pay levels are linked to the external market value of particular jobs rather than notions of internal equity. But it is clear that inflation, whether high or low, and the pay increases awarded by competitors in the same labour market, remain key factors in pay decisions.

 EXPLORE FURTHER

The details of employment legislation change fairly frequently, so the best way to check current requirements is the website of the Department for Business Enterprise and Regulatory Reform (BERR): http://www.dti.gov.uk/employment/index.html

An alternative source is the ACAS website: http://www.acas.org.uk/

To obtain a fuller understanding of the theory underpinning employment regulation and the content of the law in the UK, see Lewis, D. and Sergeant, M. (2004) *Essentials of Employment Law*, 8th edn. London, Chartered Institute of Personnel and Development.

For a fuller understanding of the role of collective bargaining, see Williams, S. and Adam-Smith, D. (2006) *Contemporary Employment Relations. A Critical Introduction*. Oxford, Oxford University Press.

For a good discussion of the debate about 'market versus equity', see Kessler, I. (2007) 'Reward choices: strategy and equity', in Storey, J. (ed.) *Human Resource Management: a critical text*, 3rd edn. London, Thomson.

PART TWO

In Part Two structures and processes for extrinsic reward determination are introduced and evaluated. Practicalities surrounding their design and operation are sketched. Over three chapters, first, basic employee reward architecture is described; secondly, pay determination and systems for pay 'progression' are specified; and thirdly, notions of variable pay – contingent on factors such as competence, skill, performance and summative 'contribution' are reviewed.

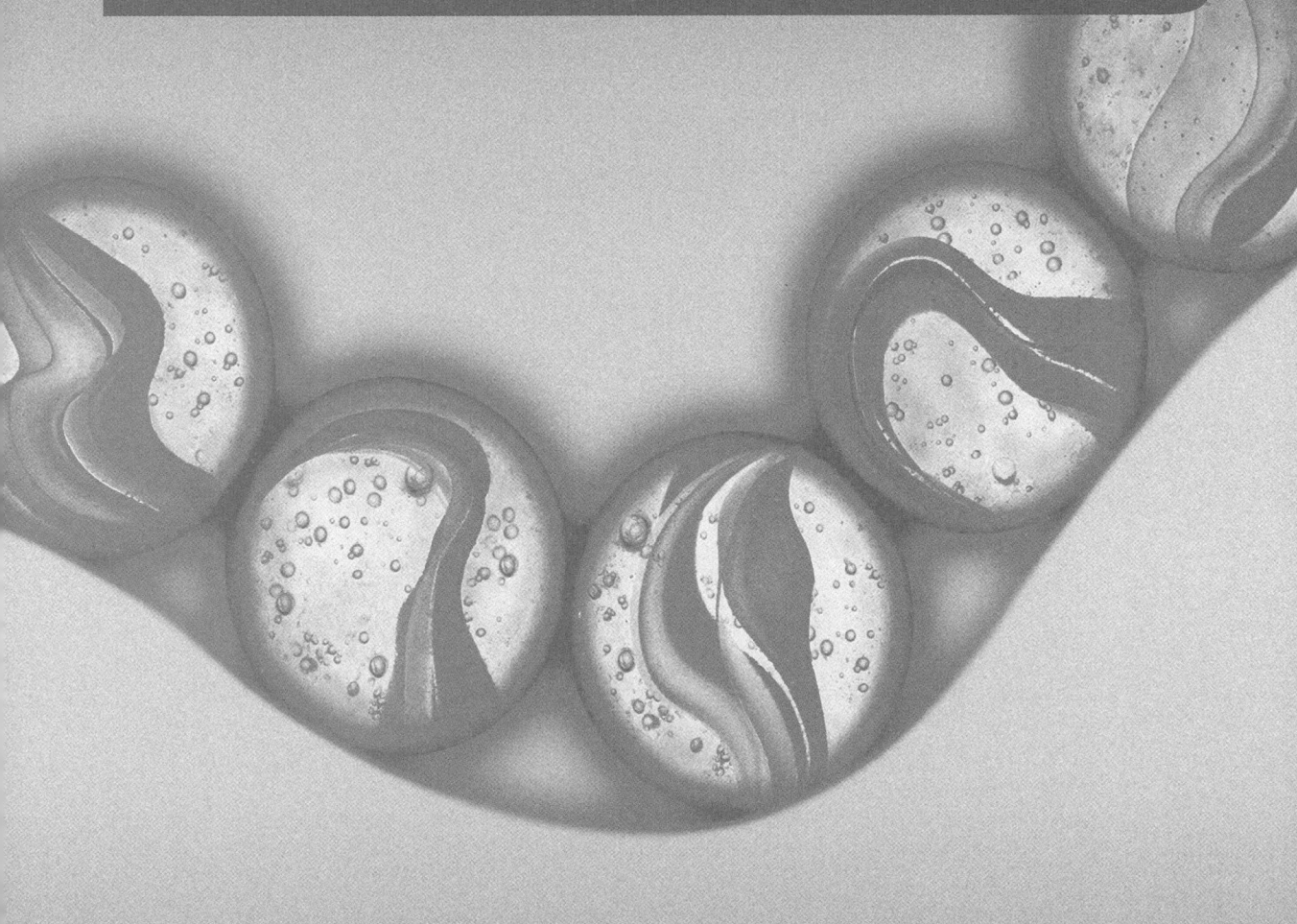

CHAPTER 4

Base Pay Structures and Relationships

CHAPTER OBJECTIVES

At the end of this chapter you should understand and be able to explain the following:

- The importance of pay structures in ensuring internal equity and providing a framework for pay decisions.

- The various types of pay structures in use and their relationship to organisational needs.

- The use of job analysis and job evaluation as a key mechanism for apportioning value to jobs and protecting organisations from legal challenges.

- The emergence of more flexible and person-based reward structures.

- The importance of maintaining a balance between internal equity and external market competitiveness.

- The use of pay intelligence sources to update reward systems.

CIPD STANDARDS COVERED IN THIS CHAPTER:

To be able to:

- Advise senior management on the design or modification of a pay structure.

- Help to analyse a pay structure to assess whether it contains sex or other discrimination and suggest ways of making a job evaluation scheme free of bias.

- Contribute to the conduct of local or national pay and benefit surveys.

- Advise senior management on whether to introduce job evaluation and advise on the design and implementation of an appropriate scheme.

- Advise senior management on policies for general and individual pay reviews and administer the implementation of policies.

To understand and explain:

- The concepts of reward system, reward structure and reward levels.

- The criteria for an effective pay structure.

- The objectives and limitations of job evaluation processes.

INTRODUCTION

As outlined in our introductory chapter, two major components of any reward system are, on the one hand, a pay structure and, on the other, methods for rewarding growth or contribution in the job or role by the individual employee – known as pay progression. We consider the issue of pay progression in the next chapter. Here we consider the former aspect – the creation of a pay structure that meets both the requirements for fairness and equity and the need to keep that structure aligned with the external market. As IDS (2006: 4) comments: 'There is a tension between seeking coherence and equity in pay and grading structures on the one hand, and seeking to change occupational pay relativities on the other.' For reward practitioners these twin requirements, and the fact that they are often perceived to be in conflict, is a major strategic and operational issue. How does one meet the needs for fairness and equity within the organisation while at the same time recognising that the external market for those jobs may differ substantially for different occupations and roles? This issue, moreover, is now increasingly subject to legal regulation through the requirement to ensure equal pay for work of equal value between males and females (see Chapter 3).

The pay and grading structure is the foundation for the architecture of a pay system and sets the framework for base pay allocation. We begin the chapter by considering the rationale for grading systems and the various options available. We then review the major method for attributing value to jobs within organisations – job evaluation. We then go on to consider how such pay structures are related to the external labour market and the various methods for benchmarking the value of individual posts against competitors.

GRADING STRUCTURES

Grading structures are the core building blocks of any organisation's human resource management system, not just for pay but often for conditions of service and career development as well. Small organisations (and even some larger ones), however, may not have any formal organisational structure. As such they may choose to pay their staff individual salaries or wage rates completely at management discretion (known as 'spot rates'), based on the owner's or manager's view of the relative merit and market value of each individual member of staff. But generally, as soon as organisations begin to grow, the need for some sort of formal organisational structure, complete with job or 'grade' levels, becomes apparent. This is especially the case where the owner of the business devolves management of the enterprise to a manager and hence no longer has a view on individual employees' strengths and weaknesses. Even if a formal grading structure is not acknowledged by management or communicated to staff, in reality some sort of employee 'hierarchy' will usually exist. This is because few employers have complete freedom to pay individuals simply what they wish. Pay structures are de facto created in these situations because different jobs usually attract different rates of pay according to their value in the external market and because employees doing higher-level work will expect to be paid more than those doing lower-level work.

'A grouping of jobs with equivalent demands which are offered the same rate or range of pay. Jobs are often allocated to grades through a formal process of job evaluation. A pay structure will typically comprise a hierarchy of grades with less demanding jobs occupying the lower grades and more demanding jobs occupying the higher.'

Heery and Noon (2001)

The creation of grading structures is closely linked to the desired shape of the organisation. Child (1985) suggests that there are two major decisions to be taken in the design of organisations. The first is the vertical dimension – the length of the organisational hierarchy – and whether the structure is tall or flat. Organisations have to decide on what degree of vertical differentiation there should be between people and jobs. The second dimension is the degree of horizontal differentiation between groups and sections, departments and divisions. Research indicates that these organisational dimensions tend to reflect the 'span of control' – the number of staff managed by a supervisor or manager. For example, if a large number of people are doing basically the same function, they can be grouped under a single manager or supervisor, leading to a fairly flat structure. If, on the other hand, there is a large number of specialised sections or departments the dissimilarity between functions and the greater need for co-ordination between these different sections will mean that each requires its own specialist supervisor or manager. This in turn leads to fewer spans of control, greater numbers of managers and a longer vertical hierarchy.

Major questions thus arise of how organisations group together staffs of similar and different functions or on what basis an organisation should be specialised. Grading structures and 'job ' or 'career' families therefore relate closely to the shape of an organisation. For example, an organisation such as a fast food company will tend to have large numbers of people doing the same or similar type of work, and hence these organisations will have fairly flat grading structures. In contrast, a large bureaucratic organisation (like a local council, a university or a hospital) will tend to have a wide range of functions, and hence grading structures will tend to be both taller and more differentiated on the horizontal level.

In Figure 4.1 we graphically portray four types of organisational shape. The first example is the traditional hierarchical pyramid, often found in manufacturing in the past, with the numbers of staff in each grade reducing the higher one rises up the structure. The second example represents, perhaps, a more modern structure where the majority of the staff will be found in the central part of the grading hierarchy. This is more likely in knowledge-worker-type organisations

Figure 4.1 Types of organisational structure

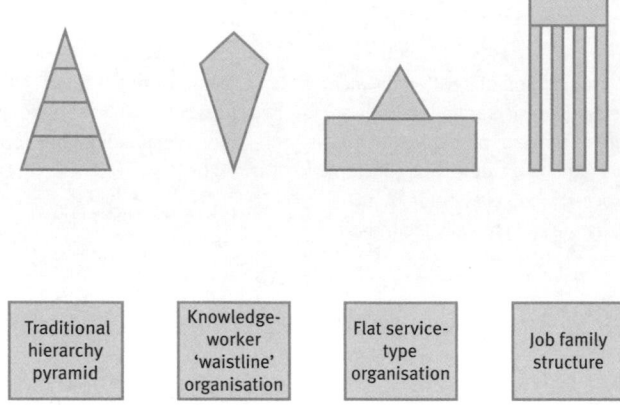

where teams of professional staff are supported by fewer, lower-grade, numbers of support administrative and clerical staff. The third example is a typical flat, service-type organisation, such as a fast food company. Here there are large numbers of fairly low-skilled workers working in a small number of grades in the restaurants but managed by a central HQ of higher-paid administrative and management staff. The fourth example is a job family structure where staff are organised in vertical silos depending on their function. Each silo will have its own hierarchy, but at the highest (management) levels roles may become more generalist and interchangeable.

Organisational shape can even vary between organisations within the same field. For example, in his report on the use of incentive pay in the civil service, John Makinson (2000) examined the organisational shape of four departments and agencies. Looking at the spread of staff by pay level, there were significant differences in shape between the four, reflecting the different vertical and horizontal influences at work. For example, the HM Revenue and Customs exhibits a traditional hierarchical pyramid – with decreasing numbers of staff the higher the level one goes. On the other hand, Customs and Excise appears to be a 'waist-line' organisation with the majority of its staff located in the middle of its structure. Interestingly, these two organisations have since merged, and it would be interesting to see how this has affected the new shape of the merged organisation.

 SELF-ASSESSMENT EXERCISE

Compare three different types of organisation – a manufacturing company, a retail chain and a university – and think about what the vertical and horizontal organisational shapes might look like.

Grading also usually reflects the value of jobs as related to the level of skill, difficulty or responsibility required for a particular task. This will often reflect the amount of investment in education and training required for the job. For example, it has been calculated that there is a 'lifetime pay premium' for those who undertake university education, whereby the investment in education at an early age positions the graduates for higher-paid jobs throughout their working careers. Armstrong and Stephens (2005) comment that a grading structure only becomes a pay structure when pay rates or ranges are attached to grades. The hierarchy of grades or different job families may therefore also reflect the demand and supply of those particular attributes in the external labour market.

How one ascribes value to a job or role is a major decision for organisations but is no easy task. As Adam Smith (Smith 1776: 134), the father of classical economics, commented in 1776: 'There may be more labour in an hour's hard work than in two hours' easy business; or in an hour's application to a trade which cost ten years' labour to learn, than in a month's industry at an ordinary and obvious employment. But it is not easy to find any accurate measure either of hardship or ingenuity.'

The value of a particular job within society, moreover, can change over time and vary between different types of society. For example, under the communist system in the old Soviet Union and in China factory workers were often paid more than medical doctors because the skills of the factory worker were seen, in economic terms, as more important to society than those of the doctors. Furthermore, technological change can rapidly change the value of a particular occupation or skill (Braverman, 1974). For example, in the past the skills of the typesetter in the printing industry were very well rewarded, but the advent of new computer-based technology largely de-skilled these jobs, with resulting reductions in the value attributed to these jobs. In general, unskilled manual labour is perceived today to be of much less value than in the days when manufacturing and the extractive industries relied on large numbers of such workers. An important aspect of this variation in the value given to different jobs in different societies and historical epochs has been the consistent undervaluing of jobs done predominantly by females (Hastings, 2000). For example, while in the past both typesetters and typists used the same keyboard technology, the typesetting role was overwhelmingly performed by males and was paid at a higher level than that of typists (Cockburn, 1991).

Another key reason why employers establish pay structures is the rational need for employees to know why they are paid at the levels they are paid. If reward practices are to be seen as equitable, fair and consistent, employees must be able to see how their position within the organisation relates to that of other staff. The traditional key to this process has been the definition of the 'job' – what is required of the employee by the employer. But in more recent times there has been decreasing emphasis upon the details of the work carried out as such and more upon the 'role' played by the employee within the organisation. As the 'new pay' writers emphasise, there has been a shift away from 'pay for the job' to 'pay for the person' (Schuster and Zingheim, 1992).

More importantly, grading structures usually provide the organisational framework for managing the employment relationship, such as recruitment entry points and career development pathways. They also indicate the wider social values that are placed on particular occupations. Grading structures therefore have much wider roles than simply providing the basis for paying staff and deciding the range of benefits on offer.

THE HISTORICAL DEVELOPMENT OF GRADING STRUCTURES

Pay structures in the UK have traditionally been separate for manual and non-manual workers. The origins of manual worker grading structures can be found in the systems established under the medieval craft guilds and perpetuated through the development of trades unions, apprenticeship schemes and collective bargaining in the nineteenth century (Hastings, 2000). Non-manual grading structures developed at a later stage in the growth of capitalism. These reflected the growth of the administrative and technical functions in the enterprise and the creation of new bureaucratic structures within organisations.

Manual work has traditionally been divided between skilled and unskilled. Skilled workers normally served an apprenticeship or training period before being allowed to join the craft guild or trade organisation. In contrast, employment of unskilled workers, such as labourers who required no training, was not regulated and most manual workers were employed on a casual, often daily, basis. The pay of skilled workers was determined through formal procedures (initially craft guilds but later through agreements between employers and unions), and was based on notions of exclusivity and restrictions on the supply of their skills. The level of skill required for the job, therefore, largely determined pay rates. In time, gradations of skill level led to the development of semi-skilled and unskilled rates. As Hastings (2000) indicates, this social construction of skill usually discriminated against females, who did not have access to guild or craft training (and initially to trade union membership) and whose jobs were considered unskilled on the grounds that they did not require physical strength.

In contrast, non-manual workers' grading systems developed with the growth of large administrative activities such as finance, the railways and the public services. Unlike manual workers, such white-collar professionals had career and status expectations. To this end, non-manual grading structures tended to be more complex and incorporate the notion of career (and hence pay) progression, both within a grade and between grades, in line with growing experience and service.

In recent times, the decline of manufacturing and its associated manual labour has led to an erosion of the 'class divide' in grading structures. The creation of more 'single status', 'integrated' or 'harmonised' pay structures for all workers within an enterprise has been noted, with the inclusion of manual workers alongside other staff (Russell, 1998). This was particularly driven by the perceived success of Japanese firms, which operated 'single status', in the 1980s and 1990s.

Despite this trend, there continue to be separate grading structures for manual and non-manual workers in many organisations. More importantly, most organisations retain separate pay and grading arrangements for their senior executives and managers (see Chapter 10) and sometimes for key functions (such as sales staff).

THE IMPORTANCE OF EQUAL-PAY LAW

An increasingly important consideration in the design of pay structures is the issue of gender discrimination. As described in Chapter 3, there has been a substantial growth in both the content of equal-pay legislation in the UK (and Europe generally) and in case law. Pay inequality between men and women has always existed and continues, despite over thirty-five years of equal-pay law. For this reason, the gender discrimination potential of any pay and grading system needs to be considered carefully.

Job evaluation (JE) has become the major tool for ensuring equity of treatment in valuing jobs or roles. An analytical JE scheme (explained later in this chapter) has become the major defence for employers facing equal-pay challenges. Some writers, however, have questioned the efficacy of JE in resolving equal-pay issues (Arnault *et al*, 2001; Figart, 2001; Gilbert, 2005; Madigan and Hoover, 1986). We discuss the critique of JE as a tool for dealing with equal pay later in this chapter.

Any choice of pay structure will require careful consideration of the equal-pay implications. Fuller details of the statutory requirements in the UK for equal pay are provided in Chapter 3. The EOC has published a good practice guide on how to avoid sex bias in JE schemes. This is available at: http://www.equalityhumanrights.com/Documents/Gender/Employment/Guidance%20note%204%20%20Job%20evaluation%20schemes%20free%20of%20sex%20bias.pdf

ISSUES IN REWARD

BOX 4.1 EOC TRUMPETS CLEANER'S PAY-GRADING WIN

Woman was paid 60p less an hour for carrying out same role. Zoe Roberts reports

The Equal Opportunities Commission has called for employers to review their pay and grading systems after a female cleaner won her tribunal claim of sex discrimination and victimisation.

Dawn Ruff was awarded £4,000 after the tribunal ruled that her employer,

Norwich-based Hannant Cleaning Services, could not justify its pay-grading systems.

Ruff had discovered that she was earning 60p less an hour than a man who worked for the same company. She was told that her job was a grade four post while the man's was grade three.

The tribunal found that Hannant Cleaning could not justify employing male employees at a higher rate. 'The grading system itself is unsupportable… it disproportionately disadvantages women who provide the bulk of the lower grade of the work force,' it ruled.

'This is a straightforward case of a woman being paid less than a man simply because she was a woman,' said Julie Mellor, chair of the EOC. 'All employers need to check their pay and grading systems do not reflect a bias of any kind.'

The tribunal also found that Ruff was bullied after her employer began to change her breaks and took away extra hours she had agreed to work on bank holidays.

Source: *PM Online*, 28 June 2002

 SELF-ASSESSMENT EXERCISE

Look at the EOC good practice guide on how to avoid gender bias in pay structures, available online. What are the key features, and how would they apply in your own organisation or one with which you are acquainted?

THE OBJECTIVES OF GRADING STRUCTURES

As described above, an organisation's shape – in terms of the deployment of its staff – is a key determinant of its grading structure, but this is not to imply that the design of such structures is mechanistic or deterministic. Organisations may redesign grading structures as a proactive device in changing or developing their human resource strategy. In doing this a number of objectives are often considered.

To paraphrase Armstrong (2002), a number of criteria may be examined when designing pay structures. These include:

- the issue of the pay relationships between staff and the achievement of equity, fairness and consistency;
- the relationship of the internal structure to the pressures arising from the external labour market;
- the degree of operational flexibility and continuous development envisaged; the scope for rewarding performance and increases in skill and competence within the structure;
- the clarity of reward and career paths;
- the ease with which they can be communicated; and
- the degree of control over pay that the structure provides to management.

The emphasis that different organisations place on these different criteria will determine the form of such structures.

One thing is clear, however. For all organisations there is a continuous and dynamic tension between, on one hand, the need for internal equity, fairness and consistency in motivating staff and, on the other, the need to meet the demands of the external labour market in recruiting and retaining staff.

TYPES OF PAY STRUCTURE

Organisations can operate a single, integrated pay structure for all employees within the enterprise (the so-called 'single status'), or there may be separate structures for different groups of employees or occupations. As mentioned earlier, a traditional divide has been between manual (often hourly-paid wage) workers and non-manual salaried staff (Hastings, 2000), but elsewhere the structures may reflect different professional or occupational job or career 'families' (eg finance, marketing and sales, research and development). Another important factor in the past has been the influence of trades unions and collective bargaining whereby different trade unions organised different groups of workers, each with their own pay structure. In the UK higher education sector, for example, 10 separate occupational pay structures, each with its own pay grades, have recently been merged on to a single pay spine under a Framework Agreement for Pay Modernisation. Similarly, the recent pay modernisation agreement for the National Health Service merged 16 pay groups.

There are a number of types of pay structure. In general, the differences revolve around whether they are individual or collective and whether they are narrow or wide in scope. The types include:

- individual 'spot rate' or rate for the job
- individual job ranges
- narrow-graded structures
- pay spines
- broad-banded structures
- 'job' or 'career' families.

The CIPD Annual Survey of Reward Management 2008 found that the most common structures are individual pay rates/ranges/spot salaries followed by broadband pay structures (CIPD 2008). Individual pay rates/spot salaries are most popular for senior management while broad bands are most popular for middle/first line management and technical/professional staff. Job families/career grades are most popular for technical/professional staff. Narrow grades are most common for clerical/manual workers.

Narrow-graded structures remain popular in the public services and voluntary sector. In some cases, local employers often link these narrow grades to a national 'pay spine' of incremental points. This provides a national framework for pay progression but allows some flexibility in level of grade (eg in UK local government, the NHS and universities). These pay spines can also form the basis for broad bands.

Table 4.1 Pay structure management, by occupation %

Type of pay structure	Senior management	Middle/first-line management	Technical/ professional	Clerical/ manual
Individual pay rates/ ranges/spot salaries	46	29	28	25
Broadband pay structures	25	31	30	26
Job families/career grade structures	17	23	25	24
Pay spines	11	14	15	15
Narrow-graded pay structures	9	13	13	16
Other	4	3	3	4

Source: CIPD Reward Management Annual Survey Report 2008

Research by IDS (2006) for the Office for Manpower Economics (the UK body that administers the Pay Review Bodies and Police Negotiating Board) on developments in occupational pay differentiation points to two parallel developments over recent years. These are a growing emphasis upon job evaluation and job weight to design equal-pay-proofed structures, on the one hand, and a renewed emphasis on market testing of pay levels through benchmarking, on the other. The source of these developments was the de-layering of organisations in the early 1990s and the creation of so-called 'broad-banded' pay structures. These broad-banded structures gave employers much more freedom to place and progress employees through the pay range. IDS also points to the growth of the job or career family concept as another means to respond to external labour market pressures.

INDIVIDUAL RATE FOR THE JOB

As discussed earlier, smaller organisations may not have formal grading structures as such but will pay each individual worker a separate 'rate for the job'. This is sometimes referred to as a 'spot rate'. Each job rate will be reviewed periodically, but no guaranteed progression is provided in the grade. Traditionally, such individual rates have been most common at the very bottom of organisational structures (for manual workers) or at the very top (for chief executives and senior managers – see Chapter 11). The latest CIPD survey (CIPD, 2007), however, finds spot rates to be least likely among clerical and manual workers, although this may be an issue of definition. A particular 'spot rate' may apply to more than one individual within the organisation and, indeed, traditional, collectively agreed grading structures for manual workers have tended to set a 'spot rate' (or rate for the job) for each skill level (skilled, semi-skilled and unskilled).

The BMW Oxford pay structure shown below is an example of such a 'spot rate' system for manual workers in a manufacturing environment. 'Spot rates' do not

Table 4.2 BMW Oxford pay structure (at 1 November 2007)

Grade	Job examples	£ per annum	£ per hour
1*	Track assembler	19,678	10.22
2	Track assembler	22,956	11.93
3	Rectifier, relief operator	24,021	12.48
4	Craftsman (single skill), team co-ordinator	25,008	12.99
5	Multi-skilled craftsman	26,176	13.60
6	Logistics officer, technician	27,516	14.30
7	Production area manager	28,812	14.97

*This grade is for new hires, starting in grade 2 jobs, and a benchmark rate for temporary workers.

Source: IDS *Pay Report 989*, November 2007.

therefore have to indicate 'individualisation', rather the lack of any guaranteed pay progression.

INDIVIDUAL JOB RANGES

A development of the individual 'spot rate' is the provision of a pay range for each member of staff. This may just be a minimum and a maximum for the grade. It provides the employee with some expectancy of pay progression (on top of any cost-of-living increase), but movement through the range may not be formalised or it may be based on some measure of the employee's performance or seniority. What is different about such individual job ranges in contrast to narrow grades or broad bands is that there is still no collective structure as such – each individual employee will have his or her own range.

NARROW-GRADED STRUCTURES

Once organisations move beyond informal, individualised pay structures, they have a choice in the degree of flexibility they wish to introduce. The narrow-grade pay structure is the traditional form of grouping employees according to their skills, competencies and responsibilities. In some cases, especially in the public services, these grades may be attached to a common pay spine. Under a narrow-grade structure, a 'career ladder' or 'stairway' of grades exists, each grade having its own 'scale', with usually a number of pay 'increments' (in the case of a pay spine these will be points on the spine) to allow pay progression. These narrow grades may or may not overlap. Where they overlap this allows employees to continue to progress up the pay scale without having to be promoted (see Figure 4.2). The grading structure for NHS nurses and other health professions is a good example of a typical narrow-grade structure (see Table 4.3).

Figure 4.2 A typical narrow-graded structure

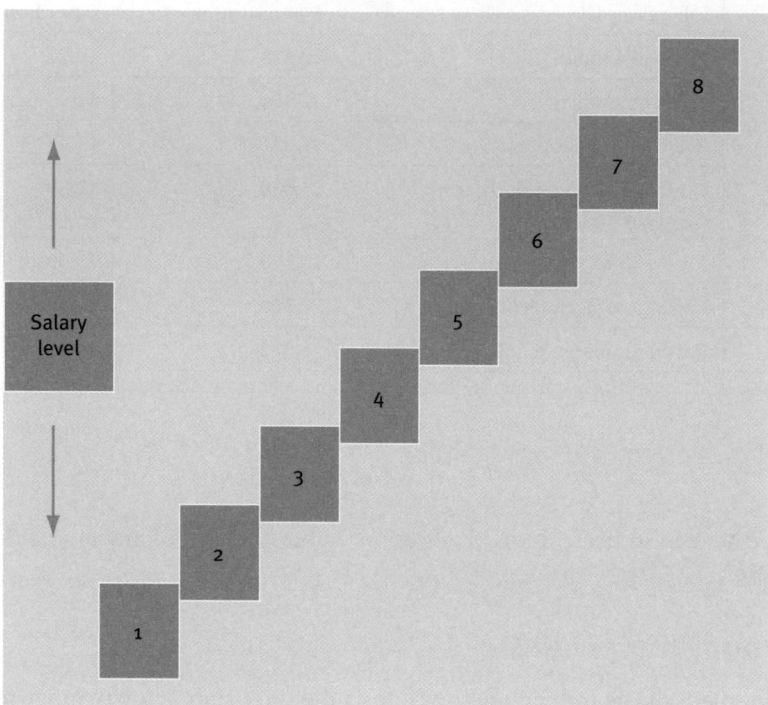

The number of grades or bands in a narrow-banded structure can vary but usually consists of more than four grades in order to accommodate the full range of jobs and levels in an organisation. The number of increments within each scale may also vary, although in recent years many organisations have reduced the number of points in each scale. This has been partly to simplify structures but has also reflected equal-pay concerns about the potential gender discrimination risks of having very long scales (ie where women take career breaks to have children they may return to a point where their male colleagues have already moved ahead). We discuss this issue in Chapter 5.

The 2008 CIPD Survey (CIPD 2008) shows that narrow-graded pay structures remain most common for clerical/manual staff but less so for other levels.

PAY SPINES

Pay 'spines' (or a column of pay points) are common in the public services. These spines provide the 'backbone' to local grading structures and are often a way of linking local pay structures to some national pay structure. Under the Framework

Table 4.3 Pay structure for NHS nurses and other health professions (at 1 April 2005)

Band	Minimum £ per annum	Maximum £ per annum	Spine points	Job examples
1	11,494	12,539	1–4	Healthcare science support worker (entry level)
2	11,879	14,739	2–9	Clinical support worker, healthcare science support worker (stage 2), phlebotomist
3	13,694	16,389	7–13	Anatomical pathology technician – mortuary (entry level), clinical support worker (higher level), dental nurse, health improvement resource assistant, healthcare science support worker (higher level)
4	16,004	19,248	12–18	Ambulance practitioner, anatomical pathology technician – mortuary, assistant/associate practitioner, cytology screener, dental nurse, health improvement resource assistant (higher level), medical engineering technician (entry level), nursery nurse, occupational therapy technician, optometrist (entry level), pharmacy technician, play specialist
5	18,698	24,198	17–25	Ambulance practitioner specialist, assistant practitioner (higher level), biomedical scientist, chaplain (entry level), clinical psychologist, counsellor (entry level), dental nurse specialist/team leader, dental technician, dietician, healthcare scientist practitioner, medical physics technician, midwife (new entrant), nurse (qualified), occupational therapist, orthoptist, pharmacist (entry level), physiotherapist, podiatrist, radiographer, speech and language therapist, theatre practitioner
6	22,328	30,247	23–31	Ambulance practitioner advanced, arts therapist (entry level), chaplain, clinical psychology trainee, counsellor, dietician specialist, district nurse, healthcare scientist specialist, health visitor, midwife, pharmacist, sexual health adviser, specialist medical photographer, specialist nurse, trainee clinical psychologist

Band	Minimum £ per annum	Maximum £ per annum	Spine points	Job examples
7	26,948	35,527	28–36	Arts therapist, clinical psychologist, dietician (advanced), health visitor specialist, midwife (higher level), nurse team manager, orthoptist (advanced), radiographer advanced/specialist/team manager, registered clinical scientist, specialist counsellor, sexual health advisory service manager
8a	34,372	41,246	35–40	Dental laboratory manager, midwife consultant, modern matron, nurse consultant, occupational therapist consultant, pharmacist advanced, principal clinical psychologist, principal clinical scientist
8b	40,036	49,496	39–44	Consultant clinical psychologist, principal clinical scientist
8c	48,176	59,395	43–48	Consultant clinical scientist
8d	57,745	71,494	47–52	-
9	68,194	86,240	51–56	Head of service

Source: IDS (2006a) *Pay in the Public Services,* p177

Agreement for Pay Modernisation in Higher Education, for example, a 51-point spine provides the starting point for local institutions to create their grading structures (see Figure 4.3). The uplift to the pay spine remains subject to national pay negotiations between the employers and unions, but which spine points are used for particular job levels is left to local determination. A model grading structure was provided at national level as a guide, but locally employers have adapted this model to varying degrees or ignored it altogether.

BROAD BANDS

The main alternative to narrow grades is so-called 'broad-banding'. Under a broad-band structure, employees are grouped into a small number (normally no more than five) of pay bands. In each band the span between the floor and ceiling of each band is wide (perhaps the maximum salary point will be between 70 and 100 per cent or more of the minimum). The concept originated in the USA and was seen as a more flexible system than the rigidity of narrow grades. It grew out of the 'downsizing' of organisations in the 1980s and early 1990s when hierarchical layers were stripped out of companies, reducing the scope for employee advancement through promotions.

Broad bands have been seen as more flexible than narrow grades in that employees can continue to be rewarded for growth in their role without

Figure 4.3 Higher education pay spine and model grading structure

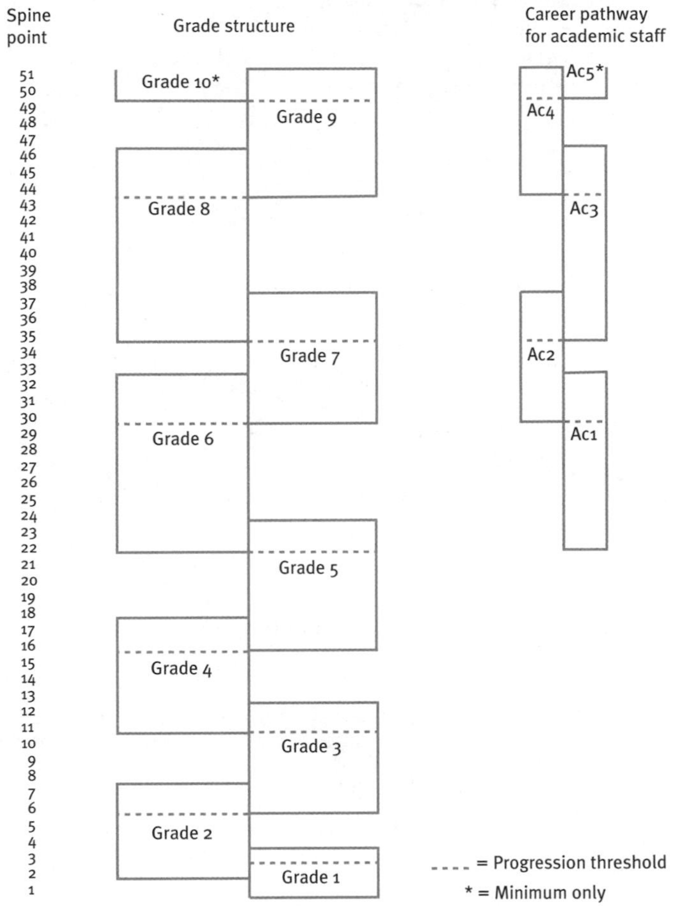

Source: Joint Negotiating Committee for Higher Education Staffs

necessarily having to be promoted into a higher grade. Such structures also provide managers with both more flexibility in progressing individual employees through the career structure and greater discretion in appointment salaries. They have been particularly useful where performance- or competence-based progression has been adopted as they provide a wide range within which individual contribution can be recognised. It has been argued that broad bands reflect the new, more flexible, career structures found in the flatter hierarchies being established in many organisations. This enables lateral career moves to take place more easily than in traditional 'narrow-grade' structures. IDS (2006: 4) comments: 'In theory, broad-banded structures provided vast distances between salary minimums and maximums and individuals could be placed more of less anywhere on the scale. Management was therefore able to exercise some degree of individual differentiation within non-transparent structures.'

> **DEFINITION**
>
> 'Broad-banding is the replacement of a graded structure comprised of multiple short grades with a small number of broad pay "bands", usually four or five in total.'
>
> Heery and Noon (2001)

Figure 4.4 Traditional graded structure – 40% grade width

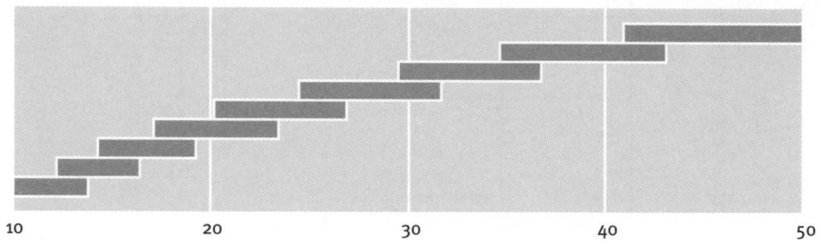

Source: IPD (1997)

Figure 4.5 Broadbanded structure – 100% band width

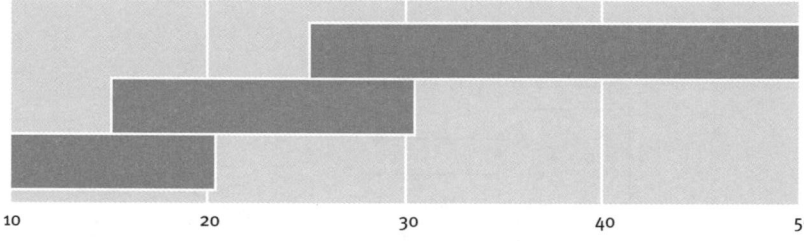

Source: IPD (1997)

The CIPD (2001) points out, however, that the term is often used loosely. Some organisations claim to have broad bands, even when they have seven or more grades and spans of only 40 to 50 per cent. The IPD (2000) suggested that these latter structures 'might be better called "fat grades", while those that are truly broad-banded could be termed "career-based" structures'. The latter term is seen as appropriate because many of the organisations reporting having such pay structures claim that they are as much about career development as the delivery of pay.

In the example above, a traditional nine-grade structure with grades spanning 40 per cent of base salary could be converted into a structure with three 100 per cent spans as shown.

A 1999 survey of broad banding by the IPD (IPD, 2000) found that such structures varied in practice between different organisational levels. Broad-banded structures with three or fewer bands were most common for senior executives, whereas those with six to nine bands were most common for staff.

Table 4.4 Reasons for introducing broad bands

Objectives	% of respondents
To provide more flexibility in reward	29
To reflect changes in organisational structure	18
To provide a better base for rewarding growth in competence	14
To replace an over-complex pay structure	12
To devolve more responsibility for pay decisions to managers	11
To provide a better basis for rewarding career progression	11
To reduce the need for job evaluation	8
To simplify pay administration	7
To eliminate the need for job evaluation	2

Source: IPD, 2000

The width of grades also varied: the most common spans were between 50 and 79 per cent. In terms of usage, the CIPD (2001) summarises various surveys of practice with broad bands.

The prevalence of broad bands ranged between 49 per cent (of staff) in the IPD 1999 survey to just 12 per cent in a survey by IRS in 2000 (IRS, 2000). According to the largest sample survey, by Towers Perrin in 1997, around 32 per cent of UK organisations were using broad bands (Towers Perrin, 1997). According to the 2008 CIPD survey, broad bands are most commonly used for middle/first-line management and technical/professional staff but were less common for clerical/ manual workers and for senior management.

Reasons given by employers in the IPD 1999 survey for adopting broad bands are shown in Table 4.4.

The IPD 1999 survey found that a majority of employers felt that their objectives for broad bands had been broadly achieved. Where they had failed the most common reasons were poor performance management systems and poor training of line managers to administer the new system.

While broad-banded structures were initially seen as an alternative to job evaluation (JE), in reality a large proportion of employers continue to use JE as the basis for assigning jobs to the bands. Employers have also been concerned about the threat of unlimited pay progression arising from these wide pay spans. As a result many have inserted performance bars into their bands while others have adopted 'zones' within bands that indicate the normal range of pay for a particular job or role (see Figure 4.6). These zones often reflect the external market reference or anchor points for a fully competent individual and are often aligned to the comparator rates in the external labour market.

An IPD report (IPD, 1997) lists the advantages and disadvantages of broad bands. Overall the advantages are that such structures allow an employer to adjust the pay of an individual more easily. This includes more freedom to set pay levels for new employees and to progress staff through a pay range without having to frequently promote them to a new grade. Such structures also allow organisations to reward lateral career movement, continuous learning and the achievement of high levels of competence and contribution.

A major disadvantage identified, however, is that broad bands may restrict promotion opportunities for employees, with resultant effects upon morale and motivation. Furthermore, those in higher grades who see their jobs 'collapsed' into new broad bands may feel that their work has been devalued. The wide pay spans may raise employee expectations that cannot in practice be realised. The possible employee perception of lack of clarity in the structure – with no clear 'career signposts' – may also concern employees. This potential lack of clear criteria for progression may lay the organisation open to the risks of discrimination and inequity.

This is exemplified by the case of the Biotechnology and Biological Sciences Research Council, which was one of the first organisations to conduct an equal-pay audit. It found that broad pay bands and low pay increases since the organisation moved away from the previous civil service pay system meant that women were clustered at the bottom of pay bands. By introducing faster progression and reducing the link between recruitment salaries and an applicant's previous salary (which had led to gender discrimination in the past) the organisation was able to make its pay system fairer (Allison *et al*, 2002). Most importantly, there may be a very real risk of pay 'drift' if progression through the bands is not closely controlled.

Figure 4.6 A broad band with zones for individual roles

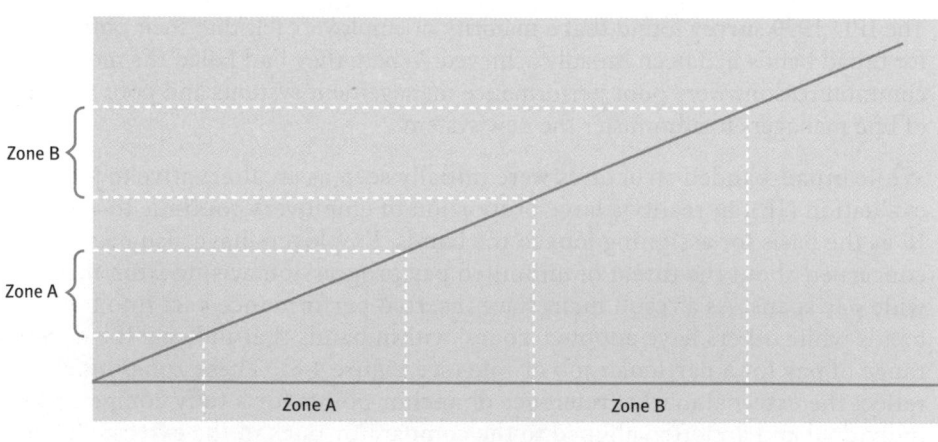

Source: IPD (1997)

According to IDS (2006: 5): 'Pure broad-banded structures had weaknesses from the start. They were harder to manage than narrower graded structures and made considerable demands on line managers who found it difficult to explain salary levels and limits on progression.' A major issue is whether broad bands match the culture of the organisation – broad bands may not suit highly hierarchical organisations. Despite this, it is worth observing that broad bands have been adopted in parts of the civil service.

More recent evidence indicates that broad-banding has become more 'structured' in recent years, with a return to more transparency and easily understood principles for band allocation and progression. According to IDS (2004a: 12), 'Broad banding has been challenged by the development of market-based pay and also by the renewed emphasis on JE and job weight in the context of equal pay reviews and pay modernisation.' Armstrong has also commented that 'the original concept of broad banding was eroded as more structure was introduced and job evaluation became more prominent to define the structure and meet equal pay requirements' (IDS, 2004b).

 SELF-ASSESSMENT EXERCISE

What are the advantages and potential disadvantages of broad bands?

JOB FAMILIES/CAREER GRADES

Another recent reward phenomenon has been the growth of 'job families' or 'career grades'. In some ways these reflect the need for organisations to link the pay of a particular occupational group (eg information technology) or business process (eg customer services) to different external labour markets. Job or career families are especially useful where the alternative would be a single structure with various ad hoc market allowances or supplements to reward particularly hard-to-fill jobs. This trend towards job families could be seen as constituting a retreat from attempts to create single, harmonised pay structures and a return to the occupational segregation of the workforce described earlier in this chapter. This may well, however, make pay progression easier for employees to understand. Moreover, unlike traditional segregated pay structures based on different 'bargaining groups' for different occupations, job families can form part of a single, integrated pay structure and can sit within job-evaluated structures or a single pay spine. As IDS (2006: 5) comments, 'Job families allow a company to maintain a clear grade structure where staff can see the internal relativities but the employer can still differentiate on the basis of pay.'

'A job family is a set of jobs based around common activities but conducted at different levels of the organisation. For instance, a finance and accounting job family could embrace junior finance officers, senior accountants, and the finance director of the enterprise. A job family may form the basis for an integrated pay structure, such that all jobs within the family are managed using a common set of rules and procedures.'

Heery and Noon (2001)

HOW DO JOB FAMILIES WORK?

Each job family will have its own number of levels with different pay ranges. The band/role/grade width may even vary within the job family. But in some job family structures all families have the same number of levels. Some organisations only operate job families for specific occupational groups – often those that attract a high market premium (such as IT) – while others have applied the concept to their whole workforce (IDS, 2006b: 3). A distinction has also been drawn between 'job families' and 'career families'. According to Armstrong (2005: 25), unlike job families, career families have common pay and grading structures and, 'in effect, a career structure is a single graded structure in which each grade has been divided into job families'. But the terms are often used interchangeably by practitioners.

Organisations may establish their job or career families on the basis of clear functional groups – eg HR, IT, finance or marketing – or they may reflect broader organisational divisions, such as administration, customer services or support services. Each job or career family will then be divided vertically into levels or grades, reflecting levels of experience, knowledge, skills and/or competencies. An example given by IDS (2006b) is Zarlink Semiconductor, which has six levels as follows: entry; developing; working; senior; specialist; principal. A feature identified by IDS of such systems is that there may be fewer levels than in traditional grading structures. Such systems may also allow greater lateral movement between job families, especially where levels are broadly comparable. At Norwich Union Central Services (see case study at the end of this chapter) there are 22 career families, each of which is relatively small. Each career family has seven levels, and all staff are allocated to a career family except heads of division. In addition, staff are placed in one of two broad bands, one covering management and the other non-management.

Although research by the IPD in 1999 (IPD, 2000) found that job family structures then existed in only 16 per cent of organisations, 17 per cent were planning to introduce them within the next two years. A high proportion of the survey respondents had fitted their job families into common broad-banded pay structures and had allocated levels in their job families by using job evaluation. A smaller proportion based their levels on competence or skill. The trend towards job families in the 1999 research has been confirmed in more recent research. The

Table 4.5 Objectives for job families

Objectives	% of respondents
To map out career paths	28
To achieve more flexibility	24
To identify market groups	22
To provide for rewards to be based on personal contribution and progress	21

Source: IPD (2000)

CIPD 2007 Reward Management survey found that the most significant change since the equivalent 2006 survey was that employers are using job families/ career grades for their senior, middle and first-line managers and their technical/ professional employees (CIPD, 2007).

Table 4.5 summarises the 1999 IPD research into the main objectives of organisations in using job families.

Research by IDS in 2006 (IDS, 2006b) suggested that a key reason for using job families was the flexibility provided to vary the pay for particular groups of jobs according to the market for those jobs. Commenting on its 1999 research, the IPD suggested that the introduction of job families into broad-banded pay structures reflected the need for organisations to find ways of demonstrating career and pay progression opportunities for staff in increasingly opaque grading systems.

However, as Wright (2004) has argued, job families can be seen as divisive in organisations seeking greater teamworking between different occupational groups and may create risks of gender pay discrimination if the job families are made up predominantly of one gender or the other. If a job family approach is adopted, regular external benchmarking will be required to justify paying some jobs more than others – particularly where they are broadly comparable in terms of job size and accountability.

As we have shown, the alternatives available to employers in creating an organisational structure are many, and each will have its own advantages and disadvantages to be considered. In recent times employers have sought to move away from traditional grading systems based on hierarchy towards more flexible systems such as broad bands and job families. In the public services, however, there have been contrary moves towards simpler, harmonised pay structures that bring different occupational bargaining groups together on to single pay spines. The consequences of decisions about organisational structure are far-reaching, not just in relation to reward.

 SELF-ASSESSMENT EXERCISE

What are the benefits of a job family system and what might be the potential problems?

JOB EVALUATION

As mentioned earlier, job evaluation (JE) has become the major mechanism for valuing the content of jobs or roles. Despite criticism by the 'new pay' writers as old-fashioned and bureaucratic, there is no sign that its popularity in the UK is diminishing. This is demonstrated by major recent JE exercises in the public services – for example, in local government, the NHS and higher education.

JE is used to establish the relative value of different jobs or roles within an organisation. It is based on a process of job or role analysis, whereby the key aspects of the work are analysed, and is widely used as the basis for creating a grading structure. According to Hills (1989: 3–32), four basic assumptions underpin the use of JE:

- jobs differ in terms of the various required contributions from the employee (eg in terms of skill, responsibility, effort etc);

- employees will accept the criteria used to assess job worth;

- JE plans assume that equity perceptions lie in the eyes of the beholders, ie the employees; and

- organisations assume that equity criteria remain stable over time.

JE is primarily used to inform decisions about pay and grading, but increasingly has found other purposes. Many organisations use JE to underpin the revision of existing pay and grading structures but it can also be a tool to assimilate new jobs into existing structures. Research by IDS (2007) found that JE was being used increasingly where completely new organisations were being created, such as Virgin Mobile, which started out with no formal pay and grading structure. Elsewhere, it has been used to equality-proof pay structures in order to reduce the risks of expensive litigation. Other organisations are using JE more as a career development tool. IDS (2007: 5) notes that 'One by-product of analytical schemes is that the factors they employ can be used to produce job profiles. These can then be used to show staff how their current position differs from or is similar to other roles in the organisation and how they might therefore progress to the next level. In flatter organisations, this can also be useful for encouraging employees to make lateral movements across the structure.'

DEFINITION

'Job evaluation is a procedure for assessing the relative demands of jobs with a view to allocating jobs to positions within a pay structure. Job evaluation involves job analysis, the production of job descriptions, and an assessment of the "size" of jobs (i.e. how demanding they are) so that they can be placed in rank order and divided into grades. The latter will thus consist of jobs with equivalent demands, which will receive the same basic rate of pay or be allocated to the same salary scale or pay range.'

Heery and Noon (2001)

THE DEVELOPMENT OF JOB EVALUATION

Given the recent critique of JE by 'new pay' writers, it is worth looking at its origins and the reasons why it became so popular. JE was closely identified with the development of scientific management and the rise of mass production industries (Figart, 2001). As Mahoney (1992: 338) comments, 'the concept of job was the unifying concept in the scientific management approach to organisation and management'. JE offered an apparently 'rational' management technique for distinguishing between the value of different jobs in handling the distribution of pay within the organisation.

The earliest record of job evaluation is the introduction of a job classification system by the Commonwealth Edison Company of Chicago in 1909, although even earlier, in 1902, the US Civil Service Commission had recommended the reclassification of pay rates on the basis of the 'duties performed' (Hills, 1989). In the USA, four major JE techniques had been established by 1926 – ranking, grade description, factor comparison and point factor. The points factor system of Edward Hay became the most common method, and the Hay system remains the pre-eminent JE scheme in the world today.

While JE was originally focused largely on establishing internal pay differentials, it was also viewed as a strategy for controlling pay costs (see Figart, 2001 for an interesting account of the history of JE). Edward Hay argued that 'job evaluation permits considerable control over salary costs' (cited in Figart 2001: 410). From its inception it was also seen as a method for constraining the effects of collective bargaining on pay levels. JE provided a seemingly scientific method of allocating value to jobs and hence could counter the pressures exerted by trade unions representing particular well-organised groups of workers. On the other hand, Mahoney (1992: 338) argues that such job-based pay structures led to the concept of 'job ownership expressed in the labor movement and collective bargaining'. Unions were therefore ambivalent about JE. JE was also seen as a means of reducing pay disparities between departments and divisions and hence lessening employee grievances and escalating wage costs through competition between groups of employees or individuals within the same enterprise.

It is interesting to note that, at the time of its introduction, economists were concerned that job evaluation would reduce the effects of the market in pay-setting and hence undermine the natural working of the labour market. While collective bargaining outcomes were considered, at the end of the day, to be susceptible to the natural pressures of the labour market, JE was not.

While in recent times JE has tended to be used more for non-manual jobs than manual, it was originally seen as a device to deal with the growth of non-craft jobs as mass production replaced craft manufacture. Whereas craft workers were seen to have individual value according to their skills (ie the person), unskilled workers were seen as more easily dealt with on a job' basis. This provides an interesting context for today's criticisms of job evaluation that it rewards the 'job' rather than the 'person'.

JE grew rapidly during the Second World War, especially in the USA where a freeze on pay increases meant that the only way to obtain a pay rise was to be regraded. In the post-war period JE became an integral part of many large corporations' remuneration practices, reinforcing the internal labour market and 'lifetime' employment practices of the period. There was a further growth in the use of JE in the 1960s and 1970s. Jacques (1964) developed a method based on the theory of the 'time span of discretion', under which jobs are ranked according to the maximum period of time a person was expected to work on their own before becoming accountable to a manager.

Pritchard and Murlis (1992) make the interesting observation that the 1960s and 1970s was a period when UK government incomes policies led to a strong concern for internal equity rather than market competitiveness. Because in reality the only form of pay progression allowed on top of the incomes policy pay limit was fixed incremental progression, organisations made little difference in practice between high- and low-performers. Therefore, in many organisations pay was driven almost entirely by job evaluation, with annual uplifts to the pay structure in line with the government-decreed incomes policy pay limit. The major way to obtain a real pay increase was to be regraded under the JE scheme.

THE CRITIQUE OF JOB EVALUATION

In recent years, however, JE has been subjected to criticism. Critiques have come from both the normative 'new pay' literature in the USA and academic research. As mentioned earlier, however, criticism of job evaluation is not new. Recent criticism of JE from management writers has focused on four issues (CIPD, 2001). First, JE can be highly bureaucratic and paper-intensive, as well as inflexible, 'time-wasting' and costly. Secondly, it reinforces the concept of a rigid hierarchy that is not in accord with the ways in which de-layered and process-based organisations function. Thirdly, it inhibits flexibility in making pay and grading decisions. Fourthly, it is inconsistent with the ways in which work is now carried out – it is important to pay for the person rather than the job.

According to Lawler (2000: 109), 'Even when job evaluation is used in conjunction with a traditional top-down approach to management, it has a number of problems. These include the fact that "job worth" can be hard to communicate and that people find the value system that underlies job worth difficult to accept because they think of *themselves* as having value to the organisation, not the work they do.' Lawler argues that the message from tying pay and benefits to job size is that higher-level individuals who hold highly evaluated jobs are the ones who matter; 'thus the key to being a success is moving to bigger and bigger jobs'. This may suit traditional hierarchical organisations but may not be appropriate where the most valuable staff in an organisation do not supervise many people and may not have responsibility for large budgets. Moreover, because job evaluation links an individual with a 'job' or 'role', it becomes difficult to change those jobs or roles if the outcome is a reduction in JE points. Staff may also see JE as a route to promotion and hence higher pay, so that regrading appeals become a constant feature of the system. Lastly, JE can create its own internal bureaucracy, with a team of staff permanently employed in keeping the JE system up to date.

The 'new pay' writers (eg Lawler, 1990; Mahoney, 1992; Schuster and Zingheim, 1992) generally see JE as a barrier to strategic reward and an obstacle to more variable and individual forms of reward. For these writers, internal equity is about individual performance and contribution, rather than job size. Research by McNabb and Whitfield (2001) gives some support to this critique. Using two large UK datasets – the Workplace Industrial Relations Survey and the employer Manpower – they found that there was a weak link between JE and 'high performance' work practices. Organisations using the full range of high-performance work practices were, in particular, less likely to have analytical JE schemes. Organisations that had both analytical JE and high-performance work practices had significantly worse financial performance than those that had one or the other of these, but not both.

The other critique of JE has come from an equal-pay perspective. Figart (2001: 405) argues that while JE has traditionally been about establishing pay equity, the 'process of reconciling equal pay as ideology with pre-existing gender wage disparities resulted in a narrow definition of equal work'. While JE has become the major practical tool for combating gender pay discrimination in the workplace, some writers suggest that the use of JE is problematic in dealing with equal value (or 'comparable worth' in the USA).

Research undertaken in the 1980s (Madigan and Hoover, 1986) subjected 206 job classifications to evaluation using six different JE schemes. The study found wide differences in the value allocated to the same job under the different schemes. Similarly, an experiment by Arnault *et al* (2001) rated the same set of 27 jobs, using three different JE schemes. The results were again different for each job. The research indicates that the choice of JE method significantly affects decisions on job hierarchies and pay equity, and that attempts to promote equal value may be quite sensitive to the JE scheme chosen. Gilbert (2005), in a review of the use of JE in UK employment tribunal cases about equal pay, concludes that in some cases JE has been used as a barrier or weapon against those making such a claim. Quaid (1993: 239), an ex-JE consultant, argues that job evaluation is in fact a 'myth' because 'it is a process based on widely held beliefs that cannot be tested objectively'.

Despite these criticisms, JE continues to be popular among HR practitioners and is being updated and adapted to cope with more flexible pay structures. As Kessler (2000: 277) has suggested, 'revision stops well short of abandonment. The majority of organisations still have job evaluation.'

 SELF-ASSESSMENT EXERCISE

Thinking about the various objectives of job evaluation described above, which of these objectives do you think is most important for (1) employers and (2) employees? Are they the same?

THE TYPES OF JOB EVALUATION

As already mentioned, there are fundamentally two types of JE – analytical and non-analytical – but there are various types of scheme under both headings. Non-analytical schemes evaluate 'whole jobs' as opposed to analytical schemes that break down jobs into factors or component elements such as the points factor method. Non-analytical schemes may use simply job titles or simple job descriptions to compare job content. While such schemes are simpler, more flexible and cheaper to implement than analytical schemes, they are also more open to charges of subjectivity and inconsistency, mainly because it is difficult for the job analyst to distinguish between the job content and the performance of the jobholder. For this reason, non-analytical JE schemes are not generally defensible against equal-pay challenges.

Analytical schemes, on the other hand, are seen as a potential defence against claims for equal pay for work of equal value because such schemes are seen as more rigorous in their analysis of job content, but this would depend on the validity of the methods used. Analytical JE schemes can still be challenged on the basis that they are in some way flawed in the factors used.

For a more detailed comparison of the various JE techniques, see Armstrong *et al* (2003), Armstrong and Barron (1995) or Pritchard and Murlis (1992).

NON-ANALYTICAL SCHEMES

The main types of non-analytical JE scheme, according to Armstrong and Barron (1995), include the following:

- job ranking
- paired comparison ranking
- job classification
- internal benchmarking.

These will be analysed in turn.

Job ranking

Job ranking is the simplest form of JE and consists of comparing jobs with one another to produce a rank order or hierarchy. As Armstrong and Barron (2000) comment, in one sense all JE schemes are about ranking jobs, but the difference between non-analytical and analytical schemes is that the latter attempt to quantify the judgments made. A list of criteria may be used in job ranking, but the weight that individual job analysts give to these criteria will differ, creating problems of consistency and uniformity.

Paired comparison ranking

An alternative to simple job ranking is a system known as 'paired comparisons' (see Figure 4.7). This is similar to job ranking but involves an element of points- scoring to give an indication of the relationship between two different jobs. Pairs of benchmark jobs are compared with points being allocated to each role according to whether the

Figure 4.7 Example of a paired comparison ranking form

Job letter	JOB TITLES	a Accounts Assistant	b Bought Ledger Controller	c Compuetr Operator	d Customer Service Operator	e Marketing Assistant	f Personnel Officer	g Postroon Assistant	h Receptionist	i Sales Executive	j Secretary	TOTAL SCORE	OVERALL RANKING
A	Accounts ledger		0	1	0	1	0	2	2	0	0	6	8
B	Bought Ledger Controller	2		2	2	2	0	2	2	0	2	14	3
C	Computer Operator	1	0		1	1	0	2	2	0	0	7	7
D	Customer Service Officer	2	0	1		2	0	2	1	0	1	9	4=
E	Marketing Assitant	1	0	1	0		0	2	2	0	2	8	6
F	Personnel Officer	2	2	2	2	2		2	2	0	2	16	2
G	Postroom Assistant	0	0	0	0	0	0		1	0	0	1	10
H	Receptionist	0	0	0	1	0	0	1		0	0	2	9
I	Sales Executive	2	2	2	2	2	2	2	2		2	18	1
J	Secretary	2	0	2	1	0	0	2	2	0		9	4=

Company: XYZ Ltd   Division   Headquarters
Evaluator   Name: J. Smith   Job Title: Company Secretary

Source: Armstrong and Barron (1995: 57)

job is of less, similar or more importance than the other (ie with a score of 0, 1 or 2 accordingly). The scores for each job are then added to produce an indicative rank order. Such paired comparisons may be used in small organisations but would not provide an effective defence against an equal-pay challenge as there is no detailed evidence of why one job is considered more important or demanding than another.

Job classification

Job classification begins from a different perspective. Unlike job ranking and paired comparisons, where the grading structure emerges from the spread of job levels identified through the JE exercise, under job classification the grading structure is designed first, along with job descriptions for each grade or level. A number of representative (benchmark) jobs are then compared against these job descriptions to validate the structure, and the remaining jobs are then slotted in to the predefined grades. Unlike job ranking and paired comparisons, job classification does lay down basic principles for comparing jobs on the basis of the skills, effort and responsibility laid down in the job descriptors. But, unlike analytical schemes, it does not quantify these differences. The problem, again, is that too much subjectivity in deciding the level of job is left in the hands of the analyst. For this reason, such schemes would not normally provide a defence against an equal-pay challenge.

In the past, some proprietary job classification schemes were available, for example, the one provided for clerical and administrative staffs by the Institute for Administrative Management (IAM), but the development of equal-pay law has led to these being no longer considered commercially viable.

Internal benchmarking

Armstrong and Barron (1995) comment that internal benchmarking has never been dignified as a formal type in the textbooks on job evaluation but is probably what people often do through intuition when valuing jobs. It is about comparing the job under review with any similar internal benchmark jobs that have already been properly graded. The job is then slotted into the appropriate grade. This comparison is usually made on a 'whole job' basis without analysing the job factor by factor, although this fact leaves the decision open to challenge under equal-pay law.

In some ways internal benchmarking is similar to job classification in that the job is compared against an existing grading structure, but it is different in that the existing grading structure is likely to be based on analytical methods. Armstrong and Barron (1995) say that internal benchmarking is perhaps the most commonly used method of informal or semi-formal JE. It is sometimes used after a formal analytical JE process has been completed to slot in similar jobs to grades without having to evaluate every single job.

ANALYTICAL SCHEMES

As mentioned earlier, the key difference between analytical and non-analytical schemes is that the former breaks down individual jobs into component parts rather than using the 'whole job' as in the latter.

The main types of analytical JE scheme are as follows:

- factor comparison
- point-factor rating
- competence-based job evaluation.

These will be analysed in turn.

Factor comparison

The factor comparison method was one of the earliest JE schemes invented (by Eugene Benge in 1941). In a traditional factor comparison scheme, jobs are broken down into their component elements or 'factors' under five headings: mental requirements, skill requirements, physical requirements, responsibilities and working conditions. The main difference between traditional factor comparison schemes and point-factor schemes is that, in the former, monetary values are related directly to factor scores. Under the point-factor method, only points are attached to factors.

Traditional factor comparison schemes are little used today but a variant – 'graduated factor comparison' – is often used in equal-value cases. This variant requires comparisons to be made on a graduated scale (eg low, medium, high), but the factors are not weighted. This can be especially useful when comparing just a few jobs (as in an equal-value case), and in some ways is a rather more sophisticated form of non-analytical job ranking.

Factor comparison entails comparing an individual job directly with another in terms of a defined factor. The rate of pay of each benchmark job is broken down and distributed among the factors, based on the relative importance of the factors. This means that the selected benchmark jobs used to arrive at the price of the various factors must be properly paid to start with.

Another method is analytical factor comparison. This technique compares the content of jobs against a set of descriptions for each factor. These are arranged in order of difficulty, but with no number score, allowing the job grade to be deduced from the overall results.

Point-factor rating

The point-factor rating method was the first quantitative form of JE and was invented by Lott in 1924. Many standalone, internally designed JE schemes are of this type. Point-factor rating breaks down each job into several factors, which are scored against a numerical scale. The sum of the factor scores gives the total job size.

The method works as follows. A number of job factors are selected and defined (eg skill, responsibility and effort). Such factors must be common to all jobs in the organisation or to clusters of jobs in job families. The levels or degrees to which each factor is present in the organisation are then defined. Each factor may be assigned a weighting, and this is translated into a maximum point score that can be given to each factor. The sum of the scores for each factor indicates the maximum score that can be given to any job.

The maximum points for each factor are then distributed between the levels or degrees of each factor. Each level thus has its own score or range of points. Benchmark jobs are then analysed in terms of the factors, and the level at which each of the factors is present in the benchmark jobs is determined by reference to the factor plan. Scores are given for each factor in line with the factor plan and added together to produce a total score for each of the benchmark jobs. This in turn produces a rank order of jobs. A grading structure is then developed from the rank order, with each grade defined in terms of the range of points attached. The job grades are then priced according to external market rates and/or existing rates of pay and relativities. The job content for each factor is usually described, and the job analyst selects the factor level most appropriate to the job.

STUDENT EXERCISE

Look at the examples of factor plans below. Why do you think the public sector schemes generally have more factors than the proprietary schemes? Which do you think is better: simplicity or the full range of potential criteria?

To summarise, point-factor rating has three main components:

- the factors
- the number of levels in each factor
- the score for each factor level.

The choice and number of factors is crucial to the success of the scheme. The number of factors will depend to a large extent on the type of organisation and the range of occupations, but the minimum number would be three and the maximum probably less than 20. The types of factors used will vary from scheme to scheme, but they should cover all the significant features of the workforce, be acceptable in terms of equal-value considerations and avoid double-counting, omission or combining of features.

Some examples of factor plans

Hay Guide Chart-Profile Method

- Knowhow
- Problem-solving
- Accountability

KPMG Equate

- Accountability
- Job impact
- Thinking demands
- Communication demands
- Knowledge skills and experience

PA

- Judgement
- Planning and management
- Communication
- Job impact
- Theoretical knowledge and application
- Skills acquisition and practice
- Effect of errors
- Manual dexterity and effort

Price Waterhouse Coopers

- Responsibility
- Knowledge
- Mental skills
- Physical skills
- Environmental conditions

Higher Education Role Analysis

- Communication
- Teamwork and motivation
- Liaison and networking
- Service delivery
- Decision-making processes and outcomes
- Planning and organising resources
- Initiative and problem-solving
- Analysis and research
- Sensory and physical demands
- Work environment
- Pastoral care and welfare
- Team development
- Teaching and learning support
- Knowledge and experience

NHS Agenda for Change

- Communication and relationship skills
- Knowledge, training and experience
- Analytical and judgemental skills
- Planning and organisational skills
- Physical skills
- Responsibilities for patient/client care
- Responsibilities for policy and service development
- Responsibilities for financial and physical resources
- Responsibilities for human resources
- Responsibilities for information resources
- Responsibilities for research and development
- Freedom to Act
- Physical effort
- Emotional effort
- Working conditions

Local Government Single Status*

- Knowledge and skills
- Effort demands
- Responsibilities
- Environmental demands

(*each factor is sub-divided – eg knowledge and skills is divided into knowledge, mental skills, interpersonal and communication skills and physical skills)

The Equal Opportunities Commission (EOC, 1994) has published guidance on the factors possibly open to gender bias. For example, length of service, experience, heavy lifting and physical hazards tend to favour male jobs while caring, dexterity and typing/keyboard skills will tend to favour females.

The number of levels for each factor is also an issue. Having the same number of levels for each factor may not be appropriate. Some factors just have a larger range of levels to be analysed and measured.

THE PREVALENCE OF JOB EVALUATION IN THE UK

Despite increasing criticism of JE in the 1990s from both the 'new pay' writers and feminist critics, JE continues to be commonly used in the UK. The Workplace Employee Relations Survey in 2004 found that 25 per cent of workplaces with 25 or more employees had a job evaluated pay structure. It established that such schemes were more common in larger workplaces and organisations, workplaces that were part of a wider organisation and workplaces in the public sector (Kersley *et al*, 2006, and Table 4.6). Three-fifths of workplaces in the public administration sector had formal job evaluation schemes compared with one-tenth in the private construction sector. JE was also more likely to be found in unionised workplaces and in workplaces where the majority of staff were female. There was also a strong correlation between the use of JE and the presence of formal policies on equal opportunities or managing diversity.

Table 4.6 Presence of a JE scheme, by workplace characteristics

	Job evaluation scheme (% of workplaces)
All workplaces	20
Workplace size	
10–24 employees	17
25–49 employees	22
50–99 employees	23
100–199 employees	35
200–499 employees	36
500 or more employees	54
All workplaces with 25 or more employees	25
Organisation status	
Standalone workplace	7
Part of a larger organisation	27

	Job evaluation scheme (% of workplaces)
Organisation size	
10–99 employees	9
100–999 employees	21
1,000–9,999 employees	30
10,000 employees or more	34
Sector of ownership	
Private	16
Public	42
Industry	
Manufacturing	14
Electricity, gas and water	(43)
Construction	10
Wholesale and retail	17
Hotels and restaurants	13
Transport and communications	15
Financial intermediation	42
Other business services	16
Public administration	59
Education	25
Health	28
Other community services	23
Union recognition	
No union recognised	12
At least one union recognised	41

Source: Kersley et al (2006: 245)

All workplaces with 10 or more employees

Table 4.7 Most common factors used in JE

Knowledge, skills, expertise and experience	Environment and work demands
Communication, contacts and interpersonal skills	Freedom to act/discretion
Decision-making, problem-solving and complexity	Responsibility for financial and other resources
Impact and accountability	Innovation and thinking
People management, leadership and team working	Planning
Various types of responsibility, demands and attributes	

Source: E-reward (2003)

Almost three-fifths of the workplaces with JE schemes used analytical points-rating schemes. These were particularly common in larger workplaces and organisations, and also within the public sector.

The previous WERS survey in 1998 did not contain questions on JE but earlier versions did, allowing some longitudinal analysis of trends. Between 1980 and 1990 there was a rise in the prevalence of JE from 21 per cent of workplaces to 26 per cent. A key change since 1990, however, has been the continuing increase in JE in the public sector (up from 27 per cent in 1990 to 44 per cent in 2004). This has been mirrored by some decline in the use of JE by the private sector (down from around a quarter of all workplaces in 1990 to a fifth in 2004) (Kersley *et al*, 2006).

A survey by E-Reward in 2003 found that around four-fifths of the sample of 39 schemes were analytical, and of these 70 per cent were point-factor rating schemes. The most common factors used in the schemes are shown in Table 4.7.

CHOOSING A JOB EVALUATION SCHEME

In choosing which type of JE scheme to use, organisations have some choice. The main options are buying 'off the shelf' from a provider of one of the proprietary schemes (eg Hay) or designing one's own, although there is the possibility of adapting an existing proprietary scheme as well. In recent times there has been a trend towards schemes specifically designed for a particular sector, especially in the UK public sector. Examples include the NHS Agenda for Change scheme, the HERA scheme used in much of higher education, and the local government 'Single Status' scheme. All of these sector-specific schemes had to deal with issues arising from the harmonisation of different occupational 'bargaining' groups on to single pay spines. Because of the range of jobs and roles covered, it was felt that 'off the shelf' schemes would not be able to reflect the wide range and scope of the organisation's functions. More importantly, remedying cases of gender discrimination was central to these exercises, and again it was felt that only a 'bespoke' approach would work in dealing with this issue. In the NHS the use of the Agenda for Change scheme is mandatory, but in both local government and higher education organisations are free to choose their own schemes. In some cases this has meant that proprietary schemes have been selected.

A first stage in any process of selecting a JE scheme is the establishment of a project team to assess the project, set the timetable and compare the various schemes available. The information collected by the project team can be used to make informed decisions about which product is most appropriate for the organisation or indeed whether a bespoke scheme needs to be designed in-house.

Project teams will often include representatives of the workforce, as well as HR staff. In unionised environments, trade union representatives are often invited to join, but even in non-union environments it makes sense to involve staff from various levels of the organisation. Their expertise can help in making the right decisions about the choice of scheme. Also, such staff participation achieves 'buy-in' from staff, building confidence in and assisting acceptance of the final outcomes from the scheme. The degree of staff involvement will vary from organisation to organisation, but the larger the project the larger the chances of staff involvement.

Clearly, if staff are involved they will need to be given time away from the their normal duties to take part in the process. This may mean providing facility time to staff representatives and may also suggest that realistic timescales are required. In addition to the actual project team (of which there may be sub-committees dealing with specific tasks), there may be a steering committee of senior managers to monitor and oversee the process.

Organisations often use external HR consultants to assist either in the selection of an appropriate JE scheme or in the actual designing of an in-house scheme.

☐	**Methodology**	Which type of job evaluation scheme would best suit your particular needs – analytical or non-analytical?
☐	**Off-the-shelf scheme**	Can an off-the-shelf or proprietary scheme meet your needs? Can such a scheme cope with the number and range of jobs that you want to evaluate?
☐	**Tailored approach**	Have you considered an off-the-shelf scheme that is tailored to reflect the jobs in your particular sector? Alternatively, do you require a scheme to be designed from scratch specifically for you?

☐ **Supplier's track record**   Can the consultant show that its system works well elsewhere? Does it have a track record of managing similar-sized projects, particularly in your sector?

☐ **Timetable**   How long does the consultant estimate it will take to design and implement your scheme?

☐ **Using appropriate factors**   Do the factors in an off-the-shelf analytical scheme and the associated weightings reflect those areas you are seeking to prioritise and reward? If there are gaps, how easy is it to put right? Can competencies, for example, be accommodated in the scheme? Are you able to express the factors in language appropriate to your circumstances? Do you wish to weight the factors?

☐ **Information-gathering**   How does the consultant propose to collect the job information? Will new job descriptions be required or will jobholder interviews be carried out? Establish who will be involved.

☐ **Union involvement**   To what extent do you want trade unions or employee representatives to be included in the steering committee or job evaluation panel? What experience does the consultant have of working with trade unions in your sector?

☐ **Level of computerisation**   What level of computerisation do you require? How easy is it to link the software to other HR systems? Is it user-friendly and easy to update? How much of the actual evaluation process do you wish to automate?

☐ **Communications**   How will the consultant help communicate details of the job evaluation exercise to your staff and keep them informed of developments? How open do you want the process to be?

☐ **Pay structure design**   If new grading arrangements are the key output required, what experience does the consultant have of developing an appropriate pay structure following on from the job evaluation exercise?

☐	**Salary survey data**	How important to you is easy access to salary surveys and other benchmark market data to support a new pay structure? What relevant data can the consultant provide directly and what will this cost?
☐	**Scheme maintenance**	What training does the consultant propose to offer your staff to help them undertake job analysis work and make the most of any software? How will it help ensure that you are in a position to operate the scheme in-house over the longer term?
☐	**Cost considerations**	What are the consultant's charging arrangements? Will it quote you a fixed price? If not, establish the hourly rates of the staff who would be working on your project and obtain an estimate of the amount of work involved. Is the provision of software part of the package?

Source: IDS (2007: 33) Reproduced by kind permission of Incomes Data Services

STUDENT EXERCISE

Thinking about the grading system in your own organisation or one with which you are familiar, what would be the major issues in taking a decision to select a JE scheme?

THE DESIGN STAGE

Deciding on the factors to be used to evaluate jobs or roles is the key decision. As mentioned earlier, this is increasingly important if the scheme is to satisfy the requirements of equal-value legislation. According to IDS (2007), the factors used in JE schemes can be divided into four broad categories:

- Inputs – what contributions are jobholders required to make?

- Processes – how are jobs done?

- Accountabilities – for whom is the jobholder responsible?

- Impact – what is the job's overall influence on the organisation's activities?

As we showed in our selection of factors used in different schemes, the number of factors can be as few as two or as many as 15. Often broad categories are broken down into sub-factors.

Organisations use a number of criteria in making a choice about the number and types of factor to be used. Factors need to be measurable, comprehensive, not unfairly discriminatory and balanced across the whole job population covered. IDS (2007) makes the point that employers will need to decide whether the factors to be used will help reward the inputs and outputs identified, and whether they will be happy to live with any consequences in terms of potential pay costs.

In order to make the factors clear to both staff and evaluators, there is usually a set of descriptions alongside each factor to explain the criteria to be used in judging them.

As mentioned earlier, factors may be weighted so that some are more important than others. These are usually expressed as percentages, which are used to calculate the total scores for each job or role. This may mean deciding whether a factor is 'essential' or 'desirable' for the job. If an organisation chooses to use a proprietary scheme the weightings will already be decided in many cases, but in the case of 'in-house' schemes decisions about weighting will usually be taken by the project team or steering group. It is at this stage in the process that the potential for gender discrimination is most apparent. If the factors themselves or the weighting applied to them is biased in favour of male occupations, the scheme may well not meet the test of an Employment Tribunal.

JOB OR ROLE ANALYSIS

Having decided on the shape of the scheme, the factors to be used and the weighting (if any) to be applied to them, the next stage is begin analysis of jobs or roles. Job or role analysis is a methodology for developing an understanding of the content of a job or role. Its outcome has traditionally been a job description, but increasingly it is a role profile. The difference between these two is as follows.

A *job description* typically provides an overview of the job and its place in the organisational structure, a detailed description of the duties and responsibilities of the job and a commentary matching the various JE factor headings. Job descriptions, however, require regular updating to reflect any changes in the work of the jobholder as they are fundamentally prescriptive documents detailing what the employer and employee expect to be accomplished. In that sense, job descriptions have a quasi-contractual nature, and some writers have commented that this tends to limit employee activity to the contract, rather than encouraging employees to work 'beyond contract'.

A *role profile*, in contrast, is seen as more flexible in that it perhaps provides a more 'psychological' approach. Role profiles are more about the type of personality required for the task and are more focused on outputs and inputs, the knowledge and skills required and expected behaviours. As Armstrong *et al* (2003: 94) comment, the concept of role focuses on 'what is needed to deliver organisation objectives, by setting out the behavioural expectations as well as the expected outcomes, rather than the minutiae of how the work needs to be done'.

An advantage of a role profile is that it does not need regular change, as there is no detailed description of how the work should be done. Role profiles are much more about setting out how the employee is expected to contribute and behave, rather than the detailed requirements of the particular job. The use of role profiles also enables a more generic approach, reducing the number of documents that need to be kept – unlike job descriptions, where there might be a separate document for every job in the organisation.

Such job or role analysis is used not just for job evaluation purposes but for a range of other HR applications, including job-matching against the external market, pay structure design, recruitment and staff development.

There are a number of techniques for conducting job or role analysis. These include interviews with jobholders and supervisors, observation of work activity or the completion of job-analysis questionnaires by the jobholder.

IDS (2007) makes the point that interviewing jobholders, though the most thorough way of collecting information, is onerous and time-consuming. For this reason this method is often limited to particularly complex jobs or roles or where only a few jobs or roles are being considered. Instead, employers are increasingly using questionnaires to gather information, often in line with the factor plan being used in the JE scheme. This more quantitative approach has the advantage that large amounts of information can be collected rapidly and in a consistent manner. Its disadvantage, as with other quantitative research techniques, is that it may miss subtle differences between jobs or roles and there is reduced opportunity to clarify ambiguities in responses. Of course, if there are existing job descriptions or role profiles these can be used in the JE exercise, but it is essential that such documents are up to date, and they may not be designed to match the factor plan.

While in smaller organisations it may be possible to evaluate all posts, in larger organisations it is usual that only a series of 'benchmark' or typical jobs or roles are analysed. Once these have been evaluated, other jobs or roles are compared with the benchmark job descriptions or role profiles and matched to the appropriate level. It is therefore vital that the benchmarks cover a fair range of jobs or roles and be selected to avoid any bias, especially in terms of gender.

 STUDENT EXERCISE

What is the difference between a job description and a role profile? Which would you say is the method used to describe grade content in your own organisation?

SCORING THE JOBS OR ROLES

Once the information about the benchmark jobs and roles has been collected and validated – usually by a supervisor and/or senior manager – the evaluations can be completed. If an analytical JE approach is being used, 'scores' or 'ranks' are usually assigned to each of the factors. These scores are then analysed using relevant software to calculate a total score for the job or role. According to the total scores, all the jobs can be ranked to produce a 'league table' of jobs or roles in the organisation. Using software usually makes the calculation of scores very easy as these can instantaneously produce the weightings and any complex algorithms required for different factors.

The next stage is to set grade or band boundaries around this hierarchy of jobs or roles. It is usual in any point-factor scheme for scores to cluster around certain points in the hierarchy. These usually indicate where the grade or band 'break points' should be. Today most organisations use pay-modelling software to review the different outcomes and costs for different grade boundaries. Some organisations may opt to set the grade or band boundaries first and then allocate jobs/roles on the basis of their scores or by comparing them to generic role profiles for each grade or band.

This stage is most important as where the grade or band boundaries fall can have a dramatic effect on the cost implications of any new grading structure for the employer. This depends on the number of employees that will benefit from the new structure (referred to as 'green circled') and the number who will be disadvantaged (referred to as 'red circled'). By moving grade or band boundaries, the numbers of these 'green' and 'red' circled staff can be reduced or increased. Clearly, the more 'green' outcomes there are, the higher the likely costs as these staff will have to be promoted or moved up the grade. But 'red circled' staff are also problematic. Apart from any motivational issues associated with being 'downgraded', there is usually a period of pay protection for these employees, which can also be costly. Keeping the number of red and green circles to a minimum, with most staff moving across on their existing level, is clearly the objective for many employers.

Once a grading structure has been agreed, the next stage is to allocate pay ranges to each grade or band. These are often set in line with external market rate reference points. Where a proprietary JE scheme is used, one advantage may be that the consultant may be able to provide such reference points from their own pay information database. For example, Hay can provide such a service. In other circumstances, employers may well need to conduct their external pay benchmarking exercise to decide on the grade or role minima and maxima. In some of the recent large-scale JE exercises in the UK public services, there has been a pay spine of incremental points against which organisations have been able to plot their grade boundaries.

THE IMPLEMENTATION STAGE

Once the JE outcomes and any new grading scheme have been agreed, the final stage is implementation. The big problem here is that there will undoubtedly be winners and losers from any JE exercise. Given the fact that most employees are particularly sensitive to their place in the organisational hierarchy, and that any changes may impact on longer-term earnings potential, changes in their rank or place in the hierarchy of jobs/roles can be very disturbing. It is at this stage that JE ceases to be a 'technical' exercise, and the employee relations aspects of reward come to the fore. All the skills of reward practitioners have to be deployed to handle the disappointments that may result from a JE exercise.

The key issues here involve communication of the results to staff, some protection arrangements for those downgraded, and the avenue for individual appeals against the results. Many organisations, according to IDS (2007), stress the importance of openness and transparency when carrying out a JE exercise. Often staff representatives are directly involved in the process alongside HR and other managers. But the amount of information that is shared with the workforce varies. It is usual for staff to be told about why the exercise is happening; what and whom it will involve; when it will take place and when results will be expected; the implications for staff; and any appeals process. Individual members of staff may be given their overall JE score, although in some cases they will only be told in which grade they have been placed. It is rare for employers to give out individual factor scores as these are seen as both too complex and potentially contentious where an individual just misses a grade by a few points.

Communication

The main methods of communication with employees are those usually utilised in the workplace, for example in-house magazines, email bulletins, staff presentations and briefings by managers and supervisors, help desks, videos and DVDs, and written guidance. Line managers need to be especially well-briefed to be able to explain any individual grading decision. It is usual to write to all staff individually with their own result.

Upgrading, downgrading and pay protection

Staff who are upgraded ('green circled') in the JE scheme are usually moved into the most appropriate pay band for the score achieved but at the minimum point of the scale (unless the grades overlap and the individual is already within the next grade range). There is usually a date agreed when all staff are assimilated to the new structure.

The situation with downgraded employees ('red circled') is more difficult. Generally, employers guarantee that nobody will receive an immediate pay cut as a result of JE. Those jobs found to have been over-graded are usually moved down to the new grade, but their pay level is protected for a period of time. During this period of protection, employees may be encouraged to undergo training and development to ensure that they can meet the needs of their old grade (by expanding their duties or role) and hence be reinstated in their old grade. Normally pay is protected at the old pay level for a period of years, usually no more than three. The EOC has issued guidance on the length of time protection can endure. Protection may involve a pay freeze or it may allow for cost-of-living increases but no pay progression within the grade. If, after the protection period expires, the employee has been unable to be redeployed or upgraded, they will revert to the salary of the grade they were originally allocated to under the JE exercise.

Appeals

Natural justice dictates that individual staff should be able to appeal against a JE exercise decision. A formal process is normally established whereby staff can appeal against the grade or banding allocated to them. Certain guidelines normally exist to control this process. Appeals may only be possible if the individual can prove that there was something wrong with their job or role description, or because the process was implemented unfairly. A deadline for appeals is usually set. As with other grievance procedures, the appeals process usually starts with an informal stage of a meeting between the individual and his or her line manager and an HR officer. At this stage, misunderstandings can be cleared up and minor complaints dealt with. The next stage is normally a formal appeals panel, chaired by an independent manager. Where an appeal is successful the job or role is usually re-evaluated by a different analyst or scoring panel.

 SELF-ASSESSMENT EXERCISE

What are the key issues to consider when implementing a JE scheme?

ALIGNING PAY WITH THE MARKET

As discussed at the beginning of this chapter (and in Chapter 3), there is a continuing tension within organisations between the internal need for equity and the demands of the external market for labour. On the one hand, a pay structure needs to be fair, consistent and transparent in terms of the internal ranking of jobs if it is to satisfy employees. On the other hand, this equity and rationality is not normally reflected in the external labour market. In the external market, the value of jobs is much more likely to reflect the supply of, and demand for, different skills and the relative power of different occupational groups to control the price of their labour. As mentioned earlier in the book, such factors change over time and may be subject to quite qualitative perceptions. Even where employees organise themselves into trade unions to enforce equity upon employers, the pressures of the labour market will often dictate the relative power of different unions and different bargaining groups.

In this section we consider how organisations manage this tension and what sources of information they use as evidence to support their decisions. While employers often refer to the 'market rate', in reality there is no such thing. While economists may speak of the point where supply and demand curves meet and the market-clearing rate is set, in reality there are a number of 'market rates' for the same job. As Armstrong and Murlis (2007: 178) state, 'People often refer to the "market rate" but it is a much more elusive concept than it seems.'

Organisations can respond to the demands of the external market in various ways. In Chapter 2, we discussed the important concept of the 'internal labour market' and how employers may seek to protect themselves from the vagaries of the external market. Prior to the 1980s, the relative global economic stability meant that many organisations, especially larger ones, could defend themselves from external competition for their labour by creating strong incentives to staff to remain loyal. These incentives included 'lifetime careers', strong grading and career development structures, pay and benefits systems that rewarded service and loyalty, and the development of firm-specific skills that were not easily transferable to other employers.

From the 1980s, however, the much more competitive global economic environment has weakened such systems so that today employers are placing much more emphasis upon 'employability' than 'lifetime employment', reward systems are linked to individual performance and acquisition of skills rather than service, and pay levels are benchmarked against external comparators rather than internal equity.

Market pricing of jobs involves collecting pay and benefits data for equivalent jobs to establish their market rate or price, the speed at which rates are changing and the direction of any changes. In considering the external market for a particular job, employers have to decide on the segment of the labour market in which such jobs are to be found. In general there are three main segments:

- the immediate local labour market surrounding the workplace (the town or suburb);
- the regional labour market (the geographical region or travel-to-work zone);
- the national (or, indeed, international) market.

In general, lower-level jobs (eg manual and clerical) are found in the local labour market; medium-level jobs (eg administrative and technical posts) in the regional market; and senior jobs (senior managers and the professions) in the national or international market. This is a generalisation, of course, and some industries recruit their manual workers from much wider labour markets (eg construction workers are highly mobile, even across national frontiers). Employers also distinguish between sectors and industries as the same role may be paid differently in different contexts. Again, it is more likely that sectoral data will be more important for some jobs than others. Some occupations are transferable across sectoral or industry boundaries while others only exist in particular types of workplace. The size of the organisations compared will also be an important issue in benchmarking.

The advantages of market-based pay are that it allows employers to respond flexibly to changes in the labour market and to target pay according to external value. It can be particularly appropriate where organisations adopt a job or career family structure (see the NUCS case study at the end of this chapter for an example), and therefore need to apply different levels of pay to different occupational groups.

But linking pay too closely to market comparisons may be problematic. It can undermine internal relativities and teamworking across different occupations. It can also break down harmonised pay structures and can lack transparency. Following the market can also create an upward spiral in pay as employers compete to stay 'ahead of the pack'. Not least, such systems can create very real problems of unequal pay where external values for occupations simply reinforce traditional gender pay gaps.

It should also be remembered that the market is only one consideration when setting pay levels (see Chapter 3). External comparisons may be irrelevant if either labour turnover reveals no problem with recruitment and retention or if the employer's ability to pay more is limited by the financial resources available.

Six ways of differentiating between different groups of employees to match the market are described by IDS (2006):

- interim ad hoc payments for specific groups;
- market supplements (this is most common in the public sector);
- separate pay structures for different groups of staff;
- job or career family structures;
- skills-based approaches whereby organisations address skill shortages by developing their own staff;
- using grading structures and/or actively encouraging grade drift (ie regrading staff where there are recruitment and retention issues).

SOURCES OF PAY INTELLIGENCE

The types of benchmarking data available to employers include the following: information on pay awards (whether negotiated or not) and actual salary scales; company-specific data; commercially produced salary surveys or pay databases held by consultants; and pay 'clubs', which share information between participants. In addition, some organisations analyse job advertisements. Such data can be broken down into two forms, non-analytical and analytical. In general, non-analytical information means data collected on the basis of job titles only or where the survey asks respondents to match their jobs to short 'capsule' descriptions of levels and functions. The former is clearly problematic in that a single job title can cover a range of different job descriptions and pay levels. The latter enables more accurate comparisons to be made, but is still based on fairly 'broad brush' criteria. Comparisons can also be made on the basis of 'whole job' comparisons or measures of responsibility.

Basic information about pay levels for particular job titles can be found in a range of published sources. Earnings data by occupation is available in various UK government statistical series, such as the Annual Survey of Hours and Earnings and the Labour Force Survey, while more specific information on named organisations is available from commercial publishers such as Incomes Data Services (IDS), Industrial Relations Services (IRS) and the Labour Research Department (LRD). In some cases, wage rates agreed in national agreements for specific occupations and levels may form the benchmark for those occupations. A good example is the national rates agreed for electricians under the Joint Industry Board in the electrical contracting industry – these rates are not just followed by electrical contractors but set the level for electricians employed elsewhere.

In contrast, the analytical job-matching method uses analytical JE techniques to determine 'job size' comparisons, in which jobs are broken down into factors and points and each benchmark scored against the factor points scale. The total score gives the 'size' each job being compared. Undoubtedly, analytical comparisons are the most accurate, but such an approach can be lengthy, labour-intensive and expensive. Where employers already use a patent JE scheme, comparisons with the external market may be made easier through access to the consultant's database of JE outcomes. Unfortunately, this can limit the type of comparisons available to those organisations using that particular JE scheme.

IDS research on market pricing (2006) came to three main conclusions: first, in pricing their jobs organisations rely on more than one source of data; secondly, reading across to data based on analytical job evaluation techniques is only part of the exercise and often is not used at all; thirdly, data-gathering exercises are ongoing and the results implemented annually, or within the year if recruitment and retention problems are severe.

SALARY SURVEYS

Surveys of pay and conditions form an important source of intelligence for organisations. The number of surveys has grown considerably over the last few decades, and the IDS Guide to Salary Surveys lists almost 300 such sources. They fall broadly into two main types: those available to anybody for a price and those only available to participants (often known as 'pay club' surveys). The type of survey available to non-participants is normally organised by job title or generic job description/level. Participants in such surveys are asked to match their own jobs to the survey level and function descriptors. The problem with such surveys is the big range in quality between survey providers and the need for fairly rigorous analysis of the data if the results are to be meaningful. Those surveys based on job evaluation generally provide better results, but they can be very expensive and are normally only available to the consultants' clients.

Another important issue to consider when judging the relative merits of surveys is the purpose for which they were designed. A number of professional institutions run their own membership surveys as a means to inform their members of their potential value. These surveys are often 'self-reported' by members and can therefore suffer from inaccurate reporting. In contrast, surveys where results are submitted by employers and based on actual payroll information are likely to be more accurate.

A key issue in considering the potential value of surveys is the sample size, as variations in sample sizes for competing surveys in the same field can lead to quite different results. As a general rule, the larger the sample the better will be the survey's accuracy. Employers also need to know about the sample organisations – their size, sector and geographical spread. Clearly, a sample based on just large organisations in the financial services sector in London would provide a very limited picture if one were seeking general data on clerical staff salaries. IDS (2004) suggests that the difficulties in interpreting the results of any survey indicate that employers should never rely on a single source of pay data but always 'triangulate' one source with a couple of others. Where the post is particularly special or unique, employers may commission their own 'bespoke' survey from a consultant.

Another problem is the issue of 'matched samples'. If a survey is conducted every year it may well be the case that the number of participants will vary from year to year. Moreover, within each participating organisation there will be turnover of individual staff throughout the year, with some staff leaving and others arriving. These changes can have quite considerable statistical effects on year-on-year comparisons. To ensure there is a comparison of the same organisations and same individuals year on year, some surveys provide a constant or 'matched' sample whereby data is provided that makes comparisons on exactly the same basis as the previous year's survey.

Surveys can provide a range of data on various aspects of reward. The most common data definitions are: base pay; cash bonuses; short-term incentives; long-term incentives; total earnings; employee benefits; and total remuneration.

Having collected sufficient market data to make a comparison, employers have to decide at what level in the range or distribution of salaries they wish to pay. This is termed 'market position' and can apply either to the whole pay structure or may be varied according to job family or even individuals. IDS (2004) makes the point that in any aggregate set of data it is normally assumed that the market rate is the median or midpoint, but most organisations claim to be in the 'upper quartile' (top 25 per cent). As IDS says, this is intriguing because some organisations must form the 'lower quartile'. Most surveys will also provide an arithmetic average or 'mean', but generally employers prefer to use the median as it cannot be distorted by extreme 'outliers' (either a few very high-paid or very low-paid staff). The UK government statistical service, the Office for National Statistics, has been keen to use the median as its benchmark, rather than the mean, and especially when making comparisons of earnings by gender. However, European data on the gender pay gap uses the mean.

Another useful statistic is the 'inter-quartile range'. This measures the range between the 25th and 75th percentile. Employers may also use the data to decide both starter rates for new recruits and target salaries after a number of years' service.

In order to check whether internal pay levels are in line with the market, employers can calculate a 'compa-ratio'. A compa-ratio of 'one' shows that the internal level and the market level are equal. A ratio of less than one would indicate that the internal level was below the market, and a ratio of more than one would indicate it was above the market.

A 'salary policy line' may also be drawn. This can be a curve or a straight line that relates internal salary points to the chosen survey target levels. A regression or 'best fit' line may then be constructed and salary ranges constructed around this.

IDS (2004) makes the important observation that medians and means should not be confused with salary mid-points. Means and medians can be lower than mid-points because either promotion, transfer or resignation leaves the remaining postholders concentrated at the bottom of the pay range or low turnover means that the majority of postholders reach their maximum point.

CAREER FAMILIES AT NORWICH UNION CENTRAL SERVICES

CASE STUDY

Norwich Union Central Services' career family framework was introduced to align a variety of arrangements used by the group's legacy companies. The business believes that this framework provides a simpler structure than a more traditional hierarchical arrangement, making it both easier to administer and for employees to understand. Staff now have a much clearer picture of the opportunities available to them and the skills they will need to progress.

Preamble

Norwich Union Central Services (NUCS) is the internal service provider for its parent company, Aviva. It covers a wide range of services, from designing and implementing new IT infrastructure to managing buildings and catering. It also houses HR shared services for the Aviva group.

Norwich Union and CGU merger

In early 2000, Aviva was formed from the merger of Norwich Union and CGU (itself a merger of General Accident and Commercial Union). The new company was divided into three distinct businesses:

- Norwich Union Life – life insurance

- Norwich Union Insurance – general insurance products

- Norwich Union Central Services – covering facilities, IT, HR shared services (eg payroll, recruitment administration) and security.

Aligning pay structures

Immediately following the merger, existing Norwich Union and CGU terms and conditions and pay models continued. Indeed, the first annual salary review after the merger, in April 2001, was carried out under these separate arrangements. Within NUCS, this meant that HR had to manage three separate pay review systems – covering former Norwich Union, former CGU and former CGU Life staff. As Nick Kennedy, Reward and Employee Relations Manager for NUCS, explains: 'By taking a "firefighting" approach and tackling issues as they arose, the pay round went relatively smoothly. However, it was clear that the old arrangements could not be maintained indefinitely and that it would be necessary to assimilate all staff on to a new pay structure. Our aim was that everyone within NUCS would be singing from the same hymn sheet by April 2002.' Work subsequently began across all three Aviva businesses to develop new pay structures.

Designing a new structure

The design work for the new pay and grading structures began in April 2001. Within NUCS, roll-out of the final framework began in August 2001 and was completed by the deadline of April 2002, in time for the annual pay review.

As the smallest of the business units and with limited HR resources, NUCS worked closely with Norwich Union Insurance (NUI) to develop its career family structure. The models in each are very similar, although some of the career families vary in line with the different functions covered by each business. For example, the 'facilities' family is peculiar to NUCS while 'claims' and 'underwriting' are only found in NUI.

Why career families?

The grading structure within the former Norwich Union had been based on a structured job evaluation exercise. This originally involved using a grading panel to position jobs. This process was found to be cumbersome and not always objective – it could depend on how well managers put forward their case for a particular job. Grading panels were therefore eventually replaced with a computer-based scoring system, which determined a grade on the basis of the information supplied.

A simpler approach

Going forward, NUI and NUCS wanted something more straightforward. As Nick Kennedy explains: 'We wanted an approach that would be simple enough for managers to use themselves and that employees would find easier to understand.' In addition, the aim was to introduce a system that would enable the businesses to have a clearer view of what resources were available in the way of skills and competencies. Moreover, the businesses wanted a solution that would make career progression more transparent and give employees a clearer view of where they fitted into the organisational structure. As a result, the decision was made to develop a career family structure, grouping roles of a similar size and aligning them on the basis of the kind of work done, not where it was done.

NUCS was confident that the final structure would enable line managers to make grading decisions independently of HR. However, in practice, HR continues to slot new roles into the framework. (Norwich Union Life, meanwhile, opted for a broad-banded approach based largely on the model that had been operated by CGU.)

Line manager input

Line managers played a central role in developing the career families framework. With the help of HR business partners, managers across NUCS were asked to provide typical role profiles. Where there were, for example, 20 separate job descriptions for employees basically doing the same job, managers were asked to apply some commonsense and create new generic profiles using standard templates.

Jobs were slotted into a career family matrix by central HR on the basis of these profiles, with the position within a family depending on the level of responsibility. The matrix now forms the basis of the career family framework.

Seeking expert support

Throughout the design process, NUCS was supported by consultants from Watson Wyatt. They were able to confirm that jobs had been slotted into the framework at the appropriate level. Subsequently, Watson Wyatt has supplied NUCS with market pay data.

The career family framework

The NUCS career family framework is designed to support staff to develop within their current roles, while also helping them to meet their future career aspirations. There are three key components:

- career families
- generic groups
- broad bands.

Career families

Each role falling within a particular career family is related through the activities carried out and the knowledge/skill set required. The families do not belong to one business but operate across NUCS. For example, individuals within the 'secretarial and administration' family could work within finance, HR or the property and facilities functions.

Within NUCS there are many small groups of staff with very specific duties – for example, there are half a dozen chauffeurs. This has resulted in a framework consisting of a relatively large number of small career families. NUCS currently has 22 separate career families:

- chauffeurs
- change management

- communications
- contract management
- corporate office operations support
- engineering
- facilities management
- finance
- human resources
- IT development
- IT technical
- occupational health
- occupational safety
- planning and management information
- projects
- property management
- purchasing
- risk management
- secretarial & administration
- security
- sports & leisure
- switchboard.

The list of career families is not static. At the corporate office in London, there is a group of around 12 or so messengers and receptionists. These staff have been incorporated into the NUCS career family framework as the 'corporate office operations support' family. More recently, the number of families has been reduced as various functions, such as postal and supply, have been outsourced.

All staff fall into a job family apart from heads of divisions.

Generic groups

Within the majority of career families, jobs are aligned to one of seven generic groups:

- managing consultant
- business manager

- consultant
- team manager
- lead adviser
- adviser
- support.

These are typically split into five levels on the basis of responsibility, complexity and accountability. Managing consultant and business manager roles are typically considered of equal value, as are team manager and lead adviser. This enables dual career paths so that employees do not have to move into a people management role to progress.

Role profiles
The accountabilities of a job at each level are set out in generic role profiles. This enables a job to be slotted into the system by simple comparison with the generic accountabilities.

However, NUCS recognises that while jobs may carry the same level of responsibility, the specific tasks carried out can be vastly different. For this reason, every member of staff also has a personal role profile. These set out everything an employee should be doing on a day-to-day basis as well as their specific objectives. These more detailed profiles are vital for effective performance management.

Therefore, while the framework is populated with a small number of generic roles, behind these are a much larger number of specific job titles.

Broad bands

The generic groups are also split into two 'broad bands'. These essentially split the groups into management and non-management roles and link to terms and conditions.

As Nick Kennedy explains: 'This split mirrors the former practice within Norwich Union of splitting management and non-management staff on the basis

of traditional negotiating arrangements – non-managers were represented by Amicus-MSF, while managers were represented by an internal staff representative forum.'

Typically, 'support' staff, 'advisers' and 'lead advisers' fall into broad band 2, while the jobs at the higher two levels fall into broad band 1. Within IT and change management, the majority of the jobs fall into broad band 1, which is broken down into five levels rather than two.

The box illustrates how the generic groups and broad bands align with market salary guides.

Pay and progression

Market salary guides

Previously, Norwich Union based its pay bands on a minimum, maximum and a mid-point, matched against the market. The new system moves away from the concept that there can be an exact 'market rate' for a job. Therefore, there is no mid-point.

Instead, for each generic group in each job family there is now a set of market salary guides, based on an entry point, a low point and a high point (see the example in the box). The entry point is the minimum salary anyone in the role should receive and is typically paid to a new recruit on probation. Most staff will fall somewhere between the low point and high point. This is where the market median should fall. The high point, therefore, is a market guide not a maximum for the pay band. In fact, NUCS does not set a maximum salary for any role.

Benchmarking market pay

While the market salary guides for jobs at the same level but in different families can be almost identical, they do vary and are set according to market data for the particular role.

The market salary guides are reviewed annually to make sure they are competitive with the external market. Watson Wyatt provides market data for all the generic groups within the career families. For example, an accountant at team manager/consultant level equates to Watson Wyatt level 12.

In terms of the broad bands, broad band 2 maps to Watson Wyatt levels 4 to 9, while broad band 1 maps across to levels 10 to 14. Heads of division map to Watson Wyatt levels 15 and 16.

Salary progression

Employees' annual pay increases are set with reference to the market salary guides, their contribution over the year and affordability.

Reviewing performance

During the year, employees' progress is monitored at regular one-to-one meetings. There are also formal mid-year and annual reviews. While these reviews are not designed specifically to centre on pay, there is inevitably a link.

Following their end-of-year review, employees are allocated one of four performance ratings on the basis of their overall contribution against the key accountabilities for their roles.

Calculating salary increase

Employees' performance ratings translate into their annual basic pay increases. The formula used in April 2005 was as follows:

NUCS looks to award its best performers the highest increases.

Employees given a rating of 'underperforming' and therefore receiving no pay increase are typically in the capability or disciplinary procedure.

Online calculator

Once employees know their performance rating, they can calculate their salary increase using an online tool. This automatically calculates their increase if they enter their rating and the lower and higher market salary guide for their role.

Performance-related bonus

The size of the bonus payment received by employees depends on their performance against their personal objectives for the year.

The bonus available to employees in each broad band differs. Those in broad band 1 can achieve a 15 per cent bonus based on individual objectives; in broad band 2, the potential is 7 per cent of salary depending on performance against either individual or team targets.

Career progression

The career family framework at NUCS illustrates to employees how they can progress. As Nick Kennedy explains: 'People tend to think of career families in terms of pay structures. But they are actually more to do with career progression.'

At NUCS there are two ways to progress:

- when an employee's job grows
- through promotion.

Performance	Pay increase
Outperforming	6% – based on 110% of high point
Performing	3.5% of high point
Developing	1.5% of low point
Underperforming	0%

Example of a career family at NUCS: Facilities Management

Broad band	Generic group/ level	Market salary guides at 1 April 2005 (£)		
		Entry point	Low point	High point
1	Business manager/managing consultant	26,800	33,500	45,000
	Team manager	18,400	23,000	30,000
	Consultant	17,350	21,700	29,000
2	Lead adviser	13,200	16,500	19,600
	Adviser	10,080	12,600	14,500
	Support	9,250	11,300	12,000

Job growth

An employee's personal role profile describes his or her job. This is not fixed and may be revised each year to take account of changing priorities and responsibilities. If an employee's role changes significantly – in terms of greater autonomy rather than merely doing more – he or she may move to a higher level. Line managers are responsible for spotting that an employee's role has changed in this manner.

Promotion

Alternatively, progression can be achieved by promotion if a suitable job becomes vacant.

Dual career paths

One of the main criticisms in the past was that when employees reached the top of broad band 2, the only way to progress further was to move into a management role.

The new career family structure was therefore designed to provide parallel paths for promotion. Those employees who do not wish to move into a management role can instead progress into senior technical roles at the same level. In this way, NUCS is able to retain staff with key skills who are unsuited to or who have no interest in people management.

Benefits of job families

The career family structure enabled NUCS to successfully align pay for staff coming together from across its pre-merger companies. Moreover, the business believes that the framework provides a number of key benefits over a more traditional grading structure:

- development can be planned that is specific to an employee's role;

- employees have a better understanding of the opportunities available to them across NUCS;

- the framework sets out clearly the skills and behaviours staff need to progress;

- salaries can be more easily reviewed against market data.

Crucially, having fewer 'grades' makes the structure easier to understand and administer. In the words of Nick Kennedy: 'The career family structure can be explained in a few words or a couple of paragraphs. This has to be better than having to read an entire manual.'

Promoting the roll-out

Effective communications were central to the successful roll-out of the NUCS career family framework. The intranet was used as the core communications channel. But because the concept of career families was so new to staff, the company also carried out roadshows to brief managers over a three-week period.

Questions and answers

At the time of the launch, NUCS produced a comprehensive list of questions and answers. Rather than being based on what HR expected employees to ask, this was based on questions actually raised by staff.

Ongoing communications

Ongoing communication efforts, particularly using the intranet, have also been key to embedding the framework as a key business tool.

Information and tools on the intranet

Employees can access information on every job family within NUCS via the intranet. This includes straightforward summaries and illustrations showing how the generic groups and broad bands align with market salary guides.

There are also useful online tools, such as the salary increase calculator.

Managers can also access a detailed set of guidelines on pay and bonus reviews, which include a summary of their role, a calendar setting out when actions need to be taken, and the distribution ranges for bonus payments and salary increases. There is also information on how to deal with reviews for new entrants, part-time staff and those on maternity leave.

Case Study Questions

1 What were the main reasons for NUCS to introduce job families?

2 What are the main components of the job family structure? How do these interrelate?

3 How does NUCS use market pay benchmarking to set job family pay?

4 How does NUCP pay progression system relate to the job families?

5 What are the main benefits of the NUCP job families system (a) to the company and (b) to employees? What might be the disbenefits?

6 Why is communication of the system so important to its success?

KEY LEARNING POINTS AND CONCLUSIONS

In this chapter we have covered the purpose of grading and pay structures. As we have shown, it is important to remember that grading structures exist for a range of organisational reasons, not simply reward, but they only become pay structures when pay is allocated to a grade. Pay structures form the foundations for any reward system by creating the architecture for all the other aspects of the system. As we have discussed, there is a range of pay structures available from which employers can choose – from quite simple and individualised systems to complex job-evaluated structures.

But employers do not have total freedom in this choice. These different structures usually reflect important contextual issues, not least the type of organisation, the range of employees employed and the span of management control. The degree to which reward is bargained is also vital. For example, where trade unions are present there is normally a stronger emphasis on internal equity, the 'rate for the job', a concern for promotion opportunities for all and less emphasis on individualised pay. In non-union settings, in contrast, employers may have more freedom to move individual employees through the grading structure as they see fit.

The consequences of these decisions also vary. While some employers have recently sought to move away from traditional hierarchical structures through the use of more flexible broad bands and job families, other employers have sought to simplify and rationalise their pay structures. More flexible organisational structures may offer employers greater discretion, but the consequences may be an absence of coherence and hence employee dissatisfaction.

The continued popularity of job evaluation is reinforced by the general acceptability of JE to trade unions and the legal requirements to ensure that pay structures are free of gender bias. While traditional job evaluation techniques have been criticised from both the managerial and academic perspectives, they continue to provide the major mechanism for assessing the value of individual jobs. One consequence, however, is that employers will have less discretion over how employees are valued within the organisation.

Whatever grading structure is adopted, there will be always be some degree of tension between maintaining the equilibrium of this structure against the external market. As we have explained, jobs that may have the same value within the internal structure may not have the same value when compared with the external market. Benchmarking the pay of job or career families, or indeed individual jobs, against the external market may assist with recruitment and retention but may lead to the entrenching of traditional pay hierarchies and can simply produce chronic 'pay drift' as employers chase their competitors.

Most importantly, grading structures of any kind can only attempt to weigh the value of one job against another – they cannot provide a means to rewarding the individual effort bargain. The major ways in which employers adjust the levels of pay to reflect the individual effort bargain are through the concept of pay progression and contribution, on the one hand, and various forms of variable pay additions, on the other. In the next chapter (Chapter 5) we consider the various forms of pay progression within and between grades, while in Chapter 6 we consider the various forms of variable pay.

EXPLORE FURTHER

For a fuller exploration of job evaluation techniques, see Armstrong, M., Cummins, A., Hastings, S. and Wood, W. (2003) *Job Evaluation. A guide to achieving equal pay*. London, Kogan Page.

For a discussion and critique of the equality issues arising from grading structures, see Hastings, S. (2000) 'Grading systems and estimating value', in White, G. and Druker, J. (eds) *Reward Management: a critical text*. London, Routledge.

For an up-to-date description of recent moves to market-based pay structures and the techniques used to compare pay levels, see IDS (2006) *Developments in occupational pay differentiation. A research report of the Office for Manpower Economics*. October 2006. London, Incomes Data Services.

For a fuller discussion of broad banding and job family structures, see IPD (2000) *Study of Broad-banded and Job Family Structures*. IPD Survey Report. January. London, IPD.

CHAPTER 5

Pay Setting, Composition and Progression

CHAPTER OBJECTIVES

At the end of this chapter you should understand and be able to explain the following:

- The setting of pay levels for individual jobs, grades or roles.
- The composition of reward and the differences between basic pay, earnings, total remuneration and total reward.
- The difference between wages and salary systems and the frequency with which reward is delivered.
- The different methods by which employees can progress through a pay structure and the various criteria used to make decisions about progression – seniority, skill or knowledge acquisition, competence, performance or by reference to market rates.
- The concept of 'pay for contribution'.
- Compensation for particular forms of work – for example, overtime and shift premiums, call-out and on-call pay, location allowances and market supplements.

CIPD STANDARDS COVERED IN THIS CHAPTER:

To be able to:

- Provide accurate and timely advice to line management, colleagues and employees on all aspects of employee reward policy and practice and the composition of an individual's reward package.
- Analyse the case for or against the introduction of a pay-for-performance system and advise on its introduction, implementation and auditing.

To understand and explain:

- The criteria for an effective pay structure and pay for performance schemes.
- The principles underlying performance management.

INTRODUCTION

As we discussed in the previous chapter, the grading structure provides the overall architecture of the reward system and usually relates closely to organisational structure. But grading structures only provide a mechanism for allocating staff to an appropriate level within the organisational hierarchy. This process does not tell an employer what pay level to assign to any grade or band or how to reward the individual effort bargain. Deciding what and how to pay the employees in these various grades or roles is a further reward decision. Pay levels have to be attached to the grades or bands to create a 'pay structure', and decisions must be made about whether or on what basis employees will progress through the pay structure.

Gerhart and Rynes (2003: 115)) argue that 'There are several reasons to believe that the decisions of organisations regarding *how* to pay are in some sense more strategic and more important to performance outcomes than decisions about *how much* to pay.' One reason is that organisations are probably more constrained in pay-level decisions – because of market comparisons – than how they pay. Research indicates that organisations differ more in how they pay than how much, and also that the differences in type of pay (eg based on performance vs not based on performance) have a stronger relationship with organisational performance than pay levels per se. In this chapter, we therefore consider the various criteria used to progress employees through the pay structure – by service, by performance, by acquisition of skills or competences.

It is also important for the student of reward management to understand some basic concepts about the composition of pay (see Box 5.1, below), pay progression and the different approaches to manual and non-manual employees' reward systems.

Most employees today have some form of pay progression built in to their pay structures. Progression between grades is normally through the process of promotion, often along the same lines as any recruitment process (ie jobs are advertised, candidates apply and interviews take place), although in rare circumstances promotion between grades may be automatic after a period of service, probation or induction. Progression within the grade, in contrast, can be contingent on a range of criteria – by service, age, performance, competence, acquisition of skills, the achievement of qualifications or, in many cases, simply a comparison with external market rates.

BOX 5.1 COMPOSITION OF PAY

An important concept in reward management is the difference between base pay, earnings, total remuneration and total reward. We provide some definitions below, but students should also see Chapter 9 where we discuss the 'total reward' concept (see Figure 9.1).

1 Base pay is the fixed part of the remuneration package and is usually the guaranteed and contractual part. This can be the hourly basic pay rate (often expressed as a weekly wage) or an annual salary.

2 Earnings include base pay and all the payments made in addition to this basic wage or salary. These may include such additional payments as bonuses, overtime pay, shift pay, market or location pay supplements, compensatory payments for on-call working or call-out, and any additional allowances for holding particular skills or working in particular circumstances.

3 Total remuneration will include base pay, all other earnings plus the various benefits provided such as holidays, sick pay and pensions.

Total reward includes both financial and non-financial rewards. This will include basic pay, all additional earnings, benefits and the wider non-financial rewards available in the workplace (such as recognition schemes, the work environment etc).

A key issue for HR managers is the gap between base pay and earnings levels, known as 'pay drift'. Traditionally, manual workers have had substantial amounts of non-guaranteed pay, such as overtime, shift and incentive bonuses, and hence their pay levels have tended to fluctuate from week to week. In comparison, non-manual workers have traditionally tended to have little in the way of additions to their base salaries. This position, however, is now changing. With the increasing spread of more variable pay systems, non-manual earnings may be subject to more variation from month to month.

This gap between growth in base pay and growth in earnings has been the subject of a study by IDS for the Office of Manpower Economics (IDS, 2006a). This study found considerable differences between the private and public sectors in terms of 'pay drift'. While private sector pay drift was higher overall than in the public sector, in the private sector drift was largely the result of performance-related progression through the grade. In contrast, the pay drift in the public sector was likely to be much more strongly related to seniority or service-related incremental progression through the grade.

WAGES VS SALARY SYSTEMS

As we mentioned in Chapter 4, some employees – usually lower-grade workers – have 'spot' rates or salaries, that is, single pay points for each job, with no provision for rewarding growth in the job or role. For example, workers in a fast food restaurant or retail outlet are normally paid on a single hourly grade rate (with their pay calculated on the number of hours worked). They may in some cases be paid a different hourly rate according the 'zone' or location in which they work (and in some cases may be able to move to a higher rate on the basis of their performance), but in general there is only one rate for each grade.

Pay structures for the lowest-paid workers tend to be relatively simple, with basic hourly rates of pay and few additions to this basic rate (LPC, 1999). The difference between manual and non-manual work has traditionally been designated by the terms 'wages system' and 'salary system'. 'Wage' normally refers to a system of single pay rates for each grade or role (eg £10 per hour), whereas 'salary' implies an annual payment (eg £25,000 per year). While salaries are normally stated as annual amounts, in reality the salary is normally delivered in 12 monthly instalments (in some countries there can be 13 instalments or more, with the additional instalments being paid as holiday pay). A salary also often implies some progression opportunities, with employees moving up through the grade or range from a minimum to a maximum.

The big difference between wages and salary systems in the past was that waged workers tended to have less security of income and more fluctuating pay levels, with large amounts of incentive pay and/or overtime or shift pay on top of low hourly rates. In contrast, salaried workers had more secure and guaranteed incomes, with little in the way of incentive pay. This situation has now been reversed, with smaller numbers of manual workers being paid by their output and a lot more non-manual workers now being paid according to their performance (Cannell and Wood, 1992; Druker, 2000).

As we discussed in Chapter 4, in a typical narrow grade structure, or where a pay spine exists, employees will usually progress through the grade in steps, or 'increments', as these are often called. These increments can be valuable additional elements to the annual cost-of-living rise and can lead to significant pay drift (we discuss this phenomenon later). In more modern, broad-band structures, however, there may not be any increments as such, and employees may move between the minimum and maximum by percentage increases based on criteria such as merit, skill acquisition or the measurement of competence. In other words, increasingly there is no guaranteed progression to the maximum of the grade.

In addition to progression 'within grade' there is also progression 'between grades'. Normally this indicates promotion to a larger job or role. In some cases, pay grades or bands overlap so that progression can continue within the grade or role without the necessity for promotion.

 SELF-ASSESSMENT EXERCISE

Ask your friends, fellow students and family members about how they are paid. What jobs are paid through wages systems and what sort are salaried? What does this tell us about the value placed on these jobs?

REWARD CONTINGENCIES

Mahoney (1989) argues that there are three reward 'contingencies' in making decisions about reward – job, person and performance. The first of these, the relationship between pay and the job, was covered in Chapter 4. In this chapter we consider the other two contingencies. As Kessler states (2005: 320): 'If job is the basis for establishing the grading structure, a pay system is the mechanism used to drive pay movements once the post and the individual filling it have been placed in the structure.'

Two main categories of pay system have been identified (Casey *et al*, 1991) – person-based or performance-based. Table 5.1 shows the range of options available within these two categories. As can be seen, as well as age and seniority, other forms of person-related progression might be based on criteria such as the acquisition of skills or knowledge (often in the form of qualifications) or the development of competencies. This might be categorised as 'pay for development' or 'pay for the right attitudes'. Apart from individual performance-related pay as a form of pay progression, we deal with all the various performance-based systems in Chapter 6 on variable pay.

The 2007 CIPD Reward Management survey (CIPD, 2007c) found that most employers adopt a 'hybrid' or combination approach to pay progression, with variations both by sector and by grade. For example, senior managers are more likely to be assessed solely by their performance than other levels of employee. By sector the public and voluntary sectors are much more likely to base progression solely on service, but this is rare in the private sector today. The 2004 WERS (Kersley *et al*, 2006) found that merit pay alone – defined as pay that is related to a subjective assessment of performance by a supervisor or manager – was used in only 9 per cent of workplaces. But a further 7 per cent used it in combination with some other form of payment by results (see Chapter 6).

Table 5.1 Categories of pay system

Person	Performance
Age	*Individual*
Seniority/experience	Commission (eg sales)
Qualifications	Piecework (eg goods produced)
Competence	Individual performance-related pay/merit bonus
Behaviour/traits	
Attitudes	*Group*
Knowledge	Profit-sharing
Skills	Gain-sharing
	Team bonuses

Source: adapted from Kessler (2005)

? SELF-ASSESSMENT EXERCISE

Looking at Table 5.1 above, which categories of pay system are used in your organisation (or one with which you are familiar)?

TIME- OR PERFORMANCE-BASED REWARD?

Brown (1989) argues that pay systems have been subject to two basic criteria: time and performance. In other words, employees may be paid for the time they spend at work (or the time taken to undertake a specific task), or they may be paid according to the quantity or quality of the work produced. The big question is how to value the work in terms of the time taken to perform a task. For a professional sportsman or entertainer (or indeed a management consultant), the value of several hours' work may be very high while for the lowest-paid workers an hour's work may be measured in a few pounds or dollars. The alternative, payment by performance – whether quantity or quality of work produced – poses other problems, not least the issue of how one measures individual output.

ISSUES IN REWARD

BOX 5.2 THE EXPERIENCE OF A LIFETIME

This extract is from the nineteenth-century libel case against John Ruskin, the art historian and critic, by the American painter, J.M. Whistler. Ruskin had accused Whistler of 'throwing a pot of paint in the public's face', to which Whistler had responded by taking a libel case against Ruskin. The following extract refers to the cross-examination of Whistler by the Attorney-General, acting as defence counsel for Ruskin. He is asking Whistler about a particular painting, 'The Falling Rocket', and the amount of time taken to complete it.

Attorney-General 'How long did it take you to knock it off?'

Whistler '... I was two days at work on it.'

Attorney-General *'The labour of two days then is that for which you ask two hundred guineas?'*

Whistler 'No; I ask it for the experience of a lifetime.'

Quoted from William Gaunt (1957), *The Aesthetic Adventure*. London, Pelican.

Time-based pay systems normally reward the worker for his or her attendance at the workplace. Such systems developed with the industrial revolution and the shift of the workforce from agricultural production to factories. Whereas agricultural workers had generally been paid by the day and the work required had fluctuated with the seasons, factory owners required their employees to be available 12 hours a day, six days a week. One sure way of ensuring that they attended work for the full hours required was to base their pay on an hourly rate. Such systems do have the advantage of predictability for both the employer and the employee – the employer can easily calculate his or her wage costs and the employee can easily calculate his or her potential weekly pay. Where additional hours were required of employees by their employers, the practice of 'overtime' developed, whereby workers are paid a higher hourly rate for each additional hour worked on top of the contracted hours. Similarly, in order to persuade employees to work unsocial working hours (ie those outside the normal working hours such as night shifts), employers developed the practice of paying additional premiums for working shifts or rotas.

Even when employees are paid according to their performance, their pay is still usually related in some way to the time spent at work, at least in the frequency with which payment is made. Employees may be paid weekly, fortnightly or monthly, although the majority is now paid by the month. With the growth of part-time and casual work, and particularly so-called 'zero hours' contracts, many employees continue to be paid by the number of hours worked each week, rather than a fixed amount. In the UK, about 70 per cent of employees are paid monthly, around 20 per cent at weekly intervals and 10 per cent at other intervals (ONS, 2006a).

Kessler (2005) points out that a pay system driven by time can also come together with all three pay contingencies – job, person and performance – in the sense that progression within the grade (job) often operates on the basis of service (person) and service is seen as some measure of performance. It is assumed in such systems that the longer a person occupies a job or role, the more skills and knowledge will have been acquired. Such systems can also act as a retention device – employees are paid for their loyalty in staying with the organisation. On the other hand, equal pay and age discrimination legislation have increasingly provided challenges to seniority-based systems of pay progression (we discuss these in Chapter 3).

The EOC recommends that long, service-based pay scales (ie longer than five years) are not conducive to equal pay, because often female employees take career breaks for maternity or child care reasons. Justification for paying such individuals less than male employees for work of equal value will depend on the demonstrable benefits of the service requirement. Similarly, age discrimination legislation also requires clear and demonstrable justification for seniority-based systems.

Time can also be used as a form of performance measure. While some employees are paid entirely by their output (eg traditional payment by the piece), most piecework systems today are based on how long a particular task takes to complete. A standard time will be agreed for the typical worker and extra pay provided if the work can be completed in less time. We cover incentive schemes of this type in Chapter 6.

Nonetheless, despite the simplicity of payment by time, seniority or service-based progression is in decline and many employers, especially in the private sector, have moved towards pay progression systems linked more to individual performance (Thomson, 2000). While seniority-based pay may pose equal-pay risks, it should be noted that individual performance or merit can still be rewarded on top of seniority or service-based pay progression. In some organisations, the highest increments in each grade may be reserved for high performers, or merit may be rewarded through one-off bonus payments rather than through the progression system. We consider the issue of incentive pay – as opposed to merit as a form of progression – in Chapter 6. It is also worth remembering that few organisations base all their reward decisions on performance or contribution – for example, the provision of benefits such as holiday entitlement is still largely related to job level/status and/or to service.

 SELF-ASSESSMENT EXERCISE

What are main advantages and disadvantages of time-based pay systems? Are there particular circumstances where an organisation may choose such a reward system?

In the next part of this chapter we consider the various criteria used for pay progression. These include the following:

- Service- or seniority-based pay
- Age-related pay
- Performance-related pay
- Competency-based pay
- Skills-based pay
- Market-based pay.

SERVICE- OR SENIORITY-BASED PAY

The traditional method of pay progression within grade for many employees has been according to length of service or seniority. The assumption is that length of service equals improved knowledge and experience, and hence improved performance. Historically, such systems were the product of strong internal labour markets and were designed to provide rewards for loyalty to the organisation. As Williamson (1975) postulated, firms rationally choose seniority-based systems because they avoid the high 'transaction cost' of specifying and measuring individual contracts based on performance. Such systems are also seen as enhancing employee commitment (Benson, 1995; Cappelli, 1995, cited in Thomson, 2000), leading to higher productivity, better quality and customer service, and lower levels of staff turnover.

Seniority-based systems operate on the basis of fixed steps or 'increments' on a scale from the minimum to the maximum of the grade. Under such progression systems, increments may be withheld for poor performance or employees may be fast-tracked up the grade by jumping increments, but the expectation of most employees is that progression to the maximum is guaranteed. Some scales have a bar under which employees may have to meet certain criteria to progress further – for example, merit or competence.

Such service-related progression is still common in many parts of the public services and voluntary sector, but is increasingly absent from the private sector. Service-related progression systems have always been popular with trade unions because they provide automatic and guaranteed progression to the maximum of the grade for all staff – and because this does not normally involve the line manager in pay decisions. Such systems can be popular with line managers too for the same reason – they do not have to become involved in individual pay decisions. Such systems also have the advantage that pay costs are relatively predictable. As long as the employer knows how many staff are located on each salary point, he or she can calculate the cost of annual progression fairly easily.

On the other hand, such systems have traditionally been unpopular with reward writers and many senior managers because they are seen as inequitable, inflexible and encourage 'time-serving' behaviour among employees. The criticism is that poor performance is treated equally with good performance, so there is no incentive to improve. Such reward writers have also pointed out that the assumption that length of service implies more experience and hence higher performance is unproven. In time of low labour turnover such systems can also become expensive as every employee moves to the maximum of the grade. Indeed, one reason why performance-related progression became so popular in the 1980s was that employers wanted to release pressure at the maximum points of grades without necessarily having to reward all staff in the same way.

As mentioned earlier, in recent years such systems have also been criticised from a gender and age discrimination perspective (see Chapter 3). Females may be doing exactly the same level of work as males but may be on a lower increment simply because they have taken a career break. While it may take four to five years to learn some jobs, longer service periods probably do not reflect a 'learning curve', and some jobs probably take much less than five years to learn. The original aim of rewarding loyalty through such systems, moreover, seems less important to organisations today.

According to Lawler (2000: 122), seniority-based pay best suits the traditional internal labour market – or 'develop and build from within' – human capital approach. It also fits organisations that are relatively stable and need to have a long-term committed workforce. Lawler cites such stable, capital-intensive organisational examples as oil and mining companies where stability of employment and long-term employment relationships are required to develop an in-depth understanding of the business. It does not suit organisations that face rapidly changing business environments and where there needs to be changes in workforce capabilities. According to Lawler, 'the seniority approach is likely to retain all employees, not just those required to deal with new technologies, markets and businesses' (Lawler 2000: 122). Moreover, 'it does nothing to

Table 5.2 School teachers' service-based pay progression (as at September 2005)*

	National	Outer Fringe	Outer London	Inner London
Main pay scale	£pa	£pa	£pa	£pa
M1	19,161	20,082	22,002	23,001
M2	20,676	21,597	23,316	24,315
M3	22,338	23,259	24,978	26,007
M4	24,057	24,981	26,697	27,756
M5	25,953	26,877	28,593	29,676
M6	28,005	28,923	30,642	31,749

* In addition there is an upper performance-related pay scale of three increments. There are separate scales according to work location (eg Inner London, Outer London etc)

Source: *Pay in the Public Services* (IDS, 2006)

facilitate the departure of employees whose skills and knowledge are no longer needed'. Lastly, Lawler argues that seniority-based rewards can contribute to an 'entitlement-oriented culture', 'in which individuals feel they are owed something simply because they are long-tenure employees...'.

Table 5.2 shows an example of a service-related pay progression system (for school teachers in England and Wales).

AGE-RELATED PAY

A linked form of pay progression to seniority is through age, whereby pay rates are attached to specific ages. Age is different to seniority in that it normally provides the progression route for younger workers, and such pay progression was traditionally linked to periods of training or apprenticeship. For example, in the early 1970s the Retail, Drapery, Outfitting and Footwear Wages Council set weekly pay rates from ages 15 to 22, with increasing percentages of the adult rate, from 52.1 per cent at age 15 to 100 per cent at age 22 (cited in IDS, 2004: 15). In recent times age-related pay progression has become rare, owing to the increase in the school-leaving age, larger numbers of young people going into higher education and a decline in apprenticeship-type training programmes. The introduction of the national minimum wage has, however, led to some resurgence. Some organisations still have separate 'youth rates', and the UK National Minimum Wage retains separate hourly rates for 16 and 17 year olds and those between 18 and 21, with the adult rate starting at 22. The main reason that the Low Pay Commission has continued to advocate age-related rates is because of concerns that paying 'adult' rates to workers under 22 would lead to higher levels of unemployment among younger age groups.

Those employers with age-related pay for younger workers argue that the lower pay levels reflect the employers' cost in contributing to training and also the

Table 5.3 Age-related pay at McDonalds (national bands)

Pay structure at 18 September 2005				
	6am to midnight		Midnight to 6am	
Band B/C (national)	Minimum £ph	Maximum £ph	Minimum £ph	Maximum £ph
Crew aged 16 and 17	4.00	5.80	-	-
Crew aged 18 to 21	4.25	6.05	4.75	6.55
Crew aged 22 and over	5.05	6.85	5.55	7.35
Training squad	5.05	7.10	5.55	7.60
Security co-ordinator/admin asst	5.10	7.85	5.60	8.35
Dining area host(ess)/party entertainer	5.15	7.80	5.65	8.30
Maintenance person	5.15	7.80	5.65	8.30
Floor manager	5.30	7.95	5.80	8.45
Shift running floor manager	6.35	8.70	6.85	9.20

Source: IDS *Pay Report 943* December 2005

'market value' of such workers in the external labour market. Other employers, however, argue that age-related progression is contrary to concepts of pay for performance or contribution. Age discrimination law, moreover, has placed a question mark over relating pay to age, although the minimum wage regulations currently allow such differentiation (see Chapter 3).

 SELF-ASSESSMENT EXERCISE

What are the advantages and disadvantages of (1) service-related pay and (2) age-related pay?

PERFORMANCE-BASED PAY

The other major method of pay progression within and between grades is on the basis of merit or performance. Performance-related pay describes a system of pay progression where advancement through the grade or band is dependent on some evaluation of a worker's individual performance by a supervisor or manager. This is usually done through the performance management system and an annual (or more frequent) appraisal. For this reason, Acas refers to this type of pay as 'Appraisal Related Pay' (Acas, 1990). While many pay for performance schemes link pay through individual appraisal to progression through the grade or band, some schemes provide annual 'one-off' merit bonuses that do not relate to pay progression and are therefore not consolidated into base pay. In this chapter we consider reward for performance only as a mechanism for progression through the pay and grading system. Incentive pay, merit bonuses and other forms of variable pay are covered in Chapter 6.

'The term performance-related pay is used in two senses. First, it can describe the broad class of payment systems which relate pay to some measure of work performance. As such, it can embrace profit-sharing, merit pay, gainsharing, piecework, sales incentives and other output-based pay systems.

Second, it can refer to individualised systems in which salary increases are related to the results of performance appraisal. This latter usage corresponds to appraisal-related or merit pay.'

Heery and Noon (2001)

There has been a lengthy and wide-ranging debate among both HR practitioners and academic commentators about the benefits and disbenefits of performance-related pay. In both the USA and the UK there has been conflicting research evidence about whether such systems work. The differences between economic and psychological theories was discussed in Chapter 2, but it is worth remembering here that psychological theory places much more importance on individual differences to explain differences in performance than does economic theory. While economists recognise the role of ability in performance (in efficiency wage theory), psychologists have found many more variables to consider, such as personality, the need for achievement and self-esteem. Gerhart and Rynes (2003) suggest that economists (and many managers) may find this complexity inconvenient, but argue that ignoring the individual and contextual differences may impede managers in seeking to improve performance. Finally, psychologists are interested in the meaning of money to employees and the part it plays in their lives. Money often provides an important measure of an individual's success and status when comparing themselves to other workers. A belief that one is not being treated equitably, furthermore, is an important factor in working life, and pay is an important mechanism for signalling value and achievement. The most important motivational theories underpinning performance-related pay are expectancy theory, goal-setting theory, equity theory, attribution theory, agency theory and tournament theory (see Chapter 2 for a discussion of relevant theory).

Kessler (2005) points out that any typology of performance management systems must address three questions. These are:

- what is being assessed?
- how is it being measured?
- how is it being rewarded?

The first of these questions concerns the unit of performance. Are we assessing the individual, the team or the organisation? Rynes and Gerhart (2000) argue that, while historically much of the emphasis on incentives has related to individuals, there is increasing interest in group or organisational incentives. The main advantage of such collective incentives is seen as their potential to foster co-operation between group members (Pfeffer 1998). On the other hand, Gerhart and Rynes (2003) provide both theoretical arguments and research evidence that there may be efficiency losses under such group schemes.

The second issue is whether pay is to be based on behavioural criteria (judgements on the effectiveness of the employee by a supervisor) or results (concrete output measures). In general, it is easier to measure results than behaviours, and there is evidence that organisations have moved towards greater use of results-based plans – or 'contracts', in agency theory terms (Rynes and Gerhart 2003: 167). This growth is explained by the spreading of results-based pay plans down from senior management to other staff, and partly from the growth of new, high-technology organisations where stock options are used to supplement below-market pay levels. It is also explained by changes in the labour market towards more flexible employment relationships, such as outsourcing, temporary employment and individual contracting. Outputs are usually defined in quantitative terms as 'results', such as the number of sales, productivity increases, quality improvements or profit growth.

Inputs are more difficult to measure as they are generally more qualitative in nature (and are therefore more likely to be individual targets rather than group or organisation). These can relate to behavioural inputs such as behaviours (eg the manner in which employees carry out their activities or tasks) or traits (eg the personality characteristics of the employee). For example, a trait might be the need to be 'professional' at work, but this is rather vague. In contrast, the behaviours expected from a professional might be 'courtesy to customers', 'submit work in a timely and accurate manner', etc. According to Heneman (1992), behaviours have two advantages over traits – first, they are more easily defined, and second, the employee has more control over them because performance expectations are usually spelled out. It is difficult for an employee to change their personality but they can change their behaviour. Nonetheless, creating behavioural measures is more complicated and time-consuming than creating trait measures. Research has shown that the decision to base pay on results instead of behaviours can have a substantial effect on the rank ordering of employees for pay purposes (Rynes and Gerhart 2003: 167). This suggests that results and behaviour-based systems yield different and often conflicting information about individual performance.

The third question relates to the performance–pay linkage. This can be automatic – for example, where the achievement of target results leads to the automatic payment of an agreed reward – or variable, where some judgement has to be made about the performance achieved and the level of reward deserved. The latter normally involves some form of individual appraisal of the employee's performance by his or her supervisor and involves some exercise of discretion by the supervisor. This appraisal can be either an informal system (without any employee involvement) or, increasingly in many organisations, a formal part of the performance management system where both supervisor and employee meet to discuss the issues.

When considering any form of incentive or merit pay, decisions have to be made

Table 5.4 Pay progression criteria used within a combination approach, by sector (%)

	All	Manufacturing and production	Private sector services	Voluntary sector	Public services
Individual performance	87	92	88	78	79
Market rates	69	73	74	64	41
Competency	54	55	55	49	54
Organisational performance	51	55	57	43	20
Skills	38	40	42	31	24
Team profit/ performance	23	26	27	17	6
Length of service	17	8	12	34	46

Source: CIPD (2008)

Table 5.5 Pay progression criteria used within a combination approach, by occupation(%)

	Senior management	Middle/first-line management	Technical/ professional	Clerical/ manual
Individual performance	90	90	87	82
Market rates	68	69	70	67
Competency	55	54	56	51
Organisational performance	64	52	44	41
Skills	36	36	41	39
Team profit/ performance	28	27	20	17
Length of service	16	16	18	19

Source: CIPD (2008)

about whether the reward is incorporated into the base salary level (known as 'consolidation') or has to be re-earned every year ('unconsolidated').

ARGUMENTS IN FAVOUR OF IPRP (INDIVIDUAL PERFORMANCE-RELATED PAY)

Lawler (2000) identifies the following advantages of individual performance-related pay. First, he argues that basing individual pay on performance has a strong motivational effect by allowing 'an almost perfect line of sight' between the behaviour of individuals and their rewards. Lawler argues that, 'with an effective individual pay-for-performance system, the potential exists to create a highly motivated workforce in which employees see a close relationship between how well they perform and how much they are paid' (Lawler 2000: 149). Secondly, IPRP enables organisations to retain high performers, who will have a higher market rate in the external labour market than average performers. Thirdly, IPRP can help remove poor performers from the organisation because, as their relationship to the external market falls (through zero or minimal pay increases), they will not be able to afford to remain as employees.

Armstrong (2002: 254) similarly argues that IPRP has three arguments in its favour. First, 'it is right and proper that those who perform better ... should receive higher financial benefits than those who do not'. Secondly, making pay contingent on individual performance can motivate employees to achieve higher levels of performance. Thirdly, linking pay to performance can communicate strong messages about organisational expectations of employee behaviour.

In the UK, Acas (1990) argues that IPRP (or appraisal-related pay, as Acas terms it) can help employers improve the efficiency and effectiveness of their workforce by emphasising the need for high standards of job performance. It can also offer the flexibility to help motivate and retain valuable employees by targeting pay at better performers. In turn, employees may welcome a system that rewards extra effort with extra pay. Acas also indicates that the introduction of IPRP is often linked to other changes in pay and personnel policies, such as greater decentralisation of responsibility for pay determination; the introduction or extension of appraisal schemes; and moves towards harmonised terms and conditions of employment.

ARGUMENTS AGAINST IPRP

There is an established critique of IPRP in the academic literature. Pearce (1987), for example, argues that individually contingent pay is based on the false assumption that market-type contracts are appropriate to the social contract between employer and employee. He argues that 'Most kinds of organisations succeed because of co-operation among their members, not because of members' discrete, independent performance' (Pearce, 1987, cited in Steers *et al*, 1996: 525). Alfie Kohn's much-cited article for the *Harvard Business Review* (Kohn, 1993) argued that incentive schemes fail for the following reasons:

- pay is not a motivator;
- they punish staff who do not receive them, leading to demotivation;
- they rupture relationships through competition and undermine teamwork;
- they are used as an alternative to managing staff performance properly;
- they discourage risk-taking; and
- they undermine intrinsic interest in the work.

Heneman (1992) identifies a number of potential pitfalls with IPRP. Most important is the decrease in intrinsic motivation identified by Deci (1972), but he also identifies decreased co-operation between employees, decreased self-esteem and decreased equity.

More recently, Jeffrey Pfeffer (1998), a strong proponent of the 'best practice' school of HRM, has argued strongly against IPRP, arguing that such schemes have been plagued by a number of problems. First, subjectivity and 'capriciousness' among managers has tended to reward employees' political skills or 'ingratiating personalities', rather than their performance. Secondly, IPRP has undermined teamworking by emphasising individual success, sometimes at the expense of peers. Thirdly, Pfeffer argues that there is often an absence of concern for organisational performance so that individual objectives ignore wider organisational needs. Fourthly, IPRP encourages a short-term focus among employees and discourages long-term planning. Fifthly, there is a tendency for such systems to produce a climate of fear in the workplace. Finally, and most importantly, Pfeffer (1998: 204) argues that 'by making pay contingent upon performance (as judged by management), management is signalling that it is they – not the individual – who is in control'. As a consequence, 'performance-related pay may lower the individual's feelings of competence and self-determination, and run counter to an intrinsic reward policy'.

Lastly, there is a view that placing emphasis on individual performance is unethical (Heery, 2000). Heery argues that IPRP is unethical because:

- it poses a threat to employee security (by putting their income at risk) and hence undermines employee commitment;

- it is potentially unjust in both terms of procedural and distributive justice, leading to possible gender and other forms of discrimination; and

- it is undemocratic in that it leaves little scope for collective employee involvement in pay decisions.

Criticism of IPRP has not just come from academic writers. Two UK government reports also concluded that IPRP had not worked well in the civil service (Bichard, 1999; Makinson, 2000). Bichard concluded that there was little evidence that the existing civil service pay arrangements had helped to confront poor performance, and that the 'performance pay system is not perceived to offer significant rewards for excellence'. He argued for more use of unconsolidated (ie not incorporated into basic salary) bonuses. Makinson too, in his review of performance rewards in national government networks, concluded that performance increases should not be consolidated into base pay, leaving scope for more meaningful annual bonus awards. He also concluded that bonuses should be based on team, rather than individual, performance and that such awards should be sufficient in size (at least 5 per cent of an individual's salary) to be a real incentive.

 SELF-ASSESSMENT EXERCISE

What are the arguments for and against individual performance-related pay? Which of these arguments do you find most convincing? What do your fellow students think?

WHAT DOES THE RESEARCH EVIDENCE TELL US ABOUT IPRP?

Several large-scale research projects in the USA have indicated that financial incentives can have a substantial impact upon employee performance. According to Gerhart and Rynes (2003), however, most of these studies have tended to be primarily focused on employees carrying out relatively simple work tasks and were conducted at the level of the individual rather than the organisational level of analysis. Moreover, most of the empirical research on the relationship between pay and performance outcomes has concentrated on how pay influences the attitudes and behaviours of individual employees (eg the motivational effects). There has been little research on how pay can influence the ability and personality characteristics of an organisation's workforce through improved recruitment, retention and turnover. Gerhart and Rynes (2003: 122) point out that the relationship between incentives and performance is complex and relates to many moderating factors, such as goal difficulty, task complexity, work interdependence and individual self-efficacy.

Milkovich and Newman (2008), in their review of a range of research studies about the effects of linking pay to employee behaviour, cite Huselid's (1995) study of HR practices in over 3,000 companies. This found a clear correlation between organisations that had appraisal-related pay and those that had higher annual sales per employee. They also cite Heneman's (1992) review of research on IPRP, which reported that 40 out of the 42 research studies examined found that performance increased when pay was tied to performance. A study of 200 companies by Gerhart and Milkovich (1990) found a 1.5 per cent increase in return on assets for every 10 per cent increase in the size of the bonus (cited in Milkovich and Newman, 2008: 272). Furthermore, they found that the variable portion of pay had a stronger impact on individual and corporate performance than did the level of base pay.

Almost of all of this research on the beneficial effects of IPRP comes from the USA. This might be explained by the fact, as Lawler (2000) has argued, that IPRP is more acceptable in a strongly individualistic national culture such as the USA than in more collectivist cultures. It interesting to note that there are few similar large-scale studies of IPRP in the UK, Europe or elsewhere that have found such strong links between IPRP and corporate performance. Recent research by Dickinson (2005), however, on employee preferences for the bases of pay differentials identified three major elements – responsibility, qualifications and performance. Dickinson comments that the level of support found for performance as a criterion in her research was surprising, given the association of performance-related pay with variability in pay and problems with performance assessment (although all of the new pay structures examined in this study had consolidated performance pay increases).

In the UK, much of the research on IPRP has been critical. In particular the UK research looking at employee attitudes to IPRP, as opposed to management perceptions of its effectiveness, has found little evidence of any motivational effect (see Heery, 1998; IRS, 2000; Kessler and Purcell, 1992; Marsden and Richardson, 1992; Thompson, 1993). Marsden and French's large-scale study of various IPRP schemes in the public services found that IPRP had failed to motivate many staff and was seen as divisive (Marsden and French, 1998). On the other hand, they identified a paradox that, despite the negative views of employees, productivity seemed to improve.

All these earlier studies of IPRP were conducted in the public services – probably because it is easier for researchers to access public sector employees than those in the private sector. In some cases, the research was conducted via trade unions. Kessler (2000) has argued that this concentration of UK IPRP research in the public sector may have biased the overall picture towards this negative outcome, as such pay systems are more likely to be problematic in a public service culture than in the private sector. This is partly because such systems often challenge collectively bargained pay arrangements and, as we discussed in Chapter 3, the public sector is much more likely to negotiate pay with unions than the private sector. It is perhaps surprising that so little research on performance-related pay has been conducted in the private sector, where one might expect the climate and circumstances to be more congenial to such pay systems.

Given this bias to the public sector, most of the UK research has found that, while in general employees favour the concept of being paid according to their individual performance, the actual experience of working under such systems for the majority of workers had been negative. Most of the problems identified with IPRP, however, appear to relate to process rather than the principle. For example, research for the CIPD (Thompson and Milsome, 2001: 36) noted that:

> Even the most committed supporters of individual performance-related pay acknowledge that it is phenomenally difficult to manage well. It has to be planned and operated with great care, and the organisation has to be prepared to be flexible – fine tuning the scheme in the light of changed circumstances and feedback from managers and employees. Certainly it is not appropriate for all organisations.

The major problems identified with IPRP processes revolve around three major operational issues:

- the setting of appropriate performance measures;
- the evaluation of performance; and
- the linking of performance appraisal outcomes to pay.

Kessler (2000) points out the problems of setting performance targets, particularly for less-skilled jobs or for certain professional jobs. He also notes concerns about subjectivity in the evaluation process and the reluctance of line managers to differentiate between employees. Research for the IPD (1998) also found that a large majority of managers surveyed said that their employees distrusted line managers to make judgements on their performance. Finally, Kessler identifies problems with the amount of performance pay being delivered as insufficient to motivate individuals. Small amounts of IPRP are particularly a problem during periods of low inflation.

One of the few studies of IPRP in the private sector (Lewis, 1998) looked at three financial services organisations. This research suggests that, even if the pay element of the performance management cycle is not accepted by employees, if conducted effectively the processes that determine the reward may 'mitigate the unacceptable impact of the pay element'. Lewis concludes that the effectiveness of the IPRP process cycle is central to the acceptance by employees of this form of payment, and that key to this are the skills and attitudes of the line managers in the process.

The linkage between organisational culture and IPRP is also a key variable (although little researched) in its success. In some organisations the introduction of IPRP has failed because the concept does not fit easily with organisational culture. A good example is the research by Randle (1997) on the use of IPRP in a pharmaceuticals research environment. This research questioned the appropriateness of such pay schemes in a 'knowledge worker' environment. While the scientists broadly accepted the fairness of pay for performance, it was one of the 'most consistently disliked management practices' (Randle, 1997: 198). As Randle suggests, 'Measuring the quality of ideas, a crucial aspect of individual performance in research, presents huge problems for managers.'

IPRP has also been used as a tool to change organisational cultures. Brown and Armstrong (1999) argue that IPRP played a particularly important role in the UK in the development of the 'reward management' paradigm, marking an important shift in the UK away from 'passive, reactive pay administration to active, strategic reward management' (Brown and Armstrong, 1999: xii).

A more recent article by Marsden (2004), revisiting his earlier research on IPRP in the public services, considers the paradox that IPRP has led to performance improvements despite employees' evident distaste for the process. He states that much of the literature on IPRP misses this point in focusing on its role as an incentive. Much of the research has therefore concentrated on whether employees feel better motivated, rather than whether performance improved as a result. Its role as a means to renegotiating performance 'norms', he argues, has been largely neglected. According to Marsden, the use of IPRP in the UK public services has actually been primarily about renegotiating the 'effort bargain' between employers and employees in order to reassert management's control, rather than seeking ways to improve motivation. As Marsden (2007: 108) states: 'Procedural justice is an important support for effective renegotiation of performance goals and standards, but the associated procedures will work better if their design fits with management's underlying agenda of change.'

BOX 5.3 KENT COUNTY COUNCIL REVIEWS REWARD SYSTEM

Performance-related pay is 'money well spent'

Date: 26 July 2007
Kent County Council has introduced performance-related pay for 25,000 staff members. Reward manager Colin Miller told delegates attending the CIPD's Reward Symposium in London earlier this month that all council employees, other than teaching staff, received an appraisal rating of between 1 and 5, based on their total contribution. Each point awarded pushes the employee half a point further up their pay scale. So a worker receiving a 'good' rating of 3 is raised one point further up the pay scale, while an 'excellent' 4 would raise them 1.5 and 'exceptional' 5 puts them up 2 points.

The 'total contribution' of staff is measured against four criteria: meeting objectives, their behaviour, personal development and any other responsibilities they take on beyond their job description that add value.

'What we are trying to do is distinguish between individuals and their performance levels throughout the council, which wasn't the case before,' said Miller. 'While we expect most (rated as "good") to make steady progress, the system allows us to reward those who are performing exceptionally well.'

There should be few surprises at the bottom end since those rated at less than 3 should have their performance addressed in the normal course of the year, he added.

Miller has also introduced an initiative whereby managers can pay £500 one-off bonuses to high-performing staff, providing the chief officer gives approval. 'That met with some resistance, along the lines that the money would be better off given to services,' said Miller. 'But if we are rewarding top performance and, as a consequence, top performance is more likely to happen in future, then that's money well spent.'

Source: People Management

IPRP AND THE PERFORMANCE MANAGEMENT SYSTEM

As indicated above, the basis of any IPRP system is an effective performance management system. This requires clear processes for establishing what performance measurements are to be used; how performance is to be measured; and how any resulting performance 'score' is to be linked to pay. It also involves important decisions about who is to undertake the measurement and when.

A useful theoretical frame for understanding the importance of the performance management process is the concept of 'procedural justice' versus 'distributive justice' (see Chapter 2). Procedural justice is defined as the fairness of the procedures for allocating rewards, while distributive justice is defined as the fairness of the actual rewards received (Folger and Cropanzano, 1998). In general, where procedures are operated fairly there is more likelihood that employees will accept the actual rewards on offer. As Marsden (2007: 111) states: 'The processes associated with performance appraisal, and the design and allocation of associated rewards all fall under the umbrella of procedural justice, and, it is argued, employees are likely to withdraw performance if they feel that management violate procedural justice norms when operating their reward systems.' In other words, employees are likely to feel that distributive justice has not been achieved if they perceive that procedural justice has been violated. This failure can result from a variety of operational problems: the inability of managers to set attainable goals and review employees' performance accurately; if managers are not acting in good faith; if the performance criteria contradict employees' own professional values and experience; and if management's concept of motivation is not in alignment with the employees' sense of value and achievement. Procedural justice is therefore not just about having the right procedures, 'but rather of having procedures that are sufficiently well-informed to lead to decisions that are considered fair' (Marsden, 2007: 112).

According to Bach (2005), with the increasing recognition of the problems that permeate many organisations' performance appraisal systems, there has been a shift from performance appraisal alone to the wider concept of performance management. This has focused attention on the broader organisational context in which appraisal takes place and the key role of the line manager, rather than the HR department, in managing individual performance.

Armstrong and Baron (2005: 17) suggest five objectives for a performance management system:

- to communicate a shared vision of the organisation's purpose and values;
- to define expectations of what employees need to deliver and how it should be delivered;
- to ensure that employees are aware of what constitutes high performance and how it can be achieved;
- to enhance motivation, engagement and commitment by providing a mechanism for recognising endeavour and achievement through feedback; and
- to enable employees to monitor their own performance and encourage dialogue about what needs to be done to improve.

Research by the CIPD (1998 and 2005) indicates that there has been a marked increase in the number of organisations using a formal system of performance management. During the 1990s, however, there was a significant shift from an almost exclusive emphasis on reward-driven systems based on IPRP and hard, quantifiable measures of performance towards more holistic systems based more on the developmental needs of the worker. The proportion of organisations linking performance appraisal to pay declined from 43 per cent in 1998 to 31 per cent in 1998 (Armstrong and Baron, 2005: 68).

According to the most recent WERS (Kersley et al, 2004), 78 per cent of workplaces reported undertaking performance appraisals compared to 73 per cent in 1998. Two-thirds of all workplaces regularly conducted appraisals for most (ie 60 per cent or more) non-managerial employees. WERS found that appraisals were typically conducted on an annual basis and a further 16 per cent conducted them on a half-yearly basis. These were done by the employee's immediate line manager or supervisor in three-quarters of those workplaces that conducted appraisals for non-managerial staff. In the vast majority of workplaces, performance appraisals resulted in an evaluation of employees' training needs whereas only in around a third of workplaces were they linked to pay.

Armstrong (2002) argues that there are four fundamental questions to be asked when introducing a performance pay system: can good or poor performance be identified?; can the causes of good or poor performance be established?; how should performance be rewarded?; and can all this be done fairly and consistently? The 1998 research for the CIPD (Armstrong and Baron, 1998) found that the most common features of performance management systems were objective-setting and review; annual appraisal; and personal development plans. The research found that less than half the respondents felt that performance-related pay was very or mostly effective, and there was a substantial minority who thought it ineffective. The research also identified a shift from more mechanistic performance management systems to more integration with other HR processes and from 'top-down' annual reviews towards a more continuous and joint process between the appraiser and the appraisee, focused more on the future than the past. This has led to more emphasis on inputs rather than outputs. The use of rating scales had also become less prominent, and there was growing interest in more varied sources of feedback, including 360-degree appraisal.

One popular method of measuring performance is the 'balanced score-card' developed by Kaplan and Norton (1996). This approach uses four related criteria in measuring performance: how should we appear to our customers?; how

Figure 5.1 The balanced scorecard

Rockwaters balanced scorecard

Financial Perspective

Return-on-Capital-Employed
Cash Flow
Projecy Profitability
Profit Forecast Reliability
Sales Backlog

Customer Perspective

Pricing Index
Customer Ranking Survey
Customer Satisfaction Index
Market Share
Key accounts perspectives

Internal Business Perspective

Hours with Customers on New Work
Contract or Tender Success Rate
Repeat Contracts
Safety Indicators
Project Perormance Index
Project Closeout Cycle

Innovation and Learning Prespective

% Revenue from New Services
Rate of Improvement Index
Staff Attitude Survey
Number of Employee Suggestions
Revenue per Employee

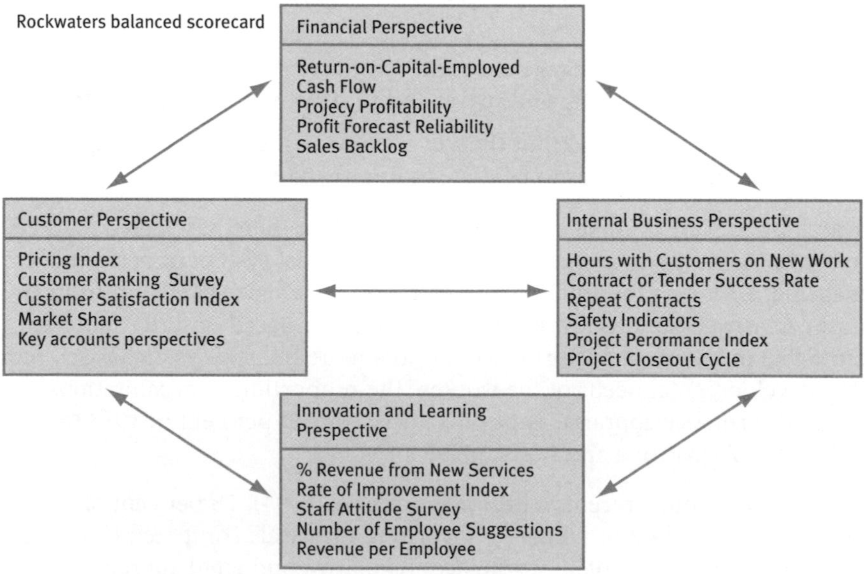

Adapted from Kaplan and Norton (1993)
Source: Wright (2004: 127)

should we appear to our shareholders?; what business process must we excel at?; and how will we sustain our ability to change and improve? (IDS, 2007a: 5). Armstrong (2002) cites several UK organisations that use this method, such as NatWest Bank, Bass Brewers and the Halifax Bank.

One final point is that performance management is clearly a managerial concept. While management may follow such principles, this is not to imply that the effort bargain – where the employee gets to exercise influence over the process and outcomes – will automatically coincide with what the textbooks say or what managers may desire.

THE PERFORMANCE MANAGEMENT CYCLE

There are essentially four stages in the performance management process. The first stage is the performance planning meeting where objectives are agreed between the manager and employee. The performance plan, agreed by both the employee and manager, establishes the framework for the process. According to IDS (2007a), there are three core elements to this plan: individual objectives; competencies and behaviours; and personal development plans.

The second stage of the process is about tracking progress. This entails formal interim reviews, regular informal feedback to the employee by the manager and, if necessary, changes to the performance plan to reflect any changed circumstances.

The third stage is the annual appraisal. This will require the collection of evidence, both by the employee and the manager, to prepare for the meeting. This evidence can include feedback from colleagues and clients or customers and self-assessment by the employee. The meeting between the manager and employee will then take place to review the evidence. As mentioned earlier, it is easier to evaluate performance against 'hard' quantitative measures of

Figure 5.2 The performance management cycle

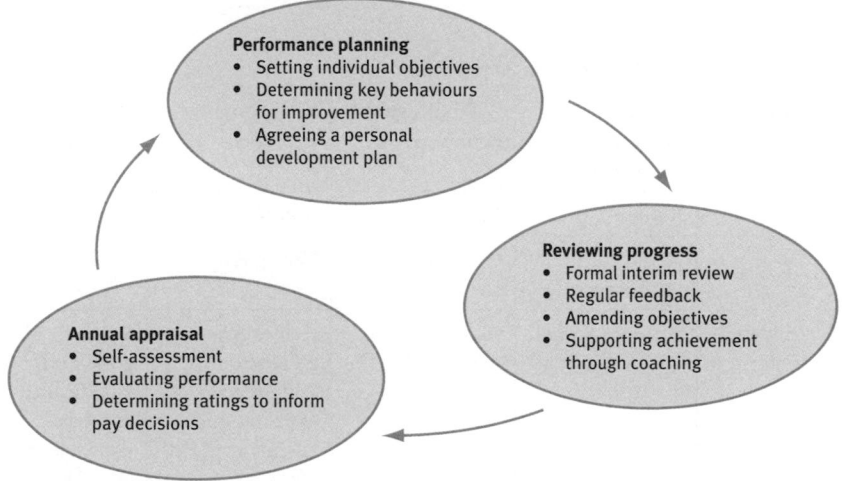

Source: IDS (2007: 3)

Reproduced by kind permission of Incomes Data Services

achievement of tasks or project-oriented goals than against competencies or behaviours. Evaluation of competencies or behaviours is primarily based on the managers' own observations or those of colleagues, but organisations often provide a checklist for this purpose.

The fourth stage is the 'rating' of individual performance. This stage is especially important if the outcomes of the appraisal are to be linked to pay progression or reward. IDS (2007a) found that there are essentially three core levels of performance used in organisations, between which there may be further 'shades' of performance. These three are:

- 'exceptional', or 'exceeds expectations';
- 'effective', or 'meets expectations';
- 'not effective', or 'below expectations'.

The number of ratings on the performance scale usually ranges from four to five (see example in Table 5.6, below). In some cases there may be separate rating scales for achievement of objectives and for competencies exhibited. Some organisations have absolute measures of performance against which an 'effective performer' is measured while others allow assessment against performance relative to other staff. Ratings can send important messages to staff about their performance but they have also been recognised as potentially demotivating. For this reason, the language used to describe the levels is important.

Following this process, the employee is normally given some opportunity to record his or her own views on the appraisal form. Both parties – the appraiser and the appraisee – then sign off the documentation. Some organisations require the employee to confirm that the appraisal is an accurate reflection of the discussion that has taken place. An adjudicator, such as a more senior manager or the HR department, normally handles any disagreements in the first place, but in the final analysis they may become the subject of formal appeals or grievance procedures.

Table 5.6 Example of a rating scale: Abbey Bank

Majority of goals not met	Under-achieved on some goals	All main goals achieved	Some goals exceeded	Majority of goals exceeded
Rating: 1	Rating: 2	Rating: 3	Rating: 4	Rating: 5
Poor	Needs improvement	Good	Very good	Excellent
Under-achieves in the majority of goals	Achieves some goals but not all	Achieves all main goals	Achieves all goals and exceeds expectations against goals in some areas	Achieves all goals and significantly exceeds expectations against goals

Source: IDS (2007a: 40)

A key aspect of any performance management system is employees' perception of its fairness and consistency. To ensure that different managers are not applying different standards organisations may use a 'grandparent' system whereby each appraisal has to be signed off by a more senior manager. This may be followed up by a more formal evaluation of the overall outcomes of the process through an audit by the HR department. Clearly, this is important to ensure that there are no grounds for future legal challenges – such as allegations of gender or race discrimination.

The fifth element in the process, where this is the case, is the linkage to pay. There are various ways in which ratings can be applied to pay progression, merit bonuses or share options for higher paid staff, as described below.

TYPES OF PERFORMANCE PAY PROGRESSION

The major ways in which pay is linked to pay progression are as follows:

- Through the award of additional 'performance-related' increments on top of an essentially service-based progression system.
- Through all incremental progression within the grade based on performance ratings.
- Through 'all merit' annual pay increases where the increase will range in size according to the individual performance rating.

A further complexity is whether performance-based increments are 'consolidated' into the base salary for eternity or whether such increments remain additional to base pay or are only consolidated after a period of some years of sustained high or satisfactory performance. Where progression is through a variable merit increase dependent on the rating given (eg zero for poor performance; 2 per cent for satisfactory performance and 3 per cent for exemplary performance), movement through a pay band or grade may be more easily controlled than under the fixed increment systems.

Clearly, there also have to be some controls over 'pay drift' under an IPRP system. If all managers choose to award high performance ratings – and there is research evidence that line managers are often reluctant to award low ratings for fear of antagonising staff – the cost of IPRP can escalate quickly. For this reason many IPRP systems operate a 'forced distribution' whereby there are limits on the number of staff who can be entered under each rating category. There will also be audits of each manager's ratings to ensure that consistent standards are being applied across the workforce. Another feature of many IPRP systems is that merit increases may be larger at the bottom of the pay range and smaller at the top. This reflects the view that performance improvements are most obvious when staff are starting in their roles and become less clear as their experience grows.

SELF-ASSESSMENT EXERCISE

From your own experience of being appraised – or indeed given feedback on your academic performance – what do you think are the major obstacles to a fair and consistent system of assessing your performance? How might these be overcome? What do your fellow students think?

COMPETENCY-BASED PAY

As doubts have increased in recent times about the effects of IPRP, there have been moves either to change the process – through improving the design of schemes – or shift to new methods of individualised pay progression. Under these alternative systems, progression still relates to the individual worker rather than everybody having guaranteed progression to the maximum of the grade or band as under a traditional seniority-based system. The criteria for progression, however, are linked to factors wider than simply target outcomes. There is some evidence that competency-based progression systems are more popular among employees (and trades unions) than IPRP because they incorporate a notion of employee development into pay progression (Industrial Society, 1998). Not only are workers encouraged to develop their skills but they are also rewarded for doing so. Whereas IPRP can appear to be simply a punitive system to penalise workers, competency-based systems can in contrast appear positive for employees' own career development.

The growth of competency-based HR systems has partly been attributed to the changing nature of white-collar work. As Mayhew and Keep (1999) argue, non-manual work is increasingly as much about behaviours and attitudes displayed at work as the possession of any particular analytic skills or skills based on understanding theoretical concepts. This change has been driven particularly by the growth of the service sector, where competitiveness is highly dependent on the social skills of the employees (Thomson, 2000). These 'people skills' are found in both private services such as retail, finance and hospitality and in traditional public services such as health and education. Such 'interpersonal skills' are often difficult to measure under traditional output-based IPRP schemes, and employers have become increasingly interested in 'competency-based' approaches. As Kessler (2005) suggests, traditional IPRP schemes have been observed to create a 'tunnel vision' situation where employees focus only on what is required to be achieved at the expense of how it is achieved. They have also been criticised for undermining teamwork. Competency-based pay, in contrast, rewards behaviours and attitudes such as co-operation, courtesy and communication.

Another attraction of competency-based pay is that it can form part of a much wider competency-based HR system, with the same competencies being used for other HR functions such as recruitment and selection, job evaluation and the design of grading systems, and employee development.

'A payment system that relates salary progression or a cash bonus to the display of "competencies" by individual employees. Systems originate in the identification of competency, understood as the key attributes and behaviours of employees that underlie good performance in a particular organisation or job.'

Heery and Noon (2001)

The growth of competencies or 'behavioural traits' as the building blocks for HR systems began in the 1980s and developed through the 1990s. Boyatzis (1982), for example, argued that it was possible to identify and define the behaviours that good performers display and hence these could be codified and used to evaluate and develop such behaviours across an organisation. Lawler (1994) says that the use of competencies reflects the shift away from HR systems built on the traditional concept of 'job' with fixed duties, accountabilities and responsibilities towards more fluid and developmental approaches. As Thomson (2000: 142) indicates, 'under these new structures, the job paradigm is seen as less effective because it leads to inflexibility, and creates a mindset that resists managerial objectives to adapt continuously to changing organisational circumstances'. According to Lawler (1994: 76), the 'challenge in a competency-based organisation is to focus on what individuals need to be able to do in order to make the work processes operate effectively'.

Competency-based systems are also often linked to the introduction of broad-banded grading systems (see Chapter 4) as they enable the absence of vertical career progression to be replaced by a new language of performance, and development within the role that is not necessarily linked to promotion. It can also provide more lateral flexibility to move employees across career boundaries as progression is no longer linked to specific skills and knowledge but to abilities and behaviours (Thomson, 2000). Brown (2001) makes the point that competency measures are often combined with more traditional performance measures, and hence a more suitable term might be 'competency-related pay'.

COMPETENCE OR COMPETENCY?

A key issue is the definition of competence. Woodfruffe (1991) has suggested that there is a difference between '*competence*' and '*competency*'. **Competence** refers to the areas of work in which the employee is competent (measurable skills). **Competency** is a wider concept and refers to the behaviours that underpin competent performance (ie an assessment of the employee's attitudes and behaviour). Furthermore, Armstrong (2002) identifies a distinction between 'work based or hard competences' – which refer to the expected standards and outputs for particular levels of performance – and 'behavioural or soft competences', which refer more to the personal characteristics that employees bring to their work (eg teamworking, strategic perspective, leadership and achievement-orientation).

Under competency-related progression individual employees will still be subject to an annual performance review, but the issues addressed will be the extent to which they have met or exceeded the expected level of competency for their role. Such systems can look, on the surface at least, very similar to traditional IPRP ratings, and there is some variation between organisations in terms of the mix of skills and behaviours required. Some competency-based schemes may emphasise the acquisition and use of particular skills (such as knowledge of particular computer software systems) more than the behaviours and attitudes required. Research by IDS (2000), however, indicates that most organisations favour more qualitative measures such as communication and teamworking ability.

ISSUES IN REWARD

BOX 5.4 NEC'S COMPETENCY FRAMEWORK

NEC's competency framework is designed to give employees a better understanding of the behaviours required to carry out their roles at a satisfactory level. A competency is defined as 'a combination of a person's skills, knowledge and attitude to a given area of the job'.

The framework ties together a number of HR activities, including:

- recruitment and selection

- personal development

- succession planning

- performance management.

Core competencies

There are ten core competency areas, which are closely related to the key job factors used in NEC's job evaluation scheme:

- leadership

- championing change

- focusing on goals

- imagination and excellence

- managing resources

- communication

- teamwork

- developing self and others

- information management

- decision-making and problem-solving.

Against each of these, a more detailed definition is provided, along with typical examples of positive and negative behaviours.

Assessing competence

The competency framework is now central to performance appraisal at NEC. Each year, employees focus on developing competencies applicable to their roles, as identified by their line manager with reference to job factors. At the end of the performance year, they are rated on their level of competency against a five-point scale, where 1 is 'outstanding', 2 is 'very good', 3 is 'fully acceptable/good', 4 is 'nearly acceptable' and 5 is 'unacceptable'. Employees are required to meet 'fully acceptable' for each competency.

Observable behaviours

To help line managers assess and benchmark the competency levels of individual employees, NEC provides examples of observable behaviours for each competency. For example, the core competencies and observable behaviours given for 'leadership' are as follows:

Leadership

The ability to 'make things happen', be encouraging, inspiring and channel the contributions of others.

Core competencies	Observable behaviours	
Elements	**Positive**	**Negative**
Creates a clear vision	Creates a picture that others can visualise and understand	Is muddled in communicating the vision
Visibly earns respect	Is valued as a result of acts and deeds	Is aloof and unapproachable
Acts decisively	Responds quickly, with a clear plan	Procrastinates, asks for more information and greater analysis
Inspires others and demonstrates loyalty	Demonstrates support to others and encourages them to achieve greater things	Openly criticises others and does not demonstrate visible support

Source: IDS HR Study 839, February 2007

Reproduced by kind permission of Incomes Data Services

BOX 5.5 EXAMPLE OF A FUNCTIONAL COMPETENCY AT INFORMA

All the jobs in a particular department are divided into four levels of functional competence. Below are examples of the indicators of proficiency at each of the levels within sales:

Sales functional competency			
Level 1	**Level 2**	**Level 3**	**Level 4**
• you have the ability to successfully identify and prospect new leads • you are able to listen attentively and highlight salient points from a conversation	• you demonstrate a high level of commercial awareness • you communicate opportunities for cross-selling to colleagues in your team and group	• you are aware of competitor activity and strategically plan to maintain advantage • you value the products you manage and nurture your team who promote them	• you are a figurehead for the industry and business; your presence and reputation in the industry commands due respect • you take ultimate responsibility for profit and loss

Source: IDS HR Study 839, February 2007

Reproduced by kind permission of Incomes Data Services

Most competence-based pay (CBP) systems will refer both to inputs (eg knowledge, skills, attitudes, attributes and abilities) and outputs (measurable achievements), but there may also be an emphasis on process – how the work is carried out.

The incidence of CBP is unclear, largely because it is often used in combination with other pay progression criteria rather than alone. Brown (2001) states that two-thirds of companies now include competencies in their performance management systems but, according to a European survey by Towers Perrin in 1997, only 13 per cent of respondents were linking pay to competence (Tower Perrin, 1997). Thomson and Milsome (2001), reviewing the range of estimates of the coverage of CBP, found a range from 12 to 38 per cent of organisations. They concluded that it had been slow to take off and that many organisations were wary of 'contaminating' their competency-based HR systems by linking to pay.

According to the more recent 2008 CIPD Reward Survey, 54 per cent of respondents based progression on competence to some extent. This was most common in the private services sector (55 per cent) and manufacturing and production industries (55 per cent). There was little difference in use between different occupational groups, with a range between 51 per cent for clerical/manual workers and 56 per cent for technical/professional. Users of CPB in the UK have included such companies as Glaxo-Wellcome, ICL, NatWest Bank, the Woolwich, the AA, Scottish & Newcastle, and Volkswagen (Brown, 2001: 132).

Research by IDS (1996) found only one example of 'pure' competence-based pay out of eight case studies. This was at Volkswagen. The other seven case studies used CPB as part of broader performance-related or other pay systems. All of the eight case studies in the IDS research agreed that CPB was about paying for performance. The research also found that the most common reason for introducing CPB was organisational change, flatter management structures, cultural change and a need to increase flexibility. CPB was often seen as a means to reward future rather than past performance.

The main arguments in favour of competency-related pay are that it can focus attention on the need for improved competence, encourage the development of competence, facilitate lateral career moves, encourage staff to take an interest in their own development, and help to integrate role and generic competences with organisational core competences (Armstrong, 2002: 301).

Critics of such progression systems have questioned the linkage of competence to pay for several reasons. Sparrow (1996) has done so from the standpoint of a professional occupational psychologist. He argues that there are two levels of competency – one that is trait-based and not amenable to change (eg it concerns the individual's own personality), and one that is open to change. Most competence-related pay schemes, he argues, are not robust enough to be able to distinguish between these two. Sparrow also cast doubt on the ability of managers to measure and evaluate complex issues like human behaviour. Strebler *et al* (1997) have also raised issues about the desired behaviours used in competence schemes, not least the risk of gender and ethnic stereotyping of the desired personality traits.

There has also been criticism from the managerial perspective. Lawler (1996) questions the ability to measure an individual's ability to perform a task, and argues that core competences may not be relevant in assessing individual roles. He argues that competencies need to be combined with other criteria for progression.

 SELF-ASSESSMENT EXERCISE

Consider the advantages and disadvantages of competency-related pay progression. Do you think that such systems are preferable to IPRP?

SKILLS-BASED PAY

Another way of linking pay to the individual is through skills-based pay. Such schemes link progression – either through the grade/band or through promotion to a new grade/band – to acquisition of designated skill levels. Such systems are also sometimes known as 'pay for knowledge' or 'knowledge-based pay'.

Skills-based pay (SBP) has been seen as promoting workforce flexibility through rewarding individuals for the type, number and depth of skills held. In some cases these systems are linked to modular training programmes. SBP is more often found among manual and clerical workers than for higher-level professional and management roles, where there is usually greater scope for individual discretion. But there can be some overlap with 'competences' where these are defined as skills or knowledge rather than behaviours. While originally used mainly in manufacturing SBP has now spread to retail, distribution, catering and other private services.

> DEFINITION
>
> 'Skills-based pay is an input-based payment system in which employees receive increases in pay for undergoing training and adding to their range or depth of skills.'
>
> Heery and Noon (2001)

Such systems have often been used in organisations that use self-managed work teams. In these organisations, individuals are required to learn a range of skills in order that the team can operate with a minimum amount of supervision and control. According to Lawler (2000: 131), such schemes were first used in the late 1960s in both the USA and Europe, 'and they remain the system of choice in manufacturing and service environments that use self-managing teams'. It has also been observed that SBP plans often require fewer classifications and grades than traditional reward systems (Recardo and Pricone, 1996). We consider team pay in Chapter 6. Skills-based pay systems are normally founded on the view that employees are only paid for the skills and knowledge the organisation needs them to acquire and that they are willing and able to use. Such schemes therefore normally provide guidance on what skills are required and for what purpose.

Five types of SBP plans have been identified by Recardo and Pricone (1996), which can be categorised as follows:

- *Vertical/skill plans* measure the acquisition of input/output skills within a single job (eg a press operator acquiring preventive maintenance skills).

- *Horizontal skills plans* reward the acquisition of complementary skills across several jobs (eg an individual learns how to do both accounts payable and accounts received).

- *Depth skill plans* reward skill specialisation (eg a computer programmer specialising in databases).

- *Basic skill systems* reward employees for developing expertise in the basic skill areas (mathematics, reading, writing and speaking English).

- *Combination plans* reward any of the skills above.

Most SBP systems are of the last category. Recardo and Pricone also point out that SBP systems normally require the redesign of jobs by shifting away from traditional Taylorist job design and towards more socio-technical approaches that 'focus on the completion of a discrete piece of work, foster task variability, promote task significance, provide on-going "realtime" feedback, and enhance decision-making autonomy' (Recardo and Pricone, 1996: 17). Once the work has been redesigned, tasks are then reconfigured into 'skill blocks'. The number and sequence of skills that an employee can learn vary significantly between organisations. In some manufacturing environments employees may have the opportunity to learn all the jobs required within a 'cell'. Learning may be accomplished through job rotation, and there are normally a minimum number of skills that an employee must acquire within a specified period. Acquisition of the required skills is rewarded by progression – either through an additional increment or pay increase or, in some cases, regrading.

Many SBP systems require some form of certification of skills. This requires clear measures of demonstrable ability, and evaluation is normally conducted through observation, oral or written tests or on-the-job performance. Workers may also be required to undergo periodic recertification, with failure possibly leading to reductions in pay.

Employers who have used SBP claim that it promotes flexible working practices. This is partly achieved through fewer and simpler job classifications and partly through the employee involvement that such systems encourage. Such systems have also improved operational problem-solving and cut the cost of supervisory and administrative overheads. There have also been claims of benefits to workers in terms of greater work satisfaction and improved perceptions of job security. Such systems also often provide pay progression routes for manual workers who traditionally may have been paid on single 'spot rates', thereby opening up opportunities for earnings growth. SPB has also been seen as a more equitable pay system because it is argued that it rewards demonstrable increases in the value of the worker to the employer.

Most of the benefits of SBP discussed above, however, link to the promotion of more flexible, less Taylorist, methods of job design. The real question is whether the linkage to pay is necessary as an incentive for employees to adopt such practices. Armstrong and Stephens (2005) are critical and argue that SBP is expensive to introduce and maintain. They state that 'Although in theory a skill-based scheme will pay only for necessary skills, in practice individuals will not be using them all at the same time and some may be used infrequently, if at all' (Armstrong and Stephens, 1996: 249).

Lawler (2000), however, concludes that paying for skills can be an effective approach to determining base pay. But, like Armstrong and Stephens, he also sees SBP as relatively high-maintenance because skills need continuous updating as the technology and structure of the organisation change and individuals change their ability to perform tasks. What happens when a worker has learned all the skills required? Lawler (2000) argues that skills-based pay, because it does not pay for ongoing performance, also needs to be combined with some form of performance-related pay if it is to be effective. He also comments that SBP may help to retain the most skilled workers because they become highly paid relative to the market rate for their jobs and because the specificity of the skills learned makes it difficult for them to find other jobs.

Thompson and Milsome's (2001) review of reward research discovered wide disparities in the prevalence of SPB in the UK. They found the incidence ranged between 14 and 32 per cent, depending on the survey, but concluded that SPB was rare in the UK. The most recent annual Reward Management Survey (CIPD, 2008) reported that progression based on skills was found in 38 per cent of organisations and that it was most common in private services, manufacturing and production and the voluntary sector. Surprisingly, this survey found little difference between levels of staff. It seems particularly surprising that a large proportion of managers appear to have their pay partly linked to skills.

PAY FOR CONTRIBUTION

Given the range of methods of linking pay to progression, the HR practitioner may be bewildered. Each method has its own advantages and disadvantages, and the choice of system, at the end of the day, is contingent on the strategy, circumstances and culture of the organisation. What has appeared in more recent times is a more 'blended' approach to reward design. This approach has been designated 'pay for contribution' by Armstrong and Brown (1999). In their book,

Paying for Contribution, they set out a new approach to pay design in which no particular progression system is advocated. Rather, they propose a return to contingency theory (see Chapter 2) and a 'pick and mix' view of reward design. This is partly a defence of individual-based reward systems in the face of strong criticism of traditional IPRP systems – and to a lesser extent competence and skills-based systems – and partly a call for a more strategic approach to the design of reward systems that emphasises strategic fit rather than best practice.

Armstrong and Brown (1999: xiii) argue that their approach is a 'manifestly distinct approach', characterised by the following:

- paying for how results are achieved as well as the results themselves, thus paying for competence as well as performance;
- paying for those skills and behaviours supporting the future success of the individual and the organisation, not just immediate results;
- rewarding a combination of organisation, team and individual performance, rather than concentrating wholly on the latter;
- the use of a wide variety of reward vehicles;
- a long-term evolutionary approach, incorporating a variety of HR systems and processes, rather than attempting a pay 'quick fix';
- addressing all aspects of reward strategy: the objectives and goals, the design and systems, the implementation and operation, rather than just focusing on the design mechanics.

These authors argue that this return to contingency is happening because:

> *Traditional categorisations such as paying for the job or paying for the person; paying in fixed base pay or paying in variable bonus; paying for the team or paying for the individual's performance; and paying for results or how those results are achieved; ... are increasingly being broken down as companies develop a series of tailored and hybrid approaches, which themselves are subject to regular modification and change. Changing a pay or bonus plan after a year of operation used to be seen as an admission of failure; ... now it is increasingly regarded as obvious and essential.* (Armstrong and Brown, 1999: 415)

They continue:

> *As the research and our experience have illustrated, there is no universal set of success criteria, just as there are no 'right' or 'wrong' types of scheme. Success is totally dependent on your pay and reward scheme objectives, and on the environment and circumstances in which you introduce and operate it. The same scheme can work brilliantly in one setting and fail disastrously in another.* (Armstrong and Brown, 1999: 416)

They identify three main features of their 'pay for contribution' paradigm:

- An acknowledgement that 'pay is potentially a highly powerful management tool'.

- An aversion to 'off-the-shelf, merit pay systems'.
- An acknowledgement of 'a strategic approach to reward.

They also provide five 'practical pointers'. These are:

- Contribution-based pay is particularly appropriate in sectors where it is recognised that employee skills and behaviours are the key to competitive success.

Table 5.7 Comparison of 1980s style pay for performance approaches with pay for contribution

	Pay for Performance	Pay for Contribution
Organising Philosophy	formulas, systems	processes
HR approach	instrumentalist, people as costs	commitment, people as assets
Measurement	pay for results, the 'whats', achieving individual objectives	multi-dimensional, pay for results and 'how' results are achieved
Measures	financial goals cost efficiency	broad variety of strategic goals: financial, service, operating etc added value
Focus of measurement	individual	multi-level: business, team, individual
Design	uniform merit pay and/or individual bonus approach throughout the organisation	diverse approaches using wide variety of reward methods, to suit the needs of different areas/staff groups
Timescales	immediate past performance	past performance, and contribution to future strategic goals
Performance management	past review and ratings focus top down quantitative	mix of past review and future development 360° quantitative and qualitative
Pay linkage	fixed formula, matrix	looser, more flexible linkages, pay 'pots'
Administration	controlled by HR	owned/operated by line/users
Communication and involvement	top down, written	face-to-face, open, high involvement
Evaluation of effectiveness	act of faith	regular review and monitoring against clearly defined success criteria
Changes over time	regarded as failure; all or nothing	regular incremental modification

Source: Brown and Armstrong (1999: xiv) Paying for contribution: real performance-related pay strategies. London: Kogan Page.
Reproduced by kind permission of Kogan Page Ltd.

- Pay generally supports the move towards a more competence- and contribution-focused organisation, rather than leading the change.

- All aspects of pay and reward need to be integrated (ie a 'total reward' approach).

- In the majority of organisations, there is still the need to consider job content and results achieved as well as competencies, base pay as well as bonus, individual as well as teams, when paying for contribution.

- Keep it simple.

There does seem to be some empirical support for Brown and Armstrong's view that organisations are using more 'blended' pay progression systems, rather than relying on one method (IDS, 2006b). IDS says that the factors driving this recent shift to more varied approaches stem from the apparent lack of transparency in pure IPRP systems and increasing concerns about equal-pay cases. IDS also notes that the fact that labour markets have remained tight has prompted more explicit linkages with the market.

 SELF-ASSESSMENT EXERCISE

Is the 'contribution-based pay' concept just 'old wine in new bottles', or do you think it is really new? To what extent do you think such a contingency-based approach is required, or do you believe that the 'best practice' approach of writers such as Jeffrey Pfeffer is more convincing?

MARKET-BASED PAY

The last method of individual pay progression considered in this chapter is market-based pay. Clearly, all pay structures have to be kept in line with the wider economy – either in terms of the pay levels of competitor buyers of the same labour or keeping the purchasing power of pay in line with inflation. We looked at these pay alignment issues in Chapter 3. Employers use a wide range of market benchmarking tools to ensure that both the whole pay structure is kept competitive within the external labour market and in setting individual salary levels. Gathering pay intelligence, such as salary survey data and relevant economic data, has become a major and ongoing exercise for the reward manager.

In this section, however, we discuss briefly how organisations use pay and benefits data to design individual pay packages and to govern the rate of progression through the grade or band. Pricing a particular job for both recruitment and retention purposes requires a clear understanding of the value of particular occupations in various labour markets (local, regional, national or international, depending on the level of the job). As we have already indicated earlier, there is in all organisations a constant dynamic tension between meeting the demands of internal equity (so that staff feel fairly paid in comparison to their colleagues) and the needs of the external labour market. These two pressures can, in reality, yield very different outcomes. For example, under job evaluation an accounts manager and a marketing manager may score at the same level in terms of job 'weight' (and hence be graded in the same grade or band). But when external comparisons are made it may well be found that accounts managers are paid considerably more than marketing managers. There may also be significant differences in pay level for the same role both between organisations in the same field, in different geographic locations and between sectors or industries.

To research the market for particular jobs employers use a range of benchmarking tools, the main one of which is the salary survey. The CIPD (2005) claims that some 75 per cent of UK organisations share information through remuneration and benefits surveys. As White (2000) has argued, over the last few decades there has been a dramatic increase in the number and range of salary survey sources available to the reward practitioner. This partly reflects the diminishing importance of industry-wide pay agreements (where all employers in a sector pay the same for the same jobs) as collective bargaining has declined as the major form of pay determination. It also reflects the increasing individualisation of reward systems, with greater emphasis on the performance or competence of the person in the role, rather than the 'rate for the job'.

Research by IDS (2004) found that employers follow market patterns and trends through a combination of comparisons: organisations in the immediate locality (often referred to as the 'local market'); organisations in the same industrial sector; and through influential firms in the economy. IDS also found that employers may use different external benchmarks to find suitable comparisons for different levels of staff. For example, staff in the lowest grades are often recruited from the immediate locality as these staff often do not wish to travel far from home to work. Moreover, these staff may be unskilled or semi-skilled and hence in a more general market for such labour, rather than the market for their current occupation. For example, a cleaner in a local council may move to a new job as a catering assistant in a hospital. For staff in the mid-range positions (eg skilled craft workers, clerical and secretarial staff, technicians) the market may be the region or 'travel-to-work' area, while for higher-level positions, such as professional and managerial staff, the market may be national or even international. IDS cites the example of Lloyds TSB, which uses the functional labour market (the whole finance sector) as its benchmark for senior staff, while clerical staff are more likely to be benchmarked against a range of occupations and sectors in the local labour market.

In some cases, the provider of the job evaluation system will also provide an annual pay benchmarking exercise for its clients. By accessing salary data collected from all its clients, the job evaluation (JE) provider can provide a good gauge of pay levels for jobs of similar weight in different organisations. The sample, however, is clearly limited to those organisations using that particular JE scheme.

One problem identified with market pay is the potential lack of transparency for employees. Employees must take on trust the benchmark estimate of the value of their job in the external market. Benchmarking the particular job will depend on the availability of good comparator data, but there will be some jobs where data is sparse and others where the data is inconclusive. In addition, the employer then needs to communicate the outcome in simple terms to the employee. In smaller organisations, individual pay levels may be set and updated solely in line with market information about the particular job or role. Others may have job families (see Chapter 4), which allow the employer to distinguish between different occupational groups in terms of their wider market value.

There are, of course, implicit dangers of gender discrimination in this process, particularly if one occupational group (eg HR) is overwhelmingly female and another (eg finance and accountancy) is overwhelmingly male. If the data used by employers is not sound, employers may leave themselves open to equal-pay claims. Equal-pay legislation does, however, recognise the 'market' as a defence for inequality in particular circumstances.

An alternative method of dealing with the market is to have *market supplements* for particular jobs or roles. These additions to base pay are often paid to compensate staff where their grade or band allocation under a job evaluation scheme places them at a disadvantage within the wider labour market. For example, IT specialists may be graded alongside other technical and administrative staff but may require a market supplement if their pay is to stay in line with the external market for such staff. Such supplements need to be regularly reviewed as the external market can change.

This was particularly the case with IT staff following the run-up to the end of the twentieth century when there were fears that a 'millennium bug' would lead to IT systems crashing on the change of century. IT staff were in great demand in this period, and many organisations introduced either market supplements or higher salaries for such staff in order to recruit and retain them. Once the millennium passed, and the fears were found to be unfounded, such a premium for IT staff dissipated rapidly.

Table 5.8 Progression types

Type	Description	Advantages	Pitfalls
Pure Types			
Service	Annual increments based on time spent in grade – still common in not-for-profit and public sectors. In private sector, likely to be modified by performance requirements	Highly transparent, with clear career paths for staff, usually based on experience	Can be a source of discrimination if scales are long, as women tend to have breaks in service
Performance	Appraisal-based payments consolidated into basic salary, on basis of overall 'pot', with individual increases varying according to performance. Commonplace for white-collar staff, much less so for manual workers	Can improve staff motivation and retention	Associated with low transparency; can demotivate, especially in periods of low inflation

Type	Description	Advantages	Pitfalls
Competency	Dimensions of behaviour that an employee must display in order to perform capably in their role in the workplace, eg analytical thinking, communications skills. Some schemes mix behavioural elements with more objective measures of skill level	Often more acceptable to staff and unions than merit-based approaches	Complex – link to pay not straightforward
Skills	Extra pay for completing each skill module in a sequence. Grew out of traditional approaches for manual and craft workers, eg apprenticeships, but now applied to lower-level white-collar staff as well	Pay differentiated more objectively, on basis of skills or experience	Need to ensure skills are being used in the job; updates necessary as work processes change
Market	Linking salary levels to what other organisations pay for similar jobs. Exact applications vary, from 'market anchors' with no floors/ceilings, to using market rates to define progression within ranges	Can assist with retention, especially in tight labour markets	If market static, no progression, which may demotivate; issues around transparency, and data availability (specialised jobs)
Contribution	New concept, sometimes defined as performance plus competency, which measures employees' achievement against both objectives and competencies	Provides ability to influence employees' behaviour	Most suited to senior management roles; needs to fit with company culture
Hybrid types			
Service plus performance	Most common hybrid – progression according to annual increments, subject to satisfactory performance. More rapid progression possible, subject to budgets	Flexibility to withhold or accelerate increments	Stronger links to performance constrained by budgets
Performance plus market	Various systems that provide accelerated progression to a market rate or zone, with slower progress once this has been achieved. Commonplace in finance	Said to speed progression to target rates, with added openness about ways pay is managed	Staff dislike lack of progression above market rates; not always as transparent as claimed

Type	Description	Advantages	Pitfalls
Performance plus skills or competency	Progression accelerated or withheld on basis of performance, but also link to skills acquisition. Common among call centre employers and some electronics manufacturers, eg Motorola	Flexibility for employers; can aid staff retention	Need to focus on use of skills, not simply on their acquisition

Source: IDS (2006b: 15–16)

Reproduced by kind permission of Incomes Data Services

COMPENSATORY PAYMENTS

Finally, in terms of the composition of pay, there may also be special 'compensatory payments' to employees working in particular circumstances. These tend to be applied to all staff in a grade or role, irrespective of their individual performance or market rate. The main examples of compensatory payments are: location allowances; overtime premiums; shift premiums; and call-out and standby payments. There are also some particular allowances paid to manual workers in particular industries – for example, tool allowances for engineering and construction crafts. While location allowances may apply to all levels of staff, overtime, shift and call-out payments are usually limited to lower-grade employees. Furthermore, in recent years there has been a concerted effort by many employers to move away from a plethora of separate allowances and premiums towards so-called 'clean remuneration' whereby these allowances are integrated or 'consolidated' into base pay.

LOCATION ALLOWANCES

Location allowances originally emerged in London in the 1970s to compensate workers for the higher cost of living within the metropolitan region. Such allowances continue to feature in many organisations' reward systems in order to be able to recruit and retain staff within the city. Moreover, within the tight labour market of the 1990s, such allowances began to spread out beyond London to the so-called 'Roseland' area (Rest of South East) and further.

Originally such allowances, or 'weightings' as they are often known, were designed to provide 'cost compensation' to staff for living and working in London (and were based on government indices showing changes in costs published for this purpose). Because of the indices, allowances tended to be similar across organisations. In more recent times, however, such allowances have become more associated with recruitment and retention issues (because the London and South East regions in the UK have the tightest labour markets) and hence more differentiated. Employers have also moved away from flat-rate allowances (eg £3,000 pa) paid to all staff irrespective of grade level towards percentage allowances or simply to regional pay bands.

The most recent research on London allowances (IDS, 2006c) showed that around two-thirds of 148 employers surveyed paid a free-standing, flat-rate inner or central London allowance to their staff. The median payment was £3,200 per annum. However, IDS notes a range of other methods of dealing with the London labour market. These include:

- separate, higher, London salary scales or ranges;
- zonal pay systems, with particular locations moving from one zone to another according to local labour market conditions;
- nationwide, broad-banded structures, providing scope to vary pay levels according to 'market salary guides';
- various forms of 'recruitment and retention' or 'hot spot' supplements; and
- the use of grading flexibilities within existing pay spines.

ISSUES IN REWARD

BOX 5.6 REPORT OF THE LONDON WEIGHTING ADVISORY PANEL 2002

An independent advisory panel appointed by the London Assembly (Greater London Authority, 2002) to review London Weighting found that:

There were increasing difficulties in recruiting and retaining public sector workers in London.

Pay levels recognising the 'additional expense of working in the capital' would be helpful.

Pay setting in the public sector had become more decentralised, leading to inconsistency in levels of allowance between different public service employers.

Direct cost compensation had not stood the test of time and was seen as complex and arbitrary in calculation. It did not take account of both the advantages and disadvantages of living and working in London. Moreover, such an approach attempted to compensate for the additional cost of living in London, while London allowances are paid to all employees on the basis of where they work, not where they live.

Instead of cost compensation, the advisory panel recommended the following approach:

London weighting in the public sector should be based on pay comparability with the private sector (in terms of the difference between public and private sector pay levels) rather than cost compensation.

The appropriate percentage differential amount should be made available for London weighting.

The City of London (the 'square mile') should be excluded from these comparisons because of its highly specialised, financial labour market.

Employers and employees should decide how the allowance should be paid (eg flat rate amount, percentage etc).

Source: Greater London Authority (2002)

OVERTIME PREMIUMS

Compensation for working more than the contractual hours for the job is often paid through an overtime premium. These premiums may vary between the times when the extra hours are worked, with higher compensation for working weekends and Bank Holidays than weekdays. There are legal limits on working hours in the UK (the Working Time Regulations), but there is no legislation laying down the overtime rates to be paid (unlike employees in the USA covered by collective agreements with trade unions). These rates are decided at industry or organisation level. Typical overtime premiums paid may be one and half times the basic hourly rate for weekdays and Saturdays (known as 'time and a half') and double the hourly rate for working on weekends (known as 'double time') (IDS, 2006d). Such premiums have been most commonly found in manufacturing and the public services and among lower-grade manual and clerical staff. IDS notes that eligibility for overtime pay may differ between manual and non-manual staff, with white-collar grades often having a cut-off point above which overtime premiums are not paid.

Recent statistics on overtime working (ONS, 2006a) show that the proportion of full-time employees working paid overtime in April 2006 was 15.6 per cent. The median number of paid overtime hours worked per week was four hours. The proportion of men working paid overtime hours was almost double that of women.

Some employers have sought to reduce the cost of overtime working by introducing so-called 'annualised hours' systems where employees are contracted to work flexibly within an overall annual limit (with any hours beyond the limit being paid extra). The annual hours total typically comprises a high proportion of 'rostered' hours and a small number of flexible hours, which are worked as and when required. Under these schemes, overtime premiums are consolidated into enhanced basic salaries.

SHIFT PREMIUMS

As well as compensating employees for working additional, overtime hours many organisations pay compensatory payments for working other unsocial hours such as shifts. In some occupations, 24/7 working is essential (ie in many continuous process industries and the public services), but elsewhere shift working may depend on demand for the goods or services. Government figures on shift working (ONS, 2006b) indicate that 15.7 per cent of all employees are working shifts regularly. The most common shift pattern is a two-shift system (two eight-hour shifts over 24 hours). Shift systems that involve a mix of day and night work are the second most common, closely followed by three-shift working (three eight-hour shifts over 24 hours) (IDS, 2007).

Shift premiums vary according to the type of shift worked (eg time of shift, length of shift, extent to which night or weekend working is required). Typical shift premiums can add a fifth to a third to basic pay (IDS, 2007b).

ON-CALL AND CALL-OUT PAY

A final common form of compensatory payment is that given for being on standby or 'on call' at home or in the workplace, and for being called out to work outside normal working hours. In many sectors, key workers may need to be available 24/7 in case of emergencies or mechanical/production breakdowns. This is most common in manufacturing and the public services, but even in other sectors there may be key workers required to be available at short notice to deal with specific contingencies – such as IT failures, security issues etc. IDS (2005) provides an overview of such payments.

IDS publishes frequent reviews of location allowances, overtime arrangements, shift pay and systems, and on-call/call-out allowances.

KEY LEARNING POINTS AND CONCLUSIONS

In this chapter we have explored the various methods of linking pay levels to grades or bands to create pay structures. As we have seen, pay structures are dynamic and progression through the structure can relate to various factors. While seniority-based pay has traditionally been the most common form of pay progression, at least for non-manual workers, this picture changed dramatically in the 1980s and 1990s. While initially there was a strong shift to individual performance-related pay, in more recent times employers have sought to find alternative, more transparent and manageable systems of pay progression. These have included competency-based, skills-based, market-based and contribution-based. The last of these provides a blended approach where different factors are combined to reflect different aspects of an employee's contribution. One thing is clear: pay progression systems have become more varied and individualised. Only in the public services and the not-for-profit sector is seniority-based pay still the most common form of progression.

As we have discussed, the major issue to be addressed is the extent to which progression is guaranteed and to what extent it is contingent on some form of individual appraisal or review of the employee's progress. Seniority-based systems have traditionally offered both employers and employees stability and predictability. Once other criteria are adopted to judge employee progress, there are clear consequences in terms of frequent renegotiation of the effort bargain; the requirement for robust systems of evaluation; and a strong reliance on line managers to 'get it right'.

Clearly, context plays a key role in the selection of a pay progression system. The predictability of seniority-based systems, both for employer and employee, coupled to resource constraints, has limited the spread of alternative progression systems in the public and not-for-profit sectors. The presence of trade unions has also acted as a barrier to change. In contrast, the private sector has had both the resources to finance new initiatives in pay progression and, in many workplaces, greater discretion to experiment. The effects of alternative progression systems will vary according to the system adopted. But these consequences are also likely to reflect the context in which the progression system is introduced. The process is vital. For this reason, robust performance management systems are a prerequisite for any contingent form of pay progression.

EXPLORE FURTHER

For a good summary of recent developments in pay progression systems, see IDS (2006b) *Understanding Reward: trends in pay progression: multi-faceted approaches gain popularity*. IDS Pay Report 945. January: 15–17. London, Incomes Data Services.

For recent research on performance management systems, see IDS (2007a) *Performance Management*. IDS HR Studies 839. February. London, Incomes Data Services.

For a full exposition of the 'Pay for Contribution' paradigm, see Brown, D. and Armstrong, M. (1999) *Paying for Contribution. Real performance-related pay strategies*. London, Kogan Page.

CHAPTER 6

Variable Pay Schemes

CHAPTER OBJECTIVES

At the end of this chapter you should understand and be able to explain the following:

- The concept of 'variable pay' and the various means by which this is achieved.

- The concept of incentive pay.

- The various types of incentive payment system: short-term and long-term; individual; team; and organisation-wide.

- Patterns and trends in incentive pay systems.

CIPD STANDARDS COVERED IN THIS CHAPTER:

To be able to:

- Advise senior management on the design or modification of a pay structure.
- Analyse the case for and against the introduction of a pay-for-performance system and advise on its introduction, implementation and auditing.

To understand and explain:

- The criteria for an effective pay structure and pay-for-performance schemes.

In the previous chapter we discussed how employers set pay levels for different levels of staff and how, for the majority of employees, there is some form of pay progression through the grade or band. In this chapter we consider the alternatives to paying a fixed basic wage or salary by adopting various forms of 'variable pay'. These variable pay components often co-exist alongside base pay, but in recent years there has been a growth in such payments for non-manual employees.

A strong message from the American 'new pay' writers is that base pay should form a diminishing part of the overall remuneration package and that reward should be composed of various separate elements, each of which should be based on specific measures of performance (Schuster and Zingheim, 1992: 154). The pretext for this view is that, if reward is to be genuinely strategic in purpose, the system must reflect the various strategic priorities and psychological levers available to the employer. Such variable payments may be individual, group or organisation-wide.

This shift to variable pay, however, may have important implications for both employers and employees. As discussed in Chapter 5, there has been a strong critique of the notion of linking pay to performance (eg Pearce, 1987; Kohn, 1993; Pfeffer, 1998). The consequences of placing stronger emphasis upon 'variable pay' can imply a shift in the employment relationship towards one where the employees carry more risk (Heery, 2000). On the other hand, they may also have the capacity to increase control over their own reward outcomes.

It is also worth remembering that such variable pay systems (which have always existed for manual workers) have a history of industrial conflict and unforeseen consequences, not least in terms of loss of management control, as employees learn to 'work the system'. In this chapter we consider the context for this new emphasis upon variable pay, the degree to which pay has become more variable, the various alternative forms of variable pay available and their particular purposes, and the consequences of such developments.

INTRODUCTION

Despite the existence of a range of critical research, both theoretical and empirical, about the motivational effects of pay (see Chapter 12 for the debate on this issue), almost all managers base their reward philosophy on the view that money motivates. They continue, therefore, to design their remuneration systems around the concept of rewards for those who achieve specified targets and penalties for those who do not. Basing pay on the level of output or production has been a part of payment systems for many hundreds of years, even in pre-industrial times. As described earlier in this book, manual workers' earnings have traditionally fluctuated from week to week, according to both the effects of incentive pay and enhanced base pay for working extra and/or unsocial hours. For this reason, incentive pay has been a long-standing contested area of the employment relationship. The employee relations literature has many examples of how management attempts to improve productivity and to use incentive pay to drive output have been halted or subverted by employees. It was especially the growth of shop-floor incentive schemes in manufacturing that led to the rise of the union shop steward and the development of workplace collective bargaining in the 1950s (Clegg, 1976). Indeed, in the 1960s the UK government sought to discourage the use of individual incentives because of these industrial relations concerns. Instead the emphasis was placed on productivity agreements that sought collective solutions to employee performance issues (Flanders, 1964; NBPI, 1967).

In contrast, the use of incentives for non-manual employees has been a more recent phenomenon but has grown rapidly over the last few decades. The large annual bonuses paid by finance and legal firms in the City of London attract critical press attention and have a major impact on the government's average earnings index. Incentive pay is now common for non-manual employees in the private sector.

From the discussion in Chapter 2, students will be aware that the first key text advocating incentives to improve productivity is the work of Taylor (1911), the father of scientific management. The history of incentives, however, goes back at least to the beginning of the industrial revolution and even to ancient history. Most early work on the effects of incentives tackled productivity improvements in manufacturing environments and among manual workers. Only with the growth of the sales function in organisations in the twentieth century did the concept of financial incentives start to be applied to non-manual occupations.

Chapter 2 provides a discussion of the motivational theory underpinning the concept of pay for performance. This chapter should be read in conjunction with Chapter 5 on pay progression systems as the conceptual differences between incentive pay, variable pay, performance-related pay and 'pay for contribution' can be confusing to the student of reward. We begin this chapter by trying to unpack some of these terms.

SOME KEY CONCEPTS

The traditional terminology used to describe payment systems designed to secure high levels of output or performance has been 'incentive scheme' or 'payment by results' (PBR). These terms were commonly used in the past to describe payment systems for manual workers in the manufacturing and construction industries (Smith, 1989). In recent times, however, incentive pay has become much more common for all types of employee. Heery and Noon, (2001: 168) define an incentive as 'a cash payment or some other reward that is offered to employees conditional on an improvement in performance'. They go on to say that the 'purpose of an incentive is to induce motivation'. In a sense, all of the payment terms listed below refer to various forms of 'variable pay'. While some, however, embrace both forms of pay progression within a grade or band and standalone payments, others are clearly only applicable to additional payments that are not consolidated into base pay.

Mitchell *et al* (1990) define incentive plans as those linking pay to individual or (small) group output, and they identify three types: piece rates, more elaborate incentives and commission. They do not consider profit-sharing or gain-sharing (which operate at the higher level of department, site or organisation) as incentive plans as such. Armstrong and Murlis (2007) argue that incentives are 'forward looking' while rewards are 'backward looking' or retrospective. In other words, an incentive is designed to provide direct effect – 'do this and you will receive this'. Incentives are therefore normally based on some form of target.

In contrast, argue Armstrong and Murlis, financial rewards are more indirect in motivational effect and more about recognition of employee efforts, rather than tied to some measurable target. They state, for example, that a bonus is a financial reward, rather than an incentive. This distinction relates to the differences between expectancy and reinforcement theory (see Chapter 2). Expectancy theory views motivation from a forward-looking perspective whereby expectations of reward are set in advance while reinforcement theory is more about retrospective recognition of past performance. In practice, however, the terms incentive and reward are often used interchangeably and often describe exactly the same type of payment.

Armstrong and Stephens (2005) use the all-embracing term 'contingent pay' to cover all these types of individual financial rewards. Armstrong and Murlis (2007: 297) define 'contingent pay' as 'payments related to individual performance, contribution, competence or skill or to team and the organisation'. Shields (2007: 348) observes that it may also be inappropriate to classify skills-based or competency-related pay systems as performance-related rewards because they focus on rewarding employees' productive inputs, rather than work behaviour or outputs. These types of individual pay relate more to forms of pay progression within base pay than incentive pay as such. Brown and Armstrong (1999), however, include both skills-based and competence-based rewards within their concept of 'pay for contribution'.

A more useful term for these types of reward may be **variable pay**. In the UK Workplace Employee Relations Survey (WERS) 'variable pay' is defined as having three main forms: performance-related pay, profit-related pay and employee share schemes. WERS defines performance-related pay ('also known as incentive pay') as payment-by-results, 'in which the level of pay is determined objectively by the amount of work done or its value' and merit-based systems, 'in which pay is related to a subjective assessment of performance by a supervisor or manager' (Kersley *et al*, 2006: 191). Armstrong and Murlis (2007) argue that variable pay, unlike base pay, has to be re-earned and is not consolidated into base pay.

The CIPD (2006: 6:24) defines variable pay as 'the practice of paying an amount of pay in addition to or instead of base pay as part of an employee's total remuneration which varies according to criteria'. It should be noted, nonetheless, that for Milkovich and Newman (2008: 629) the term variable pay is defined more closely as 'pay tied to productivity or some measure that can vary with the firm's profitability'.

In this chapter we have decided to use the term 'variable pay' as an overarching concept covering all forms of 'unconsolidated' pay separate from base pay. It is important to note, however, that we have included some forms of pay variation (as opposed to variable pay), such as location allowances or enhancements to the hourly rate for working unsocial hours, as forms of base pay.

Incentive: *'A payment, dependent on the achievement of some pre-determined target for output or performance, designed to motivate the employee to work harder.'* (Heery and Noon, 2001)

Bonus: 'A payment made in addition to the basic wage or salary usually linked to the achievement of a performance target or behavioural standard of some kind. Bonuses are separate cash payments additional to basic pay and are normally stand-alone payments that have to be re-earned in each bonus period. There is a wide range of bonus payments and they can be part of various payment systems, including merit pay, profit-related pay and sales rewards.' (Heery and Noon, 2001)

Commission: 'Commission is a form of bonus, often found in sales occupations, which links pay to the number of sales or customers served. It is often expressed as a percentage of the price of the sale or service to the customer.' (Heery and Noon, 2001)

Payment by results (PBR): 'A system of payment tied to estimates of worker output or performance (e.g. piecework, work-measured incentives and appraisal-related pay).' (Heery and Noon, 2001)

Merit pay: 'Merit pay is a system by which an individual's pay is related to an assessment of the performance in the job. Merit pay can cover a range of payment systems including performance-related pay, appraisal-related pay and "pay for contribution".' (Heery and Noon, 2001)

Individual contingent pay: 'Individual contingent pay relates financial rewards to the performance, competence, contribution or skill of individual employees. It may be consolidated in to base pay or provided as cash lump-sum bonuses.' (Armstrong and Stephens, 2005)

Variable pay: 'Variable pay is that part of total pay which varies according to some measure of individual, team or organisational output or performance. In some cases, all pay will be variable (e.g. under simple piecework systems based on individual output) but in many cases it will form a proportion of total remuneration.' (Heery and Noon, 2001)

Performance-related pay: 'Performance-related pay can either describe the broad range of payment schemes which link pay to some measure of work performance or it can simply mean individual appraisal-related or merit pay.' (Heery and Noon, 2001)

Pay for contribution: 'Pay for "contribution"' is a term coined by Brown and Armstrong to describe a holistic approach to reward design. It encompasses not simply individual performance-related or merit pay but pay based on other individual measures, such as competences or skills, and on teams or organisation-wide performance.' (Brown and Armstrong, 1999)

 SELF-ASSESSMENT EXERCISE

What is meant by 'variable pay'? What are the key aspects? What are the various forms of variable pay?

THE DIMENSIONS OF INCENTIVES

There are five major dimensions in the design of variable pay components. These are:

- What is being measured? Inputs or outputs?

- What period of performance does the payment reward: short-term (ie 12 months or less) or long-term (over a year)?

- Does the payment reward an individual's performance or does it relate to team or organisational success? Or does it operate at all three levels?

- Is measurement based on a single factor or multiple factors?

- What form does the payment take: cash, company shares or non-financial?

The first important dimension in designing variable payments is whether they will reward outputs from the work or inputs by the employee. In general terms, it is easier to measure outputs (where these are concrete products or cash outcomes) than inputs (which tend to be more based on behaviours and attitudes to work). Financial incentives are therefore more likely to be found in industries and occupations where individual or team performance can be most easily identified and measured (see Commerzbank case study below). Schemes that measure individual inputs or behaviours are more likely to be found in sectors and occupations where performance measures are less tangible (eg for health workers or in a research and development environment).

BOX 6.1

ISSUES IN REWARD

Commerzbank is an international German bank providing retail and corporate banking worldwide. Its UK operation focuses on investment and corporate banking. It employs around 700 staff in London, roughly split half and half between traders and middle- and back-office support.

The average age for middle- and back-office staff is 37, and the average length of service is six years. For traders, the average age is around 34, and the average length of service is three to four years.

Commerzbank competes for front-office staff such as sales and traders against larger investment banks by offering individuals the chance to specialise in niche products, such as exotic derivatives or providing

services to the German middle market. However, while lucrative, the lifecycle of investment products can be very short, with maturity three or four years away. Staff, including traders, then have to acquire a new expertise, or stay with it but accept that their earnings potential is unlikely to increase. Commerzbank also attracts traders by offering to be a stepping stone to the larger investment banks, or by developing a career within the bank.

While the rewards for traders can be high, so too are the expectations. To get a job as a trader, the bank is generally looking for two numeric degrees, and ideally an MBA. A second language is also normally required. Traders also have to study and pass quickly the regulator's (Financial Services Authority (FSA)) qualifications in their own time. They typically work 60-hour weeks in a pressured and competitive environment. Every conversation they have on the trading floor is taped and CCTV constantly monitors them as part of the FSA regulatory requirements.

The bank typically offers traders a £100,000 base annual salary, and a discretionary bonus with a linked share plan. The annual base salary, which it pitched using McLagan's salary data, is not seen as the major part of the package.

If their performance merits it, all staff are eligible for the firm's discretionary bonus plan awarded each year and paid in March. Important factors in deciding the bonus level include the performance of the business area in which the employee is working, the performance of the bank overall and individual performance. Employees can earn bonuses worth between zero and many multiples of salary.

As well as the bonus scheme there is a share plan, which is a conditional scheme with stock options restricted for between one-and two-year periods. The amount awarded depends on bonus level, market and economic conditions. Initially, while the plan was good at tying in staff, over time this has reduced, as many banks are now prepared to buy out talented individuals. While few traders leave because of the money, most that leave do so because they want a different challenge or to go to a bigger bank.

The reward function believes that the bonus scheme motivates staff, in particular those in the front office, to make bigger profits for the bank. There is a lot of satisfaction in being a top earner in a particular product line and pride in working for an investment house, like Commerzbank, with strong and profitable product lines. In addition, there is considerable scrutiny by analysts on the amount paid by each investment bank in bonuses as a percentage of income, so the process can be very transparent both for the banks and for staff. The reward function also believes that the bonus plan helps to align the interests of the staff with those of the shareholder.

One of the biggest challenges faced by the reward function can be managing bonus expectations. This is easier to manage for front-office staff, as the product heads knows what each of their employees is bringing into the firm and the associated costs, so they are able to indicate to them what they may expect to earn. For mid- and back-office staff, it's harder to assess the size of the bonus pot and their likely award – they read the stories in the media about the 'huge city bonuses' and some assume that they too are in line for such payments.

The reward function at Commerzbank, London, is held in high regard by both front-, mid- and back-office staff. Ian Davidson, Head of Compensation and Benefits, believes that this is based largely on getting to know what drives the business and drives its employees. 'Being able to talk to the front-office staff about such issues as the state of the markets and trading models helps establish our credibility in their eyes. They understand how we can add to the business. However, there are occasional times when we do have to be prepared to stand firm with some individual whose requests with regards to their bonus payments fall outside of the bank's payment criteria.'

This information was supplied by Ian Davidson, Head of Compensation and Benefits, Commerzbank, London.

Source: CIPD (2008)

The second dimension to consider is whether the incentive will be short-term, so that the reward follows closely behind the achievement, or long-term, where the reward may require a much longer time period of measurement. Some have argued that incentives will only work if the reward is made close in time to the achievement of the performance. Longer-term incentives have been seen as having a less powerful motivational effect. For example, work-measured incentive schemes usually relate to individual output over fairly short periods (a shift, a working day, a working week or a month) while schemes that relate the incentive to company performance targets or profitability will probably provide annual payments. Share ownership schemes (through share bonuses, share options or share purchase) will require even longer time periods to yield results. These longer-term forms of variable pay might be seen more as a manifestation of agency theory (linking the subordinate's interest to that of the owner or manager).

The third dimension is whether the incentive will relate to individual performance, group or team performance, or to some measure of organisational or corporate performance. The latter two types – group and organisation-wide schemes – focus on collective objectives rather than individual. Collective rewards are designed to encourage socially integrative behaviour (ie collaboration and co-operation), rather than the self-assertive tendencies (ie competition) found in individual approaches (Wilson and Bowey, 1989). In some organisations pay will vary according to all three of these measures. Individual workers may receive a personal bonus, a team bonus based on the success of the group or team in meeting their targets, and perhaps an annual bonus based on profits or achieved targets of the organisation. These three incentives may all be paid at the same time but more normally they are based on different frequencies of payment.

The fourth dimension relates to whether the incentive is based on a single target or objective (ie sales) or several factors. Single-factor schemes can be useful in focusing employee effort on a key objective such as profitability or productivity. For example, the scheme at Boots the Chemists is based entirely on store sales (IDS, 2007a: 4). In contrast, multi-factor schemes have a number of targets to be achieved. At Tesco Express, for example, each store's performance is measured through a combination of sales, costs, stock-level results and customer service ratings (IDS, 2007a: 4). Such multi-factor schemes may operate at several levels: individual, team, department and site. The individual factors may be weighted to reflect their importance. At ICI Paints, for example, local measures account for half the potential maximum bonus, while functional measures account for 20 per cent and overall profit 30 per cent (IDS, 2007a: 4). In terms of factors, IDS found that the key factors used in incentive schemes are: productivity, quality, safety, financial performance, customer service, cost management, attendance, sales, teamworking and individual performance.

The fifth dimension relates to what form the incentive will take. While the most common form of incentive is a cash payment, in some cases the reward will take the form of shares in the organisation or some non-financial reward (eg a gift or free holiday) (see Chapter 9). Payments may also be differentiated on the basis of an employee's grade or role. IDS (2007a: 7) gives the example of Asda, where a full-time departmental manager can earn up to £1,250 a year in bonus, compared to £300 for a full-time hourly paid employee. Paying a percentage clearly benefits the higher-paid, rather than a flat-rate amount across all employees.

Figure 6.1 illustrates the various types of variable payment available in terms of two of these dimensions – short-term or long-term and individual or collective.

The major categories of variable pay are as follows:

- individual results-based schemes (eg traditional piecework, work-measured schemes, sales commission);
- team-based rewards;
- collective short-term incentives (eg gain-sharing, goal-sharing, profit-sharing);
- collective long-term incentives (eg employee share schemes).

Each of these categories is dealt with later in this chapter.

Figure 6.1 Types of variable pay

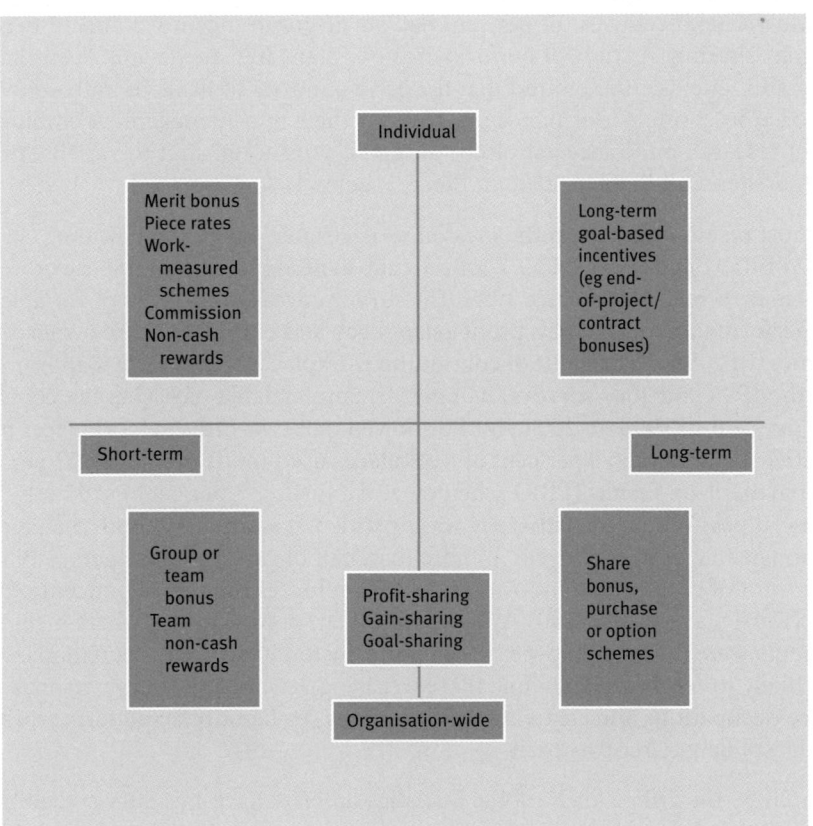

SELF-ASSESSMENT EXERCISE

What are the major dimensions to be considered when designing variable payments? How do these relate to the context of your own organisation (or one with which you are familiar)?

HOW COMMON IS VARIABLE PAY?

There has been a substantial increase in the use of variable pay in all developed countries since the 1980s. This growth has taken different forms in different countries, with a strong emphasis upon employee financial participation schemes (organisation-wide profit-sharing or share ownership schemes). In some countries, such as France, profit-sharing has been compulsory for some years in firms above a certain size. The growth of individual incentive schemes has been more patchy, but there has been a clear increase in such schemes in the USA, Canada, Australia and the UK. A 2002 survey by Lowe *et al* (2002) of 770 North American organisations found that more than two-thirds operated variable pay plans of some sort. An earlier, large-scale, survey by the American Productivity Center (O'Dell and McAdams, 1987, cited in Mitchell *et al*, 1990) found that 32 per cent of respondents had profit-sharing schemes, 28 per cent had individual incentives, 14 per cent had small-group incentives and 13 per cent had gain-sharing. A study of performance pay plans in Canada and Australia (Long and Shields, 2005) found that the great majority of firms in both countries utilised at least one performance pay plan for their non-management employees. Recent research on France has also indicated a substantial shift to variable pay (see Marsden and Belfield, 2006 in Box 6.2, below).

The most recent research on the incidence of variable pay in the UK, the 2004 WERS (Kersley *et al*, 2006), found a substantial increase in the use of performance-related pay since 1998. The survey covers three types of variable pay: performance-related pay, profit-related pay and employee share ownership schemes. In 2004, 32 per cent of continuing workplaces (ie those that appear in both the 1998 and 2004 surveys) had performance-related pay schemes, compared to 20 per cent in 1998. In 2004, WERS showed that two-fifths of workplaces had incentive pay schemes; 9 per cent of workplaces used merit pay alone; 23 per cent used payment-by-results (PBR) schemes; and a further 7 per cent used both PBR and merit pay. Where incentive pay was provided, it was paid to both managerial and non-managerial employees in more than half of cases; to managers only in 10 per cent of cases; and to non-managerial employees only in 34 per cent of cases (Kersley *et al*, 2006: 190). WERS found that, in workplaces where incentive payments were made, employees in sales and customer service occupations were most likely to receive them, while those in caring, leisure and other personal service occupations and elementary occupations (eg labourers and farm workers) were least likely to receive them.

Research by the Office for National Statistics on New Earnings Survey data from 1992 to 2002 showed that incentive pay declined as a proportion of total pay between 1987 and 1990, but since then has remained fairly constant. In 2002 one in seven employees received some incentive pay compared to one in five in 1992 (although it should be remembered that the definition of incentives in the New Earnings Survey only included direct monetary payments). These incentive payments contributed an average 22 per cent of gross pay (Grabham, 2003: 398) but males were much more likely to receive incentive pay than females.

There is a clear influence of sector on the prevalence of incentive pay. It is, according to the WERS, more common in the private sector (44 per cent of workplaces) than in the public sector (19 per cent). Incentives were also much more likely to be found in the finance sector (82 per cent of workplaces) than elsewhere. The ONS research (Grabham, 2002) found that, in the financial sector, incentive pay accounted for a quarter of gross pay in 2002. While incentive pay appears to be more common in non-unionised workplaces, this largely reflects the fact that the public sector – where incentives are less common – is more heavily unionised than the private sector. If we take the private sector alone, there is little difference between unionised and non-unionised workplaces. In fact, in manufacturing, incentives are more likely to be found in unionised than non-unionised workplaces.

ISSUES IN REWARD

BOX 6.2 WHAT THE GROWTH OF INCENTIVE PAY SCHEMES IN FRANCE CAN TEACH THE UK

Dominance of 'rate for the job' systems eroded in favour of individualised pay increases and group rewards

The use of performance-related pay (PRP) has become widespread in recent years. However, evidence for the superiority of compensation systems that incorporate elements of PRP over traditional, time-based ones is weak. Indeed, academic studies offer a remarkable variety of assessments of the relative effectiveness of PRP systems.

Our own study builds on this observation by investigating three key questions. First, we look at how far workplace context – the 'monitoring environment' – determines the impact of PRP systems on performance. Second, we consider the ways that management operates these pay schemes and what influence this has on staff motivation. Finally, we

test the idea that managers need to engage in experimentation to find the best combination of pay system and monitoring environment.

We have been investigating these questions using the British and French workplace employment relations surveys, which span the years 1980–2004 and 1992–2004 respectively. Both consist of data on pay systems, methods of employee representation and measures of plant performance.

A first glance at the two surveys suggests that incentive pay systems of various kinds are more widely used in French than in British firms. However, in both countries the dominance of 'rate for the job' systems has been eroded in favour of individualised pay increases and group rewards. In France, the use of group incentives appears to have caught up with individualised ones, whereas in the UK group incentives have overtaken individual ones.

Performance bonuses appear to be more widely used for managerial than for non-managerial employees in France. Britain has seen a comparable decline in the use of payment by results systems for blue-collar workers, and an increase in their use among white-collar staff. Preliminary comparisons of the use of incentive pay systems and the financial performance of individual establishments suggest that those operating performance pay schemes perform better. However, it is too early to draw conclusions about why this is the case. It could be, for example, that already prosperous firms offer more generous performance incentives.

Although our research is still in progress, some of the key factors driving changes to pay systems in France are already apparent. An emphasis on price competition is associated with the use of individualised incentives, whereas an emphasis on prices, innovation and quality favours adoption of group incentives in French firms. Size of firm also influences the choice of pay system, with large firms most likely to use collective bonuses. Low levels of involvement are associated with limited use of both types of pay scheme. New technology does not appear to determine what type of incentive pay is used, though it stimulates the search for new reward methods.

For UK observers, perhaps the most striking finding is the degree of change that has taken place in France over the past decade. While this is at odds with the popular view that the French labour market is rigid and over-regulated, it is not surprising given the evidence that the hourly productivity of French workers is greater than that of employees in Britain.

Key points

- Incentive pay systems have become more widespread in the past two decades.

- They appear to have spread more widely in France than in Britain.

- Important factors associated with the spread of these systems in France include size of firm, type of technology, organisational practices, product market competition and the use of employee involvement practices.

David Marsden and Richard Belfield, Centre for Economic Performance, London School of Economics

Date: 12 October 2006

The paper 'New Pay Systems, Work Organisation and Performance in Britain and France' was presented at the CIPD's Professional Standards Conference at Keele University, 26–28 June 2006.

Source: People Management

The prevalence of incentive payments also appears to relate to the degree of product market competition faced by the workplace. In the trading sector, half of the workplaces with a 'very high' degree of competition had PBR or merit pay, compared with just over a third in those facing a 'very low' degree of competition. Similarly, almost half of those workplaces facing 'many competitors' had incentive pay, compared with 28 per cent of those who said they dominated their product market and had no competitors. Incentive pay was also most likely to be found in workplaces where the demand for goods or services was highly

Table 6.1 Types of cash-based bonus or incentive plans on offer, by sector, 2008

Percentage of respondents					
Type of plan	All	Manufacturing and production	Private sector services	Voluntary sector	Public services
Individual-based	60	53	61	65	72
Scheme driven by business results	51	57	54	26	19
Combination	50	46	57	35	25
Team-based	27	24	30	26	16
Ad hoc/project-based	19	20	20	4	28
Gain-sharing	3	3	3	-	3

Source: CIPD (2008)

dependent on price rather than quality, and least likely in those workplaces where demand was not highly dependent on either price or quality. This has clear implications in terms of the balance of extrinsic and intrinsic motivation in different types of workplace.

A CIPD survey (CIPD, 2008) found that the use of cash-based bonus or incentive plans for all or some employees was common but that there was variation according to sector, size and age of the workforce (see Table 6.1). Like the WERS, the CIPD found that cash-based bonus or incentive plans were most common in private sector services (89 per cent of respondents) and manufacturing (86 per cent), but less common in the public sector (30 per cent) and voluntary sector (30 per cent). The presence of a cash-based bonus or incentive also related to organisational size. Some 78 per cent of organisations employing between 1000 and 4,999 employees had such a plan compared with 67 per cent of organisations employing 49 or fewer employees. Such plans are most common for senior management and least common for clerical/manual employees. The 2007 survey found that incentives were more likely to be found in organisations with a predominantly young workforce. Most organisations have more than one incentive scheme in operation, with a sizeable proportion of private services employers and larger organisations operating four or more (CIPDa, 2007: 14). The most common type of incentive found in the survey was a bonus payment linked to an individual's performance.

Recent research by IDS (2007a: 2) found that organisations adopted incentive or bonus schemes for the following reasons:

- to improve business performance (eg sales, productivity or profits);
- to focus employees' efforts on a number of important areas (eg safety, quality or customer care);
- to motivate staff by establishing a clear link between pay and performance;

- to give employees a share in the success of the business;
- to assist recruitment and retention by forming a key attraction of the reward package on offer;
- to help promote certain behaviours, such as teamwork or good attendance.

However, as we have argued elsewhere in this book, the exact objectives will depend on a number of variables, including corporate strategy, organisational culture and occupational norms.

INDIVIDUAL RESULTS-BASED REWARDS

Individual results-based rewards are probably the most common form of variable pay. At their most basic, in smaller organisations they may simply be one-off cash sums paid out by the owner of the business to individuals considered to have done a 'good job'. In larger organisations, however, there is usually a more formalised and structured approach.

Individual bonuses can help focus the employee on the desired results or behaviours, but they are only likely to work where those results or behaviours can be easily measured. Individual bonus schemes are therefore more commonly found where hard financial or output targets can be set, such as in sales, production, manufacturing and logistics (IDS, 2007a). Schemes can have perverse effects, however, where employees are encouraged to compete rather than co-operate. They are therefore sometimes seen as inappropriate for professional or more knowledge-based occupations where the sharing of information is key. There may also be, in line with expectancy theory, an issue about the size of the reward, with a clear link between the desired results and the amount of bonus paid. Lastly, such schemes have been found to work best where individuals or groups are able to control their own work and hence be able to vary performance or levels of output.

The major forms of results-based incentive schemes are traditional piecework schemes, commission and work-measured schemes. These normally relate the incentive in some way to output. Other forms, more common for non-manual workers, are sales 'commission' or customer service incentives, although these reflect more the 'value' of the output than the output alone. There are also various other results-based incentive schemes that relate the incentive to some measure of individual achievement of target goals. These differ from merit pay schemes that are more likely to measure behaviours.

Results-based schemes began to wane in the 1960s, partly because they were seen as encouraging 'wage drift' (ie earnings increased faster than base pay rises) and because of the industrial relations climate that they engendered. A book by William Brown of the Glacier Metal Company chronicled the damaging effects of such schemes in the workplace (Brown, 1963), and in the late 1960s the government set out to eradicate such schemes as part of economic policy. Recent research by IDS (2007b) found that organisations in the engineering industry have largely moved away from these individualised schemes towards schemes related more to collective performance in some form, such as company-wide profit-sharing or other profit-based systems. Three-quarters of the bonus schemes examined in the research were based on company-wide performance targets, rather than individual output. Elsewhere, manual workers are now subject to appraisal-based pay systems, with criteria such as training targets, safety or quality widespread. Where individual bonus schemes still exist, they may be designed to reward corporate or plant-level targets or new ways of working. Attendance bonuses – which reward target levels of attendance at work – are also common in manufacturing. These trends reflect both the shift of employment away from traditional manufacturing and extractive industries, where output was more easily measured, and the increasing focus in many manufacturing firms on quality, flexibility and efficiency rather than quantity of output. Such individual output-based schemes are therefore much rarer today but can still be found in some sectors (eg clothing and textiles).

INDIVIDUAL PIECEWORK

Individual or 'straight' piecework is the oldest form of incentive, dating back to pre-industrial times when it was the main form of payment for craft workers. After the industrial revolution it became widely used in engineering, printing, foundries, clothing and shoe manufacture. Adam Smith, the eighteenth-century economist, referred positively to pieceworking as a method of payment to encourage productivity (Smith, 1776). Under individual piecework systems, employees are paid per unit of production. Employees are therefore paid according to the number of items of items they produce or process, so pay is directly related to results. Thus, if the piece rate is £1 per item, production of 100 items will yield £100 in pay. Such work is now largely limited to low-paid and often 'hidden economy' jobs, especially 'home workers' in clothing and toy manufacture, and workers in agriculture and food processing. This decline in piecework largely reflects the fact that technological changes in manufacturing mean that workers now have little control over their own pace of work and that employers are today often more interested in quality than quantity.

Most schemes provide a minimum earnings guarantee or 'fall-back' rate, and there may be allowance for 'downtime' caused by machine failure, maintenance or shortage of materials. The fall-back rate may be set at 70–80 per cent of average earnings but, from 2004, under the National Minimum Wage (NMW) Regulations, employers must now determine a 'fair' piece rate for each piece or task accomplished, by reference to the rate of the average worker. The rate per piece must then be set so that the average worker then earns 120 per cent of the NMW, ensuring that most workers will achieve the NMW (DTI, 2004).

It is often said that piecework is an ideal form of incentive because of its simplicity and clear linkage between output and pay. It is also effectively 'self-supervising' in that it is in the employee's interest to keep busy and manage their time effectively. Employees can also easily calculate their pay from the price per piece and set their own pace of work to match their aspirations. The reason why the incidence of traditional piecework has diminished so much is that it has serious disadvantages. Taylor (1911) identified two main problems with piecework: the tendency for employees to hoard work and restrict their output, and the tendency for employers to cut the rate if production levels rose, hence defeating any motivational gain. For employers these are also potential problems with quality (because the emphasis is on output). The frequent, and sometimes acrimonious, renegotiation of the rate for the job is also seen as not conducive to good employee relations (Burawoy, 1979). For employees there can be problems in predicting longer-term earnings levels in the absence of a guaranteed weekly income.

WORK-MEASURED SCHEMES

The more common form of results-based incentive in production industries today is the so-called 'work-measured scheme'. These schemes replaced traditional piecework schemes during the twentieth century and were common in a number of industries until quite recently. One of the earliest schemes was Taylor's 'differential piece rate system' (cited in Shields, 2007), which sought to overcome the problems inherent in straight piecework. In work-measured schemes the job, or its component parts, is timed and a standard time for completion of the task established. The incentive is related to exceeding this standard time target for the task. In other words, if the task can be completed in less than the standard time the employee's pay will increase in proportion to that standard. The advantage of work-measured schemes is therefore that performance is linked to the hourly rate of pay. Under such schemes workers can often earn an extra third in pay for exceeding the standard time for the job. The downside is the potential work intensification that may result for the worker.

In order to link performance to pay, work-measured schemes require elaborate methods of timing jobs and measuring outputs. This exercise is conducted by 'work study' or industrial engineers who observe workers and time individual components of a job with a stop watch. This involves a number of timings of different workers doing the same jobs and at different times of the day or night. An 'effort-rating' is then given to each worker to fix their standard speed or output. The work study engineer identifies normal effort without financial incentive and standard effort with an incentive. In the UK, effort is normally measured using the British Standard Scale, with normal effort at 75 and standard effort at 100 (see Figure 6.2 below). The bonus is designed to raise effort by one-third, from 75 to 100, and this then translates into a pay bonus of a third.

Various allowances are made when calculating the standard values or times, such as a reasonable allocation of time for relaxation, personal needs, fatigue and down-time for machine adjustments or maintenance. A scale of payment is produced by which pay increases as output rises. These scales can either be a flat scale (progressive) or a sliding scale (regressive). Under the former arrangement, no bonus is paid until the goal is met and no extra money is paid if the goal

Figure 6.2 British Standard Scale of Rating

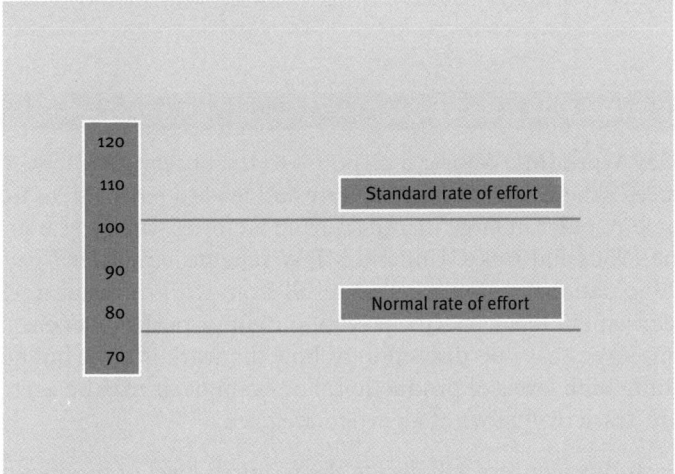

Source: Smith (1989: 33)

is exceeded. In contrast, a sliding scale means that the bonus is linked to the degree of achievement (often starting at 75 per cent of the target and rising as a proportion to 100 per cent at 120 per cent of the target).

The advantage of work-measured incentives for employers is that they are a more effective method of measuring employee performance on the job than simply counting the number of pieces produced or processed. Such schemes are best suited to short-cycle, repetitive work where changes in the work are infrequent. Such schemes, from a management perspective, may also require rigorous supervisory management if workers are not to manipulate schemes to their own advantage.

In theory, once the rate has been fixed, it should be relatively easy for workers to pace their work to meet their pay aspirations, but the use of such schemes has, like traditional piecework, also declined considerably in recent times. The major reason for this decline has been management concerns about quality and 'pay drift' whereby employees learn to operate the scheme to their advantage, rather than the employer's. This 'degeneration' in schemes arises from employees learning new and faster ways of completing tasks and negotiating additional and larger downtime allowances which were not reflected in the original timings and prices set for the jobs (Roy, 1952). The decline also reflects the fact that such schemes require considerable administration and supervisory management to operate effectively. Frequent negotiation and renegotiation with individual employees and their representatives may also be required (Burawoy, 1979). Lastly, technological changes in manufacturing have made it much more difficult for employees to influence the speed of production. Computer-aided manufacture means that many of the production jobs once done by operatives are now performed by 'industrial robots' or other automatic processes. Manufacturing systems based on 'just-in-time' philosophies, where stock is kept to a minimum, also mitigate against these schemes, which emphasise output (and hence the amount of stored stock) over quality.

MEASURED DAY WORK

Measured Day Work (MDW) was a response to the observation that work-measured schemes tend to degenerate and lead to pay drift, as noted above. MDW became popular in large manufacturing factories, such as car assembly plants, in the 1950s and 1960s. Under a MDW scheme, employees' pay is fixed (unlike the fluctuations in earnings that result from work-measured schemes), but on the agreement that a specific level of output or performance is maintained. In MDW employees have no discretion in how the work is done but are rewarded for maintaining high levels of production. For example, it may be agreed that the assembly line 'track' will move at a particular speed.

Again, work study engineers will decide the required level of production required and monitor the output, but in theory this should avoid the constant haggling between supervisors and workers over the 'rate for the job' inherent in work-measured schemes. The disadvantage identified with MDW is that the performance target set often became too easy. For this reason, MDW has now largely been abandoned and replaced by a high 'day rate' often combined with team or organisation-wide bonuses based on corporate targets.

COMMISSION

Commission on sales or customers served is one of the oldest and simplest forms of individual incentive used to motivate non-manual workers. Like traditional piecework and work-measured schemes, commission schemes are designed to motivate the worker to increase individual output. So, for example, a typical sales commission scheme might pay a 10 per cent bonus (ie 10 per cent of base salary) for every 100 sales achieved. In an estate agency, commission may be paid according the value of the property sold over a particular period of time. In hairdressing stylists are often paid on the basis of commission on the amount of money generated by the salon each week (including both customers served and sales of hair care products).

Some jobs are rewarded entirely by commission on sales (ie there is no base salary), although employers must pay at least the NMW. It is more common, however, for commission to be paid on top of base salary. Rates of commission will also need to be set at levels that ensure they are affordable. Where commission accounts for a very high proportion of total earnings, there may be resultant problems with employee behaviour. For example, sales staff may prioritise particular products where commission is highest or may indulge in 'hard sell' tactics that endanger good customer relations. As Shields (2007: 408) states: 'Commission payments may encourage aggressive, deceptive and negligent selling practices, including the sale of goods to consumers who may be unable to service a consumer credit or loan debt.' Part of the pensions mis-selling crisis of the 1990s was caused by over-indulgent financial services sales staff selling products indiscriminately to customers, whether they were suitable products for that particular customer or not. This is a good example of the unintended consequences that can arise from ill-conceived rewards.

RESULTS-BASED INDIVIDUAL BONUSES

Another form of individual incentive is the results-based bonuses that have become common for managers and other professional occupations. Unlike other types of individual results-based variable pay, these appear to be increasing. Such bonuses are common in the financial and legal services sector where end-of-financial year bonuses can be in multiples of the base salary. As in work-measured schemes, the bonus may relate to a scale of achievement and be either progressive or regressive. It may be based on a single factor or form part of multi-level schemes, where the bonus relates to individual, team, departmental and organisational targets.

SELF-ASSESSMENT EXERCISE

What are the major types of individual, results-based variable pay? Why have they fallen from favour in some industries but gained favour elsewhere?

TEAM-BASED REWARDS

One alternative to individual results-based incentives is a group or team reward. Under such schemes the reward is distributed between the members of the work group or team rather than different rewards being received by members of the same team. Team incentives for manual workers have existed for some time, but they became popular in the 1990s for non-manual workers too as employers sought new ways to encourage collaboration and knowledge-sharing between employees. In some cases, team rewards were seen as an alternative to individual performance-related pay and, in the UK civil service, there was active encouragement of and experimentation with such approaches in the 1990s (Makinson, 2000). Experiments were run in the Benefits Agency, the Inland Revenue and Customs and Excise. The Institute of Employment Studies and Hay also ran a major project on teamworking in the National Health Service.

Shields (2007) states that most team-based schemes are adaptations of multi-factor business unit gain-sharing or goal-sharing plans (see later in this chapter) and that their emergence coincided with the development of high-involvement or high-performance 'best practice' models of HRM, of which teamworking is one example. The 2004 WERS (Kersley *et al*, 2006: 91) found that teamworking was present among core employees in almost three-quarters of all workplaces. It was most likely to be found in public administration (91 per cent of workplaces), construction (89 per cent) and education (88 per cent), and least common in transport and communication (55 per cent) and wholesale and retail (51 per cent). It was also found to be most common among professional employees and least likely among sales and customer service staff. Unfortunately, WERS does not specify whether any of these staff were paid on a team basis. The latest CIPD reward management survey (CIPD, 2008), however, indicates that 27 per cent of all respondents used team rewards. They were found to be most common in the voluntary sector and private sector services.

DEFINITION

'Team rewards consist of payments or non-financial rewards provided to members of a formally established team. They are linked to the performance of the team as a whole, and are awarded in addition to the individual pay received by each team member.'

Armstrong (2000)

The rationale for team-based reward is to encourage the behaviours that encourage effective teamworking. It is often seen as an alternative to individual performance-related pay, which, it is argued, encourages individuals to focus on their own targets to the exclusion of wider priorities, and discourages managers and supervisors from developing teams (Armstrong and Murlis, 2007). Research by Thompson (1995) found that the main advantages of team pay were: it rewards teamwork and co-operation; encourages the group to improve work systems; increases flexibility and the ability to respond to changing needs; encourages information-sharing and communication; and helps to focus people on the wider organisation.

Teamworking is not, however, problem-free. There is clearly the issue of the 'free-loader' who does not perform his or her share of the team's work but is still eligible for the reward. For this reason, managers may need to ensure careful supervision. Research by academics from the University of Bath (Kinnie *et al*, 1998) found clear evidence of improvements in productivity from teamworking but also commented on the possible negative aspects. These included reduced quality of working life for workers, because of greater pressures to perform and the close monitoring of work required, and the potential for social pressures on members of the team to conform to group norms, with the possibility of harassment of weaker members of the team. An evaluation of an experiment with team-based reward within the UK civil service (Burgess *et al*, 2004) found that team incentives worked well for small teams but not for larger ones. It also found that the team incentive had a major effect on the quantity of work produced, but not quality.

Armstrong (2000: 70) argues that team-based reward can only work where teams are easily defined and of relatively long standing. He also argues that it can be demotivating for staff who prefer to be rewarded individually and that it fails to distinguish the contributions of individual team members. As mentioned above, group norms can also lead to undesirable effects in terms of social cohesion in the work group, and unco-operative attitudes can be spread from individuals to the wider team, leading to barriers to flexibility and change. Appropriate measures of team performance may also be difficult to design. This implies that any shift to team or group payments needs careful consultation with the workers and their active involvement in the design of such schemes.

TYPES OF TEAMWORKING

Like all reward initiatives, both the context and form of team reward influence its acceptability and success. It is interesting, for example, to note that the 2004 WERS found teamworking least common among sales and customer service staff, areas where individual incentives are very common. Shields (2007) points out that the decision whether to use team rewards as opposed to organisation or department-level rewards depends on the degree of inter-team dependence. Where teams operate more or less autonomously it is easier to identify individual team performance, but where teams are highly dependent on other teams, broader incentives may be more appropriate. Team rewards will also relate closely to the form of team working adopted by organisations. Three main types of team have been identified: process teams, parallel teams and project teams (Gross, 1995). Lawler (2000) adds a fourth type to Gross's typology – the management team – but here we concentrate on the original three types.

Process teams are permanent and tend to be found in manufacturing and service provision processes. Such teams tend to involve multi-skilling, with each member of the team trained to perform the full range of tasks within the team. Examples of such teams can be found in engine assembly plants, insurance claims processing and customer inquiry teams in call centres (Shields, 2007: 438). Such teams tend to be highly interdependent, both on members of the team and other similar teams, and semi-autonomous, but, according to Shields (2007: 438) 'the norm ... will be close external supervision by line managers'.

Parallel teams are part-time teams that meet to solve a particular problem and then disband, or that meet together from time to time to deal with particular issues (such as 'quality circles' or health and safety groups). These teams are likely to be cross-functional and draw members from different occupational functions. In general, such teams tend to have low to moderate autonomy.

Project or time-based teams are full-time teams committed to completing a project within a given timescale and in which membership may vary over time. Project teams are also likely to be cross-functional and require high levels of knowledge, skill and ability on which each member depends to complete the task. Typical examples of project teams would be hospital surgical teams and construction project management teams. Most project teams will tend to operate in a fairly autonomous manner, and hence team performance tends to be rewarded on a project-by-project basis. In some cases, the length of the project may mean that the team reward is only made at the end of the project period, which in some cases could be several years.

MEASURING TEAM PERFORMANCE

The measures to be used will vary according to the type of team. Those for manual workers will probably reflect both quantity and quality of output, and may also reward initiative and a good safety record. For non-manual teams the measures may include sales, accuracy and customer satisfaction. Measurement of team performance may be based on a single factor or multiple factors. Single-factor schemes tend to focus on labour productivity or labour cost savings. The scheme at BG described in the case study at the end of this chapter uses six factors.

HOW IS THE REWARD DISTRIBUTED?

A major decision to be taken in any team reward system is how to distribute any reward. Four main methods of distribution have been identified (Shields, 2007: 441):

- each member of the team receives the same cash sum;
- team bonuses are paid as a percentage of individual base pay;
- individual awards are based on individual appraisal ratings;
- non-cash recognition awards.

Clearly, the first of these takes an egalitarian approach, but is more likely to be used where members of the team are all on the same grade and hence closer together in terms of base pay levels. The second allows the differentials manifested in the grading system to be reflected in the team reward. The third approach allows individual performance ratings to be reflected in the distribution, but this may contradict the objective of creating team cohesion. Lawler (2000) suggests that organisations should be quite clear about what they are seeking to reward through team pay (shown in Figure 6.3).

The CIPD view is that team reward 'is a just and equitable way to acknowledge the contribution made by people as team members or individuals'. Nonetheless, the CIPD's own research has shown that team pay has been more 'talked up' than practised, and there are 'strong arguments against relying on team pay alone' (CIPD, 2007b).

SELF-ASSESSMENT EXERCISE

What are the perceived advantages and disadvantages of team- or group-based variable pay? In what environments have such schemes been found to work best?

Figure 6.3 Individual vs collective rewards

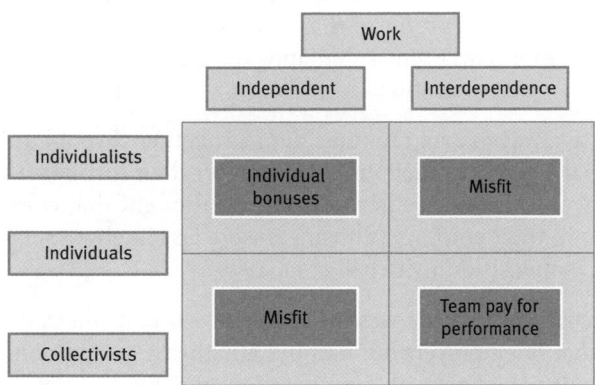

Source: Lawler (2000: 218)

COLLECTIVE SHORT-TERM REWARDS

Collective short-term rewards are those that apply at organisational level and normally deliver the reward within a year or less. Clearly, collective rewards are quite different from individual-based systems, and the decision to share the reward between employees, rather than target reward on individual performance, is normally based on the context and objectives of the organisation or workplace. Where organisations wish to encourage knowledge-sharing, co-operative behaviour and collaboration, collective rewards may be more appropriate than individual. They may also be more suited where the nature of the work or occupation means individual performance is difficult to measure or where intrinsic rewards may be more important.

Collective rewards are usually more acceptable to trade unions, because they are normally based on organisation-wide results, rather than individual, and may allow the reward to be subject to the collective bargaining process. Many productivity schemes of the 1960s and 1970s were based on such collective agreement. On the other hand, such collective rewards may also exist alongside individual (and team) rewards and, indeed, collaborative behaviour may be rewarded as part of an assessment of individual performance.

There are two main forms of short-term collective reward: profit-sharing and gain-sharing.

PROFIT-SHARING

Profit sharing has a long history, the earliest examples appearing in the mid-nineteenth century. A key objective was to establish social harmony to overcome the conflict between capital and labour that emerged with the industrial revolution. One solution suggested was worker ownership through co-operatives, but a more popular device was to encourage employers to provide workers with a share of the profits of the business. Financial participation was seen as a useful response to unions' demands for a role in management decision-making through co-determination.

A second objective was to avoid unionisation altogether through binding workers' financial interest to their employer, rather than through a trade union. A third objective was to improve efficiency – it was thought that workers who had a financial stake in their employer's business were less likely to shirk, therefore economising on supervision (Mitchell *et al*, 1990).

Under profit-sharing schemes it was thought that workers' interest would converge with that of employers but without any threat to ownership. Interestingly, Taylor, the father of scientific management, did not support profit-sharing as a pay system, believing it was too far removed from the worker to provide an incentive.

Interest in profit-sharing increased during from the First World War through to the Second World War, but it then waned until the 1980s. Martin Weitzman (Weitzman, 1984; Weitzman and Kruse, 1990), the American economist, became a major proponent of such payment systems in the USA in the 1980s. Weitzman argued that, where companies adopt profit-sharing, changes in product demand would be met by adjustments in pay and not through job losses (although this premise was based on the idea that the profit share would form part of base pay, rather than paid on top of base pay). He argued from research evidence at the level of the firm that there was a clear link between profit-sharing firms and higher productivity.

Profit-sharing is also common in many other developed countries, not least Japan. In the UK, in the 1980s and 1990s, the Conservative government also encouraged profit-sharing and share ownership as key to reducing labour market rigidity and improving flexible working. In order to encourage such financial participation schemes it passed legislation offering tax advantages to such schemes. The main vehicle to encourage profit-sharing was cash-based Profit Related Pay. By 1997 some 14,500 schemes were active, but the loss of income tax that resulted led in time to a reversal of government policy, with no further tax relief available after 2000. There was little evidence of any benefit from the scheme in terms of employment or wage flexibility (Hyman, 2000). This again perhaps demonstrates the problem of unintended consequences in adopting ill-conceived variable pay systems.

According to Armstrong and Murlis (2007), the objectives for profit-sharing include the closer identification of employees with their employer through a common concern for its progress and as a means to raising employee interest and understanding of the firm's business. These authors also see profit-sharing as a means to better co-operation between management and employees, with employers demonstrating their goodwill in concrete terms.

Types of scheme

There are two main types of profit-sharing schemes: cash schemes and stock schemes. Under a cash scheme a proportion of profits is paid direct to employees, whereas under a stock scheme a proportion of profits is paid as shares in the company. The most common form is the cash scheme.

Most profit-sharing schemes are open to all employees, although there is often a service requirement before the employee becomes eligible. The 2004 WERS (Kersley *et al*, 2006) found that in two-thirds of cases the profit-related pay scheme covered non-managerial employees, but in a minority of schemes membership was limited to management.

Three main approaches to calculating the share of profits have been identified (Armstrong and Murlis, 2007):

- A fixed percentage of profit based on a predetermined formula.
- The amount of profit share is determined at the discretion of the board of the organisation.
- A combination of the first and second approaches. A profit threshhold is fixed below which no payment is made, and maximum limits placed on the proportion of profits to be distributed.

A fourth method is for payments to be 'smoothed'. Under this arrangement, the formula produces an annual sum that is then added to the profit share pool. A fixed proportion is then distributed, with the balance carried forward to future years. This enables the scheme to pay out similar amounts each year, irrespective of the actual annual profit. Of course, this method may well defeat the purpose of linking the reward to company performance, and might not really be considered a short-term reward but rather a retention or goodwill measure.

The 2004 WERS (Kersley *et al*, 2006) found that in nearly half of the cases (48 per cent of workplaces) where profit-related pay was present, some measure of workplace profits was used, whereas in 40 per cent an organisation-based measure was used. In 8 per cent of workplaces profits were calculated at divisional or subsidiary level.

There are several mechanisms for distributing the profit shares: as a proportion of base pay with no increment for service; as a proportion of earnings with the reward linked to service; or in proportion to pay and some measure of individual performance, although this is uncommon. The percentage of pay paid out can vary between 2 and 20 per cent or more but, according to Armstrong and Murlis (2007), ideally the share should be between 5 and 10 per cent; this is meaningful but at the same time will not build up too much reliance on the payment.

Incidence of profit-sharing

The 2004 WERS (Kersley *et al*, 2006) found that 30 per cent of workplaces had some employees in receipt of profit-related payments or profit-related bonuses. The results from the trading sector, where profit is more likely to be found, indicate higher proportions. In the trading sector, 36 per cent of private sector and 15 per cent of public sector workplaces had such payments. The sectors with the highest incidence of profit-related payments were financial services (67 per cent of workplaces) and electricity, gas and water (59 per cent). Foreign-owned workplaces were more likely to have such payments than UK-owned. Profit-related pay did not seem to correlate with organisational size, but it was less common in unionised workplaces. In private services, however, it was more likely to be found in unionised workplaces than non-unionised. There was also a clear linkage between profit-related pay and product market competition, with those organisations facing very high competition most likely to have such schemes. Comparing the 2004 WERS data with the 1998 survey, there appears to have been little change in the take-up of profit-related pay.

The effects of profit-sharing

There is as yet little academic consensus on the effectiveness of profit-sharing, despite a large volume of research having been conducted. A study of the effects of profit-sharing on employee attitudes conducted for the UK Department of Employment in 1986 (Poole and Jenkins, 1990) found clear evidence of a link between such schemes and a positive set of attitudes in employees on a wide range of aspects of company policy. Similarly, research by Coyle-Shapiro *et al* (2002) found that favourable perceptions of profit-sharing served to increase organisational commitment. But other research (eg Blanchflower and Oswald, 1986, 1998) established no significant link between business performance and firms with profit-sharing schemes.

GAIN-SHARING

Gain-sharing is a form of collective short-term reward whereby the organisation seeks to share the financial benefits of any improvement in productivity or performance with its workforce. Gain-sharing differs from profit-sharing in that the latter is based on a wide range of factors that contribute to improved profitability (such as depreciation, tax and bad debt expenses), many of which the individual employee will have little control over. In contrast, the factors used in gain-sharing are likely to be more limited and be much more closely linked to employee ability to affect outcomes.

Gain-sharing plans have four defining features (Shields, 2007: 421): a focus on measurable results that are within the employees' collective control; the specification of a historical baseline of financial performance against which subsequent gains can be measured; the use of a predetermined formula for sharing the monetary gains between the organisation and participating employees; and a formal system for employees to make suggestions and decisions about ways to improve performance. Many schemes are therefore designed, implemented and administered by joint committees of workers and managers. Armstrong and Murlis (2007) argue that fundamental to gain-sharing is a sense of ownership and involvement in the scheme by the workforce. Good communications are therefore essential.

Gain-sharing is well established in the USA. There are two main types of gain-sharing plan – traditional single-factor schemes and multi-factor schemes. Traditional single-factor schemes focus on a single issue (such as labour cost reductions or productivity improvements) and are usually self-financing. In other words, the monetary gain is generated from efficiency savings. The second type, multi-factor schemes, combines a number of measures such as sales value, productivity and savings on material wastage. Such schemes can also include non-financial measures, for example, customer satisfaction or improved safety compliance, although the inclusion of factors like these rather negates the concept that the reward has to be generated from direct monetary savings.

The three traditional gain-sharing plans are the Scanlon Plan, the Rucker Plan and Improshare (Shields, 2007). The Scanlon Plan measures employment costs as a proportion of total sales. The Rucker Plan is similar in measuring employment costs against sales, but less the costs of materials and supplies. The rationale for this is that it measures 'value added' by employees and that materials and supply costs are independent variables over which the employees have no control. Improshare is based on an established standard that defines the expected hours needed to produce an acceptable level of output, based on work-measurement techniques. Any savings from the achievement of greater output in fewer hours is then shared between the firm and its employees according to a predetermined formula. Payments are made on a monthly, quarterly or annual basis.

The advantages of gain-sharing are that rewards are closely related to monetary gains that employees can directly influence. Such schemes may also improve employee commitment and reduce supervision needs. The fact that they are usually jointly administered means that they fit well with a unionised environment. The research evidence on the effects of gain-sharing is quite positive (see Shields, 2007 for a review of the evidence).

A variant of gain-sharing is goal-sharing, whereby a set of goals is established against which collective performance is measured and a monetary reward attached to the outcomes. A series of goals is set and a predetermined amount is paid for each goal achieved. In a sense, this is simply a collective form of the individual results-based incentive scheme. It is different from gain-sharing, however, in that payments are linked to future targets rather than based on benchmark historical data. Payments can be flat-rate or there may be a scale of payment according to how well the target is achieved. Such schemes, like gain-sharing, usually pay out on a monthly, quarterly or annual basis. But, unlike gain-sharing, which relies on any rewards being self-financing, the money for goal-sharing schemes has to be found from other sources.

 SELF-ASSESSMENT EXERCISE

What are the major forms of short-term collective variable pay? Consider each in turn and weigh the advantages and disadvantages of such schemes in relation to your own organisation or sector.

COLLECTIVE LONG-TERM REWARDS

Collective long-term rewards are those that reward organisational performance but where the receipt of the reward takes longer than 12 months (Shields, 2007). The main form of collective long-term reward is the employee share ownership scheme where workers own shares in their employing organisations. Such schemes usually provide shares in one of two ways: either employees are given shares in their company, or they purchase shares over time from their own funds or through a fund established by the company. In the USA such schemes are more likely to be known as stock option schemes.

Share option schemes have many of the same objectives as profit-sharing or gain-sharing schemes, and are also a form of employee financial participation. They therefore reflect the principles of agency theory in attempting to bring into alignment the aims of the principal (the organisation) and the agent (the worker). Under the share option approach, however, workers actually take a stake in the ownership of their employing organisation. In such schemes employees have a personal financial investment that is missing from most profit-sharing or gain-sharing schemes. Whereas a profit-share scheme may yield nothing in a year when the organisation has a poor performance, a disastrous fall in the share price may well wipe out any accumulated gain for the employee. The reward is therefore much more 'at risk' than short-term collective payments.

As Hyman (2000: 180) indicates, both supporters and critics of share employee share schemes tend to adopt similar arguments but from opposing perspectives. The first is that employee share schemes offer property rights to participants. For supporters this is seen as a device to encourage popular belief in capitalism, while critics see the schemes as obscuring the true nature of the relationship between capital and labour in society by creating a 'false consciousness' among workers.

The second argument is that the property nexus positively influences the behaviour of the employee towards the organisation, reinforcing identification with the employer's interest and loosening collectivist ideology. For the employers the associated benefits are assumed to be greater organisational commitment; easier recruitment of scarce staff; and better retention of employees through the fact that full tax-free benefits only accrue to employees after a qualifying period.

The third argument is that there is unilateral management control over the scheme (as opposed to profit-sharing and gain-sharing, where there is more likely to be joint control by managers and workers).

The advantages of such schemes to employees listed by the CIPD (CIPD, 2007) include the fact that, as shareholders, employees will gain a better understanding of the company's performance and directly benefit from any success (especially where the shares are provide free). Such schemes also provide a tax-efficient method of saving and an income from dividends or capital gains if the shares are sold.

In contrast, the disadvantages are that the employees become financially dependent on their employer – if the company closes down they may not only lose their jobs but the value of their savings as well. The CIPD gives the example of the firm Marconi, where employees facing redundancy in 2001 also saw the value of their shares fall by 97 per cent over the previous 12 months. Such schemes also require a reasonable length of service to see any real benefit, so employees who leave after a few years' service may not see any benefit. Such schemes may not therefore be appropriate where there is high turnover of staff.

Hubbick (2001: 3) argues that 'the performance of companies that have made a public commitment to employee ownership and to being employee-owned companies can … be demonstrated at a high level'.

A review of the research evidence (Hyman, 2008) also generally reports positive effects of employee share ownership on company performance. Cable and Wilson (1989), in a study of UK engineering firms, found enhanced productivity associated with such schemes, while Conyon and Freeman (2004) also found positive productivity effects, especially for share option schemes. Another study (Richardson and Nejad, 1986) found that movements in share prices are higher where employee share schemes are present.

However, as Hyman (2008) points out, there are issues of causality – we cannot be sure that employee share ownership is the key variable to explain the success of the enterprise. It may also be that successful firms are more likely to introduce such schemes than less successful – because they can afford to. Hyman also makes the point that few studies have been conducted on the effects of failing performance on employee ownership schemes. There is also little evidence that employee attitudes and behaviour are affected by such schemes. Numerous studies have failed to find any a causal linkage between share ownership, employee attitudes and behaviour and organisational performance (McHugh *et al*, 2005, cited in Hyman, 2008).

Evidence also indicates that the value of shares owned by employees does not tend to be high and that they are not retained for long periods (Hyman, 2008). This might suggest that the use of such schemes to build employee loyalty might be misconceived and that employees take a much more instrumental attitude towards such rewards. The small relative value of the shares may mean that employees see them as a form of bonus or gratuity rather than creating a sense of co-ownership of the enterprise. There is also a view that such schemes provide rewards so distant from individual employee performance that they serve no real incentive value. The size of worker share holdings is also probably insufficient to give them any real participative role in the firm's governance.

Pendleton *et al* (1998) found that employee commitment only increased where significant portions of equity were transferred to employees and some control over the enterprise passed to employee representatives.

INCIDENCE OF EMPLOYEE SHARE SCHEMES

The 2004 WERS (Kersley *et al*, 2006) found that 21 per cent of workplaces had some form of employee share ownership scheme. The most common type was the SAYE scheme (13 per cent of workplaces), followed by SIPs (8 per cent) and CSOPs (6 per cent). Another 4 per cent operated some other form of share ownership scheme. Where employee share ownership schemes operated, eligibility extended to non-managerial staff in 85 per cent of cases. Moreover, in 76 per cent of cases all categories of staff were eligible to join the scheme. Participation rates by workers in such schemes appear to be high: there were 100 per cent participation rates in 44 per cent of those workplaces where the schemes were open to all employees; in a further two-thirds (67 per cent) participation rates were at least 40 per cent.

Size of workplace was a major factor in whether or not an employee share ownership scheme was offered by the employer. Of those organisations with at least 250 employees, 44 per cent offered a scheme, and over three-fifths of the largest organisations (with 10,000 or more employees) had such schemes. They were more likely to be found in private services workplaces than manufacturing, and were most common in financial services, where over 80 per cent of establishments offered such schemes. Workplaces with such schemes were also more likely to be foreign-owned, and there was a strong correlation with workplaces where business competition was very high.

It is interesting to note that, despite the criticism of share ownership schemes as a mechanism to undermine collective organisation, the 2004 WERS found that workplaces with recognised trades unions were three times more likely to have such schemes than those without. This is partly explained by the size factor – such schemes are much more likely to be found in larger workplaces where unions are more common. WERS 2004 also found that there had been little change in the incidence of employee share ownership between the 1998 and 2004 surveys.

BOX 6.3 TYPES OF SHARE SCHEME

ISSUES IN REWARD

In the UK there are currently four types of employee share scheme:

• Share Incentive Plans (SIPs);

• savings-related schemes (also known as Save-as-you-earn (SAYE) or ShareSave schemes);

• Enterprise Management Incentives (EMI);

• Company Share Option Plans (CSOPs).

According to the HMRC, at April 2006 the following schemes had been approved: 830 SIPs, 960 SAYE schemes, 6,880 EMI schemes and 3,030 CSOPs.

This chapter concentrates on all-employee schemes. See Chapter 10 for executive share schemes.

SHARE INCENTIVE PLANS (SIPS)

Share Incentive Plans (SIPs) were introduced in the Finance Act 2000 and replaced the former AESOP (all-employee share ownership plan), which in turn replaced the old Profit-Related Pay scheme. The SIP is a 'tax-advantaged, all-employee scheme that gives employees the opportunity to own shares in the company they work for' (IDS, 2007c: 2). Four types of plan are available: free shares (up to £3,000 a year per employee); partnership shares (employees can use up to £1,500 a year to buy shares from gross salary); matching shares (a maximum ratio of two free shares for each partnership share purchased); and dividend shares (up to £1,500 a year may be invested in the plan as dividend shares). A survey by IFS Proshare found that 88 per cent of firms offered partnership shares, 51 per cent dividend shares, 49 per cent matching shares and 23 per cent free shares (CIPD, 2007d).

The SIPS must be set up under a trust that holds the shares for the participating employees. Shares must be offered to all employees who are eligible under the legislation, including part-time employees. A qualifying period of service can, however, apply.

SAVINGS-RELATED SCHEMES

Savings-related schemes, better known perhaps as SAYE or ShareSave schemes, were introduced under the Finance 1980 as all-employee share schemes and allow employees to be granted an option to buy shares in their employer's company at a fixed price. These shares can be purchased through amounts set aside under an SAYE contract. The price of the shares is set by the market price at the date of the grant and may be discounted by up to 20 per cent (IDS, 2005).

Employers can offer options that can be exercised in three, five or seven years from the date of grant. A tax-free bonus is paid at the end of the savings contract, when the employee has the choice of whether or not to purchase the shares. If the share price is below the exercise price, the employee can choose to keep the savings and tax-free bonus. If the employee takes the share option, they are subject to capital gains tax but they may transfer shares to a spouse or to an ISA to shelter the capital gain. There is a minimum savings amount of £5 a month and a maximum of £250 a month.

ENTERPRISE MANAGEMENT INCENTIVES (EMIS)

Enterprise Management Incentives (EMIs) were introduced under the Finance Act 2000 with the aim of encouraging small independent firms to utilise share ownership as a means to attract, retain and reward their staff. EMIs do not require HMRC approval in advance, although unlisted firms must submit a share valuation. The scheme exempts gains from NI contributions and capital gains tax, rather than giving tax relief.

COMPANY SHARE OPTION PLANS (CSOPS)

Company share option plans (CSOPs) were introduced under the Finance Act 1996. Under this scheme employees are given a share option but not an obligation to buy a certain number of shares at a fixed price at a particular time. This type of scheme is mainly used for senior managers, although some employers offer the scheme to all employees. The aggregate value of all outstanding share options must not exceed £30,000 at the market value at the time of the grant.

UNAPPROVED SCHEMES

In addition to the HMRC approved schemes, there are many unapproved schemes (meaning they do not attract tax relief).

The CIPD viewpoint is that, although employee share schemes have become increasingly popular, opinion is divided on how effective they are in reaching their objectives.

 SELF-ASSESSMENT EXERCISE

What are the main forms of long-term collective forms of variable pay and what role do they play in the reward system?

KEY LEARNING POINTS AND CONCLUSIONS

This chapter has covered the range of 'variable pay' options. We discussed how the terminology can be confusing and how there are various terms used for these forms of reward. We explained that we have adopted the term 'variable pay' to denote all the alternative methods of paying employees by unconsolidated forms of contingent reward – either as an alternative to or as an addition to base pay. We also discussed the traditional divide between manual and non-manual workers' variable pay systems and how there have been countervailing trends in recent years. Pay for manual workers has increasingly moved away from individualised systems, such as piecework and work-measured schemes, towards more collective forms of reward, such as measured day work, team-based reward, profit-sharing and gain-sharing. A major reason for this shift in emphasis has been for employee relations reasons – employers were losing control of individualised reward systems – but it also reflects the economic and social changes in the workplace in recent times. The decline of manufacturing and changes in production methods have also driven these changes in payment systems.

In contrast, for non-manual workers there has been a strong shift towards more variable pay systems, with the traditional 'commission' payments made to sales staff being spread more widely to other groups of staff. There has also been a large growth in individual bonus schemes, especially in the financial services industry.

These observations reinforce the importance of context in designing such schemes. What may work in one environment or for one part of the workforce may not work for another.

We identified the various dimensions of variable pay – both in terms of individual, team or collective rewards and in terms of short-term or long-term focus. As we discussed, there have been recent moves away from individualised forms of variable pay and towards team or other collective rewards. This change has reflected changes in context for organisations, with increasing emphasis on the need for teamwork, knowledge-sharing and quality improvement. Individual competitive behaviour may no longer be appropriate in many organisations, and hence individual forms of reward no longer work.

There has also been a growth in more long-term forms of reward. These new forms have often sought to increase employee engagement with business objectives rather than simply seeking to motivate them to increase productivity or profits. Several of these collective forms are more akin to employee participation exercises, where employees share financial ownership with the management, although such moves raise questions about employees' control over organisational strategy. Some research has indicated that such schemes work best where employees have a genuine voice in organisational strategy, rather than simply a financial stake in the organisation's future.

While some employers use only one form of variable pay, many are using several types at individual, team and organisational levels. Clearly, the consequences of using variable pay vary, and the research evidence provides both support and a critique for such practices.

CASE STUDY

TEAM REWARD AT BRITISH GAS

Service engineers at British Gas work in teams consisting of between 25 and 50 members. Since 1998, the company has operated a team reward scheme for these employees. Formed around six factors, the scheme is chiefly designed to recognise staff contribution towards business profitability and customer satisfaction. It also helps to promote a feeling of unity in field-based teams.

Preamble

British Gas – a subsidiary of Centrica – supplies gas, electricity and telecommunications services to residential customers throughout Great Britain. British Gas Home Service Operations (HSO) – the business unit responsible for service and installation – employs around 6,000 service engineers providing installation, maintenance and breakdown cover for over 4 million heating appliances.

Team composition

British Gas operates its HSO unit under a regional system for its servicing and breakdown engineers. This divides

Britain into six geographical areas, each of which is overseen by a general manager. These areas are split into a total of 19 regions, each of which has its own regional service manager. These regions are then further subdivided into a total of 144 'patches'. Each patch has its own team of service engineers and is managed by a service manager.

These teams can be one of two sizes: 'standard', where the team has around 25 engineers, or 'large', with a group of around 50. Whether a patch has a standard or large-sized team is determined by a number of factors, including the size of the patch, the number of customers it contains and the average workload.

In the patches where large teams are deployed, further assistance is often provided to the engineers in the form of operational support managers and an additional technical support engineer. The operational support managers are able to offer help with customer- or business-related issues, while the technical support engineers can be called upon whenever an engineer needs assistance.

These teams are field-based and are supported by six area service centres. The engineers are supplied with specially equipped vans, mobile phones and laptop computers. Each engineer works independently, going out to visit customers on his or her own.

Team management

The teams' service managers are responsible for all line management duties, including customer-facing issues, for improving business performance and for employee-related matters.

Staff rostering

Engineers' weekly working hours vary on a broadly seasonal basis. The average working week ranges from 33 hours in the summer to up to 43 hours in the winter. This variation reflects the increased demand for engineers during the colder months.

When rostering the team's weekly hours, the service manager must strike a balance between meeting the engineers' own preferences and ensuring that there will always be enough team members on duty to cover the incoming workload (which is highly variable owing to the prevailing weather conditions).

Communication

The vast majority of the service managers' day-to-day contact with their teams is conducted over the phone. Engineers receive their daily workload from their area's planning and deployment office throughout the day via their laptop.

Team briefs

Each team gets together once a month for a 'team brief'. A convenient, central venue is organised for these meetings, which typically last for around two hours. They provide the service manager with a chance to speak to the engineers and to discuss their general level of performance and any important business issues. Where pertinent, guest speakers will sometimes be invited to these events, and senior managers are required to attend. However, the meeting is intended to be a two-way process, with the engineers encouraged to raise any issues and ask any questions.

In addition to the regular team briefs, every engineer has a performance and development review with their service manager on a quarterly basis.

Intra-team communication

As the service engineers work almost exclusively on their own, there is little opportunity, other than at the team briefs, for face-to-face interaction between team members. Team spirit is fostered through other forms of communication, however. For instance, the service engineers at British Gas have their own audio newsletter, *BluePike*, which is mailed out to all team members on a regular basis. It features items such as interviews with senior managers, comments and ideas from other engineers and technical Q&As. In the future, British Gas is also seeking to make the company's intranet accessible via engineers' laptops.

In addition to expert systems on their laptops, service engineers also have access to a technical helpline, which they can phone if they come across a particularly difficult job.

New team members

After completing an extensive training period, focused primarily on learning the necessary technical knowledge to perform the job together with vital customer service skills, new engineers are accompanied by an experienced team member on their first few visits. This 'buddy process' is designed to give new employees the support they need when first undertaking work on their own in customers' homes.

Training

British Gas invests significant amounts of time and money in keeping its service engineers up to date with the latest technology and developments. It has six mobile training units that travel around the country, and the company has also invested in a number of new training centres nationwide.

Team reward

British Gas operates a well-established team reward system as an incentive for the workforce to achieve higher standards in terms of work quality and customer satisfaction, and to improve overall business performance.

It was introduced in 1998, following the company's move away from output-based bonus schemes and a depot-based structure to the current field-based operation. In each subsequent year, the scheme has been modified to reflect the changing nature of the company's goals and targets.

The rationale for a team-based approach

The service engineers at British Gas work independently and have little day-to-day contact with the other members of their team. Despite the individual nature of their work, however, the company adopted a team-based reward scheme rather than one based on individual performance. This approach helps to foster a supportive atmosphere within the group, together with a feeling of ownership of common goals. It also recognises the variability of the types of work and roles carried out by individual engineers.

Factors

The basic foundation of the team reward scheme is that it should be 'self-financing', that is, any rise in reward payments should be paid for from increased company performance. The reward paid to engineers is calculated against six factors:

- profitability of the team;
- customer satisfaction;
- business performance indicators;
- cost of materials used;
- business generation targets – best advice;
- reduced cancellation of new contract applications.

Profitability of the team

This is one of the key performance factors and measures how well the team as a whole has performed against budget. If a team is able to operate and organise itself so that it completes its workload more efficiently than expected, the company will make more profit; this is then reflected in the level of reward paid to the team's engineers.

Customer satisfaction

Another major element – and a key driver for the business as a whole – is customer satisfaction. This is measured through questionnaires, which are mailed out to customers following an engineer's visit. Many of the questions focus on the behaviour of the engineer, not just on the quality of the work completed. An analysis of the customers' responses results in a score for the team, which is then compared to its previous scores. Actual performance and any improvement in scores are rewarded, and thus the scheme recognises both outstanding teams and those that have made progress relative to previous performance.

Business performance indicators

This factor is based upon a matrix comprising six elements, such as number of jobs completed, number of recalls (jobs that were not completed satisfactorily and a second visit was required), the overall level of breakdowns and the availability of the engineers.

Cost of materials used

Related to the overall profitability of the team, this factor compares the cost of parts against a target price. Should the team meet the target, or beat it, then they will qualify for higher reward payments. This encourages good behaviour such as returning defective and warranty parts.

Business generation targets

British Gas as a business is growing and continues to seek new business opportunities. Its team of service

engineers is well placed to offer advice to customers about whether they may require a new boiler or if their central heating system could be improved.

The overall objective here is to provide the best advice for the customer's needs.

Targets

The actual targets set are determined independently for each of the teams, taking into account the make-up of their patch in terms of, for example, size, number of customers, average age of boilers and central heating systems. The rationale of setting the targets in this way is that all of the teams must achieve a comparable level of performance in order to meet them.

Keeping staff informed

Another important role for each team's service manager is to keep the engineers informed of how well they are performing in relation to their targets.

Service managers have access to centralised information offering an analysis of their team's performance in terms of each reward factor. They can also make comparisons with other teams to see whether performance in a certain area is low across the whole company or just within their own team.

Should their team be failing to hit targets in certain areas, it is the role of the service manager to investigate why this is happening and to introduce measures to address any problems, which may include adopting best practice from other teams. The monthly team brief offers the ideal opportunity to discuss any such difficulties.

Payments

Not all of the team reward payments can be taken as cash. Under a system known as QDOS, run for British Gas by Page & Moy, employees accumulate 'points' rather than cash in return for meeting and exceeding targets on the business generation and customer satisfaction factors. These points can then be exchanged for items such as high-street gift vouchers or catalogue purchases. They can also be exchanged for cash, although any amount converted from points in this way is non-pensionable.

Payment schedule

Payments for each factor are made at different intervals during the year:

When paid	Factor
Annually	Team profitability
Six-monthly	Cost of materials used
Quarterly	Customer satisfaction

Operating in this way allows regular payments to be made throughout the year, the aim being to incentivise the workforce to perform to a high standard at all times.

Customer and business factors contribute 80 per cent to the overall reward total, and business generation around 20 per cent. The average total reward paid out to engineers in 2002 was £1,600.

Non-financial rewards

In addition to the financial rewards available to engineers who perform well, Centrica (the parent group of the British Gas businesses) operates a group-wide 'excellence rewards' scheme. These are prestigious awards, recognised at board level, designed to acknowledge individuals or teams nominated by their colleagues as having gone beyond the call of duty in the course of their work.

Future developments

The total reward package for servicing and installation engineers at British Gas is currently under strategic review with the GMB trade union. The team reward element is likely to remain an integral part of the package but its exact components may well change, as the company further develops its business policies to meet customer and employee aspirations.

Case Study Questions

1 What is the rationale for team reward at British Gas?

2 What form does the team pay scheme take? What criteria are used to evaluate the team's performance?

3 How is team performance monitored and why is communication between the service manager and the team so important?

EXPLORE FURTHER

For a more detailed discussion of the various forms of variable pay, see Shields, J. (2007) *Managing Employee Performance and Reward. Concepts, practices, strategies*. Cambridge, Cambridge University Press.

For an up-to-date review of bonus schemes, see IDS (2007a) *Bonus Schemes*. IDS HR Studies 843. April. London, Incomes Data Services.

For practical guidance on bonus and incentive plans, see CIPD (2005) *Bonus and Incentive Plans. A development guide*. London, Chartered Institute of Personnel and Development.

For a review of current UK share schemes, see IDS (2007c) *Share Incentive Plans*. IDS HR Studies 840. February. London, Incomes Data Services.

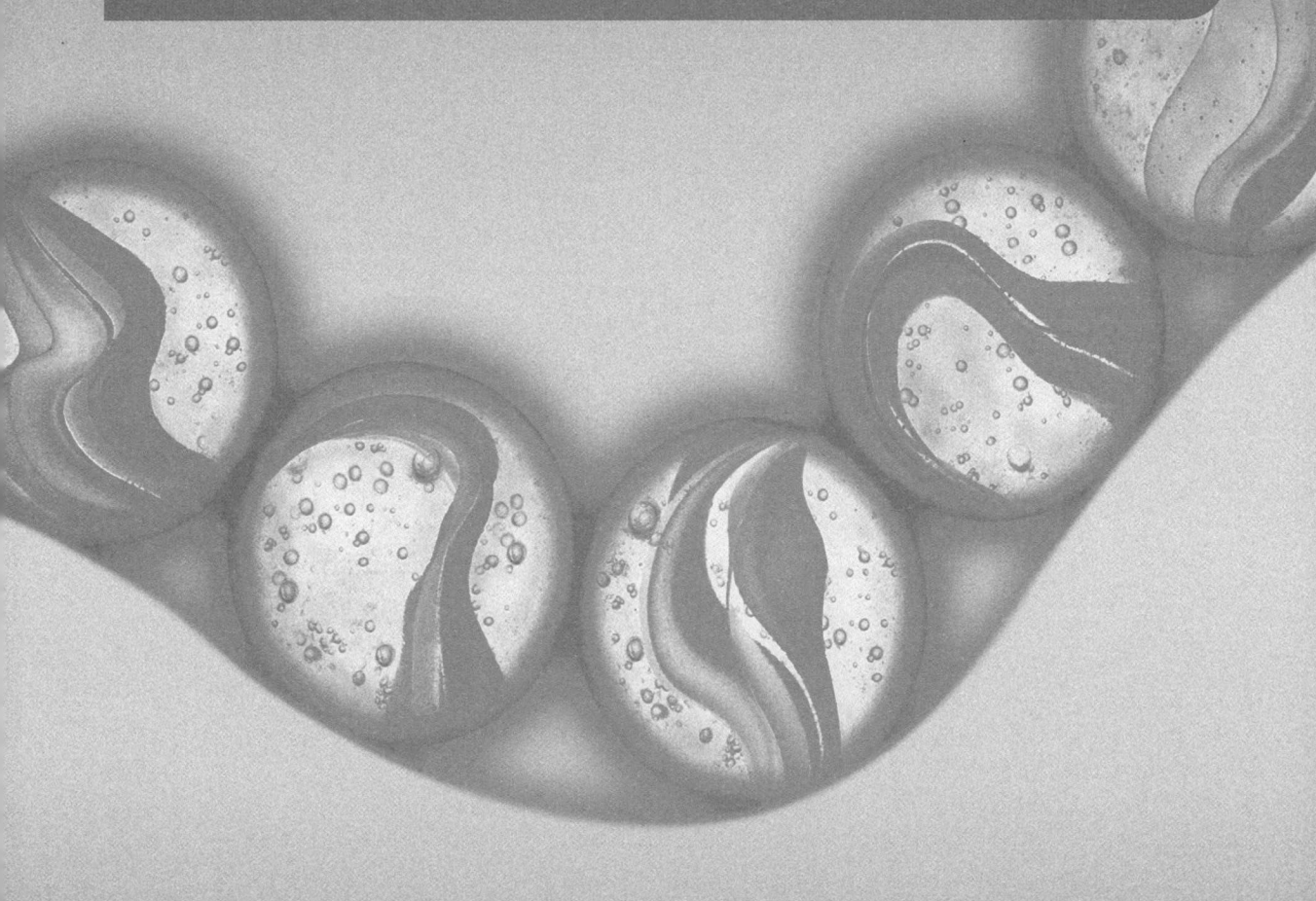

PART THREE

In Part Three we review principles, policies and frameworks for 'non-cash benefits', 'deferred remuneration, and 'intrinsic rewards'. Three chapters in this part cover, respectively non-cash employment benefits and their delivery, the increasingly contentious topic of pensions and its management, and the significant field of non-financial rewards, combining with cash remuneration, deferred compensation and material benefits under the rubric of 'total reward'.

CHAPTER 7

Benefits

CHAPTER OBJECTIVES

At the end of this chapter you should understand and be able to explain the following:

- The purpose of employee benefits within the reward system.
- The origins of and influences upon the provision of employee benefits.
- Benefits strategy and the role of tax and national insurance in the design of benefits.
- The various types of employee benefit and their different roles.
- Single Status and harmonisation.
- The major benefits provided.
- Flexible or 'cafeteria' benefits.
- Voluntary benefits.
- Salary sacrifice schemes.

CIPD STANDARDS COVERED IN THIS CHAPTER:

To be able to:

- Evaluate the case for flexible benefits.

To understand and explain:

- The basis upon which flexible benefit systems work.

Employee benefits (or 'conditions of service' or 'fringe benefits', as they are sometimes termed) are those additional parts of the remuneration package that are not cash pay. While these benefits may not be part of the monthly or weekly pay statement, they clearly have a cost to the employer and a value to the recipient. Smith (2000) estimates that employee benefits can comprise up to half the cost of the total remuneration package for some staff. In some cases, despite being seen as non-cash items, they are received in cash form (such as sick pay, maternity pay or redundancy pay). In the case of pensions, they are often viewed as a form of 'deferred remuneration' in that the employee saves part of his or her annual income towards a guaranteed future income when retired. We deal with pensions, which are of increasing importance within reward systems, in Chapter 8.

In this chapter, we consider first the current absence of both theory and research on employee benefits before proceeding to look at their historical growth and the contextual issues driving benefits provision. We then consider a number of typologies of benefits to enable some theoretical analysis before reviewing the decisions required of managers. We then consider three main categories of benefit: welfare, work-related and status. Finally, we consider three recent developments in benefit practice: flexible or 'cafeteria' benefits, voluntary benefits and salary sacrifice systems.

INTRODUCTION

The role of employee benefits within the reward system varies between countries. In some countries, such as the USA, the absence of a 'welfare state' has meant that employers have been expected to bear the burden of employee health care, whereas in many European countries the state plays a much more central role in the provision (and regulation) of benefits. Another key variable is the tax regime used in each country, which can affect the value of the benefit to both employer and employee.

While benefits have been a growing part of the remuneration package in the UK since the Second World War, there have been some significant developments in recent years, especially in the provision of pensions and so-called 'family-friendly' benefits. Both developments reflect wider changes in society. There has also been increasing employer concern about the escalating costs of such benefits (especially, but not solely, in the USA) and a perception that employees do not recognise the value of what is on offer and take such benefits for granted. This in turn has led to both a 'budget' approach to benefits based on the concepts of flexibility and choice and to an increasing emphasis on the 'total remuneration' concept (see Chapter 9), where employers talk about the value of the whole pay and benefits package.

This has shifted the rationale of many employers' benefits policies from an emphasis on the welfare 'safety net' nature of the benefit to an emphasis on the 'value for money' approach. Increasingly employers are seeking to discover whether benefits can play a more strategic role in wider human resource policy, such as recruitment, retention, motivation and performance. On the other hand, legislation is also playing an increasing role in defining both the content and the boundaries for employee benefits.

'Employee benefits or "fringe benefits" form part of remuneration and consist of a broad range of special payments or benefits in kind. ... An important function of benefits is to provide for employee security in the event of disruption to regular earnings, while in other cases benefits may confer status or serve as an aid to recruitment and retention.'

Heery and Noon (2001)

AN ABSENCE OF THEORY

Many employers view benefits as a key part of the employment contract, and a number of objectives are often mentioned as the explanation. For example, Armstrong and Murlis (2007) argue that: benefits increase commitment; provide for the actual or perceived personal needs of employees; demonstrate a 'good employer' image; attract and retain staff; and provide a tax-efficient method of remunerating staff. Unfortunately, unlike some other components in the reward system, there has been very little research or development of theory concerning benefits. In most cases, we simply do not know if benefits work or not.

As Milkovich and Newman (2008) point out, there are no clear answers to the questions of whether effective benefit management contributes to organisational effectiveness and performance or whether benefits impact upon an organisation's ability to attract, retain and motivate employees. They say that a 'similar lack of research surrounds each of the other potential payoffs to a sound benefits programme' (Milkovich and Newman, 2008: 399). Employer strategy in the past has been largely reactive, either to particular labour market pressures or to legislative requirements.

The only clear issue is that benefits account for an increasing proportion of the total payroll, rising in the USA from 25 per cent in 1959 to 40 per cent in 2004 (US Chamber of Commerce Annual Benefit Surveys, cited in Milkovich and Newman, 2008: 405). Over the period from 1955 to 1975, employee benefit costs in the USA rose at a rate almost four times greater than employee wages or the consumer price index, largely driven by the costs of healthcare and pensions (Milkovich and Newman, 2008: 405). Overall non-wage costs account for between 15 and 40 per cent of total labour costs in OECD countries (OECD, 1997, cited in Wright, 2008). The CIPD reports that the median cost to employers for their benefits is 15 per cent of the pay bill, within an inter-quartile range of 10–24 per cent. From a survey of 522 employers, Thomson-on-line (2007) reports that some 45 per cent of employers did not know how much their benefits were as a proportion of the pay bill.

Wright (2008) suggests two theoretical perspectives for benefits policy, economic and psychological. Forth and Millward (2000) indicate that, from the economic perspective, some employers may choose to provide more generous benefits to compensate for lower base pay and earnings levels. This is partly confirmed by the fact that many public service employers provide more generous benefits than their private sector competitors in the labour market to compensate for less competitive salaries for similar jobs. On the other hand, research has found that benefits tend to be better in higher-paying organisations than lower-paying (Dale-Olsen, 2005). In other words, the entire pay package is pitched at a more competitive level.

Research has also shown that low-paid workers are likely to have fewer and less generous benefits than the higher-paid (Forth and Millward, 2000; Green *et al*, 1985; White *et al*, 2007). Forth and Millward (2000: 50) suggest that efficiency wage theory (see Chapter 2) may also be of relevance. Better benefits and higher wages may go together as part of a policy to elicit worker loyalty and effort. Or it may be a result of unions pressing for benefits as well as higher wages. Forth and Millward comment that, in representing the preferences of their typical members, unions tend to favour the preferences of older, relatively permanent workers who have a greater desire for fringe benefits, especially those that increase with service.

Barringer and Milkovich (1998) suggest that institutional theory, resource dependency theory, agency theory and transaction cost theory might all be useful avenues to explore the effects of benefits on employee behaviour (see Chapter 2 for explanations of these theories), but that as yet there has been little attempt to explore the field using such theory. Milkovich and Newman (2008) refer to two US studies that support the view that benefits reduce the mobility of staff (Mitchell, 1982; Schiller and Weiss, 1979). But more detailed studies (Even and Macpherson, 1996; Mitchell, 1983) found that in reality this was due to just two benefits: pensions and health care. Virtually no other benefit has been found to influence rates of turnover. There is also little research evidence to date to support the view that benefits contribute to improving employee performance and hence the company 'bottom line'. There is, however, some indication that employers who provide work/life balance benefits have experienced improved productivity (Lambert, 2000).

In terms of psychological theory, Cole and Flint (2003) use organisational justice theory to investigate employee perception of flexible benefits compared to traditional benefits systems. Through testing the self-interest and relational models of organisational justice, they found that employees with flexible benefits systems had significantly higher perceptions of procedural justice than those in traditional systems, although there were no significant differences in perceptions of distributive justice between the two plan types. The effect of benefits on employee satisfaction might also be an avenue for research, although currently in the USA only 32 per cent of workers appear to be satisfied with their benefits plans (Bates, 2004, cited in Milkovich and Newman, 2008: 417). One reason for this might be the recent reduction in benefits as organisations seek to cut costs (Dreher *et al*, 1988, cited in Milkovich and Newman, 2008: 417).

SELF-ASSESSMENT EXERCISE

To what extent do employee benefits motivate staff or are they just tools to recruit and retain staff? If you think they do, which benefits would motivate you to higher performance?

THE GROWTH OF EMPLOYEE BENEFITS

The provision of employee benefits began in the nineteenth century in the UK. While pensions were provided for army and naval officers and for civil servants from an early date, the development of welfare provision in the workplace went hand in hand with the development of the personnel function in the final decades of the century. It was enlightened employers such as the Rowntree family, Cadbury and Lever Brothers who were the first to develop on-site healthcare facilities, sick pay, subsidised meals and housing. The provision of such benefits was partly driven by philanthropic motives and partly by the view that such welfare benefits would yield a healthier and hence more productive workforce. They were also seen as important elements in employer strategies to resist trade union organisation in their workplaces.

Pensions began in the 'poor relief' established in the reign of Richard II (Smith, 2000: 154) and were developed in the nineteenth century through the provision of insurance benefits through friendly societies and some trade unions. Working men's societies also played an important role in supporting aged and disabled workers no longer capable of working. One, the Northumberland and Durham Miners' Permanent Relief Society, was paying significant pension benefit to 4,000 workers by 1901 (Hewitt Associates, 1991).

The company pension began in the second half of the nineteenth century, with schemes being established for clerical staff in the civil service, banking and the railway companies. State provision began in 1908 under Asquith's Liberal government with the first state pension scheme. This was improved in 1925, when for the first time the poorest two-thirds of the UK population were able to contribute and draw a guaranteed pension on retirement. The establishment of trust law to govern the administration of such schemes, and the introduction of tax relief on pension contributions in 1921, encouraged many larger employers to establish schemes. This development was given further impetus following the industrial conflict between employers and unions of the 1920s, when employers sought to insulate themselves from union organisation through adopting more humane conditions for workers.

It was not, however, until the election of a Labour government following the Second World War in 1945 that the 1946 National Insurance Act introduced a universal contributory state pension for all citizens.

State sickness benefit, paid to workers unfit for work through accident or ill health, had been introduced through the National Insurance Act of 1911, but paid maternity leave did not arrive until the 1975 Employment Protection

Act. Paid holidays were rare until the Holidays with Pay Act 1938, which gave workers covered by collective agreements and wages boards the right to holidays. The growth of holiday entitlement followed the spread of collective bargaining between employers and unions, and holiday entitlements were incorporated into collective agreements. It was not until the 1998 Working Time Regulations, however, that for the first time there was a statutory holiday entitlement for all workers in the UK (20 days per year).

As this short history of the development of benefits shows, the growth in the range of employer-provided benefits has largely been driven by responses to external initiatives. Growth in both the range and level of benefits provided has been strong since the 1960s. Between 1964 and 1981 benefits in UK manufacturing industry increased from 11 per cent of average pre-tax remuneration to 19 per cent (Green *et al*, 1985). As Smith (2000: 166) indicates:

> *uneven distribution of these benefits – with high-paid employees receiving absolutely and proportionately much more than the low-paid – has been a consistent characteristic for decades. Until the 1970s the provision of benefits to manual workers was unusual, apart from annual holiday entitlement and some compensatory payments (i.e. for travel and subsistence).*

Several factors have changed this situation. In the USA, Milkovich and Newman (2008) identify five factors: wage and price controls; labour unions; employer initiatives; cost-effectiveness; and government policy.

First, during both the Second World War and the Korean War, the federal government's strict wage and price controls allowed more latitude in benefits provision than base pay and earnings. Both employers and unions therefore sought to introduce new or enhanced benefits to satisfy workers' demands. This led to a growth in pensions, health care and a broad spectrum of welfare benefits not available before 1950.

Secondly, the growing power of the labour unions following the 1935 Wagner Act generated demands for pensions, supplementary unemployment benefit and improved holiday entitlement.

Thirdly, employers' increasing realisation that there was a linkage between a healthy workforce and productivity led to the growth of rest periods, leave and medical services in the workplace. There was also a perceived need to create a climate in which employees believed that management was genuinely concerned for their welfare, not least as part of a defence against union organisation.

Fourthly, there was an increasing awareness of the cost-effectiveness of benefits. This related to two cost advantages. The first is that most benefits are not taxable in the USA, so provision of a benefit rather than the equivalent in salary avoids federal and state income tax. A second advantage is that group-base benefits (such as life, health and legal insurance) can be purchased more cheaply through group discounts than could easily be achieved by individual employees.

Lastly, the introduction of three mandatory benefits by the US government – workers' compensation, unemployment insurance and social security – increased pressure on employers to improve benefits.

In the UK, as we have seen above, there were similar developments to those in the USA. Smith (2000) argues that there were two key developments in the UK. The first was the passing of the 1975 Social Security Pensions Act, which allowed employers and employees to 'contract out' of the state secondary pension and join employers' schemes. The second was the repeal of the Truck Acts in 1986, which abolished the right of manual workers to be paid 'cash in hand' and allowed employers to pay them by credit transfer arrangements. This in turn led to manual workers moving on to salary systems and paved the way for the 'harmonisation' of their benefits with other staff.

In the 1980s, there was a big growth in the range of benefits provided as employers sought to profit from the tax advantages of providing certain benefits as opposed to the cash alternative (eg company cars). A large industry of benefits consultants developed to advise employers on how best to use the tax and National Insurance rules to their advantage. In the 1990s, these tax and National Insurance loopholes began to be closed by the UK government and the emphasis shifted to cost containment. While there are still avenues to explore in terms of 'tax efficiency', some employers today have cut back their entitlement to a range of core benefits and prefer to emphasise the cash part of the total reward package, especially where large bonuses are available.

The Hay Survey of Employee Benefits, which has been charting benefit trends for over 30 years, has recently shown a decline in defined benefit pensions schemes (see Chapter 8), a big rise in the number of organisations offering childcare, and a fall in the level at which company cars are provided (ie more staff are eligible) (cited in Armstrong and Murlis, 2007: 470). There are also indications of a continuing simplification of benefits packages, increased emphasis on individual employee choice, and further attention to improving communication of the value of the benefits on offer to employees.

The 2004 WERS found that while the pay advantage of unionised employees over non-unionised had fallen in recent years, there continues to be a benefits premium among employees who are represented by a union (Kersley *et al*, 2006: 199). Core employees in unionised workplaces were significantly more likely to be entitled to an employer pension scheme and to have more than statutory entitlement to paid annual leave and sick pay, both in the whole economy and in the private sector. Employees in non-union workplaces were slightly more likely to have a company car and be entitled to private health insurance.

 SELF-ASSESSMENT EXERCISE

Why do you think unionised organisations have better benefits than non-union?

TYPOLOGIES OF EMPLOYEE BENEFITS

As mentioned above, there is now a wide range of benefits provided to employees by employers. The major ones are listed in Table 7.1 below. But different benefits have different organisational objectives:

- some are required by law (eg minimum holiday entitlement, statutory sick pay);

- some are provided to compensate employees for expenditure incurred in the performance of their work or to assist in that work, often known as 'expenses' (eg travel and subsistence expenses, essential user company cars or vans);

- some are welfare benefits designed to retain employees or to create an image of a caring employer; and

- some are 'status' benefits provided as 'perks' to retain and incentivise more senior staff (e.g. non-essential user company cars).

Table 7.1 The major types of benefit

Sick pay	Personal accident insurance
Holidays	Travel and subsistence
Private health care	Personal accident insurance
Life assurance	Permanent health (long-term sickness) insurance
Maternity leave	Season ticket loans
Paternity leave	Discounts on company goods or services
Compassionate leave	Sports or social club membership
Pensions or 'superannuation'	Subsidised canteen or luncheon vouchers.
Childcare vouchers	Health screening
Counselling (career, financial or personal)	Above statutory redundancy pay
Subsidised mortgages	Company loans (eg for computers)
Relocation expenses	Company car
Long-term disability/permanent health insurance	Car mileage allowance
Parental leave	Sabbaticals
Adoption leave	Pre-retirement planning
Career breaks	Early retirement options
Training and education fees	Company credit cards
Time off work for public duties, trade union duties etc	Work clothing allowances and laundering

Table 7.2 Typologies for categorising benefits

Author(s)	Typology
Armstrong and Murlis (2007)	• 7 categories:
	• pensions
	• personal security (eg health insurance and redundancy or life insurance)
	• financial assistance (eg loans, relocation expenses)
	• personal needs (eg holidays, childcare, retirement counselling)
	• company cars and petrol
	• other benefits (eg subsidised workplace restaurants or meal vouchers and gym membership)
	• intangible benefits (eg pleasant working environment; easy access to transport and shops).
Hume (1995)	3 categories:
	• financial security (pensions, life assurance, personal accident insurance, above statutory sick pay, private health insurance, above statutory redundancy pay)
	• financial assistance (subsidised mortgages, company loans, relocation expenses, company cars)
	• personal needs (annual leave, maternity/paternity leave, career breaks and sabbaticals, counselling, medical services, childcare, subsidised catering, sports and social facilities, clothing/laundry services, training and education.
Smith (1983)	3 categories:
	• security (eg pensions, sick pay, life insurance)
	• goodwill (eg holidays, early retirement, relocation)
	• performance (eg company cars, health insurance).
Wright (2004)	4 categories:
	• personal security and health (eg pensions, above-statutory sick pay)
	• job, status and seniority-related (eg cars, holidays above statutory minimum)
	• family-friendly (eg childcare, elder care, above statutory maternity/paternity leave)
	• social or 'goodwill' or lifestyle benefits (eg subsidised catering, sports/social facilities).

In some cases it is not easy to classify the purpose of a benefit easily. For example, private healthcare can be seen as both a 'welfare' benefit and a 'status' benefit as it is usually only available to higher-paid employees. Similarly, a company car might be seen as essential in some cases (such as mobile sales staff and maintenance engineers) but as a 'status' benefit where it is non-essential to carry out the job.

There have been a number of attempts to create a typology of benefits (see Table 7.2 above). For example, Armstrong and Murlis (2007) suggest benefits can be divided into seven categories: pensions schemes; personal security; financial assistance; personal needs; company cars and fuel; 'other benefits'; and intangible benefits. This appears to be a rather unnecessarily complex typology from an analytical perspective. In contrast, Smith (1983) suggests just three categories: security, goodwill and performance. Hume (1995) also suggests just three main categories: financial security, financial support and personal needs. Wright (2004) provides four categories, adding a category for family-friendly benefits separate from goodwill or personal needs.

Smith (2000) has also attempted to analyse the impact of various benefits on organisations by considering them under three headings: contribution to the HRM function; contribution to performance/goodwill/security; and role as motivator or 'hygiene' factor. Smith sees some benefits, such as enhanced leave, sick pay and life insurance, as 'hygiene' factors – that is, their presence may not motivate but their absence may have a negative effect. In contrast, he sees such benefits as pensions, cars and expenses as motivators. Smith argues that some benefits will have a more direct impact upon motivation than others, but that the majority of benefits can have implications for performance and motivation.

Perkins (1998) argues that benefits will only link to company performance if the workforce values them.

A very different approach to categorising benefits is adopted by Flannery et al (1996). These Hay consultants suggest that benefits can be categorised according to the type of organisation in which they are found. From a strategic perspective, the Flannery et al typology makes some sense, with its emphasis upon contingency theory. It is worth remembering, however, that employers in the USA – the context for Flannery et al – have more freedom in the design of benefits packages than in Europe, first because of the different tax regimes and secondly because the requirements for statutory benefits are fewer in the USA.

Flannery et al's model envisages four main types of organisational culture: functional, process, time-based and network. **Functional cultures** are highly organised and bureaucratic, with clear lines of authority and accountability. They provide secure employment and have a strong sense of equity. The benefits of a functional culture are epitomised by the values of longevity and security, reflecting the aspirations of the career-focused employees employed. There is a strong emphasis on generous pension entitlement, and life and health insurance.

In contrast, while security is still important for **process-based cultures**, the performance of the team or group is more important. Pensions in process cultures may be linked to profit-sharing plans tied to organisational performance.

Healthcare and life insurance benefits are less important, reflecting the fact that there is less expectation that employees will stay with the organisation in the long term, and there may be more choice in benefits than in a functional culture.

A **time-based culture** aims to maximise the return on fixed assets and requires flexibility and technical agility. Employees are encouraged to be multi-skilled and are often engaged short-term. In time-based cultures the emphasis is on portability of benefits, as employees tend to move around a lot, sometimes from team to team but also from one business unit to another. Benefits therefore tend to be highly flexible and moveable, with lots of choice for employees. Employees may also be expected to share the cost of their benefits.

Finally, in the **network culture** work is designed around alliances for specific projects. Such organisations are propelled 'by innovation, mobility and market creation and penetration' (Flannery *et al*, 1996: 39). Benefits in such organisations tend to be very dissimilar to those of other cultures. In general, there are far fewer benefits and those that do exist tend to be very flexible. Employees are also expected to shoulder a significant share of the cost of their benefits.

 SELF-ASSESSMENT EXERCISE

To what extent do you think the various categorisations of benefits make sense in practice? What do your fellow students think? Thinking about your organisation – or one with which you are familiar – try to apply these models.

EMPLOYEE ATTITUDES TO BENEFITS

Research has indicated that equity is an important consideration among employees in relation to benefits. For this reason, an employer policy of basing the allocation of benefits upon individual performance or contribution is very rare. Even where there is individual choice available to employees, it is unlikely that overall entitlement will vary for those on the same grade or pay range. Trade unions will tend to hold the view that all staff should have the same entitlement and range of benefits, irrespective of status or rank.

Another way of assessing employee views on benefits is to conduct some analysis of their preferences. It is often assumed that these preferences will relate to demographics, with younger workers having different preferences from older ones, and males different from females, married people different from single, and manual workers different from non-manual. Research from the USA, however, appears to show that this is only partially true (Milkovich and Newman, 2008). While there is evidence that older workers have a stronger preference for pensions and those with families for family benefits, differences based on gender, marital status and social class seem less important. In contrast, there was a great deal of similarity across these groups in terms of preferences. The most popular benefits were health/medical insurance and stock plans, and the least favoured were options such as early retirement, profit-sharing, shorter hours and counselling services. Whether these preferences would be replicated in Europe or Asia is a moot point.

BENEFITS POLICIES AND DECISIONS

Like all aspects of reward, many employers have clear and transparent policies concerning entitlement to benefits, but in smaller businesses these may be less formalised. Some organisations choose to operate a 'single status' policy whereby all staff receive the same range of benefits. Even in 'single status' or harmonised workplaces, however, some status benefits such as company cars will be limited to senior staff. Other employers offer different benefits for different groups of staff, with the range and/or value of the package normally increasing the higher up the organisational hierarchy one is graded. In some cases these variations may reflect different collective agreements for different groups of employees. In recent times in the UK public services there has been some movement towards harmonised benefits as part of moves to 'single pay spines' and concerns about equal pay for work of equal value (eg the NHS Agenda for Change and Local Government 'Single Status' agreements).

Milkovich and Newman (2008) provide a useful list of issues that have to be considered when designing a benefits package. These are:

- Who should be protected or benefited?
- How much choice should employees have?
- How should benefits be financed?
- Are the benefits legally defensible?

The first decision to be taken is the range of benefits to be offered to staff. Some benefits are now expected by prospective employees (such as pensions and season ticket loans) and are seen as a hygiene factor in recruitment and retention, while others are required by law (such as sick pay and maternity leave). Will all staff receive the same range of benefits or will some only be available to certain levels of staff? What will be the implications in terms of both cost and employee relations?

Secondly, employers have to decide on the scale of the benefits provided. What values will they attach to each benefit, and what will be the cost of each? Increasingly employers are seeking to use a budget approach to benefits and to control the amounts they are prepared to pay for particular benefits. This is particularly important if an employer wishes to introduce an element of choice of benefits or benefit scale. Some benefits are linked to seniority or service – for example, annual leave often increases with service. While this might be seen as a breach of age discrimination law, the 2006 Employment Equality (Age) Regulations include an exemption for all 'benefits' awarded by service as long as the service period required is five years or less. Employers who wish to have a service period longer than five years must demonstrate a 'business need'.

Thirdly, employers will need to decide on the overall 'spend' on benefits compared to total remuneration. How much of the total pay costs will benefits account for? Clearly, the costs will be more significant in labour-intensive organisations than in capital-intensive, where labour costs form a minor proportion of total costs. Some organisations have adopted a 'total remuneration' approach and will only discuss the total 'spend' with employees rather than the value of basic pay alone. Emphasising the value of the benefits on offer, however, is particularly difficult where pay levels are negotiated separately from local conditions of service (as in some industry-wide collective agreements).

In the USA, there is an increasing tendency for employees to make a contribution to the cost of their benefits. This is viewed as advantageous in two ways: first it makes employees more aware of the cost and hence they place greater value on the benefits provided and, secondly, employees are more likely to control their usage of the benefits if this affects their cost. In the UK, however, the only major benefit where employees are expected to make a contribution is pensions, although sometimes the benefit entitlement can be increased by employees making additional contributions (eg where employees make contributions to private medical insurance plans to cover their family members). Voluntary benefits, where employees can purchase additional benefits out of their own income, are also now available (with 'salary sacrifice' allowing employees to gain tax advantages from this choice).

The fourth decision is how benefits might be allocated to staff. Will all staff be treated the same or will there be a hierarchy of benefits according to grade? Employers should be aware that the benefits provided to a particular grade or level of worker, however, cannot vary according to whether they are full-time or part-time. In Europe employees working on permanent part-time contracts are entitled to the same benefits (pro rata) as full-time. Clearly, those on short-term contracts may not be eligible for those benefits where there is a service requirement, but once they have completed the required service period they must be offered the opportunity to join. The other issue is whether there will be 'single status' whereby all employees receive the same benefits or whether there will be different arrangements for different groups of employees.

'Harmonised' approaches to managing human resources were particularly popular in the 1980s and 1990s when an influx into the UK of Japanese companies, where single status is the 'norm', led to a growth in single status (Druker, 2000; Price and Price, 1994; Russell 1998). In recent times, however, this trend has slowed and organisations have been more interested in containing the costs of the existing arrangements rather than incurring additional costs by extending some benefits to lower-level staff. Where harmonisation has been implemented it has been more to do with mergers and acquisitions – the need to bring the reward systems of two separate organisations together – rather than between different groups of workers in the same organisation. Concerns about the status divide between manual and non-manual employees appear less important today, probably because they are often less likely to be different in practice.

A fifth and final consideration is the degree of choice that employees will have in their allocation of benefits. A recent trend has been towards 'cafeteria' or 'flexible benefits' whereby each employee is given a personal budget to spend on a 'menu' of possible benefits. We consider flexible benefits later in this chapter.

Whatever decisions are made by employers on the benefits provided, external comparisons with the market will be essential to ensure that the level of benefits on offer is, and remains, competitive. This involves careful research on market comparisons. As Armstrong and Murlis (2007) indicate, however, in some cases the principle of equity of treatment may be abandoned because of the requirement to provide particularly attractive benefits to key staff. There are considerable variations in benefits practice between organisations, and particularly between sectors or industries. In general, the private sector tends to provide more 'status' benefits, such as company cars, than the public sector, but increasingly the public sector tends to provide more generous pensions, holiday entitlement and family-friendly benefits.

In the section below we review some of the major benefits available. First, we consider the 'welfare' benefits, those expected by employees and often where there is a statutory minimum entitlement fixed by government. We then consider those benefits provided to attract applicants for jobs and to enable employees to undertake their jobs (recruitment and retention measures or compensatory benefits), which we term work-related benefits. Finally, we consider status or 'perk' benefits (eg company cars).

 SELF-ASSESSMENT EXERCISE

Thinking about your own organisation – or one with which you are familiar – what are the issues driving the benefits programme? How do the benefits fit with the business strategy of the organisation?

WELFARE BENEFITS

HOLIDAYS

As mentioned above, until the European Working Time Directive in 1998, there was no statutory requirement to offer holidays other than standard bank holidays, although many workers were covered by collective agreements. From the passing of the Working Time Regulations on 1998, workers have been entitled to 20 days' holiday per year. From 1 October 2007, following a successful challenge to the UK interpretation of the Directive, this entitlement is being increased to 24 days (based on a five-day week) and from 1 April 2009 to 28 days. Entitlement to bank or public holidays is subject to individual employment contracts.

In reality, few UK organisations gave less than 20 days prior to the Directive. According to IDS (IDS, 2007a), average basic holiday entitlement (excluding public and bank holidays) is 25 days per year for non-manual staff and 23.8 days for manual

Table 7.3 Average basic holiday entitlement by sector

Industry sector	Days
Energy and water	26.6
Public services	25.9
Finance	25.5
Glass, ceramics and building materials	25.4
Mining and quarrying	25.3
Oil, chemicals and pharmaceuticals	25.1
Paper, print and packaging	25.1
Food, drink and tobacco	25.0
Not-for-profit	24.8
Engineering (inc. electronics)	24.7
IT, telecoms and media	24.6
Textiles, clothing and footwear	24.5
Transport, storage and distribution	24.4
Agriculture and forestry	23.8
Other manufacturing	23.5
Retail	23.2
Construction	22.7
Hotels and leisure	21.5
Overall average	**24.6**

Source: IDS (2007a)

staff. For employees on harmonised conditions, the average is 25 days per year, and the overall average for all employees is 24.6 days. Holiday entitlement varies between sectors, with the lowest entitlement in hotels and leisure (21.5 days) and the highest in energy and water (26.6 days).

Over half the 437 organisations surveyed by IDS (2007a) gave service-related additional leave. This often provides for a further five days after 5 to 10 years' service.

The management of holidays is a major issue for managers in order to ensure that, on the one hand, there is equity of treatment in allocating holidays in the annual rota and, on the other, ensuring that not all staff take holiday at the same time. In some cases, however, employers may decide to fix the weeks of holiday and close the plant or offices for that period. This not only overcomes the problem of holiday rotas but also allows the employer time to carry out essential annual maintenance work on the plant.

There are also various provisions in many organisations for special leave. This is most commonly for compassionate leave for close relatives who are bereaved. It is normally paid leave for a fixed period, with the option of further unpaid leave if necessary. Special leave may also be granted for other reasons, such as time off for public duties, to carry out trade union duties or to deal with urgent family commitments. In the UK, there are statutory rights to particular types of special leave.

SICK LEAVE

The provision of sickness benefit by the state in the UK goes back to the National Insurance Act of 1911. In 1993, statutory sick pay (SSP) replaced state sickness benefit for most employed people, and for the first time employers were required to provide a minimum level of sick pay. This change was largely driven by the government's wish to transfer the financial burden of sickness benefit from the public purse to employers, although initially employers were able to recoup most of the cost from their NI contributions.

The full weekly SSP rate from April 2007 is £72.55. Employees have to have been sick for at least a period of four calendar days and have average weekly earnings of £87 (April 2007) in order to claim SSP. Some SSP may be recoverable by employers under the percentage threshold scheme designed to help employers who have a high proportion of employees sick at any one time. SSP is payable for up to 28 weeks. Employers who provide contractual pay equal or above the SSP rate for each day of sickness may opt out of the SSP regulations. They are then free to determine their rules on sick pay (see Table 7.4).

Most employers top up this minimum level of statutory sick pay with 'occupational sick pay' schemes. The most recent research on sick pay schemes – albeit on quite a small sample of only 29 schemes – shows that most organisations have one scheme for all workers (IDS, 2007b). Where there is more than one scheme, this usually relates to differences between manual and non-manual employees or, where a new scheme has been introduced, between new and existing members of staff. Employees are usually covered as soon as they join an organisation, but IDS found that 40 per cent of organisations operate a service-related qualifying period, for example, after the probationary period has been completed. Some organisations differentiate between different types of employee in terms of this qualifying period, for example, between manual and staff employees. Under European law, part-time and fixed-term contract staff are required to receive no less favourable treatment than full-time permanent staff.

Sick pay is usually based on basic pay, inclusive of SSP. Maximum sick pay entitlement varies greatly between organisations, with some offering up to a year on full pay. Around a third of organisations were found to reduce sick pay after a specific period of absence, typically by half. Sick pay entitlement often improves with service, with a service period of up to 20 years in some organisations before employees reach the maximum entitlement. IDS found that the most common service period required was five years. UK age discrimination law requires that

Table 7.4 Some examples of sick pay entitlement

The following is intended only as a brief summary of each organisation's main sick pay scheme. A number operate more than one scheme. Full details are provided in IDS HR Study 852.

Organisation	Entitlement after 1 year's service	Maximum scheme entitlement	Service required for maximum
Age Concern England	8 weeks' full pay + 8 weeks' half pay (3 months to 15 months' service)	18 weeks' full pay + 18 weeks' half pay	5 years +
Airbus UK	24 weeks' full pay 3 months' full pay + 3	52 weeks' full pay	> 5 years
Allianz Insurance	3 months' full pay + 3 months' reduced pay	6 months; full pay	> 3 years
Avon Cosmetics	8 weeks' full pay	26 weeks' full pay	> 5 years
The Body Shop	13 weeks' full pay	28 weeks' full pay	> 5 years
Bombardier Aerospace	144 hours (4 weeks' full pay)	144 hours (4 weeks' full pay)	On entry (white-collar) 12 months (manual)
British Library	6 months' full salary + 6 months' half pay	6 months' full salary + 6 months' half pay	on entry
Calor Gas (employees who joined after 1.1.00)	16 weeks' full pay	26 weeks' full pay	> 2 years
Kimberly-Clark	360 hours' full pay (up to 3 years)	1,728 hours' full pay	> 10 years
Kodak	26 weeks' pay	52 weeks' pay	> 5 years
London Underground	24 weeks' pay	39 weeks' pay	> 6 years
Mersey Docks & Harbour Company (weekly-paid staff)	4 weeks' full pay + 4 weeks' half pay	26 weeks' full pay + 26 weeks' half pay	> 25 years
Merseyside Fire and Rescue Service (uniformed personnel)	6 months' full pay + 6 months' half pay	6 months' full pay + 6 months' half pay	On entry
Messier-Dowty	15 weeks' full pay	52 weeks' full pay	> 5 years
Nissan Manufacturing UK	12 months' full basic salary	12 months' full basic salary	1 year +

Organisation	Entitlement after 1 year's service	Maximum scheme entitlement	Service required for maximum
Norwich & Peterborough Building Society	4 weeks' full pay + 4 weeks' half pay	13 weeks' full pay + 13 weeks' half pay	> 5 years
OKI (UK)	8 weeks' full pay	26 weeks' full pay	> 5 years
Panasonic (white-collar staff)	8 weeks' full pay 2 months' full pay + 1 month's half pay (3 months to 3 years)	4 months' full pay + 4 months' half pay	6 years +
Peabody Trust	3 months' full pay (up to 5 years)	3 months' full pay + 8 months' full pay + 2 months' half pay	20 years or more
PSA Peugeot Citroën Automobiles UK (staff)	28 weeks' full pay	52 weeks' full pay	4 years +
Port of London Authority	6 months' full pay + 6 months' half pay	6 months' full pay + 6 months' half pay	On entry
SAS Institute	8 weeks' full pay + 18 weeks' reduced pay (75 per cent of basic pay)	8 weeks' full pay + 18 weeks' reduced pay (75 per cent of basic pay)	On entry
Standard Life Assurance Company	No maximum period that the company pays sick pay	No maximum period that the company pays sick pay	-
Tate & Lyle (excluding union represented groups)	26 weeks' pay	26 weeks' pay	On entry
Tate Galleries	16 weeks' full pay (up to 3 years)	6 months' full pay + six months' half pay	> 3 years
Toshiba Information Systems (UK)	2 weeks' basic pay	16 weeks' basic pay	5 years +
Waterstones Booksellers (staff employed after 1.6.07)	40 days' full pay	65 days' full pay	> 3 years
Woolworths (retail and clerical)	4 weeks' pay	26 weeks' pay	10 years and over
Wyman-Gordon (staff employed after 1.3.06)	1 month at 90 per cent + 1 month at 45 per cent	6 months at 90 per cent + 6 months at 45 per cent	> 3 years

Source: IDS HR Study 852, August 2007

a service period more than five years has to be justified in terms of a 'business need', and IDS found several organisations reducing their service requirement to comply with this requirement. In some organisations (eg PSA Peugeot Citroen, cited in IDS, 2007b), sick pay entitlement varies according to the individual employee's sickness absence record.

Employees who are long-term sick or injured may exhaust their sickness benefits entitlement. IDS found that fewer than 40 per cent of schemes extend entitlement beyond the maximum in these circumstances. The alternative is to offer long-term permanent health insurance to those unable to return to work within the entitlement period or, if they are members of a pension scheme, to offer early retirement pensions with enhanced provision.

MATERNITY AND PARENTAL LEAVE

All UK female employees have been entitled to statutory maternity leave since 1975. In response to the 1996 EU Parental Leave Directive, however, the UK introduced new statutory rights to parental leave and time off for family emergencies, under the Maternity and Parental Leave Regulations 1999 and the Employment Relations Act 1999. The Employment Act 2003 further developed the legal framework by providing new or enhanced employee rights or support (Stanworth *et al*, 2006). These included: the extension of maternity leave to 26 weeks (regardless of service); rights to paternity leave; paid adoption leave; the right for parents to request flexible working arrangements; and the right to unpaid parental leave to care for a child.

The Work and Families Act 2006 has further improved entitlement. A woman expecting a baby has the right to 26 weeks of 'Ordinary Maternity Leave' and 26 weeks 'Additional Maternity Leave', making one year in total. Provided certain notification requirements are met, this can be taken no matter how long the employee has been with the employer, how many hours are worked or how much the employee is paid. Statutory maternity pay (SMP) is payable for up to 39 weeks and is payable by the employer. The employer pays 90 per cent of the employee's average weekly earnings for the first six weeks, then up to £112.75 for the remaining 33 weeks. Employees pay tax and National Insurance (NI) in the same way as on normal earnings. The employer reclaims the majority of SMP from their NI contributions and other payments. To qualify for SMP employees must pay tax and NI as an employee (or would pay if they earned enough).

Fathers who have worked for at least 26 weeks ending in the 15th week before the expected birth are entitled to one or two consecutive weeks' paternity leave. Most fathers are entitled to statutory paternity pay (SPP) during this period (the rate being the same as SMP). Fathers can take either one or two weeks off, but this cannot be taken as odd days off. If the two weeks are taken they must be taken together. If paternity leave is taken, as long as the employee is earning at least the lower earnings level for tax and NI contributions, they will receive statutory paternity pay (SPP) during the leave. The amount of SPP is currently (as at 2007) £112.75 per week or 90 per cent of average weekly earnings if this is lower.

Employees pay tax and NI in the same way as on normal pay. The employer reclaims the majority of SPP from their NI contributions.

Statutory adoption leave is for 52 weeks, with statutory adoption pay payable for up to 39 weeks. Paid adoption leave is available to employed people who are adopting a child on their own, or for one member of a couple who are adopting together. The couple can decide who will take the paid leave. The other member of the couple, or the partner of the adopter, may be able to take paid paternity leave.

Employees are entitled to 13 weeks' 'parental leave' (in total, not per year) for each child, up to their fifth birthday (or up to five years after the placement date of an adopted child), or 18 weeks for each disabled child, up to the child's 18th birthday. Parental leave is usually unpaid, unlike maternity or paternity leave, which is related to the birth of a new baby, or adoption leave, which applies when an employee adopts a child.

Employees are also entitled to ask their employer for flexible work arrangements, but the government has introduced a statutory right in order to encourage applications. An employee (but not an agency worker or in the armed forces), who has worked for his or her employer for 26 weeks continuously before applying, has the statutory right to ask for flexible working arrangements if they have a child under six or a disabled child under 18; are responsible for the child as a parent/guardian/special guardian/foster parent/private foster carer or as the holder of a residence order; are the spouse, partner or civil partner of one of these and are applying to care for the child. Employees also have the statutory right if they are a carer who cares, or expects to be caring, for a spouse, partner, civil partner or relative or who lives at the same address as the person being cared for.

Many UK employers provide maternity and paternity leave in excess of statutory requirements (in terms of pay but not necessarily length of leave), especially in the public services. The 2004 WERS found that, overall, 57 per cent of workplaces provide fully paid maternity leave (84 per cent of public sector workplaces) (Kersley *et al*, 2006: 31). Fully paid paternity leave or discretionary leave was provided in 55 per cent of workplaces (84 per cent of public sector workplaces). The survey indicates that extra-statutory leave arrangements are more likely to be found in larger workplaces and organisations and in workplaces where trade unions are recognised. On average, 16 weeks of fully paid maternity leave were provided, and on average eight days of fully paid paternity leave.

In contrast, however, a recent survey in South East England (Corby *et al*, 2005) found that, while 25 per cent of employers paid above the statutory minimum for maternity leave, only 14 per cent allowed more than the statutory minimum leave period.

LIFE INSURANCE

While there is no statutory requirement to provide life insurance, many employers choose to do so. This can either be provided as part of the pension scheme benefits or separately. It normally provides for a multiple of the employee's salary (eg up to the HM Revenue and Customs limit of four times the annual salary) in the event of death-in-service. Entitlements may vary between different categories of employee. This is a relatively cheap benefit, and applies only if the employee dies in service. Benefits are normally free of income and inheritance tax.

PERSONAL ACCIDENT COVER

Another relatively cheap benefit is insurance providing accident compensation. Employers are legally required to hold insurance against accidents in the workplace (should they be sued for damages), but many also provide this benefit, especially where the work is hazardous or involves frequent travel.

PERMANENT HEALTH INSURANCE

As mentioned above, permanent health insurance (PHI) is often provided to cover employees who are long-term sick or injured, when their sick leave entitlement ends. It is normally payable after the first six months of sickness absence. Cover can be provided either through the pension scheme or through a separate insurance policy. There are usually substantial discounts from insurance companies for group schemes – where there is a guaranteed number of staff covered – and it can be much cheaper than individual employees insuring themselves. Employees are only taxed on the benefits in payment and not on any premiums paid by the employer.

EXTRA STATUTORY REDUNDANCY PAY

While employees are entitled to a minimum level of statutory redundancy pay if they have to be dismissed through no fault of their own, many employers provide additional compensation. This is sometimes referred to as a 'severance package'. This can be set down in a policy or provided on an ad hoc basis in particular circumstances. Such extra-statutory compensation can cover additional service-related payments (eg two weeks per year of service instead of the statutory one), or paying above the statutory maximum weekly pay limit. It may also involve ex gratia payments – so-called 'golden handshakes'.

CHILDCARE

An increasingly popular benefit among employees is employer assistance with childcare. Employers have three main ways of supporting staff with childcare costs: childcare vouchers; payments to childcare providers; and workplace childcare provision (Daycare Trust, 2007). All three of these methods can attract exemptions from tax and NI contributions (NICs). Employees pay no tax or NICs on the benefit, and employers pay no NICS. The amount depends on the type of support provided – whether it is in addition to or instead of the employee's salary. The latter is so-called salary sacrifice, whereby the employee forgoes part of their salary in exchange for this non-taxable benefit. For a parent given £55 worth of childcare vouchers per week in addition to salary, the actual gain is £2,860 per annum as they pay no tax or NICs on the amount. For a parent given £55 worth of support per week after taking an equivalent salary sacrifice, the annual savings on tax and NICs is likely to be between £962 and £1,195 per annum, depending on the rates of tax and NICs paid. Employers would save £300 a year in NICs for each employee given the benefit (Daycare Trust, 2007). With workplace nurseries the saving for employers and employees can be much higher because the exemption is on the whole of the subsidy.

Average childcare costs in England are £141 a week, on which the saving would be in the range from £30 to £58 per week or £1,500 to £3,000 per year. A child qualifies for the tax and NIC exemptions up to the 1 September following their 15th birthday. The number of children in the family makes no difference to the amount of exemption. The childcare utilised must be registered or approved, and all staff with children must be eligible for the benefit. Only around 5 per cent of employers currently provide workplace nurseries (Bestbear, 2006). In their research in the South East of England, Corby *et al* (2005) found that only 13 per cent of employers offered help with childcare and, of those, the most popular measures were workplace nurseries and childcare vouchers.

SELF-ASSESSMENT EXERCISE

Do you think the improvements in family-friendly benefits for fathers will lead to better take-up of such benefits among fathers? What might be the barriers?

WORK-RELATED BENEFITS

ACCOMMODATION

Some employees may be required to live 'over the shop' or in company-provided housing. Such employees include caretakers or janitors, publicans and hotel staff, and those working in residential care homes. In the past it was also common for nurses, police officers and firefighters, but less so today. In some cases, accommodation may only be provided when the employee is required to be on site (such as doctors in hospitals). In other cases, the accommodation is provided so that the employees can be close to their jobs (eg in agriculture). Such accommodation can be a substantial benefit to the employee, either in areas of high-cost housing (eg London) or in rural areas where work is located a long way from areas of habitation. But is also provides a substantial benefit to the employer in having staff readily available on site.

Under the National Minimum Wage (NMW) legislation, employers are entitled to offset the cost of accommodation provided to employees against the calculation of entitlement to the minimum wage, but only up to a statutory limit. Research for the Low Pay Commission (LPC) (White *et al*, 2007) found that in fact low-paid employees are less likely to be found in 'tied accommodation' than higher-paid employees. The LPC research found that in 2005 around 290,000 people were living in tied accommodation (1.1 per cent of all employees). The sectors where such accommodation is most likely to be found are agriculture, hospitality, retail, social care and leisure, travel and sport.

Employers may also provide subsidised or free catering services to employees in the workplace but, unlike tied accommodation, such subsidies cannot be offset against the NMW. In some organisations the employer provides 'luncheon vouchers', which can be exchanged in particular restaurants and outlets.

MORTGAGE ASSISTANCE, LOANS AND DISCOUNTS

A key benefit to attract and retain employees is assistance with home ownership. An alternative to tied or subsidised accommodation may be assistance with house purchase. Subsidised mortgages are a considerable benefit, although they are largely confined to the finance sector. The subsidy is usually limited to a particular level but tends to be available to all staff, irrespective of grade, service or age. Housing assistance can also be given in the form of bridging loans or a guaranteed selling price, sometimes as part of a relocation agreement.

In recent years the tight labour market in London and South East and East of England has led to problems of recruiting key workers into the public services (eg teachers and police officers). This in turn has seen the government introducing housing assistance schemes for 'key workers'.

The 'Key Worker Living Programme' provides help with home ownership for those who are eligible. Eligible workers must be a first-time buyer; a homeowner who needs to buy a larger property to meet their household needs (eg family-sized homes); a worker who needs to take part in shared ownership schemes; or who needs to rent at affordable prices. The scheme is only open to specific key workers in London and the South East and East of England.

The programme offers three different kinds of help:

- A loan to help buy a home on the open market. Key workers are expected to raise a mortgage of around 75 per cent of the property's value.
- If eligible, employees can buy at least 25 per cent of the cost of their home and pay a reduced rent on the remaining share.
- Rent is set at a level between that charged by social and private landlords. The accommodation is provided by a landlord registered with the Housing Corporation (Registered Social Landlord).

Organisations can also provide smaller loans interest-free or at favourable interest rates. These can be used for specific purchases such as personal computers.

HM Revenue and Customs places a limit on when such loans can be tax-free. Repayments are normally made through payroll. Another common loan is the season ticket loan for commuters. These are normally interest-free.

RELOCATION

Another important benefit necessary to recruit and retain staff is relocation expenses. Where employees are required to move from one part of the country to another by an existing or a new employer, the employer often provides a subsidy towards this cost. This normally covers the costs of removal as well as some contribution to legal and estate agent fees. HM Revenue and Customs places a tax limit on what can be provided tax-free.

TRAVEL AND SUBSISTENCE

Most employers will provide reimbursement of reasonable travel and subsistence costs incurred by employees in carrying out their work. This can apply to flights, rail and bus journeys, hotel charges and meals taken en route. Organisations normally have policies setting out the monetary limits on what can be claimed. There may also be clothing allowances and laundry tokens for those who are required to wear a company uniform. A benefit that has seen recent growth is the refunding of home or mobile telephone/broadband connections made in the employer's interest.

 SELF-ASSESSMENT EXERCISE

What are the major forms of work-related benefits? What is the purpose of such benefits in the reward system?

STATUS BENEFITS

COMPANY CARS

The provision of cars for employees by organisations grew from the 1970s but has shown a recent downturn. While the great majority of company-owned cars are found in the private sector, in recent years some public sector employers have begun to provide cars through leasing or assisted purchase schemes. Armstrong and Murlis (2007) comment that the company car appears to be a uniquely British phenomenon that is found in few other countries. There are basically two types of provision: where staff require the use of a car (or van) to undertake their work, such as travelling sales staff and mobile maintenance engineers; and cars provided as a status symbol for senior staff. The great majority of large private sector organisations provide cars, either for essential users or as a status benefit or both.

There is evidence that the prevalence of the benefit has fallen in recent years, probably reflecting changes in its tax treatment and partly a reflection of growing environmental concerns. According to the Department of Transport (DoT, 2004, cited by CIPD, 2006) in 2004, 5 per cent of household cars were owned by companies, a fall of 9 per cent since 1992/4. There are also onerous administrative systems necessary to operate a company car fleet, which is why many organisations outsource this job to an external provider. Lastly, HR managers often find that entitlement to a car can be a rather conflict-prone issue in the workplace.

With increasing use of flexible or 'cafeteria' benefits policies (see below), some employers are leaving the choice to employees of whether they have a car or take another benefit or cash instead. The 2006 Hay Group Benefits Survey (cited in Armstrong and Murlis, 2007) indicates that 72 per cent of organisations allowed their staff to take a cash alternative to a status car and 33 per cent allowed this for essential user cars. The survey also showed an increasingly flexibility in the size of car available, encouraging more environmentally friendly vehicles. A recent IDS survey of car policies found that the minimum qualifying level salary for a company car ranged from £25,000 to £49,500 per annum, with the most common level being between £30,000 and £35,000 (IDS 2006).

Cars provided are usually taxed, insured and maintained by the employer. Clearly, where employees are expected to travel between work locations on a regular basis (eg to visit clients or customers), and particularly where the employee has to carry a large load (eg tools, parts or samples), cars are usually provided from within a fleet and may not be personally allocated. Where they are provided as a status benefit the employee is often given some choice of vehicle within a specified budget, although in some cases companies will specify a particular make and model.

The value of a company car as a benefit can be between £5,000 and £10,000 a year (or more), depending on the model (Armstrong and Murlis, 2007), and therefore there is usually a clear level or grade at which the employee becomes eligible. The advantage to the employer of providing such a status benefit is that cars are a highly visible reward and can therefore play an important role in recruitment and retention of staff. It was also, until the mid-1990s, a relatively cheap benefit to provide when the tax and NI implications were taken into account. Since then the government has closed various tax loopholes for company cars, partly to collect more revenue and partly as a measure to discourage the use of cars for environmental reasons.

Between 1992 and 2002, cars were taxed on the basis of the number of business miles driven each year, with the tax paid reducing as business miles increased. This was seen as a perverse incentive to drivers to abandon public transport and use their cars instead. In 2002, the government therefore changed the policy to one based on the carbon dioxide emissions produced by the vehicle, with lower tax rates for more environmentally friendly cars.

The advantage to the employee is also less now than some years ago as the tax treatment for the employee has changed. There is, however, still a financial advantage to having one's car insured, taxed and maintained by one's employer.

A company car can also be a very visible sign of status. For this reason, organisations trying to develop a more harmonised or 'single status' culture may decide not to provide such a benefit.

Most company car policies stipulate when and to whom the entitlement applies, the rules governing the use of company vehicles and choice of the make and model of car provided. Most company cars today are leased, rather than purchased, but some companies still prefer to purchase the vehicles and may allow the employee to buy it when its period of use is over. In some cases, employees may be allowed to add their own cash to purchase a higher-specification model. Cars are commonly replaced after three or four years or 80,000 miles, whichever comes first. Clearly, essential user cars will probably experience more 'wear and tear' than status vehicles, and so these may replaced earlier.

One alternative to car leasing is the Personal Contract Plan (PCP). This entails the employer making regular payments over an agreed period to finance the car, with the option of final purchase at the end of the contract or returning the car and starting a new plan. Some of these plans include insurance and maintenance costs. PCPs can be offered to the whole workforce or limited to particular levels or groups of employees.

Another alternative is the Employee Car Ownership Scheme, whereby the employee enters into an agreement with a leasing firm for the purchase of the vehicle, rather than the employer, over an agreed period or mileage. This allows the employer to transfer ownership of the car to the employee so that they are not taxed on the benefit as a company car.

When considering the provision of company cars it is imperative to decide whether fuel will also be provided for private use. If this is the case, there are further tax implications. Since April 2003, the tax on car fuel benefit has been based on the carbon dioxide emissions of the car.

Where employees use their own cars for work purposes, they must be insured for this purpose. Car mileage allowances are usually based on some assessment of the maintenance, depreciation and other running costs as well as reimbursement of the actual cost of the fuel used. There may be a ceiling on the mileage allowed for any single journey to encourage the use of public transport for longer journeys. Car mileage allowances are usually expressed as pence per mile.

OTHER STATUS BENEFITS

Employers may also provide credit cards or fuel cards if employees are expected to make purchases on the employers' behalf. In addition, where employees are engaged on international assignments (see Chapter 11 on International Reward Management), the organisation may pay the fees for the private education of an expatriate manager's children. One could also consider private medical insurance as a status benefit as it is usually limited to more senior levels of staff.

SELF-ASSESSMENT EXERCISE

What are the main forms of status benefits? What purpose do they serve and to what extent do they conflict with other reward principles such as transparency, equity and performance?

FLEXIBLE BENEFITS

While some organisations have always allowed some limited degree of flexibility in the employee's choice of benefits, it is only over the last two decades that flexible benefits programmes have begun to develop in the UK. Flexible benefits schemes are systems that allow employees to vary their pay and benefits package to meet their personal requirements.

The concept, like so many reward ideas, is an import from the USA where the first plans were introduced in the 1970s. In the late 1990s, Barringer and Milkovich (1998) reported that around 70 per cent of firms in the USA offered flexible benefits. In contrast, the 2007 CIPD reward management survey (CIPD, 2007a) found that just over 1 in 10 employers were allowing some choice to employees. It also found that such benefits were more common among larger organisations (5,000-plus) in the private sector with young workforces. The much greater popularity of such plans in the USA is partly explained by the more benign attitude towards such flexibility by the US Internal Revenue than the UK Inland Revenue.

> **DEFINITION**
>
> 'Flexible benefits systems allow for a degree of employee choice over the form of remuneration.'
>
> Heery and Noon (2001)

Heery and Noon (2001) identify two main forms of flexible benefits. The first is 'within benefit flexibility', which allows employees to take more of a particular benefit by surrendering cash rewards and vice versa (eg better holiday entitlement). The second form is 'across-benefit flexibility', also known as 'cafeteria benefits', where an employee is given a personal budget or points and then asked to select the benefits they want from a menu (up to the maximum points or budget ceiling).

In the USA, as mentioned above, the definition is easier as Section 25 of the Internal Revenue Code sets one out. This defines flexible benefit plans as those plans that offer employees a choice between qualified (non-taxable) benefits and cash (Beam and McFadden, 1996 cited in Barringer and Milkovich, 1998). If a plan does not offer the cash option, then in the USA it is not considered a flexible benefit plan, whereas one that offers the option of paying for a benefit with pre-tax wages is. Barringer and Milkovich (1998) identify four general types of design that range from salary reduction through to mix and match, with the cost to the employer rising as one moves through this range.

Armstrong and Murlis (2007) state, however, that UK employers have adopted three approaches to flexible benefits:

- the introduction of new 'voluntary' or discounted benefits funded by the employee out of post-tax income or by salary sacrifice;

- variation in the level of existing benefits with a compensatory adjustment to cash pay; and

- defining the benefits package in terms of a 'flex fund' to be spent as the employee wishes.

According to the Hay Group (cited in Armstrong and Murlis, 2007), the great majority of flexible benefits plans are limited in scope, with only certain benefits open to choice.

MEETING EMPLOYEE NEEDS OR CUTTING EMPLOYER COSTS?

The concept of flexible or 'cafeteria' benefits schemes originated in the USA and was an employer response to the escalating cost of benefits, especially private healthcare. The concept also fitted well with the American 'new pay' paradigm, with its advocacy of more individualistic reward systems, and with discussions about the need for more variable pay. Giving employees some choice in their benefits was seen as both meeting changing demands from employees and assisting in limiting the cost of benefits provision (Employee Benefits Research Institute, 1995). Flexible benefits have also been promoted as a good recruitment and retention measure and as part of employer branding as an 'employer of choice'. IDS (2003) also points out that flexible benefits can be useful in mergers and acquisitions where two organisations' benefits systems have to be harmonised. If individuals' benefits packages cannot all be standardised, flexibility offers some consistency of approach.

ADVANTAGES AND DISADVANTAGES OF FLEXIBLE BENEFITS

As long ago as the 1970s, Lawler advocated the use of flexible benefits to raise employees' awareness of the cost of benefits to the employer (Lawler, 1971), but a number of other advantages (and disadvantages) have been identified.

The advantages of flexible benefits cited (CIPD, 2007b) include the following:

- employees choose benefits that they want and value, rather than having to accept unwanted and under-valued benefits;

- if a budget system is adopted, the cost of benefits is better controlled;

- employers and employees share the responsibility for benefits;

- employees can change their benefits as their lifestyle changes (eg from single to married status, from childless to family-oriented and from family to retirement-oriented);

- employees participate in the design of their reward package;
- dual-career couples avoid duplication of benefits;
- employers are seen as responding to employee demands for flexibility.

The disadvantages of flexible benefits are as follows:

- such schemes can be complex and difficult to administer as records of the benefits selected must be kept on each individual employee and updated regularly;
- employees need good financial counselling to ensure that they do not make financially risky decisions (eg choosing to withdraw from a pension scheme);
- discounts on some benefits may be lost if coverage ceases to be blanket and employees withdraw from schemes (and hence costs may rise);
- employees may feel that a budget system limits the value of what is on offer, and unions may claim that the scheme is designed to cut costs rather than assist employees.

External benefits consultants, who will design and administer the scheme on behalf of the employer, can supply 'off-the-shelf' flexible benefits systems. This can reduce the amount of onerous administration required and reduce costs. Increasingly, the process of selecting benefits can be done by employees online.

To avoid employees taking risky decisions, many organisations insist that certain core benefits are not flexible below a certain level. On the other hand, research by IDS (2003) found less emphasis on limiting employees to a nominal flex fund. The most common benefits that are flexed, according to IDS (2003), are childcare vouchers, critical illness insurance, dental insurance, holidays, life insurance, permanent health insurance, personal accident insurance, private medical insurance and travel insurance (leisure). Other fairly common flexible benefits were cars, health cash plans, health screening, pensions and retail vouchers. The least common flexible benefits were car breakdown cover, financial planning advice, health club membership, legal protection, lifestyle management services, personal computer leasing, pet insurance and a will-writing service.

INTRODUCING FLEXIBLE BENEFITS

Most flexible benefits schemes are initially based on an organisation's existing benefits provision, but the range of benefits on offer may either be reduced or increased once the scheme is in operation. The CIPD (2007b) recommends that certain benefits, such as sick pay and maternity leave, should be excluded from any scheme. Some employers also exclude the flexing of pension entitlement.

The employee is given a menu of benefits from which to make a choice. There is usually a budget limit on what can be flexed and some baseline provision that must be taken (such as a minimum level of life cover and permanent life insurance). In the case of holidays, employees cannot flex their entitlement below the statutory minimum required. In some cases employers provide their menu in cash terms, showing the cost of each benefit so that employees can calculate the impact of any choices. This helps to convey to employees the cost (and value) of their benefits, but can also have the disadvantage that employees are encouraged to think they are spending their own money, rather than the employer's. In other cases, employers use a points system for allocating choices. Regardless of which method is used, all schemes make a clear distinction between notional salary and the final value of the salary actually paid.

Schemes have to be costed on the basis of predicted take-up of particular benefits. To stop employees making 'adverse selections', the relative values of benefits are usually set so as to avoid too many such choices.

Despite the fact that flexible benefits schemes remain the exception rather than the rule in the UK, the CIPD states that they are 'an ideal way of addressing diversity in benefits, as reinforcement of cultural change, harmonisation of reward practices, especially during merger and acquisition, and an effective means of cost management' (CIPD, 2007b: 5). They are not, however, a 'magic solution', says the Institute, and need careful management if they are to work.

Academic research on the effects of flexible benefits schemes, as opposed to descriptions of how schemes operate, is sparse in the UK, and most of the research has been conducted in the USA.

 BANK BOOSTS TAKE-UP OF BENEFITS DEAL

CASE STUDY

Total reward programme has direct effect on employee engagement levels (Katie Hope reports from the Hay Group conference, Making Reward Work, 2005)

Lloyds TSB has increased take-up of its flexible benefits by 10 per cent since introducing them two years ago. When it was launched in 2003, the participation level of the flex scheme was 50 per cent. However, the latest figures show that it has increased to 60 per cent among the bank's 70,000 employees. From this October, Lloyds TSB has segmented the marketing of its total reward package according to participation levels, and aims to achieve 75 per cent involvement as a result of this approach.

It has also introduced 'people champions' in areas such as telephony where take-up is low, to advise colleagues about the offers available. 'Base pay is imperative and if you get that wrong then staff won't stay

for long, but I don't believe you can change the culture in your organisation without changing your add-ons,' said Paul Farley, group compensation and benefits director.

Farley said the total reward programme, which was introduced in 2003, has had a direct effect on employee engagement levels and emphasised that low take-up rates did not indicate that the scheme had been a failure. 'The point is it provides employees with choice whether they exercise it or not. This sense of opportunity is key to employee engagement,' added Farley.

Currently, Lloyds TSB has an employee turnover rate of 10 per cent a year. Farley said that if the bank's total reward offering could reduce this figure by as little as 0.25 per cent it would save the organisation £2.8 million annually. He based this figure on an estimated cost of £16,000 to replace an employee.

People Management, 13 October 2005

SELF-ASSESSMENT EXERCISE

What are the key features of a flexible benefits scheme?

What are the advantages and disadvantages of such schemes – for both employers and employees?

What lessons might be learned from the experience of Lloyds TSB?

VOLUNTARY BENEFITS

Voluntary benefits are a low-cost method of enhancing the benefits on offer to employees. There has been some recent interest among employers in this concept. Crucially, the difference between voluntary benefits and 'core' benefits is that the employee pays rather than the employer.

> **DEFINITION**
>
> 'In contrast to conventional employee benefits packages, which they complement, voluntary benefits are not funded by the employer. Instead, the company arranges preferential rates on a variety of products and services that employees can take advantage of as they see fit. Similar packages may be available to particular occupational groups, such as teachers, or to union members.'
>
> IDS (2004)

Employers can either negotiate directly with the supplier of the service or product, or they can outsource this role to a third-party organisation. Research by IDS (2004) indicates that increasingly organisations are signing up to pre-arranged benefits packages, often in the form of online 'portals'. Some of these external providers charge an annual subscription fee for access to the portal, while others offer free access and make their money from advertising and commission on sales.

The range of typical voluntary benefits products includes financial products (such as personal loans and mortgages); holidays and travel (discounted flights and holiday packages, travel insurance); health (healthcare cash plans, dental plans, optical care, gym/health club membership); motoring (car purchase, rental, insurance, breakdown cover); home and garden (discounts on garden equipment); entertainment (discounts on CDs, DVDs, reductions on tickets for events and entry charges at a range of attractions); and gifts (jewellery, confectionery, floral gifts).

Employees can either pay online for the benefits or, in some cases, employees' payments are deducted through payroll (eg for healthcare).

SALARY SACRIFICE SCHEMES

One adjunct of a flexible or cafeteria benefits scheme may be salary sacrifice arrangements. Salary sacrifice schemes allow employees to give up part of their taxable pay in return for a non-cash benefit that is treated in a more beneficial manner for tax and/or National Insurance contributions (NICs) purposes (IDS, 2007c). Both employer and employee must agree in writing to such an arrangement. Following any amendments to the employment contract, the employee becomes liable for tax and NICs on the lower salary and any non-cash benefits. As many of the benefits offered through such schemes are wholly or partly exempt from tax and NICs, there is a clear incentive to enter into such an arrangement. For example, by making a contribution of £1,000 to a pension scheme through such a scheme an employee can save £110 in NICs per year (and the employer will also reduce its share of NI contributions).

Guidance from the HM Revenue and Customs (cited in IDS, 2007c: 17) states that:

> Employers and employees have the right to arrange the terms and conditions of their employment and to enjoy the statutory tax and NIC treatment that applies to each element in the remuneration package. Arrangements, which are designed to make use of these exemptions, should not be regarded as avoidance.

The major benefits commonly offered through salary sacrifice schemes are: pension contributions; annual leave; childcare vouchers; workplace nurseries; other employer-provided childcare; and employer-provided bicycles or cyclist safety equipment.

There are clearly important issues to be considered by both employer and employee under such arrangements, and employers may provide financial counselling to employees to explain the details. One important point is that employees cannot reduce their pay below the NMW through such schemes. Further details of the tax and NIC rules concerning salary sacrifice schemes can be found on the HMRC website, www.hmrc.gov.uk/manuals/eimanual/EIM42750.htm.

KEY LEARNING POINTS AND CONCLUSIONS

In this chapter, we have considered a further component within the reward system, employee benefits. As we have discussed, the major reasons for the growth of such benefits were external pressures from government and from the labour market, but such rewards have also been seen as important for recruitment and retention as well. Government regulation remains an important driver for occupational benefits policies in terms of requiring minimum levels of benefits. Research on benefits is sparse, but what exists is inconclusive as to what effects such rewards have upon employees, either in terms of loyalty to the organisation, in motivational terms or on organisational performance.

We identified three main categories of benefits: welfare benefits, work-related benefits and status benefits. Each of these categories serves a different function within the reward system. As we discussed, the range and level of benefits offered by employers varies between sectors and between organisations. In general, the higher-paid the employee the more likely they are to have more and more generous benefits. Attempts to reduce the status divide between manual and non-manual workers through 'harmonisation' or 'single status' were common in the 1980s and 1990s, but these moves appear to have slowed as other management priorities have come to the fore, not least the growing cost of benefits.

Employers' concerns about the increasing cost of benefits have led them to increasingly consider a 'budget' approach, rather than blanket provision, and to launch new communications initiatives aimed at making employees more aware of the value of the benefits provided. The major initiative has been the development of flexible or cafeteria benefits, but the spread of such schemes remains limited in the UK, not least because of the tax implications of swopping one benefit for another. We also noted both the growth of voluntary benefits, whereby employees contribute towards the cost of their benefits, and the option of salary sacrifice schemes, which offer employees tax and NIC reductions.

The context of any benefits policy remains vital. The alternative forms of benefit available to organisations provide a large range of options, but the consequences of each need careful consideration. This is particularly important where employees are being required to make financial decisions such as flexible benefits and salary sacrifice schemes.

EXPLORE FURTHER

For a detailed review of the various benefits available and their tax and NIC treatment, see Armstrong, M. and Murlis, H. (2007) *Reward Management. A handbook of remuneration strategy and practice*, rev. 5th edn. London, Kogan Page.

For reviews of current benefit levels and policies, see various IDS HR Studies.

CHAPTER 8

Pensions

CHAPTER OBJECTIVES

At the end of this chapter you should understand and be able to explain the following:

- The purpose and role of pensions in employee reward systems.

- The origins of pension schemes and the differing role of the state in pension provision in different countries.

- The different types of pensions, and their respective advantages and disadvantages to employers and employees.

- The main provisions of an occupational pension scheme.

- The factors affecting choice of scheme.

- The role of HR in administering and managing pension choices.

- The current trends in pension provision and debates about the future provision of occupational pensions.

CIPD STANDARDS COVERED IN THIS CHAPTER:

To understand and explain:

- The significance of relevant statutory interventions including limitations on providing advice on pensions

INTRODUCTION

Pensions are a major part of many organisations' benefits packages and have become a key issue for organisations in recent years. Britain's pension system is unique within Europe, and the legal constraints on the design and running of schemes are stringent. As Armstrong (2002) comments, pension arrangements are probably the most complex element within the reward system and require specialist advice. This may not be an area where the professional expertise of human resources staff may be sufficient, but it remains an important area of knowledge for those specialising in reward management. All HR staff should understand at least the basic architecture of pension schemes, the major options available to employers and the basic legal requirements.

Pensions may be seen as 'deferred pay' – employers set aside some of the regular pay received by the employee for the future payment of an income when they retire. In some cases, the employer does not require a contribution from the employee, but in most schemes the employee is required to make a (usually smaller) contribution to the pension fund. Because pensions are seen as part of reward, even if the reward is deferred until after the employee finally retires from working, it is a contested area and, where trade unions are present, they will see pension entitlement and contributions as a negotiable item. In recent years there have been several examples in the UK of industrial action by trade unions concerning changes in their employees' pension entitlements (eg in local government, the Post Office and at British Airports Authority).

Over the last decade there have been major changes in both the legal requirements concerning UK occupational pensions and in employer practice in terms of types of provision offered. Indeed, most developed countries are facing a pensions crisis that is leading to a radical overhaul of existing provision. Because of the growing importance of pensions, especially in terms of the political debate about their future, we devote an entire and separate chapter to pensions. It should be remembered, however, that pensions are just one of several benefits provided by organisations and may form part of any flexible benefits option.

DEFINITION

'A regular payment to those who have retired from work due to age or ill health paid by the state or an employer.'

Heery and Noon (2001)

This chapter begins by looking at the origins of pensions and their purpose and role within an organisation's benefits system. We then consider the different roles of the state and occupational schemes. We move on to describe the main types of pension and their respective advantages and disadvantages to employers and employees, and consider the major elements provided and methods of funding. We also consider briefly the major legal constraints upon employers in the provision of pensions, the options available and the role of human resources staff in administering schemes and providing advice to employees. Lastly, we discuss the current debates about the continuation of pension schemes and their future provision.

THE ORIGINS OF UK PENSION SCHEMES

Pension schemes originated in the form of local community relief funds for the elderly, the sick and destitute during the reign of Richard II (Smith, 2000). Even in pre-industrial times there were local funds available to citizens who fell upon hard times. The first real pension scheme was that provided for navy officers in the 1670s. From the nineteenth century pensions were also made available to senior civil servants. This initiative was followed by some of the larger private sector enterprises such as the railway companies and banks. These schemes were primarily provided for managers and clerical staff, and manual workers were not usually included. For this reason, another source of early retirement benefits was the friendly societies and trades unions established by workers in the nineteenth century. Some trades unions continued to provide this benefit until quite recently.

It was not until the start of the twentieth century, however, that the state began to provide some minimum pension entitlement for citizens. The first, non-contributory, state scheme in the UK was introduced by the Liberal government in 1908, which was then improved in 1925, when a contributory scheme was introduced for manual workers and others earning up to £250 a year. For the first time a majority of the poorest two-thirds of the UK population could contribute to and draw a pension (Smith, 2000). This development was followed by many large private sector companies introducing their own occupational pension schemes, especially after tax relief was granted on contributions to such schemes from 1921. The introduction of such schemes was partly an attempt by employers to move away from the 'hire and fire' employment methods of the nineteenth century to an approach that emphasised the need for employee loyalty and retention. Pensions were seen as a useful method to attract good workers and assist in creating a compliant and happy workforce. It was also a move intended to counter trade union organisation in their workplaces.

Not until after the Second World War, though, were pensions provided for all citizens. The Labour government of 1945 introduced a contributory flat-rate pension scheme for all under the 1946 National Insurance Act. This remained the major source of retirement income for most workers until a second, additional state pension based on individual earnings (known as graduated pension) was introduced under the 1959 National Insurance Act. The next big change was the Social Security Pensions Act 1975 (the so-called 'Castle Plan' after the Labour minister Barbara Castle). This Act introduced the State Earnings Related Pension Scheme (SERPS) and allowed employers and employees with occupational schemes to 'contract out' of the state scheme under certain circumstances and pay lower National Insurance contributions.

The cost of pensions to both the state and employers has always been an issue, and in 1980 the Conservative government of Margaret Thatcher sought to reduce the cost of the state scheme. It did this by cutting the link between increases in the state pension and increases in average earnings (linking them to price inflation instead). In 1986 the Conservative government also sought to reduce costs by making it easier for workers to opt out of the state SERPS scheme into a private pension. The 1990s saw both a major pensions scandal at the Mirror Group of newspapers and a pensions 'miss-selling' scandal among private pension providers, the latter partly a result of the 1986 changes, which encouraged the growth of the private pensions industry. As a result there was a significant tightening up of the UK pensions legislation. The 1995 Pensions Act set up regulatory and compensation schemes for those whose pension schemes go into liquidation.

It is worth commenting that the UK pension system is rather different from that of most other developed countries. Occupational pension schemes are quite rare in most European countries, and where they exist they tend to be exclusive to senior staff. In Germany, for example, workers and employers contribute about 20 per cent of salary to a government scheme, with the state adding a further 10 per cent, providing a final salary pension of up to 70 per cent of earnings (Schifferes, 2005). The USA, in comparison, has been more similar to the UK, with a minimum state provision and employer-sponsored occupational schemes. The US social security system is in deep trouble, however, and the US government has suggested privatisation of the federal scheme (Schifferes, 2005). In Australia, there is a means-tested pension provided by the state, but from the 1990s compulsory private pensions have been required for everyone earning more than a fixed monthly amount. Employers are obliged to pay contributions into these private pensions (to which employees are encouraged to contribute through tax incentives). Most schemes in Australia are run on an industry basis, rather than at company level, and 95 per cent of employees are members of such schemes, including 75 per cent of part-time workers (Schifferes, 2005).

In comparison to other developed countries, the UK's state pension scheme is one of the least generous in the world, providing incomes of just 37 per cent of national average earnings (Pensions Commission, 2004). When private provision is taken into account, however, the difference in total retirement income is much less.

THE UK STATE PENSION SCHEME

The UK State Pension is made up of the basic state pension and the additional state pension. All UK citizens are entitled to the full basic state pension (£87.30 per week for a single person and £139.60 per week for a married couple as at 9 April 2007), if they have built up enough qualifying years during their working life. Men currently need 44 qualifying years by the age of 65, and women (who reach the age of 60 before 2010) need 39 qualifying years. Those without the requisite number of qualifying years may receive a reduced pension. The minimum qualifying period for a state basic pension is 10 or 11 years' National Insurance contributions (NICs), and the minimum pension is a quarter of the full amount. Women who do not have their own NIC record may be entitled to a pension based on their husband's contributions. The Pensions Act 2007 has reduced the qualifying period for a full basic pension to 30 years for those who reach state pension age on or after 6 April 2010.

The State Pension age for men is 65 and is between 60 and 65 for women. The State Pension age for women will increase gradually from 2010, so that by 2020 it will be 65. The State Pension age for both men and women is to increase from 65 to 68 between 2024 and 2046. Most occupational pension schemes tend to use the same retirement ages as the state scheme, but some still provide a full pension from age 60 (for both men and women).

From 1978 to 2002 the additional State Pension was paid from the State Earnings Related Pension Scheme (SERPS) and was only available to employees. From 6 April 2002, SERPS was reformed to provide a more generous additional state pension for low and moderate earners, and to extend access to include certain carers and people with long-term illness or disability. This is called the State Second Pension.

Employees who work for an employer and earn more than a specified annual amount (£4,524 in 2007/8) are automatically included in the additional State Pension scheme. But employees may choose to 'contract out' of the additional State Pension and join a contracted-out occupational pension if they think it will give them a higher income, or other benefits, when they claim it. Where a person joins a 'contracted-out' occupational scheme, the employer provides the additional pension instead of the state. Other employees may choose to do this by setting up a personal pension arrangement with an independent pension provider.

UK OCCUPATIONAL PENSION SCHEMES TODAY

Around 46 per cent of all employees are members of pension schemes additional to the state scheme, although the figure is slightly less in the private sector than the public sector. There are around 13 million people saving in workplace pension schemes, of which 5 million are public servants and 8 million are private sector workers, according to the Annual Survey of Hours and Earnings (ASHE) (ONS, 2006, cited in NAPF, 2007a). The ASHE shows a higher proportion of pension scheme membership in the private sector than other sources. According to the Government Actuary, there are 69,000 private sector occupational schemes with 4.7 million members (Government Actuary's Department, 2005: 94).

There is, however, some evidence that the coverage of pension schemes in the UK is declining. The peak of pensions coverage was reached in 1967, when they covered 12.5 million members, but by 2005 the figure was down to 9.1 million, having lost 1.4 million members alone since 1995 (Pensions Commission, 2004; Government Actuary's Department, 2006). Figure 8.1 below shows the decline in the number of private sector employees contributing to a non-state pension.

Data from the Department of Work and Pensions (DWP, 2005/06) shows that almost 60 per cent of all pensioner households have income from an occupational pension, although among recently retired pensioner households the figure is lower, confirming the decline in private sector occupational pension scheme coverage. On the other hand, the recently retired appear to have higher levels of

Figure 8.1 Public and private sector participation in non-state pension schemes: millions

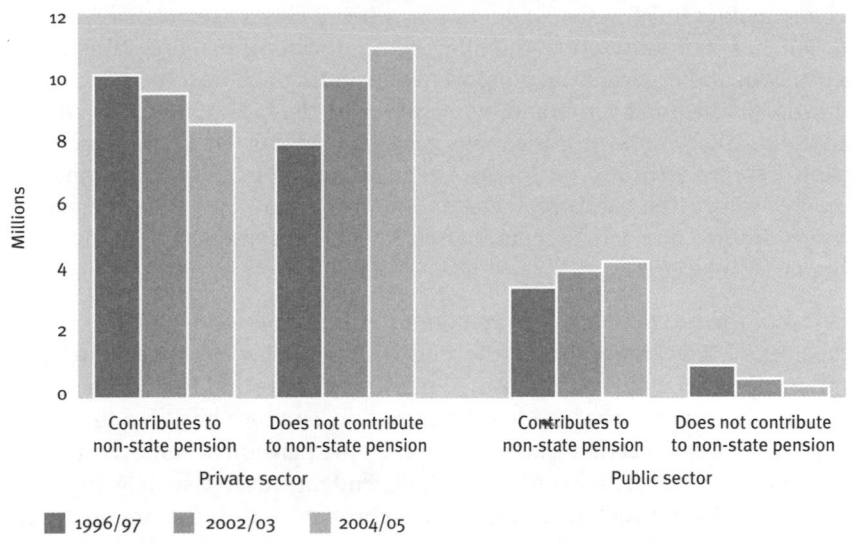

Source: Pensions Commission estimates based on FRS, ONS employment data and Occupational pension scheme surveys, GAD

Note: Data from 1999/2000 onwards are not directly comparable with earlier data. Those individuals with personal pensions that are only receiving contracted-out rebates have been counted among non-contributors since they will only accrue pension rights equivalent in value to the SERPS/S2P rights foregone (assuming that GAD calculations of appropriate rebates are fair). Definition of public and private sector may differ between sources used. Self-employed workers are included in the private sector. Analysis assumes that if an employee in the public sector is not a member of an occupational pension scheme they have no non-state alternative provision. Figures are for GB only. Analysis based on working age people defined as all adults aged 16–59/64. Individuals aged 16–18 who are in full-time education are not included in the analysis. In a small number of cases the contributions referred to will be solely provided by employers and not the employee themselves.

pension than all pensioner households (an average £188 compared to £146 per week).

WHY DO EMPLOYERS PROVIDE PENSION SCHEMES?

The introduction of employer-sponsored occupational schemes is closely linked to the development of personnel management. As suggested above, the growth of pension schemes was closely linked to changes in employment practices at the start of the twentieth century. Employers viewed pension schemes as a useful aid to rewarding the loyalty of those staff they wished to retain – initially managers and white-collar senior staff but later other workers. Pensions developed hand in hand with the concept of an internal labour market (see Chapter 2), in which employers sought to protect themselves from having their employees recruited by competitors. As already discussed in Chapter 8, pensions are one of only two benefits identified in the US literature as being closely correlated with retention and staff satisfaction, the other being stock options. Providing access to a pension, and especially an employer contributory scheme, has been seen in the past as 'good employer' branding. A survey by the CBI (CBI, 1994, cited in Armstrong, 2002) found that the major reasons given for offering an occupational pension were to: provide a competitive edge in the labour market; enhance the company's image as a good employer; and motivate staff. HM Revenue and Customs-approved pension schemes also provide a very tax-efficient method of saving for employees.

A review of the econometric research on the effect of pensions (Taylor, forthcoming 2008) argues that all the studies show a close correlation between membership of an employer-sponsored pension scheme and low labour turnover. Taylor, however, questions whether there continues to be a basis for this belief. Taylor (2000) argued earlier that it may not be the pension scheme as such that causes retention, but rather some other independent variable such as higher pay or better HR management, which often correlate with those organisations providing pensions. Taylor also points out that most of these studies pre-dated legislation that stopped schemes having rules that heavily penalised early leavers. In the UK the limit on full vesting rights (the date at which the employee becomes entitled to accrued benefits) is now two years, so employers cannot use this device to 'trap' employees into staying longer than they wish.

In terms of the effect of pensions as recruitment devices there is even less research evidence. Research by the NAPF (2007b) indicates that while a pension scheme can be attractive to job candidates and act as an important element in their decision to apply for jobs, there seems to be less concern about the type of pension on offer. Moreover, research for the CIPD (2007) indicates that the recent change from the more generous 'defined benefit' schemes to the less generous 'defined contribution' schemes has had no obvious impact upon labour turnover in the private sector. The ending of 'defined benefit' schemes has not led to any observable increase in employee mobility. Research by Loretto *et al* (1999), looking at undergraduate student views on pensions, found that many, especially males, did not rate pensions highly in terms of employment choice, preferring individual decisions on how to spend their money. Similarly, research by Hales and Gough (2002) on employee perceptions of occupational pensions found that the attraction of these schemes was not the security they provided but rather the opportunity for cost-effective saving and the possibility of early retirement. Hales and Gough conclude that company pension schemes are seen more as contingent private transactions than as part of long-term stable commitments by and to an employer.

A final factor that may influence employer provision of pensions is the presence of collective bargaining. In other words, through their unions, employees demand the establishment and/or continuation of good pension schemes. The 2004 WERS (Kersley *et al*, 2006) found that core employees in workplaces with some collective bargaining were significantly more likely to be entitled to an employer pension scheme than those not covered by collective agreements. This held true both for the whole economy and the private sector data. It is also interesting to note, however, that entitlement to an employer pension scheme was associated with lower pay satisfaction. This suggests 'either that employees face a pay penalty in order to obtain pension rights or else that, when offered as a supplement to pay, employees may prefer a cash equivalent' (Kersley *et al*, 2006: 201).

SELF-ASSESSMENT EXERCISE

To what extent do you think employees still value an occupational pension? From discussion with colleagues and friends, do you think younger employees prefer to have a larger disposable income than a smaller income and a guaranteed pension on retirement?

TYPES OF OCCUPATIONAL PENSION SCHEME

Most occupational pension schemes are administered under trust law, with the control of their funds vested in a board of trustees. This is designed to ensure some independence from the employer and has become even more important as a safeguard following the Maxwell pensions scandal referred to above. The advantages of setting up a scheme under trust law are that: HM Revenue and Customs approval of schemes is dependent on this; the assets of the scheme are separate from those of the employer; and it provides protection for those beneficiaries who are not employees (ie spouses and dependants).

Tax relief on contributions is available to employee members of those schemes approved by HM Revenue and Customs. The Revenue lays down limits on the maximum benefits available with this tax relief. The employer can also recover the tax on its contributions and the income tax payable on investment income from UK investments. Until recently, under the Revenue limits, a pension could not exceed two-thirds of final earnings after 40 years' service, and there was a ceiling on the annual pension amount payable.

This changed with the Pensions and Finance Act 2004, which was designed to make pension schemes simpler to understand and easier to invest in. The changes, which came into effect on 6 April 2006, removed Revenue restrictions on pension contribution levels. Employees can now invest up to 100 per cent of earned income in any tax year, up to a maximum amount, and receive tax relief. A 'lifetime cap' was also established, which allows employees to hold up to a total investment of £1.5 million (as at 2006) in a pension scheme. Up to 25 per cent of the pension fund may be drawn as a tax-free lump sum. The minimum normal retirement age was also raised from 50 to 55 by 2010. The full details of the Revenue limits are available from the Pensions Schemes Office of the HMRC (http://www.hmrc.gov.uk/PENSIONSCHEMES).

As mentioned above, under the 1975 Social Security Pensions Act employers were allowed to contract their schemes out of the requirements of the State Earnings

Related Pension Scheme (SERPS) under certain conditions. The employer had to provide a guaranteed minimum pension (GMP) roughly equivalent to what the employee could expect from SERPS. The advantage of contracting-out was that the tax relief on contributions was higher than for not contracted-out schemes. From 2002, the SERPS scheme was reformed to provide an additional pension entitlement to some of those who were not employed as well as the employed. Occupational schemes may still 'contract out' of this additional pension, although from 2010 this will depend on the type of pension scheme offered.

There are two main types of occupational pension scheme: 'defined benefit' (DB) and 'defined contribution' (DC), which will be examined in turn.

DEFINED BENEFIT (DB) SCHEMES

Under a DB scheme, contributions are made by employers, employees or both into a pension fund (although in some public sector schemes there is no actual fund as such), which is then invested and pensions paid out of the investment income. When a scheme member retires, his or her pension is calculated on the basis of the number of years' membership of the scheme. The pension has traditionally been based on some proportion of the final salary or earnings received, or the best year's earnings of the most recent service period (normally three years). The proportion per year is normally 1/60th in the private sector and 1/80th in the public services, although in the past some schemes have given more generous proportions than these.

So, for example, somebody in the private sector with 40 years' service would be entitled to 40/60ths (two-thirds) of their final salary (similarly, a public servant would be entitled to 40/80ths or half their final salary). In addition, employees can exchange part of the pension amount for a tax-free lump sum (in the public sector it is common for employees to receive a tax-free lump sum of 3/80ths of salary per year of service).

The reason such schemes are known as 'defined benefit' schemes is because the employee (and employer) will be able to project exactly today, given the requisite number of years' service will have been completed on retirement, the amount of the final benefit to be received (calculated at today's value). The value of the final pension is therefore guaranteed to the employee.

DEFINED CONTRIBUTION (DC) SCHEMES

A DC scheme also operates on the basis of contributions paid into a fund, which is then invested to pay the pensions of retired members, but, unlike the DB scheme, the value of the pension at retirement age is not guaranteed. The amount of pension finally received will be based on the return on investment on the individual's pension 'pot' at the time of retirement, which cannot be known until the individual pension account is traded in for an annuity on retirement. For this reason, such schemes are often known as 'money purchase' schemes. It is also the case that, unlike a 'final salary' pension scheme, if the pension is deferred or 'frozen', the employer does not have to guarantee any minimum annual increase in its value. In other words, the employee's pension will be based upon what the money saved in the fund will buy when the employee reaches retirement.

Under a DC scheme, employees may have the option to decide where their fund is invested, whereas under a DB scheme the fund is normally centrally controlled and invested. Employer contributions can be a fixed percentage of salary or the contribution may increase with service. An alternative is that the employer agrees to match whatever the employee puts in (or may agree to a multiple of the employee contribution). From April 2010, defined contribution schemes and personal pension schemes will no longer be able to contract-out. All contracted-out members of such schemes will be contracted back in to the Second State Pension.

THE PROS AND CONS OF THE TWO TYPES

The original employer justification for DB schemes was that they helped to recruit and retain good staff. They also had the benefit of fixing a retirement age so that employees could both be encouraged to stay until the scheme retirement age was reached, but no longer, thus dealing with any possible declining performance issues (Taylor, 2008 forthcoming).

The disadvantage of a DB scheme for an employer is that they have to take responsibility for any risk to the fund and pay for the guaranteed pension amount, even if the fund is in deficit. The cost of a scheme may exceed its liabilities if salaries grow faster than expected, the age at which pensioners die increases (because the pension has to last for longer), or the fund investments do not perform as well as projected. These potential risks may mean the employer has to provide a substantial additional contribution to keep the scheme solvent.

On the other hand, if the fund is in surplus, the employer can stop making contributions on the employee's behalf until the fund is in balance again (as many employers did in the 1980s and 1990s). It is because of the escalating cost of DB schemes that there has been a recent substantial decline in employers offering such schemes.

In some cases employers are changing their DB schemes to a salary calculator based on 'career average' earnings rather than 'final salary'. This method adds together the salary/earnings received in each year of service and then divides this figure by the number of years' service to create an average. The result is usually a lower retirement basic pension. While such a system may benefit lower-paid workers, whose earnings may decline as they approach retirement, it clearly reduces the final pension for those whose salary is at its highest at retirement age.

Clearly, the great advantage of the DB scheme for employees is that their future retirement income is guaranteed. Moreover, because the final pension received is based on the most recent salary or earnings, employees benefit from any promotions during their work careers. The disadvantage for employees is that such schemes were designed to reward loyalty and service with a single employer.

If the employee does not work for that employer for his or her entire working career then the resulting pension will be smaller than the maximum entitlement (eg an employee who worked for five years would only receive 5/60ths).

Moving a DB pension entitlement from employer to employer is difficult, and schemes usually levy a substantial charge for transferring accrued pension rights to another scheme. The pension can be deferred or 'frozen' (ie left in the scheme but not collected until retirement age), but the 'frozen pension' will only increase in line with the legal requirement for protection of the value of the pension. Under the Pensions Act 1995 schemes were obliged to provide for an annual increase in deferred pensions of 5 per cent per year or the retail price index, whichever is the lower figure (this figure was reduced to 2.5 per cent from 6 April 2005). So DB schemes do not suit those who regularly change employer.

In contrast, the advantage of a DC scheme to an employer is that, there being no guaranteed pension, they will not have to make good any deficit in the pension fund. All the employer needs to guarantee is their level of contribution, not the final benefit. If their contribution buys less pension entitlement in the long run for the employee, then there is no problem for the employer.

The great advantage to the employee is that such DC pensions are usually much easier to transfer to another employer as one is simply transferring a sum of money, not a guaranteed right to a specific level of pension. The disadvantage for the employee is that they will have no clear idea of what the pension fund will yield in the final pension amount until they retire (although schemes usually provide projections based on current fund performance and various investment return scenarios).

According to the ASHE (ONS, 2006), there were 3 million people saving in private sector DB schemes in 2006, and all 5 million public sector members were in DB schemes. There were 4 million people paying into private sector DC schemes and 1 million paying into undefined private sector schemes. Even where DB schemes exist in the private sector, however, they may no longer be open to new members.

The NAPF Annual Survey (NAPF, 2006) found that around a third of private sector DB schemes surveyed were still open to new members in 2006 (accounting for over half the active members of private sector defined benefit schemes). Over 4 in 10 members in private sector DB schemes have 'frozen' or deferred pensions (ie they are no longer making contributions to the scheme, but will have an entitlement when they finally retire). Some 26 per cent of private sector DB scheme members are pensioners.

 SELF-ASSESSMENT EXERCISE

What are the major advantages and disadvantages of defined benefit and defined contribution pension schemes?

OTHER TYPES OF SCHEME

Another alternative is the hybrid pension scheme. This combines features from both the DB and DC schemes. The most common hybrid is where a final salary scheme has an underpinning DC arrangement. Under this arrangement, if the final salary figure is lower than that that could be obtained through 'money purchase', an employee can convert the final salary pension into a more financially attractive option by purchasing an annuity on retirement instead of taking the final salary pension. These types of schemes are more common for senior executives.

Another method used for senior executives, where they are often employed for short contract periods, is the 'top hat' scheme. This enables the executive's occupational pension to be topped up with a separate executive pension plan.

Another alternative is the Group Personal Pension Scheme. Under these schemes, all employees have their own personal pension contract. These pensions are contract-based rather than governed by trust law and are administered by an insurance company. In many ways these schemes are really the same as a private pension plan taken out by an individual with a bank or insurance company. There are, however, advantages in that the employer normally makes a contribution to the scheme on the employee's behalf, and there may be a significant discount on the cost of the same plan taken out individually. According to the NAPF (2007a), over a quarter of private sector organisations now use such group schemes.

EQUALITY ISSUES

One of the key findings of the Pensions Commission (2004) was that women pensioners in the UK are significantly poorer than men. This reflects the fact that females have a lower employment rate than men, with lower average earnings, and more work part-time. It also reflects the fact that many women take time out from employment to have a family and hence, coupled to a lower retirement age, have fewer years in which to earn a pension. It also relates to the fact that the state pension system has tended to assume that females receive their retirement income through their husbands, and assumptions have been made about family structure that are no longer valid. On the other hand, women are generally more expensive to pension as they often retire earlier than men and live longer in retirement.

THE MAJOR BENEFITS AVAILABLE

Most pension schemes provide a number of basic benefits. These are:

- an annual pension on retirement;
- the facility to 'commute' pension for a tax-free lump sum;
- dependants' benefits;

- the ability to enhance a pension through making additional voluntary contributions (AVCs);
- the ability to purchase 'added years' to enhance the final pension;
- benefits on death in service and death in retirement;
- benefits on leaving the employer before normal retirement age.

ANNUAL PENSION

The major benefit from any pension scheme is the actual monthly pension amount received by the employee. As explained above, the final sum received will vary – according to the number of years the employee has been a member of the scheme in DB schemes, and according to the size of the final pension fund and the annuity it will buy in the DC scheme.

Both DB and DC schemes were obliged under the Pensions Act 1995 to provide increases on pensions in payment of 5 per cent per annum, or in line with the Retail Prices Index (RPI), whichever the lower figure. From 6 April 2005, however, this figure has been reduced to 2.5 per cent or the RPI, whichever the lower, and money purchase schemes do not have to increase pensions that come into payment after 6 April 2005. While employees receive tax relief on pension contributions, pensions in payment are taxable as income.

TAX-FREE LUMP SUM

Scheme members can usually convert part of the final pension sum into a tax-free lump sum. This is known as 'commutation'. The HMRC places limits on the amount of any lump sum that can be commuted tax-free. In public sector schemes, which are normally based on an accrual rate of 1/80th per year of service, a lump sum is usually provided as one of the fixed benefits, and the final pension received will consequently be smaller than in a scheme based on 60ths. Public sector schemes usually provide a lump sum of 3/80ths per year of service (eg for an employee with the full 40 years' service the lump sum would be 40 x 3/80ths = 120/80ths (one and a half times) final salary).

AVCS

Most schemes will allow employees to make additional voluntary contributions (AVCs) to increase the value of the final pension benefits. Contributions are usually made into a separate fund, and the schemes operate in effect as an additional 'money purchase' element. The additional pension entitlement will be based on the value of the fund and the annuity that it will buy on retirement, rather than on service.

ADDED YEARS

A more expensive option in some DB schemes (especially the public sector schemes) is for the employee to purchase additional years in the scheme. This has the advantage that the employee can guarantee to increase the size of the final pension, but is expensive because the employee is normally expected to pay the full cost of the added year (ie the employer's contributions as well as their own employee contributions).

BENEFITS ON DEATH

The main benefits available if the scheme member dies before reaching retirement age are a death-in-service lump sum; pensions for spouses (if married); and pensions for dependants (if there are any). The death-in-service lump sum is similar to a life insurance policy and provides an amount to the deceased member's estate of between two and four times salary. Schemes will normally also provide for a pension based on the deceased member's expected pension on retirement, usually half the sum that would have been paid to the member had they lived to normal retirement age. Where children are left, the scheme may also provide dependants with an income until they reach adulthood at 18.

LEAVING AN EMPLOYER BEFORE RETIREMENT

As discussed above, one disadvantage of a pension scheme based on service (ie a DB scheme) is that it discriminates in favour of those who stay with the same employer for their entire working life. Because a DB scheme's intention is to reward those who remain loyal to the employing organisation, there are usually penalties for those who leave that employer's service before retirement age. Where employees wish to retire early (other than through ill health), there are often provisions for 'early retirement' whereby the employee can take the pension accrued to date. However, under this early retirement arrangement, the pension is normally actuarially reduced to compensate the scheme for the fact that the pension will be paid for a longer period and is based on a shorter period of investment growth.

Early retirement has been a very useful device over the last few decades in redundancy or 'downsizing' exercises, allowing workers close to retirement age to leave the organisation and take their pension, often with some form of enhancement to encourage this move. This has happened in both the private and public sectors in the past, but such early retirement options currently appear to be reducing – partly because of the costs involved by the scheme and partly because of the introduction of later retirement ages to deal with the demographic changes. As the article from *People Management* in Box 8.1 below indicates, however, early retirement remains a popular option for employees.

Where employees choose to leave their employer's service to move to a new employer, employees can either seek to transfer their accrued pension to the new employer; have a refund of their contributions to date; or defer collection of the pension until they reach retirement age. Transfer is usually much easier to arrange with a DC or 'money purchase' scheme as the transfer is simply of a fund, not an entitlement to a guaranteed level of pension. As already explained, any deferred DB pension must be increased each year by at least 2.5 per cent or the RPI (whichever is the lower).

SELF-ASSESSMENT EXERCISE

What are the major benefits available from a typical occupational scheme?

ISSUES IN REWARD

BOX 8.1 RETIREMENT NEEDS A FLEXIBLE APPROACH

Most UK workers remain determined to retire as soon as possible

Flexible working and retirement policies will fail unless they are tailored to individual employees, according to the Employers Forum on Age (EFA).

Its research found that regardless of how much they enjoy work, more than half of UK workers (52 per cent) want to retire as soon as they can. Less than a third of those questioned who hadn't saved enough for their retirement were willing to consider working for longer.

The report, Attitudes on Age, based on 1,600 interviews with a cross-section of the working population, coupled with analysis of the 2003–04 Office for National Statistics' Labour Force Survey, indicates that the government's attempt to address the UK's early retirement culture is failing.

'The oft-repeated message that we all need to keep working is too simplistic.

Employers need to tailor HR policies to meet individual needs and make working for longer a realistic and appealing option for everyone,' said Sam Mercer, director of the EFA.

The research identified four types of worker based on their attitude to work and retirement. It found no correlation between these attitudes and workers' ages.

Heather Staff, media and research director at Penna Recruitment Communications, a recruitment advertising agency, said the message that age did not determine someone's attitude to work was welcome. 'Clients often start a brief saying that they want a person of a certain age. This research gives us a comfortable and logical perspective on targeting certain people, whereas age does not,' said Staff.

Source: *People Management*, 15 September 2005

BT

CASE STUDY

BT has decided to abolish fixed retirement ages before age discrimination legislation is introduced next year.

The telecommunications company had originally considered the removal of its fixed retirement age of 60 'a step too far' because very few people stayed on until that age. Since then the company has changed its retirement policy.

Previously the business was able to retain people beyond 60 if they were needed. Now, all employees have the option of staying on past 60 unless there is a clear business reason against it.

'It's about providing a level of choice for our people,' said Becky Mason, people networks manager and leader of the age action team at BT. 'We are not forcing them to stay on, but they can if they want to.'

Currently, 83 per cent of BT employees who will have reached 60 by March next year have expressed a desire to stay on, compared to only 43 per cent two years ago.

Source: People Management, 15 September 2005.

STAKEHOLDER PENSIONS

From October 2001, employers who do not offer an occupational pension scheme to their employees have been obliged to offer their workers a government-sponsored stakeholder pension (Scrimshaw, 2000). There is, however, no requirement for employers to contribute to these schemes, but they must set up arrangements for the deduction of employee contributions from payroll and pay them direct to the pensions provider. In effect the scheme was designed to encourage workers not currently saving for a pension to start doing so. The target audience for these schemes is those earning between £10,000 and £20,000 per annum, although it was expected that such schemes would have wider appeal.

Such schemes operate on a DC 'money purchase' basis. Employers required to offer access to a stakeholder scheme must offer all employees with more than three months' service the option of joining such a scheme. Schemes must be registered by the Occupational Pensions Regulatory Authority. Before establishing such a scheme, the employer must consult all relevant employees and their representatives. The introduction of compulsory, minimum employer pension contributions under the Pensions Act 2007 may see these schemes become more attractive to employees.

THE ROLE OF HR IN PENSIONS

While specialists, either employed by the organisation or under contract normally administer pension schemes, the HR department will be the first point of contact for scheme members, and will normally manage communications with members. It should be remembered, however, that under the Financial Services Act 1986 and the Pensions Act 1995, there are restrictions on who can give financial advice to employees. HR staff can, however, give information on their organisation's occupational pension scheme, including the basic details of the benefits and contributions and the rights of staff leaving the organisation's employment, as long as this simply relates to information. Any form of advice on options (eg on buying added years) is, however, prohibited. HR staff may also be involved in pre-retirement planning for those retiring, and information about pension rights will be a major item on any such programme.

THE PENSIONS CRISIS

Until recently, defined benefit 'final salary' schemes were the most common form of occupational pension provided by employers. Until the 1990s 'defined contribution' schemes were very much a minority of schemes, but over the last decade this picture has changed dramatically. There has been both a rapid decrease in the number of organisations offering an occupational scheme and a shift from DB to DC schemes. This has led to a significant reduction in the number of employees saving in an occupational pension scheme – down from 40 per cent in 1995 to 32 per cent in 2005 (Pensions Commission, 2004: 81; Government Actuary's Department, 2006: 9). Moreover, as mentioned above, there has been a huge fall in the number of employers offering a defined benefit, 'final salary' scheme.

DB schemes are increasingly only made available in the public sector, where membership has remained stable. Even here, where such schemes continue, employers may have switched to the 'career average' system of calculating the final basic pension, reducing the cost. The withdrawal of defined-benefit, 'final salary' schemes has led to a number of major industrial disputes as workers, through their trade unions, take action to protect their entitlements (see, for example, the extract from *People Management* in Box 8.2 below). This pension crisis is also affecting the future of the UK state retirement provision as well.

A number of reasons have been put forward for these important changes. These include:

- The escalating cost of employer pension scheme contributions has deterred employers from providing pensions or at least led to less generous schemes being offered.

- Long-term demographic trends – namely, pensioners are living much longer, which means that the pension has to provide for a much longer period of retirement.

- The return on pension fund investments has reduced significantly in recent years.

- The increasing state regulation of pensions, following the pensions scandals of the 1990s, has deterred employers from establishing or maintaining schemes.

- A decision of the UK Accounting Standards Board in 2000, through Financial

Reporting Standard 17, changed the way pension scheme assets are valued. This change, effective from 2005, requires organisations to value pension fund assets and liabilities in annual accounts on a market-related basis, meaning that the fluctuations in fund assets are now shown in the company balance sheet, affecting the perceived value of the company among investors.

- The size of the pensioner population is projected to grow significantly, such that the proportion of the working population paying in to pension schemes will be unable to support the enlarged retired population.

In order to deal with this important issue of public policy, the government established the Pensions Commission, chaired by Adair Turner. The 'Turner Commission', as it became known, produced three reports, which in turn led to new government legislation in 2007.

ISSUES IN REWARD

BOX 8.2 BRITISH GAS ENGINEERS STRIKE OVER PENSION PLANS

Firm to close final-salary scheme to new employees

British Gas engineers went on strike today, in protest over proposed changes to the firm's pension scheme. Workers are angry that the company will close its final-salary pension scheme to new employees from next April. The GMB union, which represents staff, said that 6,000 engineers had voted four-to-one in favour of industrial action when they were balloted in November. The union wants British Gas to reconsider its plans.

'GMB sought a suspension of the action by British Gas to close the pension scheme to new starters,' said Brian Strutton, the GMB national secretary. 'This could last for a period of 12 months to allow a re-evaluation of the scheme. We made it clear that we would call off the industrial action if British Gas would agree to this suspension.'

David Kendle, director of British Gas Services, said that the company was standing by its decision. 'Around 75 per cent of the UK's final-salary schemes are already closed to new members and we're facing a similar pensions challenge,' he said.

Further one-day strikes are planned for 19 and 21 December and 6 and 9 January. The company said it has contingency plans to help vulnerable people who might be caught up in the strikes.

Source: *People Management*, 12 December 2005

THE TURNER REPORTS

Turner's first report (Pensions Commission, 2004) provided an analysis of the problems faced. Turner posed four options for the future:

- Pensioners will have to get poorer compared to the rest of society.
- A greater share of taxation will have to be spent on pensions.

- People will have to save more for their retirement.
- People will have to work longer.

The first report's key conclusions were that:

1 Growing life expectancy, coupled to a declining birth rate, mean that by 2050 the proportion of the population aged 65 and over will have doubled and will continue to increase thereafter. The 'baby boom' of the last 30 years has delayed this effect, but will now produce 30 years of very rapid increase in the dependency ratio (the number of pensioners to those of working age). Given this fact, society faces four options: pensioners will become poorer relative to the rest of society; taxes/NICs devoted to pensions must rise; savings must rise; or average retirement ages must rise.

2 Raising retirement ages and increasing the number of elderly people in employment is one solution, but this will insufficient alone to deal with the problem.

3 The UK state pensions system has been one of the least generous in the developed world. This deficiency, however, has been compensated by the fact that the UK had the most developed system of voluntary private funded pensions, so that the overall percentage of GDP transferred to pensioners has been comparable to other countries. The government plans to cut back on state provision, however, to deal with the demographic and cost projections, and expects the private sector to develop to offset the state's declining role. The underlying trend in private sector employer contributions has been downwards since the early 1980s, but the outcomes of this trend were not appreciated until the late 1990s. Since then, defined benefit schemes have been closed to new members and replaced by less generous defined contribution schemes. This means that the underlying level of pension saving is falling rather than rising to meet the new challenges.

4 Given present trends, many employees will face 'inadequate' pensions in retirement, unless they have large non-pensions income or intend to retire much later than current practice. Three-quarters of all DC scheme members have contribution rates below the level required to produce adequate levels of pension.

5 Non-pension savings and housing assets will be insufficient for most people to use in retirement as a replacement income.

6 There are considerable barriers to encouraging more voluntary retirement income provision, but this situation has been made worse by the complexity of the UK pension system, state and private combined. Means testing within the state system both increases complexity and reduces the incentives to save via pensions.

7 To achieve adequacy, three possible options were offered:

- a major revitalisation of the voluntary system;
- significant changes to the state system; and/or

- an increased level of compulsory private pension saving beyond that already implicit within the UK system.

The first report was followed by a second (Pensions Commission, 2005), which laid out recommendations for change. This report laid out four key dimensions for a future integrated approach. These were:

- Reform the state scheme to deliver a more generous, more universal, less means-tested and simpler state pension.

- Strong encouragement to individuals to save for earnings-related pensions through automatic enrolment at a national level.

- A modest minimum level of compulsory employer contributions to ensure that savings are beneficial for all savers.

- The creation of a National Pension Savings Scheme, where there is no good employer-sponsored pension provision, with the state taking on the role of organiser of pension savings and bulk buyer of fund management to ensure low costs and hence higher pensions and better incentives to save.

The third and final report (Pensions Commission, 2006) reiterated the recommendations of the second report but provided more detailed proposals on the latter two recommendations – the employer contribution and the size of the National Pension Savings Scheme.

GOVERNMENT RESPONSE

The government responded to the Turner Commission with a White Paper outlining a number of proposals based on the Commission's recommendations. Following consultation on this White Paper the government introduced new legislation, the Pensions Act 2007. The major changes included in the Act were as follows:

State Pension

- The age at which people can receive their state pensions will rise to 68 by 2046.

- The Basic State Pension will rise in line with earnings from the latest by 2015.

- The minimum income guaranteed by the means-tested Pension Credit will continue to rise in line with earnings each year.

- The State Second Pension will become less valuable for higher earners.

- It will be easier for people with interrupted work patterns (eg those with caring responsibilities) to qualify for contributory state pensions.

Private pensions

From 2012 all employees aged between 22 and State Pension age will be automatically enrolled into a pension scheme, although they will have the freedom to opt out. Where individuals choose to stay in a scheme their employer will be required to make a modest contribution to their pension fund (3 per cent of any earnings between £5,000 and £33,000 per annum) on their behalf. Employers who do not have, or do not wish to establish, their own pension schemes will be able to pay contributions into Personal Accounts, a new occupational pension scheme being set up by the government. A body entitled the Personal Accounts Delivery Authority is to be set up to do the preliminary work necessary for the establishment of personal accounts from April 2012.

 SELF-ASSESSMENT EXERCISE

Is there a moral obligation on employers to provide pensions for their workers? Or should the state be the major provider, as in other European countries, with a consequent increase in taxation on both employers and employees to pay for this scheme? What do your fellow students think?

KEY LEARNING POINTS AND CONCLUSIONS

In this chapter we have considered the role of pensions within the overall reward package as a form of 'deferred pay'. Occupational pensions clearly provide an important and valuable part of the reward package. In the past they have been an integral part of employer recruitment and retention strategies, and a common feature of internal labour market-type organisations, but research indicates that employees may place less value on this benefit today than in the past. This is intriguing, as a pension scheme is one of the most tax-efficient forms of saving and, where the employer makes a contribution, a very valuable benefit for the employee.

The state pension scheme provides a minimum level of entitlement for all citizens, but many, although a diminishing number, of employers also provide private occupational pension schemes. There are two major types of occupational pension scheme – defined benefit and defined contribution. Both these types of scheme have advantages and disadvantages for employers and employees, but the disadvantages of defined benefit schemes appear uppermost in most employers' minds today. The withdrawal of defined benefit schemes has led to some major employee relations problems as unions have mobilised their members in defence of such schemes.

There are a number of pressures encouraging employers to either close their pension schemes or reduce the benefits from them. At the same time there is an increasing demand for adequate retirement incomes in the future, and the question of who should pay for these – government, the employer or the worker – is a major debate at present. The government has commissioned three major reports on this issue. In response to these concerns, the government is introducing legislation providing for new obligatory membership by employees of a private pension scheme and mandatory minimum contributions from employers.

EXPLORE FURTHER

For a detailed review of the issues currently affecting pensions, see the first Turner report: Pensions Commission (2004) *Pensions: Challenges and Choices. The First Report of the Pensions Commission*. London, The Stationery Office.

For basic facts and figures on pensions, see the website of the National Association of Pension Funds, www.napf.co.uk/policy/keyfacts/workplacepensions.cfm

For a more detailed description of current pension options, see Chapter 35 in Armstrong, M. and Murlis, H. (2007) *Reward Management. A handbook of remuneration strategy and practice*, rev. 5th edn. London, Kogan Page.

CHAPTER 9

Non-financial Reward

CHAPTER OBJECTIVES

At the end of this chapter you should understand and be able to explain the following:

- The meaning, constitution and role of non-financial reward within reward systems.

- Debates in the literature around 'total reward', 'employee engagement', the 'value proposition', and related phenomena in commentary and reported practice.

- How a major employer has embarked on a journey to design, communicate and enact a reward strategy that includes attention to 'what it's like to be here'.

CIPD STANDARDS COVERED IN THIS CHAPTER:

To be able to:

- Advise on the management of change when introducing or modifying elements of the reward system.
- Evaluate the case for introducing flexible benefits.
- Promote fairness in reward practices.

To understand and explain:

- The process of reward management, its components and aims.
- The part that financial and non-financial rewards play in attracting, retaining and motivating people.
- The factors that influence employee satisfaction with their rewards and the reward system, such as equity, fairness, consistency and transparency.
- The skills line managers need to implement reward practices and policies and how these skills can be developed.
- New developments in employee reward and their application within the organisation.

INTRODUCTION

In Chapter 7 we described and appraised elements of the employee reward 'package' comprising non-cash 'benefits', as summarised in the list in Table 7.1, and grouped into categories in Table 7.2. We also provided commentary on 'flexible benefits' practices. The present chapter is designed to extend thinking and practice around employee reward and its management, moving into the interesting if sometimes vague and frequently complex realm of non-financial reward. Not so long ago it seems:

> Compensation was the primary 'reward' and benefits, still in their infancy, were a separate and seemingly low-cost supplement for employees. The concept of combining these things – let alone using them with still other 'rewards' to influence employee behavior on the job – was decades away. (Davis, 2007: 1)

Evolution in employment systems, their contexts and reward sub-systems may be perceived as having prompted rethinking of the alternatives available when designing and managing the effort–reward bargain, especially when, as hinted in the final part of the quote above, the intention is to have an influence on how employees *behave* at work. In a recently reviewed book speculating on 'the future of management', co-authored by 'management guru' Gary Hamel, readers are reminded that while 'human beings were not born to be employees', management orthodoxy during the previous century appears to have been founded on the premise that, to achieve discipline and efficiency, people should be 'enslave[d] … in quasi feudal top-down organisations', with the result that 'human imagination and initiative [have been] … squandered' (Johnson, 2007). In the context of a perceived shift towards 'an intelligence economy', in which to become valuable 'worthless … [r]aw information … needs to be processed by a thinking and feeling being' (Coyle, 2001: 33), the argument has been made that employees are recognised 'as drivers of productivity, rather than as relatively interchangeable cogs in a larger wheel' (Davis, 2007: 2).

Under this scenario, rather than through 'a capacity to labour' for an employer, potential employee contribution is seen as frequently vested in tacit knowledge (eg Slaughter, Ang and Boh, 2007). Given the perceived 'shift in the economics of value creation … footloose … workers in possession of the most desirable skills …' are making 'more complex and more subtle demands' on the employment relationship – especially if the employer wishes to 'entice' them 'along the extra mile' (Reeves and Knell, 2001: 41). Such 'engaged' input to organisational performance is 'something the employee has to offer: it cannot be "required" as part of the employment contract' (CIPD, 2007b: 1). One response has been development and popularisation of a discourse under the term 'total reward', something we will define and discuss below.

Employers may choose to apply 'total reward' as a medium to balance and complement extrinsic rewards offered to employees with more intrinsically oriented elements, in pursuit of what has been described as an 'engaged' workforce (CIPD, 2007b; Purcell, 2006). It is possible to attribute to the total reward rubric recognition that, amplified by changes not only to types of work and work settings but also to workforce composition, reward management approaches may not have the same effect on all employees, even assuming consistent application.

If complex organisations employ a diversity of people, it follows logically that employees may be responsive to equally heterogeneous HR policies (Kinnie *et al*, 2005). Specifically in the case of reward policies, while there may be significant scope to standardise *pay* administration (Vernon, 2006), as explained in Chapter 7, this is less likely to be the case in relation to non-cash benefits, particularly in relation to institutional factors, such as variation in tax treatment of perks and other benefits between jurisdictions resulting in marked differences in 'value' conveyed to employees.

Moreover, although '[a]t present, most organizations' compensation practices appear to mimic those of other organizations', and despite the attractions of standardisation to achieve efficiency gains, Gerhart and Rynes point to 'recent evidence...' implying that 'firms might achieve competitive advantage by being "as different as legitimately possible"' (2003: 261). While other organisations within a perceived 'competitor' group may be able to replicate pay and benefits 'packages', a more distinctive 'employee value proposition' (Lawler, 2005; Ulrich and Brockbank, 2005) may be desired to succeed in the so-called 'war for talent' (Michaels *et al*, 2005). Extending the emphasis to intrinsic rewards, subject to variations in how individuals and groups perceive value, contingent on their varying aspirations, beliefs and needs (Kinnie *et al*, 2005), consequences at the effort–reward nexus are likely to be even more marked.

Against this background, we will seek to clarify in this chapter concepts and associated debates in the literature concerned with non-financial (or non-material) rewards, accounting for context. To ground the discussion in practice, balancing theoretical considerations, we will follow one prominent UK-headquartered organisation, Lloyds TSB Group, on a 'journey' the organisation's management have embarked on, inviting customers and employees alike to accompany them, aligning marketing and people management posture, with consequences for the employee value proposition or total reward offering.

DEFINING NON-FINANCIAL REWARD

While the increasingly popular umbrella term 'total reward' may be used to label non-financial reward, its meaning is not straightforward to specify: 'it is easy to see how people can use the term ... only to find that they are referring to very different notions' (Davis, 2007: 2). Reflecting on initial definitions on offer, a relationship may be discerned between 'total reward' and ideas such as 'high investment work systems' (Lepak *et al*, 2007), 'mutual gains' (Bacon and Blyton, 2006) and 'high involvement work practices' (Huselid, 1995); 'employee involvement programmes' (Cox *et al*, 2006; Marchington and Cox, 2007), notions of 'employee voice' and 'partnership at work' (eg Ackers *et al*, 2003); as well as 'emotionally intelligent' leadership (Brown *et al*, 2006; Goleman, 2002; Palmer *et al*, 2001), coupled with attention to 'employee well-being' and the 'psychological contract' (eg Guest and Conway, 2004).

Adopting a broad definition, and using it interchangeably with the term 'employee value proposition', or 'total value', total reward 'can expand to encompass everything that is "rewarding" about working for a particular employer or everything employees get as a result of their employment' (Davis, 2007: 2). In the spirit of this approach, in a Factsheet on the topic, the CIPD refers to 'a mindset that enables employers to look at the bigger picture' (Richards and Hogg, 2007: 2). The implication is that, by going beyond the extrinsic elements of the effort–reward bargain, employers will 'actively manage … aspects of the work experience' that may have been 'taken for granted' (Richards and Hogg, 2007: 3).

Inherent in the total reward concept here, then, is the expectation of managerial proactivity, with the consequence that 'embedded' managerial attitudes towards effort–reward management and the part they have to play need to be factored in to considerations of total reward design and process (Marchington and Cox, 2007). The 'CIPD viewpoint' concluding its Factsheet is that 'total reward has the possibility of being a very powerful management tool'; as a 'change catalyst'

Figure 9.1 An inclusive view of total reward

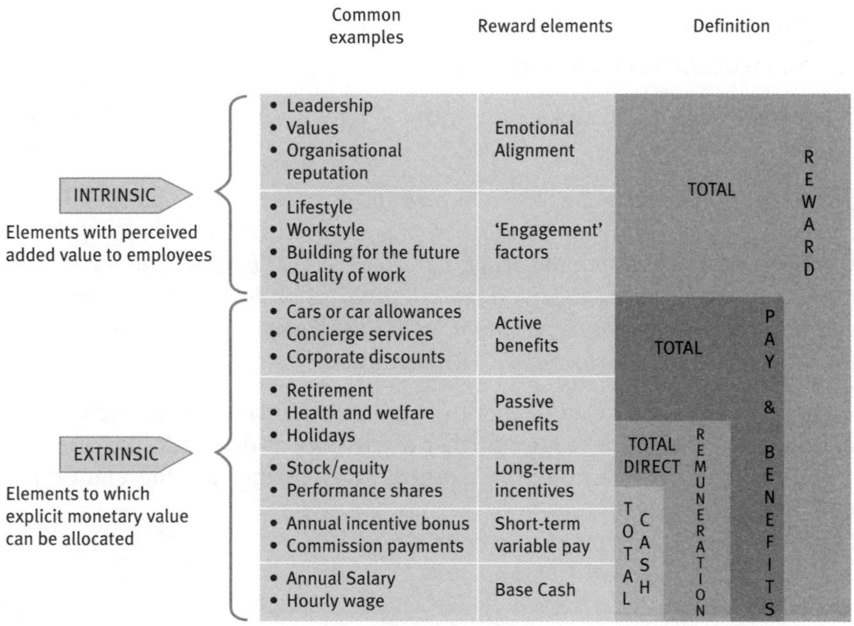

Source: Adapted from Helen Murlis and Clive Wright (personal correspondence)

it 'is fairly simple to understand but very complex in operation' owing to the 'wide-ranging implications for ... reward management' (Richards and Hogg, 2007: 4).

In the World at Work's handbook on total rewards (notice the added 's' in this US label), the emphasis is on employees' perception of value. In short: 'For a total rewards strategy to be successful, employees must perceive monetary and nonmonetary rewards as valuable' (Davis, 2007: 4).

CIPD Reward Faculty members Helen Murlis and Clive Wright use a diagram like the one in Figure 9.1 to help communicate visually the types of phenomena the various total reward definitions appear to comprise, depending on breadth of approach adopted. But active management of total reward is not a one-way, employee-centric enterprise. The notion of an effort–reward exchange is emphasised, albeit implicitly, in the World at Work definition. In combination, extrinsic and intrinsic rewards are 'provided to employees in exchange for their time, talents, efforts, and results': five key elements are 'artfully tailored' into a package intended, on the one hand, to secure and retain talented employees, as well as, on the other hand, to motivate them optimally to achieve business results (Davis, 2007: 4). The five components of World at Work's total rewards are summarised as follows:

- compensation
- benefits
- work–life
- performance and recognition
- development and career opportunities.

The itemisation is broadly in keeping with the total reward definition offered by the CIPD:

> The term ... adopted to describe a reward strategy that brings additional components such as learning and development, together with aspects of the working environment into the benefits package. It goes beyond standard remuneration by embracing the company culture, and is aimed at giving all employees a voice in the organisation, with the employer in return receiving an ngaged employee performance. (Richards and Hogg, 2007: 1)

The latter description may go further in making reference to terms such as 'culture' and 'voice' that require further discussion, as do 'work–life' and 'recognition' for performance in the World at Work listing, and the 'emotional reward' cited in Figure 9.1.

CASE ILLUSTRATION 1
INTERPRETING TOTAL REWARD IN PRACTICE

We locate this discussion in the context of the rolling company case we are using to ground discussion of the total reward concept in specific practice, in the words of Tim Fevyer, Head of Pay Policy & Market Intelligence at Lloyds TSB:

> *Historically, we defined reward and talked about our package (internally and to prospective employees) in terms of salary (or 'base pay') alone. However, recognising that people can, and do, receive much more than just base pay, we set the goal of moving understanding along a spectrum.*

> *At the first stage of the journey, we began to talk in terms of the 'total cash' an individual receives each year combining base pay and bonus or other incentive payments. Talking about the 'employment offer' in terms of total cash began to better represent how people are actually rewarded. However, we also invested a considerable amount in non-cash benefits and, in the same way, it was clear that there was a gap between what people received and how we talked about it.*

The diagram in Figure 9.2 illustrates the stages in the Lloyds TSB total reward journey.

Figure 9.2 Lloyds TSB's reward management journey

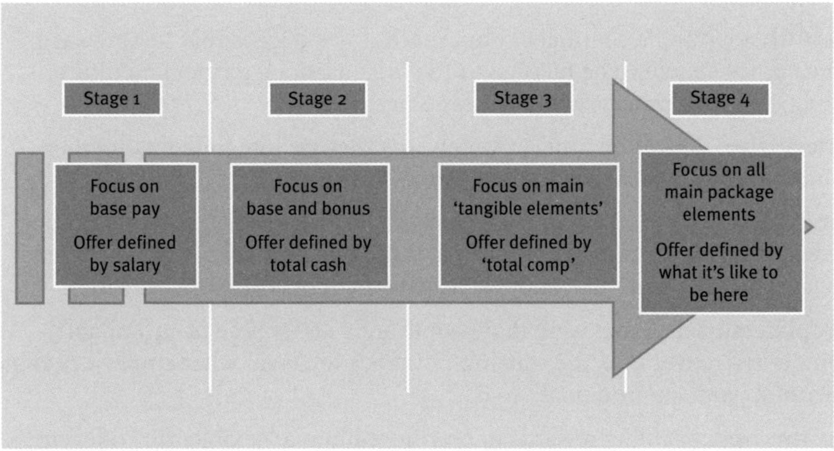

Stage 1	Stage 2	Stage 3	Stage 4
Focus on base pay / Offer defined by salary	Focus on base and bonus / Offer defined by total cash	Focus on main 'tangible elements' / Offer defined by 'total comp'	Focus on all main package elements / Offer defined by what it's like to be here

Source: Adapted from Tim Fevyer (personal correspondence)

Fevyer continues:

> *We were missing out on a significant part of our 'employment deal'. Partly in terms of the investment, partly in terms of people not being able to calculate the true worth of their package, and partly because there was a range of elements that people might really value but that weren't really 'communicated'. We realised the importance of process, reflecting the dynamism involved: while*

we might talk about pay and benefits, as though these were static, the real difference was being made through flexibility in how they were applied. As a result, we formed a deliberate plan to move along the spectrum – to talk to our existing people and to prospective employees in much broader terms about the total package.

This next stage also brought a conscious change of voice. Firstly we moved from communicating to 'marketing' – introducing a new and different colourful employee reward brand. This brand served to create a reward identity: it stimulated 'anchors' and 'hooks' for people. For the first time, we could talk about one element of reward and automatically encourage people to make connections with other elements of the package. The initiative helped us in getting people to take notice of the broader elements of the Lloyds TSB reward proposition and over time became a type of self-fulfilling prophecy.

To round off this 'definitional' section of the chapter, an analysis of various models of total reward (Thompson, 2002) may help to establish a sense of the aspirations that may be observed as characterising this area of commentary and reported practice. The review of practice echoes the discourse outlined above, but is usefully expressed below in précis form, finding that total reward combines the following features. It is:

- **Holistic**: with a focus on how employers attract, retain and motivate employees to contribute to organisational success using an array of financial and non-financial rewards.

- **Best fit**: adopting a contingency approach, the advice is that total reward approaches should to be tailored to the organisation's particular culture, structure, work process and business objectives.

- **Integrative**: delivering innovative rewards that are integrated with other human resource management policies and practices.

- **Strategic**: aligning all aspects of reward to business strategy – total reward is driven by business needs and rewards the business activities, employee behaviour and values that support achievement of corporate priorities.

- **People-centred**: recognising that people are a key source of sustainable competitive advantage, the starting-point is a focus on what employees value in the 'total work environment'.

- **Customised**: enabling rewards to be tailored into a 'flexible mix' offering choice and improved design to match employees' needs, their lifestyle and stage of life.

- **Distinctive**: using a complex and diverse 'employment experience' to create an idiosyncratic 'employer brand' to differentiate the organisation from its rivals.

- **Evolutionary**: a long-term approach to effort–reward determination is adopted, based on incremental rather than on radical change.

The strategic and integrative aspects associated with the total reward concept, along with developments in 'employment branding' are subjects of specific and detailed attention in Chapter 12, 'Employee Reward within HRM'.

STUDENT EXERCISE

The 2007 CIPD Annual Reward Survey reports that nearly 4 in 10 employers had adopted or are implementing a total reward approach, with a higher proportion among larger private sector firms (CIPD, 2007c). Search online for some company annual reports statements and look at the section dealing with 'our people' or a similar term:

- For instance, access the discussion on 'people development' at retail group Kingfisher plc, authored by Tony Williams, Group Human Resources Director, at: http://www.kingfisher.com/ managed_content/files/reports/annual_report_2007/index.asp?pageid=16.

- Another example appears on pages 6–7 of Unilever plc's 2006 Annual Report and Accounts, under the heading 'our employees'. Follow the online link using the URL: http://www.unilever. com/Images/ir_06_annual_report_en_tcm13-88803.pdf?linkid=dropdown, and then use the search facility with the search term 'employees'. Some examples are provided of initiatives to enable people employed by the group company in roles at various levels around the world to 'develop', illustrating particular features of their employment offer.

Using these examples or others you identify, try to reach a consensus with a group of fellow students on the kinds of issues that 'total reward' thinking might address. The kinds of criteria included in the definitions section above may guide your judgements.

A HIGH-INVESTMENT EMPLOYMENT EXPERIENCE

In this section, we explore the non-financial aspects of 'total rewards' positioned in terms of deliberate managerial initiatives to align employees and work systems by moving beyond monetary-style 'incentives' to contribute to organisational performance. Relating the practices involved back to the discussion of 'efficiency wage' theory in Chapter 2, the underlying thinking may be viewed as investment-rather than cost-oriented, based on the assumption that 'investment returns' will follow, to be evaluated using 'HR metrics' such as 'improvement of the workforce mindset' (Beatty *et al*, 2007: 364).

At a first-stage process level, 'flexible' administration of non-cash benefits with a monetary value may itself be counted as a *non-financial* benefit: empowering employees to tailor a portfolio of employment terms to match preferences that, as sketched above (citing Kinnie *et al* (2005)), may differ among individuals and groups, and change over time. The employer may also be better able to highlight the financial value delivered to employees, when individuals are afforded the flexibility to construct a benefits portfolio, making trade-offs between the various facets making up the whole, so building understanding of the 'benefit' received from both active and passive benefits exemplified in Figure 9.1, comparing themselves with others, and how they are rewarded, inside and outside the organisation.

CASE ILLUSTRATION 2
CUSTOMISING TOTAL REWARD IN PRACTICE

Indicative of the learning that takes place at each stage of the Lloyds TSB journey, Tim Fevyer observes that:

> *Relying on pay to achieve the things we want our line management to do was only abdicating line management to pay. What we found was that, in reality, the impact of pay is limited ... unless you get it wrong – in which case it can have a significantly negative impact. Therefore, get pay right; then focus on the things that really do make a difference.*

> *We started to treat people on a much more individualised basis. With some 65,000 people, with a rich diversity of backgrounds and aspirations, it no longer made sense to treat them like one homogeneous group. We undertook detailed investigation into take-up trends across our flexible benefits programme (introduced in 2003). We found that there were some very clear patterns across particular groups of individuals (differentiated, for example, by age, length of service, and income). We cross-matched the data to our customer segmentation model and found that there were five main groupings that could be regarded as distinctive. Specific groups of people were responding to different things in different ways, in terms of what they valued, where they 'spent their money' and how they liked to be communicated with.*

> *From this it was a small step to conclude that we ought to be talking to key distinctive groups in different ways. Using the expertise developed in the Group's marketing function, under an umbrella brand, we radically changed our communications, tailoring them to the characteristics of each broad segment. The result was a disproportionate increase in take-up within our specifically targeted segments (those where take up had previously been lower than trend).*

The Lloyds TSB case provides an insight into managerial thinking that, while skilful calibration is important (as we discuss in Chapter 5), on its own pay is unlikely to be sufficient to achieve corporate goals through the employment relationship. And, although marking a progressive initial step, flexible administration of employee benefits may not go far enough for employers who wish to create a distinctive 'employment value proposition'. Workforce members may regard flexible benefits as 'little more than an extension to the existing salary package and something, therefore, that can be matched by rival companies' (Richards and Hogg, 2007: 2). For 'maximum effect', defined in terms of obtaining competitive advantage – in sourcing talented people and through them achieving profitable high performance – the advice is to align organisational strategy with employee aspirations and needs into something that is hard for others to replicate.

This thinking is consistent with the resource-based theory of the firm, especially in industrial contexts where 'the human element is fundamental to the business' (Jackson and Schuler, 2007: 27). High-investment human resource (HIHR) systems may be defined as a set of 'practices to enhance employee skills and motivation for the attainment of competitive advantage' (Lepak *et al*, 2007: 223). A range of research conducted during the period 1995–2001 is cited by Lepak *et al* (2007) to argue that application of HIHR systems is positively related to a variety of outcomes important to employers, including employee turnover, organisational commitment, operational performance and financial performance.

A decision to invest in policies and practices purposely intended to shift the 'employment experience' over and above extrinsic rewards is not, of course, an issue limited to employers in the private sector. In a report prepared for the Office of Manpower Economics, to investigate suggestions that had been made to members of UK public sector review bodies that the quality of recruits to public sector organisations had declined in recent years, PA Consulting Group cite prior findings by HMG's Audit Commission that people join the public sector for an interdependent bundle of reasons. These are to '"make a difference", in a job that satisfies them, and with a reward package that meets their needs' (2007: 33). The deciding factor for accepting employment was professionally grounded, the report stated, rather than linked to the sector in which the role may be located; PA said this echoed the consultants' own experience 'working with a range of organisations in both sectors' (2007: 33). Key 'push' factors in driving employees away from the public sector factors were 'dissatisfaction with organisational culture and the ways of working', in particular, '"bureaucracy", paperwork and targets, and a feeling that ... managers did not understand or value them' (2007: 33).

The view offered by PA was that extrinsic 'reward is only one of three principal factors that determine the ability of employers to attract, retain and motivate quality employees. The other factors, employer reputation or brand (including culture, values and environment) and job content/career prospects, are at least as important in determining job choices' (2007: 33). Although the relative weighting given to each factor may be a matter of individual employee preference and circumstances, the perceived consequence was that 'high calibre' employees, likely to have the most choice in labour markets, will be able to seek the best overall combination of the extrinsic and intrinsic total reward elements specified.

 SELF-ASSESSMENT EXERCISE

Consider the argument outlined above that industry sector is less important to employees in assessing the prospects for a rewarding employment experience than the profession or role they occupy. If you were seeking to make a business case to top management to migrate consciously to a high-investment HR system, where would you begin? Repeat the exercise in the guise of a HR professional, (a) in private sector manufacturing, (b) in private sector services, (c) in the voluntary sector, and (d) in the public or government service sector.

While the total reward ethos is holism, given the complex nature of the range of potentially interconnected parts, we will examine in this section of the chapter the total reward factors that combine to comprise 'the work experience' (Davis, 2007: 5), namely, acknowledgment; balance (of work and life); career or professional development; workplace environment and culture. Each element will be taken in turn – for description and reflection on accompanying positive and negative argument in the literature – before weighing the candidacy of the bundle as 'greater than the sum of its parts'.

ACKNOWLEDGEMENT

> *The promise of public recognition for exceptional performance can be a considerable stimulus, even if recognition is only the award of a certificate that has no monetary value whatsoever.* (Kressler, 2003: 43)

Handel (2001) reports Greg Boswell, executive vice-president of the National Association for Employee Recognition (NAER), as attributing 'strategic initiative' status to employee recognition. Some organisations have indeed invested in developing fairly sophisticated employee recognition schemes that go beyond acknowledgment by management representatives of what an employee has done, to include a tangible 'award'. Tracking the return on managerial investment, however, a sober assessment of the effects of formalised employee recognition appeared in a report published in the USA in February 2007 by the Institute for Corporate Productivity (i4cp), stating:

> *While 73% of recently surveyed companies said that they have an employee recognition program in place ... 37% of respondents said they do not know how satisfied their employees are with the program, and more than 15% said their employees are not satisfied at all.* (i4cp, 2007)

A spokesperson for i4cp implied that managerial processes were at fault. Employee recognition was rated a key factor in the motivation of employees, linked to organisational outcomes, but it was argued that a system of checks and balances needed to be in place to make sure formal employee recognition arrangements did what management intended. The implication is that, where employee recognition is formalised, at least, holistic thinking is needed backed up by formal processes so that recognition is firmly located within the overall reward management system.

When surveyed about the structure and types of employee recognition investment (where recognition attracts 'a dollar value', based on an aspiration to create 'a culture of recognition'), 89 per cent of some 600 US compensation specialists cited length of service awards as the most common type of recognition programme (NAER and World at Work, 2005). This compares with the (2007) i4cp survey findings that 'personal performance' formed the top criterion for recognition awards at (49 per cent), followed by 'extra effort' (35 per cent) and 'corporate performance' (26 per cent).

Almost 70 per cent of respondents to the NAER/World at Work (2005) survey stated that their organisations had a specific budget for employee recognition, with a majority (57 per cent) locating responsibility for managing the programme in the HR function. While a majority (55 per cent) also reported a positive view of formal employee recognition among senior management, 13 per cent said it was judged as an expense. According to these respondents, the success of the programme is assessed based on evidence such as participation rates and the number of employee nominations, although the most common method is via surveys of 'employee satisfaction' (45 per cent).

One US consultant whose firm assists organisations with this aspect of the reward portfolio argues that the rationale is 'to create an environment that goes above and beyond the minimum expectations, which has a positive impact on employees and creates the reputation of a company that people choose to work for' (Dermer, 2005: 40).

The case of NBC Universal is offered to illustrate necessary managerial actions if employee recognition is to be more than simply another tangible award (Dermer, 2005). The company had a history of recognising employee efforts with cash-based spot bonuses – however, awards were reportedly presented 'without fanfare'. A cross-functional group of managers reviewed principles for recognising employee contribution that was seen as demonstrably linked with overall organisational improvement goals, to achieve 'a synergistic effect' (Dermer, 2005: 40). The new initiative was branded 'Ovation', suggesting that individuals were being explicitly applauded before their peers and others in the organisation. The review panel developed guidelines based on '"voice of the customer" input from operations managers' (Dermer, 2005: 40). They concluded that recognition should be:

- visible: public presentation of awards is encouraged;

- prevalent: smaller-size awards are given more frequently, to more employees;

- memorable: rather than just cash, recognition awards may offer employees a specially branded Gift Certificate Award;

- personal and spontaneous: Internet technology is used by NBC Universal to enable a wide variety of choices (merchandise, travel packages, airline miles and phone cards, as well as cash) to appeal to a large and diverse employee audience, while suiting different occasions calling for recognition.

In an attempt to reinforce NBC Universal's corporate values, employees are recognised for a variety of things, 'including successful launches, extraordinary effort, cost containment, customer service, imagination, initiative, innovation, leadership, teamwork, project support, safety and volunteerism' (Dermer, 2005: 40). Recognition budgets are held at division levels and managed by HR specialists in conjunction with operations managers. Administration is outsourced and uses technology for ordering, delivering and tracking.

Hansen *et al* (2002) sound a cautionary note regarding the assumption that employee recognition can be organised managerially into an administrative procedure. They criticise commentary in which reward and recognition are treated as synonymous, arguing instead that the results of each approach reflect a dualistic impact on human motivation. Hansen *et al* (2002) ground their argument in theoretical commentary on human motivation, as discussed in Chapter 2 above. Citing Herzberg's 'two-factor' approach and Maslow's 'needs hierarchy', Hansen *et al* (2002) draw a distinction between extrinsic and intrinsic motivation stimuli. Relating this to reward and recognition, they argue that rewards should only be viewed instrumentally, as 'means-to-end' for 'doing chores' (2002: 65). This contrasts with the 'appreciating', 'honouring' and 'noticing' that they say should apply to recognition, even if that recognition is perceived managerially as encouraging and supporting an action.

Hansen *et al* (2002) cite Deci's (1975) argument that intrinsic motivation is derived from an individual's changed perception related to competence – intrinsically motivating recognition is thus associated with an emphasis on 'competence feedback'. This compares with actions predicted to decrease intrinsic motivation, which for Hansen *et al* are those 'administered controllingly'.

> *Recognition that is perceived to be superficial or frivolous will be seen as a veiled attempt to manipulate. It will undermine rather than support the intrinsic motivational processes it is designed to support.* (Hansen *et al*, 2002: 69)

To avoid praise being viewed by an employee as attempted behavioural control, in the way that 'money or threats' may be perceived, so communicating to employees that their response should be similarly instrumental, the process needs to 'provide people with positive information about their self-competence' (2002: 66). Hence, following this line of reasoning, the actions that management plan for the various units of total reward need to be organised against the presence of two motivational sub-systems.

Intended employee recognition should be organised in accordance with the intrinsic motivational sub-system, delineated from the other half of the reward–recognition duality associated with extrinsic motivation. Whereas reward programmes that support extrinsic motivation have a finite life and desired behaviours may fall away as the programme degrades over time, Hansen *et al* (2002) argue that properly handled attention to recognition – whether the behaviours are specifically recognised or not – will ensure that how employees operate at work are continuously motivated 'from the inside out' (Hansen *et al*, 2002: 72).

Respecting the employee heterogeneity argument by Kinnie *et al* (2005), as well as the foregoing encouragement to provide forms of 'competence development feedback', active acknowledgement may offer managements an important means by which to build positive relationships with specific employee communities. For example, Bergmann and Gulbinas Scarpello cite research scientists as likely to regard 'aspects of their work [as] more important than money' (2001: 584). The commentators argue that for such an employee group 'freedom to create and to discover' (2001: 584) is likely to encourage commitment to an employing organisation. We will return to these considerations when discussing career/professional development and workplace 'culture' below.

SELF-ASSESSMENT EXERCISE

You are the HR director of a large pharmaceutical company. Devise a set of criteria to evaluate the extent to which formal and informal employee recognition is appreciated by workforce members, (a) in research and development roles, and (b) in sales force roles.

BALANCE OF WORK AND LIFE

Work–life balance is a term associated [on the one hand] with individual choice and responsibility; on the other hand, the term stands accused of obscuring global and interconnected issues that require reciprocal negotiation and changes between men and women, in their families, their workplaces, their communities and wider society. (Shearn, 2007: 601)

That dichotomy provides a setting for discussion of this element of total reward thinking that has become the subject of extensive commentary.

A decade ago, few employers would have said 'Work–life benefits really make a difference to our current employees or our prospective employees when it comes to recruitment and retention'. A decade later, employers are offering work–life carrots at every chance. (Federico, 2007: 109)

Notions of 'employee wellbeing', and concomitant managerial initiatives to combat workplace and work–life stress, may also be considered under the 'work–life' rubric, although running the risk of being perceived as little more than 'a clever re-labelling of traditional absence management, occupational health and good management practice' (CIPD, 2007d: 1). The UK government has adopted a more positive orientation to the topic, arguing in a 2004 Department of Health white paper, cited by the CIPD (2007d), that employers who linked 'healthy choices' for their employees recognised that this made 'good business sense', as well as being the corporately socially responsible thing to do.

The CIPD interprets the evidence in case studies assembled to inform a 'change agenda' report as indicative of employee wellbeing 'steadily rising up the business agenda', in the context of 'an overarching aspiration to create an equal, healthy and vibrant society where people enjoy what they are doing whether in or out of work, in turn leading to individuals being more productive in their working lives' (2007d: 2–3).

At the European level, work–life balance has been perceived as a central theme of the EU gender equality framework, although standards vary across member states with different welfare regime traditions (Idil Aybars, 2007). The 2004 WERS findings, however, suggest caution in generalising around managerial attention to balancing the demands of work and other commitments, accounting for firm sector and size:

Managers in the private sector were more likely to consider that employees had the sole responsibility for ensuring their own work–life balance, especially those managers located in small workplaces. (Kersley *et al*, 2006: 51)

Messersmith (2007) reviews research findings on 'work–life conflict', which he defines as 'a construct referring to the general interference that work life tends to have on an employee's personal life' (Messersmith, 2007: 430). The construct is 'a more general form of work–family conflict', defined by Greenhaus and Beutell (1985: 77, in Messersmith, 2007: 430) as 'a form of interrole conflict in which the role pressures from the work and family domains are mutually incompatible in some respect'. An imbalance between work and employees' other activities can be exemplified as intrusions of work into family time and leisure activities. It may also be manifested in a general inability to stop thinking about employment-associated work even when physically moving out of the workplace to the home and personal environment.

While appearing to readily meet Knell's (2001) definition of the 'footloose worker' on whom employers have come to depend in the intelligence economy, peopled by Coyle's (2001) 'thinking feeling beings' whose labour converts the raw information to valuable organisational knowledge, Messersmith (2007) argues that employees in the information technology sector are more prone than most to work–life conflict. Consequently, learning to manage this conflict is posited as an important corporate challenge. The business case for managerial action is expressed in stark cost terms: as the experience of work–life conflict increases, especially among key professional employees, research suggests that both job satisfaction and commitment to organisational objectives decrease, leading to unplanned employee wastage among employees with high 'career mobility' potential (Messersmith (2007):

This revolving door can prove to be quite costly to organizations, with one estimate suggesting that it costs a company approximately 120% of annual salaries when high-performing IT workers leave organizations. (Vitalari and Dell, 1998, in Messersmith, 2007: 431)

One possible management response to work–life conflict within the total rewards portfolio is to establish 'family-friendly' and 'life-friendly' policies. Evaluators publishing lists of 'best place to work' organisations are reported to demand the 'big three' of on-site childcare, flexible work arrangements and 'accommodating' time off policies (Federico, 2007: 110). Other features observed characterising organisations' work–life/wellness programmes include 'domestic-partner benefits' (ie not just for legal spouses), health screenings, fitness benefits, tuition reimbursement, on-site convenience/concierge services and sabbaticals.

Federico (2007) also draws attention to publicity associated with a 'Best Employers for Workers over 50' list, in tune with perceived demographic shifts in workforce composition. With large numbers of 'mature' employees acting as primary care-giver for aging parents, a demand for elder care support services, as well as flexible work arrangements is listed as increasingly recognised by employers. Oates reports the prediction that 'eldercare [will] replace childcare as the major work–life issue by 2020' (2007: 40).

Policies to enable employees to work 'virtually' may also be introduced, enabling employees with children and elder carers to meet these calls on their time while working full- or part-time. In addition, Messersmith argues:

Virtual work reduces time-based conflict by reducing the number of hours an employee is asked to commute each week. Employees may enjoy significant time-savings in major metropolitan areas, allowing them to engage in more non-work-related activities. (2007: 437–9)

While there appears to be a case in favour of virtual work as a form of 'family flexibility' employment, there are reported downsides. First, if the once-present boundary between work and personal life is severed, virtual work is actually predicted to increase levels of work–life conflict. Secondly, virtual work may not successfully reduce work–life conflict unless accompanied by a willingness on the part of employers to invest in establishing the technical infrastructure to facilitate it at both the organisation and the employee's home. Thirdly, there is a risk that isolation will cause 'virtual workers' to lose touch with informal intra-organisation networks, ultimately leading to a loss of promotion and advancement opportunities (Pinsonneault and Boisvert, 2001, cited in Messersmith, 2007).

Widening the critique still further, Eikhof *et al* call for 'analysis that explores the back-story to work–life balance debate as well as the operation of work–life balance policies' (2007: 325). There is little, they argue, in the work–life debate that challenges work per se, especially the *over-work* phenomenon 'identified as a problem throughout the modern world' (Roberts, 2007: 334); and 'life' is too narrowly perceived, equating it with women's care work, hence the emphasis on 'family-friendly' polices (Eikhof *et al*, 2007). For Gambles, Lewis and Rapoport (2006, cited by Shearn, 2007) work–life balance is no more than a myth arising from 'three critical tensions: the invasiveness of paid work, the need for time and energy to care about each other, and gender roles' (2007: 601).

CASE ILLUSTRATION 3
WORK–LIFE BALANCE CONSIDERATIONS IN PRACTICE

In Lloyds TSB, work–life balance policies are seen as 'a critical way of engaging people and harnessing talent', according to Tim Fevyer:

Reflecting what I've already said about taking notice of the diversity of wants and needs among the people we employ, the view is that by accommodating these differences it helps us to recruit, retain, and 'engage' the people we need.

We know (for example, from internal surveys of employee opinion, and from option take-up through flexible benefits), that people really do value the opportunity to balance their work and home life – a third of our staff now work reduced hours, and many more work flexibly in various patterns on an informal basis. So, again, if we provide people with the flexibility to create more balance, it is very likely that it will positively impact on their engagement in the organisation. Which, in turn, will ultimately feed through to bottom line results.

If it's managed properly, flexible working is also a clear investment. Giving people the flexibility they need (as long as it's balanced with the needs of the organisation), we find, invariably leads to the individual giving more to the company – through greater flexibility and commitment on the part of the individual, as well as the fact that people tend to work more 'smartly' making much more effective use of time. Many individuals across the organisation will say that, by providing greater flexibility to balance their work and home life, it means they can actually give more to both.

STUDENT EXERCISE

Conduct a straw poll among people you know from your network of professional and wider contacts on what respondents say they understand by the terms 'work–life balance' (and its opposite); 'wellness'; and flexibility around working life. Using the range of definitions you assemble, draw up a plan specifying ways in which business needs for committed and 'available' people can be achieved while satisfying employee aspirations.

CAREER OR PROFESSIONAL DEVELOPMENT

We have no intention of duplicating commentary properly developed at greater length in specialist texts on employee resourcing and learning and development. Such material may, however, be complemented by examining arguments suggesting that the signals and benefits perceived by employees from managerial investment in their career and/or professional 'development' should be positioned within the total reward envelope, while being mindful of Kinnie *et al*'s (2005) caveat on workforce heterogeneity. Access to learning opportunities – both formalised 'training' and through a range of planned and corporately supported experience – may be perceived among workforce members as a form of 'progression', and so potentially valued as an intrinsic benefit. This is particularly the case where flatter organisational structures, designed to enhance lines of communication and responsiveness to market demands, limit traditional 'promotions' and accompanying extrinsic reward 'progression'.

Rather than a experiencing work as something mechanical 'within an incomprehensibly huge machine', Kressler argues that employees will feel 'rewarded' and enabled to attain personal development and self-actualisation if work is experienced 'as [making] a contribution to business objectives, as recognized performance, as … confirmation of personal and professional competence' (2003: 33). Thus, it is argued that work should be managed so as to fulfil the individual's 'desire for personal growth' as well as 'a need for belonging – to a business, a group or a profession, at least to something that imparts a positive value, including status and prestige' (2003: 33).

As a minimum, having a clear understanding of one's role eliminates wasted time and energy spent trying to work out the tasks that need to be completed and the internal and external customers with whom the employee is expected to communicate. This is particularly noteworthy during new employee induction/ socialisation processes. Messersmith (2007, citing King *et al*, 2005) contends that, as a result, workers (particularly those in 'knowledge-intensive' roles) feel less role conflict and therefore are more likely to be committed to the organisation and have higher levels of job satisfaction. Actions may include allocating mentors, so connecting new entrants, for example, to more experienced employees.

A reality check on this upbeat line of argument is offered, however, by Marchington and Wilkinson, who contrast reports of the emergence of 'learning organisations', and 'knowledge management' with the view that 'it remains the case that in many workplaces access to training and development remains inadequate and partial' (2005: 218). Citing Herriot (1998), Marchington and Wilkinson (2005) argue that the foundation of the contemporary 'psychological contract' is based on the principle that employees will offer the organisation 'flexibility, accountability and long hours' (2005: 34) in return for provision of 'a good job' (as well as a high salary). A 'good' job is here understood, using criteria outlined by Marchington and Wilkinson (2005), as providing employees with:

- scope to exercise a range of skills and talents;
- a requirement to see an identifiable job through from start to completion;
- a sense of a significant role to perform, measured in terms of impact on others;
- autonomy and discretion in selecting methods and working time; and
- clear feedback on how performance is judged by supervisors.

Maximising these characteristics is expected to result in workforce members:

- experiencing meaningful work;
- having a sense of being responsible for outcomes; and
- gaining knowledge of the results of work activities.

Focusing in particular on high 'growth-need strength' workforce segments, the conclusion is that employees are more likely to secure a positive work experience (assessed in terms of their psychological state) if these principles are in evidence in work design and career management practices (Marchinton and Wilkinson, 2005).

Bergmann and Gulbinas Scarpello (2001) also single out specific workforce segments for attention. Workers in creative sectors and research and development roles are cited as exemplars of employee groups 'for whom aspects of their work are often more important than money'. Thus a work environment needs to offer a setting – eg access to the latest technology, as well as room for autonomy – that will enable these people to create and discover (Bergmann and Gulbinas Scarpello, 2001: 584). Another route by which to 'reward' specialists ('creatives' and innovators) non-financially is through 'the creation of career paths that recognize members' particular skills' (2001: 584).

This rehearses a long-standing argument whereby standard career ladders are criticised on the ground that they lack the flexibility to accommodate routes to advancement for some workers other than moving into 'management'. Although offering tangible rewards commensurate with equivalent managerial levels, operating 'dual career ladders' permits 'researchers to continue to do what they do best, creating and innovating', something 'often more beneficial to both the researchers and the organization' (2001: 584).

The general thrust of this argument may apply not just to particular occupational groups but also to public sector workers, noted earlier as actively seeking 'public service' employment because they wish 'to do something worthwhile' (PA, 2007). Another group, possibly emerging in all sectors, is one for whom 'worthwhile employment' may represent career management that is socially responsible relative to the natural environment, creating a minimal 'carbon footprint'. In the case of innovators, a more tangible recognition may of course be opportunities to share in the success of realisation and commercialisation of their inventiveness, so that patent rights and royalties do not simply pass to the employer, as has traditionally been the case (Bergmann and Gulbinas Scarpello, 2001).

Reflecting a 'resource-based' theoretical stance, Dyer and Ericksen argue that more than 'heavy investments in cutting-edge training and development' (2007: 275) are necessary if organisations are to be 'dynamic', in the sense of being flexible and ready to adapt to constantly changing business environments, and to build capabilities among a 'fluid' workforce that is not only valuable but also hard for competitors to replicate. Following this line of reasoning, one of the actions managements need to take is to 'provide unwavering support for employees who move from opportunity to opportunity in pursuit of smart risks that sometimes pay off in a big way but always result in highly valuable future oriented-learning even when they fail' (2007: 275–6).

Employees likely to succeed in such environments are perceived as expecting to be supported in this way, and to be assigned to roles that are not simply bundles of regular tasks with scope for innovation limited to 'other duties as assigned': instead core tasks are reduced to a minimum, with wide discretion to be constantly on the look-out for new challenges as well as new ways of meeting familiar ones. Creating a mind-set attuned in this way, it is argued, will create an enriched talent pool as well as retaining talented individuals and groups who otherwise might pursue more rewarding job design elsewhere or at best not perform to corporate expectations.

UK evidence, however, suggests the existence of a principles/reality gap. While WERS 2004 findings are that employee wellbeing is 'positively related to the degree of job influence' (Kersley *et al*, 2006: 103), Felstead (2007) reports that, when surveying people about the degree of choice available to them over how they perform their job, he found 'a marked decline in task discretion' over a fifteen-year period (2007: 129). Asked about the degree of choice over how they perform their job, in 1986, 52 per cent of respondents reported 'a great deal' of discretion; the figure fell to 39 per cent in 2001.

'Strategic workforce planning' has been advocated by The Conference Board under the rubric of 'forecasting human capital needs to execute business strategy'

(Young, 2006). But Isles criticises a 'dearth of formal internal succession plans for even senior positions' (2007: 107). He argues that a propensity among talented people to switch organisations, enhanced by 'broadening geographic mobility', among other things, to improve their 'employability and earnings potential' (2007: 107) might help explain the interest in 'talent management'. Here 'talent' is not only a form of trait, 'the sum of a person's abilities'; it is also vested in 'opportunity', 'because talent requires opportunity to be displayed' (2007: 107). Talent management initiatives may not only exist to extract the value of talent for the organisation's benefit; the result may be viewed under the total reward rubric as another way in which to retain key workforce segments who might otherwise depart in response to offers of 'the right culture [providing] self-fulfilment, a sense of accomplishment and emotional attachment in their employment' (2007: 107).

Isles (2007) identifies a combination of talent management practices, including work design initiatives, actions to foster relationships via mentoring and coaching, and encouragement for networking between individuals and their functional areas for mutual benefit. Of course, yet again rehearsing Kinnie *et al*'s (2005) diversity argument, different talent segments (eg 'player managers' in financial services, compared with research and development specialists in manufacturing) may need different talent management initiatives to enable them to add value and so feel recognised.

Career and professional development as features within total reward may thus be seen as aligning reward management with employee resourcing policies and practices: one aspect of providing skilled people with the sense that the organisation is an 'engaging' place to be compared with alternatives on offer. While tangible reward in the short run may not be the issue, employees may make connections between actions taken to mange their professional careers that they value immediately while perceiving the link with longer-term higher earnings potential. In a 'letter from the chair' in the CIPD Reward Forum Newsletter, Clive Wright has argued that actively securing connections between employee reward and initiatives like 'strategic workforce planning' helps HR specialists to demonstrate direct 'business' support for the organisation, consequently making it difficult for managers to 'opt out'.

 STUDENT EXERCISE

Argument in support of making explicit connections between a range of HR policies and practices, including career and professional development, under the total reward rubric has been exemplified in the preceding section of the chapter. Discuss the ways in which HR specialists might adopt the role of 'business partner' to help line mangers in identifying and acting on such potential 'high-investment workplace' initiatives.

WORKPLACE ENVIRONMENT AND CULTURE

A range of commentary under this heading may be found in the employee relations literature, as well as wider HRM writing, discussing managerial style and the contexts in which employees may individually and collectively participate in managerial decision taking at work (eg Ackers *et al*, 2003; Marchington *et al*, 2001). This non-financial form of 'partnership' differs from, although may complement, employee financial participation, for example, through profit share schemes and employee share option plans, described in Chapter 6. As in the case of career and professional development, the intention is not to replicate specialist material developed elsewhere at greater length, but to briefly consider the ways in which this strand of the total reward framework may be understood, standing in proximity to other organisation and people management activity.

When surveying levels of employee engagement, CIPD (2006c) identified 'the two most important drivers' as being:

- having opportunities to feed upwards, and

- feeling well informed about what is happening in the organisation.

Workplaces characterised by 'good communication', which the CIPD regards as 'very much a feature of a good psychological contract', mean an environment where more than 'simply about passing information down; it is also about trusting people to interpret that information, and listening to what people say (and then, if necessary, acting on what has been said or explaining why no action has been taken' (2007e: 1).

Cox *et al* (2006) observe a statistically significant link between addressing these kinds of issues directly, in ways that have a close and immediate impact on employees, and both workforce commitment and reported satisfaction. Embedding the principle of involving employees in workplace activity in ways that may become valued by them as a non-financial benefit of their employment, however, does not rely exclusively on the activities of employee communication specialists (CIPD, 2007e). The spotlight falls specifically on line mangers.

Marchington and Cox (2007) point to possible problems if line managers do not share the principles adopted by employee communications and involvement policy architects, or lack the skills to handle related procedures and their consequences in terms of employee response. This may help explain why senior management intentions for this aspect of the non-financial rewards bundle may not be precisely translated into practice. In looking for ways to close the gap some organisations invest significantly in developing line management capability. At the 2007 Annual 'Voice and Value' conference at the LSE, Natalie Lode, Senior Communications Manager, Lloyds TSB, explained:

> *It is of great importance that people are provided with information to get the 'big picture' of where the company is heading. But information alone is not enough. Line managers need the competences and skills required to translate that information into implications for their teams – that is, 'what does it all mean for me?' ... We are developing our training offerings on core*

communication skills such as active listening, managing difficult situations and involving people, through one-to-one coaching and team communication workshops. (Uhe and Perkins, 2007)

During the same proceedings, Fiona Webster, a management consultant with ORC, pointed out that training was good but not enough if employee involvement was to be seen as meaningful, 'since *consultation* is much more than just communication' (Uhe and Perkins, 2007). The need to make business decisions quickly stood in tension with the demand to follow consultation procedures, she observed, a comment echoed by Marchington and Cox (2007) in counting the perceived 'cost' of employee involvement in terms of slowing down managerial decision-taking.

Informed by leader-member exchange theory, Sparrowe and Linden (1997) position 'vertical dyad' interactions between the manager and subordinate within a wider system of network of relationships in the organisation. The leader–member exchange involves reciprocal exchange of loyalty, information, emotional support and respect, representing 'intangible resources' (1997: 526) associated with the employment relationship. Those who obtain more resources may reciprocate with higher levels of commitment and performance. (There are parallels here with the idea of paying an 'efficiency wage', as discussed in Chapter 2.) The organisation has been characterised as depending on the leader for management of these resources and the consequences flowing from their application.

Sparrowe and Linden (1997) argue that attention is required not only to vertical leader–member exchange dyads but also, especially in the more complex contemporary organisations where organisation and work process boundaries are more 'permeable' to informal and horizontal interrelations between employees and others in their social network.

While increasing employee commitment and satisfaction levels (Cox *et al*, 2006), creating the conditions for an inclusive workplace environment and a culture in which employees have a 'voice' under the total reward rubric is not without risk (Richards and Hogg, 2007). A significant ideological and practical commitment is required from management at all levels. There are risks for employees too. Messersmith (2007) balances the argument that 'high-involvement work practices' may serve as 'buffering mechanisms' that reduce the negative consequences of work–life conflict with a possible downside:

despite the importance of involvement in sustaining job satisfaction and organizational commitment, involvement can have negative consequences [with] several studies linking career identity salience with the number of hours worked and ultimately to work–life conflict. (Messersmith, 2007: 433)

 STUDENT EXERCISE

Discuss perceived priorities and risks in locating workplace culture and environment within the total reward portfolio in fast-paced, knowledge-intensive organisations.

TOTAL REWARD, EMPLOYEE ENGAGEMENT: MANAGING WORK(ER) IDENTITY?

So what may be discerned from the unravelling and review of elements attributed to the total reward bundle over the preceding pages of this chapter? Is it reasonable to assume that the whole is greater than the sum of the parts?

Singly, the experience of being acknowledged, enabled to address work–life conflicts, trained, located in a skills-matched career path, or involved in workplace decision-making, may have a functional role. But, taken together, *experiencing* HR practices may have 'a non-instrumental role in both reflecting and reinforcing organisational climate' (Kinnie *et al*, 2005: 11). Informed by social exchange theory, the researchers argue that, when positive, these reactions constitute a sensation among employees of a personal commitment to them by the employer, mediated in particular through the relationship with the individual's immediate supervisor. The organisation is rewarded, in turn, by reciprocal 'affective' commitment (Purcell, 2006), that is, the employee shares the organisation's values and is likely to offer discretionary behaviour and task performance helpful to achievement of organisational goals. (Affective commitment contrasts with 'continuance' commitment (Legge, 1995) where the employee remains in post only because the alternatives are constrained or severing the particular employment relationship carries socio-economic costs.)

CASE ILLUSTRATION 4
ALIGNING 'BUSINESS CASE TOTAL REWARD' STRANDS IN PRACTICE

Having 'got the basics right', Tim Fevyer says, 'we've moved on to focus on what really does make a difference' in the relationship between Lloyds TSB and people employed across the group company. The 'basics' involved: (1) creating market-informed 'salary zones', balancing internal and external equity; (2) creating a sense of distributive justice by giving people a share in business success with meaningful variable pay, funded by business performance and then distributed according to individual achievement over the relevant performance cycle; and (3) enabling flexible benefits choices.

> Our focus is on the complementary themes of diversity, choice and flexibility. We're making progress in managing total reward through branding, communication, and marketing. At this stage in the journey, total reward is still in the domain of the more tangible elements. Moving further along the spectrum [Figure 9.2] means having an answer to the question – What's it like to work here? What do we stand for? What does our employment brand comprise?
>
> We tested hypotheses that once pay is managed properly, the drivers of people's performance, motivation, and engagement are much more likely to be founded in the non-pay arena. Our internal research was consistent with this proposition. For example, we talked to people about what they really valued and found that an overwhelming number of people came back stating

that they would really value greater flexibility. This was perhaps unsurprising. However, more importantly, behind this, we found that an equally large proportion of our people (some 85 per cent) were also saying that if we gave them more flexibility it would change the way they felt about Lloyds TSB for the better. This formed the base for one of the strands of our business case: we have measured the take-up – and the attitudinal change – and shown really positive results.

Also, if you are spending a significant amount of money on benefits (to give an example, £100 million p.a.) and people are only valuing part of this – or may not even be aware of all that is there – then there is a risk of a significant value loss. We tested this with our employees and found out that, on an extrapolated basis, people were only valuing 80 per cent of the true spend. Now, on the one hand, by helping raise people's awareness of the total spend and, on the other hand, making sure that people have access to things that they actually want, we reasoned that closing this gap by just two percentage points, offered a saving worth £2 million in otherwise destroyed value.

The summary position is illustrated in Figure 9.3.

Figure 9.3 Business case total reward strands in Lloyds TSB

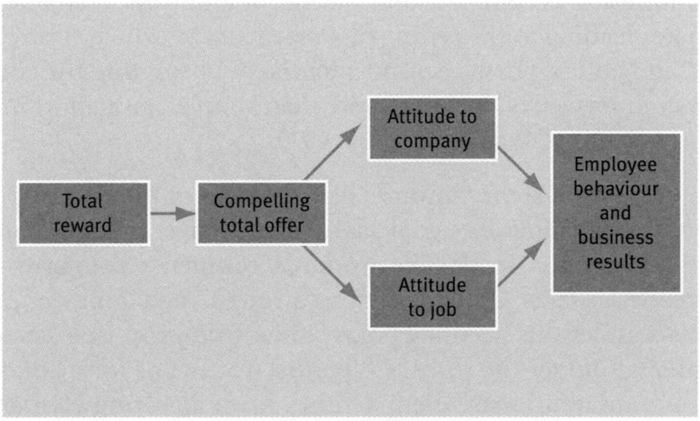

Source: Adapted from Tim Fevyer (personal correspondence)

The 'CIPD viewpoint' in its 'employee engagement' Factsheet (CIPD, 2007b) argues that, despite research findings of a significant gap between UK workforce engagement levels and those that would produce optimum performance:

Engaged employees are more likely to act as organisational advocates than disengaged employees and can play a powerful role in promoting their organisation as an employer of choice. (2007b: 3)

Benkhoff applies social identity theory to explain that, although employee 'commitment' – defined as 'an attitude ... which links or attaches the identity of the person to the organisation' (1997: 45) – is a desired managerial outcome, this requires an integrated organisational strategy congruent with the employee's own values. However, 'once employees feel part of the company ... their sense of identification shows in a cognitive positive bias towards the in-group and a negative bias towards out-groups. People who identify with their organisations are more likely to believe in the quality of the products, the competence of management and the ethical standards of the business' (1997: 45).

Informed by empirical research in a service sector company, Benkhoff concludes that 'the presence of a superior who endorses company policy' (1997: 52) is an important link in the values-identification chain so that, in terms of policy implications, 'companies have to ensure consistency *between policies and among managers*' while also respecting 'the importance of business ethics and generally a high reputation' (1997: 56, emphasis added).

Operating in this psychologically complex terrain, some organisations are reported as seeking 'emotionally intelligent' leaders capable of meeting these kinds of challenges, and of demonstrating 'the ability to monitor emotions in oneself and others and the ability to manage emotions in oneself and others' (Palmer *et al*, 2001: 6). The managerial challenge is complicated further by argument suggesting that, adopting a post-structuralist perspective, 'ethical norms differ from those usually discussed in organization studies because they often involve a democratic formulation, albeit one which is constrained by the power relations inherent in capitalist enterprises' (O'Mahoney, 2007: 480). Empirical research findings based on a telecommunications company indicate 'negotiation' between managers and subordinates leading to the setting of 'precedents by which future activities were assessed and ethical norms became identified', prompting the conclusion that 'moral encounters [may] become more than simple conflicts of interest' in employment situations (O'Mahoney, 2007: 491).

Adopting a more critical stance towards management of the contemporary labour process, Degiuli and Kollmeyer signal caution regarding strategies intended to secure 'voluntary coercion' in 'flexible' work environments 'primarily through ideological means' (2007: 498). Engagement through 'managing emotions' could be located under this headline proposition. Compromise between capital and labour interests under the so-called 'Fordist' regime or forms of 'welfare capitalism' prevalent in mid-twentieth-century manufacturing plants involved paying efficiency wages (ie above market rates), for example, in return for workers' acceptance of monotonous assembly line working. While ideologically driven workplace control may be typically associated with the effort–reward bargain applied to 'highly paid professionals', Degiuli and Kollmeyer are concerned at the ethics of applying such 'hegemonic' techniques in industrial sectors 'dominated by low-wage workers' (2007: 498). Engagement is thus not merely complex but contested.

 SELF-ASSESSMENT EXERCISE

Draw up a total reward 'balance sheet'. What would you include on the side of 'assets' to the effort–reward bargain derived from the application of total reward thinking and consequent 'progressive' managerial practice? What would you include as questions that might feature on the 'liabilities' side of the balance sheet? Account for issues discussed in this chapter such as workforce identification gains, enhanced awareness of 'benefits spend', total reward 'costs' to management, work–life conflict management, the ethics of employee engagement initiatives, etc.

KEY LEARNING POINTS AND CONCLUSIONS

It may be concluded from the foregoing review that non-financial rewards are multi-faceted, and may be interpreted differently depending on the recipient. As such, policy design and application informed by 'total reward' principles is complex, and demands careful reflection as well as a willingness by senior managers and HR specialists to involve employees and the line managers on whom successful practice largely depends. Choices are necessary to commit to investment in non-financial rewards, accepting as a consequence the need for management time allocation to be built in to the process – accepting the need to address possible tensions where the priority seems to be a swift response to environmental context beyond the organisation.

In reflecting on non-financial rewards, thinking HR performers will wish to consider:

- Evolution in employment systems is reported as creating the conditions under which what is included in the effort–reward bargain needs to be rethought, especially when managements wish to secure discretionary effort and a sense of identification among employees for whom 'pay and benefits' provide only part of the employer's consideration.

- While flexible benefits may go some way to addressing workforce diversity issues, ideas grouped under the logic of 'total reward' are promoted by commentators as building blocks for still further customisation, with the prospect of achieving a distinctive employment proposition.

- Definitions of non-financial reward are multi-faceted and often complex, requiring dissection of the elements to facilitate detailed cost–benefit analysis while simultaneously seeking to promote holistic 'employment experience' value greater than the sum of the parts.

- To interpret and evaluate the alternatives and possible consequences of a total rewards approach, it is helpful to apply multidisciplinary theoretical lenses.

- Research findings suggest that senior managers and total rewards policy designers need to pay particular attention to the role of front-line mangers if expectations from investment in employee engagement using total rewards are not to be misplaced.

- Unpacking the total reward portfolio may bring to tensions to the surface between the reward elements and their management, which managements need to reflect on carefully, to be clear about what may be necessary to mitigate and compromise on before committing to strategic decisions that may be deemed unsuitable for the organisation, its principals, and/or workforce members.

- The ethical and moral dimensions of ideological initiatives intended to secure voluntary identification between individual employees and the organisation need to be understood and acted on in framing policy choices and their detailed application.

EXPLORE FURTHER

For a straightforward description and CIPD viewpoint on 'employee engagement', see CIPD (2007) *Employee Engagement*. Factsheet. London, Chartered Institute of Personnel and Development. Copies may be accessed from the CIPD web pages: http://www.cipd.co.uk/subjects/empreltns/general/empengmt.htm.

A comprehensive perspective on total reward, developed and published in the USA is available from Davis, M.L. (ed.) (2007) 'Total rewards: *everything* that employees value in the employment relationship', in *World at Work Handbook of Compensation, Benefits, and Total Rewards*. New York, John Wiley and Sons: 1–13.

A more critical orientation towards debates around employee wellbeing and work–life balance is provided in the following article: Eikhof, D.R., Warhurst, C. and Haunschild, A. (2007) 'What work? What life? What balance? Critical reflections on the work–life balance debate'. *Employee Relations* 29(4): 325–33.

Combining psychological contract thinking and evidence on employee wellbeing is a CIPD Research Report by Guest, D.E. and Conway, N. (2004): *Employee Well-Being and the Psychological Contract*. London, Chartered Institute of Personnel and Development.

PART FOUR

In the three chapters making up Part Four, specific attention is focused on approaches to rewarding employees who have a direct influence on corporate governance, as well as the employee reward implications of organisational expansion requiring transnational knowledge mobilisation. Finally, attention turns specifically to questions around alignment between organisational strategy, HRM and employee reward management.

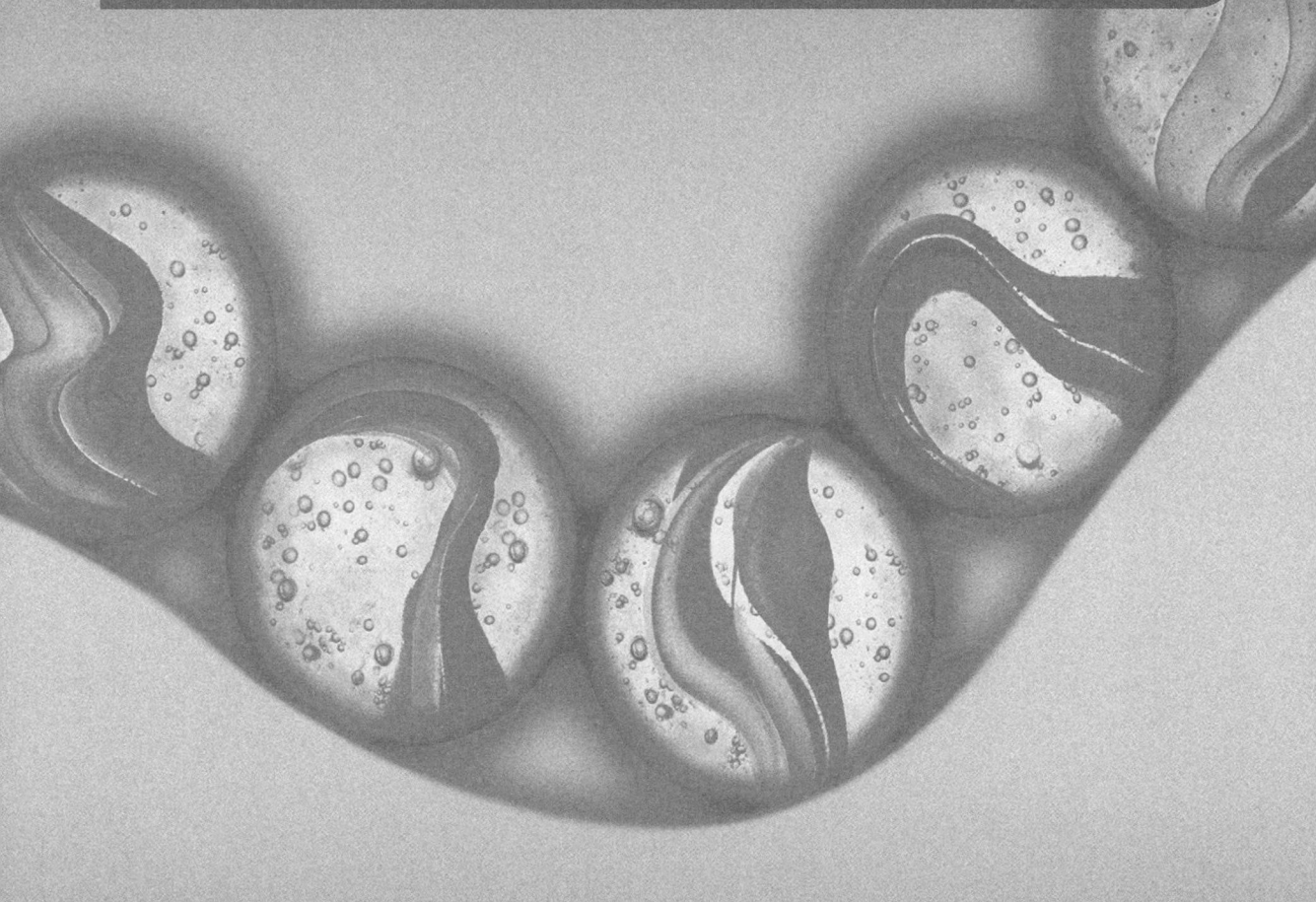

CHAPTER 10

Rewarding Directors and Executives

CHAPTER OBJECTIVES

At the end of this chapter you should understand and be able to explain the following:

- The nature of reward for directors and other senior executives, together with developments in institutional practices surrounding executive reward management design and practice.

- Detailed design and reporting considerations associated with rewarding directors and other senior executives.

- Argument and evidence to facilitate sober assessment of debates surrounding this high-profile, politically sensitive field of employee reward activity.

CIPD STANDARDS COVERED IN THIS CHAPTER:

As a contribution to corporate policy making and practice, to be able to:

- Contribute to the identification of appropriate reward strategy from an analysis of an organisation's corporate strategy and take part in the preparation of reward plans.

- Promote fairness in reward practice.

- Take part in processes related to managing the reward system for special groups to advise on methods of achieving transparency through communication on reward issues and practices.

- Contribute to the administration of employee reward policies and processes, and evaluate effectiveness and value for money.

To understand and explain:

- The process of reward management, its components and aims.

- The criteria for an effective pay structure and contingent pay schemes.

- New developments in employee reward and their application within the organisation.

- The use of modelling facilities and the skills line managers need to implement policies and practices, and how these skills can be developed.

INTRODUCTION

In this chapter, attention will focus on an area that occupies a significant proportion of the energies of large numbers of corporate reward specialists, as well as the managerial decision-makers they advise and support. Evidence for this claim can be obtained by turning the pages of the annual report and accounts of any FTSE top 250 company. A separate and detailed section will be found reporting on – and accounting for – the pay and other forms of remuneration and benefits received by the company's directors, frequently accompanied by commentary on reward factors related to other senior executives too. (See Box 10.1 for a brief description of the special status of directors – who may combine the role of officeholder and employee.) Beyond stock market-listed corporations, it is possible that a 'transparency' imperative will see information being placed in the public domain detailing rewards enjoyed by top managers in other organisations, in both public (state-owned agencies and related institutions) and voluntary service sectors.

With these issues in mind, we discuss below the, sometimes emotionally charged, context against which developments in executive reward and its management are to be interpreted and appraised. We then outline and comment on the ways reward for directors and other executives may be approached, in particular the role and accountabilities of specialist 'remuneration committees' that boards either have to (or if outside stock exchange regulations may choose to) establish with the aim of bringing independence to the setting, monitoring and rationalisation of executive reward – and communicating to interested parties how these accountabilities have been discharged. Complementing the descriptive material, we draw on relevant theory and published research findings to weigh issues under consideration, illustrating the kinds of consequences that may follow specific choices that feature in executive reward and the corporate governance system with which it interacts.

The generic term 'executive reward' will be used throughout the chapter to cover reward issues at corporate director level as well as related to other senior organisational managers. Where regulation, for example, is exclusively applicable to company directors, this will be signified. It should be noted that while company board officeholders share equal legal accountability for oversight of the business, the non-executives elected to the board have been charged with playing a particular role in governing the reward arrangements applicable to their 'executive' colleagues employed by the company.

BOX 10.1 THE COMPANY DIRECTOR

In approaching reward arrangements specifically for directors, it is necessary to appreciate that a company director is an officer (ie someone who works for the company) charged with the conduct and management of its affairs. A director may be an 'inside' or 'executive' director (a director who is also an officer of the company, such as the finance director or marketing director) or an 'outside', or non-executive director (sometimes referred to as an 'independent, director'). The directors collectively are referred to as a board of directors. In the UK and the USA, a so-called unitary board is constituted, whereas in continental European companies operational and supervisory aspects may be formally separated by the constitution of two-tier board arrangement.

While the (normally full-time) executive members of a company board also tend to be covered by an employment contract, they are a special class of company 'employee', with an officeholder's service agreement distinguishing the appointee from others employed to work for the firm. While their obligations were until recently subject to common law provisions (in the UK), since the Companies Act 2006 received Royal Assent, directors' duties have been specified in a statutory statement included as part of the Bill that was presented to Parliament 'in place of the corresponding equitable and common law rules' (Linklaters, 2006: 1).

The duties of directors include provisions that require them to act in ways likely to promote the company for the benefit of members of the company as a whole; to exercise reasonable care, skill and diligence; to exercise independent judgement; and

to avoid conflicts of interest. It is the latter statement that holds relevance in the case of the actions the board members take in settling directors' remuneration. Arguably, this places directors – as managers of corporate assets – in a situation where their interests (in achieving employment benefits) may conflict with their duties to promote the benefits of the company and its members, in particular those who have a claim on residual assets. The appointment of an independent remuneration committee (composed exclusively of non-executive members) to oversee and account for the determination of executive directors' rewards, featuring in corporate governance guidelines, is derived specifically from this position.

Individuals may be part of a senior management team established and led by the chief executive whose collective function is to oversee the firm's operations, but these officers may not necessarily be a company director. (In practice this suggests an informal parallel with the two-tier governance structure referred to above.) However, good practice guidance suggests that the remit of remuneration committees include reward policy applicable to the senior corporate executive team and possibly other senior managers, in the interests of good governance and consistency of approach.

A further point to bear in mind when considering approaches to directors' and other executive-level rewards, compared with other employee groups, is the relative impact on organisational performance attributable to executives. Dive (2002) explains that, while all work in organisations will have an 'operational' side, towards the top of the hierarchy, the emphasis is on 'strategic' action, that is, where discretion over decision-taking and attendant resource allocation is such that attainment of corporate purpose may be significantly influenced. Trade-offs are determined here, based on interpretation of opportunities and threats to the organisation's future health overall. And at executive level the average time necessary to complete the portfolio of tasks for which the individual is accountable is relatively greater than at subordinate levels, providing a rationale for performance incentives similarly targeted over the longer term. The effects are likely to be comparatively externally orientated rather than inwardly focused – having the scope directly to effect changes in the value of financial investors' stakes in the business, for example, through dividend payments and share price movement. A practical illustration of this situation appears later in the chapter (Table 10.3), where the directors' remuneration report published by the example organisation contains a section intended to illustrate the nature and timeframe over which executive performance, aligned with incentive plans, is tracked.

WHAT DO EXECUTIVES EARN; HOW DOES IT COMPARE WITH OTHER EMPLOYEE REWARD LEVELS; IS IT JUSTIFIABLE?

CIPD President Vicky Wright has been reported as stating that discovering the details of executive reward 'is a bit of a forensic exercise … partly because it is split into different elements and partly because there is no disclosure on share options or performance shares sold. Oddly enough, there is a view that directors make more than they actually do' (Newing, 2007). Tyson (2005) advises looking to data residing in surveys such as those produced by large management consultancies to help answer the questions. Findings from a survey of Financial Times Stock Exchange-listed (FTSE) top 350 directors published in autumn 2006 by Incomes Data Services reveal just over a half of all FTSE 350 chief executives earning over £1 million annually, with five receiving total packages valued at more than £10 million gross.

Among FTSE top 100 chief executive officers (CEOs), a survey report by KPMG, published in October 2007 using data to March 2007, indicates that compared with corresponding figures for 2006, median total remuneration (ie pay, bonus and long-term incentives) increased by 12 per cent. To avoid the distorting effect on the average of exceptional payments attributable to severance compensation, only those individuals remaining in the same post over the accounting period were included in the calculation. Average pay among this group of executives was reported at £2.6 million (up from £2.3 million). The 2007 rate of increase was somewhat less than that reported in the same survey the previous year, when the year-on-year increase quoted was 27 per cent, at which time some commentators cited this as evidence of 'out of control' executive reward levels (Watts and Roberts, 2006). Such judgements do of course raise questions about the benchmarks for judging reward levels; what 'control' mechanisms might involve; and who would do the controlling – a topic discussed in the next section of the chapter.

COMPARING VERTICALLY

One approach to obtain a sense of perspective is to compare executive reward levels relative to those of other employee segments. IDS (2006) reports CEOs in the FTSE companies earning on average 98 times more than all full-time UK employees over the year to July 2006. The report is accompanied by the judgement that this represents the biggest pay gap recorded since the beginning of the decade. And in the same survey analysis, the consultants highlight an ever-widening pay gap between executives and other employees over time. Since 2000, FTSE 100 CEO total earnings have increased by 102.2 per cent, on average, compared to an average rise of 28.6 per cent for all employees in the UK working full-time (IDS, 2006).

Findings from another survey the previous year confirm the trend longitudinally, adding additional comparative indicators: in 2005, CEO pay in a UK listed company had risen 208 per cent since 1998, while the average all-employee earnings increase over the same period had been 33 per cent. A fall in the FTSE share price index of 13 per cent acted as a proxy pay-performance indicator (IRS, 2005). Variable pay levels arising from, for example, cash bonus and share-related earnings are often cited as major contributors to high pay for executives.

New Bridge Street Consultants reported in September 2007 that variable pay linked to performance now accounts for more than 55 per cent of a typical pay package. Around 60 per cent of this variable pay relates to long-term performance – reported by *The Independent* (2007) as up from around 50 per cent in four years. FTSE 350 directors' salary increases also outpaced those received by shopfloor employees, however. Over the year surveyed, directors' salaries increased on average by 9.6 per cent, contrasting with IDS Pay Databank figures showing wage settlements for employees generally across the UK economy running at 3 per cent (IDS, 2006).

INTERNATIONAL PEER-LEVEL COMPARISONS

In the interest of balance, making a transatlantic point of comparison, Tyson (2005: 21) comments that UK executive pay levels 'may seem beyond the dreams of most ordinary working people'. But rewards achieved by the top ten earners among US executives reported by *Forbes* add a further dimension before absolute judgements are arrived at. 'The lowest of the [*Forbes*] top ten earners was Seibel System's CEO on $88 million' (Tyson, 2005: 22). Conyon and Murphy (2000) show that, controlling for size, sector and other firm and executive characteristics, CEOs in the USA earn 46 per cent higher direct cash remuneration and 190 per cent higher total reward (accounting for 'package' elements such as share options) than their UK counterparts. And, comparing pay at the top of US corporations with wage levels among other workers, based on data from an Associated Press survey of 386 Fortune 500 companies, Anderson *et al* reported in 2007:

> *CEOs of large U.S. companies last year made as much money from just one day on the job as average workers made over the entire year. These top executives averaged ... total compensation over 364 times the pay of the*

average American worker ... Workers at the bottom rung of the U.S. economy have just received the first federal minimum wage increase in a decade. But the new minimum wage of $5.85 still stands 7 percent below where the minimum wage stood a decade ago in real terms. CEO pay, over that same decade, has increased by roughly 45 percent. (Anderson *et al*, 2007: 5)

Table 10.1 Europe's top 20 CEOs by total remuneration (excl. LTIPs)

Executive	Position	Organisation	Pay level ($m)
Carlos Ghosn	President/CEO	Renault, France	45.5*
Jean-Paul Agon	CEO	L'Oréal, France	19.3
Alessandro Profumo	CEO	Unicredit, Italy	18.1
Arun Sarin	CEO	Vodafone, UK	15.2
Antoine Bernheim	Chairman	Assicurazioni Generali, Italy	14.2
Josef Ackerman	Chairman/CEO	Deutsche Bank, Germany	12.4
Henri de Castries	Chairman	AXA, France	12.1
Thiery Desmarest	Chairman/CEO	Total, France	10.8
Daniel Bouton	Chairman/CEO	Société Génerale, France	10.7
Alfredo Saenz	CEO/vice-chairman	Banco Santander, Spain	10.6
Marcel Ospel	Chairman	UBS, Switzerland	10.5
Xavier Huilard	CEO	Vinci, France	9.1
Sergio Marchionne	CEO	Fiat, Italy	8.7
Benoit Potier	Chairman	Air Liquide, France	8.0
Donald Shepard	Chairman	Aegon, Netherlands	8.0
Frederick Goodwin	CEO	Royal Bank of Scotland, UK	7.8
Martin Bouygues	Chairman, CEO	Bouygues, France	7.8
Franck Riboud	Chairman/CEO	Danone, France	7.3
Franz Humer	Chairman/CEO	Roche, Switzerland	6.9
Patrick Kron	Chairman/CEO	Alstom, France	6.7

Source: Gumbel, P. (2007) 'Europe's fattest cats', *Fortune* 156(3): 8–9 Reproduced by kind permission of *Fortune*/Time Inc. The remuneration figures are based on companies on the Fortune Global 500 list, but it is understood that calculations, while including the value of share option awards, did not take account of long-term incentive plans (LTIPs), that is, vested stock associated with certain performance conditions. This may explain the apparent divergence between the data in Table 10.1 and the IDS (2006) reported picture applicable to UK FTSE top 350 chief executives described earlier, given the inclusion of LTIP values in that assessment.
*A correction was subsequently published by Fortune magazine stating that BoardEx, a consultancy that had compiled the figures in the table, had incorrectly calculated Carlos Ghosn's pay figure. This was attributed to a misunderstanding about how Renault reported their CEO's pay. The correct figure was given as $6.0m – the remainder was attributed to LTIP.

By way of further comparative benchmarks, the details listed in Table 10.1 suggests that, at least before the effects on 'total remuneration' derived from stock-grant-based long-term incentive awards, British top executives are not necessarily in the vanguard of pay trends across Europe. In this 'top 20' listing published in 2007 by *Fortune* magazine, only two UK chief executives feature: Arun Sarin of Vodafone and Frederick Goodwin of RBS, respectively occupying third and fifteenth position. Wray (2007) reports that the strong showing of French executives on the list may be explained by a greater use of share options there than in other European countries.

THE CASE FOR

A gap is evident too in judgements on the justification for executive pay rates. Drawing on his testimony to the US House of Representatives Committee on Financial Services, Kaplan (2007) answers with an unequivocal 'no' to the question 'are CEOs overpaid?' Resting his case on the 'market forces' argument discussed later in the chapter – although not specifically furnishing evidence that executive talent is actively traded between the various sectors – Kaplan contends that 'while CEOs earn a great deal, they are not unique ... the increase in pay at the top seems to be systemic' (2007: 23). The peer-level comparison ('other groups with similar talents and backgrounds' (2007: 23)) is used to defend a view that rather than causing general increases in economic inequality, executive reward escalation is merely being carried along as part of the trend. Rather than reward inflating consultancy advice and self-serving board relationships, as he says critics have suggested, Kaplan believes that CEO reward is 'bid up' as firms get larger, and the size of returns to the employer increases as a function of hiring a more productive CEO.

To substantiate the claimed benefits to investors derived from paying more for stewardship of the firms in which they have placed finance capital, using 'average' (or idealised?) data illustrations, Kaplan contends that since 1980 the market values of large US firms have increased 'by a factor of four to seven times' (2007: 28). And, as 'the CEO job has become increasingly difficult and less pleasant', as well as 'riskier today than it has been in the past' (2007: 23), if 'compensation' is not pitched high, then temptations for plc leaders to defect, for example, to high-paying private equity-owned firms freed from public scrutiny, may be acted on.

Kaplan concludes: 'Rather than being irrationally exuberant [in the celebrated term used by Alan Greenspan, when head of the US Federal Reserve], the US stock market and US companies have benefited from unexpectedly good productivity growth.' And 'while pay abuses have occurred, those examples are not typical and are likely to become less common' (2007: 36).

THE COUNTER-CASE

Representatives of British workers, for example, seem unconvinced by arguments like those made by Kaplan (2007). TUC General Secretary Brendan Barber is quoted in a press release commenting on the IDS Directors' Pay Report 2006, as follows:

> It is hard not to conclude that this further huge rise in executive pay is more about greed than performance. No one should now have any illusions that executive remuneration has been brought under control. Giving shareholders a vote on boardroom pay has failed to rein in excess, as remuneration committees have simply found new ways to keep pushing up pay. The stratospheric levels of directors' pay compared to average wages mean that executives now live in a class apart, even from employees in their own companies. It is not just socially divisive, but bad for the economy. (TUC, 2006)

We may surmise from the material in this section that debates around the substance of 'top pay' are far from concluded. However, a further sense of context may be gained by reflection on the relative position among the world's wealthiest (Box 10.2).

ISSUES IN REWARD

BOX 10.2 WHO IS THE RICHEST OF THEM ALL?

Topping the 'Sunday Times Rich List' 2007, the Walton family (retail group Wal-Mart) is reported with wealth of £42.6bn, with Bill Gates (Microsoft) coming in at number two, but as the richest individual listed, with £28.7bn. Below these two entries from the USA is Mexican, Carlos Slim Helu (deriving reported wealth of £27.2bn from telecommunications interests).

The richest man in Britain (and in Europe), placed at position seven on the 'Sunday Times Rich List' 2007, is Lakshmi N. Mittal, an Indian-born steel magnate who it is reported has recently bought a 20 per cent stake in football club Queen's Park Rangers (QPR) from the club's owners, Formula One racing tycoons Bernie Ecclestone and Flavio Briatore. *Time Magazine* reports Arcelor Mittal as the world's largest steel company. Google co-founders Sergey Brinn and Larry Page tie for position 34 with £8.5bn each (sharing this position with the Swiss Oeri/Hoffmann family whose interests are reported as in pharmaceuticals).

Contrasting with the 'new money' listers, the UK's aristocratic or 'old money' Duke of Westminster is reported at position 48, with attributed wealth of £7bn. With retailing interests (Arcadia and BhS), Sir Philip and Lady Green appear at position 76 (£4.9bn). A newcomer to the 2007 'Sunday Times Rich List' among UK residents is Nasser David Khalili, described by *Forbes Magazine* as 'art maven and real estate investor' born into a Jewish family of art dealers in Iran, now occupying position 61 with wealth of £5.8bn.

Outside the top 100 'listers' worldwide (lowest reported wealth value £4.1bn), but among the richest UK residents in 2007, well-known entrepreneurs Sir Richard Branson has wealth the *Sunday Times* reports as £3.1bn, and Sir Alan Sugar £0.83bn. Norfolk turkey magnate Bernard Matthews has attributed wealth totalling some £0.17bn.

Recent stories of 'celebrity' pay in the sports world, of course, include that reportedly awarded to England manager Fabio Capello after the

Football Association directors made him 'the highest-paid coach in international football'. According to *The Times*, Capello 'commands a salary commensurate with his reputation'. He will receive £4.8 million per year, before tax, rising incrementally throughout a contract scheduled to run for 4½ years, open to termination by either party after the 2010 World Cup. If England wins the World Cup, the new coach will earn a £5 million bonus. According to the newspaper report, the FA have 'learnt the hard way from the expensive mistake they made with Sven-Göran Eriksson, whom they were still paying 12 months after his dismissal': a severance package of £2.5 million has been agreed from the outset, should Capello depart mid-contract.

Crossing the showbiz/sports stage, in December 2007 *The Times* carried a story on agent Simon Fuller, who discovered the Spice Girls, as developer of the £128 million deal (over five years) to take David Beckham to the US Los Angeles Galaxy team – reportedly placing 'Becks' 'on the road to the most lucrative contract in football' (Eason, 2007). According to a related story, 'in financial terms it's the jackpot: Beckham will receive a salary of £5m (more than the rest of the team put together); a share in club profits expected to generate another £5m a year; and sponsorship deals worth another £12m or so'. The average US soccer player's salary is reported to be 'about £45,000 a year' (*Sunday Times*, 2007). For a comparative UK club player example, the *Sunday Times* reported in November 2006 that Manchester United player Wayne Rooney had signed a new contract committing him to remain at Old Trafford until 2012, on a package that 'will increase his wages from £55,000 to around £100,000 a week, making the deal worth more than £30m in salary alone. With bonuses and commercial deals, he could earn £10m a year' (*The Times*, 2006).

SO MUCH FOR SUBSTANCE: WHAT ABOUT THE PROCESS?

While the comparative data summarised above are important, it is easy to become ensnared in 'the numbers' surrounding executive reward management, possibly losing sight of the processes involved. Still focusing on CEOs, Lawler and Finegold (2007: 38) observe that discussion tends to revolve not just around the question of whether their reward levels are too high. The other priority for commentators is 'the degree to which it is tied to performance'. And, contrary to Kaplan (2007), Lawler and Finegold's evidence leads them to conclude that '[m]any board members think CEO compensation is too high and should be more closely tied to performance' (2007: 46). This raises the issue of how 'performance' may be understood beyond the 'average' comparators used by Kaplan (2007). Jensen *et al* (2004) argue that, for reasons discussed below, executive reward needs to be evaluated in close interaction with concerns summarised under the rubric of 'corporate governance'.

THE GOVERNANCE REGIME

While there is no single model of the company – and thus how it should be governed – in the Anglo-American tradition, the relationship between the company and its shareholders is a proprietary one. Shareholders, deemed to be part-owners of a business in which they have invested finance capital, are entitled to expect the company to be governed exclusively in their interests (Parkinson, 2003). This argument is used 'to defend the fundamentals of the current [Anglo-American] governance structure', under which shareholders-as-owners elect directors 'to run the business on their behalf and hold them accountable for its progress' (Parkinson, 2003: 482).

While subject to critical debate – and alternative traditions, for example, in mainland European countries – it is fair to say that these sentiments form the basis on which both mainstream analysis and policy interventions related to directors/executive employment contracts and concomitant reward determination are constituted. It is probably the case that the UK has led thinking worldwide over much of the past two decades regarding corporate governance and executive reward management (see the chronology of corporate governance regulation summarised in Table 10.2).

A seminal report from a committee chaired by Sir Adrian Cadbury, published in 1992, contains guidance regarded as 'highly influential in the UK and abroad' (Point, 2005: 61), and this initiative was followed in 1995 by a second committee of enquiry chaired by another then-serving large public limited company (plc) chairman, Sir Richard Greenbury. While Cadbury had plenty to say about executive pay as a feature of corporate governance, Greenbury focused even more specifically on tackling what by the mid-1990s had become a subject of sustained popular concern (at least as represented in media and political circles where 'almost frenzied attention' (Tyson, 2005: 20) had been visible. But this issue does not seem to be targeted at the substantive level: prominent voices calling for intervention were not proposing a general reduction in what executives receive as appointees and employees of large stock market-listed firms. The exercise was 'theoretically designed to ... make high pay levels acceptable' (Point, 2005: 61).

REGULATION OF EXECUTIVE REWARD

Consistent with prevailing interest in aligning employee reward directly to performance contribution, as discussed at length in Chapters 4 and 7, the argument was that while 'market forces' under globalisation might require high rewards paid by organisations competing in a so-called 'war-for-talent', the overall level of reward should be defensible by reference to measures that shareholders at least, and possibly other organisation stakeholders too, would recognise as appropriate. A 'legion of academic articles' (Baden-Fuller, 2000: 475), written by economists, in particular, has surfaced, especially on the western side of the north Atlantic, in which sophisticated models are described and tested in an attempt not only to catalogue executive reward trends, but also to *explain* what is observable with special attention to the variety of instruments adopted with the intention of regulating total reward levels.

One sustained focus has been on discovering economic relationships between top management pay, firm size and corporate performance (Veliyath, 1999). CEO remuneration has also been studied in relation to organisational strategy (Balkin and Gomez-Mejia, 1990); length of tenure (Hill and Phan, 1991); the structure of internal incentives (Lambert, Larcker and Weigelt, 1993); the dimensions of board structure and control (Conyon, 1997); and information disclosure (Conyon and Sadler, 2001; Conyon, Mallin and Sadler, 2002). In spite of all this industry, prominent writers such as Martin Conyon have suggested that attention be paid to a richer set of social and political explanations' of the problems that have been articulated (Conyon and Peck, 1998: 146). However, there is relatively little analysis that examines the processes of executive reward management: see Bender and Moir (2006); McNulty and Pettigrew (1999); Perkins and Hendry (2005); Pye (2001); Roberts *et al* (2005).

 SELF-ASSESSMENT EXERCISE

You have considered debates around executive reward. Now read the story below, based on media accounts, and draw up a list of questions you would wish to have answered, first as a company shareholder representative (fund manager), secondly as an adviser to government on corporate governance regulation, and thirdly as the leader of a trade union in the sector. What themes are common to each of these groups? What if anything might differentiate their interests in this topic? What would be the top three points you would emphasise in a brief to the chair of the remuneration committee due to meet stakeholders to discuss the controversy?

Hard-wired 'telecompensation'

> Cable and Wireless has become a byword for its controversial 'private equity' incentive plan (Burgess, 2008).

Shareholders welcomed the appointment of Richard Lapthorne as chairman of Cable and Wireless in 2003. BBC News reported at the time that following a series of profits warnings, leading to a "hammering" for shares, the new non-executive chairman's brief was to secure "a major restructuring of its global business".

In 2006, Mr Lapthorne announced to shareholders that he intended to offer an incentive to executives to turn round Cable and Wireless that he likened to what might apply in a private equity firm. Consultation with the investment community concluded with an agreement to cap individual bonus payments at £20m. Shareholder opinion was divided. According to the Financial Times, Legal & General Investment Managers, one of the largest shareholders, found the incentive plan "original and innovative". By comparison, the Association of British Insurers said the plan did not go far enough in linking reward to long-term value creation. At that stage the chairman, who receives "an annual fee of £386,000" (Cable and Wireless Annual Report), was excluded from the scheme.

After a year, and the recovery of the share price, Cable and Wireless announced plans to lift the bonus caps. Defending the decision at the 2007 annual shareholder meeting, Mr Lapthorne admitted that he had not anticipated the speed of recovery but pointed out that, compared with executives in the four-year scheme, shareholders could cash in their stake at any time. If the company's share price reached roughly 228p by 2010 a 100% bonus payout would be triggered (Wray, 2007). The company's top 60 executives would share a bonus pool of up to £216m (Burgess, 2007). A Cable and Wireless spokesperson cited by the Financial Times said that the concern was that capping could encourage risk aversion among the senior management team, inhibiting further growth in shareholder value.

Based on the perception of his pivotal role in the recovery, Mr Lapthorne was also to be offered an incentive reward plan. In a Cable and Wireless press release dated 6 June 2007, it was announced that, after three years, he was to be awarded "up to 5.5 million shares on demanding performance criteria": total returns to shareholders in the top 10% of peer companies in the FTSE Global Telecoms Index. The scheme was to supplement the 3.5m Cable and Wireless shares already owned by Mr Lapthorne, resulting in a potential overall £11m reward (Wray, 2007). It is unusual for non-executive office holders to participate in corporate incentive plans, due to shareholder disapproval (Burgess, 2007). According to a Guardian report following the Annual General Meeting held on 20 July 2007, Cable and Wireless shareholders were not given an opportunity to vote directly on the revised arrangements, only to register an indirect protest by refusing to re-elect Mr Lapthorne on to the board of directors (which "11% of those voting" did).

Sources:

BBC News Online, January 2003. 'Chairman boost for Cable & Wireless', accessed 12.09.07 from http://news.bbc.co.uk/1/hi/business/2646557.stm.
Cable and Wireless Remuneration Committee Report, Annual Report and Accounts 2006-07.
Cable and Wireless Press Release: 'Cable and Wireless announces revisions to Chairman's contract and proposed changes to the long term incentive plan (LTIP)', June 6 2007.
Kate Burgess 'C&W chair urges approval of pay plan', Financial Times, June 5 2007.
Kate Burgess 'The UK: Investors disagree over private equity-style pay', March 25 2008.
Richard Wray 'C&W bosses to get unlimited bonuses, The Guardian, July 21 2007.

THE CORPORATE GOVERNANCE CONTEXT

By way of a footnote to the case exercise (above), the situation at Cable & Wireless has been labelled as 'among the most contentious shareholder votes this year' (Burgess, 2007). While it may rate highly in the 'contention' stakes, it seems this is not an isolated case. Placing reward issues in the foreground, 'shareholder activists' Robert Monks and Allen Sykes argue that corporate governance problems on both sides of the Atlantic have become so acute as to represent a systemic problem (Monks and Sykes, 2002). While the most serious effects are being felt in the USA, Sykes (2002) argues, Britain is demonstrating the same underlying weaknesses.

As well as having an appreciation of the debates surrounding executive reward practice, then, HR thinking performers need to be aware of the successive waves of regulatory initiatives that the state has taken mindful of the contention surrounding this aspect of organisational affairs. Rather than passively accepting the logic of regulation, however, specialists again need to be aware of entrenched positions adopted by interested parties: while governments may feel obliged to act for political reasons, those like Kaplan (2007) advise against legislation (which he says is sometimes termed 'say on pay') given the potential he believes such policy intervention may have to impose cost on companies and boards, where it is possible to 'imagine politically oriented shareholders attempting to make political statements' when enfranchised to vote on executive pay decisions, rather than remaining bounded by economic considerations.

The UK government has acted directly to regulate, or else co-opted policy-related initiatives by institutions such as the London Stock Exchange and representative bodies such as the Association of British Insurers (ABI), the National Association of Pension Funds (NAPF), etc). Corporate governance regulations from Cadbury onwards enshrine the principle that executive reward should contain 'strong incentives for executives to act in shareholder interests' (Ogden and Watson, 2004: 35). And the UK government appears to hold the view that '... directors deserve high rewards for good performance' (Patricia Hewitt, then Secretary of State for Trade and Industry, recorded in Hansard, 2004: 51–52 WS).

To repeat, the governance prescriptions 'were never intended specifically to hold down pay levels' (Ogden and Watson, 2004: 35), but to ensure that executive reward determination complies with sanctioned governance standards, or else decision-making is accompanied by detailed explanation for departures from 'best practice'. A statement of principles exemplifying core values and expectations surrounding executive reward, expressed on behalf of the finance capital investment community, appears in Figure 10.1, extracted from recent guidelines published by the ABI. The simple phrase 'comply or explain', enshrined in the 'Combined Code', a document specifying corporate governance expectations, which originally appeared in 1998 and with updating and extending was republished in 2003 and (revised again) in 2006, carries significant meaning that corporate managers and their advisers need to be mindful of in discharging their accountabilities.

Two lines of scrutiny are expected to assure this process. Rather then rely on board executive directors to regulate their own reward against the governance principles, first, remuneration committees of company boards are expected to be populated exclusively by 'independent' (or non-executive) directors, charged with designing performance-based reward systems covering their executive colleagues, and accounting for their decisions to shareholders. (Non-executives are not

Figure 10.1 Extract from ABI guidelines on executive remuneration policies and practices (published December 2006)

PRINCIPLES

Boards are responsible for adopting remuneration policies and practices that promote the success of companies in creating value for shareholders over the longer term. The policies and practices should be demonstrably aligned with the corporate objectives and business strategy and reviewed regularly.

Remuneration Committees should be established in accordance with the provisions of the Combined Code. They should comprise independent directors who bring independent thought and scrutiny to all aspects of remuneration. It is important to maintain a constructive and timely dialogue between boards and shareholders regarding remuneration policies and practices.

Executive remuneration should be set at levels that retain and motivate, based on selection and interpretation of appropriate benchmarks. Such benchmarks should be used with caution, in view of the risk of an upward ratchet of remuneration levels with no corresponding improvement in performance.

Executive remuneration should be linked to individual and corporate performance through graduated targets that align the interests of executives with those of shareholders. The resulting arrangements should be clear and readily understandable.

Shareholders will not support arrangements which entitle executives to reward when this is not justified by performance. Remuneration Committees should ensure that service contracts contain provisions that are consistent with this principle.

Source: http://www.ivis.co.uk/pages/gdsc2_1.html, accessed 10.09.07

---

only 'governance scrutineers', however: they are expected to work hand in hand with the executive team to set corporate strategy, a possible source of tension.) Secondly, in turn, shareholders are called on to challenge 'situations where directors enjoy rich rewards whilst companies perform poorly and shareholders and employees suffer' (Hansard, 2004: 51–52 WS).

Although the regulatory environment has stiffened considerably over the past decade, alleged laxity on the part of remuneration committees has been subject to criticism in oversight of the process. Reilly and Scott (2005) give as an example situations in which executives have been authorised to exercise large grants of stock option awards just prior to a share price collapse, when the losses experienced by shareholders may be perceived as the fault of poor performance by the executive(s) concerned.

Publicly expressed disquiet over 'rewards for failure', especially when these involve 'severance' terms when an executive is being removed from office, is rooted in the view that 'such payments reflect an inappropriate culture at the top of organisations and can have a strong influence in wider society, making the issue one in the public interest' (ACCA, 2005). Compensation granted to underperforming executives at the time of departure seen to be over-generous might, it was felt, damage the image and reputation of British business as a whole, in the words used in a government consultative document published in June 2003.

To try to remedy problems encountered in the past, the latest guidance is premised on an expectation that remuneration committees (working in association with the board 'nominations' committee) will take steps at the time executives are initially contracted to the organisation to ensure that terms and conditions connected with possible future severance are seen to be fair and reasonable. If a situation arises, the logic is that termination will be capable of resolution transparently and satisfactorily (ACCA, 2005). Again a two-pronged governance strategy has been adopted by legislators for the time being at least: an express desire to see 'increased activism by institutional investors, and the promotion of best practice' to remedy the situation, rather than add further to regulatory instruments (Hewitt, 2004).

To set the standard against which this kind of scrutiny is exercised the Combined Code states that remuneration committees should as a rule set directors' notice or contract periods at one year or less, to avoid the accrual of large compensation for loss of office entitlements. In addition, the Financial Reporting Council (FRC), a body responsible for maintaining and promulgating the Combined Code, calls on remuneration committees to 'take a robust line on reducing compensation to reflect departing directors' obligations to mitigate loss … in the event of early termination' (FRC, 2006: 12).

Policy intervention to regulate executive reward is beginning to occur on a pan-European basis. In July 2007, the European Commission published a report on member states' application of the EU recommendation of 14 December 2004 on the remuneration of directors of listed companies. The terms of the recommendation are broadly similar to UK provisions governing disclosure of directors' remuneration introduced in a 2002 Statutory Instrument (No. 1986) requiring quoted companies to produce a directors' remuneration report and allow shareholders to vote on it (Linklaters, 2007). A summary chronology of key corporate governance regulatory developments since the early 1990s impacting on executive reward is presented in Table 10.2.

Table 10.2 A chronology of corporate governance regulation

Initiative	Emphasis
Cadbury Committee, 1992	Separation of chair and CEO role.
	Standing committees for matters such as audit and directors' remuneration.
Greenbury Committee, 1995	Specification of best practice in determining and publicly accounting for directors' remuneration.
	Remuneration committee independence.
	Decision-makers to weigh merits of alternative forms of long-term incentive to stock options: LTIPs 'subject to challenging performance criteria'. Shareholder votes on new schemes.
Hampel Committee, 1998 (set up to review implementation of Cadbury and Greenbury recommendations)	Promoting 'principles' in place of 'the more detailed guidelines of the Cadbury and Greenbury codes':
	Remuneration committee reports on behalf of unitary board (not 'independently').
	Less prescription on LTIPS – judgement by remuneration committee regarding best fit and explanation to shareholders.
	More gradual shift to one-year director notice periods/calculation for loss of office payments, given existing contractual norms.
	Accrued pension rights reporting as value of company liability. not element in individual's total remuneration.
	Shareholder voting on remuneration committee report at company discretion.
Turnbull Report, 1999 (Flint Report, 2004)	Specification of best practice on embedding internal control and risk management for UK listed companies to safeguard shareholders' funds and corporate assets.
	Guidance on avoiding unnecessary financial risks and exposing fraud and reporting on actions taken to shareholders annually.
	Includes monitoring the board and its committees to assess effectiveness of controls.
	In July 2004, the FRC set up a group chaired by Douglas Flint (Group Finance Director, HSBC Holdings plc) to review the guidance and update it where necessary, in the light of experience in implementing the guidance and developments in the UK and internationally since 1999.

Initiative	Emphasis
Myners Report, 2001	Reviewing UK institutional investment practice to encourage active engagement of shareholders in monitoring and communicating with directors of companies in which they hold shares, including exercising votes on governance-related issues (consistent with the various guidance listed in this table).
	The Institutional Shareholder Committee (ISC) published 'Principles' setting out strengthened responsibilities on the part of institutional shareholders and fund managers in respect of publishing policies on how they will actively engage with the companies in which they place capital funds, evaluating and reporting to clients or beneficiaries on the effectiveness of practice – including intervening where necessary where they are concerned about managerial actions. In 2007, the ISC has been reviewing the position.
Directors' Remuneration Report Regulations 2002 Statutory Instrument No. 1986	Obliging directors of a quoted company to prepare a directors' remuneration report for each financial year, containing specific information including details of remuneration committee, policy on directors' remuneration, and its detailed application to individuals.
	Updated as DRRR 2008 (part of implementation of Companies Act 2006) to include a requirement to report information enabling comparison of directors' and employees' pay. (According to HMG guidance, the manner will be not 'overly burdensome'.)
	Requires the information to be set out in the report to meet particular criteria.
Higgs Report, 2003 (published simultaneously with the Smith Report on audit committees) Tyson Report, 2003	**Higgs**
	Review of appointment, role, remuneration and effectiveness of non-executive directors.
	Identification of a senior independent director to be available to shareholders for discussion of corporate governance-related concerns.
	Broaden pool of candidates for non-executive appointments.
	Minimum of three non-executives on remuneration committee.
	Delegated responsibility for setting chairman and executive directors rewards, plus level and structure for (other) senior executives.
	No single non-executive to sit on the three principal board committees: audit, nomination and remuneration.
	Chief executive not to become chairman of the same company (so as to be judged 'independent'); board to agree separated chair/CEO role statements.
	Tyson
	Intended to complement Higgs, with a specific focus on enhancing board effectiveness via a range of different backgrounds and experiences among board members, exploring how a broader range of non-executive directors can be identified and recruited (including internationally).

Initiative	Emphasis
DTI Report: 'Building Better Boards', 2004	Product of discussions with academia, business and executive search consultants.
	Best-practice guide to help companies improve recruitment and performance in the boardroom and to make a business case for effective diversity and better practices in the boardroom.
Combined Code on Corporate Governance, 2006 (originally published in 1998 and revised in 2003 to incorporate Higgs and Smith guidelines): expected to have been applied by UK stock market-listed companies from second quarter 2007 onwards	Setting out standards of good practice in relation to issues such as board composition and development, remuneration, accountability and audit, and relations with shareholders, drawing on each of the various corporate governance exercises undertaken since 1992.
	Contains the statement: 'Whilst recognising that directors are appointed by shareholders who are the owners of companies, it is important that those concerned with the evaluation of governance should do so with common sense in order to promote partnership and trust, based on mutual understanding.'
	All companies incorporated in the UK and listed on the main market of the London Stock Exchange are required under the Listing Rules to report on how they have applied the Combined Code in their annual report and accounts.
	2006 amendment permits chairman to sit on the remuneration committee where considered independent on appointment as chairman, but recommended that he or she should not also chair the committee.
	During 2007 the FRC has been reviewing the impact and implementation of the Combined Code. Intention announced (October 2007) to consult on 'limited' additional amendments.
Company Law Reform Bill as introduced in the House of Lords on 1 November 2005, and given Royal Assent on 8 November 2006. The Companies Act 2006 revises and consolidates UK company law, following the recommendations of the Company Law Review, which reported on the modernisation of UK company law in 2001. Implementation expected to be phased in over the period to October 2009.	Among the key areas covered by the Act are:
	Setting out directors' duties (including corporate social responsibility expectations), allowing companies to indemnify directors, and providing for corporate governance rules implementing EU directives.
	Overriding reported aim: to 'enhance shareholder engagement and a long-term investment culture'.

MARKETS

Commentary in the academic and related literature attempting to theorise executive pay and the contingencies against which it is determined reveals a range of views. On the one hand, consistent with classical macro-economic theory 'market forces' have been cited by those offering a defensive rationale for executive reward management practice (eg Kaplan, 2007). And the viewpoint is not an exclusively 'academic' one. Stiles and Taylor (2002: 76) report on discussions with company directors in which the latter judge 'market factors' as 'very important in determining executive pay', constituting 'a central factor in recruitment, retention and motivation'.

Pepper (2006: 15) cites an even more unequivocal remark by a large UK stock market-listed company CEO made in response to a question at a shareholders' meeting. The individual apparently declared: 'My remuneration is determined by market forces.'

Using more measured terms, the report of the committee on governance chaired by Sir Ronald Hampel states that to attract business executives 'of the required calibre' their remuneration will be '*largely* determined by the market' (1998: 4.3, emphasis added). The predecessor Greenbury Committee also referred to market forces, but acknowledged 'imperfections' so that:

> *While market forces set a broad framework ... remuneration committees for the most part have quite a wide range of discretion in setting levels and forms of remuneration.* (Greenbury, 1995: 6.4)

Explaining 'why the market doesn't work' in relation to executive reward determination, Pepper (2006: 15), who is a partner in a 'Big Five' accountancy/ professional services consultancy with a special interest in executive reward, argues that 'practically none' of the conditions for a perfect economic market to operate are visible. Rather than free market entry and exit, there are limitations on the numbers of executive jobs open and suitable candidates to fill them at any one time. Executive are not homogeneous commodities: no two individuals are the same. The same difficulty applies to systematic comparative evaluation of 'unique' executive roles to be filled (Hijazi and Bhatti, 2007).

Moreover, 'despite claims that high levels of boardroom pay are essential to prevent a management brain drain ... only a handful of top companies in continental Europe and the US are led by UK executives' (Milner and Seager, 2007: 26). Citing the author of a recent study into management practices at 4,000 companies, a question mark was raised as to 'whether British executives could cut it overseas [suggesting the basis for international executive market flows] if ... disenchanted with pay levels in Britain'. According to the director of the Centre for Economic Performance, Professor John Van Reenen, who co-authored the report:

UK management is not in the premier league. Management aspires to pay as well as the US, but our study finds that average management quality in the US far outstrips that in the UK. Only one in every 50 American firms in our sample can be described as 'very badly managed', compared with roughly 1 in 12 in the UK. (Milner and Seager, 2007: 26)

Finally, even if the market position were to be accepted, while (proxy) market comparisons have been encouraged by more comprehensive disclosure of total executive rewards, information on how to 'price' executive experience and skills is far from perfect. A sample of FTSE 100 remuneration committee members interviewed by Perkins and Hendry (2005) voiced barriers to calibrating price-value norms objectively: idiosyncrasies arise between executives and the roles they are asked to undertake that require 'artful' assessments (Noldeke and Samuelson, 1996). The price-value placed on a specific executive may depend more on the characteristics and preferences of the recruiter than on the 'talent' (perceived capability and potential to perform) being acquired. In conceptualising executive reward outcomes, thinking performer HR specialists must give consideration to institutional factors and socially contextualised decision-taking as much as to economic factors, it seems.

PERFORMANCE

Given severely mixed views regarding the 'market forces' justification for executive reward regulation, to what extent is the faith regulators have vested in performance contingencies well placed? The adequacy of alignment between the executive reward levels and 'corporate performance' (eg 'total shareholder return' – ie share price appreciation and dividend yield) has been 'a central theme within the UK debate' (Conyon and Sadler, 2001: 141). Kaplan's (2007) macro-economic assessment again faces a challenge in the face of a wide-ranging review of evidence from a series of studies in both the UK and USA over the late 1980s and early 1990s, which concludes that even where a statistical link is identifiable between executives' direct rewards (salary and cash bonuses) and the stock market performance of their firms, this is small.

Conyon (1998) finds a more robust correlation between company size and pay level. Conyon and Sadler examine evidence from studies since the end of the 1990s that reflect the changing composition of executive reward packages shifting the balance away from 'current cash compensation' to emphasise non-cash (share-based-related) incentives (2001: 146), consistent with the 2007 New Bridge Street Consultants survey findings reported earlier, and the observation in the 2007 KPMG report that the bulk of the increases received by FTSE 250 executives over the preceding year came 'through variable pay linked to performance' (2007: 3). Conyon and Sadler conclude that taking account of a reward portfolio calibrated in favour of 'changes in the value of the stock and equity options held by the CEO ... the pay–performance link may be becoming stronger' (2001: 151).

Jensen *et al* (2004) attack equity-based reward policies currently in operation, however. The commentators argue that the latter types of performance-based executive reward initiatives compound a problem of overvalued corporate equity.

When executives recognise that the position is not sustainable, the risk is that they attempt to artificially manipulate short-term equity prices. The worst-case scenario is an Enron-style corporate scandal (see Box 10.3). Even in less high-profile cases, however, shareholder capital suffers 'value destruction' over the long run.

Jensen *et al* (2004) do not limit their criticism to executives and remuneration committees. The also adopt a negative attitude towards financial investment market managers, who 'are not acting as shareowners' (2004: 239). In the UK, as observed above, state policy-makers have called on institutional shareholders to play a more 'engaged' role. The 2001 government-commissioned Myners Report explicitly sought to encourage greater 'shareholder activism' – especially in the stance taken towards underperforming companies, 'exercising their votes in a considered way' (Mallin, 2004: 239). This is something vociferously advocated for some time by long-standing activists representing the beneficial owners of company shares, such as Monks and Sykes (2002).

SOCIO-POLITICAL INTERACTION

If thinking performers are not satisfied with economic market explanations for executive reward decision-taking or attempts to find an unequivocal reward–performance link, the allusions reported in the media to the need for some control to be exercised suggests attention may be needed on socio-political phenomena. The nature of relations between the parties to executive reward contracting comes to the fore. A major strand of the theoretical literature on executive reward focuses on debates around the value of 'agency' considerations (Jensen and Mecklin, 1976; Jensen *et al*, 2004). The notion of 'power-dependency' (Pfeffer and Salancik 2003; Wright and McMahan, 1992) also surfaces when considering interpersonal and intra-organisational relationships, as does the role of 'tournament'-based interaction between actors close to the top of corporate hierarchies (Conyon, Peck and Sadler, 2001; Conyon and Sadler, 2001). And social constructionist accounts provide another conceptual lens through which to view relations between executive agents and their 'principals' (Roberts, 2001). We briefly review this commentary next.

AGENCY THEORY

Analysis of corporate governance has been significantly influenced for over 30 years by Jensen and Mecklin's (1976) theorisation of the firm, its management and managers' relationship with the firm's 'owners', using the concept of 'principal–agency' relations (Buck, Filatotchev and Wright, 1998). An agency relationship is defined as a contract: a principal (ultimately, the beneficial owner(s) of shares in productive capital) engages an agent to perform some service on the principal's behalf. The 'shareholders are seen as the focal group whose interests are furthered through crafting executive pay arrangements that cause a top management team motivated by self-interest to maximize shareholder value' (Bruce *et al*, 2005: 1493).

Agency problems may arise for shareholders when evaluating whether they are getting the best value return from the executives to whom corporate management is delegated. If it were easy to assure alignment between payments (inputs) to executives and performance (outputs), shareholders could simply pay their executives a fixed salary (in effect, a form of insurance payment), and then assess whether that agent is supplying optimal effort in the shareholder's interest (Perkins and Hendry, 2005). Jensen *et al* (2004) contend that the agency problem cannot be eliminated, only mitigated. And if inappropriate, there is a risk that reward arrangements will actively give rise to agency problems, leading to value-destroying agency on the part of executives entrusted with the running of the firm (Jensen *et al*, 2004).

The mediated agency relationship is a further source of disquiet. Sykes (2002: 256) alleges 'widespread conflicts of interest', derived from the complicated sets of interrelations involving institutional investment managers concerned with widely dispersed share portfolios managed on behalf of beneficiaries and non-executive directors. Sykes's (2002) criticism is aimed at 'largely passive shareholders' and 'complacent and ineffective non-executive directors' (2002: 256).

There is executives' own role too. Members of a unitary board of directors, although formally delegating administration to a remuneration committee, ultimately sanction their own reward and may influence the way it is accounted for. The issue to which regulatory interventions have been especially targeted is that, in the final analysis, 'directors have power to influence their own rewards and to affect the performance of their firms, probably to a greater extent than other employees, at lower levels' (Tyson and Bournois, 2005: 7).

In her written introduction to the consultative document on directors' remuneration, then Secretary of State for Industry, Patricia Hewitt, observed that this is 'the issue above all others, on which directors face a conflict of interest' (DTI, 2001: 4). This view explains the legal obligation placed on UK publicly traded companies, under the Directors' Remuneration Report Regulations (2002), not only to require extensive disclosure in a remuneration committee report accompanying company annual reports and accounts. The report must also be submitted for approval at the annual general meeting. Arguably the ambition is to locate executives as stakeholders in the firm and its fortunes alongside other interested parties.

POWER-DEPENDENCY THEORY

Pfeffer and Salancik (2003) draw attention specifically to the impact of power in relations between organisational actors, arguing that, if organisations are to be controlled and managed (as well as understood), account needs to be taken of the actions of 'core interests' groups. Emphasising context, they argue that academic literature tends to overlook – or take as a given in modelling economic transactions – the apparently obvious point that behaviour in organisations is environmentally adaptive behaviour. Senior managers are not just acted on by institutions – they are themselves actors with intentions and wants as they seek to 'orchestrate the affairs of the corporation' (Tyson, 2005: 16). Using the language of agency theory, principals must acquire and maintain the resources necessary to develop and enact strategy and operations. And the more the principal depends on the resources the more leverage the resource-holder (manager-agent) may exercise in the transaction around whether or not and to what extent to perceive their interests as aligned with those of the the principal interest-holders.

'No one stakeholder can speak with unchallenged authority for the corporate interest' (Tyson, 2005): managers require delegated authority to take initiatives based on information they have access to (unlike shareholders, or indeed employee groups lacking corporate oversight) in order to be able to act on opportunities and avoid being ensnared by operational difficulties. However, this latitude includes the freedom for managers 'to align [their] interests with the "interests' of the corporation"' (2005: 16), or not to do so. Sykes (2002: 257–8) perceives consequential problems such as remuneration committees lacking independence; management choosing the consultants to advise on their pay setting; managerial action motivated by pressures to produce value over impossibly short time periods – and stock option gains to be made.

Managerial agents 'control' the capability (experience and skills) necessary for value-creating activity. And they need to be induced voluntarily to put it to work for the principal. The *relative* power of principals and their agents in determining the effort–reward contract, for example, may be perceived as derived from mutually dependent relations (Molm *et al*, 1999). Festing *et al* (2007) argue that the extent to which behavioural adaptation occurs, with outcomes that more or less favour principals or agents, is therefore moderated by existing power relationships within the firm. Consequently, the relationship between the parties to corporate governance relationships may be theorised as 'the product of ongoing interaction and discussion' (Roberts, 2001: 1549). While Conyon (1998) finds that the threat of dismissal may discipline young CEOs, Bebchuck and Fried argue that executives may be able to mobilise embedded power resources to 'entrench themselves in their positions, making it difficult to oust them when they perform poorly' (2003: 72).

TOURNAMENT THEORY

Rosenbaum (1989: 336) defines tournaments as 'systems for selecting the most talented individuals by a series of progressively more selective competitions', in which the declared winners of each tournament are allowed to climb the career ladder and later compete in a new tournament for the next higher career position. The so-called tournament effect has been cited as an explanation of why a significant gap exists between CEO and other executives' reward levels, restricting the ultimate economic 'prize' to the incumbent CEO.

O'Connell (2006) notes arguments that CEOs receive the highest relative reward owing to the increased level of responsibility they shoulder, with demand for CEOs outstripping supply. As noted earlier, arguments have also been put forward that changes in corporate performance and executive reward increases may be matched (Kaplan, 2007). However, when examining published data from FTSE companies over the period 1990–2004, O'Connell (2006) finds is no strong case to suggest that responsibility at CEO level has become relatively greater over that timeframe. Moreover, he can offer no obvious reason why fewer CEO candidates are available to fill the job slots. And from this data series, when looking at performance alignment it seems that the rate of increase in CEO cash reward has continued to run ahead of increases in corporate performance.

Under tournament theory, the prediction is that locating a distinctive 'prize' at the top of the organisation motivates agents in contention for CEO positions, for example, to compete by out-performing fellow executives, with the result that the organisation and its principals benefit from the sum of individual contributions. However, once there are 'no tomorrow aspects of the final stage of the game' (Rosen, 1986, cited by Conyon and Sadler, 2001), the predicted benefits may not be sustained. O'Connell's (2006) analysis also finds no obvious evidence that, compared with other board-level executives CEO pay is more strongly a reflection of performance.

Greater transparency not only in terms of rewards obtained but also levels of performance makes pay–performance alignment easier to observe in non-business settings, in which the majority of testing predictions derived from tournament theory has taken place, such as among racing drivers, jockeys or professional golfers (Conyon and Sadler, 2001). Conyon *et al* (2001) test tournament predictions using data on 100 large stock market companies, and find 'some confirmatory evidence' that 'the ratio of pay increases as one moves up the hierarchical level' (2001: 155). They also observe a positive relationship between the CEO reward premium and the number of tournament contenders. However, empirical work informed by the tournament approach specifically focused on business and related organisations is limited: caution is required, therefore, before drawing general conclusions.

AN ALTERNATIVE ORIENTATION (STAKEHOLDER AGENCY THEORY)

Calling for a return to first principles, Roberts (2001) challenges the dominant agency orientation in corporate governance literature and policy. Agency theory, he argues, is predicated on an essentialist perspective of human nature: accordingly, employment relationships are no more than a series of implicit and explicit socio-economic contracts with associated rights.

A more relativist perspective, on the other hand, introduces the possibility of learned and reinforced trust. Buck *et al* (1998), for example, extend agency theory beyond its 'traditional financial version' to propose a Stakeholder Agency Theory (SAT). As an heuristic for structuring enquiry into corporate governance complexities in more volatile environments (such as Russia post-privatisation), SAT draws attention to the possible existence of organisational cultures in which trusting relationships encourage stakeholders to suspend opportunistic actions in favour of an ethic of co-operation (Buck *et al*, 1998).

BOX 10.3 CORPORATE SOCIAL RESPONSIBILITY AND SHAREHOLDER VALUE DISCOURSES

In considering the context for executive reward determination, attention might be paid to recent debate contrasting notions of 'corporate social responsibility' (CSR), on the one hand, and 'shareholder value', on the other hand. 'The rational economic notion of "shareholder value" [locates] the interests of the shareholder as paramount and encourages managers to privilege only those strategies and decisions that directly benefit shareholders in the short term' (Michelson and Wailes, 2006: 239). Simultaneously, CSR 'speaks of a range of legitimate claims on the organisation and suggests social, ethical and moral considerations ought to play a more significant role in corporate strategic planning and decision-making' (Michelson and Wailes, 2006: 239).

Kessler (2007) observes that for some years 'strategic' reward management has been advocated as the overriding concern of progressive human resource management, but draws attention to the argument that this does not imply a binary alternative to more traditional concerns around the effort–reward bargain to do with equity and fairness. Consequently, it may be proposed that 'effective' executive performance and reward management, aligned with more corporately responsible organisational stewardship, may imply consideration of factors that go beyond the shareholder value dimension.

Emphasising the need to pay attention to the dynamics of power in organisational affairs, Michelson and Wailes (2006) argue, however, that in the struggle for dominance between what they term the 'meta-discourses' of CSR and shareholder value, the power shift to those whose priority is shareholder value results in 'bounded rationality' on the part of executive management such that, even when nominally pursuing CSR-inclined policies and practices, the 'effectiveness' benchmark ultimately will be: is this 'good for the business' measured relative to those whose capital stake is financial?

Michelson and Wailes (2006) chart changes beginning in the late 1970s in the purpose attributed to organisations and their management, which the analysts attribute to a shift in socio-economic power. They argue that the changes constitute a reaction to the governance of organisations observable in the mid-twentieth century against principles sometimes referred to as 'managerial capitalism' (Jacoby, 2006). That is, the senior managers of corporations 'owned' by shareholders in western economies were able to accumulate power to secure their status relative to shareholders who during that period were dispersed, providing managers with a dispositional advantage in power-dependency terms. Corporate managers could engage in so-called 'empire building', accumulating business units that reduced the firms' competitive exposure, but allegedly at the cost of delivering returns rightly due to financial investors. It also enabled managers allegedly to transfer a higher than justified share of retained earnings to increase their own remuneration.

However, during the final decades of the twentieth century, increased concentration of shareholdings under fund managers – for example, major insurance and/or retirement funds

– reduced the room for managerial manoeuvre, and increased the leverage that shareholders (or institutional managers acting on the part of beneficial interest holders) could apply. While initially adopting a defensive stance towards the challenge to their autonomy, a new generation of corporate managers during the 1980s and 1990s appeared to make common cause with the 'shareholder value' ideology, as initiatives derived from principal–agency-based theorising on the relationship between investors and management took hold, holding out the prospect of wealth accumulation opportunities for individual executives, via stock options and other forms of long-term incentive payments (Jacoby, 2006).

Michelson and Wailes describe the scope for dysfunctional behaviour on the part of executives to arise consequent on following a shareholder value orientation and concomitant reward strategy, manifested most dramatically in the collapse of energy company Enron where, until the company filed for bankruptcy in 2001, a public face was conveyed by the corporate leadership, for example, in a letter sent to shareholders by the chief executive in 2000, 'portraying the organisation as perfect in every way' (2006: 257).

The same analysts contend that those concerned with regulation of corporate governance and executive behaviour have taken 'the wrong lesson' (2006: 257) from corporate scandals such as this. Rather than judging the problem as systemic – that is, an inevitable consequence of 'shareholder value'-based management – opening the way for a less bounded CSR discourse to take root, Enron's failure was presented 'as the outcome of a series of unfortunate and complex events … "special" or "unusual" circumstances' (Michelson and Wailes, 2006: 257).

The evidence discussed in the preceding section is indicative of the lack of consensus justifying the quantum of executive reward, absolutely and relatively; how it should be set; and who should take the lead role in controlling this corporate governance aspect. Each of these factors may be perceived as creating a context, in open systems terms, within which executive reward may be observed, interpreted and appraised. Now we turn attention to the particulars of designing executive reward, and to the associated task of accounting for outcomes and process to satisfy compliance requirements.

 STUDENT EXERCISE

Working in groups, discuss the comparative merits of the corporate social responsibility and shareholder value discourses. What actions are open to thinking HR performers to navigate the tensions outlined in the literature reviewed in this chapter? Are you able to reach a 'professional' consensus view comparing different groups' conclusions?

DESIGNING AND REPORTING ON EXECUTIVE REWARD

We have reviewed debates around the substance and process of executive reward, including the corporate governance context, and associated theoretical orientations shaping interpretation and analysis. Attention now turns to the fabric of executive reward portfolios, which may help in discerning whether or not there is evidence of a distinctive employment relationship between organisations and the executives contracted to lead and manage them.

Veliyath (1999: 124) arranges the primary variables as follows: '(1) fixed compensation independent of firm performance, versus variable reward [tied to a performance measure], and (2) current compensation accruing at the end of the year, versus deferred compensation accruing in later years'. When considering executive reward design and administration attention is required also to account for choices made and consequences flowing from them. Beyond the bargain agreed between the employer (mediated by the appointments and remuneration committees) and employee (executive/director), increased public scrutiny of executive reward arrangements accompanying corporate governance regulatory developments requires companies to report on how corporate governance standards have been met – or, as noted earlier, to explain departures from 'best practice'. The features of executive reward design, administration, and reporting will be described below with that basic architecture in mind, drawing on current published evidence.

THE AGENT'S INTEREST

It is important also not to overlook the executive's own viewpoint when seeking to interpret executive reward determination. Individuals are likely to evaluate the worth of pay and benefits offered under the rubric of an executive employment relationship, measured against their own perceptions of an acceptable return on the investment of human capital (ie the experience and skills the individual brings to the employment relationship in addition to a willingness to apply these on the employer's behalf). Whether or not the executive's assessment is warranted by the remuneration committee, and in turn shareholder representatives, depends on the criteria applied (and power-dependency balance). It may be unwise to assume uncritically that the positions may be objectively verified – the indeterminate nature of the effort–reward bargain introduces subjective factors that are difficult to control for – it may be argued, therefore, that designing and rationalising executive reward portfolios represents an artful as much as a scientific process.

The search for an executive employment relationship to satisfy the aims of both employer (or 'principal') and employee (or 'agent'), as well as to comply with standards of public reporting, have led to the establishment of executive reward 'package' norms. Three principal elements may be observed payable either directly in cash or ultimately convertible to cash: the salary traditionally afforded to a 'staff' employee (someone whom it is assumed the employer anticipates can have an impact on the organisation beyond the hour or the day of hire);

a 'bonus' payment for meeting short-term performance requirements beyond contributing attendance and capability to perform; and forms of deferred reward, specifically long-term incentives for meeting objectives of strategic significance over an extended period (generally beyond one year), and a retirement pension. An additional element of the executive reward package may comprise perks and other non-cash benefits such as insured benefits, company-funded cars, etc.

EXECUTIVE REWARD PORTFOLIOS

In constituting the 'package', an increasingly proactive orientation on the part of decision-makers is in evidence, justified by the combined pressure of 'competition for scarce talent in an international market' (House of Commons Trade and Industry Committee, 2003: 17), and the corporate governance regulatory developments summarised in Table 10.2. As we have already seen, these phenomena are each subject to robust debate in the literature. Notions surrounding what the package should involve, qualifying conditions (Buck *et al*, 2003) to satisfy the multiplicity of goals and interests involved, as well as contextual dynamics, mean the process is not straightforward.

Payment of a salary may continue to anchor the executive reward package, but its relative position has been subordinated as 'good practice' guidelines have shifted the focus increasingly towards 'at risk' reward, intended as an incentive for executive agents to perceive their interests aligned with shareholder principals – sharing the risk and potential reward (Norris, 2005; Pepper, 2006). This has been further refined so that executive reward should combine not only incentives to perform individually in making a short-term contribution to the profitable

Figure 10.2 Accounting for executive reward

The Directors' Remuneration Report Regulations 2002 (UK Government Statutory Instrument No. 1986) apply to quoted companies (defined as UK-incorporated companies that are UK, EU or Nasdaq/NYSE- listed but not AIM-listed companies). They apply to all directors – not just remuneration committee members – and require quoted companies to publish a report on directors' pay as part of the annual reporting cycle on which shareholders will vote at each AGM. The vote of shareholders is advisory only, but a failure to obtain approval effectively amounts to a vote of no confidence in the remuneration committee.

The report must include:

- details of individual directors' pay packages;
- explanations for any compensation packages awarded in the preceding year;
- details of the board's consideration of directors' pay;
- membership of the remuneration committee;
- the name of any remuneration consultants used;
- a performance graph on the company's performance compared with an appropriate share market index;
- a forward-looking statement of policy on directors' pay, including details of any share-based incentives.

Source: Linklaters (2006); Freshfields Bruckhaus Deringer (2007)

Note: In accordance with the Large and Medium-sized Companies and Groups (Accounts and Reports) Regulations 2008 (to come into force on 6 April 2008), quoted companies must include in their directors' remuneration report a statement of how pay and employment conditions of employees of the company and of other undertakings within the same group as the company were taken into account when determining directors' remuneration for the relevant financial year.

organisation. In addition, a longer-term element has been factored in: to retain executives in post, and to focus their attention on value-creating agency over the longer term. While it is true to say that at risk (or incentive) elements have become increasingly common across all employee groups, in the case of executives, the logic articulated is that as the group most able to impact positively or negatively on corporate success, the bias in the guaranteed (basic) elements of their pay should be shifted towards the variable (incentive) elements.

Pepper (2006: 14) posits 'a strong prima facie case' for keeping the three elements in balance. The conclusion to be drawn is that, at least in theory, decision-makers anticipate that the reward amalgam will motivate behaviour on the part of executives acting together to represent shareholder interests, and sometimes those of wider stakeholders (Jensen *et al*, 2004), beyond the separate effects of the elements comprising the package taken singly. As we have seen, analysis within the empirical literature as to whether or not this aim is achieved in practice remains inconclusive.

EXECUTIVE REWARD COMPLIANCE/DISCLOSURE ISSUES

Expectation and prescription has given rise to complexity in executive reward design, administration and reporting, as illustrated by the reference in the chapter's opening paragraph to the resource-intensive activity to produce compliance statements included in plc annual reports. Remuneration committee reports have become a sizeable part of the documentation publicly quoted companies now regularly produced for reporting purposes, running to several pages in length, with cross-references to other parts of the annual report, to make explicit connections between executive reward and corporate commercial performance, and in future to make some comparison between executive reward and the arrangements applicable to all other employees (see Figure 10.2 on Accounting for executive reward).

Table 10.3 is derived from part of a 2007 remuneration committee report included in a FTSE 100 company's annual report and accounts, detailing the reward portfolio applicable to directors. Actual reported values will of course vary from firm to firm. In addition to describing the substance of executive rewards, to meet regulatory standards an account is provided also of what the board intends to reward executive directors for, assessed against a variety of reward contingencies. The report itself further contains detailed (audited) information on the pay levels and other employment benefits received by named individuals covered by these arrangements. This includes details of the timing of exercise of outstanding share options, share grant values, individual shareholdings and trading in company shares.

The detailed account may be perceived as carefully crafted to 'tell the story' behind actions taken to order the relationship between the agents and principals in corporate governance and employment relations, enshrined in reward content and processes. Underscored by a statement of guiding principles, the aim may be understood as an attempt to demonstrate objectively how gains from employment received by executives, financed from resources that might otherwise pass to shareholders, represent a legitimate share in the value created by the individual and collective action of the executives on behalf of shareholders.

Detailed statements on executive reward – and indeed remuneration committees – would have been an exceptional feature of companies' annual reports and accounts only a few years ago. Deloitte (2004: 19) note that shareholder representatives consulted by them report that the requirement in the Directors' Remuneration Report Regulations (2002) to vote on whether or not to accept the remuneration committee report has had a 'very significant impact upon [shareholder] attitudes and behaviours'. More comprehensive disclosure is perceived as having been vital in enabling informed review and decision-taking: the complex task facing boards, in reporting, and shareholders, in acting on, this detailed information, in compliance with regulation and good-practice standards is not about to recede. However, political regulation (mediated through stock market listing requirements), including the time invested by remuneration committee members and their specialist internal advisors and those outside the organisation, incurs a significant corporate cost to achieve enhanced transparency in reward administration limited to a minority segment of the corporate workforce.

Table 10.3 Example FTSE 100 company executive reward framework

Reward component	Purpose	Award details	Policy context
Salary	To reflect the value of the role and the individual occupant, and to recognise skills and experience.	Payable monthly in cash and counted as salary for pension accumulation purposes.	Subject to review annually, with changes usually taking effect from a set date. Benchmarked against a selected cohort of FTSE 100 firms and others as appropriate. Individual salary level positioned against the relevant comparator group for each role.
Annual performance incentive bonus	To offer an incentive to achieve short-term performance targets year on year.	A performance-related cash payment awarded annually; [normally] not counted for pension accumulation purposes.	Based entirely on the plc's overall financial performance, with a major proportion based on profit measures, targets for which are set by reference to the company's annual operating plan. Payment can be up to 100% of salary earned for 'on target' performance; 200% of salary for performance deemed 'outstanding', as a maximum award.

Reward component	Purpose	Award details	Policy context
Share options	To offer an incentive in relation to share price earnings growth over three years, discounted for the cost of capital, above a threshold level, thereby providing focus on increasing the plc's share price over the medium to longer term.	A parcel of share options is granted with an exercise price set at the market value on date of grant. The value received by individuals is subject to meeting financial performance targets and the share price increasing above the grant value. The discretionary annual award is to offer a performance incentive over the long term.	At the maximum, 375% of salary may be granted in share options annually. Performance is judged against plc earnings per share (eps) performance measured on a sliding scale. For an international business, adjustments are made to offset exchange rate movements affecting eps performance. After negative assessment in corporate governance guidance since October 2004 a retest facility* has been removed for options grants.
Share awards Long-Term Incentive Plan (LTIP)	To offer an incentive to achieve levels of 'total shareholder return' (TSR) over three years relative to a selected peer group of companies, thereby focusing executive attention on delivering 'superior returns' to shareholders. [TSR is assessed by combining share price movements and dividend payments.]	Parcels of shares are awarded to individuals. The value of awards is highly variable owing to the vesting schedule over which ownership of the shares is confirmed. This is a discretionary annual award to offer a performance incentive over the long term. LTIPs became popular following the 1995 Greenbury Report.	A maximum annual initial award of 250% of salary may be granted. TSR performance is tested against a peer group of companies. Performance below the median results in no element of the award being confirmed: a sliding scale is applied to improvements in the ranking above median. For achieving first or second position, 150% of the initial award vests.

Reward component	Purpose	Award details	Policy context
Pension	To provide competitive post-retirement reward.	Pension is counted as deferred income, which is payable on retirement in the form of a monthly pension with the option to receive part as a lump sum.	Pension benefit accrues at 1/30 of annual salary, payable at a fixed 'normal retirement age' [usually between 60 and 65]. The maximum pension payable will not exceed 2/3 of final remuneration minus retained benefits. From 1 April 2006, a pension employee contribution payable by executive directors was introduced following governance guidance revisions. Subject to election by individuals, benefits in excess of the Lifetime Allowance permissible under income tax regulations for 'approved schemes' are provided through an 'unfunded' non-registered arrangement.

*Regulatory provisions have been revised to prevent 'retesting' of the so-called strike price at which an option has been granted in relation to its current fair market value. Previously, where a share price had fallen below the value at which it had been granted downward adjustment was possible to restore the 'incentive' value. However, the practice was outlawed for UK Inland Revenue-approved schemes, given the view that retesting (reducing) the value at which executives can exercise options to acquire shares, following adverse market assessments of the plc's value possibly arising from executive under-performance, was not consistent with aligned executive and shareholder interests.

UNPACKING THE PORTFOLIO

The total remuneration available to executives in the FTSE 100 example plc 2007 reward portfolio summarised in Table 10.3 is based on a basic amount guaranteed once it has been determined (reviewed from time to time, normally annually), taking account of comparisons with other employees inside and outside the firm at peer level and below, and the individual executive's perceived contribution potential. The balance between fixed and variable elements of remuneration changes with performance. It is reported that the anticipated 'normal' mix between fixed and variable remuneration may be anticipated so that, dividing the 100 per cent of remuneration earned, 33 per cent will be fixed remuneration and 67 per cent will be performance-related, excluding pensions and other benefits. Pension provision 'to provide competitive postretirement reward' is described separately in Table 10.3.

The variable performance-related proportion is reported as dividing 33 per cent short-term bonus and 34 per cent long-term incentive opportunity. The commentary notes that: 'in some years, the performance-related remuneration may be higher or lower depending on the performance of the business'. The proportions are consistent with those Pepper (2006) identifies as the idealised balance of total remuneration applicable in the contemporary environment. Long-term sustained performance is presented as forming 'the heart of [plc's] corporate strategy', a claim evidenced by reference to a consistent 'above median' positioning during the preceding three-year performance and reporting cycles, as measured relative to a selected peer group of companies, in the total shareholder return (TSR) plan, reflected in financial returns to shareholders and rewards paid to the plc's executives.

Changes in the nature of long-term incentive arrangements have been common recently among stock market-listed companies (Deloitte, 2004; IDS, 2006). A rise in incentive scheme potential payments at the maximum, justified in terms of action to align directors' and shareholders' interests, is reported by IDS (2006), leading to a shift in the balance between fixed and variable pay towards performance-related remuneration (although no corresponding reduction in salary increase levels is reported – as noted earlier, these continue to rise above the general average in the employment system).

There is a range of potential outcomes from operation of an executive reward framework such as the one illustrated in Table 10.3, taking account of the combination of fixed and variable elements intended to cohere as the basis for recognising against stated criteria how senior executives create value for shareholders over the short and longer term. In setting levels of reward, the remuneration committee reports that members have considered the total remuneration packages paid in the top 30 companies in the FTSE 100 by market capitalisation, excluding those in the financial services sector. The committee states a belief in the appropriateness of positioning total remuneration between the median and upper quartile of this group, given the corporation's size and complexity globally.

Complex calculations often attach to the estimated value arising from awards to be made to executives in accordance with incentive plans, forming part of the information companies are expected to disclose in accordance with good practice. With LTIPs, mathematical models (eg 'Black Scholes' or 'Binomial') may be used to indicate future outcomes. While the principles of shareholder-aligned performance may be theoretically sound, in practice wide deviations between the estimates and eventual outcomes are reported. And declaration of performance targets against which executives are to be assessed is further complicated by corporate concern regarding making public details of operating plans that may be commercially sensitive (Deloitte, 2004).

Policy governing executive reward management in the case of a plc is reported as having been introduced three years previously. Its underlying premise is stated as 'to attract and retain the best global talent to deliver [plc's strategy] within a framework of good corporate governance'. A set of interdependent principles supports the policy, summarised in the remuneration committee report as follows:

- The belief that pay should vary significantly with performance over both the short and long term.

- Salary levels generally set 'to ensure market competitiveness' around the median of the relevant market for each role, although with discretion to position a salary above the median if justified by the requirement to recruit or retain key executives.

- Annual bonuses paid in cash after the end of each financial year, determined by performance in the year 'against pre-set stretching business targets'.

- Long-term incentives comprising a combination of share option grants and share awards in each year, varying respectively with three-year earnings per share (eps) and TSR performance.

- A requirement on senior executives to hold shares in [plc] to participate fully in the share option and share award plans.

THE REMUNERATION COMMITTEE'S ROLE

In the FTSE 100 case, it is reported that the remuneration committee, consisting of 'all the independent non-executive directors', is 'responsible for making recommendations to the board on remuneration policy as applied to [plc's] senior executives'. This category is defined as 'the executive directors and the executive committee' (senior individuals who report to the CEO but do not have a seat on the board of the directors).

In the course of the evolution of the corporate governance regulations, opinion has shifted between making the remuneration committee wholly accountable for executive reward determination and subordinating that role ultimately to the corporate board of directors, albeit to ratify the detail decided among the non-executives sitting as the remuneration committee (see Table 10.2). The remuneration committee report continues that:

> The board of directors continues to set stretching performance targets for the business and its leaders in the context of the prevailing economic climate. To achieve these stretching targets requires exceptional business management and strategic execution to deliver performance. This approach to target setting reflects the aspirational performance environment that [plc] wishes to create.

Not only does the remuneration committee maintain a watching brief over the administration of extant executive reward policy, more long-term review and revision appears to apply. The long term now seems to match the cycle over which LTIP plans operate, with 'long-term' defined as three years, something that may be open to reflexive debate. In the FTSE 100 plc case, whose remuneration committee report is drawn on to illustrate the discussion here, it is announced in the remuneration committee report that:

to ensure our incentive arrangements continue to have stretching performance targets that will drive the business and its leaders over the medium to long term, the committee intends to review the current remuneration arrangements during the next financial year.

A review in 2008 will coincide with the renewal of the FTSE 100 plc's LTIP, following expiry of the previous three-year cycle. As part of this process, it is reported, the remuneration committee members intend 'to engage with our major investors on any significant changes that may result from the review' – to align with good-practice guidelines, but with a sub-text of heading off any possible negative reaction when shareholders are called to vote on the proposed plan at an annual general meeting.

SELF-ASSESSMENT EXERCISE

Source a recent FTSE 350 plc annual report and turn to the remuneration committee report section. Study the content and see if you can work out how the 'comply or explain' principles underlying current UK corporate governance regulations have been interpreted.

THE REWARD SPECIALIST'S ROLE IN EXECUTIVE REWARD MANAGEMENT

Developments surrounding design, management and accounting for executive reward have given rise to specific consequences for the part the HR specialist may play in this complex and politically sensitive organisational sphere. Based on recent conversations with leading corporate reward specialists, the role has shifted over the past decade so that more than reward technician's skills are deemed necessary. Knowledge of a range of disciplines – actuarial, finance, legal – in addition to reward management know-how is required, as well as a capacity to play the part of skilled diplomat or 'go-between' in relation to members of remuneration committees and senior corporate executives. Effective liaison may also be called for in dealings with consultants appointed not only by the specialists' employer but also by the remuneration committee, and with other external parties such as the ABI and NAPF, whose guidance non-executive directors are perceived as wary of contradicting, given possible risks to individuals' reputation as competent corporate supervisors acting on the shareholders' behalf in their dealings with management.

Attention to detail in the preparation of remuneration committee papers and in the records of decisions is important: as one reward director put it: 'With so many moving parts it's easy to overlook something that may have consequences later.' The instance was given of where, during a significant organisational change, the need to consult shareholders concerning an aspect of an already existing long-term incentive plan was recognised at a late stage, having been overlooked to that point by external advisors. Project management skills are thus called for to ensure that the process runs to time and cost (given the sheer range of activity demanded, the latter can be significant).

The reward specialist may also need to draw on other skill sets with further resource consequences internally – for example, to obtain support from colleagues (eg finance function) to undertake complex financial modelling to meet remuneration committee demands for systematic evaluation of projected outcomes from applying certain performance measures with goal-setting and computation of executive bonus and related incentive awards. Given the scale and complexity of disclosure reporting annually in the directors' remuneration report, excellent drafting skills are necessary, as well as awareness of the latest regulatory developments requiring compliance action, most likely working in co-operation with the company secretariat and finance function.

Competence in communicating, accurately and diplomatically, orally as well as in writing is viewed as a prerequisite. Non-executive directors do not expect to be 'lectured' by a specialist operating below their peer level, but offered a précis briefing on an issue to be debated or in response to a question to inform their decision-making. It has been observed in our conversations that an employment relations background – building experience in understanding the views of the parties and engaging in negotiating outcomes – as well as in representing the organisation in determining terms and conditions related to individual senior appointments, may be useful developmental experience to prepare an aspirant future head of reward for exposure to remuneration committee activity.

While addressing corporate expectations, ensuring that the individual's professional integrity is safeguarded has also been noted as critical: in the politically sensitive arena of contemporary executive reward management the answer may not always be 'yes'. Thus, in summary, the role of the contemporary senior-level corporate reward specialist has become one of skilful expert across a range of interconnected disciplines: efficient and effective project manager and corporate governance steward; accomplished communicator; and social diplomat able to preserve personal and professional integrity.

EXECUTIVE REWARD IN THE PUBLIC SECTOR

Discussion in this chapter is primarily informed by commentary regarding executive reward determination in for-profit enterprises. However, a new management ethos directed towards the public/not-for-profit sector of the economy (Cabinet Office, 1999) means we should not neglect to mention the implications for executive-level reward. Cahan, Chua and Nyamori (2005: 441) argue: 'the purpose of public sector reforms is to make public sector entities more like private sector firms, including the use of private sector-style boards as the primary internal corporate governance mechanism'. However, in terms of reward management in the absence of an externally determined share price, determining changes in the public entity's value is more difficult, complicating attempts to apply traditional agency-based reward systems to align executive incentives with the interests of owners (ie the state and ultimately citizens) and managers (Cahan, Chua and Nyamori, 2005).

The same researchers report 'limited, if any, empirical research examining, for example, the relationship between CEO compensation and board structure in the public sector' (2005: 441). They argue that public sector board effectiveness is particularly important given the reduced substitute control mechanisms compared with the private sector (ie 'market monitoring'). Although the gap between executive pay and lower levels in 'liberal market economy' private sectors, most notably in the USA, is not open to replication on a similar scale in an environment where 'wealth accumulation' instruments like stock options are not available, then, the position is noteworthy where a new generation of public sector executives may be instrumentally inclined to embrace a more contingent approach to reward, given potential to manage it in their favour.

For example, Brickley *et al* (2003, cited by Cahan, Chua and Nyamori, 2005) researched a sample of just over 300 not-for-profit hospitals in the USA, examining the relation between chief executive reward and board structure. The researchers found, first, higher levels of chief executive reward when the chief executive was a voting member of the board; and, secondly, some evidence that chief executive reward was positively related to board size and the percentage of 'inside' (or executive) directors.

The situation is not confined to the size or rate of increase in reward levels: the so-called 'rewards for failure' debate in the media received a fillip in the UK, surrounding the fate of Paul Gray, former chairman of HM Revenue and Customs, who resigned in November 2007 over an 'extremely serious failure' of security, but reportedly would retain his entitlement to final earnings-linked pension benefits (Gilmore and O'Connor, 2007).

KEY LEARNING POINTS AND CONCLUSIONS

In this chapter, a range of contemporary literature has been drawn on to inform the understanding of the thinking HR performer regarding the alternatives and consequences associated with executive reward and its management, as well as the context in which executive reward systems interact dynamically between elements and actors within and outside the organisation. One conclusion prompted is that executive reward design and management may be interpreted as combining to delineate a distinctive employment relationship between an organisation and those to whom leadership and management is entrusted by those with a beneficial stake in its effective governance.

With reference to stock market companies, in a strictly legal sense within Anglo-American business systems the beneficiaries are limited to shareholders. However, although commentators disagree on the merits of widening the zone of interests to be served by corporate leaders (see Jensen *et al*, 2004), expectations may be perceived in some quarters that stakeholders more generally should expect to see their interests served in corporate organisation, as reflected in forms of incentive and recognition afforded to organisational stewards. This may be especially the case as public service and voluntary sector organisations are brought into consideration. As has been illustrated using the literature reviewed for this chapter, the position is complex and controversial – and may be subject to contradiction (Perkins, 2008).

Thinking performer HR specialists may wish to approach executive reward bearing in mind the need to accommodate the requirement to align executive reward with business strategy; to be able to demonstrate this achievement to the extent required by corporate governance codes of practice, ensuring that practice is fully compliant with transparency and disclosure standards. Simultaneously, it is necessary to design and operate reward arrangements for executives that are aligned with trends in appropriate employment markets, bearing in mind the possible influence of international considerations, and that the substance and processes involved act to communicate clearly the priorities for outcomes and behaviours desired corporately. In all this, given 'almost daily headlines in the mainstream media' (world@work, 2007) executive reward system architects need to be able factor in attention to what world@work (2007) labels 'community concerns'. A 'questionary' of factors executive reward designers and decision-takers may wish to take into account, expressed in headlines, includes:

- The internal environment unique to each organisation – not only the enterprise and its aims but also its human capital resources to achieve them, including people's expectations, and the philosophy to guide action to address these phenomena.

- The range of stakeholders with a financial and (perhaps more qualitative) interest in the organisation, its governance and consequences.

- The external environment (domestic and international economic trends, industry sector developments, impact of government and special interest groups, etc) that is likely to comprise factors outside the control of the organisation and its management, but need to be accounted for when designing executive reward arrangements.

- Disclosure and transparency, and how forms of socio-political regulation interact with the organisation's values and priorities and strategy for engaging with economic threats and opportunities, impacting on the extent to which the organisation provides complete and comprehensible information – or explains exceptions to compliance provisions.

EXPLORE FURTHER

For an extended review in historical perspective, as well as comment on contemporary problems in executive reward determination, see Jensen, M.C., Murphy, K.J. and Wruck, E.G. (2004) *Remuneration: where we've been, how we got to here, what are the problems, and how to fix them.* ECGI Working Paper 44/2004. Social Science Research Network Electronic Paper Collection: http://ssrn.com/abstract=561305.

For a development of the arguments suggestive of dysfunctional effects arising from executive reward management and theory explicitly or implicitly underpinning it, see Perkins, S.J. (2008) 'Executive reward: complexity, controversy, and contradiction', in White, G. and Drucker, J. (eds) *Reward Management: a critical text*, 2nd edn. London, Routledge (in press).

For a useful sole-authored guide to thinking through theory and practice on executive reward, see Pepper, S. (2006) *Senior Executive Reward: key models and practices*. Aldershot, Gower.

For a collection of readings on executive reward with some mainland European as well as UK material, see Tyson, S. and Bournois, F. (eds) (2005) *Top Pay and Performance: international and strategic approach*. London, Elsevier.

CHAPTER 11

International Reward Management

CHAPTER OBJECTIVES

At the end of this chapter you should understand and be able to explain the following:

- The current context multinational employers encounter influencing their aims and choices in determining employee reward across international operations.

- The various types of employees for whom employee reward strategies, policies and processes need to be designed and administered.

- The use of theory and knowledge derived from empirical research in weighing opportunities and problems in rewarding employees in an international context.

CIPD STANDARDS COVERED IN THIS CHAPTER:

In the context of the multinational employer, to be able to:

- Contribute to the identification of an appropriate employee reward strategy from an analysis of an organisation's corporate strategy, and take part in the preparation of reward plans.

- Assist in preparing an employee reward policy statement and the process for its continuous review.

- Promote fairness in reward practice.

- Advise on the management of change when introducing or modifying elements of the reward system.

In the context of the multinational employer, to understand and explain:

- The process of reward management, its components and aims.

- The factors affecting reward philosophies, strategies and policies, and their potential for supporting change when integrated with organisation and personnel strategies and policies.

- New developments in employee reward and their application within the organisation.

INTRODUCTION

To gain a sense of the significance of international organisation and the consequences of transnational organisational activity for employment and reward management, one need only turn to the 2007 World Investment Report (UNCTD, 2007). Here we find 78,000 transnational companies, with 780,000 foreign affiliates, employing nearly 73 million people worldwide. During 2006, UNCTD (2007) reports growth in foreign direct investment (FDI) inflows occurring in all three groups of economies: developed countries, developing countries and the transition economies of South-East Europe and the Commonwealth of Independent States. In total (in US dollars), the reported sum involved was $1.306bn. These financial investment flows are attributed to significant mergers and acquisitions activity, but also to 'greenfield' investment – especially in developing and transition economies.

While this context implies plenty of scope for policy and practice work, human resource specialists' 'critical responsibility' for the design and maintenance of employee reward systems becomes 'much more complex and difficult' when set in the context of 'the conduct of international business' (Briscoe and Schuler, 2004: 305). For one thing, practical considerations – clearly articulated by a practising HR specialist well over 30 years ago – challenge the 'equal pay for work of equal value' principle taken as self-evident in respect of employee reward content and administration in jurisdictions such as the UK. While it may represent 'a compensation manager's nightmare ... we can have equal compensation only when we live in an equal world' (Krutz, 1972: 30).

REWARDING EXPATRIATION – REWARDING MULTI-LOCAL TALENT

The HR specialist faces problems to be solved, first, in supporting a multinational's wish to employ 'parent country nationals' (PCNs) not only in the organisation's country of origin, drawing from domestic employment sources. PCNs may be expatriated to work in other countries to resource business development and operations there. And these transfers may be more than an isolated 'out-return' cycle but require multiple assignments over time as the multinational and its strategy-structure arrangements evolve. The assignments may vary in terms of duration, as well as giving rise to different considerations around the effort–reward bargain, bearing in mind that the employee's circumstances, like those of the organisation, are unlikely to remain static.

Secondly, there is the question of employing individuals sourced from the 'host' country where the multinational sets up operations, to support the enterprise in that jurisdiction. If 'host country nationals' (HCNs) are working alongside PCNs – possibly occupying positions of superiority in leading regional operations – according to the equal pay for work of equal value principle, it may be hypothesised that they should be subject to PCN reward management terms and conditions. Or do other considerations apply?

Thirdly, as multinationals increase their presence, and develop confidence in the potential of talented employees in countries around the world to transfer corporate practice embedded in their experience and knowledge beyond their country of origin, corporate management may choose to widen the source from which to assign managers and specialists transnationally. These 'third country nationals' (TCNs) may have been recruited and rewarded on terms embedded in their country of origin employment system. But if they are expected to contribute to corporate performance, working transnationally, in the same way as PCNs, again, is there a case that their reward should be synchronised with that of the PCNs?

CONVERGENT TRANSNATIONAL CAPITAL POWER – DIVERGENT BUSINESS SYSTEMS

By way of context for addressing such issues, as discussed in Chapter 1, prevailing wisdom may be to theorise a convergence between employment systems worldwide – even if this involves two capitalist 'varieties' (Hall and Soskice, 2001): a deregulated 'liberal market'-oriented variant, on the one hand, and a more politically 'co-ordinated' type, on the other hand.

In liberal market economies, the tendency is for active stock market regulation of business, with unitary boards and decentralised industrial relations: typical examples cited are the UK and USA.

In co-ordinated (sometimes 'social') market economies, stock markets may be balanced by direct engagement in business governance by banks and other long-term-oriented financial interests. Industrial relations tends to be centralised, with legislation on occupational categorisation sometimes specifying a hierarchy of pay rates; and trade unions may sit on the supervisory part of a two-tier board structure along with capital investors, overseeing top management appointments and strategy. Typical examples cited include Germany, Japan and the Scandinavian countries (albeit with variation between them, just as there are between the UK and USA, in terms of detailed business system characteristics – eg in Japan, industrial relations tends to be highly decentralised). These are very simplified descriptions, and the reader is directed to sources such as Hall and Soskice (2001) for a more comprehensive specification.

From the point of view of the multinational management wishing simply to follow a common recipe for rewarding workforce members irrespective of the operating environment, however, as Brookes *et al* (2005) argue, diverse 'business systems constitute mechanisms and structures for regulating market relations. While, at least partially, they may be backed up by coercive power, they are most visible in shaping, moulding and making possible everyday exchange relationships through imitation and network ties' (2005: 406–7). The multinational's dispositional advantage as the source of FDI capital may suggest potential on the part of the inward investor to mobilise coercive power. But although 'use of coercion as a means of backing up and enforcing practices' is feasible, this constitutes 'a relatively inefficient and resource-intensive mechanism that is unlikely to deployed in day-to-day social transactions' (2005: 407). Observable underlying cultural and institutional factors continue to vary (Sparrow, 1999; 2000), reflecting differences in tax and social insurance regulations, as well as social considerations affecting work orientations that, in practice, enable and constrain reward management choices in the multinational organisation (Bloom *et al*, 2003).

NOT FOR PROFITS ALONE

By way of a final preamble point to open the chapter, it needs to be emphasised that, while much of the literature (and therefore its discussion in this chapter) reports on developments in profit-seeking enterprises, many of the considerations around employee reward and its management apply equally to not-for-profit organisations, such as transnational and supranational government institutions and voluntary sector bodies. Such organisations also operate across a variety of international locations, and compete for talented people to run them – both indigenous and expatriate.

Moreover, not-for-profit enterprises face employee reward management issues just as, if not more, pressing than those encountered by commercial trading entities. While people may be perceived as joining voluntary or regulatory organisations for reasons different from those attributed to people recruited to business firms, it is easy for these assumptions to cloud the universal problem of getting scarce people resources into place – when often those places not only demand highly skilful capabilities; they may also represent especially challenging environments in which to deploy people. We will include case evidence with that in mind, as well as using the generic term 'multinational' in references to organisations that form the types of employers under consideration in this chapter.

The chapter will explore the literature on employee reward in an international context to help the HR thinking performer to understand and evaluate approaches that might be used to advise corporate managers in relation to PCN, HCN and TCN workforce members under three principal headings, as follows:

- What are the problems to be addressed, adopting a strategic orientation?

- How can the theories such as those discussed in Chapter 2 assist in specifying the issues to be determined?

- How can published research be used to help weigh the merits of predictions about the outcomes from following particular international reward and recognition approaches, bearing in mind open systems contextual influences?

MULTINATIONAL CONTEXTS FOR EMPLOYEE REWARD MANAGEMENT

We begin the review with a specification of 'context' within which employee reward problems may arise when organising to support corporate activity across international boundaries. In the case of commercially governed businesses (although much the same could be argued to apply to other forms of organisation), operations in countries outside the multinational's country of origin are reported to have become increasingly significant as the balance of commercial emphasis has shifted, compared with domestic activities, under conditions of economic globalisation (Farashashi, Hasi and Molz, 2005). Revenue streams from devolved manufacturing and/or trading across the multinational, once limited compared with domestic country operations, have taken on 'strategic importance', as the UNCDT (2007) evidence cited earlier indicates. Geppert (2005: 1) reports that economists tend to regard decisions 'to move from the early internationalisation stage of exporting, licensing and franchising towards foreign direct investment strategies and ... the establishment of host country subsidiaries ... as driven [mainly] by economic calculations to improve [a multinational's] profitability, cost efficiency and innovativeness'. Non-domestic activities now command an increasingly large proportion of corporate resources that all need to be deployed so that the multinational can compete profitably on a global scale.

Specifically, corporate management teams are to focus on 'the generation and transfer of knowledge across national settings, organizations and *networks*' (Goodherham and Nordhaug, 2003: 1, emphasis added).

The reference to networks is significant: 'a multinational's ability merely to enable the flow of knowledge from its headquarters to its national subsidiary units no longer represents a sufficient competitive advantage' (Nohria and Ghoshal, 1997: 1–2). Traditional scale economies have been eroded, it is argued, and competitors are no longer limited to domestic firms. Multinationals face other giant-sized multinational corporations in 'head-to-head' competition for profitable revenues. Accordingly, multinationals have been encouraged to migrate from HQ-led and hierarchical organisation structures to the 'multi-headed' (Morgan and Whitley, 2003), or 'trasnational' (Ghoshal and Bartlett, 1998) or 'differentiated network' (Nohria and Ghoshal 1997) structure. This model is consistent with the shift from an emphasis on exploiting sources of cheap labour to one of tapping tacit knowledge, embedded in new strategic assets around the globe, such as multi-local industry districts, with the accent on what Nohria and Ghoshal (1997) describe as 'prolific innovation'.

Offering a reality check to this strategy discourse, however, Edwards *et al* (2005: 1261) observe that, while ideas about the networked transfusion of knowledge may appear as corporate imperatives, 'there is little evidence on this phenomenon'. In fact, bringing our focus back to people management, what Edwards *et al* (2005) describe as 'reverse transfusion' of employment practices to support multi-headed organisation may be inhibited by the difficulties of dislodging institutional structures and practices. This implies that, for example, people in internationally facing roles located at corporate HQ may experience difficulty in changing, undermining the basic premise of the model.

Illustrating this in practice, Perkins (2006) reports evidence at the European regional level of a large, well-known information technology company. In the past, scope had existed to influence, and possibly reinterpret reward policies to meet transnational operating conditions, where lessons learned were fed back to HQ in the USA to enrich corporate policy. Now the US-based 'central hub' exclusively undertook development of reward management programmes and governance processes: activity in the regions had shifted to enabling the corporately mandated framework to work effectively across the various countries involved. Regional specialists said they accepted the logic behind the drive for centralisation and rationalisation, in response to the problem of remaining profitable in a tight globally competitive market. But they felt the new strategy of 'minimising differences' required a 'mindset change' at the corporate level. And this is not an isolated case. Perkins (2006) reports evidence suggesting efforts more generally on the part of multinational corporate reward designers to 'reduce differences', contrasting with trends discernible half a decade earlier that implied 'dispersed network' theory was being acted on in practice (Perkins and Hendry, 2001).

Edwards *et al* (2005) argue that, contrary to its ascribed flexibility as a liberal market economy, institutional legacies in the US employment system may inhibit innovation when co-ordinating activities at the multinational level. They specifically cite the example of businesses, like the IT case example, which started out under the direct management of founders with a paternalistic managerial style. One emphasis was on keeping trade unions out, translating among other things to relatively generous reward levels –consistent with the principles of efficiency wage theory described in Chapter 2. While, as in the case outlined, a fundamental break with legacy employment conditions may occur, necessitated by changing commercial conditions, the institutionally embedded mindset of 'the way we do things around here' may prevail among US corporate HQ members, influencing their dealings with other parts of the multinational, undermining the notion of a 'networked structure'.

As the reward head for Europe, Middle East and Africa expressed it in the IT company case, in the face of US-mandated reward policies, a problem arises if:

> *... you are mentally working on one model, while the Company [ie HQ in the USA] is working another ... The challenge of making that global programme achievable is a complicated challenge. This change that the Company is going through is adjusting to that and trying to start to make the words match the actions. It's clear that the Company can act in a new way before it starts to talk in a new way. And that kind of discrepancy between what you're saying and what you're doing creates huge problems for managers, for employees, and – from a professional point of view – for the rewards team. Really challenged people professionally – challenged their integrity. They were starting to complain that 'we're saying one thing and doing another'. When we feed that issue back up the organisation, the message we always get back is 'the business*

*reality' – which is fair, which is correct. But that business reality, which is
about cost minimisation, is not what the words were around our programmes.*
(cited in Perkins, 2006)

SELF-ASSESSMENT EXERCISE

Consider the division of labour and policy-based authority among HR specialists in a large
multinational with a network of regionally located operations. To what extent should members
of HR specialist teams working from regional offices around the world defer to HQ in the
detailed interpretation and application of reward policies and practices in support of their line
management 'business partners'? What might be ways of sharing experience in working with
corporate reward strategies across the network? What would be the prerequisites in terms
of working relationships between line and senior corporate management and between HR
specialists possibly working to a matrix reporting line?

CHOICES FOR MULTINATIONAL MANAGEMENT AND THEIR REWARD CONSEQUENCES

Notwithstanding sensible notes of caution not to accept idealised prescriptions
uncritically, Harvey *et al* (2002: 285) hold out the prospect that 'organizations
may become unique competitively [on a global basis] if their human resources
and their system for managing human resources are efficient and effective'.
Choosing to alter the role, organisation and priorities of multinationals and
associated people management has important consequences for employee reward
considerations.

First, use of the term 'international reward', as it has appeared in the HRM
literature, may need to be revisited when considering treatment of employee
segments subject to management in the contemporary international context
(Perkins and Hendry, 2001). Secondly, the ascription of a strategic role for
international operations and to the profitable generation and networked transfer
of knowledge may be interpreted as requiring more corporate managerial
attention to employee reward across the enterprise than may have been the
case previously. While, on the one hand, acknowledging diversity in the
character of the multinational population, giving rise to segmented employment
administration issues, on the other hand, the emphasis in the corporate strategy
literature on transnationally networked resource management implies a
requirement for more integrated policy-making.

If a multinational's human resource strategy shifts from one of exploiting cheap
labour sources, to securing '[t]acit knowledge of local markets [as] perhaps the
ultimate source of value and ... the basis for developing unique competitive
strategies' (Harvey *et al*, 2002: 285), reward management choices will need to
avoid consequences the actors perceive as unfair and so divisive, undermining
multi-headed team structures working to a common set of aims. This is
consistent with Kessler's (2007) argument that reward designs should not be

informed by business strategy in isolation from considerations of internal and external equity. If the people to be employed and managed internationally are counted as 'strategic' resources (thereby demanding top corporate management attention), then it follows logically that purposeful, co-ordinated and context-sensitive employee reward policy and practice interventions will be required.

In keeping with HRM-style people management, employee reward across international operations offers one focal point for alignment – vertically and horizontally – to achieve organisational effectiveness (see the discussion in Chapter 12). However, the spread of activities and people to be co-ordinated – taking into account not only geography but also diverse cultural and institutional environments – implies that the task to be achieved will be even more complex than that experienced in domestic operational settings.

Cazurra *et al* (2007) argue that a lack of complementary resources required to operate abroad, that is, people and their interaction with other corporate resources including operating systems and processes, represents an important cause of difficulties inhibiting internationalisation in search of new and profitable revenues. And even if corporate management seek to achieve a balance between global strategy and local sensitivity the design and application of 'employee engagement' approaches to facilitate profitable knowledge mobilisation does not occur in a vacuum.

Other multinationals will be seeking to acquire retain and align these 'strategic capabilities' also. Assuming individuals will be aware of the demand for their particular skills and willingness to put them to work, talented people are likely to bring expectations to the kind of employment relationship – and its terms – on offer for their voluntary co-operation with a corporate project that also demands accommodation within international reward design. Mamman *et al* (1996) advocate that, despite surprisingly few studies investigating the issue, multinational managements pay attention to employees' preferred criteria for pay systems to which they will be subjected, accounting for cultural factors, demographics and industry type.

 STUDENT EXERCISE

Working in groups, identify multinational organisations known to you and share ideas on what their approach to 'doing business abroad' seems to be. It may be helpful to prepare for this exercise by looking on the Internet for marketing material, corporate governance reporting information and/or other documents released into the public domain on initiatives to develop and win support from shareholders, donors, customers and other sources of capital and revenue.

How extensive do operations appear to be worldwide? Is the organisation 'mature' internationally or at an earlier stage of development? What are the implications of what you find out and synthesise in your discussion? List the top three priorities for setting terms and conditions for employing people consequent on your conclusions.

FACTORS AND TRENDS IN REWARDING *EXPATRIATED* KNOWLEDGE MOBILISATION

We agree with Edwards *et al* (2005) that commentary on networked multinational organisation should not be taken at face value – organisation practice is not the same as what academics and consultants, or even practising managers, may say it is. However, following Harvery *et al*'s (2002) suggestions, mindful of Cazurra *et al*'s (2007) challenge, the idea of mobilising key capabilities to achieve organisational goals is a promising one to focus consideration of approaches to international employee reward. If we go along with the proposition that active reward management offers employers one route by which to communicate what they value (Lawler, 1995), then there is a role in getting the message across about prioritising mobilisation of employees' knowledge so as to put it to work in situations (and places) where this can create profitable outcomes. As a first step, the types of 'mobilisation' involved within multinational networks need to be identified. This may help in thinking about the implications for reward design and practice specifically applicable to the various categories of employee making up the multinational workforce. It may also assist in clarifying what is meant by 'international reward' for the multinational pursuing a strategy of purposeful knowledge mobilisation.

Lowe *et al* (2002) are critical of the 'expatriate myopia' in literature concerned with managing people in international contexts. As indicated above, when addressing reward system issues multinationals are being encouraged to pay greater attention to how they build relationships with *all* the people they employ, with a strategic focus on organising them across globally integrated networks. So when discussing international reward and recognition, a tendency in some international HRM commentary to equate 'global reward' design with considerations pertaining to the terms and conditions applicable to expatriate assignments (eg Watson and Singh, 2005) needs to be regarded critically. In practice, multinational reward considerations encompass the terms and conditions applicable to the three principal employee categories referred to earlier: HCNs, PCNs and TCNs. Commonalities and interactions between the categories in pursuit of alignment deserve attention, but there are also reasons to unscramble international reward management approaches applied in each case.

Special considerations arise in the case of expatriated PCNs and TCNs, taking account of the fact that a prevalent approach multinationals adopt to mobilise the knowledge capabilities they offer is by relocating employees (possibly accompanied by family members) across national borders. Issues follow specific to the act of relocation between employment (and residential) systems not applicable in the case of HCNs. For this reason, policies and practices specific to expatriate mobilisation have evolved, giving rise to issues that differentiate geographically mobile employees from those retained in the territory and employment system where they were recruited. Such arrangements – and accompanying costs and complexity – are not easily set aside. But the focus in corporate strategy prescription on networking knowledge implies that reward practices that have in the past isolated expatriates from co-workers, inhibiting knowledge networking, may be part of the 'complementary resourcing' difficulties implied by Cazurra *et al* (2007). Thus not only is proper attention desirable to reward management of the multinational workforce as a whole, but even when specifically addressing expatriate reward management, account must be taken of the corporate goal of integration if the distributed network model of international organisation is pursued. Rewards for expatriate employees are discussed next, after which trends in international employee reward generally are reviewed.

DEFINING EXPATRIATES

A preliminary task in considering expatriate employees is to clarify who these people are; we will then describe the forms and durations over which they are deployed beyond their country of origin.

PCN expatriates have been defined as 'experts and managers' who are citizens of the country in which the multinational's corporate headquarters is located, assigned to work in a foreign country, tasked with transplanting corporate culture, competence and strategy to local units (Harris, Brewster and Sparrow, 2003; Moore, 2006; Phillips and Fox, 2003). In turn, TCNs may be defined as 'citizens of a country other than the headquarters or host country' (Phillips and Fox, 2003: 466). TCNs represent a 'hybrid' choice for managing international subsidiaries, residing between PCNs and HCNs. TCNs 'combine the advantages and disadvantages of the use of expatriates and host country nationals' (Tan and Maloney, 2006: 480). In theory, TCNs may have more local knowledge than PCNs and yet have less local knowledge than HCNs. And TCNs may have a deeper understanding of corporate policies than HCNs, but may be less familiar with the parent organisation's 'culture, competence, and strategy' than expatriates from the corporate centre. Resourcing decisions to populate transnational operations are therefore strategic in nature, with clear consequences for the capabilities and likely performance outcomes being invested in.

But is there evidence not only of an increased demand for managers with international experience as more organisations join the multinational marketplace? Has the character of international employee mobilisation become more strategic? Martin and Bartol (2003) answer in the affirmative, citing an argument by Gregersen *et al* (1998) that leadership experiences obtained from completing international assignments have been recognised as impacting positively on longer-term senior executive career development. Calls for more systematic management of expatriate performance imply consequences for the ways in which this is rewarded and recognised, paying attention to issues around incentive rewards (reviewed in Chapter 6).

EXPATRIATE ASSIGNMENTS

The typical expatriate assignment lasts two or three years (Harris and Dickmann, 2005), generally with a five-year limit (Briscoe and Schuler, 2004). Recent

Figure 11.1 The international mobility continuum

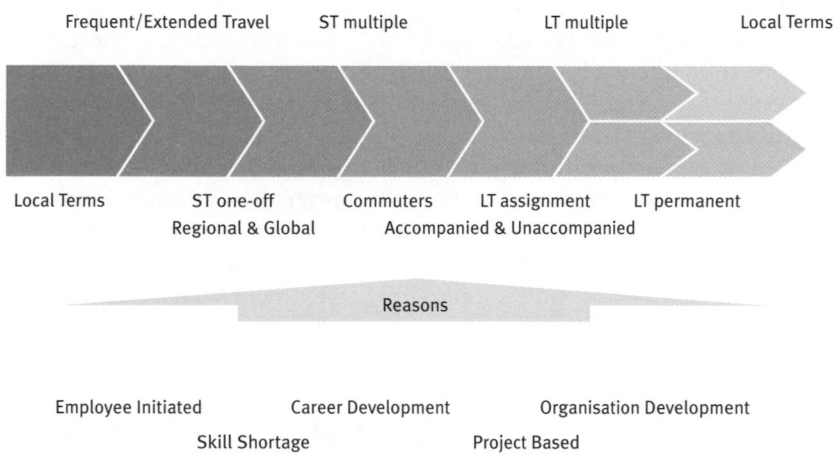

Based on a review undertaken by Shell

Source: Perkins (2006)
Reproduced with permission of CIPD.

survey evidence suggests that alternatives are emerging, including permanent migration, short-term assignments, cross-border job swaps or membership of multicultural project teams (Forster, 2000). Energy multinational Shell spent some two years recently exploring the definition of international mobility applied across the business (Perkins, 2006), concluding that rather than polarise notions of expatriation, policy-makers might find it more helpful, given the changing nature of international organisation and the accompanying developments in expatriation, to think about employee mobility in terms of a continuum, as illustrated in Figure 11.1 above. Here the variety of reasons for requiring expatriation could be set against assignment duration, facilitating a match in turn to appropriate expatriate policy terms.

A survey of policies for employees on short-term expatriate assignments, typically lasting between three and 12 months, indicates that short-term assignments are becoming more popular. Just over 60 per cent of respondents surveyed by Organization Resource Counselors Inc (ORC) signalled an increase in short-term expatriation in their organisations (ORC, 2006). The same survey findings contrast short-term expatriate assignments with 'commuter assignments', popular where home and host location are close. Companies like Unilever may appoint an individual to work weekly in London, while retaining a family home in, say, Geneva to which the assignee returns each weekend. One reason offered for why the variety of expatriate assignments has been widening is reluctance on the part of individuals to accept assignments over the traditional duration in view of dual-career commitments where both partners are following professional careers, or when children's schooling or eldercare mean that long-term absences from the country where an employee has social ties would be unacceptable (ORC, 2004).

Short-term assignments enable knowledge mobilisation across geographies, without unsettling the individual's core lifestyle and relationships. There may, however, be hidden costs beyond the provision of serviced accommodation and supplemental travel and subsistence reimbursements, where the transnational commuter experiences even more barriers to becoming embedded in the local business environment, reinforcing the 'outsider' stereotype with attendant barriers to integrated performance referred to earlier. (For a detailed discussion, see the technical appendix to chapter 5 of Perkins and Shortland, 2006). Notwithstanding these trends in use of alternatives, the most common reported form of expatriation worldwide is 'a one-time assignment with a planned repatriation' (ORC, 2004: 8).

ACCOUNTING FOR EXPATRIATION REWARD MANAGEMENT

The 'keeping the expatriate whole' principle (Phillips and Fox, 2003: 470) has governed reported thinking and practice on expatriate reward design. It is not merely a case of semantics to argue that this line of reasoning has downplayed the 'reward' aspect in favour of providing 'compensation' for accepting 'changes in lifestyle, enduring 'hardship', etc.' (Perkins and Shortland, 2006: 185). The sense of an 'exchange relationship' (we introduced this notion in Chapter 1) is still in

Figure 11.2 Example of an expatriate 'salary build-up' or 'balance sheet' plan

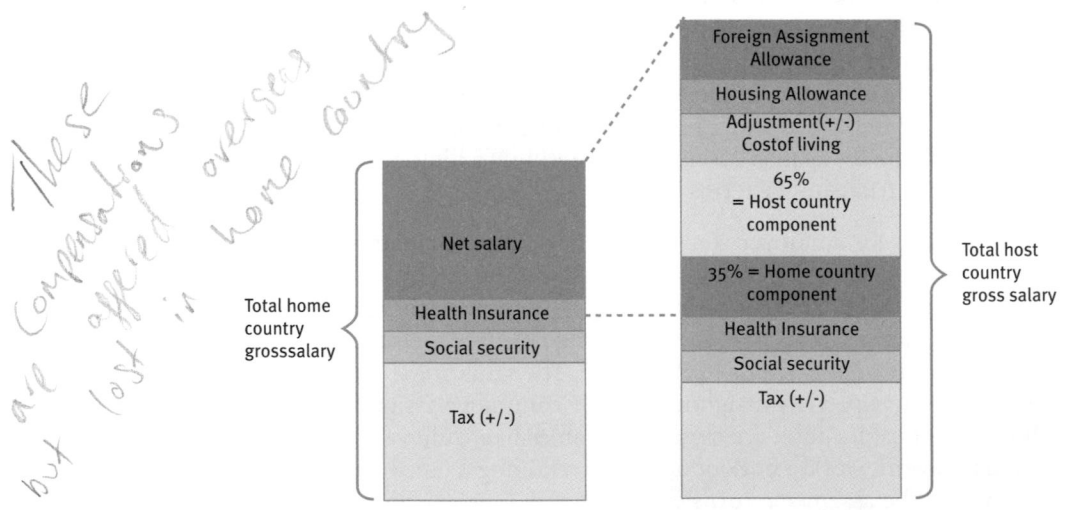

Source: Festing and Perkins (2008) *Rewards for Internationally mobile employees*, figure 8.2, p. 153. Reproduced by kind permission of Routledge.

focus, but the underlying rationale appears to veer away from the tradition of an 'effort bargain'.

This change of orientation is expressed, first, in terms of pay package design intended to preserve existing relativities with PCN peers, or at least to preserve consistency with reward levels for the employee's occupational group and level in their country of origin in the case of TCNS. Secondly, the express ambition is to maintain 'purchasing parity' – so that the expatriate may enjoy the same living standards as at home (Dowling, Festing and Engle, 2007; Fenwick, 2004).

The approach aligned to this policy orientation, known as the 'home-based/salary build-up', or 'balance sheet' (ORC, 2004), augments basic pay with a 'foreign service premium' (Dowling, Festing and Engle, 2007), as well as cash supplements to compensate for 'hardships' (eg working in remote or politically unstable locations, or those with limited social infrastructure). Housing and children's education costs are reimbursed, extending the 'kept whole' principle to the employee's family members. In addition to salary adjustments to neutralise cost of living differences, other allowances may include home leave, relocation, spouse assistance/dual career allowances and so on (Fenwick, 2004; Perkins and Shortland, 2006).

Adding complexity to expatriate 'compensation' administration, accompanying this traditional 'build-up' plan, consistent with the kept-whole principle, 'tax equalisation' generally accompanies balance sheet expatriate compensation. What this means is that the value of tax and social insurance contributions the employee would hypothetically have paid at home is deducted from the home base pay to arrive at a 'net' salary. Allowances and premiums are then added to that amount, and the organisation pays any tax falling due within host jurisdiction on the compensation package total amount.

An illustrative example of such an expatriate compensation scheme, sourced from a German multinational, is set out in Figure 11.2 above. The total salary payable in the host country is built up from the net salary that would have been payable for the same job in the individual's home country. The net 'home country salary' serves as the comparative base line for calculating the expatriate salary. In that calculation, differences in cost of living, living standards and housing standards are taken into account. In the case of the illustrative organisation, the employee is guaranteed the calculated net expatriate salary, subject to an annual exchange rate adjustment converting between home and host currency values. A tax and social insurance 'grossing-up' is undertaken and the host organisation unit pays the taxes and social insurance in the host country.

The **cost-of-living adjustment**, undertaken based on a home country 'basket' of items and the currency exchange rate used for the salary calculation, is designed to balance differences in cost of living between the home country and the host country. The intention of applying this cost-of-living index is to allow the consumption of goods and services of the same type, quality and amount as would apply in the host country. In this multinational, the cost-of-living allowance is applied to 65 per cent of the comparative net domestic salary. This percentage corresponds to a statistical value of the typical proportion of income required for daily expenses.

The cost-of-living allowance (COLA) has been reported as a source of dissatisfaction among expatriates (Suutari and Tornikoski, 2001). To determine a rate regarded as independent, multinationals may use the services of consultants who specialise in providing COLA information on a global basis, regularly updated, to their clients (Festing and Perkins, 2008).

The **housing allowance** means that the host organisation either settles rental costs directly or authorises a host rental budget, which the expatriate receives in the expatriate salary calculation. In return, an amount equivalent to the normal housing cost in the home country may be deducted as part of the expatriate salary calculation. In some cases, for example in developing countries where infrastructure is not in line with western expectations, the organisation may own a 'township' associated with operational facilities, supplying company-provided housing. In other cases a fixed allowance for accommodation may be paid or an assessment made based on a portion of income, out of which actual housing costs are paid. 'Housing issues are often addressed on a case-by-case basis, but as a firm internationalizes, formal policies become more necessary and efficient' (Dowling, Festing and Engle, 2007).

The **foreign assignment allowance** is an incentive for an employee to accept assignment requiring international mobility, and may also recognise intangible difficulties as well as material hardships, where individuals and family members experience a lifestyle different from that enjoyed in the home country, not accounted for in the COLA payment. Issues intentionally covered by what may be termed a 'hardship' payment, such as personal safety, distance, language, cultural and climatic differences, economic conditions as well as the political and social environment are included in this element.

PREVALENCE OF THE EXPATRIATE BALANCE SHEET

According to one large-scale survey, some 70 per cent of European multinationals continue to favour the balance sheet approach to expatriate compensation; in the USA and Japan the percentage rises to 85–95 per cent (ORC, 2002). There are reports, however, that multinationals find funding expatriate balance sheet packages incompatible with corporate cost containment goals (Wentland, 2003). Those experimenting with movement away from 'topping up' home-based compensation without any reference to local market conditions may attempt destination-based expatriate reward planning, using host country market benchmarks instead. This may be judged especially appropriate in 'developed' countries; in 'developing' countries, expatriates at middle and senior executive levels still tend to expect some compensation for 'hardship'.

Among a newer generation of globally mobile professionals, even in the latter territories a more 'bare-bones' approach may be tried, especially where there is agreement between the parties that the assignment has a more 'developmental' focus, as part of longer-term career management for corporate executives

(Perkins and Shortland, 2006). In its purest form 'host-benchmarked' expatriates are rewarded at the same rates as their local counterparts. Although this approach may be used for permanent transfers (so-called 'localisation'), on the whole the use of pure host-based approaches is rare. As Perkins and Shortland (2006: 187) explain:

> ... net to net comparisons need to be calculated to determine the feasibility of this approach and the rationale for the assignment needs to be considered carefully. Even if the net to net calculation provides the basis for this approach to succeed (in host reward policy terms), international assignees who are expected to return home or move on to another location are likely to have issues that set them apart from locals – most notably housing and schooling. They are also likely to require some assistance with home leave to maintain home country ties and ease repatriation. International assignees may wish to retain home country housing (assuming they are home owners) and, with the exception of very young children, are most likely to wish to keep their children in either a school of their own nationality or an international school, so that children's education is not compromised. In addition, assignees are likely to require assistance with taxation – from the very basics of completing tax returns in the foreign jurisdiction to ensuring that additional tax liabilities are met.

Region-based arrangements represent a variant of this 'destination-' rather than 'home'-facing orientation (Fenwick, 2004). Here the equity benchmark is between the assignee and local/regional peers, with the emphasis on integration (Watson and Singh, 2005), although if the location is in a low-pay country, the multinational usually supplements base pay with additional benefits and payments (Perkins and Shortland, 2006). Hybrid systems (Suutari and Torkowski, 2001), combining elements of home and host approaches, as well as individually tailored packages, apply in some multinationals.

Short-term assignment terms are generally intended to be less complex, and less expensive, than arrangements applied to long-term expatriation, although there is evidence that militates against generalising in this regard (Festing and Perkins, 2008). While those assigned for six months or less tend to receive reduced terms compared with long-term assignees, for those abroad for between six months and a year (after which long-term assignment terms generally apply), 'services, incentives, hardship compensation, housing, transportation, relocation allowances [and] trips home' continue to be provided to assignees (ORC, 2006: 12).

Commuter assignments, which Mayerhofer et al (2004) label 'flexpatriation', tend to fall outside the traditional policy categories covering expatriate reward. As already noted, commuters' international mobility tends to involve stays of weekly (or monthly) intervals, or some other duration, leaving family members at home. Expenditure will be less on household provisions and in situ transportation but more on restaurant meals and home/host/home round trips. Commuter packages therefore tend to be home-based and contain elements primarily relating to reimbursement of travel (air fares paid) and serviced accommodation costs.

While simplifying international mobilisation, on the one hand, complications in taxation (as well as visa issues) may arise in administering policies applicable to this group of international workers (Perkins and Shortland, 2006). And the trend may militate against 'transnational' organisational designs, signalling a return to ethnocentric management that inhibits expatriate enculturation into host environments (Phillips and Fox, 2003) and the concomitant sense of interdependency between expatriate and key local employees.

International assignments are important investments for multinationals. Brewster *et al* (2001) estimate that the costs of sending someone on an expatriate assignment are at least three times higher than those of domestic appointments. A PriceWaterhouseCoopers (2006) study states that, on average, costs per annum for an expatriate amount to US$311,000. This includes direct pay and benefits costs and the costs to the organisation of managing the international assignments programme. The latter accounted for 7 per cent of the total assignment costs (US$22,378).

Specifically, the direct costs of employee salaries, taxes, housing, shipment of household goods, children's education, (sometimes) spouse support, cross-cultural training, goods and service allowances, repatriation logistics and reassignment costs, are further inflated by the administrative costs of running an international assignment programme. Administrative aspects include home-based HR support (assignment planning, selection and reward management, assignment location- or host-based HR support, post-assignment placement costs as well as post-assignment career tracking costs (Festing and Perkins, 2008). Furthermore, intangible factors such as 'adjustment' costs of the expatriates have to be accounted for. Added to this, managing non-domestic operations through the medium of expatriates exposes multinationals to risk attributable not only due to direct and indirect costs associated with assignment reward packages: 'Indirect costs of a failed assignment may include loss of market share and damage to international customer relationships' (Brewster *et al*, 2001: 27).

It is therefore not surprising that more and more organisations claim to be interested in measuring a return on investment in international assignment; however, to date there is evidence that only 14 per cent are addressing this complex task, mainly looking at the definition and respective fulfilment of assignment objectives (GMAC, 2006).

Despite the controversy surrounding expatriate reward debates, an argument can still be made, informed by institutional economics theory, that expatriation remains a cost-effective solution (Bonache and Fernández, 2005). In short, corporate management may be unwilling to entrust safeguarding the value of the corporate brand to individuals recruited from local external labour markets, where attitudes to corporate governance and wider cultural values may contrast with corporate governance and trading imperatives. And if the organisation is pursuing a strategy that requires skill sets fully conversant with distinctive corporate knowledge and ways of applying it beyond the country of origin, corporate management may regard appointment of an individual long socialised into the corporate culture as a prerequisite.

The transaction costs associated with expatriate compensation packages may thus be equivalent to or even lower than those accompanying an external hire (Bonache and Fernández, 2005). The time and other resources consumed in integrating a manager recruited from one of the local economies in which subsidiary operations are located may be incompatible with the need to achieve early returns on the investment in subsidiary operations. As noted earlier, the halfway-house TCN, with a balance of global/local know-how, may offer multinationals scope to meet resourcing demands while not compromising core values, at least until such time as mutual confidence and trust has been established between all parties to a differentiated network operation.

HR ROLE: SCOPE FOR TENSION WITH THE LINE

Risks around expatriation-dependent multinational management may bring corporate HR specialists and line managers into potential conflict in meeting expectations around their respective roles (Perkins and Daste, 2007). Tensions may arise between an aim to achieve successful transnational performance across knowledge networks, limiting differences under competitive trading conditions, and the traditional principle of 'keeping expatriates whole'. Those carrying devolved responsibility for supervising expatriate managers unsurprisingly are likely to wish to smooth assignment conditions so that failure risks – that may have adverse consequences for supervisors' own reputations as well as for expatriates themselves – are minimised.

While corporate HR specialists may adopt the role of 'corporate policy integrity guardian', supervising managers in a direct line relationship may feel less constrained by what may be labelled 'personnel' issues, relying on 'the business case' to vary policy to accommodate individual expatriates' demands. We can theorise this problem using commentary on social situations giving rise to 'strategic contingency' in organisations (Pfeffer and Salancik, 1977). Supervisors in multinationals must achieve results but they depend on others (expatriates) to do so. The result is that the 'doers' accrue power to influence the terms of the relationship (see the parallels with the 'agency' and 'power-dependency' arguments discussed generally in Chapter 2, and, in relation to executive reward, in Chapter 10). The greater the dependency, the greater leverage may accrue to expatriates in bargaining around the terms of their co-operation (effort–reward).

HR specialists *depend* on expatriate supervisors to apply corporate policy consistently and cost-effectively in managing expatriate managers – their influence may be limited to *guiding* expatriate supervisors' action. Pfeffer and Davies-Blake (1987) argue that an individual's salary (and by extension other employment terms) is contingent not only on the role they occupy but is also how this 'resource' is embedded in organisational context. An expatriate supervisor may be influenced to interpret corporate policy on expatriation biased towards satisfying an expatriate manager's expectations of a package that will suitably 'compensate' their willingness to accept an assignment abroad.

This practical imperative may stand in tension with HR specialists' ambition to satisfy corporate priorities around rationalisation and standardisation of employment terms and conditions, including expatriation packages, to contain costs accumulated corporately across the expatriate managerial population. Despite a common goal, in principle, of serving corporate interests, reflection on the problem of expatriating managers, informed by analysis of empirical evidence gathered among a sample of large western multinationals, leads Perkins and Daste (2007) to predict tensions comparing influences on expatriate supervisors, in contrast to the viewpoint corporate HR specialists project in describing their feelings towards line management receptiveness to 'professional' advocacy.

One consequence may be that a more critical reading of the expatriation literature, moving beyond a simple focus on the administrative aspects, to account for political interaction between interested organisational actors is necessary to assist HR specialists in diagnosing this strategic issue. It is one with significant implications for their credibility with expatriates, their supervisors and corporate top management, as corporate policy quality assurance guardians. The HR team in a global banking and financial services corporation sum up the problem by reference to a traditional culture of individual 'deals', accompanying active steps to migrate towards more 'mature' expatriate reward management practices (Perkins, 2006).

Nurney (2001) argues that multinationals should 'stop negotiating individual packages for international assignees' when a multinational's transnational presence increases, and with it the diversity of nationalities (country start-through-and-end points) becomes significant. At this time, core reward management factors need to be weighed in formulating and applying policy that go beyond getting someone to accept a foreign posting. The message needs skilful communication, supported by the HR function, but underlined by top management, so that expatriates, their supervisors and fellow workforce members alike understand key principles surrounding mobilisation of individual 'knowledge carriers', requiring cross-border postings. If policy development, refinement, review and learning-based adaptation processes involve these key stakeholders then policy legitimisation may be enhanced too.

Practical considerations of numbers, types, duration, as well as cost-effectiveness of expatriate assignments need to be balanced against socio-political factors including trust and equity considerations (Nurney, 2001). However, interpreting standardisation in ways that imply rigidity is inconsistent with the need for nimbleness to meet competitive demands, as Baruch (2004: 220) observes '… while general guidelines should lead to a "fair" and constructive system, situational factors will force companies to be inventive and flexible in setting and managing the remuneration system across borders'.

The implication for HR specialists is not simply to hold up the standard of what 'should be', but capability to participate in what Festing and Perkins (2008) describe as social exchange negotiations around expatriation, informed by theoretical as well as situated empirical reflection. The social exchange involves not only resolving issues around material considerations, but also clarifying the kind of 'psychological contract' on offer (see Chapters 2 and 9). Care is needed before generalisation, but it may be tentatively suggested that 'relational' contracts that enable expatriates to locate assignments within a longer-term career plan may encourage the behaviours favourable to distributed network organisations, requiring give and take between all the members wherever they may be located.

If a more 'transactional' relationship is enshrined in the expatriate 'deal' then specialists and line managers should not be surprised if employees adopt a more insular and instrumental orientation to the organisation and their peers across the multinational network. In short, when approaching expatriation reward: 'Attention is required to examining not only the "how" (primary approaches) but also the "why" (salient contextual or situation factors) firms should consider when determining how to assemble an appropriate package' (Sims and Schraeder, 2005: 107).

 STUDENT EXERCISE

An international assignment policy for regional expansion

Taipei-headquartered Taiwanese multinational Hiqual-locost Automotives aims to build a world-wide assembly manufacturing and trading presence. An initial target was a successful trans-European operation, establishing a regional office in Frankfurt and operating facilities in cities in France, Italy and the UK, before extending further into Central and Eastern Europe. The Frankfurt office has responsibility for contributing towards the company's corporate performance and people resourcing within the region. While seconding senior Taiwanese managers from headquarters, a managerial cadre of Western Europeans has been groomed, not only to succeed to regional leadership roles, as the Taiwanese expatriates complete what are regarded as costly assignments. High-potential European managers are to be mobilised to work in the first two regional expansions beyond Western Europe: new manufacturing plans in Bulgaria and Romania.

Having socialised these key recruits into corporate ways of managing the enterprise, it is felt that they will be well equipped, as TCN expatriates, to transplant this knowledge to support the further international expansion. In addition, as part of PCN succession arrangements some mobility is planned between the existing European offices to fill positions requiring expertise that has emerged concentrated in particular countries. Corporate HR have advised the board that a policy will be developed to underpin these further expatriations – with the proviso that significant cost savings will be made over those anticipated if a further HQ assignment were countenanced.

The Frankfurt-based HR team has been charged with advising the HQ function on considerations to be taken into account in designing the new pan-European assignment policy to address these four types of international assignments. Based on what you have learned in this chapter, flesh out the details of the brief to the Frankfurt HR team, including the kinds of information needed to guide corporate policy-making. List and justify the individuals and groups who should be invited to take part in the exercise.

FACTORS AND TRENDS IN REWARDING *NON-EXPATRIATED* KNOWLEDGE MOBILISATION

CONSIDERATIONS AT THE EXPATRIATE–LOCAL INTERFACE

By way of a bridge between the 'big but narrow' topic of expatriate compensation and discussion of international reward issues applicable to the other 90 per cent of the multinational core headcount (Perkins and Shortland, 2006), let us briefly consider what the research literature reports regarding issues to be accounted for in reward design sensitive to interaction between PCNs, TCNs and HCNs:

> As multinational companies operate across nations and continents at vastly different levels of economic development, disparity in employee compensation is unavoidable. The disparity is most salient in the remarkable gap between the compensation received by the local employees of international joint ventures in developing countries and foreign expatriates from developed countries. (Chen *et al*, 2002: 807)

On average, the compensation delivered to western expatriates, deemed necessary to get individuals to work in nations where pay and living conditions are significantly lower, has been estimated to be not only considerably above that received by their home country counterparts; it is a great deal more than that received by the local nationals in the developing countries (Reynolds, 1997). Adding a further twist to this inequality issue, it has been reported that international joint ventures (IJVs) pay more to locals than do domestic enterprises in the countries where the IJVs are established, and reward may be 'packaged' in different ways too (Chen *et al*, 2002). However, there is evidence to support a case that, while needing careful handling, straight expatriate–local comparisons are not always problematic. Again we turn to theory to seek clarification.

Equity theorists indicate that people are egocentric – they make judgements about equity on the basis of how favourable the outcome is to them. Judgements are based on social referents. Following this line of reasoning, the question becomes how do locals compare themselves with expatriates? Chen *et al* (2002) argue that people compare themselves against 'similar others' – this may be people undertaking similar work tasks at a similar organisational level. It may also depend on factors such as age, gender, race and tenure. The question for corporate policy designers becomes: are the expatriates so different from their local counterparts that they are not meaningful social referents for one another?

Chen *et al* (2002) conducted a study of IJV employment practices in China, and found that comparisons between local national employees in IJVs and those of other IJVs were an important source of moderating feelings of injustice between their own reward levels and those of expatriates. Building an understanding of local comparators, investigating employee preferences, sensitive to culture and industry, as Mamman *et al* (1996) advocate, and adopting a 'premium' pay posture (an 'efficiency wage' orientation – see Chapter 2) relative to the market for local recruits may, therefore, assist efforts by multinational managements to build team-cohesion between locals and expatriates, even where the latter receive higher absolute levels of reward.

Chen *et al* (2002) found that the mitigation effect was the same irrespective of the level of disparity between the expatriates and locals. The effect was *offsetting*, not just moderation of a negative effect. Local elite status counts, then. The ability to set premium pay will depend on the level of investment (and anticipated profitability) of the local subsidiary, and of the local human capital influence over open market rates – dependency theory signals that employee leverage will accrue based on managerial perceptions of how much these people are needed. Chen *et al* (2002) emphasise the importance for HR specialists of developing reasonable explanations and justifications for the inequities – as well as offering alternative non-financial recognition such as fast-track management development for key locals. Demonstrating a caring and sensitive attitude itself may have positive benefits, showing local core workforce members the extent to which corporate management are interested in their feelings and general welfare, as valued members of the organisation seeking competitive success in local markets and delivering returns for other stakeholders. While attention to cultural considerations, as surfaced in Chapter 1, is important the more salient issue may be overcoming economic disparities mindful of *relative* equity considerations.

The issue may go beyond horizontal alignment of HR–reward practices, however, bearing in mind vertical influences flowing between employment relations management and corporate strategy. Based on the knowledge mobilisation imperative, attempted shifts to the multi-headed transnational organisation may trigger a chain of events that further alter the context for assessing reward relativities across the multinational. Milkovich and Bloom (1998) argue that the organisational goal should be to rethink international reward to develop 'global mindsets' across all the workforce members, one outcome of which could be to shrink perceived social differences between the expatriate and local population. 'A global work environment may … stimulate social comparisons with otherwise dissimilar co-workers when employees from diverse social backgrounds interact with each other to perform joint tasks' (Chen *et al*, 2002: 808).

STRATEGY, DOMINANT LOGIC AND OPPORTUNISM

Vernon argues that the pay element of international reward has more 'standardisation' potential than other aspects of HRM, owing to 'the relative simplicity of administering pay across national borders' (2006: 217). This raises the prospect of opportunities to use pay 'strategically' in multinational organisations, or, as Gomez-Mejia (1993: 4) puts it: 'as an essential integrating and signalling mechanism to achieve overarching business objectives'. While highlighting its strategic potential, Vernon (2006) counsels that unthinking ethnocentric application of western normative reward management principles is to be avoided, however. Factors applicable across multi-local settings at least need to be systematically appraised and 'managed' before applying universalistic reward 'solutions'. In other words, while avoiding the trap of stereotyping, attention to culture (Sparrow, 1999; 2000) as well as institutional values and traditions between business systems (Whitley, 2000) is necessary.

Referring to contexts for employment relations such as Germany, where on the face of it managerial prerogative is constrained by institutional practice whereby, for example, structures of employee representation are codified to a greater extent than in, say, the UK and USA, Edwards *et al* (2005: 1283) argue that 'practices negotiated through this route may be received with less scepticism by employees than those that are imposed'. Also, as considered earlier by reference to the IT case organisation, while administratively it may be possible to enact changes initiated by the corporate centre, vertically aligned with revisions to business strategy, reorienting workforce expectations – horizontally aligning reward decision-taking with related processes such as employee communications – offers a more complex managerial challenge.

Bloom *et al* (2003) argue that the 'dominant logic' for managing the reward system adopted by multinationals may vary across a number of recognisable types, reflecting competing pressures for consistency of approach in pursuit of global alignment with organisational aims and local conformance pressures. What Bloom *et al* (2003) term 'export oriented' reward strategies aim to transfer wholesale the parent firm's reward system to the overseas affiliates, in pursuit of a 'common mindset', driven by headquarters thinking. An 'adapter' group, by contrast, chooses practices designed to match as closely as possible the conditions of the local context. Within these extremes, 'integrationists' may attempt what at worst may be little more than a cobbling together of a diverse array of practices, but at best suggests efforts to craft a coherent and comprehensive transnational reward management regime mindful of the mutually interdependent nature of the multinational management and workforce members. In keeping with the 'distributed network' proposed by Ghoshal and Nohria (1997), policies may flow as easily between subsidiaries and from subsidiaries to headquarters, as from headquarters 'down' and outwards to operations located worldwide.

In practice, Bloom *et al* (2003) suggest that multinationals tend to be opportunistic across their international operations in the adoption of practices that reflect one or more of the approaches described theoretically. They identify three complementary features that may reflect or influence multinational reward strategies under particular conditions.

First, the weight of institutionally generated pressures to conform to the conditions of local jurisdictions and markets may be deemed overwhelming – representing an 'investment cost' of choosing to trade in a particular economy. Secondly, multinational managements may identify scope to avoid or forestall acquiescence with local conformance pressures – where the application of regulatory and market practices is lax, for example. Thirdly, if the multinational is bringing investment capital that host governments regard as significant, active resistance to local conformance pressures may be initiated, mediated through attempts to challenge or change (at least in some way to influence) factors in the local host context, using access to legislators and other key opinion formers. The framework is usefully summarised as a matrix (Table 11.1).

Table 11.1 Context-related multinational reward management factors

	Conform	Avoid	Resist
Adapters	Generally	Where possible	Rarely
Exporters	Rarely	Generally	If cost-effective
Globalisers	If necessary	Sometimes	Where feasible

Source: Perkins (2006), summarising Bloom et al (2003)

Again, then, the situation is dynamic and universal prescriptions require cautious interpretation (Brookes et al, 2005). As Perkins (2006: 11) observes:

> The insight from the analysis is that the degree of variation in contextual factors – between and within – local host contexts rather than just the type of host contexts (cultural norms, economic conditions, regulatory pressures, etc.) may be what matters most when multinational managements consider how to balance corporate versus host influences on reward strategy design.

An investigation by Lowe et al (2002), measuring the current position on various reward management approaches in 10 countries around the world (although notably excluding Europe), supplemented by managerial perspectives on what practices 'should be' applied, indicated a degree of consistency the researchers found surprising given the range of cultural and institutional contexts surveyed (from China to the USA). In terms of managerial perceptions of the extent to which reward practices were related to the employment of high performers, satisfied employees and an effective organisation:

> Collectively, these findings suggest that there is a high degree of cross-cultural consistency in the perceived utility of compensation plans as a method for achieving organisational effectiveness. However, the mix of appropriate compensation practices is likely to vary across these same countries. (Lowe et al, 2002: 69)

In the case of future focused preferences, the researchers argued that the data set indicated thoughtful item-by-item responses by managers surveyed, rather than any 'within-country scale-anchor preferences' (Lowe et al, 2002: 71). Managers generally expressed a bias in favour of increasing the incidence of incentives, benefits and long-term pay focus compared with the current practice. Consistent lines between the results of 'cultural programming' variances across countries and regions and the practice and preferences of organisational managers are not in evidence from this research, therefore. The implication is that systematic 'due diligence' analysis on the part of multinational corporate reward policy architects to match reward and recognition plans for employees in countries around the world may be a worthwhile investment, when expanding their overseas operations. (The discussion of contingency theory in Chapter 2 may be helpful in thinking through this proposition.) Lowe et al (2002) contend that, by enhancing understanding of 'best practices' in other countries, their findings serve to challenge the extreme positions reported by Bloom et al (2003), whether ethnocentric exportation of reward management designs or 'locally responsive' adoption of the status quo in a given locale.

SELF-ASSESSMENT EXERCISE

Sparrow (1999) lists five groups of factors that may be influenced by national culture with possible consequences for how employees respond to reward management: (1) attitudes to what makes an 'effective' employee; (2) orientations to giving and receiving work performance feedback; (3) career anchor preferences – eg seniority versus performance; (4) expectations of manager–subordinate relationships; and (5) conceptions of what makes 'socially healthy' pay distribution between individuals and groups.

Based on the research evidence presented above regarding organisational aspirations to achieve transnational work team cohesion, some measure of pay system standardisation and the factors employees appear to deploy when making comparisons horizontally and vertically about equitable reward treatment, what priorities would you emphasise in counselling a new transnational team leader about their role?

Brown and Perkins (2007) report on recent CIPD survey findings, where HR specialists in multinationals were asked to define the level of influence that proactive components of the business strategy, such as increasing total shareholder returns and customer satisfaction, actually had on reward practices in their organisation. Respondents were also asked to rate the influence of external and less controllable factors on rewards, such as the rates of price and wage inflation, external labour markets and the activities of their competitors for staff, as well as trade unions.

According to the results obtained, a more reactive (traditional personnel administration-style) approach appears to feature in more of the organisations than those claiming to be proactive. When asked about the influence of parent country reward principles compared with local differentiators, and in turn compared with a mix-and-match approach of the kind Bloom *et al* report, the picture was almost evenly balanced 33:33:33 between responses obtained. The inference may be one of 'good old muddling through' or, by reflecting more deeply on these findings, one of sophisticated opportunity management recognising that global–local balancing will be a constant challenge to be addressed, requiring skilful handling.

The findings reported imply that multinational reward decision-takers are not simply reading from a common template at the level of specific practice. Using more in-depth interview data, Perkins (2006) reports that large multinationals do appear to be attempting to increase the degree of co-ordination in transnational reward management. The first case study below illustrates the action long-established multinationals may take to restructure business operations in ways that use employee reward interventions to emphasise accountability, beyond membership of a federation of geographically situated units to corporate brand development opportunities. Some multinationals have made a significant investment in new information technology-based infrastructure to rationalise and standardise reward management practice across the enterprise (for details, see the Honeywell case study in Perkins, 2006: Part Three). While no doubt these shifts will be the subject of debate among organisational members, the explicit commercial focus means the new focus has a logic that most will acknowledge.

This contrasts with the issues corporate management have encountered in the second case below, where a voluntary sector organisation has taken steps to increase the common focus on performance by introducing a pay-related recognition element. A diversity of voices – right up to the highest policy-making levels – has engaged in a debate on whether or not, despite an economic logic, the approach 'fits' what the organisation stands for and how it goes about meeting corporate aims and objectives.

CASE STUDY 1

Branded goods multinational Unilever employs 234,000 people in around 100 countries. A restructuring operation under a new group chief executive, bringing with it a change in management style, is expected to have important consequences for how reward is managed for junior managerial jobholders and above.

The new corporate strategy design is to capitalise more effectively on corporate brands than may have been the case previously over Unilever's more than 75 years in business. Group-wide influence on explicit 'reward management' is constrained, according to corporate specialists, in the case of the 200,000 people around the world occupying roles such as plantation workers, manufacturing workers, salespeople, etc, whose employment terms and conditions are often subject to collective bargaining.

In the case of managers, however, the orientation to employee reward has shifted. While the trinity of attracting and retaining and motivating these employees remains, the focus is on finding ways in which reward management may be used more explicitly to align what people do, and the way their contribution is recognised, with corporate governance goals.

Accenting transnational integration, the HR function itself has been reorganised, combining reward management policy-making within a single corporate unit with activities focused also on 'talent management', 'organisational effectiveness' and 'learning'. Thus an aspiration may be discerned to integrate people management at both the vertical level (with corporate strategy and governance) and horizontally across the HR function.

The reward system architecture is not being altered as such under the new regime: instead, the emphasis is on improving its execution, aligned with the new corporate strategic priorities. The challenge is seen as one of articulating the idea of 'corporate value creation' as something that Unilever people see as 'relevant' to them, while accommodating diversity in economic conditions affecting regionally dispersed operations. On the one hand, helping the company to benefit from emerging market growth opportunities has to be recognised without inflating results, taking account of fluctuation in currency values. On the other hand, in the 'mature' economies, such as those of Western Europe and the USA, the managerial task is perceived as achieving targets associated with *retaining* profitable market share.

A 'talent management listing process' intended to integrate the identification of high-potential employees has been implemented with actions to increase what the system architects refer to as 'performance accountability'. The incentive reward management system is to be operated in ways that differentiate the distribution of extrinsic rewards: while differentiation might be anticipated as a self-evident feature of individual incentive reward arrangements, past practice was to emphasise consistency in applying market-leading levels of reward. Instead, the plan is 'to ensure at least some of our money goes to where it is supposed to', according to the head of reward who participated in the new scheme design.

The importance of 'accountability' in 'One Unilever', as the new CEO has termed it, is to remove barriers to the networking of knowledge between the multinational's branded 'lines of business' and geographical regions, to support the corporate value-creation priority. Initiatives have been launched to address unnecessary 'complexity and intellectualism' that risks resource inefficiencies through duplication of effort across business operations (eg in managing product development or marketing activity).

Clarifying accountability across corporate networks, on the one hand, is expected to reduce misalignment with corporate policy and cost-effective mobilisation of skill sets. On the other hand, there is an attempt to make people management more than reading-off detailed rules from functionally policed templates.

In reward management terms, detailed decisions about policy application in individual cases are being devolved to line managers, to increase transparency. This is perceived as a culture change accompanying the new accountability, requiring local managerial judgement within the performance-oriented corporate principles. 'Managers are no longer asked to just fill in a spreadsheet box only for corporate HR to change the numbers afterwards,' the researcher was told.

Source: Adapted/extended from Perkins (2006)
Reproduced by kind permission of CIPD.

CASE STUDY 2

Explicit pay for performance management remains controversial, especially beyond the commercial sector. The charity HelpAge International is a very diverse organisation, with 'over 70 nationalities employed right up to senior management level', according to the head of HR interviewed for the CIPD international reward and recognition research. Trustees are similarly diverse – the board is 'incredibly diverse', with a majority of members female and from developing countries. There is an emphasis on building up local capacity, employing people from the regions concerned, reducing a reliance on expatriates and keeping the London head office slim.

The guiding principles for reward management are 'consistency and fairness within and across the organisation'. Modest changes have been made to the reward system but have been the subject of 'hot debate' among management decision-makers. Limited performance contribution recognition has been introduced over a two-year period, at the time of annual salary reviews. In addition to the across-the-board inflation-linked salary increases, two additional employee assessment categories have been introduced to determine increase levels for 'good' and 'exceptional' contributors.

The scheme is not a (forward-calibrated) formal incentive programme. It is a (retrospective) recognition arrangement, intended to signal acknowledgement of particular contribution levels (see Chapter 6). It is recognised that the levels involved are not likely to act as a retention device in the case of people leaving for higher material rewards elsewhere.

While top management's intention has been to communicate a positive message, there has been some negative reaction. Dissatisfaction has centred on things like who is included and why and, at an individual level, debate on issues such as 'why rate me *only* "good" not "exceptional"?' Some senior management team members have voiced anxieties about differentiation: pay-for-performance may run counter to the overriding principles considered typical of not-for-profit multinationals.

Source: Adapted/extended from Perkins (2006)
Reproduced by kind permission of CIPD.

KEY LEARNING POINTS AND CONCLUSIONS

International reward and its management may be approached from a variety of angles, as the chapter has illustrated. If Ghoshal and Bartlett's (1998) 'transnational solution' to multinational business strategy is adopted, reward may be viewed as an important managerial resource for profitable knowledge mobilisation supported by an effort to encourage a shared 'global mindset' across the workforce (Milkovich and Bloom, 1998). While aspiration may be voiced, we have seen that although administratively reward may offer scope for consistent administrative practice, reverse diffusion of learning may be inhibited, but less for technical reasons than political.

Consistent with our open systems conceptual framework, we have considered rewards for the international workforce segmented between expatriates and others, on the one hand, in order that nuances of expatriate 'compensation' administration may be appreciated. On the other hand, we have drawn attention to the need for policy design mindful of the interaction between the segments that, as Chen *et al* (2002) have shown, does not break down simply in terms of an expat–local dichotomy, but demands local–local comparisons too.

With a reported accent on standardisation to support a performance orientation, reward architects in the multinational also need to draw on theoretical and empirical knowledge of practices that may be discovered in the generic reward literature, which commentators such as Lowe *et al* (2002) suggest managers are reflecting on rather than reading from a template or at least, as argued by Bloom *et al* (2003), and Brown and Perkins (2007), are approaching 'strategically', accounting for in-country as well as transnational enablers and constraints to 'best practice'.

SELF-ASSESSMENT EXERCISE

Managing employee reward in a multinational context is a highly complex endeavour. The perennial issue is balancing corporate ambition to conjoin knowledge where it produces profitable outcomes – however 'profitable' may be defined, depending on the sector involved. Identify and prioritise the steps thinking performers in HR specialist roles may take to use theoretical frameworks, complemented by reported empirical experience among multinationals, to manage this complexity and diversity of ideas and expectations. What are the opportunities and risks for multinationals, and how may the latter be minimised?

The competitive context has amplified the problems for multinationals, but reward system design may still be usefully informed by some overriding principles articulated a decade and a half ago (Carey and Howes, 1993), which we have interpreted and slightly extended, in summary form, below:

- As companies establish themselves globally, corporate strategies are called for that can accommodate both unity and diversity: this surfaces issues such as how to allocate rewards and to tie reward outcomes to corporate goals.

- Specifically, multinationals need to develop reward system characteristics that fit with overall corporate strategy but are tailored to the needs not only of business operations but also of employees in specific locations. Flexibility not only regarding the quantum but also in terms of how employees receive their material rewards may be increasingly expected. This may apply not just in home markets and other developed country settings but also across discerning knowledgeable 'global talent' populations. On the other hand, where socio-economic infrastructure remains limited, some guarantees may remain a priority expectation.

- Purchasing power parity (the rate of exchange at which general price levels are equalised) may work more effectively than the more volatile spot rates for currency conversion when setting long-term pay levels.

- Reward comparator groups may need to comprise a combination of both other multinationals in the same industrial sector and other industry groupings. Account needs to be taken also of local–local comparisons that HCNs may make when recruited to international joint ventures as well as organisations wholly funded by foreign direct investment sources.

- When creating a global reward regime, the total pay and benefits mix in various countries requires measured evaluation: decisions are required here as to the role allocated to salaries, short-term bonuses, long-term incentives and other material benefits, and to whether these should be measured in pre-tax or post-tax terms. Given pressures to reduce tax burdens, jurisdictions have been cutting back government-provided benefits, raising the question of the extent to which these should be factored in to 'total reward' calculations (see Chapters 7, 8 and 9 for detailed consideration of these issues).

- While enabling choice may appear contrary to standardisation and unifying initiatives through reward management, allowing choice when migrating from multi-local to a more globally integrated system may support communication, education and understanding-building among workforce members, as well as facilitating acceptance and ownership of new corporately branded frameworks.

EXPLORE FURTHER

A review of relevant theory summarised in a heuristic model to help interpret approaches to expatriate reward management appears in Festing, M. and Perkins, S.J. (2008) 'Rewards for internationally mobile employees', in Brewster, C., Sparrow, P. and Dickmann, M. (eds) *International HRM: contemporary issues in Europe*, 2nd edn. London, Routledge.

For an empirically informed review of the role HR specialists play, and the scope for tensions with other categories of management in handing expatriation contracts, see Perkins, S.J. and Daste, R. (2007) 'Pluralistic tensions in expatriating managers', *Journal of European Industrial Training* 31(7): 550–69.

CIPD-commissioned research on trends in international reward among multinationals (primarily large mature companies but also considering the challenges faced by voluntary sector organisations operating across national borders) is published in Perkins, S.J. (2006) *International Reward and Recognition*. Research Report. London, Chartered Institute of Personnel and Development.

For an economist's perspective on pay system management internationally, see Vernon, G. (2006) 'International pay and reward', in Edwards, T. and Rees, C. (eds) *International Human Resource Management: globalization, national systems and multinational companies*. London, Prentice Hall: 217–41.

CHAPTER 12

Employee Reward within 'HRM'

CHAPTER OBJECTIVES

At the end of this chapter you should understand and be able to explain the following:

- Ideas grouped under the rubric of 'HRM' and their interaction with thinking about employee reward design and management.

- Critical appraisal of HRM/strategy/reward commentary, as one recipe for managing the employment relationship, located in open systems contexts.

- Implications of adopting a strategic reward or 'new pay' orientation for roles and competency requirements among line managers and specialists.

CIPD STANDARDS COVERED IN THIS CHAPTER:

As a contribution to corporate policy-making and practice, to be able to:

- Contribute to the identification of appropriate reward strategy from an analysis of an organisation's corporate strategy and take part in the preparation of reward plans.

- Participate as a team member in consultation or bargaining about the design, implementation and operation of a pay system.

- Advise senior management on the design or modification of a pay structure and methods of introducing it.

- Advise on the management of change when introducing or modifying elements of the reward system.

To understand and explain:

- The factors affecting reward philosophies, strategies, policies, practices and levels of pay in organisations.

- The criteria for an effective pay structure and contingent pay schemes.

- New developments in employee reward and their application within the organisation.

- The skills line managers need to implement reward practices and how these skills may be developed.

INTRODUCTION

If we situate employee reward as a phenomenon governed as a sub-function of human resource management, then it follows that choosing to act in accordance with ideas about human resource management – and the concept of 'HRM' in particular – will have consequences for how employee reward and its management is approached. In this chapter we discuss the ways in which commentators have defined 'HRM' and how this set of ideas about people management may be seen interacting with developments in thinking about employee reward.

Of course, thinking about employee reward and the way it may be regulated is not limited to 'HRM': the latter concept may be viewed critically from perspectives that, for example, do not limit the focus to the firm and its management, but recognise their systemic interaction with other political economic institutions (see Chapter 3 for a discussion of the contextual issues). Drawing from perspectives emerging both under the 'HRM' rubric and those with wider conceptual roots, systemic interaction between HRM and employee reward may, however, be framed for critical appraisal. In the course of such consideration the implications for roles to be played by parties to employee reward determination (HR specialists, line managers, individual employees and collective employee institutions, as well as regulators in particular jurisdictions) may be subjected to review.

DEFINING HRM

At the CIPD annual conference in 2007, HR professionals were challenged by two senior practitioners, Neil Roden, Group HR Director at RBS, and David Fairhurst, Vice-president People at McDonald's, to overcome what they labelled as an obsession with technical aspects of HR work. According to the report in *People Management*, HR specialists need to become part of the 'team that fuels the organisation's engine', based on 'a deep understanding of the organisation's work', so as to 'contribute to the bottom line' – the only way to be 'taken seriously by the top team' (Evans and Brockett, 2007: 9). Ideas about 'HRM' might be seen as offering a conceptual lens for seeing how to take up this challenge related to employee reward.

Ideologically presented as '*the* alternative to pluralistic employee relations' and 'how employees ought to be managed' (Keenoy, 1999: 2, emphasis in original), 'HRM' adopts the principles of *strategy* from the business management literature (Marchington and Wilkinson, 2005). HRM is contrasted with what may be positioned as more 'passive' people management (perhaps labelled as personnel management/administration). Organisational strategy, defined in terms of choices about where and how resources are to be deployed in pursuit of corporate aims relative to competitors for stakeholder commitment (Zeckhauser, 1991), is however contested terrain. Competing perspectives on 'strategy' will be discussed below.

For Storey (2001), HRM is a recipe – one among several alternatives – for the management of the employment relationship. HRM is also the basis for a 'discursive' practice. 'HRM-ism' (Keenoy, 1997; 1999) has been branded an attempt to manage meaning between the members of work organisations (Storey, 2001). Initiatives such as 'changing the organisation's culture' may be cited as one illustration of this argument – in reward terms, say, shifting expectations on pay progression from a fixed increments system based on seniority to a performance-contingent regime, as though the latter were an axiomatic choice rather than one based on debatable principles reflecting particular interests and socio-economic goals. These HRM 'rhetorics' contrast with a 'reality' (Legge, 1995) in which 'high-commitment' employment practices have been recorded in the large-scale WERS findings as comprehensively diffused to no more than 14 per cent of British workplaces (Cully et al, 1999).

Ideas prompting debates around HRM as a strategic approach to people management may be traced back to commentary emerging in the USA at the end of the 1970s. Two strands of argument have been identified as characterising the initial phase of HRM development. A 'matching model' of HRM (Fombrun et al, 1984) encourages managers to 'read off' choices about managing people at work directly from the organisation's strategic objectives. Depending on the corporate emphasis, it is reasoned that there will be one right way of workforce management.

For example, Delery and Doty (1996) present evidence from the banking industry in the USA, which they argue indicates a universal logic for implementing employee profit-sharing arrangements to secure high-performance outcomes. Their premise, explicitly underlined by agency theory, is that, 'by definition all banks strive for profit' and 'by tying individual compensation to organizational profit, the organization is rewarding behavior that is consistent with its overall performance' (1996: 826).

In addition to matching HRM to business strategy, for organisational effectiveness to be secured, it has been argued that alignment is required also between the various elements that comprise the HRM 'bundle' (Purcell, 1999). Hence attention is required at sub-functional and sub-policy level (to employee reward management and attendant processes, for example).

A second foundational approach, known as the 'Harvard model' (Beer et al, 1985), encourages attention not only to strategy: implying more 'open systems' thinking, greater account is to be taken also of the interaction between organisational strategy and factors from outside the individual firm. Rather than perceiving HRM as determined exclusively by organisational structure, practices are tailored contingent on factors such as management's leadership philosophy, and interpretation of workforce characteristics, as well as external factors such as labour market circumstances. Compromises and trade-offs may be necessary as management seeks to balance owner interests with those of other interest groups (including employees and society at large).

This more pluralistic orientation is in contrast to the apparent assumption by

Fombrun *et al* (1984) of unity among organisational interests: that is, what is good for owners will also benefit other stakeholders. Under the Harvard approach, matching HRM practices to the specificities of each organisation is more nuanced. The scope for strategic choice informed by ideological considerations alluded to by Beer *et al* (1985) also factors in the likely outcomes and longer-term consequences of managerial policy and practice. The Harvard model's 'feedback loop' again appears to reflect assumed interaction between organisational systems and external systemic features – for example, the political economy and employment system – which may enable fine-tuning and adaptation by decision-makers as the context changes during strategy implementation, that is, a more emergent approach.

A case study (Malmaison Hotels) illustrates the proactive investment strategy reportedly adopted by one organisation to align HRM policies and practices with what the business aims to achieve, derived from predictions about how, in turn, people management and development should inform the business strategy. The case study further illustrates actions that may be taken along the lines advocated by Delery and Doty (1996) to synchronise elements of people management and development so that, for example, succession planning aligned with commercial brand promotion interconnects with performance management, training and development, and efforts to motivate employees giving them a voice in the brand-building linked to personal development and associated incentives.

EFFORTS TO LINK HR STRATEGY VERTICALLY AND HORIZONTALLY (MALMAISON HOTELS)

CASE STUDY

Malmaison Hotels operates a portfolio of 21 UK hotels, with plans to increase this to 35 by 2009, doubling its staff to more than 3,000 in the process. The group company is working towards achieving a target set by management in 2004 of becoming the largest boutique hotel chain in the UK. The declared business strategy is to build a brand focusing not only on Malmaison as a group enterprise – but to retain the 'one-of-a-kind feel' attached to each individual unit, reflecting the 'boutique' offering to guests in a competitive market for hotel accommodation. According to a report in *People Management* magazine, a people development strategy has played a central role founded on the managerial belief that Malmaison's workforce will act as 'guardians of the brand',

maintaining its identity and values as the group company grows.

Recognising the possible tensions between corporate growth and marketing strategy, Sean Wheeler, Malmaison's director of people development, initiated a people development strategy and associated performance management online 'talent toolbox', used during appraisals. Applied to managers and supervisors initially, when launched in 2005, the company has since extended the facility to include employees at all levels.

Individuals and their managers 'fill in information about their career aspirations and satisfaction', complementing assessment of what individuals have done. Training plans and career progression actions are devised informed by this intelligence. For example: 'If someone has an issue with leadership, the tool comes up with options on how they can develop that skill.' *People Management* report: 'Wheeler has also negotiated deals with suppliers so they offer training or incentive schemes to staff as part of their contract.'

The strategy carries the endorsement of Robert Cook, Malmaison chief executive, reported as describing the 'talent toolbox' as the 'cornerstone' of the company's future people development strategy. Corporately, it is believed the facility enables management to grasp the ' "health" or happiness of the business', while also identifying management potential. Wheeler set a target of 30 per cent of staff in each new hotel to be recruited from within the company, and to ensure this happened he convinced a group of finance investors to invest in the company's people through better

training and improved succession planning. According to the report, reflecting on the outcome of the strategy: 'As a result ... about 70 per cent of Malmaison's general managers are now promoted from inside the company.'

In the past, more than half of Malmaison's general managers had come from outside. Mobilisation of employees across the various hotels within the group is reported as also slowly building up momentum, with the aspiration that leadership and knowledge will be diffused, balancing group brand value with boutique brand at operating unit level. The initiative won the company first place in the 'talent management for business benefit' category of the 2007 *People Management* Awards.

Source: Emma Clarke (2007) 'Grand reserve', *People Management* 13(20): 30

SELF-ASSESSMENT EXERCISE

The Malmaison case briefly refers to employee 'incentives' featuring in the group company's strategy and 'HRM bundle'. Based on your reading of the data, would you expect Sean Wheeler to 'read off' the kinds of material and other incentives that should be extended to secure and reinforce employee 'brand-guardianship'? Would these be universally applied irrespective of where employees are located? To what extent does the strategy outlined in the case imply the need for corporate management to act sensitively to exogenous system factors, on the one hand, and in relation to 'boutique' tailoring, on the other?

Make a business case for your answer framed using the HRM models summarised above. How would you deal with the question, derived from the line of reasoning in the debates around motivation, summarised in Chapter 2, that to incentivise Malmaison employees for what they may have regarded henceforth as a source of intrinsic satisfaction may undermine, not enhance their brand-guardianship?

Paauwe (2004) reports an explosion of interest in HRM during the 1990s after a seminal 1995 paper by American HRM commentator, Mark Huselid, making a claim for a link between what Huselid (1995) terms 'high-performance work practices' and high organisational performance. Paauwe (2004) notes the readiness of practitioners to embrace this apparent link, but with limited consideration as to what 'performance' implies. In fact, since its inception, HRM commentary has been subject to criticism for being under-theorised (Martín-Alcázar *et al*, 2005): located in a longer-established strand of social science commentary, writers such as Guest (1987) initially framed the debate in terms of 'human resource management and industrial relations'. Guest's stated aim was to overcome the alleged looseness with which the term had been applied, by defining HRM so as 'to differentiate it from traditional personnel management' (1987: 503), to aid development of testable hypotheses about its impact (see WERS 1998 findings above). Guest remained undecided a decade and a half later, however, as to 'whether [HRM] theory is sufficiently precise to point to the kind of empirical testing that results in convincing support or refutation' (2001: 1094).

Hatch (2006) argues that it is useful to bear in mind the stage of social development when different ideas about organisation and organising emerge. Paauwe (2004) argues that HRM as a 'high-performance work system' recipe is a product of its time and place. Again, attention to context helps to avoid the deterministic 'closed system' trap. Unprecedented mid-1990s stock market growth, following in the wake of the managerial 'excellence' movement of the 1980s (eg Peters and Waterman's 1982 book on 'lessons from America's best-run companies'), putting the USA 'back on top' in comparative political economy terms, following the Japanese threat to global competitive dominance. Neo-liberalism was the era's received wisdom – the 'dot com' crash and corporate scandals were yet to emerge.

Paauwe (2004) concludes: so why would one debate the meaning of performance? It followed axiomatically from the contemporary corporate governance paradigm and ('Anglo-Saxon') managerial priorities. Rather than accept uncritically an HRM reflective of its place and time of inception, however, Paauwe (2004) advocates greater pluralism in specifying 'performance' to include indicators that may sit more comfortably with a social market economy variant of capitalism (Hall and Soskice, 2001). Emphasising that his position is not anti-profit, Paauwe (2004) agues that paying attention to a wider stakeholder base is required to promote sustainable organisational success reflecting performance through people.

Boxall and Purcell (2008) also emphasise that if sustainable organisational effectiveness is the desired goal of strategic HRM, the social legitimacy of managerial actions needs to be placed alongside workforce productivity and organisational flexibility.

In a similar vein, Bach (2005) perceives a 'new HRM', where preoccupations with competing 'managerialist' models within idealised closed systems have been moderated, recognising that, while HRM may constitute a management-oriented perspective on regulation of the employment relationship, choices and consequences will always be conditioned by the structural, institutional and ideological context. This more open systems approach may help overcome criticism of an overly rationalised and static HRM, accounting for mediating values (Martín-Alcázar *et al*, 2005).

First, Bach (2005) argues, globalisation and information and communications technology have combined not only to enable multinational organisations to devolve production to employment systems where costs are perceived to be lower, as well as to match goods and services to the demands of diverse multi-local consumers. ICT may also be used to enable surveillance of local operators from a central vantage point. Technological 'hardware' operates alongside the 'software' of performance management systems and processes. We further discuss these trends and their implications for employee reward in Chapter 11.

Secondly, Bach (2005) argues, in liberal market economies such as the UK (Hall and Soskice, 2001), there has been some political 're-regulation', admitting a role for trade unions – not as champions of social justice, but as 'partners' in securing organisation effectiveness fit to compete in the 'globalised' world economy. State policy-making has also sought to discipline employers – especially those in small and medium-sized enterprises – to invest in human capital, not just 'sweat' labour commodities.

Thirdly, rapid and continual corporate restructuring, shifting organisational boundaries, has changed the nature of 1980s debates around 'core–periphery' workforce members, with the new accent on who 'owns' the workforce and deserves its commitment. The Malmaison case serves to illustrate that, where corporate brand 'guardianship' is a managerial preoccupation, investment may follow to encourage employees to become individually enjoined in corporate projects. This evolving context for and character of HRM raises interesting issues for employee reward if the intention remains to align the organisation's people and strategy vertically and horizontally – in particular, the extent to which it is logical to privilege 'strategic' managerial priorities over employee concerns for equitable treatment (Kessler, 2007).

STRATEGY PERSPECTIVES AND EMPLOYEE REWARD CHOICES

If HRM is synonymous with (proactively defined) strategy, it appears to be a logical progression that, consequent on choosing a 'HRM approach' to people management, there will be a 'strategic' approach to reward as an HRM sub-system. As Kessler (2007) observes, advocacy for a strategically driven reward approach was in evidence over a decade and a half ago (eg Gomez-Mejia, 1992). Placing the foregoing contextual concerns to one side, an obvious question, then, is to ask whether widespread take-up may be evidenced. Looking at recent studies – as in the case of HRM diffusion – the indication seems to be that strategically aligned reward management may remain an aspiration among commentators rather than the practice norm. Or at least, the approach is more nuanced than the prescriptive literature may suggest, when we do take account of context (capability, culture, institutional factors, etc).

For example, in the sixth annual UK Reward Survey, the CIPD (2007: 6) reports as follows:

It would appear from our findings that employers are more willing, or able, to try and get horizontal alignment between their financial and non-financial offering than vertical alignment between their business and reward strategies. This indicates that HR and reward professionals may still be struggling to understand the business in which their organisation operates and/or are still bogged down in the transactional, rather than transformational, activities.

Nearly half (41 per cent) of the 466 respondents described their approach as already governed by 'total rewards' thinking (interpreted as 'horizontal alignment' in this area of practice), and another 32 per cent said they were expecting to implement total rewards during 2007. But in respect of 'vertical alignment', defined in terms of having 'a written rewards strategy' in place, only 35 per cent responded in the affirmative; another 40 per cent said they intended to address this issue in 2007 (CIPD, 2007: 3).

Widening the lens to a European angle, a late 2006 survey conducted by management consultants Towers Perrin, drawing responses from 250 companies across the continent, indicates 'a tactically focused and piecemeal' scene and a 'say/do gap' (Crawley, 2007: 6). Again, aspirations may be couched in strategic terms, but 'it seems [respondents] struggle to convert these strategic intentions into meaningful actions' (2007: 6). Both the CIPD and Towers Perrin surveys report that stated top priorities among respondents are to:

- reward/retain the best performers;
- attract key talent; and
- link pay to the organisation's success.

PROACTION—REACTION

Of course, as Wright (2005: 1:1) observes: 'The term "strategy" is much abused throughout organisations. It is often used when what people are really talking about is a series of programmes or a set of objectives.' Looking a little deeper at what counts as strategy and its drivers, as perceived among a group of specialists in large multinationals, the position is more nuanced than some commentary might suggest. Drawing on UK and international empirical research, Brown and Perkins identify hints of 'a shift in the concept of what a reward strategy is and how it is practised' (2007: 85).

The point is illustrated by reference to a CIPD research study of international reward and recognition practices (Perkins, 2006). Just over 60 respondents from a range of large, mature multinational companies were asked to define the level of influence that business strategy components such as increasing total shareholder returns and customer satisfaction actually had on reward practices in their organisations. The results are shown in the left-hand distribution in Figure 12.1 below, with the strength of influence shown on the horizontal axis, and number of organisations on the vertical.

Respondents were also asked to rate the influence of external and less controllable factors on rewards, such as the rates of price and wage inflation, the activities of their competitors for employees influencing external labour markets, as well as intermediating institutions in the employment relationship, such as trade unions. The responses are profiled on the right-hand graph (Figure 12.1) and, as can be seen, this more *reactive* approach appears to carry greater weight in more of the organisations.

The pattern that emerges is similar to that reported in a US study of international reward management practice carried out by Bloom *et al* (2003), a pattern they describe as 'pragmatic experimentalism'. As Brown and Perkins (2007: 85) conclude:

> *The traditional, idealised reward strategy model assumes business-goal directed and unified rational organisations, and presents a theoretical choice between globally integrated strategies or locally divergent practice. In reality, in the complex and socially constructed world of large multinationals we are seeing an opportunistic mix of the two, with reward management as a dynamic, flexible and emergent phenomenon.*

For possible explanations of the reported empirical trends, which Brown and Perkins (2007) summarise under the rubric of 'reward pragmatism', it may help to look to the alternative ways in which strategy has been considered in the theoretical literature. The rationale is to help position lenses for assessing advocacy among 'strategic reward' commentators, whose prescriptions will be described below, accompanied by critiques informed by reference to social factors beyond managerial strategy in organisations. Adding a further pragmatic qualifier, Hendry signals that 'implementation costs' need to be factored in to any appraisal of an organisation's 'power to purchase skills in the labour market and its ability to support sophisticated forms of HRM' (2003: 1451) to convert these to profitable performance. The role of influences on reward design and practice may be understood in this way, accounting for factors such as equity, as well as ethical and moral considerations beyond unquestioning acceptance of 'strategic reward' as a self-evident choice (Kessler, 2007).

Figure 12.1 Global reward strategy: comparing influences

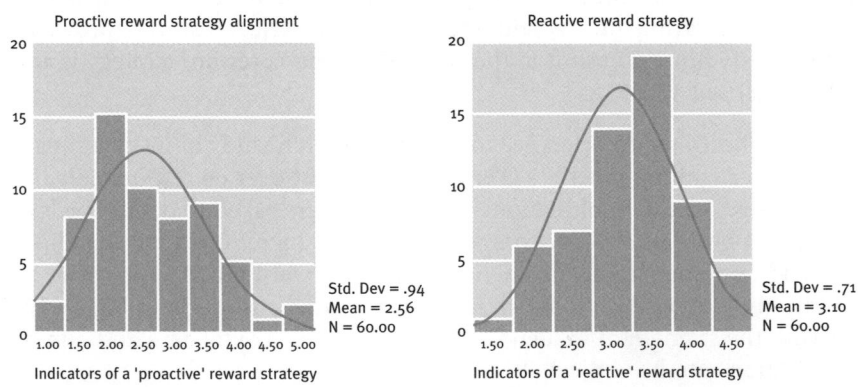

Source: Brown and Perkins 2007
Reproduced by kind permission of Worldatwork.

SELF-ASSESSMENT EXERCISE

Reflect on the factors you would draw on to develop a reward strategy – that is, meeting the aim of being vertically aligned to organisation goals and horizontally aligned with wider HRM sub-functional activities. Keep these 'common-sense brainstorming' outputs to compare and contrast with the theoretically derived influences considered below.

STRATEGY CONTESTED

Just like HRM, notions of strategy as 'proactive management' are contested: deliberate managerial choices are located at one end of a spectrum, with 'emergent' strategy at the other (Whittington, 2001). Rather than perceiving strategy as an objective phenomenon, it may be regarded as a social construction, as such reflecting and encapsulating a range of influential factors (Marchington and Wilkinson, 2005). Moving beyond economic determinism, the HR thinking performer may ask: if strategy is emergent and socially constructed, does this render problematic the idea of unitary relations between the social actors involved, or is it necessary to account for a plurality of interests in dynamic interaction around the effort–reward bargain?

Moving beyond simply defining strategy, Whittington (2000) asks whether strategy matters. It does matter, he argues, given that different commentators attach different levels of importance to what managers attempt to do in organising competitively. Some ascribe to management a planning role, to comprehend and master the external environment. The task is to gather information about economic market conditions and apply techniques in a rational and calculative way, so positioning the organisation to achieve competitive advantage. Managers as 'strategic planners' must master the organisation's environment as well as the organisation itself: the environment is seen as pliable, and the strategist knows how to handle it.

The rational approach may be viewed in the manner of some early institutionalist approaches discussed in Chapter 2, where, for example, efficiency wage theory is adopted to drive reward investment, possibly delivered using mediums that seek to balance intrinsic with extrinsic reward in pursuit of an internalised market relationship with employees intended to insulate both the organisation and its core workforce from external market vagaries. Applying such techniques, it is predicted, will secure the goodwill and high performance from the workforce on the assumption that they will perceive a unity of interest with managerial goals.

In other words, the aim is to achieve closed system conditions at least to some extent separate from open (economic/employment) system pressures derived from the application of universal 'best practice' from a central location (irrespective of cultural and institutional influences beyond the enterprise). Commentary specifically advocating 'strategic reward' interventions is likely to share these assumptions, as discussed below.

Whittington (2000) contrasts what he labels this 'rational' approach to strategy, which tends to occupy the mainstream of managerial literature, with three other broad classifications of how strategy and its role significance may be understood: the 'fatalistic', 'pragmatic' and 'relativist' perspectives. While each approach can offer a plausible rationale for mangers to act in certain ways, the prescriptions are fundamentally opposed to one another.

The **fatalist** school regards organisational survival and prosperity in economic markets as simply a matter of chance or luck. The environment, not managerial action, is what will select out winners and losers – the best the manger can do is hope to hit on a profit-maximising strategy that will enable the organisation to survive the ruthless process of 'natural selection'. Impersonal markets, not managers, make the important choices – and, as indicated in Chapter 2, adopting this theoretical stance implies a limited role for active reward management beyond environmental scanning, which may enable the strategist to spot the patterns that if imitated may aid survival (Hatch, 2006).

The prescription for management is to attempt to match market supply and demand considerations (both in terms of product and service offerings), and in securing labour with the accent on efficiency: the rationale for offering work organised under an employment contract is to optimise the transaction costs, which are expected to be higher if the choice is to get work done by self-employed contract workers, involving a series of trading exchanges. Economies of scale can be made through avoiding the need for continual renegotiation of terms, while shared knowledge about expectations between the parties is expected to speed up output delivery times – that is, getting the work done without needing repeated socialisation into the specifics of an organisation's operations.

The reward contingency in this instance might relate to the example of a firm with a single-product strategy in which the design and management of employee reward would be paternalistic and unsystematic (Marchington and Wilkinson, 2005: 4). In contrast, for a diversified firm following the more rationalist orientation, 'best practice' could be to rely on large bonus payments based on profitability and subjective assessments about contribution to company performance.

Pragmatic strategy commentators agree with fatalists that rational-type long-range planning is largely futile. However, the viewpoint is less pessimistic and more politically sensitised. Organisational settings are imprecise and 'sticky' – despite rationalist advocacy, organisational managers have too little knowledge and too limited a capacity to deploy it proactively to make a difference. Managers and their competitors in economic markets are too careless and inattentive to plans to optimise their execution – things change as time progresses. Market selection processes are just as sub-optimal: no one knows what the optimal strategy is, and if they did they would be too lax to stick to it. Consequently sub-optimal strategic planning and execution is unlikely to be fatal in terms of competitive advantage.

Here approaches such as power-dependency theory may help understand reward management outcomes – those who gain episodic advantage around politically contested organisational control frontiers (Edwards, 1990), including having knowledge that organisation managers have come to depend on them until such time as they can substitute people with alternative technologies, can expect to negotiate individually oriented reward 'deals'. In Chapter 11, we exemplify the way this line of reasoning may play out in practice when discussing approaches associated with employment terms in some forms of expatriation.

In common with rationalists, the **relativist** school of thought, as characterised by Whittington (2000), regards strategy as important and something managers should be concerned with. However, whereas rationalists – in common with mainstream HRM ideas – anticipate a unitary interest among the parties to organisation, relativist theory draws attention to the embeddedness of organisational action and hence to the need to understand organisations – and their leaders – as products of the social as well as economic contexts in which they are situated.

This chimes with the viewpoint expressed by Boxall and Purcell (2008), and Paauwe (2004), as well as in Bach's (2005) 'new HRM', outlined above. The world is viewed as a social construction, and hence open to reconstruction: not only profit maximisation to benefit finance capital shareholders under neoliberal market conditions may be prioritised: trade-offs and compromises may be required in recognition of pluralistic interests in organisation. Thus attention is needed to the social system in which strategy is to be formed and enacted: it also implies that universalistic approaches and the attempted transplantation of 'strategic' or 'best' practice between socio-economic settings is problematic.

Perhaps disguised, a rational approach is nonetheless the driving force: so a willingness exists to adapt not only the content but also the delivery mechanisms associated with employee reward, to accommodate variety in what will be regarded as an equitable distribution and forms of value, for example, among organisational stakeholders. This point will be developed in more detail when discussing recent critiques of strategic pay commentary below.

 STUDENT EXERCISE

A brightly branded future?
The case

Mobile phone company, Orange, has been reported as relaunching its 'employer brand'. The rationale offered in news reports is to enable the organisation to stand out in a competitive market for talented employees. While the idea may be traced back to work on the idea in British Airways during the late 1980s, 'it was the emerging talent struggle in the mid-1990s that encouraged professional firms in the US to look more closely at what made them distinct as employers and then to think of their employment proposition as a brand similar to their corporate or customer brands'.

Orange employs 12,500 people in the UK, in contact centres, retail outlets, in technical functions or at head office, and has attempted 'to understand what each of these talent pools wants from us', according to a quote attributed to David Roberts, Employer Brand Manager at Orange. Remarks by Mr Roberts were further quoted situating the employer brand HR initiative alongside competitive strategy the company applies to shape its approach to a range of corporate functional activities.

'Whether it's down to marketing, PR, HR or internal communications, we need to ensure that our employment offer is defined and communicated consistently,' Roberts was reported as stating, adding: 'It makes HR think in terms of why it is doing certain things and what's important to the people we are trying to attract, retain, motivate and inspire.'

In common with 'total reward' principles, Orange has divided the employee brand between 'the emotional' and 'the rational'. Rational factors include pay and benefits, work–life balance, professional contribution and impact on the business, and possibilities for career development. Emotional factors might include company image, leadership and social responsibility. Orange management have been trying to understand how different groups of workers respond to each set of factors. 'We are able to adjust the emotional and rational offer. We can segment the message to meet the aims of different groups,' Mr Roberts told *People Management* magazine.

According to Paul Walker, Head of Brand Development at recruitment firm Barkers, and author of a CIPD guide on employer branding, the brand concept gives HR a way to demonstrate its value using 'language that the rest of the business can understand'. Rebecca Clake, CIPD Adviser, Organisation and Resourcing, appears to agree:

> There are some helpful things that people can take from employer branding in the way we think about our people and our organisation. … Although many of these ideas existed before the term was coined, it can be useful to apply some of the principles that business applies to researching its customers to researching employees.

Helen Rosethorn, of integrated talent solutions provider Bernard Hodes Group, told the magazine interviewer: 'your employer brand is essentially the deal between the organisation and its people', with the sole purpose of 'becoming the employer of choice for the employee of choice', that is, determining what makes an employer distinct from labour market competitors.

According to Graeme Martin, at the Centre for Reputation Management at Glasgow University, employer branding can offer HR a useful perspective. 'Marketing people have an ability to understand their customers in a way that HR doesn't understand employees,' he says. Just as marketing people use their customer data to target particular groups and develop a more personal customer proposition, HR could use staff data to develop an individualised employee proposition.

In the interests of presenting a balanced view, *People Management* reports concerns that HR strategic planners need to weigh before recommending branding to the employer, saying: 'For many in HR, employer branding is a somewhat glitzy, unsubstantial concept.' Further:

> The argument goes that, for a brand to work, an employer has to deliver what's promised, and this has serious implications for every element of HR policy – from reward to career development, and from organisational culture to management competence. It can represent an opportunity for HR managers to shake things up, but they have to be certain that it is the needs of the business – rather than the needs of the brand – that drive their efforts.

And to avoid another possible pitfall, the organisation's employer brand and customer brand have to reinforce each other. At retail group Marks & Spencer, 'aspirational' brand statements have been drafted, which include making employees feel valued and proud to work for the company, keeping them informed about corporate performance and rewarding workers well (compared with competitors).

In the magazine report, Shirley Jenner, an academic at Manchester Metropolitan University Business School, is quoted as suggesting that the development of employer branding and ideas on 'living the brand' are, 'at best, controlling, rather creepy and possibly unethical'. She adds: 'Employer branding represents a shift from a traditional psychological contract that embodies mutual obligation and reciprocity. By viewing employment as a consumer good, we reduce a person's sense of responsibility to their employer.'

Employer branding may work for recognisable 'brands'. But, *People Management* cautions:

> *Smaller organisations can come unstuck when attempting to define their employer brand ... in a meaningful way. Ask most employers to articulate their employer brand and they are likely to use motherhood-and-apple-pie phrases such as 'fair reward', 'trusting environment' or 'opportunity to develop'. But for employees and job hunters, these are often merely the basics – the 'hygiene' factors that they expect from a job.*

The report points out that there is a contradiction between building 'brand loyalty' among employees and the widely accepted idea that there are no more jobs for life. Beyond this, the implications for workforce diversity need to be thought through in terms of an emphasis on recruiting people who can 'share the brand values' and 'fit the brand image'.

There is a commercial angle too. Graeme Martin argues that, if firms want to invest in employer branding, they should be able to put a figure on the employer brand value, just as they can on their corporate or customer brand value. Only a few businesses are thinking along these lines. Martin is reported as expressing concerns about the lack of hard evidence to back up the various claims made for employer branding

People Management gives the final word to Orange's David Roberts, saying that he understands the limits of employer branding when it comes to developing HR strategy:

> *Describing it as a tool, not a philosophy, he says: 'The employer brand doesn't drive HR strategy at Orange. Rather, it is the creative platform that helps glue the different elements – reward, talent management and so on – together.'*

Questions for Review

1 Consider the details of the Orange case and accompanying commentary. Where would you locate the strategy of employer branding as described within Whittington's (2000) four-part categorisation? Give reasons for your assessment.

2 Based on the outline of this concept provided in the magazine article, would you say that there is more than one strategic orientation that could be associated with this approach?

3 Given some of the reservations articulated about employer branding, how could organisation managements mitigate potentially negative consequences? Pay specific attention to extrinsic reward on the one hand and the 'psychological contract on the other (refer to Chapter 9 for some ideas).

4 Would your answer be the same depending on whether the organisation concerned was located in the private, public or voluntary sector; was large or SME?

Case material source: Lucie Carrington (2007) 'Designs on the dotted line'. *People Management* 13(21): 36

In summary, strategy and HRM may be considered from multiple angles, each chosen path implying a set of predicted consequences, and HRM as an ideology carrying with it the character of the context(s) from which it emerged. Armed with these insights, we may examine the ways in which, in tandem or parallel with HRM discourse, ideas about approaches to employee reward may be described and subjected to appraisal.

STRATEGIC REWARD (AKA 'THE NEW PAY'): ADVOCATES AND CRITICS

Kessler (2007) observes that early 'strategic reward' commentary privileged reward among HRM initiatives as the means by which corporate performance was to deliver competitive 'success'. He points out, citing Gomez-Mejia that, under this managerial orientation, 'issues of internal equity and external equity are viewed as secondary to the firm's need to use pay as an essential integrating and signalling mechanism to achieve overarching business objectives' (1992: 4). As will be noted below, in considering criticism of the strategic reward discourse, Kessler (2007) questions the plausibility of a statement that views equity and business strategy as competing principles in employee reward determination, arguing that the view has been overtaken by a perspective that regards them as closely related.

In 1992 a book was published in the USA entitled 'The New Pay', a label that University of Southern California academic Edward E. Lawler III had coined (1986) to underscore the terms of 'a strategic approach' to reward management (1995). The authors of the 1992 publication, management consultants Jay R. Schuster and Patricia K. Zingheim, set out to popularise Lawler's thinking. Their challenge was stark: 'To survive, American industry must have a new view of the future' – a future in which 'the responsibility and rewards for success' would be shared between organisations and employees (1992: 4).

Heery (1996) notes that the new pay architects specified the problem by reference to a perceived dichotomy. Arrangements applied to manage the employment relationship, including the effort–reward bargain, functional in stable environments and organisations designed around hierarchy and scientific mass production systems informed by the 'scientific management' principles that an earlier consultant, Frederick W. Taylor, had advocated early in the twentieth century (Taylor, 1911), had to give way to a new regime. New pay, demanded by the new employee–organisation relationship, matched the more fluid organisational form applicable under a less certain environment, demanding modification of 'attitudes, plans and approaches to both how we work and how we are paid' (Schuster and Zingheim, 1992: 4).

In keeping with the rationalistic principles associated with mainstream HRM ideas, Lawler explains that the ideas he and his associates outline are intended to integrate work and employee reward arrangements with each other and with business priorities so that individuals will engage in 'the kind of performance that contributes to overall organizational effectiveness rather than simply making the individual look good' (1996: 196). Under this 'new logic' organisational design and management style flow from the business strategy, and both drive reward systems. 'New pay' is not an alternative form of pay nor a set of techniques (eg broad bands, pay-for-performance), but a different way of thinking about the role of reward systems in complex organisations (Lawler, 1995).

Six foundational factors support Lawler's (1995) 'strategic' reward management recipe:

First, an emphasis on attracting people whose expressed and actual behaviour is congruent with the kinds of attributes specified in describing the human resource aspects of the business strategy. This idea does, of course, imply that characteristics can be specified and that individuals can have fixed traits that can be deployed in ways that match organisational demands.

Second, attention is drawn to the role reward systems can play in employee motivation. Lawler uses expectancy theory to stress the need for a 'line of sight' matching reward to the conditions applicable to the individual targeted and its delivery. The assumption is that employees' 'mental maps' enable them to orient their assessment of signals from organisations and to reach conclusions as to how they will respond. There is an onus on management to offer reward giving off signals to which employees are likely to respond positively, given the context and their priorities from the employment relationship.

Third, the reward system is to be directed in ways that reinforce employees' tendency to learn from experience and to turn that learning into skills the organisation wishes to pay for. Some organisations have therefore implemented skills-based pay – that is, pay increases for skills acquisition. The issue is akin to motivating employees to perform, but this time the emphasis is on ongoing development of the employee's capacity to be valuable to the organisation. Rewards need to be packaged so as to encourage employees to develop skills and competencies the organisation's strategy has specified as necessary to its successful achievement.

A fourth element in strategic reward architecture is culture. Carrying the implication that managers *can* act on it by direct intervention, culture, as an objective phenomenon, is to be shaped using reward forms and processes to promote behaviour types that become dominant patterns of behaviour in the organisation and influence employee perceptions of what the organisation believes in, stands for and values. Given the old/new change imperative, the assumption is that how the organisation develops and administers its reward system can communicate a cultural offering that is different from the culture the reward system practices create in another organisational setting. The employer branding initiative sketched earlier in the case study exercise may be one indication of how 'culture management' may be approached as a central strategic reward tenet.

Fifth, strategic reward commentary stresses that reward systems reinforce and define organisation structure, something Lawler (1995) claims few executives recognise during reward system design. The impact may be significant even if not intentional. The reward system can reinforce hierarchy and impact on decision-making structures. And integration among workforce members can be positively or negatively affected by reward structure and delivery modes. Differentiation in rewarding employees requires careful handling. It may be counterproductive if unity between organisation members is the goal.

Sixth, reward system designers are exhorted to factor in to their thinking how much the proposed reward system and its relative components will cost, and to review the extent to which costs should be fixed or varied with the organisation's ability to meet them. Lawler (1995) argues that one indicator of a well-designed reward system is that it leads to cost increases when the firm can afford it and containment when it cannot.

Zingheim and Schuster (2000) extrapolate from these foundations six principles to ensure the organisation will 'pay people right!' These are:

1 Create a 'positive and natural' reward experience: employees are to be involved and 'educated' as to the reasons and shared benefits for changing reward systems, guidance that assumes unitary interests between employer and workforce, or at least the basis on which rational management can 're-educate' individuals and groups who may not perceive interest overlap.

2 Align rewards with business goals to create 'a win-win partnership': clear managerial direction is to be provided that individual employees must continue to 'add value', in ways that the company will then recognise with rewards.

3 Extend people's line of sight: managers are to encourage all workforce members to become 'knowledgeable stakeholders', showing how an individual's efforts impact on the team, business unit and company, including the need to adapt to customer needs.

4 Integrate rewards: each reward tool is to be used for what it does best, integrating each element of total reward to offer a customised 'deal'.

5 Reward individual ongoing value with 'base pay', applying three elements: employee salary is to reflect increases in competencies the firm finds useful; consistent performance over time; and the individual's value in the external labour market.

6 Reward results with variable pay: it is uncritically accepted that the firm must 'meet shareholder expectations' (reasonableness is not discussed) and 'provide a compelling future'; variable pay is deemed suitable as part of the total reward offer to recognise these 'results' (as well as enjoining employees in the corporate project).

The consultants argue that 'total reward strategies are becoming more global and less industry-specific', as 'global talent can migrate from company to company because of their success in global business, rather than industry-specific success' (2000: 334). Convergence on a universalistic set of reward management norms, read off from corporate managerial strategy predilections, appears the logical outcome, for which reward designers must prepare.

Heery acknowledges the potential value of the 'new pay' model. But he also looks critically at the consequences of its application, and specifically the assumption on the part of strategic reward commentators that linking pay and performance is axiomatic, carrying with this choice 'the intention to increase employee risk' (1996: 58). Under the 'new pay' reasoning, the proportion of guaranteed pay and benefits is reduced in favour of 'at risk' payments – commissions, merit pay and bonuses, which may not be consolidated into permanent, let alone pensionable total remuneration.

Not only variable performance pay, but also basic pay progression over time follows the logic of employee compliance with corporate strategy. And what Heery (1996) refers to as 'soft' measures of performance may be applied managerially to determine contingent reward outcomes; measures that may not be directly controlled by employees (in the way, for example, piece-rate pay/ production is calibrated).

Tying reward outcomes to team contribution, or group/business unit performance, customer satisfaction ratings or financial measures (which may be subject to managerial fine-tuning for other purposes over specific time periods not set by employees) generates uncertainty for workforce members. The indicators may be subjective or susceptible to influences outside an individual's sphere of influence in the workplace.

Moreover, so-called 'nimble reward management' processes (Ledford, 1995), where line managers are called to make 'rapid but necessarily rough and ready judgements about employee entitlement to reward' (Heery, 1996: 59) may combine with the substance of 'new pay' in ways that harm employee wellbeing, standing in contradiction to employees' needs for stable and secure income from selling their labour. (Refer to Chapter 9 for discussion on employee wellbeing and total reward.)

Under conditions where employment systems have been deregulated and trade unions' capability to support resistance to injustice severely weakened Heery (1996), the transfer of risk from employer (to secure performance returns on investment in labour) to employee through variable and contingent forms of reward represents an issue carrying potentially negative consequences when evaluated on ethical and moral grounds.

Heery (1996) warns about more explicit forms of injustice arising from the scope inherent in 'strategic', business-aligned reward management for inconsistent treatment of employees, in contradiction to 'equal pay' principles designed to avoid direct and indirect discrimination on grounds related to demography. Issues arise here when considering the relative capacity of line managers and HR specialists to govern reward management in ways that do not contravene regulatory provisions and/or good practice in relation to fair treatment and human dignity at work.

As part of his critique, Heery points to 'the attachment of new pay writers to the principle of employee involvement in the management of pay' so as to secure not only understanding but also 'acceptance of the system' (1996: 61). Lawler himself (1996) argues that, when building 'from the ground up', an organisation's strategic reward choices may fall on stony ground if it fails to account for the propensity of the workforce to feel similarly positive about the approach.

Employees have exercised a strategic choice in selecting an organisation to work for on criteria such as reward arrangements. Heery cites 'evidence that employees have separate and opposing interests regarding remuneration to those of employers' (1996: 61), which he feels may best be channelled through collective representation. Accepting a shift of onus to secure pay based on their performance as judged by managers, rather than on managers to secure performance in return for guaranteed pay, may run contradictory to the basic interests Heery (1996) describes for income stability and security.

There is thus scope for employee–employer conflict around the enduring bases of pay systems long ago juxtaposed by Gowler and Lupton (1969) – pay for time (reporting for work) versus pay for performance (what happens when at work). While the assumption of unitary interests between employers and employees sits at the core of HRM ideology, a more pluralistically oriented perspective suggests that the interface of strategic choices between the parties to the effort–reward bargain needs to be considered.

Another core feature of the 'new pay' recipe is the requirement for managerially led change, to adjust to the 'new logic' of organisation (Lawler, 1996). The assumption that managers know best is challenged in remarks by Marc Thompson expressed during a debate about the interaction of reward management with notions of trust between employees and organisational leaders, where the latter hope to combine trust in 'a virtuous trinity' with commitment-building and employee motivation to work productively.

Thompson's suggestion was that perhaps organisations should go with the grain of employees' thinking around work practices and interrelationships rather than engaging in perennial attempts to change that thinking. Instead of assuming that the onus is on managers to lead the educational process, he argued, '[i]n future organisations may have to re-educate themselves to get the performance they want' (Perkins and Sandringham, 1998: 6).

Heery (1996: 63) proposes an alternative 'new pay' prescription aimed at creating a situation of 'acceptable risk', in which the interest of the employer in contingent and variable pay is balanced against the interest of the employee in reasonably stable and predictable income. Principles he believes could secure that balance are as follows:

- the use of variable pay as a supplement and not a replacement for a 'fair' base salary;
- commitment to maintaining the value of employee benefits and particularly those that provide for economic security;
- basing contingent pay systems on rigorous measures of performance that are subject to employee control;
- regulation of management decision-making about pay, supported through training, strict guidelines and review;
- transparency and full communication of pay system rules;

- regular monitoring and periodic audit of pay systems to ensure consistency of application and an absence of discrimination;

- effective 'due process' mechanisms for employees to appeal against management judgements;

- full involvement of employee representatives in the design, application and review of payment systems (Heery, 1996: 63).

Judging the content of his list as running contrary to the dominant trends in mid-1990s employee reward management practice, Heery anticipated that 'very few organizations are likely to adopt it' (1996: 63), recommending recourse to legislation to enshrine the right of employees to bargain for their reward.

Pursuing a different line of critique, just over a decade on, Kessler (2007) takes the 'strategic reward' prescriptions to task on the grounds of an underlying assumption that what have been labelled 'contribution based pay' practices (Brown and Armstrong, 1999), perceived as 'second generation' strategies for aligning reward and performance management, will generate the necessary worker attitudes and behaviours in a mechanistic and unproblematic way, so that any concern with equity, which might affect such employee responses, becomes incidental. It is only when attempts are made to theorise the relationship between pay and the achievement of business goals that issues of equity, process and meaning re-emerge as important, Kessler (2007) argues.

Thinking about the importance of equity may be developed paying attention to externally oriented equity benchmarks as well as those that may be identified between employees inside the organisation. Kessler (2007) cites reported evidence over recent years where, especially in industrial sectors such as finance, reward systems have been effected combining payment of performance-related sums with 'premium rates' in response to tight markets for certain kinds of employees to acquire the skills needed to meet organisational goals. Rather than the clinical distinction in the Gowler and Lupton (1969) pay-for-performance versus pay-for-time dualism, hybrid reward 'solutions' are being selected. Resource dependence theory (Pfeffer and Salancik 2003) may help in interpreting these kinds of trends where, as Festing *et al* explain, resources that are 'scarce or controlled by a few actors ... may affect strategic organisational behaviour [and] the stronger the dependencies the more power the focus actor has in terms of influencing organisational behaviour' (2007: 123).

Paying attention to peer reward comparisons beyond the organisation may be strategically astute not only at private industry flashpoints involving specialist labour market segments. Kessler (2007) shows that, for example, uneven external labour market pressures have influenced public sector pay-setting, leading to the award of pay supplements tied not only to occupation types but also to regional geography. External equity considerations are further observed in employer actions to establish grading structures and 'job families' that clarify and enhance employee 'total reward' progression opportunities. Kessler sees such moves as an echo of the development of internal labour markets (discussed in Chapter 2 above), originally designed as a hedge against competitive pressures in tight labour market circumstances.

Turning to internal reward comparisons, the re-regulation impacting on HRM that Bach (2005) refers to impacts on the equity between employees within the same organisation. Kessler (2007) notes that the UK government has enacted legislation intended to regulate reward management outcomes to narrow differentials between employees at the extremes of the labour market. As discussed in Chapter 3, the National Minimum Wage provisions have been designed to secure a minimum protective floor, on the one hand, while not detrimentally affecting competitiveness, productivity, employment levels or wage inflation, on the other hand. In the case of 'top pay', as discussed in Chapter 10, the government has intervened to increase transparency related to directors' and executives' reward – not necessarily to modify outcomes, but to assure the justifiability of high payouts based on a demonstrable link to corporate performance.

A further significant public policy concern that Kessler (2007) highlights, in tune with the Labour government's 'Fairness at Work' agenda, is the particular issue of equality of treatment between women and men. Pressure on the government and employers to address this issue from a range of interest groups has been observable – exacerbated by evidence that despite the elapse of over three and a half decades since the Equal Pay Act 1970, the gap between male and female employees remains stubbornly wide. Accounting not only for the substance of employee reward determination but also issues of process, paying attention to procedural justice and psychological contract considerations, Kessler (2007) concludes that, contrary to early 1990s commentary, equity factors, far from being alternatives to strategic imperatives in employee reward management, may be central to whether or not strategic goals are achievable in practice.

 STUDENT EXERCISE

Consider the statement that an existing workforce is 'not a *new pay* workforce': employees were recruited to an organisation where the terms and conditions were expressly those of a regular salary and progression by gradual movement through fixed increments. In the event that management wish to shift to a performance-contingent *modus operandi*, it could be argued that horizontally aligned HRM sub-system factors may imply the need to repopulate an organisation with a workforce attuned to the 'new logic'.

Working in groups, consider your position on these claims, informed by 'new pay' advocacy and critique, and evaluate choices and consequences of (1) 're-profiling' the workforce, or (2) re-educating the workforce, or (3) re-educating management to align performance management with the resources already in place honouring the existing 'psychological contract'.

ACTORS AND THEIR ROLES IN EMPLOYEE REWARD MANAGEMENT UNDER THE HRM RUBRIC

Elevating HRM and with it employee reward policy and practice to the level of corporate strategy implies changes not only in thinking but also a shift in the roles played by specialists and line managers in administering the reward system.

If recent arguments have salience, emphasising the crucial role of process, so as to avoid undermining strategic aspirations, education of management as much as workforce members assumes importance.

Storey (1995) argues that the impetus for HRM (and, one might reason, by extension 'strategic reward') came not from the welfare-oriented or IR-oriented specialists but from line managers. The latter wanted to focus attention on business – as noted above, reflecting the 'enterprise culture' and growing managerialist confidence that emerged in the 1980s. They were impatient with proceduralism around the employment relationship and wished to force the pace of change, acting over the heads of traditional trade union and personnel specialists alike.

Under this change imperative, HRM is not some idealised human relations paradigm. Thinking HR performers may thus need to weigh the nature of expectations about people and the role expected and tolerance for procedure or ambiguity when advising specific organisation managements. On the other hand, even in the most hard-edged individualised contexts, line management aspirations willing pluralism to go away in relations with employees may not be enough.

An exhortation to 'help managers to be strategic' (Dalziel and Strange, 2007: 45) recognising that, at first-line level in particular, there is a 'vital' role to play in managing the effort–reward bargain (Purcell and Hutchinson, 2007) prompts reflection on HR specialists' role as well. Dalziel and Strange counsel HR specialists to take opportunities to help both 'the senior team' and line managers at the organisation–workforce interface.

In the case of top-down strategy, the assistance may be mapping the strategy process to facilitate its communication to others in ways that enable them to see the relevance of their job in achieving it. Where strategy 'emerges from lower levels', the HR specialist should 'find ways to get the key information to the people at the top' (2007: 45).

The implication is that HR practitioners need to move beyond traditional concerns with designing and administering pay structures and/or incentive arrangements, salary market survey and review planning, in reaction to internal or external stimuli, to a more proactive engagement in strategy development synchronised with people management at the organisation-wide level. As mentioned in Chapter 11, in some cases organisations are making significant investments in information technology-enabled transnational employee reward administration, to enable self-service among line managers.

But although this may permit HR specialists to raise their sights, external regulatory compliance stipulations, as well as pressure to assure return on corporate investment in increasingly complex reward 'portfolios' matched to organisation and employee preferences, necessitate attention to setting, communicating and auditing line management performance against clear corporate standards, and supporting their interpretation in given circumstances.

In the case of line managers, Brown and Purcell (2007) note the burgeoning levels of responsibility over the past 10 years to appraise employee performance, determine pay and bonus adjustments, and explain flexible benefits plans, while fewer, more distant HR specialists are available to support them. In spite of this evidence suggesting the crucial role to be played, front-line managers are perceived as constituting the 'Achilles heel' at the level of strategy implementation.

Brown and Purcell draw on CIPD research indicating that while one consequence of HR functional restructuring is further devolution of more pay and people management responsibilities to the line, 'HR does not seem to be devoting enough resources to training and equipping line managers to handle these responsibilities, despite the increasingly rapid rates of change in reward methods and the spread of more sophisticated and complex scheme designs' (2007: 30–1).

These research findings inform a recommendation that HR specialists should do more to involve line managers in reward management system design and modification, for example, in the way that one retail organisation named in the research report successfully implemented a new competency-based reward framework following a focus group programme during the development phase. People reportedly like the new system because, citing a senior manager in the case organisation, 'it uses our language' (Brown and Purcell, 2007: 32).

A second recommendation relates to the support line managers receive to help them shoulder their reward management accountability – at the most practical level, a willingness to invest corporate resources in assuring competence in ways that are visible to workforce members, imbuing them with confidence in the proficiency of their supervisor to act in a manner that combines organisational efficiency and justice prerequisites. The example is given of an insurance company that accompanied introduction of a new pay-for-performance programme covering call centre operatives with provision of a minimum of two days' training and practice in its operation. Line managers were viewed by the corporate HR functional leadership as needing "'to live and breathe [the pay system] ... to own it and realise how important it is to the business strategy to make it work' (Brown and Purcell, 2007: 32).

KEY LEARNING POINTS AND CONCLUSIONS

In this chapter, the interplay between employee reward and the ideas and practices that have become associated with 'HRM' has been considered. Debates around HRM, reaching back to the early 1980s, have been reviewed, to identify the ways the concept has been defined and the expectations that have been raised concerning active alignment between organisational strategy along one dimension and between the variables in the HRM bundle along the other. Having emphasised the 'strategy' factor, attention has been paid to the multiple perspectives available to approach this concept and in turn to shape HRM thinking.

A 'strategic HRM' approach is neither simple nor self-evident, once it is recognised that a multiplicity of choices exist in this aspect of people management, each imbued with assumptions regarding the location of managerial action within systemic contexts, and each accompanied by sets of consequences for organisational outcomes and members. These foundations have been deployed to assist in considering 'strategic' commentary directed at employee reward – both advocacy for the merits of 'new pay' and caution regarding accepting the universal application of such prescription uncritically.

In summary:

- HRM can be understood as ideology as much as a set of people management practices, and empirical evidence indicates that while the term may have mainstream discourse status, comprehensive application remains quite rare.

- HRM prescriptions may be understood as reflecting the time and place in which the concept originated, and as such need to be weighed against specific situational factors encountered by contemporary practitioners.

- Not only HRM ideas but also orientation to strategy are contested, and so require the exercise of caution, accounting for the complexity of socio-economic relations around organisation, and the shifting influences on interactive outcomes, before choosing to apply universal HRM recipes in particular contexts.

- Strategic reward management commentary carries the marks of the wider HRM and strategy debates: evaluation of the merits of advocates' claims benefits from attention to arguments drawing on a wider social science literature, including ethical considerations.

- Application of strategy when designing and implementing employee reward policies and practices at the least demands attention to the character of the workforce concerned and to the managers required to take the lead role. A significant role opens up for thinking HR performers to take the lead in addressing the organisational needs diagnosed for attention.

EXPLORE FURTHER

To gain a full appreciation of their tripartite HRM strategy as efficiency, organisational-flexibility and legitimacy model, see Boxall, P. and Purcell, J. (2008) *Strategy and Human Resource Management* 2nd ed. Basingstoke, Palgrave Macmillan.

For contrasting statements for and in critique of 'the new pay', see (1) Lawler, E.E. (1995) 'The New Pay: a strategic approach'. *Compensation & Benefits Review* 27 July–August: 14–22; and (2) Heery, E. (1996) 'Risk, representation and the new pay'. *Personnel Review* 25(6): 54–65.

For an answer to Whittington's question on whether or not strategy 'matters' applied to ideas about HRM and high performance work systems, see Paauwe, J. (2004) *HRM and Performance: achieving long term viability*. Oxford, Oxford University Press.

Recent empirical research on the relative reward management roles attributable to HR specialists and line managers is presented in Purcell, J. and Hutchinson, S. (2007) *Rewarding Work: the vital role of front line managers*. Change Agenda. London, Chartered Institute of Personnel and Development.

References

ABERCROMBIE, N., HILL, S. and TURNER, B.S. (2000) *Penguin Dictionary of Sociology*, 4th edn. London, Penguin

Acas (1990) *Appraisal Related Pay.* Advisory Booklet 14. London, Acas

ACCA (2005) *Executive Pay.* Policy Briefing Paper, June. London, Association of Chartered Certificated Accountants

ACKERS, P., MARCHINGTON, M., WILKINSON, A. and DUNDON, T. (2003) *Partnership and Voice, With or Without Trade Unions: changing UK management approaches to organisational participation.* Research Series Paper 2003: 4. Loughborough University Business School

AIDT, T. and TZANNATOS, Z. (2002) *Unions and Collective Bargaining. Economic effects in a global nnvironment.* Washington, DC, The World Bank

ALBERT, M. (1993) *Capitalism against Capitalism.* London, Whurr

ALLISON, N., BRETT, S. and HATCHETT, A. (2002) 'A square deal'. *People Management.* July

ANAKWE, U.P. (2002) 'Human resource management practices in Nigeria: challenges and insights'. *International Journal of Human Resource Management* 13(7): 1042–59

ANDERSON, S., CAVANAGH, J., COLLINS, C., PIZZIGATI, S. and LAPHAM, M. (2007) *Executive Excess 2007: the staggering social cost of U.S. business leadership.* 14th Annual CEO Compensation Survey. Washington, DC, Institute for Policy Studies and Boston, MA, United for a Fair Economy

ARMSTRONG, M. (2000) *Rewarding Teams.* London, Chartered Institute of Personnel and Development

ARMSTRONG, M. (2002) *Employee Reward*, 3rd edn. London, Chartered Institute of Personnel and Development

ARMSTRONG, M. (2002) *Employee Reward*, 3rd edn. London, Chartered Institute of Personnel and Development

ARMSTRONG, M. (2005) 'Career family structures', *IDS Executive Compensation Review* 290, April

ARMSTRONG, M. and BARON, A. (1995) *The Job Evaluation Handbook.* London, IPD

ARMSTRONG, M. and BARON, A. (2005) *Managing Performance: performance management in action.* London, Chartered Institute of Personnel and Development

ARMSTRONG, M. and MURLIS, H. (2007) *A Handbook of Remuneration Strategy and Practice*, rev. 5th edn. London, Kogan Page

ARMSTRONG, M. and STEPHENS, T. (2005). *A Handbook of Employee Reward Management and Practice*. London, Kogan Page

ARMSTRONG, M., CUMMINS, A., HASTINGS, S. and WOOD, W. (2003) *Job Evaluation. A guide to achieving equal pay*. London, Kogan Page

ARNAULT, E.J., GORDON, L., JOINES, D.H. and PHILLIPS, G.M. (2001) 'An experimental study of job evaluation and comparable worth'. *Industrial and Labor Relations Review* 54(4) July: 806–15

ARROWSMITH, J. and SISSON, K. (1999) 'Pay and working time: towards organisation-based systems?' *British Journal of Industrial Relations* 37(1): 51–75

ATKINSON, J. (1984) 'Manpower strategies for flexible organisations'. *Personnel Management* 16(8): 28–31

BACH, S. (2005) 'New directions in performance management', in Bach, S. (ed.) *Managing Human Resources. Personnel management in transition*, 4th edn. Oxford, Blackwell

BACON, N. and BLYTON, P. (2006) 'Union co-operation in a context of job insecurity: negotiated outcomes from teamworking'. *British Journal of Industrial Relations* 44(2): 215–37

BADEN-FULLER, C. (2000) 'Editorial: Executive compensation in Europe'. *Long Range Planning* 33(4): 475–7

BALDAMUS, W. (1961) *Efficiency and Effort*. London, Tavistock

BALKIN, D.B. and GOMEZ-MEJIA, L.R. (1990) 'Matching compensation and organizational strategies'. *Strategic Management Journal* 11: 153–69

BARRINGER, M. and MILKOVICH, G. (1998) 'A theoretical exploration of the adoption and design of flexible benefit plans: a case of human resource innovation'. *Academy of Management Review* 23(2) April: 305–24

BARUCH, Y. (2004) *Managing Careers: theory and practice*. London, FT-Prentice Hall

BATES, S. (2004) 'Employees not as happy with benefits as employers believe'. *HR Magazine* 49(2) February: 12

BEAM, B.T. and McFADDEN, J.J. (1996) *Employee Benefits*. Chicago, Dearborn Financial Publishing

BEATTY, R.W., HUSELID, M.A. and SCHNEIER, C.E. (2007) 'New HR metrics: scoring on the business scorecard', in Schuler, R.S. and Jackson, S.E. (eds) *Strategic Human Resource Management*, 2nd edn. Oxford, Blackwell: 352–65

BEBCHUCK, L.A. and FRIED, J.M. (2003) 'Executive compensation as an agency problem'. *Journal of Economic Perspectives* 17(3): 71–92

BEER, M., SPENCER, B., LAWRENCE, P., MILLS, Q. and WALTON, R. (1984) *Managing Human Assets*. New York, Free Press

BEHREND, H. (1957) 'The effort bargain', *Industrial and Labour Relations Review*, 10(4): 503–515.

BENDER, R. and MOIR, L. (2006) 'Does "best practice" in setting executive pay in the UK encourage "good behaviour"?' *Journal of Business Ethics* 67(1): 75–91

BENKHOFF, B. (1997) 'A test of the HRM model: good for employers *and* employees'. *Human Resource Management Journal* 7(4): 44–60

BENSON, J. (1995) 'Future employment and the internal labour market'. *British Journal of Industrial Relations* 33(4) December: 38

BERGMANN, T.J. and GULBINAS SCARPELLO, V. (2001) *Compensation Decision Making*, 4th edn. Orlando, FL, Harcourt College Publishers

BESTBEAR (2006) www.bestbear.co.uk

BICHARD, M. (1999) *Performance Management. Civil Service Reform – A Report to the Meeting of Permanent Heads of Departments, Sunningdale. 30 September–1 October 1999*. London, Cabinet Office

BLACK, J. (2002) *Oxford Dictionary of Economics*, 2nd edn. Oxford, Oxford University Press

BLANCHFLOWER, D. and BRYSON, A. (2003) 'Changes over time in union relative wage effects in the UK and the US revisited', in Addison, J.T. and Schnabel, C. (eds) *International Handbook of Trade Unions*. Cheltenham, Edward Elgar

BLANCHFLOWER, D. and OSWALD, A. (1987) *Profit Sharing – can it work?* LSE Discussion Paper 255. London, London School of Economics

BLANCHFLOWER, D.G. and OSWALD, A.J. (1988) 'Profit-related pay: prose discovered'. *Economic Journal* 98: 720–30

BLOOM, M., MILKOVICH, G. and MITRA, A. (2003) 'International compensation: learning from how managers respond to variations in local host contexts'. *International Journal of Human Resource Management* 14(8): 1350–67

BONACHE, J. (2005) 'Job satisfaction among expatriates, repatriates and domestic employees: the perceived impact of international assignments on work-related variables'. *Personnel Review* 34(1): 110–24

BOWEY, A. and THORPE, R. (2000), in Thorpe, R. and Homan, G. (eds) *Strategic Reward Systems*, London: FT-Prentice Hall

BOXALL, P. and PURCELL, J. (2008) *Strategy and Human Resource Management*, 2nd edn. Basingstoke, Palgrave Macmillan

BOYATZIS, R. (1982) *The Competent Manager. Model for effective performance*. Hoboken, NJ, Wiley

BRAVERMAN, H. (1997) *Labor and Monopoly Capital. The degradation of work in the twentieth century.* New York, Monthly Review Press

BREWSTER, C., HARRIS, H. and SPARROW, P. (2001) *Globalising HR.* London, Charted Institute of Personnel and Development

BRISCOE, D.R. and SCHULER, R.S. (2004) *International Human Resource Management,* 2nd edn. New York, Routledge

BROOKES, M., BREWSTER, C. and WOOD, G. (2005) 'Social relations, firms and societies: a study of institutional embeddedness'. *International Sociology* 20(4): 403–26

BROWN, D. (2001) *Reward Strategies: from intent to impact.* London, Chartered Institute of Personnel and Development

BROWN, D. and ARMSTRONG, M. (1999) *Paying for Contribution: real performance-related pay strategies.* London: Kogan Page

BROWN, D. and PERKINS, S.J. (2007) 'Reward strategy: making it happen'. *World at Work Journal* 16(2): 82–93

BROWN, D. and PURCELL, J. (2007) 'Reward management: on the line'. *Compensation & Benefits Review* 39 May–June: 28–34

BROWN, F.W., BRYANT, S.E. and REILLY, M.D. (2006) 'Does emotional intelligence – as measured by the EQI – influence transformational leadership and/or desirable outcomes?' *Leadership & Organization Development Journal* 27(5): 330–51

BROWN, W. (1963) *Piecework Abandoned: the effect of wage incentive schemes on managerial authority.* London, Heinemann

BROWN, W. (1989) 'Managing remuneration in the UK', in Sisson, K. (ed.) *Personnel Management in Britain.* Oxford, Blackwell

BRUCE, A., BUCK, T. and MAIN, B.G.M. (2005) 'Top executive remuneration: A view from Europe'. *Journal of Management Studies* 42(7): 1493–1506

BUCK, T., BRUCE, A. and MAIN, B.G.M. (2003) 'Long term incentive plans, executive pay and UK company performance'. *Journal of Management Studies* 40(7): 1709–27

BUCK, T., FILATOTCHEV, I. and WRIGHT, M. (1998) 'Agents, stakeholders and corporate governance in Russian firms'. *Journal of Management Studies* 35(1): 81–9

BURAWOY, M. (1979) *Manufacturing Consent.* Chicago, University of Chicago Press

BURGESS, K. (2007) 'C&W wins approval for senior pay plans'. *Financial Times* 22–3 July: 15

BURGESS, S., PROPPER, C., RATTO, M. and TOMINEY, E. (2004) *Incentives in the Public Sector: evidence from a government agency.* CMPO Working Paper Series 04/103. University of Bristol, Centre for Market and Public Organisation

BURRELL, G. and MORGAN, G. (1979) *Sociological Paradigms and Organisational Analysis*. London, Heinemann

CABINET OFFICE (1999) Cm 4310: *Modernising Government*. London, The Stationery Office

CABLE, J. and WILSON, N. (1989) 'Profit-sharing and productivity: an analysis of UK engineering firms'. *The Economic Journal* 99(396): 366–75

CADBURY, SIR A. (1992) *Report of the Committee on the Financial Aspects of Corporate Governance*. London, Gee Publishing

CAHAN, S.F., CHUA, F. and NYAMORI, R.O. (2005) 'Board structure and executive compensation in the public sector: New Zealand evidence'. *Financial Accountability & Management* 21(4): 437–65

CALMFORS, L. and DRIFFILL, K. (1988) 'Centralisation of wage bargaining and macroeconomic performance'. *Economic Policy* 6: 13–61

CANNELL, M. and WOOD, S. (1992) *Incentive Pay. Impact and evolution*. London, IPM/OECD

CAPPELLI, P. (1995) 'Rethinking employment'. *British Journal of Industrial Relations* 33(4) December: 46

CAREY, D.J. and HOWES, P.D. (1993) 'Developing a global pay program'. *Compensation & Benefits Review* 25 July–August: 78

CASEY, B., LAKEY, J., COOPER, H. and ELLIOTT, J. (1991) 'Payment systems: a look at current practice'. *Employment Gazette* August: 53–8

Chartered Institute of Personnel and Development

CHEN, C.C., CHOI, J. and CHI, S.C. (2002) 'Making justice sense of local–expatriate compensation disparity: mitigation by local referents, ideological explanations, and interpersonal sensitivity in China–foreign joint ventures'. *Academy of Management Journal* 45(4): 807–17

CHILD, J. (1975) 'Managerial and organizational factors associated with company performance. Part 2: a contingency analysis'. *Journal of Management Studies* 12(1): 12–27

CHILD, J. (1984) *Organization. A guide to problems and practice*, 2nd edn. London, Harper & Row

CIPD (2001) *Reward Determination in the UK*. Research Report. London, Chartered Institute of Personnel and Development

CIPD (2003) *The Psychological Contract*. CIPD Factsheet. London, Chartered Institute of Personnel and Development

CIPD (2005) *CIPD Reward Management*. CIPD Reward at Work. London, Chartered Institute of Personnel and Development

CIPD (2006) *Company Car Policies.* CIPD Factsheet. London, Chartered Institute of Personnel and Development, available at http://www.cipd.co.uk/subjects/empbnfts/compcars/ccarpolicy?cssversion=printable

CIPD (2006) *Reward Management.* Annual Survey Report 2006. London, Chartered Institute of Personnel and Development

CIPD (2006a) *Pay and Reward: an overview.* CIPD Factsheet,

CIPD (2006b) *How Engaged are British Employees?* Survey Report. London, Chartered Institute of Personnel and Development

CIPD (2007) *Recruitment, Retention and Turnover.* London, Chartered Institute of Personnel and Development

CIPD (2007a) *Guidelines to PDS Assessment.* London, Chartered Institute of Personnel and Development

CIPD (2007b) *Reward Management Survey 2007.* London, Chartered Institute of Personnel and Development

CIPD (2007c) *Employee Engagement.* CIPD Factsheet. London, Chartered Institute of Personnel and Development

CIPD (2007d) *Flexible Benefits.* CIPD Factsheet. London, Chartered Institute of Personnel and Development, available at http://www.cipd.co.uk/subjects/empbnfts/flexbens/cssversion=printable

CIPD (2007e) *Team Reward.* Factsheet. London, Chartered Institute of Personnel and Development, www.cipd.co.uk/subjects/pay/teampay/tmreward?cssversion=printable

CIPD (2007f) *Employee Share Ownership.* CIPD Factsheet. London, Chartered Institute of Personnel and Development, www.cipd.co.uk/subjects/pay/empbnfts/empshares?cssversion=printable

CIPD (2007g) *What's Happening with Well-being at Work?* Change Agenda. London, Chartered Institute of Personnel and Development

CIPD (2007h) *Employee Communication.* CIPD Factsheet. London, Chartered Institute of Personnel and Development

CIPD (2008) *Reward Management.* Annual Survey Report 2008. London, Chartered Institute of Personnel and Development

CLEGG, H.A. (1976) *The System of Industrial Relations in Great Britain*, 3rd edn. Oxford, Blackwell

CLG (2007) *Towards a Fairer Future. Implementing the Women and Work Commission recommendations. Executive Summary.* April. London, Department for Communities and Local Government

COATES, D. (2000) *Models of Capitalism: growth and stagnation in the modern era.* Cambridge, Polity Press

COCKBURN, C. (1991) *Brothers. Male dominance and technological change.* London, Pluto Press

COLE, N. and FLINT, D. (2003) 'Perceptions of distributive and procedural justice in employee benefits: flexible versus traditional plans'. *Journal of Managerial Psychology* 19(1): 19–40

CONYON, M. and FREEMAN, R (2004) 'Shared modes of compensation and firm performance', in Card, D., Blundell, R. and Freeman, R. (eds) *Seeking a Premier Economy.* Chicago, University of Chicago Press

CONYON, M. and PECK, S.I. (1998b) *Corporate Tournaments and Executive Compensation: UK evidence.* Warwick Business School Working Paper (EIASM workshop)

CONYON, M.J. (1997) 'Corporate governance and executive compensation'. *International Journal of Industrial Organization* 15(4): 493–509

CONYON, M.J. (1998) 'Directors' pay and turnover: an application to a sample of large UK firms'. *Oxford Bulletin of Economics and Statistics* 60(4): 485–507

CONYON, M.J. and MURPHY, K.J. (2000) 'The prince and the pauper? CEO pay in the US and UK'. *Economic Journal* 110: 640–71

CONYON, M.J. and PECK. S.I. (1998a) 'Board control, remuneration committees and top management compensation'. *Academy of Management Journal* 41(2): 146–57

CONYON, M.J. and SADLER, G.V. (2001) Executive pay, tournaments and corporate performance in UK firms. *International Journal of Management Reviews* 3(2): 141–68

CONYON, M.J., MALLIN, C. and SADLER, G. (2002) 'The disclosure of directors' share option information in UK companies'. *Applied Financial Economics* 12(2): 95–103

CONYON, M.J., PECK, S.I. and SADLER, G.V. (2001) 'Corporate tournaments and executive compensation: evidence from the U.K.' *Strategic Management Journal* 22(8): 805–15

CORBY, S., STANWORTH, C. and GREEN, B. (2005) *Gender and the Labour Market in South East England. Volume 2: Employers' Policies and Practices.* SEEDA/ESF/ University of Greenwich, London

COX, A., ZAGELMEYER, S. and MARCHINGTON, M. (2006) 'Embedding employee involvement and participation at work'. *Human Resource Management Journal* 16(3): 250–67

COX, A.L. (2004) 'Managing variable pay systems in smaller workplaces: the significance of employee perceptions of organisational justice', in *Employment Relations in SMEs.* London, Routledge

COYLE-SHAPIRO, J., MORROW, P.C. and RICHARDSON, R. (2002) 'Using profit sharing to enhance employee attitudes: a longitudinal examination of the effects on trust and commitment'. *Human Resource Management* 41(4) Winter: 423–39

COYLE, D. (2001) *Power to the People*, in *The Future of Reward*. Executive Briefing. London, Chartered Institute of Personnel and Development: 33–7

CRAWLEY, J. (2007) 'Facing the challenges: reward management in Europe'. *Workspan Focus: special supplement to Workspan* September: 5–8

CROUCHER, R. (1999) 'The Coventry Toolroom Agreement, 1941–1972. Part 1. Origins and operation'. *Historical Studies in Industrial Relations* 8: 1–41

CROUCHER, R. and WHITE, G. (2007) 'Enforcing a National Minimum Wage: the British case'. *Policy Studies* 28(2) June: 145–61

CUERVO-CAZURRA, A., MALONEY, M.M. and MANRAKHAN, S. (2007) 'Causes of the difficulties in internationalization'. *Journal of International Business Studies* 38(5): 709–25

CULLY, M., WOODLAND, S., O'REILLY, A. and DIX, G. (1999) *Britain at Work: as depicted by the 1998 Workplace Employee Relations Survey.* London, Routledge

DALE-OLSEN, H. (2005) 'Using linked employer–employee data to analyse fringe benefit policies. Norwegian experiences'. Institute for Social Research Norway. Paper presented to Policy Studies Institute seminar, July 2005

DALZIEL, S. and STRANGE, J. (2007) ' How to become strategic'. *People Management* 13(5): 44–5

DAVIS, M.L (ed.) (2007) 'Total rewards: *everything* that employees value in the employment relationship', in *WorldatWork Handbook of Compensation, Benefits, and Total Rewards.* New York, John Wiley and Sons: 1–13

DAYCARE TRUST (2007) *Employer-supported Childcare.* www.daycaretrust.org.uk/mod.php?mod=userpage&menu=2801&page_id=123)

DECI, E.L. (1972) 'The effects of contingent and non-contingent rewards and controls on intrinsic motivation'. *Organisational Behaviour and Human Performance* 8: 217–29

DEGUILI, F. and KOLLMEYER, C. (2007) 'Bringing Gramsci back in: labor control in Italy's new temporary help industry'. *Work, Employment and Society* 21(3): 497–515

DELERY, J.E. and DOTY, D.H. (1996) 'Modes of theorizing in strategic human resource management: test of universalistic contingency, and configurational performance predictions'. *Academy of Management Journal.* 39(4): 802–35

DELOITTE (2004) *Report on the Impact of the Directors' Remuneration Regulations: a report for the Department of Trade and Industry.* London, Deloitte & Touche LLP

DEPARTMENT FOR WORK AND PENSIONS (2002/3 to 2005/6) *Family Resources Survey.* London, DWP

DEPARTMENT FOR WORK AND PENSIONS (2005/6) *Pensioners' Income Series*. Table 3.7. London, DWP

DEPARTMENT OF TRANSPORT (2004) *Section 6: other factors affecting travel* available at http://www.dft.gov.uk/stellent/groups/dft_transtats/documents/page/dft_transtats_039335.pdf

DERMER, M. (2005) 'Ovation: NBC Universal's recognition program sparks employee engagement'. *Workspan* 05/05: 39–42

DICKENS, R. and MANNING, A. (2003) 'Minimum wage, minimum impact', in Dickens, R., Gregg, P. and Wadsworth, J. (eds) *The Labour Market under New Labour*. Basingstoke, Palgrave Macmillan

DICKINSON, J. (2006) 'Employees' preferences for the bases of pay differentials'. *Employee Relations* 28(2): 164–83

DIVE, B. (2002) *The Healthy Organization: a revolutionary approach to people and management*. London, Kogan Page

DOERINGER, P. and PIORE, M. (1971) *Internal Labour Markets and Manpower Analysis*. Lexington, MA, D.C. Heath

DONALDSON, L. (2003) 'Organization theory as a positive science', in Tsoukas, H. and Knudsen, C. (eds), *The Oxford Handbook of Organization Theory: meta-theoretical perspectives*. Oxford, Oxford University Press: 39–62

DOWLING, P.J., FESTING, M. and ENGLE, A.D. (2007) *International Human Resource Management: managing people in a multinational context*, 5th edn. London, Thomson

DREHER, G., ASH, R. and BRETZ, R. (1988) 'Benefit coverage and employee cost: critical factors in explaining compensation satisfaction'. *Personnel Psychology* 41: 237–54

DRUKER, J. (2000) 'Wages systems', in White, G. and Druker, J. (eds) *Reward Management: a critical text*. London, Routledge

DTI (2001) *Directors' Remuneration: a consultative document*. URN 01/1400. December. London, Department for Business Enterprise and Regulatory Reform

DTI (2003) '*Rewards for Failure': directors' remuneration – contracts, performance & severance: a consultative document*. URN 03/652. June. London, Department for Business Enterprise and Regulatory Reform

DTI (2004) *National Minimum Wage: a detailed guide to the National Minimum Wage (Revised October 2004)*. London, Department of Trade and Industry

DYER, L. and ERICKSEN, J. (2007) *Workforce Alignment and Fluidity May Yield a Competitive Advantage*. ILR Impact Brief 22. Cornell University

E-REWARD (2003) *Survey of Job Evaluation*. Manchester, E-Reward

EDWARDS, P.K. (1990). 'Understanding conflict in the labour process: the logic and autonomy of struggle', in Knights, D. and Willmott, H. (eds) *Labour Process Theory*. Basingstoke, Macmillan: 125–52

EDWARDS, T., ALMOND, P., CLARK, I., COLLING, T. and FERNER, A. (2005) 'Reverse diffusion in US multinationals: barriers from the American business system'. *Journal of Management Studies* 42(6): 1261–86

EIKHOF, D.R., WARHURST, C. and HAUNSCHILD, A. (2007) 'What work? What life? What balance? Critical reflections on the work–life balance debate'. *Employee Relations* 29(4): 325–33

EMPLOYEE BENEFIT RESEARCH INSTITUTE (1991) *Flexible Benefits Plans and Changing Demographics*. EBRI Issue Brief 113. Washington, DC, Employee Benefit Research Institute

EOC (1994) *Job Evaluation Schemes Free of Bias*. Manchester, Equal Opportunities Commission

EVAN, W. and MACPHERSON, D. (1996) 'Employer size and labor turnover: the role of pensions'. *Industrial Relations and Labor Review* 49(4): 707–29

EVANS, R. and BROCKETT, J. (2007) 'Put organisations first to kick off HR's finest hour'. *People Management* 13(20): 9

FEDERICO, R F. (2007) 'The work–life impact: a best list retrospective'. *Workspan* 50(1): 109–12

FENWICK, M. (2004) 'International compensation and performance management', in Harzing, A.W. and Van Ruysseveldt, J. (eds) *International Human Resource Management*, 2nd edn. London, Sage: 307–32

FESTING, M. and PERKINS, S.J. (2008) 'Rewards for internationally mobile employees', in Brewster, C., Sparrow, P. and Dickmann, M. (eds) *International HRM: contemporary issues in Europe*, 2nd edn. London, Routledge

FESTING, M., EIDEMS, J. and ROYER, S. (2007) 'Strategic issues and local constraints in transnational compensation strategies: an analysis of cultural, institutional and political influences'. *European Management Journal* 25(2): 118–31

FIGART, D.M. (2001) 'Wage-setting under Fordism: the rise of job evaluation and ideology of equal pay'. *Review of Political Economy* 13(4): 405–25

FLANDERS, A. (1964) *The Fawley Productivity Agreements. A case study of management and collective bargaining*. London, Faber & Faber

FLANNERY, T.P., HOFRICHTER, D.A. and PLATTEN, P.E. (1996) *People, Performance and Pay: dynamic compensation for changing organizations*. New York, Free Press

FOLGER, R. and CROPANZANO, R. (1998) *Organisational Justice and Human Resource Management*. Thousand Oaks, CA, Sage

FOMBRUM, C., TICHY, N. and DEVANNA, M.A. (1984) *Strategic Human Resource Management*. New York, Wiley and Sons

FORSTER, N. (2000) 'The myth of the 'international' manager'. *International Journal of Human Resource Management* 11(1): 126–42

FORTH, J. and MILLWARD, N. (2000) *The Determinants of Pay Levels and Fringe Benefit Provision in Britain*. Discussion Paper 171. London, National Institute of Economic and Social Research

FOX, A. (1974) *Beyond Contract: work, power and trust relations*. London, Faber & Faber

FRANKLIN, D. (2006) *The World in 2006*. London, The Economist

FRC (2006) *The Combined Code on Corporate Governance*. London, Financial Reporting Council

FRESHFIELDS BRUCKHAUS DERINGER (2007) *Directors' Remuneration Report Regulations: checklist, commentary, and best practice*. London, Freshfields

FRIEDMAN, A.L. (1977). *Industry and Labour: class struggle at work and monopoly capitalism*. London, Macmillan

FRIEDMAN, A.L. (1984). 'Management strategies, market conditions and the labour process', in Stephen, F.H. (ed.) *Firms, Organization and Labour*. London, Macmillan

FURÅKER, B. (2005) *Sociological Perspectives on Labor Markets*. London, Palgrave Macmillan

GENNARD, J. and JUDGE, G. (2002) *Employee Relations*, 3rd edn. London, Chartered Institute of Personnel and Development

GEPPERT, M. (2005) 'The local–global dilemma in MNCs revisited: institutionalist contributions'. Summary of Presentation at the Research Seminar of the School of Management and Organizational Psychology at Birkbeck, University of London, 16 June

GERHART, B. and MILKOVICH, G. (1990) 'Organisational differences in managerial compensation and financial performance'. *Academy of Management Journal* 33: 663–90

GERHART, B. and RYNES, S.L. (2003) *Compensation: Theory, evidence, and strategic implications. Foundations for organisational science*. Thousand Oaks, CA, Sage

GHOSHAL, S. and BARTLETT, C.A. (1998) *Managing Across Borders: the transnational solution*. London, Random House

GILBERT, K. (2005) 'The role of job evaluation in determining equal value in tribunals. Tool, weapon or cloaking device?' *Employee Relations* 27(1): 7–19

GILMORE, G. and O'CONNOR, R. (2007) 'Paul Gray: family, football and sheep give comfort to "a really affable guy"'. *The Times,* 21 November

GMAC (2006) *GMAC Global Relocation Trends: 2005 survey report*. Global Relocation Services in conjunction with US National Foreign Trade Council Inc and SHRM Global Forum

GOLEMAN, D. (2002), 'Leaders with impact'. *Strategic HR Review* 1(6): 3

GOMEZ-MEJIA, L. (1993) *Compensation, Organization and Firm Performance*. San Francisco, Southwestern

GOODHERHAM, P.N. and NORDHAUG, O. (2003) *International Management: cross-boundary challenges*. Oxford, Blackwell

GOVERNMENT ACTUARY'S DEPARTMENT (2005) *Occupational Pension Schemes 2005*. London, GAD

GOVERNMENT ACTUARY'S DEPARTMENT (2006) *Occupational Pension Schemes: The 13th Survey by the Government Actuary*. London, GAD

GRABHAM, A. (2003) 'Composition of pay'. *Labour Market Trends*. August: 397–405

GRAINGER, H. and CROWTHER, M. (2006) *Trade Union Membership 2006*. London, National Statistics and Department for Trade and Industry

GREATER LONDON AUTHORITY (2002) *Report of the London Weighting Advisory Panel*. June. London, GLA

GREEN, F., HADJIMATHEOU, G. and SMAIL, R. (1985) 'Fringe benefits and distribution in Britain'. *British Journal of Industrial Relations* 23(2): 261–80

GREENBURY, SIR R. (1995) *Report of the Study Group on Directors' Remuneration*. London, Gee Publishing

GROSS, S. (1995) *Compensation for Teams*. New York, American Management Association

GUEST, D.E. (2001) 'Human resource management: when research confronts theory'. *International Journal of Human Resource Management* 12(7): 1092–1106

GUEST, D.E. (1987) 'Human resource management and industrial relations'. *Journal of Management Studies* 24(5): 503–21

GUEST, D.E. (1997) 'Human resource management and performance: a review and research agenda'. *International Journal of Human Resource Management* 8(3): 263–7

GUEST, D.E. (2004) 'The psychology of the employment relationship: an analysis based on the psychological contract'. *Applied Psychology, An International Review* 53(4): 541–55

GUEST, D.E. (2007) 'Don't shoot the messenger: a wake-up call for academics'. *Academy of Management Journal* 50(5): 1020–6

GUEST, D.E. and CONWAY, N. (2004) *Employee Well-Being and the Psychological Contract*. Research Report. London, Chartered Institute of Personnel and Development

GUMBEL, P. (2007) 'Europe's Fattest Cats'. *Fortune* 156 (3): 8–9

HALE, D. (2007) 'Labour disputes in 2006'. *Economic and Labour Market Review* 1(6): 25–36

HALES, C. and GOUGH, O. (2002) 'Employee evaluations of company occupational pensions. HR implications'. *Personnel Review* 32(3): 319–40

HALL, P. and SOSKICE, D. (2001), *Varieties of Capitalism: the institutional foundations of comparative advantage*. Oxford, Oxford University Press

HAMPEL, SIR R. (1998) *Committee on Corporate Governance: final report*. London, Gee Publishing.

HANDEL, J. (2001) 'Recognition: "pats on the back motivate employees"'. Workspan, December 2001, 44(12).

HANSEN, F., SMITH, M. and HANSEN, R.B. (2002) 'Rewards and recognition in employee motivation'. *Compensation & Benefits Review* 34(5): 64–72

HARRIS, H. and DICKMANN, M. (2005) *Guide to International Management Development*. London, Chartered Institute of Personnel and Development

HARRIS, H., BREWSTER, C. and SPARROW, P. (2003) *International Human Resource Management*. London, Chartered Institute of Personnel and Development

HARVEY, M., SPIER, C. and NOVICEVIC, M. (2002) 'The evolution of strategic human resource systems and their application in a foreign subsidiary context'. *Asia Pacific Journal of Human Resources* 40(3): 284–305

HASTINGS, S. (2000) 'Grading systems and estimating value', in White, G. and Druker, J. (eds) *Reward Management: a critical text*. London, Routledge

HATCH, M.J. (2006) *Organization Theory: modern, symbolic, and postmodern perspectives*. Oxford, Oxford University Press

HEERY, E. (1996) 'Risk, representation and the new pay'. *Personnel Review* 25(6): 54–65

HEERY, E. (1998) 'A return to contract? Performance-related pay in a public service'. *Work, Employment and Society* 21(1): 73–95

HEERY, E. (2000) 'The new pay: risk and representation at work', in Winstanley, D. and Woodall, J. (eds) *Ethical Issues in Contemporary Human Resource Management*. Basingstoke, Macmillan Business

HEERY, E. (2000) 'Trade unions and the management of reward', in White, G. and Druker, J. (eds) *Reward Management: a critical text*. London, Routledge: 54–83

HEERY, E. and NOON, M. (2001) *A Dictionary of Human Resource Management*. Oxford, Oxford University Press

HENDRY, C. (2003) 'Applying employment systems theory to the analysis of national models of HRM'. *International Journal of Human Resource Management* 14(8): 1430–42

HENEMAN, R.L. (1992) *Merit Pay. Linking pay increases to performance ratings*. Reading, MA, Addison Wesley

HERRIOT, P. and PEMBERTON, C. (1995) *New Deals: the revolution in managerial careers*. Chichester, Wiley

HEWITT ASSOCIATES (1991) *Total Compensation Management*. Oxford, Blackwell

HIGGS, D. (2003). *Review of the Role and Effectiveness of Non-executive Directors: consultation paper*. London, Department of Trade and Industry

HIJAZI, S.T. and BHATTI, K.K. (2007) 'Determinants of executive compensation and its impact on organizational performance'. *Compensation & Benefits Review* March–April: 58–68

HILL, C.W.L. and PHAN, P. (1991) 'CEO tenure as a determinant of CEO pay'. *Academy of Management Journal* 34: 707–17

HILLS, F.S. (1989) 'Internal pay relationships', in Gomez-Mejia. L.R. (ed.) *Compensation and Benefits*. ASPA-BNA Series 3. Washington, DC, Bureau of National Affairs

HM REVENUE & CUSTOMS (2007) *HM Revenue & Customs National minimum Wage pages*, http://www.hmrc.gov.uk/nmw/#b, accessed 22.12.07

HMSO (2002) Statutory Instrument No. 1986: The Directors' Remuneration Report Regulations 2002. London, The Stationery Office

HOLLYFORDE, S. and WHIDDETT, S. (2002) *The Motivation Handbook*. London, Chartered Institute of Personnel and Development

HOLMWOOD, J. (2006) 'Social systems theory' in Turner, B.S. (ed.) *The Cambridge Dictionary of Sociology*. Cambridge, Cambridge University Press: 587–8

HORSMAN, M. (2003) 'Continuity and change: Public Sector Pay review bodies, 1992–2003'. *Public Money & Management* 23(4) October: 229–36

HOUSE OF COMMONS TRADE AND INDUSTRY COMMITTEE (2003) *Rewards for Failure: Sixteenth Report of Session 2002–2003*. London, The Stationery Office

http://www.cipd.co.uk/subjects/pay/general/payrewrdovw.htm, accessed 12.03.06

HUBBICK, E. (2001) *Employee Share Ownership*. Executive Briefing. London,

HUME, D.A. (1995) *Reward Management. Employee performance, motivation and pay*. Oxford, Blackwell

HUSELID, M.A. (1995) 'The impact of human resource management practices on turnover, productivity, and corporate financial performance'. *Academy of Management Journal* 38(3): 635–72

HYMAN, J. (2000) 'Financial participation schemes', in White, G. and Druker, J. (eds) *Reward Management: a critical text*. London, Routledge

HYMAN, J. (2008) 'Employee share ownership', in White, G. and Druker, J. (eds) *Reward Management: a critical text*, 2nd edn. London, Routledge

i4cp (2007) 'Organizations struggle with employee recognition programs., Institute for Corporate Productivity Knowledge Center, www.i4cp.com, accessed 08.11.07

IDIL AYBARS, A. (2007) 'Work–life balance in the EU and leave arrangements across welfare regimes'. *Industrial Relations Journal* 38(6): 569–90

IDS (1996) *Paying for Competency*. IDS Management Pay Review Research File 39. London, Incomes Data Services

IDS (2000) *Performance Pay*. IDS Focus 96. Winter. London, Incomes Data Services

IDS (2003) *Flexible Benefits*. IDS StudyPlus 762. Autumn. London, Incomes Data Services

IDS (2004) *IDS Executive Compensation Review*. May. London, Incomes Data Services

IDS (2004a) *IDS Pay Report* 906: 12. June. London, Incomes Data Services

IDS (2004b) *Understanding Reward. The long-term decline and surprising re-birth of age-related pay*. IDS Pay Report 912. September: 15–17. London, Incomes Data Services

IDS (2004c) *Understanding Reward. The pros and cons of market-related pay*. IDS Pay Report 907 June: 8–9. London, Incomes Data Services

IDS (2005) *SAYE Schemes*. IDS HR Studies Update 795. April. London, Incomes Data Services

IDS (2005a) *Standby and Call-out Pay*. IDS HR Studies 798. May. London, Incomes Data Services

IDS (2006) *An Assessment of the Causes of Pay Drift in UK Organisations*. Research Report for the Office of Manpower Economics. December. London, Incomes Data Services

IDS (2006a) *Company cars and business travel, IDS study 817*. London: Incomes Data Services

IDS (2006b) *Directors' Pay Report 2006*. London, Incomes Data Services

IDS (2006c) *Job Families*. IDS Study 814. London, Incomes Data Services

IDS (2006d) *London Allowances*. IDS HR Studies 827. August. London, Incomes Data Services

IDS (2006e) *Overtime*. IDS HR Studies 813. January. London, Incomes Data Services

IDS (2006f) *Pay in the Public Services*. London, Incomes Data Services

IDS (2006g) *Understanding Reward: trends in pay progression: multi-faceted approaches gain popularity*. IDS Pay Report 945. January: 15–17. London, Incomes Data Services

IDS (2007) *Bonus Schemes*. IDS HR Studies 843. April. London, Incomes Data Services

IDS (2007a) *Hours and Holidays*. IDS HR Study 854. September. London, Incomes Data Services.

IDS (2007b) *Job Evaluation + guide to suppliers*. IDS HR Studies Plus 837. London, Incomes Data Services

IDS (2007c) *Pay and Conditions in Engineering 2006/7*. London, Incomes Data Services

IDS (2007d) *Performance Management*. IDS HR Studies 839. February. London, Incomes Data Services

IDS (2007e) *Share Incentive Plans*. IDS HR Studies 840. February. London, Incomes Data Services

IDS (2007f) *Shift Pay*. IDS HR Studies 838. January. London, Incomes Data Services

IDS (2007g) *Sick Pay*. IDS HR Study 852, August. London, Incomes Data Services

IDS (2007h) *Understanding Salary Sacrifice*. Employee Benefits. IDS HR Study 856: 17–18. London, Incomes Data Services

INDEPENDENT, THE (2007) 'Executive pay "linked to results"'. *The Independent,* 17 September: 44

Industrial Society (1998) *Competency-Based Pay*. Managing Best Practice 43. London, Industrial Society

INGRAM, P., WADSWORTH, J. and BROWN, D. (1999) 'Free to choose? Dimensions of private-sector wage determination, 1979–1994'. *British Journal of Industrial Relations* 37(1) March: 33–49

IPD (1997) *The IPD Guide on Broadbanding*. London, IPD

IPD (2000) *Study of Broad-banded and Job Family Structures*. IPD Survey Report. January. London, IPD

IRS (2000) *Pay Prospects for 2001 – a survey of the private* sector. Pay and Benefits Bulletin 510. December. London, Industrial Relations Services

IRS (2000a) *The Truth about Merit Pay. Pay and Benefits Bulletin 501*. August. London, Industrial Relations Services

IRS (2005) *Executive Directors' Total Remuneration Survey 2005*. London, Independent Remuneration Solutions and Manifest

JACKSON, S.E. and SCHULER, R.S. (2007) 'Understanding human resource management', in Schuler, R.S. and Jackson, S.E. (eds) *Strategic Human Resource Management*. Oxford, Blackwell.

JACOBY, S.M. (2006) 'Corporate governance and employees in the United States', in Gospel, H. and Pendleton, A. (eds.) *Corporate Governance and Labour Management*. Oxford, Oxford University Press: 23–48

JACQUES, E. (1964) *Time Span Handbook*. London, Heinemann

JENSEN, M. and MURPHY, K. (1990) 'CEO incentives – "It's not how much you pay, but how"'. *Harvard Business Review* 68(3): 138–49

JENSEN, M.C. and MECKLING, W.H. (1976) 'Theory of the firm: managerial behavior, agency costs and ownership structure'. *Journal of Financial Economics* 3(4): 305–60

JENSEN, M.C., MURPHY, K.J. and WRUCK, E.G. (2004) *Remuneration: where we've been, how we got to here, what are the problems, and how to fix them*. ECGI Working Paper No. 44/2004. Social Science Research Network Electronic Paper Collection: http://ssrn.com/abstract=561305

JOHNSON, R. (2007) 'Why passion and humanity are the keys to unlocking innovation', *People Management* 13(22): 48

Kalleberg, A.L. (2003) 'Flexible firms and labor market segmentation: effects of workplace restructuring on jobs and workers'. *Work and Occupations* 30(2): 154–75

KAPLAN, R. and NORTON, D. (1996) *The Balanced Scorecard*. Boston, MA, Harvard Business School Press

KAPLAN, S.N. (2007) 'Are CEOs overpaid?' *World at Work Journal* 16(3): 22–37

KATZ, H.C. and DARBISHIRE, O. (2000) *Converging Divergences: worldwide changes in employment systems*. London, Cornell University Press

KEEF, S.P. (1998) 'The causal association between employee share ownership and attitudes: a study based on the Long framework'. *British Journal of Industrial Relations* 36(1): 73–82

KEENOY, T. (1997) 'HRMism and the languages of re-presentation'. *Journal of Management Studies* 34(5): 825–41

KEENOY, T. (1999) 'HRM as hologram: a polemic'. *Journal of Management Studies* 36(1): 1–23

KERR, C., DUNLOP, J.T., HARBINSON, F.H. and MYERS, C A. (1964) *Industrialism and Industrial Man*, 2nd edn. Oxford, Oxford University Press

KERSLEY, B., ALPIN, C., FORTH, J., BRYSON, A., BEWLEY, H., DIX, G. and OXENBRIDGE, S. (2006) *Inside the Workplace: findings from the 2004 Workplace Employment Relations Survey*. London, Routledge

KESSLER, I. (2000) 'Remuneration systems', in Bach, S. and Sisson, K. (eds) *Personnel Management in Britain: a comprehensive guide to theory and practice*, 3rd edn. Oxford, Blackwell

KESSLER, I. (2001) 'Reward systems choices', in Storey, J. (ed.) *Human Resource Management: a critical text*, 2nd edn. London, Thomson: 206–31

KESSLER, I. (2005) 'Remuneration systems', in Bach, S. (ed.) *Managing Human Resources: personnel management in transition*. Oxford, Blackwell Publishing: 317–45

KESSLER, I. (2007) 'Reward choices: strategy and equity', in Storey, J. (ed.) *HRM: a critical text*, 3rd edn. London, Thomson Learning: chapter 9

KESSLER, I. and PURCELL, J. (1992) 'Performance-related pay: objectives and applications'. *Human Resource Management Journal* 2(3): 34–59

KESSLER, S. and BAYLISS, F. (1995) *Contemporary British Industrial Relations*, 2nd edn. Basingstoke, Macmillan

KINGSMILL, D. (2001) *Report into Women's Employment and Pay*. Women and Equality Unit, Government Equality Office

KINNIE, N., HUTCHINSON, S. and PURCELL, J. (1998) *Getting Fit, Staying Fit: developing lean and responsive organisations*. London, Chartered Institute of Personnel and Development

KINNIE, N., HUTCHINSON, S., PURCELL, J., RAYTON, B. and SWART, J. (2005) 'Satisfaction with HR practices and commitment to the organisation: why one size does not fit all'. *Human Resource Management Journal* 15(4): 9–29

KLEINGINNA, P.R. Jr and KLEINGINNA, A.M. (1981) 'A categorized list of motivation definitions, with a suggestion for a consensual definition'. *Motivation and Emotion* 5(3): 263–91

KOHN, A. (1993) 'Why incentive plans cannot work'. *Harvard Business Review*. September–October: 54–63

KOHN, A. (1993) *Punished by Rewards: the trouble with gold stars, incentive plans, A's, praise and other bribes*. Boston, MA, Houghton Mifflin

KPMG (2007) *Survey of Directors' Compensation 2007*. London, KPMG LLP

KRESSLER, H.W. (2003) *Motivate and Reward: performance appraisal and incentive systems for business success*. Basingstoke, Palgrave Macmillan

LAMBERT, R.A., LARCKER, D.F. and WEIGELT, K. (1993) 'The structure of organizational incentives'. *Administrative Science Quarterly* 38: 438–61

LAMBERT, S. (2000) 'Added benefits: the link between work–life benefits and organizational citizenship behavior'. *Academy of Management Journal* 43(5): 801–15

LAWLER, E.E. (1971) *Pay and Organizational Effectiveness*. New York, McGraw-Hill

LAWLER, E.E. (1990) *Strategic Pay: aligning organizational strategies and pay systems*. San Francisco, Jossey-Bass

LAWLER, E.E. (1996) 'Competencies: a poor foundation for the new pay'. *Compensation and benefits Review*. November–December

LAWLER, E.E. (2000) *Rewarding Excellence. Pay strategies for the new economy*. San Francisco, Jossey-Bass

LAWLER, E.E. and FINEGOLD, D. (2007) 'CEO compensation: what board members think'. *World at Work Journal* 16(3): 38–47

LAWLER, E.E. III (1986) *The New Pay*. CEO publicationG84-7(55). Los Angeles, Center for Effective Organizations

LAWLER, E.E. III (1995) 'The New Pay: A strategic approach'. *Compensation & Benefits Review* 27 July–August: 14–22

LAWLER, E.E. III (1996) *From the Ground Up: six principles for building the New Logic Corporation*. San Francisco, Jossey-Bass

LAWLER, E.E. III (2000) *Rewarding Effectiveness: pay strategies for the New Economy*. San Francisco, Jossey-Bass

LAWLER, E.E. III (2005) 'Creating high-performance organizations'. *Asia Pacific Journal of Human Resources* 43(1): 10–17

LAZEAR, E.P. (1995) *Personnel Economics*. Cambridge, MA, MIT Press

LAZEAR, E.P. (1999) 'Personnel economics: past lessons and future directions'. *Journal of Labor Economics* 17(2): 199–236

LEDFORD, G.E. (1995) 'Designing nimble reward systems'. *Compensation & Benefits Review* July–August: 46–54

LEGGE, K. (1995) *Human Resource Management: rhetorics and realities*. Basingstoke, Macmillan

LEPAK, D.P., TAYLOR, M.S., TEKLEAB, A.G., MARRONE, J.A. and COHEN, D.J. (2007) 'An examination of the use of high-investment human resource systems for core and support employees'. *Human Resource Management* 46(2): 223–46

LEWIS, D. and SERGEANT, M. (2004) *Essentials of Employment Law*, 8th edn. London, Chartered Institute of Personnel and Development

LEWIS, P. (1998) 'Managing performance-related pay based on evidence from the financial services sector'. *Human Resource Management Journal* 8(2): 66–77

LINKLATERS (2006) *The Matrix: an overview of corporate governance*. London, Linklaters LLP

LINKLATERS (2007) *European Commission: report on the application of the EU recommendation on directors' pay*. UK Corporate Update. July. Linklaters LLP

LONG, R. and SHIELDS, J. (2005) 'Best practice or best fit? High involvement management and best pay practices in Canadian and Australian firms'. *Asia Pacific Journal of Human Resource Management* 16(1): 1783–1811

LORETTO, W., WHITE, P. and DUNCAN, C. (1999) '"Thatcher's children" pensions and retirement. Some survey evidence'. *Personnel Review* 30(4): 386–403

LOW PAY COMMISSION (1999) *Pay Structures and the Minimum Wage.* Low Pay Commission Occasional Paper 3. September. London, Low Pay Commission

LOWE, K., MILLIMAN, J., DECIERI, H. and DOWLING, P. (2002) 'International compensation practices: a ten-country comparative analysis'. *Human Resource Management* 41(1): 45–66

LPC (2003) *The National Minimum Wage. Building on Success.* Fourth report of the Low Pay Commission. Cm5768. March. London, The Stationery Office

LUPTON, T. and GOWLER, D. (1969) *Selecting a Wage Payment System.* London, Kogan Page

MABEY, C., SALAMAN, G. and STOREY, J. (1998) *Human Resource Management: a strategic introduction*, 2nd edn. Oxford, Blackwell

MACHIN, S. (1999) 'Wage inequality in the 1970s, 1980s and 1990s', in Gregg, P. and Wadsworth, J. (eds) *The State of Working Britain.* Manchester, Manchester University Press

MADIGAN, R.M. and HOOVER, D.J. (1986) 'Effects of alternative job evaluation methods on decisions involving pay equity'. *Academy of Management Journal* 29(1): 84–100

MAHONEY, T.A. (1992) 'Multiple pay contingencies: strategic design of compensation', in Salamon, G. (1992) (ed.) *Human Resource Strategies.* London, Sage

MAKINSON, J. (2000) *Incentives for Change. Rewarding performance in national government networks.* Public Service Productivity Panel. HM Treasury. London, HMSO

MALLIN, C. (2004) 'Trustees, institutional investors and ultimate beneficiaries'. *Corporate Governance* 12(3): 239–41

MAMMAN, A., SULAIMAN, M. and FADEL, A. (1996) 'Attitudes to pay systems: an exploratory study within and across cultures'. *International Journal of Human Resource Management* 7(1): 101–212

MARCHINGTON, M. and COX, A. (2007) 'Employee involvement and participation: structures, processes and outcomes', in Storey, J. (ed.) *Human Resource Management: a critical text*, 3rd edn. London, Thomson: 177–94

MARCHINGTON, M. and WILKINSON, A. (2008) *Human Resource Management at Work: people management and development*, 4th edn. London, Chartered Institute of Personnel and Development

MARCHINGTON, M., WILKINSON, A., ACKERS, P. and DUNDON, A. (2001) *Management Choice and Employee Voice.* London, Chartered Institute of Personnel and Development

MARSDEN, D. (1999) *A Theory of Employment Systems: micro-foundations of societal diversity*. Oxford, Oxford University Press

MARSDEN, D. (2007) 'Pay and rewards in public services: fairness and equity', in Dibben, P., James, P., Roper, I. and Wood, G. (eds), *Modernising Work in Public Services. Redefining roles and relationships in Britain's changing workplace*. Basingstoke, Palgrave Macmillan

MARSDEN, D. and FRENCH, S. (1998*) What a Performance: performance-related pay in the public services*. London, Centre for Economic Performance

MARSDEN, D. and RICHARDSON, R. (1994) 'Performance pay? The effects of merit pay on motivation in the public services'. *British Journal of Industrial Relations* 32(2): 243–61

MARTÍN-ALCÁZAR, F., ROMERO-FERNÁNDEZ, P.M. and SÁNCHEZ-GARDEY, G. (2005) 'Strategic human resource management: integrating the universalistic, contingent, configurational and contextual perspectives'. *International Journal of Human Resource Management* 16(5): 633–59

MARTIN, D.C. and BARTOL, K.M. (2003) 'Factors influencing expatriate performance appraisal system success: and organizational perspective'. *Journal of International Management* 9: 115–32

MAYHEW, K. and KEEP, E. (1999) 'The assessment: knowledge, skills and competitiveness'. *Oxford Review of Economic Policy* 15(1): 1–16

McHUGH, P., CUTCHER-GERSHENFELD, J. and BRIDGE, D. (2005) 'Examining structure and process in ESOP firms'. *Personnel Review* 34(3): 277–93

McNABB, R. and WHITFIELD, K. (2001) 'Job evaluation and high performance work practices: compatible or conflictual?' *Journal of Management Studies* 38(2) March: 293–312

McNULTY, T. and PETTIGREW, A. (1999) 'Strategists on the board'. *Organization Studies* 20(1): 47–74

MESSERSMITH, J. (2007) 'Managing work–life conflict among information technology workers'. *Human Resource Management* 46(3): 429–51

MICHAELS, E., HANDFIELD-JONES, H. and AXELROD, B. (2005) *The War for Talent*. Boston, MA, Harvard Business School Press

MICHELSON, G. and WAILES, N. (2006) 'Shareholder value and corporate social responsibility in work organisations', in Hearn, M. and Michelson, G. (eds) *Rethinking Work: time, space, and discourse*. Cambridge, Cambridge University Press: 239–62

MILKOVICH, G. and NEWMAN, J.M. (2004) *Compensation*, 8th edn. New York, McGraw-Hill

MILKOVICH, G. and NEWMAN, J.M. (2008) *Compensation*, 9th edn. Boston, MA, McGraw-Hill International Edition

MILKOVICH, G.T. and BLOOM, M. (1998) 'Rethinking international compensation'. *Compensation & Benefits Review* 30(1): 15–23

MILKOVICH, G.T. and NEWMAN, J.M. (2008) *Compensation*, 9th edn. Boston, MA, McGraw-Hill

MILLWARD, N., BRYSON, A. and FORTH, J. (2000) *All Change at Work? British employment relations 1980–1998, as portrayed by the Workplace Industrial Relations Survey series.* London, Routledge

MILNER, M. and SEAGER, A. (2007) 'Executive pay: UK bosses: are they worth the money? Evidence scant that big salaries stop brain drain'. *Guardian,* 31 August: 26

MILNER, S. (1995) 'The coverage of collective pay-setting institutions in Britain, 1895–1990'. *British Journal of Industrial Relations* 33(1) March: 69–91

MITCHELL, D.J.B., LEWIN, D. and LAWLER, E.E. (1990) 'Alternative pay systems, firm performance and productivity', in Blinder, A.S. (ed.) *Paying for Productivity: a look at the evidence.* Washington, DC, Brookings Institution

MITCHELL, O. (1982) 'Fringe benefits and labor mobility'. *Journal of Human Resources* 17(92): 286–98

MITCHELL, O. (1983) 'Fringe benefits and the cost of changing jobs'. *Industrial Relations and Labor Review* 37(1): 70–8

MOLM, L.D., PETERSON, G. and TAKASHINI, N. (1999) 'Power in negotiated and reciprocal exchange'. *American Sociological Review* 64(6): 876–90

MONKS, R. and SYKES, A. (2002) *Capitalism without Owners will Fail: a policymaker's guide to reform.* London, CSFI Publications

MOORE, F. (2006) 'Recruitment and selection of international managers', in Edwards, T. and Rees, C. (eds) *International Human Resource Management: globalization, national systems and multinational companies.* London, FT-Prentice Hall: 195–216

MORGAN, G. and WHITLEY, R. (2003) 'Introduction to special edition on multinational companies'. *Journal of Management Studies* 40(3): 609–16

MORRISON, E.W. and ROBINSON, S.L. (1997) 'When employees feel betrayed: a model of how psychological contract violation develops'. *Academy of Management Review* 22(1): 226–56

NAPF (2006) *NAPF Annual Survey 2006.* London, National Association of Pension Funds

NAPF (2007a) *Key Facts on Pensions.* London. National Association of Pension Funds, www.napf.co.uk/policy/keyfacts/workplacepensions.cfm

NAPF (2007b) Workplace Pensions in Demand. Press Release. 25 May. London, National Association of Pension Funds

NATIONAL ASSOCIATION OF EMPLOYEE RECOGNITION (2005) *Trends in Employee Recognition 2005*. Scottsdale, AZ, World at Work

NBPI (1967) *Productivity Agreements*. Report No. 36. Cmnd. 3311: 1. National Board for Prices and Incomes

NEWING, R. (2007) 'Executive remuneration: quality over quantity'. *Financial Times,* 12 October

NOHRIA, N. and GHOSHAL, S. (1997) *The Differentiated Network: organizing multinational corporations for value creation*. San Francisco, Jossey-Bass Wiley

NOLDEKE, G. and SAMUELSON, L. (1996) 'A dynamic model of equilibrium selection in signaling markets'. ELSE Working Papers 038. ESRC Centre on Economics Learning and Social Evolution, http://econwpa.wustl.edu:8089/eps/game/papers/9410/9410001.pdf

NORRIS, P. (2005) 'Shareholders' attitudes to directors' pay', in Tyson, S. and Bournois, F. (eds) *Top Pay and Performance: international and strategic approach*. London, Elsevier: 29–56

NURNEY, S.P. (2001) 'When to stop negotiating individual packages for international assignees'. *Compensation & Benefits Review* 33 July–August: 62–7

O'CONNELL, V. (2006) 'The CEO's share of total directors' cash compensation: U.K. evidence'. *Compensation & Benefits Review* 38 September–October: 28–34

O'DELL, C. and MCADAMS, J. (1987) *People, Performance and Pay*. Houston, TX, American Productivity Center

O'MAHONEY, J. (2007) 'Constructing habitus: the negotiation of moral encounters at Telekom'. *Work, Employment and Society* 21(3): 479–96

OATES, A. (2007) 'Flexible working: making good time'. *People Management* 18 October: 40–3

OECD (1997) *Employment Outlook 1997*. Paris, Organisation for Economic Cooperation and Development

OGDEN, S. and WATSON, R. (2004) 'Remuneration committees and CEO pay in the UK privatized water industry'. *Socio-Economic Review* 2(1): 33–63

OLKKONEN, M.-E. and LIPPONEN, J. (2006) 'Relationships between organizational justice, identification with organization and work unit, and group-related outcomes'. *Organizational Behaviour and Human Decision Processes* 100(2): 202–15

ONS (2006) *Annual Survey of Hours and Earnings*. London, Office for National Statistics

ONS (2006a) *Labour Force Survey. Quarter 2*. Office for National Statistics

ONS (2006b) *Annual Survey of Hours and Earnings 2006*. Office for National Statistics

ONS (2006c) *Labour Force Survey, Spring 2006*. Office for National Statistics

ONS (2007) 'Analysis by occupation'. 2007 *Annual Survey of Hours and Earnings*. London, Office for National Statistics

ONS (2007a) *Income Inequality. Rise in inequality in 2005/6*. Office for National Statistics. 17 May. www.statistics.gov.uk

ONS (2007b) Low Pay Jobs. Office for National Statistics. 7 November. www. statistics.gov.uk

ONS (2007c) *Gender Pay Gap. Narrowest since records began*. 7 November. http://www.statistics.gov.uk/cci/nugget_print.asp?ID=167

ORC (2002) *Worldwide Survey of International Assignment Policies and Practices*. New York, Organization Resource Counselors Inc.

ORC (2004) *2004 Worldwide Survey of International Assignment Policies and Practices*. New York, Organization Resource Counselors Inc.

ORC (2006) *Survey of International Short-term Assignment Policies*. New York, Organization Resource Counselors Inc.

PA CONSULTING GROUP (2007) *Report Commissioned by the Office of Manpower Economics: practices in assessing employee 'quality'*. London, OME

PAAUWE, J. (2004) *HRM and Performance: achieving long term viability*. Oxford, Oxford University Press

PALMER, B., WALLS, M., BURGESS, Z. and STOUGH, C. (2001) 'Emotional intelligence and effective leadership'. *Leadership & Organization Development Journal* 22(1): 5–10

PALMER, S. (1990) *Determining Pay: a guide to the issues*. London, Chartered Institute of Personnel and Development

PARKINSON, J. (2003) 'The company and the employment relationship'. *British Journal of Industrial Relations* 41(3): 481–509

PEARCE, J.L. (1987) 'Why merit pay doesn't work: implications from organizational theory', in Balkin, D.B. and Gomez-Mejia L.R. (eds) *New Perspectives on Compensation*. Englewood Cliffs, NJ, Prentice Hall

PENDLETON, A., WILSON, N. and WRIGHT, M. (1998) 'The perception and effects of share ownership: empirical evidence from employee buy-outs'. *British Journal of Industrial Relations* 36(1): 99–124

PENSIONS COMMISSION (2004) *Pensions: Challenges and Choices. The First Report of the Pensions Commission*. London, The Stationery Office

PENSIONS COMMISSION (2005) *A New Pension Settlement for the Twenty-First Century. The Second Report of the Pensions Commission*. London, The Stationery Office

Pensions Commission (2006) *Implementing an Integrated Package of Pension Reforms. The Final Report of the Pensions Commission.* London, The Stationery Office

Pepper, S. (2006) *Senior Executive Reward: key models and practices.* Aldershot, Gower

Perkins, S.J. (1998) *Communication and the Reward Strategy Agenda.* Croner's Pay and Benefits Briefing 151, October. Kingston-upon-Thames, Croner Publications

Perkins, S.J. (2006) *International Reward and Recognition.* Research Report. London, Chartered Institute of Personnel and Development

Perkins, S.J. (2008) 'Executive reward: complexity, controversy, and contradiction', in White, G. and Drucker, J. (eds) *Reward Management: a critical text*, 2nd edn. London, Routledge (in press)

Perkins, S.J. and Daste, R. (2007) 'Pluralistic tensions in expatriating managers'. *Journal of European Industrial Training* 31(7): 550–69

Perkins, S.J. and Hendry, C. (2001) 'Global champions: who's paying attention?' *Thunderbird International Business Review* 43(1): 53–75

Perkins, S.J. and Hendry, C. (2005) 'Ordering top pay: interpreting the signals'. *Journal of Management Studies* 42(7): 1443–68

Perkins, S.J. and Sandringham, St J. (eds) (1998) *Trust, Motivation and Commitment: a reader.* Faringdon, SRRC

Perkins, S.J. and Shortland, S.M. (2006) *Strategic International Human Resource Management.* London, Kogan Page

Peters, T.J. and Waterman, R.H. Jr (1982) *In Search of Excellence: lessons from America's best-run companies.* New York, Harper & Row

Pfeffer, J. (1998) 'Six dangerous myths about pay'. *Harvard Business Review* 76 May–June: 108–19

Pfeffer, J. (1998) *The Human Equation. Building profits by putting people first.* Boston, MA, Harvard Business Press

Pfeffer, J. and Salancik, G.R. (1977) 'Who gets power – and how they hold on to it: a strategic contingency model of power'. *Organizational Dynamics* Winter: 3–21

Pfeffer, J. and Salancik, G.R. (2003) *The External Control of Organizations: a resource dependence perspective.* Stanford, Stanford University Press

Philips, L. and Fox, M. (2003) 'Compensation strategy in transnational corporations'. *Management Decision* 41(5): 465–76

Pinder, C.C. (1987) 'Valence-instrumentality-expectancy theory', in Steers, R.M. and Porter, L.W. (eds) *Motivation and Work Behavior*, 4th edn. San Francisco, McGraw-Hill: 69–89

POINT, S. (2005) 'Accountability, transparency and performance: comparing annual report disclosures on CEO pay across Europe', in Tyson, S. and Bournois, F. (eds) *Top Pay and Performance: international and strategic approach*. London, Elsevier: 57–84

POOLE, M. and JENKINS, G. (1990) 'Human resource management and profit sharing: employee attitudes and a national survey'. *International Journal of Human Resource Management* 1(3) December: 289–328

PORTER, L.W. and LAWLER, E.E. (1968) *Managerial Attitudes and Performance*. Homewood, IL, Irwin

PRICE, L. and PRICE, R. (1994) 'Change and continuity in the status divide', in Sisson, K. (ed.) *Personnel Management: a comprehensive guide to theory and practice in Britain*, 2nd edn. Oxford, Blackwell

PRICEWATERHOUSECOOPERS (2006) *Measuring the Value of International Assignments*. London, PriceWaterhouseCoopers

PRITCHARD, D. and MURLIS, H. (1992) *Jobs, Roles and People. The new world of job evaluation*. London, Nicholas Brearley

PURCELL, J. (1999) 'Best fit and best practice: chimera or cul-de-sac?' *Human Resource Management Journal* 9(3): 26–41

PURCELL, J. (2006) 'Building better organisations'. *Reflections on Employee Engagement*. Change Agenda. London, Chartered Institute of Personnel and Development: 3–4

PURCELL, J. and AHLSTRAND, B. (1994) *Human Resource Management in the Multi-divisional Company*. Oxford, Oxford University Press

PURCELL, J. and HUTCHINSON, S. (2007) 'Rewarding work: the vital role of front line managers'. Change Agenda. London, Chartered Institute of Personnel and Development

PYE, A. (2001) 'Corporate boards, investors and their relationships: accounts of accountability and corporate governance in action'. *Corporate Governance, An International Review* 9(3): 186–95

QUAID, M. (1993) 'Job evaluation as institutional myth'. *Journal of Management Studies* 30(2) March: 239–60

RANDLE, K. (1997) 'Rewarding failure: operating a performance-related pay system in pharmaceutical research'. *Personnel Review* 26(3): 187–200

RECARDO, R.J. and PRICONE, D. (1996) 'Is skill-based pay for you?'. *SAM Advanced Management Journal* 6(4) Fall: 16–22

REEVES, R. and KNELL, J. (2001) 'All these futures are yours', in *The Future of Reward*. Executive Briefing. London, Chartered Institute of Personnel and Development: 39–46

REILLY, M. and SCOTT, D. (2005) 'An inside look at compensation committees'. *World at Work Journal* second quarter: 34–40

REYNOLDS, C. (1997) 'Expatriate compensation in historical perspective'. *Journal of World Business* 32(2): 118–32

RICHARDS, J. and HOGG, C. (2007) *Total Reward*. CIPD Factsheet. London, Chartered Institute of Personnel and Development

RICHARDSON, R. and NEJAD, A. (1986) 'Employee share ownership schemes in the UK – an evaluation'. *British Journal of Industrial Relations* 23(2): 233–50

ROBERTS, J. (2001) 'Trust and control in Anglo-American systems of corporate governance: the individualizing and socializing effects of processes of accountability'. *Human Relations* 54(12): 1547–72

ROBERTS, J.D., McNULTY, T. and STILES, P. (2005), 'Beyond agency conceptions of the work of the non-executive director: creating accountability in the boardroom'. *British Journal of Management* 16(S1): S5–S26

ROBERTS, K. (2007) 'Work–life balance – the sources of the contemporary problem and the probable outcomes: a review and interpretation of the evidence'. *Employee Relations* 29(4): 334–51

ROE, M.J. (2003) *Political Determinants of Corporate Governance: political context, corporate impact*. Oxford, Oxford University Press

ROSENBAUM, J.E. (1989) 'Organization career systems and employee misperceptions', in Arthur, M.B., Hall, D.T and Lawrence, B.S. (eds), *Handbook of Career Theory*. New York, Cambridge University Press: 329–53

ROUSSEAU, D. and TIJORIWALA, S. (1998) 'Assessing psychological contracts: issues, alternatives and measures'. *Journal of Organizational Behaviour* 19(7): 679–95

ROUSSEAU, D.M. (1995) *Psychological Contracts in Organizations: understanding written and unwritten agreements*. Thousand Oaks, CA, Sage

ROUSSEAU, D.M (2006) 'Is there such a thing as "evidence-based management"?' *Academy of Management Review* 31(2): 256–69

ROUSSEAU, D.M. and GRELLER, M.M. (1994) 'Human resource practices: administrative contract makers'. *Human Resource Management* 33(3): 385–401

ROY, D. (1952) 'Quota restriction and goldbricking in a machine shop'. *American Journal of Sociology* 5(5): 427–42

RUBERY, J. (1997) 'Wages and the labour market'. *British Journal of Industrial Relations* 35(3): 337–66

RUBERY, J. and GRIMSHAW, D. (2003) *The Organization of Employment: an international perspective*. Basingstoke, Palgrave Macmillan

RUSSELL, A. (1998) *The Harmonisation of Employment Conditions in Britain. The changing workplace divide since 1950 and the implications for social structure.* Basingstoke, Macmillan Press

SCHIFFERES, S. (2005) 'Pension reform: What other countries do'. BBC News, 24 November. http://news.bbc.co.uk/go/pr/fr/-/1/hi/business/4462404.stm

SCHILLER, B. and WEISS, R. (1979) 'The impact of private pensions on firm attachment'. *Review of Economics and Statistics* 61(3): 369–80

SCHUSTER, J.R. and ZINGHEIM, P. (1992) *The New Pay. Linking employee and organisational performance.* New York, Lexington Books

SCRIMSHAW, A. (2000) *Stakeholder Pensions. A guide to implementation and practice.* London, Chartered Institute of Personnel and Development

SHEARN, M. (2007) 'Book Review: The Myth of Work–Life Balance: The Challenge of Our Time for Men, Women and Societies'. *Work, Employment and Society* 21(3): 601–2

SHIELDS, J. (2007) *Managing Employee Performance and Reward: concepts, practices, strategies.* Cambridge, Cambridge University Press

SIMPSON, B. (1999) 'A milestone in the legal regulation of pay: the National Minimum Wage Act 1998'. *Industrial Law Journal* 28(1): 1–32

SIMS, R.H. and SCHRAEDER, M. (2005) 'Expatriate compensation: an exploratory review of salient contextual factors and common practices'. *Career Development International* 10(2): 98–108

SKIDMORE, P. (1999) 'Enforcing the minimum wage'. *Journal of Law and Society* 26(4): 247–8

SLAUGHTER, S.A., ANG, S. and BOH, W.F. (2007) 'Firm-specific human capital and compensation-organizational tenure profiles: an archival analysis of salary data for it professionals'. *Human Resource Management* 46(3): 373–94

SMITH, A. (1776) *The Wealth of Nations.* London, Penguin Books [1970 edn]

SMITH, I. (1983) *The Management of Remuneration: paying for effectiveness.* London, IPM

SMITH, I. (1989) *Incentive Schemes: people and profits.* London, Croner

SMITH, I. (2000) 'Benefits', in White, G. and Druker, J. (eds) *Reward Management: a critical text.* London, Routledge

SMITH, I. (2005) 'Pay, motivation and a re-think'. *Croner Pay and Benefits Briefing.* Issue 293: 4–6

SMITH, I.G. (1989) *Incentive Schemes: people and profits.* Kingston-upon-Thames, Croner Publications

SPARROW, P. (1996) 'Too good to be true'. *People Management.* 5 December: 22–7

SPARROW, P. (1999) 'International reward systems: to converge or not converge?', in Brewster, C. and Harris, H. (eds) *International HRM: contemporary issues in Europe*. London, Routledge: 102-19

SPARROW, P. (2000) 'International reward management', in White, G. and Drucker, J. (eds) *Reward Management: a critical text*. London, Routledge: 196–214

SPARROWE, R.T. and LINDEN, R.C. (1997) 'Process and structure in leader–member exchange'. *Academy of Management Review* 22(2): 522–52

STANWORTH, C., WERGIN, N.E. and WHITE, G. (2006) 'Work–family integration in the UK – a review'. *International Employment Relations Review* 12(2): 19–31

STEERS, R.M. and PORTER, L.W. (1987) 'Reward systems in organizations', in Steers, R.M. and Porter, L.W. (eds) *Motivation and Work Behavior*, 4th edn. San Francisco, McGraw-Hill: 203–9

STILES, P. and TAYLOR, B. (2002) *Boards at Work: how directors view their roles and responsibilities*. Oxford, Oxford University Press

Storey, J. (ed.) (1995) *Human Resource Management: a critical text*. London, Routledge

Storey, J. (ed.) (2001) *Human Resource Management: a critical text*, 2nd edn. London, Thomson

STREBLER, M., THOMPSON, M. and HERON, P. (1997*) Skills, Competencies and Gender: issues for pay and training*. Report 333. Brighton, Institute of Employment Studies

SUUTARI, V. and TORNIKOSKI, C. (2001) 'The challenge of expatriate compensation: the sources of satisfaction and dissatisfaction among expatriates'. *International Journal of Human Resource Management* 12(3): 389–404

SYKES, A. (2002) 'Overcoming poor value executive remuneration: resolving the manifest conflicts of interest'. *Corporate Governance* 10(4): 256–60

TAN, D. and MAHONEY, J.T. (2006) 'Why a multinational firm chooses expatriates: integrating resource-based, agency and transaction cost perspectives'. *Journal of Management Studies* 43(3): 457–84

TAYLOR, F.W. (1911) *The Principles of Scientific Management*. New York, Harper Bros

TAYLOR, S. (2000) 'Occupational pensions and employee retention'. *Employee Relations* 22(3): 246–59

TAYLOR, S. (forthcoming 2008) 'Pensions', in White, G. and Druker, J. (eds) *Reward Management: a critical text*, 2nd edn. London, Routledge

TEPPER, B., DUFFY, M.K., HENLE, C.A. and SCHURER LAMBERT, L. (2006) 'Procedural injustice, victim precipitation and abusive supervision'. *Personnel Psychology* 59(1): 101–23

THOMPSON, M. (1993) *Pay and Performance: the employee experience*. IMS Report 258. Brighton, Institute of Manpower Studies

THOMPSON, M. (1995) *Team Working and Pay*. Brighton, Institute of Employment Studies

THOMPSON, M. (2000) 'Salary progression systems', in White, G. and Druker, J. (eds) *Reward Management: a critical text*. London, Routledge

THOMPSON, M. and MILSOME, S. (2001) *Reward Determination in the UK*. Research Report. London, Chartered Institute of Personnel and Development

THOMSON-ON-LINE (2007) *Employee Rewards Watch 2007*. Available at http://www.thomsononlinebenefits.com/Employee-Rewards-Watch-results

THUROW, L. (1975) *Generating Inequality*. London, Macmillan

TOWERS PERRIN (1997) *Learning from the Past: changing for the future*. London, Towers Perrin

TREGASKIS, O. and BREWSTER, C, (2006) 'Converging or diverging? A comparative analysis of trends in contingent employment practice across Europe over a decade'. *Journal of International Business Studies* 37(1): 111–26

TUC (2006) Press Release: Reaction to IDS Directors' Pay Report 2006. 3 November. London, Trades Union Congress

TYSON, S. (2005) 'Fat cat pay', in Tyson, S. and Bournois, F. (eds) *Top Pay and Performance: international and strategic approach*. London, Elsevier: 12–28

TYSON, S. and BOURNOIS, F. (2005) 'Introduction', in *Top Pay and Performance: international and strategic approach*. London, Elsevier: 1–11

UHE, M. and PERKINS, S.J. (2007) 'Messages from the 2007 Voice and Value conference focusing on the current state and future of collective voice'. CIPD Event Report http://www.cipd.co.uk/NR/rdonlyres/7316CE36-DC97-4B9E-B447-3D9C54B50BDE/0/futcollvoic.pdf

ULRICH, D. (1997) *Human Resource Champions: the next agenda for adding value and delivering results*. Boston, MA, HBS Press

ULRICH, D. and BROCKBANK, W. (2005) *The HR Value Proposition*. Boston, MA, Harvard Business School Press

UNCDT (2007) *World Investment Report 2007: transnational corporations, extractive industries and development*. New York/Geneva: United Nations

VELIYATH, R. (1999) 'Top management compensation and shareholder returns: unravelling different models of the relationship'. *Journal of Management Studies* 36(1): 123–43

VERNON, G. (2006) 'International pay and reward', in Edwards, T. and Rees, C. (eds) *International Human Resource Management: globalization, national systems and multinational companies*. London, Prentice Hall: 217–41.

VON BERTALANFFY, L. (1969) *General System Theory: foundations, developments, applications.* New York, George Braziller

VROOM, V.H. (1964) *Work and Motivation.* New York, Wiley

WALBY, S. and OLSEN, W. (2002) *The Impact of Women's Position in the Labour Market on Pay and Implications for UK Productivity.* Women and Equality Unit, London. Department of Trade and Industry

WALLERSTEIN, I. (1983) *Historical Capitalism with Capitalist Civilization.* London, Verso

WATSON, B.W. Jr and GANGARAM SINGH, G. (2005) 'Global pay systems: compensation in support of a multinational strategy'. *Compensation & Benefits Review* 37 January–February: 33–6

WATSON, M. (2005) *Foundations of International Political Economy.* Basingstoke, Palgrave-Macmillan

WATTS, R. and ROBERTS, D. (2006) 'FTSE pay spirals out of control'. *Sunday Telegraph,* 24 September: 1

WEITZMAN, M.L. (1984) *The Share Economy: conquering stagflation.* Cambridge, MA, Harvard University Press

WEITZMAN, M.L. and KRUSE, D.L. (1990) 'Profit sharing and productivity', in Blinder, A. (ed.), *Paying for Productivity: a look at the evidence.* Washington, DC, Brookings Institution

WENTLAND, D.M. (2003) 'A new practical guide for determining expatriate compensation: the comprehensive model'. *Compensation & Benefits Review* 35(3): 45–50

WHITE, G. (2000) 'Determining pay', in White, G. and Druker, J. (eds) *Reward Management: a critical text.* London, Routledge

WHITE, G. (2000a) 'The Pay Review Body system: its development and impact'. *Historical Studies in Industrial Relations* 9 Spring: 71–100

WHITE, G. and HATCHETT, A. (2003) 'The Pay Review Bodies in Britain under the Labour Government'. *Public Money & Management* 23(94) October: 237–44

WHITE, G., KEHIL, M. and HOLT, H. (2007) 'The pay composition of the low-paid: an analysis from 1997–2006'. Paper presented to the BJIR Conference on the National Minimum Wage at the Centre for Economic Performance, London School of Economics and Political Science, London. 13–14 December

WHITLEY, R (2000) *Divergent Capitalisms: the social structuring and change of business systems.* Oxford, Oxford University Press

WHITTINGTON, R. (2000) *What is Strategy and Does it Matter?,* 2nd edn. London, Thomson Learning

WILLIAMSON, O. (1975) *Markets and Hierarchies.* New York, Free Press

WILSON, F. and BOWEY, A.M. (1989) 'Profit- and performance-based systems', in Bowey, A.M. (ed.) *Managing Salary and Wage Systems*. Aldershot, Gower.

WOODRUFFE, C. (1991) 'Competent by any other name'. *Personnel Management* September: 30–3

WORKSPAN 44(12): http://www.worldatwork.org/waw/adimLink?id=15799, accessed 08.11.07

WORLDATWORK (2007) *Executive Rewards Questionary*. Scottsdale, AZ, World@Work

WRAY, R. (2007) 'French take the spoils in European pay league'. *Guardian Unlimited,* 25 July, http://www.guardian.co.uk/business/2007/jul/25/6, accessed 22.12.07

WRIGHT, A. (2004) *Reward Management in Context*. London, Chartered Institute of Personnel and Development

WRIGHT, A. (forthcoming, 2008) 'Benefits', in White, G. and Druker, J. (eds) *Reward Management: a critical text*, 2nd edn. London, Routledge

WRIGHT, C. (2005a) 'Linking reward and business strategy', in Childs, M. (consultant ed.) *Reward Management*. Loose-leaf. London, Chartered Institute of Personnel and Development: 1.1–1.1.4

WRIGHT, C. (2005b) 'Reward strategy in context', in Childs, M. (consultant ed.) *Reward Management*. Loose-leaf. London, Chartered Institute of Personnel and Development: section 1.2

WRIGHT, P.M. and McMAHAN, G. C. (1992) 'Theoretical perspectives for strategic human resource management'. *Journal of Management* 18(2): 295–320

YOUNG, M.B. (2006) *Strategic Workforce Planning: forecasting human capital needs to execute business strategy*. The Conference Board Report R-1391-06-WG

Zeckhauser, R.J. (ed.) (1991) *The Strategy of Choice*. Cambridge, MA, MIT Press

ZINGHEIM, P.K. and SCHUSTEr, J.R. (2000) *Pay People Right! Breakthrough reward strategies to create great companies*. San Francisco, Jossey-Bass

ZWEIMÜLLER, J. and BARTH, E. (1992) *Bargaining Structure, Wage Determination and Wage Dispersion in Six OECD Countries*. Institute of Industrial Relations Working Paper Series, University of California, Berkeley

Index